MW01711560

ORIENTALIA LOVANIENSIA
ANALECTA
——— 220 ———

THE ANCIENT NEAR EAST, A LIFE!

Festschrift Karel Van Lerberghe

edited by

TOM BOIY, JOACHIM BRETSCHNEIDER,
ANNE GODDEERIS, HENDRIK HAMEEUW,
GRETA JANS and JAN TAVERNIER

UITGEVERIJ PEETERS en DEPARTEMENT OOSTERSE STUDIES
LEUVEN – PARIS – WALPOLE, MA
2012

Note by the editors
The abbreviations in this volume follow those by the *Assyrian Dictionary of the Oriental Institute of the University of Chicago* (hereafter CAD) and *Northern Akkad Project Reports* 8 (1993) 49-77.

A catalogue record for this book is available from the Library of Congress.

© 2012, Peeters Publishers & Department of Oriental Studies
Bondgenotenlaan 153, B-3000 Leuven/Louvain (Belgium)

All rights reserved, including the rights to translate or to reproduce this book or parts thereof in any form.

ISBN 978-90-429-2662-2
D/2012/0602/115

CONTENTS

A LIFE IN ANCIENT NEAR EAST IS SOMETHING NOT TO BE FORGOTTEN …

After the conclusion of his studies in Near Eastern Languages and History at Ghent University in 1973, Karel deepened his acquaintance with Old Babylonian under the guidance of F. R. Kraus in Leiden. He scanned through the entire corpus of Old Babylonian contracts, looking for references to royal edicts for Kraus's magnum opus "Königliche Verfügungen in altbabylonischer Zeit". This project gave him a sound basis for the rest of his career. From 1978 onwards, Karel held a position at the KU Leuven, first as project-assistant of E. Lipiński, later as a lecturer. His doctoral dissertation, on some hundred tablets recovered from the house of Ur-Utu in Tell ed-Dēr[1], has given us a foretaste of the Ur-Utu archive.

Karel married Gabriella Voet. Both were students at Ghent University, meeting regularly in 'Café Den Engel' in their hometown Antwerp. Their marriage is one of great happiness and scholarly co-operation. In all his work, in the field and in the 'office', Karel was most ably helped by his wife. Gabriella, an archaeologist in her own right, has researched intensively the glyptic art of the Old Babylonian Period.

People know Karel as a jolly man and a dedicated teacher, who was able to teach his students what they had to know to become good Assyriologists and/or archaeologists, but who could also insert in these serious matters some side-information on his colleagues, famous Assyriologists as well as non-famous Assyriologists. In his courses on the Sumerian and Akkadian languages he transmitted in a pleasant way his vast knowledge of both languages to his pupils, while the courses on Mesopotamian history and archaeology were very fascinating (though the early hour of the master course on Mesopotamian archaeology could pose a problem for some students). In his courses, he used a loose, somewhat less structured style to tell his audience how interesting this text or that inscription could be, while the next moment he would talk about some tower in Eben Ezer, a house full of miniature trains, or something else.

Next to his talents as teacher and researcher, Karel also organized various conferences, the most important of which is undoubtedly the

[1] Oudbabylonische documentaire teksten uit het archief van Ur-Utu, opperklaagpriester van Annunītum te Sippar-Amnānum (defended on 12 December 1980, summa cum laude).

Rencontre Assyriologique Internationale, the yearly venue of Assyriologists and archaeologists of the Ancient Near East. The KU Leuven, with Karel and Gabriella as representatives, hosted the 42nd edition from 3-7 July 1995. The topic was called "At the Cross-Roads of Civilizations in the Syro-Mesopotamian Realm — Languages and Cultures in Contact". The organizational work for a conference of this size (about 400 participants) is immense and Karel and Gabriella, helped by a team of researchers and students, put a lot of energy in what was to become one of the best *Rencontre Assyriologique Internationale* ever, if one may believe the comments afterwards. Basically, an international conference consists of two main parts: the academic one (lectures, communications, discussions, etc.) and the social one (receptions, trips, L.I.P.-parties, etc.). The Leuven edition of the Rencontre proved to be excellent on both levels, with various high-quality lectures and a social activity each day: a reception at the Inner Court of the Maria Theresia College, the official celebration of Prof. Lipiński at the Faculty Club, a trip to Antwerp, and last but not least, the now famous L.I.P-party organized by the students at their Fakbar. This party has become a much-commented activity and was apparently that successful that the day after (during the trip to Antwerp on Wednesday) various participants asked Karel if it would be possible to organize another such party on Thursday evening. In other words, a remarkable and unforgettable Rencontre Assyriologique Internationale, thanks to Karel, Gabriella and their assistants.[2]

On the occasion of its 175th birthday, the "Generale Maatschappij van België" (Brussel) organized an exhibition on the origin of writing. They invited Philippe Talon and Karel Van Lerberghe to put their back into the undertaking. Philippe and Karel were able to persuade the Syrian authorities to lend them some of their most exquisite and unique artifacts. The project resulted in a very successful exhibition (December 1997-March 1998) and a detailed catalogue, not only containing meticulous descriptions of all the objects, but also extensive contributions by the most renown international colleagues.

[2] Other conferences, in the organization of which Karel played an important role, are (1) "The Languages of the Bilad al-Sham" (1994, organized in the frame of the Med-Campus Project in cooperation with the Yarmouk University of Irbid - Jordan) (2) "Power and Architecture" (2002, organized by KU Leuven in collaboration with UC Louvain and W.W.U. Münster), (3) "Intercultural Contacts in the Ancient Mediterranean" (2008, organized by the Netherlands-Flemish Institute in Cairo in collaboration with the KU Leuven) and (4) "Palaeography and Scribal Practices in Syro-Palestine and Anatolia in the Late Bronze Age" (2009, organized by the KU Leuven and the University of Leiden).

For Karel, as for many of us, research stays abroad were the most invigorating aspect of his job as an Assyriologist. Many of the contributors to this Festschrift volume have met him in Philadelphia, London, Chicago or recently Cornell. The contact with colleagues from all over the world combined with the exploration of cuneiform material in the museum collections has motivated him throughout his career. His contribution to the Chicago Assyrian Dictionary was a very stimulating intermezzo as well. Through his excellent copies, we all enjoy the benefit of his stays.

Indeed, Karel was never merely an insular researcher locked up in his 'ivory tower'. He craved to travel; not only regarding academic projects, Karel and his wife took full advantage of more peaceful times to travel extensively through the entire Near East on their legendary motorcycle tours. He participated in and later on organized himself several archaeological expeditions. In Iraq, at Sippar-Amnānum (modern Tell ed-Dēr) in the Baghdad Governate, where a Belgian team led by L. de Meyer excavated several Old Babylonian houses with distinct archives. Karel studied and published the texts found in room 17 of the house of Ur-Utu. He also worked one season at Petra, unearthing a betyl, bearing his name — 'Karelke' — in the excavation report.

With the Iraq war, near eastern archaeologists redirected their efforts toward excavation of sites in Syria. In 1991 the KU Leuven, represented by Karel, was one of the initial organizers of the joint Syro-European archaeological mission at Tell Beydar, in the Al-Hasakeh Governate, under the direction of M. Lebeau (and afterwards under the co-direction of A. Suleiman). Until 2001, Karel was — together with Ph. Talon, W. Sallaberger, F. Ismail and L. Milano — assigned the task of working on the tablets found at Tell Beydar.

In 1999 Karel was invited to start his own excavation project by and in cooperation with the Syrian Directorate-General of Antiquities at Tell Tweini at the Syrian coast. He was director of this project until 2008, when he was succeeded by J. Bretschneider. The members of the excavation teams in Beydar and Tweini will particularly remember his 'critical' approach of excavated features, how he flabbergasted them with groups of journalists and TV reporters on the field and his indefatigable communicative qualities late at night with a glass of beer or wine.

By directing or co-directing several series of interdisciplinary projects related to and based on the excavations of Tell Beydar and Tell Tweini or on the study of Mesopotamia's ancient environments, political entities and socio-economic systems in general, Karel's approach has always been an interdisciplinary one. By exploring, introducing and combining the input and output of a large variety of various sciences, challenging research topics could be addressed. To accomplish this, funding was provided by the *Interuniversity Poles of Attraction* (IUAP), *Fonds voor Wetenschappelijk Onderzoek-Vlaanderen* (FWO), *Onderzoeksfonds KU Leuven* (OT), *Nationale Bank van België*, *Interdisciplinaire Onderzoeksprogramma's* (IDO) and *Herculesstichting*. Moreover, Karel took a prominent role as copromotor in the Centre for Archaeological Sciences, founded in 2005; the Leuven based centre for expertise on interdisciplinary studies related to archaeology. With *Tell Beydar, Environmental and Technical Studies*, Karel and Gabriella edited a publication containing a wide variety of papers by experts who worked on the Tell Beydar excavations. More recently, environmental interdisciplinary studies were again addressed by combining several disciplines in the frame of the Tell Tweini Project. This research led to joined publications in renowned journals such as *The Holocene*, *Proceedings of the National Academy of Sciences* and *Quaternary Research.*

As an epigraphist Karel has always paid special personal attention to the supporting discipline of imaging. Already in the mid 90's he experimented in the expedition house of Tell Beydar with digital photography of the tablets using the Agfa *ActionCam* and applying visualization tools in the first software packages of Photoshop.[3] During a visit to Karel's excavations in Syria former Rector Oosterlinck of the KU Leuven suggested the usage of new techniques pioneered at the ESAT-labs of their home university. This collaboration resulted in the so-called Portable Light Dome system, a method thoroughly tested by Karel and Gabriella in their first large publication on the Dūr-Abiešuḫ texts in the CUSAS-series.

Administration and bureaucracy have never been Karel's preferred pastimes. Nevertheless, he took on his fair share of administrative duties at university. Already in 1979 he was ombudsman for the students during the examination period. He served in the permanent teaching commission for Oriental Studies as secretary (1983-1990) and chair (1990-1996). From 2001 until 2005 he headed the department of Oriental and Slavonic Studies and immediately afterwards he coordinated the section Near Eastern

[3] Honesty obliges us to mention that computers have not always been Karel's favorite 'furniture'. On regular basis the inhabitants of the neighboring offices were gently but compellingly asked again (and again) for assistance in his love-hate relationship with the digital world.

Studies for the maximum period of five years. National and international cooperation to further research on Mesopotamia by researchers and students alike lay nearer to his heart. In Belgium the University of Leuven took part in the prime minister's initiative on the Interuniversity Attraction Pole dealing with the land of Sumer and Akkad together with the universities of Gent and Liège. In line with his other activities in Syria a MedCampus program, sponsored by the European Union, was set up for exchanges with Yarmouk University (Jordan) and Aleppo University (Syria). Both students and professors have gratefully seized the opportunity to participate in this program. For Leuven students of Assyriology and Arabic the Arabic language courses at Aleppo University and the immersion in the daily city life turned out to be an unforgettable experience. The Bologna Bachelor-Master reforms led Karel to set up a cooperation with the universities of Leiden and Münster to the profit of all students.

The editors, long-time friends and colleagues in the field, hope that they will be able to continue the intellectual tradition of Near Eastern Studies at their beloved university of Leuven.

Tom Boiy, Joachim Bretschneider, Anne Goddeeris, Hendrik Hameeuw, Greta Jans & Jan Tavernier

TABULA GRATULATORIA

Abraham Kathleen - Ramat-Gan
Akkermans Peter - Leiden
Al-Maqdissi Michel - Damas
Baeteman Cécile - Brussel
Beckman Gary - Ann Arbor
Berlejung Angelika - Heidelberg
Bertrem Kurt - Leuven
Broekmans Tom - Leuven
Bunnens Guy - Liège
Cassiman Jean-Jacques - Leuven
Charpin Dominique - Paris
Charvát Petr - Pilzen
Cooper Jerry - Baltimore
Cunliffe Emma - Durham
De Breucker Geert - Groningen
Debruyne Michel - Leuven
Decorte Ronny - Leuven
De Cupere Bea - Brussel
Degryse Patrick - Leuven
Devecchi Elena - München
De Vos An - Würzburg
Dietrich Manfried - Münster
Dittmann Reinhard - Münster
Driessen Jan - Louvain-la-Neuve
Durand Jean-Marie - Paris
El-Desouky Hamdy - Leuven
Farber Gertrud - Chicago
Farber Walter - Chicago
Frame Grant - Philadelphia
Gabbay Uri - Jerusalem
Gadotti Alhena - Towson
Gorris Elynn - Louvain-la-Neuve
Gubel Eric - Brussel
Heyvaert Vanessa - Brussel
Ishaq Eva - Beyrouth
Janssen Caroline - Gent
Kaniewski David - Toulouse
Kleinerman Alexandra - Ithaca
Krispijn Theo - Leiden
Kühne Hartmut - Berlin
Kuhrt Amélie - London
Lebeau Marc - Brussel
Lebrun René - Louvain-la-Neuve
Linseele Veerle - Leuven / Brussel
Lipiński Edward - Leuven
Lodewijckx Mark - Leuven
Marinova Elena - Leuven
Masetti-Rouault Maria Grazia - Paris
Matoïan Valérie - Lyon
Matthiae Paolo - Roma
Mattila Raija - Helsinki
Mayr Rudolf - Ithaca
Michalowski Piotr - Ann Arbor
Muchez Philippe - Leuven
Neumann Hans - Münster
Nieuwenhuyse Olivier - Berlin
Oates Joan - Cambridge
Owen David - Ithaca
Paulissen Etienne - Leuven
Pfaelzner Peter - Tübingen
Poblome Jeroen - Leuven
Preys René - Leuven
Pruss Alexander - München
Rich Sara - Leuven
Richardson Mervyn - Leiden
Roobaert Arlette - Liège
Roth Martha - Chicago
Rouault Olivier - Lyon
Sallaberger Walther - München
Saleh Saraa - Leuven

Schoep Ilse - Leuven
Schoors Antoon - Leuven
Spaey Johanna - Leuven
Sténuit Marie-Eve - Brussel
Stol Marten - Leiden
Stone Elizabeth - Stony Brook
Tanret Michel - Gent
Toonen Marianne - Leuven
Tunca Önhan - Liège
Van Buylaere Greta - Cambridge
Van De Mieroop Marc - New York
Van der Stede Véronique - Liège
Van der Valk Jan - Brussel
Vanhaecke Frank - Gent
Van Hecke Pierre - Leuven
Van Koppen Frans - London
Van Neer Wim - Leuven/Brussel
Van Peer Philip - Leuven
van Soldt Wilfred - Leiden
Vandendriessche Mia - Leuven
Vandorpe Patricia - Basel
Vansteenhuyse Klaas - Leuven
Veenhof Klaas - Leiden
Vermeersch Pierre - Leuven
Vervenne Marc - Leuven
Vita Juan-Pablo - Madrid
Waelkens Marc - Leuven
Waerzeggers Caroline - London
Waetzoldt Hartmut - Heidelberg
Weiss Harvey - New Haven
Wilhelm Gernot - Würzburg
Wilkinson Tony - Durham
Willems Harco - Leuven
Zimansky Paul - Stony Brook

BIBLIOGRAPHY OF KAREL VAN LERBERGHE (UNTIL 2012)

Books Authored

2009

A Late Old Babylonian Temple Archive from Dūr-Abiešuḫ (Cornell University Studies in Assyriology and Sumerology 8), Bethesda. (co-author: G. Voet)

2007

Tell Tweini: the Syro-Belgian excavations; Tell Tweini: les fouilles Syro-Belges; Tell Tweini: de Syro-Belgische opgravingen (*Documents d'Archéologie Syrienne* X), Damascus. (co-authors: M. Al-Maqdissi, J. Bretschneider, M. Badawi)

2004

Third Millennium Cuneiform Texts from Tell Beydar (seasons 1996-2002) (Subartu XII), Turnhout. (co-authors: L. Milano, W. Sallaberger, Ph. Talon)

1996

Administrative Documents from Tell Beydar (seasons 1993-1995) (Subartu II), Turnhout. (co-authors: F. Ismail, W. Sallaberger, Ph. Talon)

1991

Sippar-Amnanum, The Ur-Utu archive (Mesopotamian History and Environment. Series III Texts I), Ghent. (co-author: G. Voet)

1986

Old Babylonian Legal and Administrative Texts from Philadelphia (Orientalia Lovaniensia Analecta 21), Leuven. (collaborators: G. Voet, M. Stol)

Books Edited

2010

Tell Tweini. Onze Campagnes de Fouilles Syro-Belges 1999-2010, Damas. (co-editors: Al-Maqdissi M., J. Bretschneider, M. Badawi)

2008

In Search of Gibala, An Archaeological and Historical Study based on Eight Seasons of Excavations at Tel Tweini (Syria) in the A and C Fields (1999-2007) (Aula Orientalis-Supplementa 24), Barcelona. (co-editor: J. Bretschneider)

2007

Power & Architecture. Monumental Public Architecture in the Bronze Age Near East and Aegean (Orientalia Lovaniensia Analecta 156), Leuven. (co-editors: J. Bretschneider, J. Driessen)

2001

Tell Beydar, Environmental and Technical Studies (Subartu VI), Turnhout. (co-editor: G. Voet)

1999

Languages and Cultures in Contact. At the Cross-Roads of Civilizations in the Syro-Mesopotamian Realm (Orientalia Lovaniensia Analecta 79), Leuven. (co-editor: G. Voet)

Omtrent Beydar. De Talen en Culturen van Noord-Syrië, Leuven. (co-editors: G. Voet, M. Debruyne)

1997

En Syrie, aux origines de l'écriture, Turnhout. (co-editor: Ph. Talon)

1995

Immigration and Emigration within the Ancient Near East (Orientalia Lovaniensia Analecta 65), Leuven. (co-editor A. Schoors)

Series and Journals Edited — Advisor

2007-

Cornell University Studies in Assyriology and Sumerology 1- (editorial committee)

1995-2007

Subartu I-XX (editorial board)

1989-1997

Mesopotamian History and Environment, Series II-III (advisory board)

1987-1996

Northern Akkad Project Reports 1-10 (advisory board)

1984-2005

Orientalia Lovaniensia Periodica 15-31 (editor as member of department Orientalistiek/Oosterse Studies Katholieke Universiteit Leuven)

1984-

Orientalia Lovaniensia Analecta 16- (editor as member of department Orientalistiek/Oosterse Studies Katholieke Universiteit Leuven)

Articles

2012

"Strontium Isotopic and Tree-Ring Signatures of *Cedrus brevifolia* in Cyprus", *Journal of Analytical Atomic Spectometry* XX, forthcoming. (co-authors: S. Rich, S.W. Manning, P. Degryse, F. Vanhaecke)

2011

"The Jebleh Plain through History: Tell Tweini and its Intercultural Contacts in the Bronze and Early Iron Age", in K. Duistermaat and I. Regulski (eds.) *Intercultural Contacts in the Ancient Mediterranean* (Orientalia Lovaniensia Analecta 202), 183-203. (co-author: J. Bretschneider)

"Medieval coastal Syrian vegetation patterns in the principality of Antioch", *The Holocene* 21(2), 251-262. (co-authors: D. Kaniewski, E. Van Campo, E. Paulissen, H. Weiss, T. Otto, J. Bakker, I. Rossignol)

"The Sea People, from Cuneiform Tablets to Carbon Dating", *PLoS One* 6(6), e20232. (co-authors: D. Kanwieski, E. Van Campo, T. Boiy, K. Vansteenhuyse, G. Jans, K. Nys, H. Weiss, T. Otto, J. Bretschneider)

2010

"Tell Tweini à Travers les Millénaires: L'Histoire er l'Archéologie", in M. Al-Maqdissi et al. (eds.) *Tell Tweini. Onze Campagnes de Fouilles Syro-Belges (1999-2010)*, Damas, 15-76. (co-author: J. Bretschneider)

"Description Topographique de Tell Tweini", in M. Al-Maqdissi, J. Bretschneider, K. Van Lerberghe, M. Badawi (eds.) *Tell Tweini. Onze Campagnes de Fouilles Syro-Belges (1999-2010)*. Damas, 9-14. (co-authors: M. Al-Maqdissi, M. Badawi, J. Bretschneider)

"Late Second-Early First Millennium BC Abrupt Climate Changes in Coastal Syria and their Possible Significance for the History of the Eastern Mediterranean", *Quaternary Research* 74, 207-21. (co-authors: D. Kaniewski, E. Paulissen, E. Van Campo, H. Weiss, T. Otto, J. Bretschneider)

"Kassite Mercenairies at Abieshuh's Fortress", in A. Kleinerman and J. M. Sasson (eds.) *Why Should Someone Who Knows Something Conceal it?*, Bethesda, 181-187. (co-author: G. Voet)

2009

"Klimaatverandering was ondergang voor Midden Oosten", *EOS* 2009 (12), Antwerpen, 70-73.

"Wild or cultivated Olea europaea L. in the Eastern Mediterranean during the middle-late Holocene? A pollen-numerical approach", *The Holocene* 19(7), 1039-1047. (co-authors: D. Kaniewski, E. Paulissen, E. Van Campo, J. Bakker, M. Waelkens)

"Living with the dead, Tell Tweini: Middle Bronze Age Tombs in an Urban Context", in J. M. Córdoba et al. (eds.) *Proceedings of the 5th International Congress on the Archaeology of the Ancient Near East - Madrid 2006*, Madrid, 140-144. (co-authors: H. Hameeuw, K. Vansteenhuyse, G. Jans, J. Bretschneider)

"Late Helladic Ceramics at Tell Tweini and the Kingdom of Ugarit", in J. M. Córdoba et al. (eds.) *Proceedings of the 5th International Congress on the Archaeology of the Ancient Near East - Madrid 2006*, Madrid 2009, 359-364. (co-authors: K. Vansteenhuyse, M. Al-Maqdissi, P. Degryse)

2008

"Tell Tweini, Ancient Gibala, between 2600 B.C.E. and 333 B.C.E.", in J. Bretschneider and K. Van Lerberghe (eds.) *In Search of Gibala, An archaeological and historical study based on eight seasons of excavations at Tel Tweini (Syria) in the A and C fields (1999-2007)* (Aula Orientalis-Supplementa 24), Barcelona, 11-68. (co-author: J. Bretschneider)

"The Syro-Belgian 'Tell Tweini' Project", in J. Bretschneider and K. Van Lerberghe (eds.) *In Search of Gibala, An archaeological and historical study based on eight seasons of excavations at Tel Tweini (Syria) in the A and C fields (1999-2007)* (Aula Orientalis-Supplementa 24), Barcelona, 1-3. (co-author: J. Bretschneider)

"Middle East coastal ecosystem response to middle-to-late Holocene abrupt climate changes", *Proceedings of the National Academy of Sciences* 105(37), 13941-13946. (co-authors: D. Kaniewski, E. Paulissen, E. Van Campo, M. Al-Maqdissi, J. Bretschneider)

"The Late Bronze and Iron Age in the Jebleh Region: A View from Tell Tweini", in H. Kühne, R. Czichon and F. Kreppner (eds.) *Proceedings of the 4th International Congress on Archaeology of the Ancient Near East-Berlin,* Wiesbaden, 33-46. (co-authors: J. Bretschneider, K. Vansteenhuyse, M. Maqdissi)

"Tell Tweini", in G. De Nutte et al. (eds.) *Syria Incognita? Het verborgen verleden van de Syrische kuststreek*, Leuven, 7-11. (co-author: J. Bretschneider)

"The Occupation Levels of Tell Tweini and their Historical Implications", in R. Biggs, J. Myers and M. Roth (eds.), *Proceedings of the 51st Rencontre Assyriologique Internationale - Chicago* (Studies in the Ancient Oriental Civilization 62), Chicago, 341-350. (co-authors: M. Al-Maqdissi, M. Badawy, J. Bretschneider, H. Hameeuw, G. Jans, K. Vansteenhuyse, G. Voet)

2007

"Power and Monument: Past and Present", in J. Bretschneider, K. Van Lerberghe and J. Driessen (eds.) *Power & Architecture. Monumental Public Architecture in the Bronze Age Near East and Aegean* (Orientalia Lovaniensia Analecta 156), Leuven, 3-9. (co-authors: J. Bretschneider, G. Jans)

"Environmental Changes in the Jebleh Plain (Syria). Geophysical, Geomorphologic, Palynological & Archaeological Research", *Res Antiquae* 4, 3-10. (co-authors: M. Al-Maqdissi, J. Bretschneider, P. Degryse, H. Hameeuw, D. Kaniewski, E. Paulissen, S. Van Simaeys)

2006

"The Clergy and Religion Institutions of Nippur in the Late Old-Babylonian Period", in G. Haayer, R. J. van der Spek and F. A. M. Wiggermann (eds.) *Studies in Ancient Near Eastern Weltanschauung, presented to Marten Stol on the occasion of his 65th birthday, 10 November 2005, and his retirement from the Vrije Universiteit Amsterdam*, Leiden - Boston, 127-131.

2005

"Tell Tweini, Ancient Gibala, in the Bronze Age", *Agypten und Levante. Egypt and the Levant. International Journal for Egyptian Archaeology and*

Related Disciplines XIV, 215-30. (co-authors: J. Bretschneider, M. Al-Maqdissi, K. Vansteenhuyse, J. Driessen)

"Digitizing the Cuneiform Tablets from Beydar", in A. Bowman and M. Brady (eds.) *Images and Artefacts*, Royal Society/Britsh Academy, 85-96. (co-authors: C. Vandecasteele, L. Van Gool, J. Van Rompay, P. Wambacq)

"Easy and cost-effective cuneiform digitizing", in M. Mudge, N. Ryan and R. Scopigno (eds.) *The 6th International Symposium on Virtual Reality, Archaeology and Cultural Heritage (VAST2005)*, Pisa, 73-80. (co-authors: G. Willems, F. Verbiest, W. Moreau, H. Hameeuw, L. Van Gool)

2004

"Tell Toueini", in Y. Calvet (ed.), *Le Royaume d'Ougarit: aux origines de l'alphabet*, Paris, 60-61. (co-authors: Al-Maqdissi M., M. Badawi, J. Bretschneider)

"More Old-Babylonian Soldiers at Sabum", in H. Waetzoldt (ed.) *Von Sumer nach Ebla und zurück, Festschrift Giovanni Pettinato zum 27. September 1999 gewidmet von Freunden, Kollegen und Schülern* (Heidelberger Studien zum Alten Orient, Bd 9), Heidelberg, 313-325.

"Texts from Seasons 1996-2002", in L. Milano et al. (eds.), *Third Millennium Cuneiform Texts from Tell Beydar (seasons 1996-2002)* (Subartu XII), Turnhout, 83-121. (co-authors: L. Milano, W. Sallaberger, Ph. Talon, K. Van Lerberghe,

2003

"Private and Public: The Ur-Utu Archive at Sippar-Amnānum (Tell ed-Der)", in M. Brosius (ed.) *Ancient Archives and Archival Traditions*, Oxford, 59-77.

2002

"Bronze and Iron Ceramics from Tell Tweini (Syria): Some Preliminary Results", *Orient Express: Notes et Nouvelles d'Archeologie Orientale* 2, 39-44. (co-authors: K. Vansteenhuyse, M. Al-Maqdissi)

"Nabada Potters: Masters in Clay Preparation or Just Plain Clay Importers?", in V. Kilikoglou et al. (eds.) *Modern Trends in Scientific Studies on Ancient Ceramics* (BAR Int. Series 1011), Oxford, 343-349. (co-authors: T. Broekmans, A. Adriaens)

2001

"A Phoenician Site at Tell Tweini, Jebleh in Syria", *American Journal of Archaeology* 105(1), 274-274. (co-authors: T. Cunningham, J. Bretschneider)

2000

"Gibala. The first two Excavations - 1999-2000", *Ugarit-Forschungen* 31, 75-131. (co-authors: J. Bretschneider, T. Cunningham)

1999

"Naturwissenschaft und Archäologie - Das Interdisziplinäre Projekt Tell Beydar", in J. Bretschneider and G. Jans (eds.), *Beydar. Mitteilungen über die Erforschung eines urbanen Zentrums im Norden Alt-Syriens 3*, Münster, 79-82.

"Tell Beydar: K.U.Leuven Project: Talen en Culturen van Boven-Mesopotamië", in K. Van Lerberghe, G. Voet and M. Debruyne (eds.) *Omtrent Beydar. De Talen en Culturen van Noord-Syrië*, Leuven, 1-12. (co-author: G. Voet)

"Het archief Ontdekt te Beydar", in K. Van Lerberghe, G. Voet and M. Debruyne (eds.) *Omtrent Beydar. De Talen en Culturen van Noord-Syrië*, Leuven, 39-42. (co-author: G. Voet)

1998

"Old-Babylonian Soldiers at Sabum", in M. Dietrich and O. Loretz (eds.) *dub.sar anta-men. Studien zur Altorientalistik* (AOAT 253), Münster, 447-456.

1997

"Ausgrabungen in der Kranzhügelstadt Tell Beydar", *Antike Welt* 28(4), 289-296. (co-author: J. Bretschneider)

"L'écriture cunéiforme classique, le deuxième millénaire", in Ph. Talon and K. Van Lerberghe (eds.) *En Syrie, aux origines de l'écriture*, Turnhout, 71-76.

"L'épigraphie, quelles perspectives?", in Ph. Talon and K. Van Lerberghe (eds.) *En Syrie, aux origines de l'écriture*, Turnhout, 97-102. (co-author: P. Wambacq)

"Les nouvelles recherches environnementales", in Ph. Talon and K. Van Lerberghe (eds.) *En Syrie, aux origines de l'écriture*, Turnhout, 171-178. (co-author: R. Decorte)

"La place de Tell Beydar dans le monde mésopotamien", in Ph. Talon and K. Van Lerberghe (eds.) *En Syrie, aux origines de l'écriture*, Turnhout, 179-183. (co-authors: J. Bretschneider, M. Lebeau, Ph. Talon)

"A Poor Man of Sippar", *Altorientalische Forschungen* 24, 148-157. (co-author: G. Voet)

1996

"The Livestock", in F. Ismail et al. (eds.) *Administrative Documents from Tell Beydar (seasons 1993-1995)* (Subartu II), Turnhout, 107-118.

"The Beydar Tablets and the History of the Northern Jezireh", in F. Ismail et al. (eds.) *Administrative Documents from Tell Beydar (seasons 1993-1995)* (Subartu II), Turnhout, 119-122.

1995

"Kassites and Old Babylonian Society: A Reappriaisal", in K. Van Lerberghe and A. Schoors (eds.) *Immigration and Emigration within the Ancient Near East* (Orientalia Lovaniensia Analecta 65), Leuven, 379-393.

"Tell Beydar: 'The Missing Link'?", *Phoenix* 41(1), Leiden, 27-42. (co-author: G. Voet)

1994

"An Old Babylonian Clone", in H. Gasche et al. (eds.) *Cinquante-deux réflexions sur le Proche-Orient ancien, offertes en hommage à Léon De Meyer* (Mesopotamian History and Environment, Occasional Publications II), Ghent, 159-168. (co-author: G. Voet)

"The Ladies Amat-Aja and Šat-Aja, Business Associates under Hammurabi", *Orientalia Lovaniensia Periodica* 25, 5-25.

1993

"Rituals and Profits in the Ur-Utu Archive", in J. Quaegebeur (ed.), *Ritual and sacrifice in the Ancient Near East* (Orientalia Lovaniensia Analecta 55), Leuven, 435-449. (co-author: M. Tanret)

"On Storage in Old-Babylonian Sippar", *Orientalia Lovaniensia Periodica* 24, 29-40.

"Sealing in Philadelphia and elsewhere", *Acta Archaeologica Lovaniensia* 32, 43-58. (co-author: G. Voet)

1991

"On "Quasi-Hüllentafeln"", *Northern Akkad Project Reports* 6, 3-8. (co-author: G. Voet)

"Tell ed-Der 1985-1987. Les vestiges Meso-Babyloniens: III. Les découvertes épigraphiques de Chantier E3", *Northern Akkad Project Reports* 6, 73-74.

1990

"Language in Sumer and Akkad", in P. Swiggers and A. Wouters (eds.) *Le langage dans l'Antiquité* (La pensée linguistique 3), Leuven, 47-55.

1989

"A Long Lasting Life", in H. Behrens et al. (eds.) *Dumu-E2-Dub-ba-a, Studies presented to A. Sjöberg*, Philadelphia, 525-538. (co-author: G. Voet)

"Une tablette administrative paléobabylonienne de Nippur", in M. Lebeau and Ph. Talon (eds.) *Reflets des Deux Fleuves. Volume de Mélanges Offerts à André Finet* (Akkadica Supplementum 6), Leuven, 177-180.

"Copper and Bronze in Ebla and in Mesopotamia", in H. Waetzoldt and H. Hauptmann (eds.) *Wirtschaft und Gesellschaft von Ebla* (HSAO 2), Heidelberg, 253-255.

1986

"Un élamite à Sippar-Amnanum", in L. De Meyer et al. (eds.) *Fragmenta Historiae Elamicae, Mélanges offerts à M.-J. Stève*, Paris, 151-155.

"Kish: Première ville royale après le déluge", *Dossiers Histoire et Archéologie* 103 (mars), 62-64.

"The Role of the City of Babylon in the Old-Babylonian Periods", *Sumer* 41, 108-109.

1984

"Note sur les tablettes en métal du palais de Sargon à Khorsabad", *Orientalia Lovaniensia Periodica* 15, 247-248.

"Contribution à l'étude des métaux de Tell ed-Dēr", in L. De Meyer (ed.) *Tell ed-Dēr IV, progress reports*, Leuven, 97-117. (co-author: L. Maes)

"Nieuwe problemen in verband met de identificatie van tin en lood in Mesopotamië", *Belgisch Tijdschrift voor Filologie en Geschiedenis* 61, 1068.

1983

"Immobiliëntransacties en eigendomstitels in de oudbabylonische periode", in K. R. Veenhof (ed.), *Schrijvend Verleden*, Leiden, 143-149.

1982

"New Data from the archives found in the House of Ur-Utu at Tell ed-Der", in H. Berger (ed.) *Vorträge gehalten auf der 28. Rencontre assyriologique internationale in Wien, 6.-10. Juli 1981* (Archiv für Orientforchung, Beiheft 19), Wien, 279-283.

"À propos d'un outil agricole, la habuda", in J. Quaegebeur (ed.) *Studia Paulo Naster Oblata II* (Orientalia Lovaniensia Analecta 13), Leuven, 279-286.

"L'arrachement de l'emblème šurinnum", in G. van Driel et al. (eds.) *Zikir Šumim: assyriological studies presented to F. R. Kraus on the occasion of his seventieth birthday*, Leiden, 245-257.

"Sumer en Akkad", *Nieuwe Tijdingen* 7, 19-23.

1979

"An Enigmatic Cylinder Seal Mentioning the *ushūm*-Tree in the Royal Museum of Art and History, Brussels", in M. Stol, *On Trees, Mountains, and Millstones in the Ancient Near East*, Leiden, 31-49.

"Une tablette de Drehem et le fonctionnaire Šu-Irra", *Orientalia Lovaniensia Periodica* 10, 109-123.

1978

"De slaven en hun werk in de Oud-Babylonische periode", *Akkadica* 7, 2-13.

Reviews

2003

"On a Recent Review by L. De Meyer", in Akkadica 124, 239-241. (co-authors: M. Stol, N. Yoffee)

1994

"Siegelabrollungen auf frühaltbabylonischen Tontafeln in der Yale Babylonian Collection, 1992, by F. Blocher", in *BiOr* 51, 441-442. (co-author: G. Voet)

1986

"Isin-Išān Bahrīyāt II. Die Ergebnisse der Ausgrabungen 1975-1978, 1981, by B. Hrouda", in *AfO* 33, 86-92. (co-author: H. Gasche)

1981

"Hammurapi von Babylon und seine Zeit, 1977, by H. Klengel", in *BiOr* 38, 634-535.

1981

"Early Old Babylonian Documents (Yale Oriental Series - Babylonian Texts XIV), 1978, by S. D. Simmons", in *OrNS* 50, 203-209.

1978

"Ancient Mesopotamian Art and Selected Texts: The Pierpont Morgan Library, 1977, by W. W. Hallo, E. Paroda, B. L. Schlossman (eds.)", in *BiOr* 35, 261-262. (co-author: G. Voet)

1977

"Die Schlussklauseln der altbabylonischen Kauf- und Tauschverträge (Münchener Beiträge zur Papyrusforschung und antiken Rechtsgeschichte 4), 1922/1974, by M. San Nicolo", in *BiOr* 34, 194-196.

Collaboration

2005

M. T. Roth, *The Assyrian Dictionary Volume 12: P*, Chicago. (as CAD Resident Staff)

1984

F. R. Kraus, *Königliche Verfügungen in altbabylonischer Zeit*, Leiden. (as Wetenschappelijk Ambtenaar)

Doctoral Thesis

1980

Oudbabylonische documentaire teksten uit het huis van Ur-Utu, opperklaagpriester van Annunītum te Sippar-Amnānum, Gent. (promotor L. De Meyer)

EXPENDITURES BY THE GU-ZA-LÁ OFFICIAL AT MAŠKAN-ŠAPIR FROM THE TIME OF RIM-SIN OF LARSA

Kathleen ABRAHAM and Uri GABBAY
Bar-Ilan University, Ramat-Gan and Hebrew University, Jerusalem

While cataloguing a group of 341 tablets from the Shlomo Moussaieff collection that were on temporary loan to Bar-Ilan University for roughly two years until January 2008, we came across a group of tablets that list expenditures by an official at Maškan-šapir.[1]

The thirteen tablets published here belong to one dossier in which the principal figure is a man by the name of Warad-Nanna, a gu-za-lá-official.[2] He was stationed at Maskan-šapir where he administered the disbursals of beer, flour and barley to various destinations. This is clear from the phrase that concludes all but one of the tablets (no. 11; but this tablet surely belongs to the same group). It stands before the date formula and reads:

> ki ìr-^{d}nanna gu-za-lá šà maš-kán-šabra^{ki} ba-zi
> (Commodities) expenditured by Warad-Nanna, the gu-za-lá official, at Maškan-šapir

The main destination of these expenditures was the *naptānum* ceremonial banquet. It occurs in eleven of the thirteen cases, dated between Rim-Sin's sixth and eighth year. Nos. 1 and 13, which lack a reference to *naptānum*, happen to be the earliest and latest texts in the dossier.

In this paper we will first edit the tablets in chronological order and then discuss their content in broad outline, touching upon matters of typology,

[1] We thank Dr. Shlomo Moussaieff for giving us the opportunity to study the tablets and publish them. The administrative texts, which are the majority of this collection, were catalogued by Kathleen Abraham, Uri Gabbay and Marcel Sigrist. We are grateful to Marcel Sigrist for his help in the preliminary identification and reading of the tablets. We would also like to thank Aage Westenholz and Yuval Levavi who were in charge of baking and restoring the tablets.

[2] For gu-za-lá, cf. Goodnick-Westenholz and Westenholz 2006, 124-127. Note that the *gu-zal-lu* mentioned in relation to Maškan-šapir in an OB text probably from Larsa dating to Rim-Sin's reign (Goodnick-Westenholz and Westenholz 2006, 122, ii:3-5), is probably to be understood as *kuzallu*, a profession connected to sheep (Stol 2007, 410).

chronology, and history. We hope with this publication of Old Babylonian tablets to honor Karel Van Lerberghe, who is to be credited, among his many achievements, for having identified hundreds of Old Babylonian legal and administrative tablets in the Rosen Collection at Cornell University and having provided exhaustive editions of the tablets (Van Lerberghe and Voet 2009).

Edition of the Texts

1. SM Tablet 281 (27/vi/6 Rim-Sin)

Obv. 10 gur zì-gu
10 + x gur še
⸢šu-ti⸣-a *ka-ra-na-tum*
(*vacat*)
ki ìr-^{d}nanna gu-za-lá
⸢šà⸣ maš-kán-šabra^{ki}
ba-zi
Rev. (*vacat*)
iti ⸢kin-^{d}inanna⸣ ud-27-kam
mu é ⸢^{d}bára-ul⸣-e-ĝar-⸢ra⸣
šà ad[a]b^{ki} mu-un-dù-⸢a⸣
⸢*ù* alan⸣ kù-⸢si$_{22}$⸣ ^{d}EN.ZU-*i-din-nam*
lugal lars[a^{ki}-m]a mu-dím-ma

2. SM Tablet 282 (10^{+}/vii/6 Rim-Sin)

Obv. [2 gur] d[abin]
[0;3.1] z[ì-gu]
[0;0.2 níĝ-àr]-⸢ra še⸣-bi [0;0.3]
⸢*na-ap-ta*⸣-*nu-u*[*m*]
0;1 dabin lú ur-^{d}[ ]
0;2.3 še šà-gal [anše kúnga]
0;1.2 dabin sá-du$_{11}$ $^{lú⸢}$kin⸣-[gi$_{4}$-a]
⸢2;2.2⸣ gur dabin
0;3.1 zì-gu
0;3 še
(*vacat*)
Rev. ki ìr-⸢^{d}⸣[nanna] gu-za-lá
šà maš-[kán-ša]bra⸢^{ki}⸣
ba-zi

(*vacat*)
iti du$_6$-kù ud-10+x-[kam]
[mu] é-^{d}bára-ul-⸢e-ĝar⸣-[ra]
[šà ada]b$^{⸢ki⸣}$ [mu-dù-a]

3. SM Tablet 312 (7/viii/6 Rim-Sin)

Obv. 3 gur dabin
0;2.1 zì-gu
0;0.2 níĝ-àr-ra še-bi 0;0.3
na-ap-ta-nu-um
0;2.3 še šà-gal anše kúnga!
0;1.3 dabin 0;0.1 zì-gu
sá-du$_{11}$ ^{lú}kin-gi$_4$-a
3;1.3 gur dabin
0;2.2 zì-gu
0;3 še
Rev. [k]i ìr-⸢^{d}nanna⸣ gu-za-lá
šà maš-kán-⸢šabra⸣^{ki}
ba-zi
(*vacat*)
iti ^{ĝiš}apin-du$_8$-a ud-7-kam
mu é ^{d}bára-ul-⸢e⸣-ĝar-ra
šà adab^{ki} mu-dù-a

4. SM Tablet 300 (13/viii/6 Rim-Sin)

Obv. 3 gur dabin
0;2.1 zì-gu
0;0.2 níĝ-àr-ra še-bi 0;0.3
na-ap-⸢ta⸣-nu-⸢um⸣
0;2.3 še šà-gal anše kúnga
⸢2⸣ gur dabin *a-na u-bar*-$^{d⸢}$utu⸣
0;2 dabin 0;0.3 zì-gu dumu-munus lú-^{d}dumu-zi-da
0;2 dabin sá-du$_{11}$ ^{lú}kin-[g]i$_4$-a
5;4 (erasure) gur dabin
0;2.⸢4⸣ zì-gu
0;3 še
Rev. ki ìr-^{d}nanna gu-za-lá
ba-zi
(*vacat*)

iti ^{ĝiš}˹apin-du$_{8}$˺-a ud-13-kam
mu é ^{d}bára-ul-e-ĝar-ra
šà adab^{ki} mu-un-dù-a
ù alan kù-gi ˹^{d}˺EN.ZU-*i-din-na*[*m*]
lugal larsa^{ki}-ma
mu-un-dím-ma

5. SM Tablet 329 (10/vii/7 Rim-Sin)

Obv. ˹1$^{?}$ gur˺ ˹kaš˺-ĝin *na-ap-ta-nu-um*
0;4 sá-du$_{11}$ érin˹$^{ḫi.a}$˺ lú unug^{ki}
˹0;3$^{?}$ sá-du$_{11}$˺ érin$^{ḫi.a}$ lú *ì-si-in*^{ki}
0;0.1 ˹^{d}EN.ZU˺-*na-wi-*˹*ir*˺
0;0.1 x x (x)-*la*-AN
˹0;0.1˺ *ik-*˹*ka*$^{?}$˺*-nu*
[0;0.1] (x x) mi$^{?}$ x
lú murgu^{ki}
0;0.1 ^{d}EN.ZU-*iš-me-*[*an-n*]*i*
0;0.1 *i-*[*din*]-^{d}[nan]na$^{?}$
lú [UD$^{?}$].UNUG^{ki}
0;0.1 ^{d}EN.ZU-*i-din-nam*
0;0.1 *ḫa-am*$^{!?}$*-sú-um*
lú *an-za-an*
0;0.1 *bur-ri-ia*
0;0.1 *ta-ri-bu-um*
0;0.1 *la-qí-pu-um*
0;0.1 ^{d}IM-*am-mar*
0;0.1 ^{d}EN.˹ZU˺-*ga-mil*
Rev. 0;0.1 *mi-in-*[ ]
lú *ì-si-*˹*in*˺$^{[ki]}$
0;0.1 DINGIR-*šu-ba-ni*
0;0.1 *i-lu-qí*$^{?}$*-ba*
0;0.1 *a-da-ia-tum*
0;0.1 *a-bu-wa-qar*
0;0.1 *ì-lí-ma-a-ḫi*
0;0.1 *a-bu-*^{d}*we-er*
0;0.1 *iḫ-bi-it-ìr-ra*
0;0.1 *da-aq-qum*
0;0.1 *ìr-ra-ba-ni*
0;0.1 *i-ri-ba-am*

0;0.1 *a-ḫu-ni*
lú *èš-nun*^{ki}
0;0.1 *ta-ak-ku-ú-a*
˹lú˺ *ak-za-a*^{ki}
3;1.˹2$^{?}$˺ gur kaš-ĝin
ki ˹ìr-^{d}nanna˺ gu-za-lá
šà maš-kán-šabra$^{˹ki˺}$
ba-zi
U.E. iti du$_6$-kù ud-10-kam
mu abul-a 2-bi maš-kán-˹šabra˺^{ki}
mu-dù-˹a˺

NOTES

14. *An-za-an* (see also no. 9:7) is the common spelling for Anšan in Elamite sources (Vallat 1993, 14-15). Note, however, that most references are later than our tablet (Middle Elamite period). The Elamite writing with ZA in our line and in no. 9:7 (rather than the regular writing with ŠA), points to the close connection between Maškan-šapir and Elam.

29. For this name see Zadok 1987, 12 (no. 95): *daq-qum* lú Elam^{ki}, and cf. Hinz and Koch 1987, 248-249, 271: *da-ak-ki-ya* (derived from *da-ak* "deponiert" or "lebendig").

34. For a similar name construction, see perhaps *ta-at-tu-ú-a* (Hinz and Koch 1987, 257-258).

35. For *ak-za-a*^{ki} (also in no. 11:10), see Groneberg 1980, 10. Note that the occurrence of this toponym in TIM 2, 14:24 should probably be dated to the reign of Rim-Sin of Larsa (Cagni 1980, 11, n. 14a). We suggest that this is a variant syllabic writing for Akšak. For the use of the sign ZA instead of ŠA, cf. the writing of Anšan as *an-za-an*^{ki} (see note to line 14 above). Note also other syllabic spellings of Akšak without the final consonant (Groneberg 1980, 7-8).

6. SM Tablet 262 (12/vii/7 Rim-Sin)

Obv. ˹3 gur˺ dabin
0;2.3 zì-gu
0;0.2 níĝ-àr-ra še-bi ˹0;0.3˺
na-ap-ta-˹nu˺-um
0;2.1 (še) šà-[ga]l anše kúnga
1 gur zì-gu 1 gur dabin ˹dumu$^{?}$˺ é-dub-ba
0;3 dabin 6 érin ^{lú}má-lá *ša* $^{˹gi˺}$pisaĝ-im-sar-ra
0;0.5 dabin kurum$_6$$^{˹ḫi-a˺}$ MÍ nam-ra *ù* 3 érin *a-sí-ru*
2 gur dabin 2 gur še
sá-˹du$_{11}$˺ érin$^{ḫi-a}$ lú *ì-si-in*^{ki}

2 ⸢gur⸣ da[bin] 2 gur še
sá-du$_{11}$ érin$^{ḫi-⸢a⸣}$ lú unug^{ki}
0;2 dabin 0;0.1 zì-gu
sá-du$_{11}$ ^{lú}kin-gi$_{4}$-a
Rev. 9;0.5 gur dabin
1;2.4 gur zì-gu
4;2.4 gur še
ki ìr-^{d}nanna gu-za-lá
šà maš-kán-šabra^{ki}
ba-zi
(*vacat*)
iti du$_{6}$-kù ud-12-kam
mu abul-a 2-bi maš-kán-šabra^{ki} / mu-un-dù-a
ù ⸢e⸣ a-šà <šà>-túm-ma
⸢4⸣ [d]anna mu-⸢un⸣-si-ga

NOTES

6. For dumu é-dub-ba in administrative and military context, see Stol 2004, 780 with n. 961.

7. SM Tablet 339 (1/vii/8 Rim-Sin)

Obv. 0;3 dabin
0;2 zì-gu
0;0.1 2 sìla níĝ-àr-ra še-bi 0;0.1 8 sìla
na-ap-ta-nu-um
0;1.5 še šà-gal anše kúnga
0;2 dabin dam ^{d}EN.ZU-*mu-pa-še-er*
0;0.1 9 sìla dabin 8 sìla zì-gu
sá-du$_{11}$ ^{lú}kin-gi$_{4}$-a
1;0.1 9 sìla gur dabin
0;2 8 sìla zì-gu
0;2 8 sìla še
(*vacat*)
Rev. [ki] ìr-^{d}nan[n]a⸢gu⸣-z[a-lá]
šà maš-kán-šab[ra^{k}]^{i}
ba-⸢zi⸣
(*vacat*)
iti du$_{6}$-ku ⸢ud-1⸣-kam
mu é ⸢^{d}en-ki šà úri⸣^{ki}-ma

ù ⸢é ^{d}nin-é-nim⸣-ma
šà é ^{d}⸢nin-mar-ki⸣
mu-dù-a

8. SM Tablet 286 (3/vii/8 Rim-Sin)

Obv. 0;2.4 kaš-ĝin *na-ap-ta-nu-*⸢*um*⸣
0;2.4 kaš-ĝin
ki ìr-^{d}nanna gu-za-lá
šà maš-kán-šabra^{ki}
ba-zi
Rev. (*vacat*)
iti du$_{6}$-kù ud-3-kam
mu é ^{d}en-ki šà úri^{ki}-ma
ù é ^{d}nin-é-nim-ma
šà é ^{d}nin-mar-ki
mu-dù

9. SM Tablet 324 (2/viii/8 Rim-Sin)

Obv. ⸢0;3.3⸣ kaš-ĝin *na-ap-*⸢*ta-nu-um*⸣
0;0.1 x x [ ]
0;0.1 ^{d}EN.ZU-[ ]
lú x (x x)$^{⸢ki⸣}$
0;0.1 ìr-^{d}nanna
0;0.1 ^{d}EN.ZU-*ma-lik*
lú *an-za*$^{!}$(A)-*an*
0;4.⸢2⸣ kaš-ĝin
(*vacat*)
⸢ki⸣ ìr-^{d}nanna gu-za-lá
šà maš-kán-šabra$^{⸢ki⸣}$
ba-zi
Rev. (*vacat*)
iti ^{ĝiš}apin-du$_{8}$-a
ud-2-kam
mu é ^{d}en-ki šà úri^{ki}-ma
⸢*ù*⸣ é ^{d}nin-⸢é-nim-ma⸣
šà é ^{d}nin-mar-ki ⸢mu-un-dù⸣-a

NOTES

4. Probably read murgu (for Malgium).
7. For an-za-an, see note to no. 5:14 above.

10. SM Tablet 319 (9/ix/8 Rim-Sin)

Obv. ⸢0;3⸣ kaš-ĝin *na-ap-⸢ta-nu⸣-um*
0;0.1 *a-bi-a-sa-ad*
0;0.1 ^{d}utu-*a-bi*
0;0.1 *šu-ni-ia*
lú *èš-⸢nun⸣*^{ki}
    0;3.⸢3 kaš⸣-ĝin
(*vacat*)
⸢ki⸣ ⸢ìr-^{d}nanna⸣ ⸢gu-za-lá⸣
⸢šà⸣ maš-kán-[š]abra$^{⸢\text{ki}⸣}$
⸢ba⸣-zi
(*vacat*)
Rev. iti ⸢gan-gan-è⸣ ud.9.kam
mu é $^{⸢d⸣}$en-ki šà úri^{ki}-ma
mu-un-dù-a

11. SM Tablet 293 (20/ix/8 Rim-Sin)

Obv. 0;3 kaš-ĝin *na-ap-ta-nu-um*
0;0.1 *i-lam*?*-du-⸢du⸣*
0;0.1 *a-da-a-a-tum*
0;0.1 *a-bi-a-sa-ad*
0;0.1 ^{d}utu-*a-bi*
0;0.1 *šu-ni-ia*
0;0.1 x x-*bi*
lú *èš-nun-na*^{ki}
Rev. 0;0.1 lú *ì-si-*[*in*^{ki}]
lú *ak-za-a*^{ki}
    0;4.1 kaš-gin
(*vacat*)
iti ⸢gan-gan-è?⸣ ud-20-kam
mu ⸢é⸣ ^{d}en-ki šà úri^{ki}-ma
mu-un-dù-a

NOTES

10. For *ak-za-a*^{ki}, see note to no. 5:35.

12. SM Tablet 291 (21/ix/8 Rim-Sin)

Obv. [0;4] dabin
0;2 zì-gu

0;0.1 5 sìla níĝ-àr-ra še-bi 0;0.2 2 sìla
na-ap-ta-nu-um
0;1.5 še šà-gal anše kúnga
0;0.2 dabin 7 (sìla) zì-gu
sá-du$_{11}$ ^{lú}kin-gi$_4$-a
  0;4.2 dabi[n]
  0;2.0 7 (sìla) zì-g[u]
  0;2.˹1˺ 2 sìla še
(*vacat*)
ki ìr-^{d}nanna gu-za-lá
šà maš-kán-šabra^{ki}
ba-zi
Rev. iti gan-gan-è ud-21-kam
mu é ^{d}en-ki šà úri^{ki}-ma
˹*ù*˺ é ^{d}nin-é-nim-ma
[*ù*] ˹é˺ ^{d}nin-mar-ki
mu-dù-a

13. SM Tablet 332 (30/ix/13^{a} Rim-Sin)

Obv.

0;2.3 še	0;1.0 dabin	0;0.1 5 sìla zì-gu	˹0;1.5˺ kaš-sig$_5$ še-bi 0;2.4 5 sìla	0;2.3 (še) kaš-ĝin	˹*a*? *-na*˺ *la-*˹*wi*!?*-la*?˺*-an*
0;0.3	0;0.1		˹0;1.0˺ kaš-ú-sa še-bi 0;0.1	0;0.1	dingir-˹*na*˺*-ṣir*
0;0.3	0;0.1		˹0;1.0˺ kaš-ú-sa še-bi 0;0.1	0;0.1	*puzur*$_4$-^{d}mar-tu
0;0.1 5 sìla	5 sì[la]			0;0.1	˹*a*˺*-a-ba-aš-di-*˹*nu*˺*-um*
0;0.1 5 (sìla)	5 (sìla)			0;0.1	^{d}EN.ZU-*i-ri-ba-am*
0;0.1 5 (sìla)	5 (sìla)			0;0.1	^{d}*we-er-a-bu-šu*

0;0.1 5 (sìla)	5 (sìla)			0;0.1	*ma-a-*⸢*ga*⸣
0;0.1 5 (sìla)	5 (sìla)			0;0.1	*ḫa-zi-ru-um*
0;0.1 5 (sìla)	5 (sìla)			0;0.1	*ḫa-am-mu-ra-pi*
0;0.1 5 (sìla)	5 (sìla)			0;0.1	*a-ḫu-wa-qar*

Rev. 2;2.2 še gur
0;1.5 5 sìla dabin
0;0.1 5 sìla zì-gu
sá-du$_{11}$ ^{lú}kin-gi$_{4}$-a *èš-nun*^{ki}
ki ìr-^{d}nanna gu-za-lá
šà maš-kán-šabra^{ki}
ba-zi
iti gan-gan-è ud-30-kam
mu bàd-gal ⸢*iš*⸣*-ku-un-*^{d}nè-iri$_{11}$-gal ba-dù

NOTES

1. If the reading of the PN *la-wi-la-an* in the last column is correct, this would perhaps be the same messenger from Ešnunna mentioned as a recipient of a sheep in a tablet dated to the year Rim-Sin 7 (Ali 2009, 16, no. 1:2-3).

Related Texts

A group of similar texts was recently published by M. Ali (2009). These texts, dated to Rim-Sin 7-9 and 21, list expenditures for the *naptānum*, for various individuals and for messengers from Ešnunna and Uruk.[3] Unlike the texts published here, they record expenditures of sheep and lambs and not of barley and beer.[4]

Another group of tablets that may be relevant to the texts published here is TLB I, nos. 50-54, edited by Leemans (1954, 76-90).[5] This is a

[3] One of the messengers from Ešnunna mentioned in this group may occur in our tablet 13, see note to no. 13:1 above.

[4] Note the term é-^{ĝiš}gu-za in some of these texts (Ali 2009, 16-20, nos. 1:3, 3:3, 4:3, 6:3), which may be connected to the profession gu-za-lá of Warad-Nanna in our texts. Note especially the related writing lú-^{ĝiš}gu-za in some texts (Goodnick-Westenholz and Westenholz 2006, 124).

[5] For no. 54, see also Robson 2004, 132.

group of expenditures of barley and flour for *naptānum*, animal fodder (šà-gal), maintenance (šuku *ṣuḫārē,* šuku PN [no. 51], šuku é [no. 54]) and named individuals. The texts in this group are set in non-tabulated (nos. 50-51) and tabulated (nos. 52-54) form. None of the texts has a year date, but it is generally assumed that they are from the later years of Rim-Sin (Leemans 1954, 71; Robson 2004, 131-132).

A group of ten small tablets was found in house B.59 in Larsa (Charpin 2003, 314). They record an amount of flour (dabin), followed by *naptānum* and the name of the month and day, but not the year. D. Charpin suggests to compare the *naptānum* in these Larsa tablets to the *naptān šarrim* from Mari, but previously he linked them to texts from Tell-ed-Dēr where the same kind of disbursals are categorized as "food provision" (šuku lú) (Charpin 1996, 222).

Lastly, an unpublished text related to our group is mentioned by Civil (2000, 675). During a discussion of a different issue, Civil refers to an unpublished administrative text, dated to Rim-Sin 7: "Among supplies for the *naptanu* of Kudur-Mabuk, and other ritual occasions, the tablet lists several equids, among them the 'horse of Inanna'."[6]

Text Typology

Type A: Flour expenditures (nos. 2-4, 6-7, 12). These documents mention types of flour and groats (dabin, zì-gu, níĝ-àr-ra) for the ceremonial banquet (*naptānum*) and for the regular supplies to the messengers (sá-du$_{11}$ ^{lú}kin-gi$_4$-a), as well as barley (še) for the fodder of the mules (anše kúnga). Texts nos. 3 and 12 mention these three destinations. The other texts in this group are more elaborate than texts nos. 3 and 12. They add to the above mentioned destinations also disbursals to named and unnamed individuals, workmen, and prisoners.[7]

Text no. 1 is also a flour and barley expenditure by Warad-Nanna, but the only beneficiary mentioned is a woman named Karānatum.[8] It is therefore different from the above texts in that no banquet, mules or messengers are mentioned. It is also the earliest text in the dossier.

Type B: Beer expenditures (nos. 5, 8-11). These documents mention beer for the *naptānum* and for various individuals from different localities (PN lú GN).

[6] Or is this another reference to anše kúnga[!] as in our texts?
[7] For details on the beneficiaries, see below.
[8] For this feminine personal name, cf. *CAD* K, 202b.

Type C: Tabular expenditure of flour and beer (text 13). The latest text in the dossier mentions both beer and flour expenditures which were dispensed "for the regular deliveries of the messengers from Ešnunna." The nine recipients in question are listed by name. The "landscape" orientation of the tablet, as well as its tabular nature, are characteristic to the early years of the reign of Rim-Sin (Robson 2004, 128-130). Unlike other tabulated tablets of this period, there is no heading to the table in text no. 13. The first row functions as heading to the first five columns by naming the types of commodities that are dispensed, but also specifies the amounts that are dispensed to the persons who are mentioned in the sixth and final column.

Chronological Framework

Warad-Nanna administered the disbursal of beer, flour and barley at Maškan-šapir in the reign of Rim-Sin. All but one of the texts are dated in autumn or early winter (months vi-ix) of this king's sixth, seventh and eighth year. The table below orders the texts in chronological order and summarizes the evidence that they provide regarding the types of disbursals that fell under Warad-Nanna's responsibility and the date on which he reported about them.

Text No	Disbursals from Maškan-šapir	*naptānum*	day	Month	year	King
1	flour + barley (Type A)	–	26	vi	06	Rim-Sin
2	flour + barley (Type A)	+	10+	vii	06	Rim-Sin
3	flour + barley (Type A)	+	07	viii	06	Rim-Sin
4	flour + barley (Type A)	+	13	viii	06	Rim-Sin
5	beer (Type B)	+	10	vii	07	Rim-Sin
6	flour + barley (Type A)	+	12	vii	07	Rim-Sin
7	flour + barley (Type A)	+	01	vii	08	Rim-Sin
8	beer (Type B)	+	03	vii	08	Rim-Sin
9	beer (Type B)	+	02	viii	08	Rim-Sin
10	beer (Type B)	+	09	ix	08	Rim-Sin
11	beer (Type B)	+	20	ix	08	Rim-Sin
12	flour + barley (Type A)	+	21	ix	08	Rim-Sin
13	flour + barley and beer (Type C)	–	30	ix	13a	Rim-Sin

As can be seen, Warad-Nanna's first attested report on an expenditure took place in Rim-Sin's sixth year, on the 27th day of month vi (no. 1). It is exceptional in that it mentions only one individual as beneficiary, whereas all future expenditures of barley or flour (also) refer to a banquet (*naptānum*), mules and messengers. Soon afterwards, namely on the 10⁺th day of month vii, another expenditure followed (no. 2), this time of the usual type A. About 3-4 weeks later two more expenditures of type A were organized by Warad-Nanna, separated from each other by six days, namely on the 7th and 13th days of month viii (nos. 3 and 4).

In Rim-Sin's seventh year Warad-Nanna is in charge of two expenditures which are separated from each other by two days. On the 10th of month vii he dispensed beer (no. 5, type B), and on the 12th — flour and barley (no. 6, type A). The beer was for the *naptānum*, as well as for workers and individuals from a variety of cities; the flour and barley were for the usual Type A beneficiaries (*naptānum*, fodder for mules, and messengers), as well as for a scribe, a team of workers in charge of rafts carrying tablet containers, workers from Isin and Uruk, prisoners and captive women.

The first two expenditures in Rim-Sin's eighth year are separated from each other by two days, namely on the 1st and 3rd days of month vii (nos. 7 and 8). The first of these two expenditures is of flour (type A) and the second is of beer (type B). One month later, an additional expenditure of beer takes place (type B), namely on the 2nd day of month viii (no. 9). This time men from various cities are mentioned besides the banquet. Five weeks later, a similar expenditure of beer is recorded (type B), namely on the 9th day of month ix (no. 10). The next expenditure, of beer as well (type B), occurs eleven days later, namely on the 20th of month ix (no. 11), for the *naptānum* and for people from various localities, including six individuals from Ešnunna, three of them identical to the ones listed in no. 10. Finally, one day later, an expenditure of flour and barley (type A) is recorded, namely from the 21st day of month ix (no. 12), destined for the usual banquet, mules and messengers.

A gap of five years occurs before the next known tablet of expenditures by Warad-Nanna. No. 13 (Type C), from the end of month ix of Rim-Sin's 13th year, is different from the previous texts not only in chronological terms, but also in its format (tabular) and to some degree even its content. It combines expenditures of barley, flour and barley for beer[9] on

[9] That barley for the preparation of beer is meant also in the column that only mentions kaš-ĝin is seen by the total amount of barley noted at the end of the tablet, which also includes the amounts for kaš-ĝin beer.

one and the same tablet and organizes the relevant data in a six-column table. The beneficiaries are ten men, messengers of Ešnunna.

Historical Framework

The noun *naptānum* may refer to various types of banquets: cultic banquets to the gods, royal banquets, military banquets and private banquets.[10] In some cases there is only a fine line separating disbursals for a "banquet" from those for the so-called "maintenance" of certain individuals,[11] even to the point that the former are simply categorized as "food provisions" (šuku lú) (Charpin 1996, 222). It is quite possible that the *naptānum* banquets for which Warad-Nanna had to supply various kinds of flour were held in honor of members of the royal family and their entourage. Maškan-šapir is known to have been the residence of members of the royal family of Larsa. Kudur-Mabuk had probably already taken up residence in Maškan-šapir during the end of the reign of Sin-iddinam and he remained firmly in control of Maškan-šapir until the end of Warad-Sin's reign and the beginning of the reign of Rim-Sin (Steinkeller 2004a, 33). Kudur-Mabuk must have died during the first years of Rim-Sin's reign. Since an inscription of Rim-Sin, dealing with the building of Enki's temple in Ur, does not mention Kudur-Mabuk (Frayne 1990, 278-279, no. 6), and since the eighth year name of Rim-Sin mentions the same act (Sigrist 1990, 40-41), Frayne (1990, 270, 278) concluded that Kudur-Mabuk was dead by Rim-Sin 8. According to Steinkeller (2004a, 41, n. 77), Kudur-Mabuk died even earlier, since the installation of statues of Kudur-Mabuk in the year names of Rim-Sin 3 and 5 (Sigrist 1990, 38-39), may indicate that he was dead by then, at least in Rim-Sin 5 which mentions that the statues were brought into é-gal-bar-ra, perhaps a royal funerary chapel (George 1993, 87, no. 311). Therefore, Steinkeller concludes that Kudur-Mabuk died not later than the year Rim-Sin 5.[12]

Our group of texts (excluding no. 13) range between Rim-Sin 6 and 8. Although this may be a coincidence, perhaps one should connect this to the possible death of Kudur-Mabuk just before or during this period. The termination of the *naptānum* texts in Rim-Sin 8 may indicate the decline of Maškan-šapir as a place of political residence in these years,

[10] For *naptānum*, cf. *CAD* N/I, 319-324; Glassner 1987-1990, 259-267; Charpin, 1996, 222; Lafont 2008, 93-98; Ali 2009, 8-27.

[11] Cf. *CAD* N/I, 323.

[12] Steinkeller gives the date as Warad-Sin 5, but this must be a mistake for Rim-Sin 5.

and therefore the royal *naptānum* did not take place there anymore. Later, Rim-Sin seems to have assigned his brother Sin-muballiṭ to be in charge of Maškan-šapir (Steinkeller 2004a, 28-29).[13]

The dates of the Maškan-šapir expenditures may have other historical implications. It may be mere coincidence, but Warad-Nanna's most active years in Maškan-šapir (Rim-Sin 6-8) concur with fortification and irrigation works at Maškan-šapir done by Rim-Sin in this period. Thus, the seventh year of Rim-Sin's reign was named after such works: "Year: He had two large doors built in Maškan-šapir and had a four mile long canal dug for the fields and the pastures" (Sigrist 1990, 40).

Beneficiaries

The following destinations and beneficiaries are found in the texts:

(1) ***Naptānum*** (all texts, except nos. 1 and 13)
The ceremonial banquet (*naptānum*) for which Warad-Nanna had to supply various kinds of flour, barley and beer were probably held in honor of members of the royal family and their entourage. The flour and barley transactions (Type A) always contain three ingredients: dabin (semolina), zì-gu flour, and groats of barley (níĝ-àr-ra). In the three documented expenditures in months vii-viii of Rim-Sin 6 (nos. 2-4, all Type A) and in the only Type A transaction of the year Rim-Sin 7 which occurred in month vii (no. 6), the amounts of these ingredients are equal or similar, ranging between 2-3 *kor* of semolina, 130-190 *sila* of zì-gu flour, and 30 *sila* of barley for the production of 20 *sila* of groats. The amounts change in the two *naptānum* Type A documents of year 8 of Rim-Sin (nos. 7 and 12): the amount of semolina ranges only between 180-240 *sila*, the amount of zì-gu flour is only slightly smaller than in the previous years (120 *sila*), and the amount of barley goes down to 18-22 *sila* for the production of 12-15 *sila* of groats.

One tablet lists beer expenditures for the *naptānum* (Type B) in year Rim-Sin 7 and four tablets list this for year 8. In the document from year Rim-Sin 7 (no. 5), dated to month vii, probably 1 *kor* of beer is listed. Again, the amounts in year 8 of Rim-Sin (nos. 8-11) seem to be considerably smaller, ranging between 160-210 *sila* of beer.

[13] Van de Mieroop (1993, 51) raises the possibility that a brother of Rim-Sin, perhaps Sin-muballiṭ, succeeded their father Kudur-Mabuk in Maškan-šapir after his death.

Is it possible that the diminishing quantities of flour and beer seen in the chronological framework of the various expenditures should be connected to the death of Kudur-Mabuk and consequently to the decline of Maškan-åapir as a place of royal and political residence (see above)?

(2) Messengers (^{lú}kin-gi$_4$-a)

Messengers are listed in the corpus in two ways:

- in general, namely in the form of "regular deliveries to the messengers" (sá-du$_{11}$ ^{lú}kin-gi$_4$-a, nos. 2-4, 6-7, 12)
- in particular, namely in the form of "regular deliveries to the messengers from Ešnunna" (sá-du$_{11}$ ^{lú}kin-gi$_4$-a *èš-nun*^{ki}, no. 13)[14]

In the general listing, without the mention of the toponym, the messengers receive various amounts of semolina (ranging between 10-120 *sila*), as well as zì-gu flour (ranging between 7-10 *sila*). In tablet no. 13 the ten messengers of Ešnunna receive rations of semolina, zì-gu flour, barley and beer.

(3) Fodder for mules

The amounts of barley for fodder for mules decline from year to year during the three years such transactions are attested. The three tablets from the year Rim-Sin 6 (nos. 2-4) list the same amount of barley for fodder for mules: 150 *sila*. The tablet from the year Rim-Sin 7 (no. 6) lists a slightly smaller amount: 130 *sila*. Both transactions of fodder from year Rim-Sin 8 (nos. 7 and 12) list the amount of 110 *sila*.

(4) Individuals

Six individuals, three women and three men, are mentioned in the tablets as receiving flour, four of whom are not identified by name but rather by their affiliation to other named individuals (man of PN, daughter of PN, and wife of PN), or by their affiliation to an administrative or military establishment (dumu é-dub-ba):[15]

- Karanātum (no. 1; she receives flour and barley)
- Ubar-Šamaš (no. 4)
- Man (lú) of Ur-^{d}[...] (no. 2)

[14] Note sà-du$_{11}$ ^{lú}kin-gi$_4$-a *èš-nun-na*^{ki} in a document dated to Rim-Sin 22 (TCL 10, 54:4-5). Further note lines 6-9 in the same document: *i-nu-ú-ma* érin$^{\text{ḫi-a}}$ *ia-mu-ut-ba-lum i-na* maš-kán-šabra^{ki} *a-na* kaskal *èš-nun-na*^{ki} *ip-ḫu-ú-ru*, cf. Edzard 1987-1990, 448.

[15] See note to no. 6:6 above.

- Daughter (dumu-munus) of Lu-Dumuzida (no. 4)
- Wife of Sin-mupaššer (dam PN, no. 7)
- Scribe (⌜dumu?⌝ é-dub-ba, no. 6)

(5) Group of men from various localities (lú GN)
Individuals identified by their place of origin, and often also by their personal name, are mentioned in four tablets (nos. 5, 9-11) as recipients of beer (Type B), always 10 *sila*. The three named individuals from Ešnunna in no. 10 are also listed in no. 11 (both from month ix of year Rim-Sin 8). One of the persons from Ešnunna mentioned in no. 11 (month ix of year Rim-Sin 8) is also mentioned more than a year earlier in no. 5 (month vii of year Rim-Sin 7). Following are the various topographic affiliations mentioned in the corpus:

- from Akša(k) (nos. 5, 11)
- from Anšan (nos. 5, 9)
- from Ešnunna (nos. 5, 10, 11)
- from Isin (nos. 5, 11)
- from Malgium (no. 5 and possibly no. 9)
- from Larsa(?) or Uruk(?) (no. 5)

The mention of Akšak, Anšan, Ešnunna and Malgium, all in the Babylonian (north-)eastern frontier, as well as the central and southern Babylonian cities of Isin and Uruk, and perhaps Larsa, reflect the geographical and strategic importance of Maškan-šapir, situated on the road from Larsa to Dēr, Ešnunna and Elam.

Note that Isin, as well as Uruk, were not yet part of the kingdom of Rim-Sin when the documents mentioning the expenditure of commodities to some of the persons associated with them were written. According to the year name of Rim-Sin 14, he defeated a coalition of forces, among them from Uruk and Isin (Sigrist 1990, 43-44; Van de Mieroop 1993, 51), and according to the year names of Rim-Sin 21 and 29, he captured Uruk and Isin respectively (Sigrist 1990, 49, 58-59; Van de Mieroop 1993, 53). As mentioned, these events occurred after the documents were written.

(6) Workmen (érin)
Workmen from Uruk and Isin are mentioned in two tablets of Type A and B dated to month vii of year Rim-Sin 7 (nos. 5-6), as receiving regular deliveries (sá-du$_{11}$) of beer, semolina and barley. For the mention of these two cities, see above.

Tablet no. 6 also lists deliveries of semolina to a team of six raft-men in charge of the transportation of reed tablet containers (6 érin lú má.lá *ša* ^{gi}pisaĝ-im-sar-ra).

(7) Prisoners

- female prisoners of war (^{munus}nam-ra) (no. 6)
- prisoner-workmen (3 érin *a-sí-ru*) (no. 6)

Origin of the tablets

The tablets were written in Maškan-šapir, where the transactions occurred, as indicated by the remark šà maš-kán-šabra^{ki} towards the end of the tablets, before the date formula. It is therefore possible that the tablets originated from illicit excavations in Tell Abu Duwari, the modern site which was identified since 1989 as Maškan-šapir (Stone and Zimansky 2004).[16] Charpin (1994, 214) has already speculated, based on prosopography, that some of the texts considered to stem from Larsa, actually originated in illicit excavations in Tell Abu Duwari.

However, it is possible that the tablets published here, although surely written in Maškan-šapir, were found in Larsa rather than Tell Abu Duwari. Indeed, they could have been removed from the archives of Maškan-šapir already in antiquity, in order to have them shipped to Larsa, where the central administration was located, especially after the death of Kudur-Mabuk in the beginning of the reign of Rim-Sin (see above), when royal residence in Maškan-šapir seems to have ended. In fact, there is a slight possibility that tablet no. 6 published here may contain a clue to such a transfer. Line 7 of this document mentions a group of six workmen in charge of a raft carrying tablet containers (6 érin lú má-lá *ša* ^{gi}pisaĝ-im-sar-ra). Could this be an indication of the transfer of the discussed tablets?[17]

Index of Personal Names

(Note the following abbreviations: An = Anšan; Ak = Akšak; E = Ešnunna; I = Isin; L = Larsa; M = Malgium; U = Uruk)

Abī-aśad (E)
a-bi-a-sa-ad no. 10: 2; 11: 4

[16] The only texts from this site which originated in an excavation are royal building inscriptions (Steinkeller 2004b).

[17] Note that the pairing of boats (má) with tablet containers (^{gi}pisaĝ-im-sar-ra) occurs also in some Ur III administrative texts, e.g., Ozaki and Sigrist 2006, 140, no. 362:3.

Abu-waqar (E)
a-bu-wa-qar no. 5: 25
Abu-Wēr (E)
a-bu-^{d}*we-er* no. 5: 27
Adad-ammar (I)
^{d}IM-*am-mar* no. 5: 18
Adayātum (E)
a-da-ia-tum no. 5: 24
a-da-a-tum no. 11: 3
Aḫūni (E)
a-ḫu-ni no. 5: 32
Aḫu-waqar (E)
a-ḫu-wa-qar no. 13: 10
Ay-abâš-dīnum (E)
a-a-ba-aš-di-nu-um no. 13: 4
Burriya (I)
bur-ri-ia no. 5: 15
Daqqum (E)
da-aq-qum no. 5: 29
Erra-bani (E)
ìr-ra-ba-ni no. 5: 31
Ḫammu-rāpi (E)
ḫa-am-mu-ra-pi no. 13: 9
Ḫamsum$^{?}$ (An)
ḫa-am$^{!?}$*-sú-um* no. 5: 13
Ḫāzirum (E)
ḫa-zi-ru-um no. 13: 8
Iddin-*Nanna* (U/L?)
i-[*din*]-^{d}[nan]na no. 5: 10
Iḫbit-Erra (E)
iḫ-bi-it-ìr-ra no. 5: 28
Ikkanu$^{?}$ (M)
ik-˹*ka*$^{?}$˺*-nu* no. 5: 6
Ilam-dudu$^{?}$ (E)
i-lam$^{?}$*-du-*˹*du*˺ no. 11: 2
Ilīma-aḫi (E)
ì-lí-ma-a-ḫi no. 5: 26
Ilu-nāṣir (E)
dingir-*na-ṣir* no. 13: 2
Ilū-*qibâ* (E)
i-lu-qí$^{?}$*-ba* no. 5: 23
Irībam (E)
i-ri-ba-am no. 5: 31
Ilšu-bāni (E)
dingir-*šu-ba-ni* no. 5: 22
Karānatum
ka-ra-na-tum no. 1: 3

Lā-qīpum (I)
  la-qí-pu-um no. 5: 17
Lawilan$^{?}$ (E)
  la-˹*wi*$^{!?}$*-la*$^{?}$˺*-an* no. 13: 1
Lu-Dumuzida
  lú-^{d}dumu-zi-da no. 4: 7
Māga (E)
  ma-a-˹*ga*˺ no. 13: 7
Min[...] (I)
  mi-in-[...] no. 5: 20
Puzur-Amurru (E)
  puzur$_{4}$-^{d}mar-tu no. 13: 3
Šamaš-abī (E)
  ^{d}utu-*a-bi* no. 10: 3; 11: 5
Sin-[...]
  ^{d}EN.ZU-[...] no. 9: 3
Sin-erībam (E)
  ^{d}EN.ZU-*i-ri-ba-am* no. 13: 5
Sin-gāmil (I)
  ^{d}EN.˹ZU˺-*ga-mil* no. 5: 19
Sin-iddinam (An)
  ^{d}EN.ZU-*i-din-nam* no. 5: 12
Sin-išmeanni (U/L?)
  ^{d}EN.ZU-*iš-me-*[*an-n*]*i* no. 5: 9
Sin-mālik (An)
  ^{d}EN.ZU-*ma-lik* no. 9: 6
Sin-mupaššer
  ^{d}EN.ZU-*mu-pa-še-er* no. 7: 6
Sin-nawir (M)
  ˹^{d}EN.ZU˺-*na-w*[*i*]-˹*ir*˺ no. 5: 4
Šuniya (E)
  šu-ni-ia no.10: 4; 11: 6
Takkūa (Ak)
  ta-ak-ku-ú-a no. 5: 34
Taribum (I)
  ta-ri-bu-um no. 5: 16
Ubar-Šamaš
  u-bar-^{d}˹utu˺ no. 4: 6
Ur-[...]
  ur-^{d}[...] no. 2: 5
Warad-Nanna
  ìr-^{d}nanna no. 1: 4; 2: 11; 3: 11; 4: 12; 5: 36; 6: 18; 7: 12; 8: 3; 9: 9; 10: 7; 12: 11; 13: 15
Warad-Nanna (An)
  ìr-^{d}nanna no. 9: 5
Wēr-abušu (E)
  ^{d}*we-er-a-bu-šu* no. 13: 6

[...]
[...]-*la-an* no. 5: 5 (M)
[...]-*mi*-[...] no. 5: 7 (M)
[...]-*bi* no. 11: 7 (E)
[...] no. 9: 2

Bibliography

ALI, M. 2009: "Naptanu Term in the Texts of Rim-Sin I", *Sumer* 59, 8-27.

CAGNI, L. 1980: *Briefe aus dem Iraq Museum* (AbB 8), Leiden.

CHARPIN, D. 1994: "Contribution à la redécouverte de Maškan-šapir", in H. Gasche, M. Tanret, C. Janssen and A. Degraeve (eds.), *Cinquante-deux réflexions sur le proche-orient ancient offerts en hommage à Léon De Meyer* (MHE Occasional Publications 2), Leuven, 209-214.

— 1996: "Maisons et maisonnées en Babylonie de Sippar à Ur", in K. R. Veenhof (ed.), *Houses and Households in Ancient Mesopotamia (Papers read the 40th RAI, Leiden, July 5-8, 1993)* (PIHANS 78), Leiden – Istanbul, 221-228.

— 2003: "La politique immobilière des marchands de Larsa à la lumière des découvertes épigraphiqes de 1987 et 1989", in J.-L. Huot (ed.), *Larsa. Travaux de 1987 et 1989*. Beyrouth, 311-322.

CIVIL, M. 2000: Review of H. Behrens, *Die Ninegalla-Hymne: Die Wohnungnahme Inannas in Nippur in altbabylonischer Zeit* (FAOS 21), Stuttgart 1998, *JAOS* 120, 674-676.

EDZARD, D. O. 1987-1990: "Maškan-šāpir", *RlA* 7, 447-448.

FRAYNE, D. R. 1990: *Old Babylonian Period (2003-1595 BC)* (RIM Early Periods 4), Toronto.

GEORGE, A. 1993: *House Most High: The Temples of Ancient Mesopotamia*, Winona Lake, Indiana.

GLASSNER J. J. 1987-1990: "Mahlzeit. A. In Mesopotamien," *RlA* 7, 259-267.

GOODNICK-WESTENHOLZ, J. and A. WESTENHOLZ 2006: *Cuneiform Inscriptions in the Collection of the Bible Lands Museum Jerusalem: The Old Babylonian Period* (Cuneiform Monographs 33), Leiden.

GRONEBERG, B. 1980: *Die Orts- und Gewässernamen der Altbabylonischen Zeit* (RGTC 3), Wiesbaden.

HINZ W. and H. KOCH 1987: *Elamisches Wörterbuch*, Berlin 1987.

LAFONT, B. 2008: "À propos des repas collectifs et banquets (*naptanum*) à l'époque d'Ur III," in P. Michalowski (ed.), *On the Third Dynasty of Ur: Studies in Honor of Marcel Sigrist* (Journal of Cuneiform Studies: Supplemental Series 1), Boston, 93-98.

LEEMANS, W. F. 1954: *Legal and Economic Records from the Kingdom of Larsa* (SLB I/2), Leiden.

OZAKI, T. and M. SIGRIST 2006: *Ur III Administrative Texts from the British Museum*, Part 1 (BPOA 1), Madrid.

ROBSON, E. 2004: "Accounting for Change: The Development of Tabular Bookkeeping in Early Mesopotamia", in M. Hudson & C. Wunsch (eds.), *Creating Economic Order. Record-keeping, Standardization, and the Development of Accounting in the Ancient Near East*, Bethesda, Maryland, 107-144.

SIGRIST, M. 1990: *Larsa Year Names*, Berrin Springs.
STEINKELLER, P. 2004a: "Chapter 3: A History of Mashkan-shapir and Its Role in the Kingdom of Larsa", in Stone and Zimansky 2004, 26-42.
— 2004b: "Chapter 7: A Building Inscription of Sin-iddinam and Other Inscribed Materials from Abu Duwari", in Stone and Zimansky 2004, 135-152.
STOL, M. 2004: "Wirtschaft und Gesellschaft in Altbabylonischen Zeit", in: D. Charpin, D. O. Edzard and M. Stol, *Mesopotamien: Die altbabylonischen Zeit* (OBO 160/4), Fribourg and Göttingen, 643-975.
— 2007: Review of Goodnick Westenholz and Westenholz 2006, *BiOr* 64, 408-411.
STONE, E. C. and P. E. ZIMANSKY (eds.) 2004: *The Anatomy of a Mesopotamian City: Survey and Soundings at Mashkan-Shapir*, Winona Lake, Indiana.
VALLAT, F. 1993: *Les noms géographiques des sources suso-élamites* (RGTC 11), Wiesbaden.
VAN DE MIEROOP, M. 1993: "The Reign of Rim-Sin", *RA* 87 (1993), 47-69.
VAN LERBERGHE, K. and G. VOET 2009: *A Late Old Babylonian Temple Archive from Dūr-Abiešuḫ* (CUSAS 8), Bethesda, Marlyland.
ZADOK, R. 1987: "Peoples from the Iranian Plateau in Babylonia during the Second Millennium B.C.", *Iran* 25, 1-26.

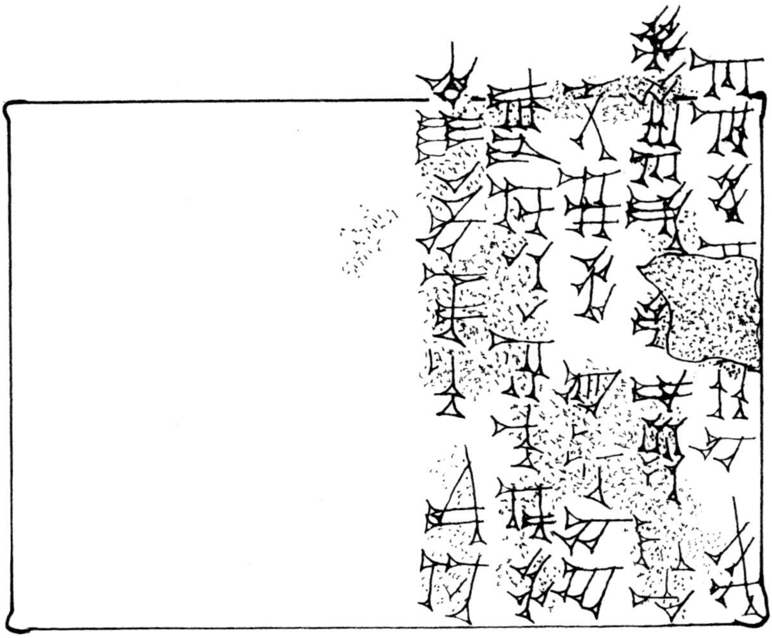

no. 1 rev.

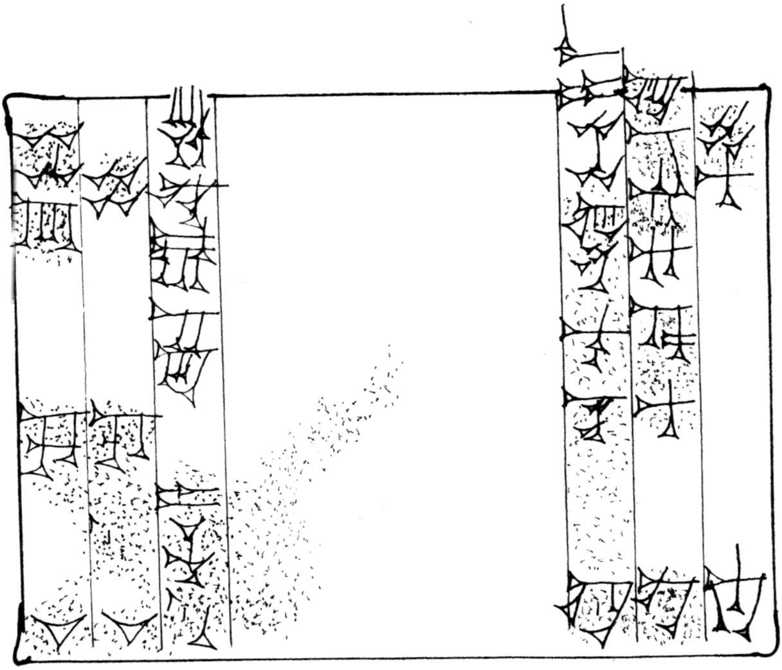

no. 1 obv.

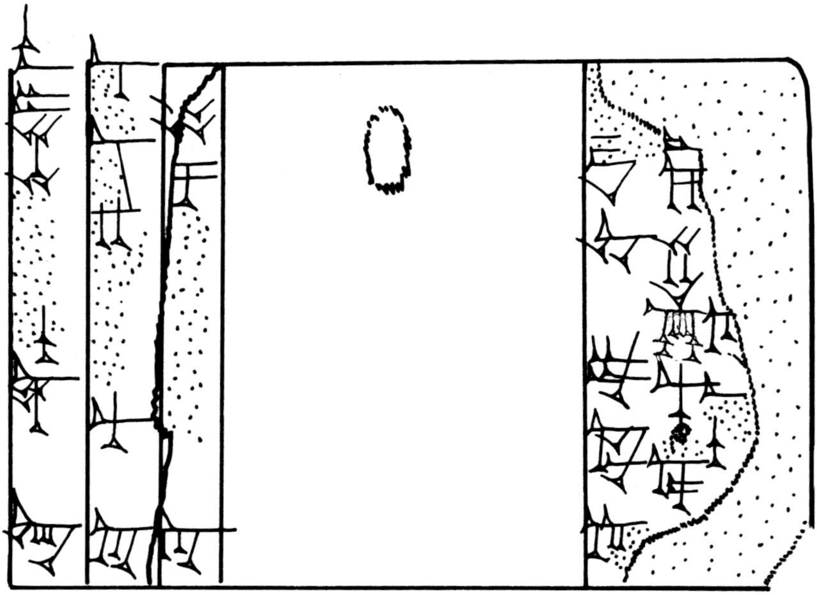

no. 2 rev.

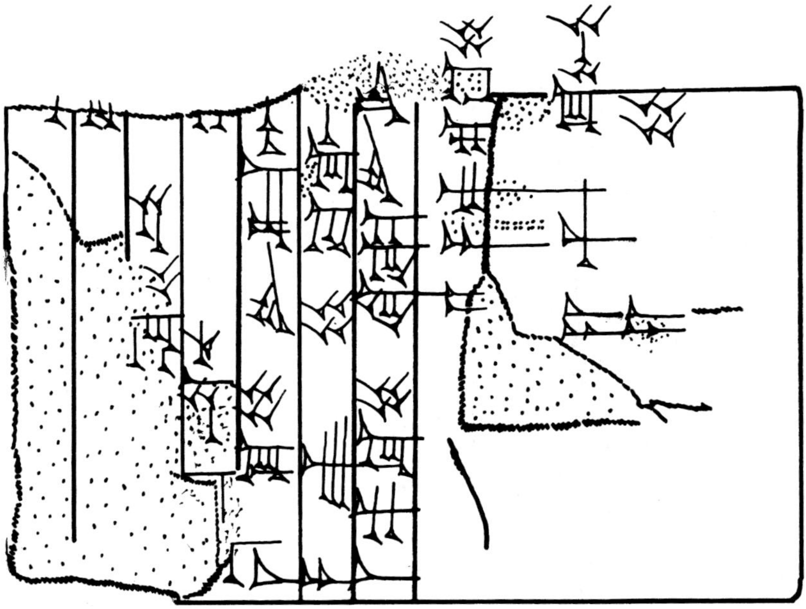

no. 2 obv.

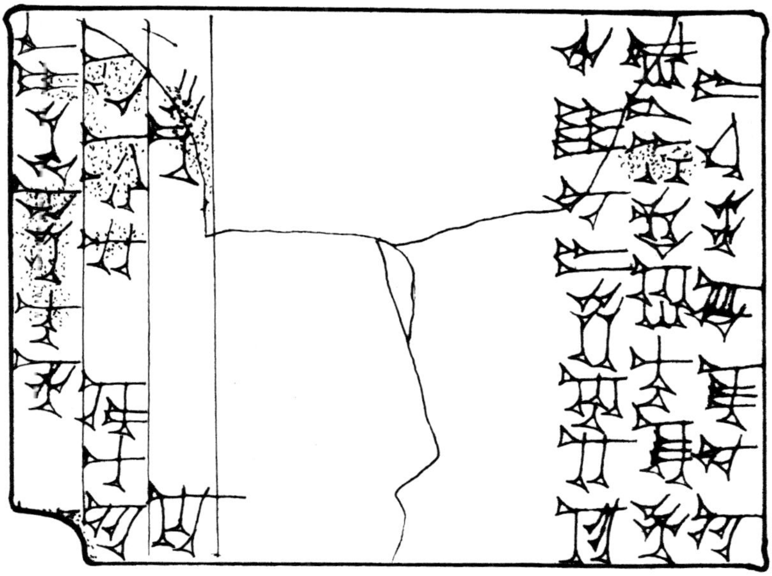

no. 3 rev.

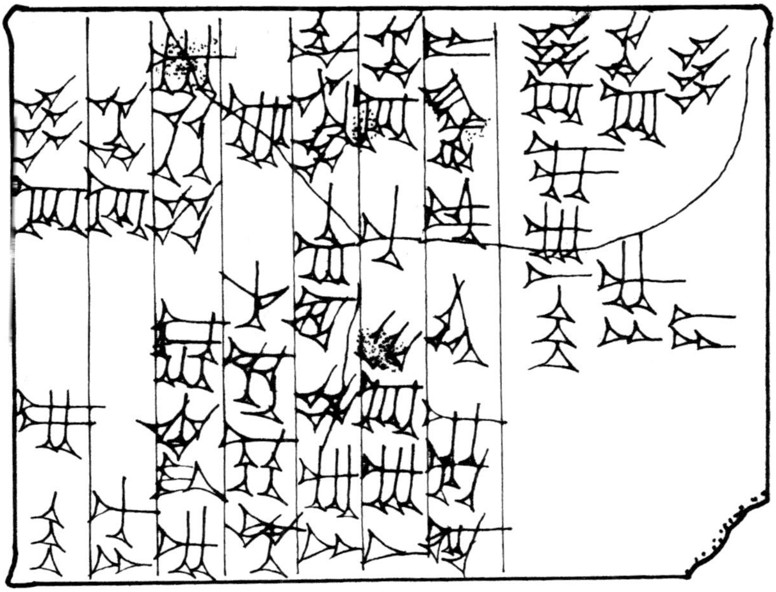

no. 3 obv.

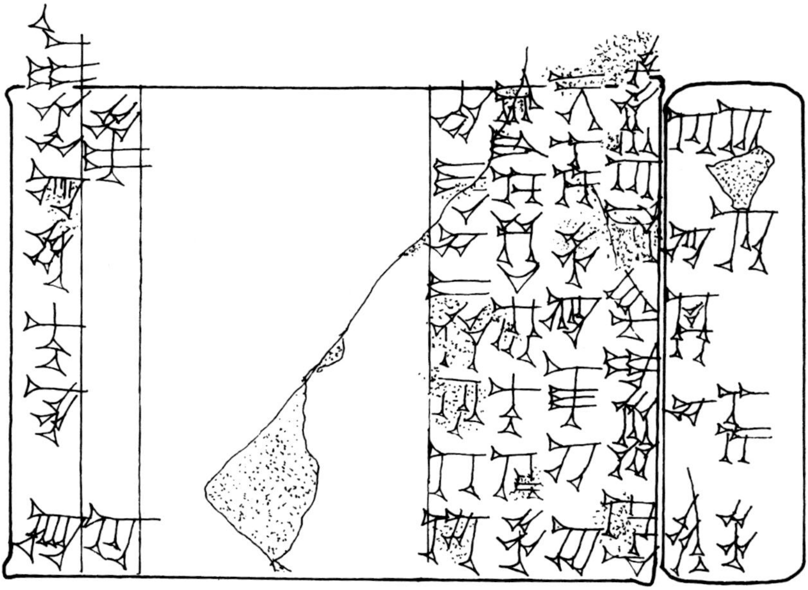

no. 4 rev.

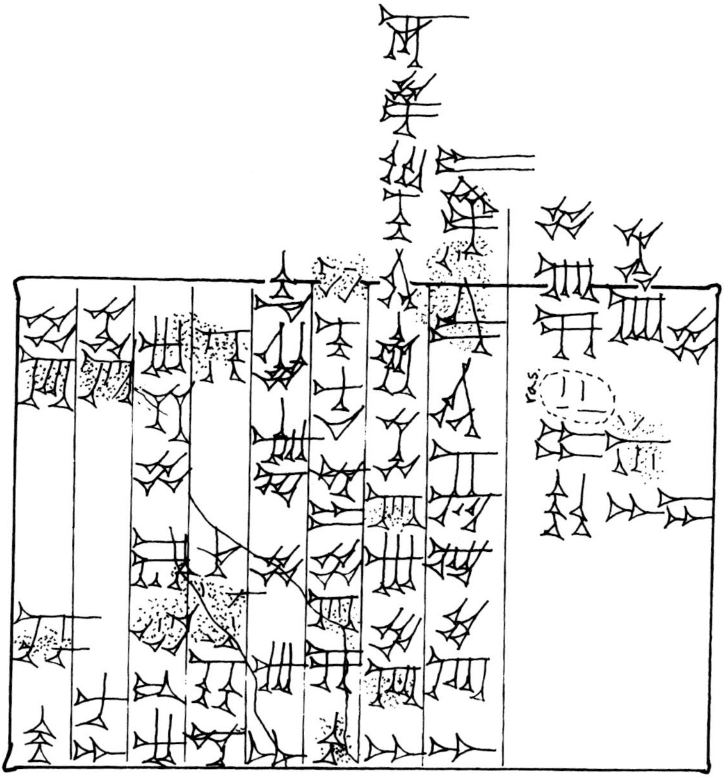

no. 4 obv.

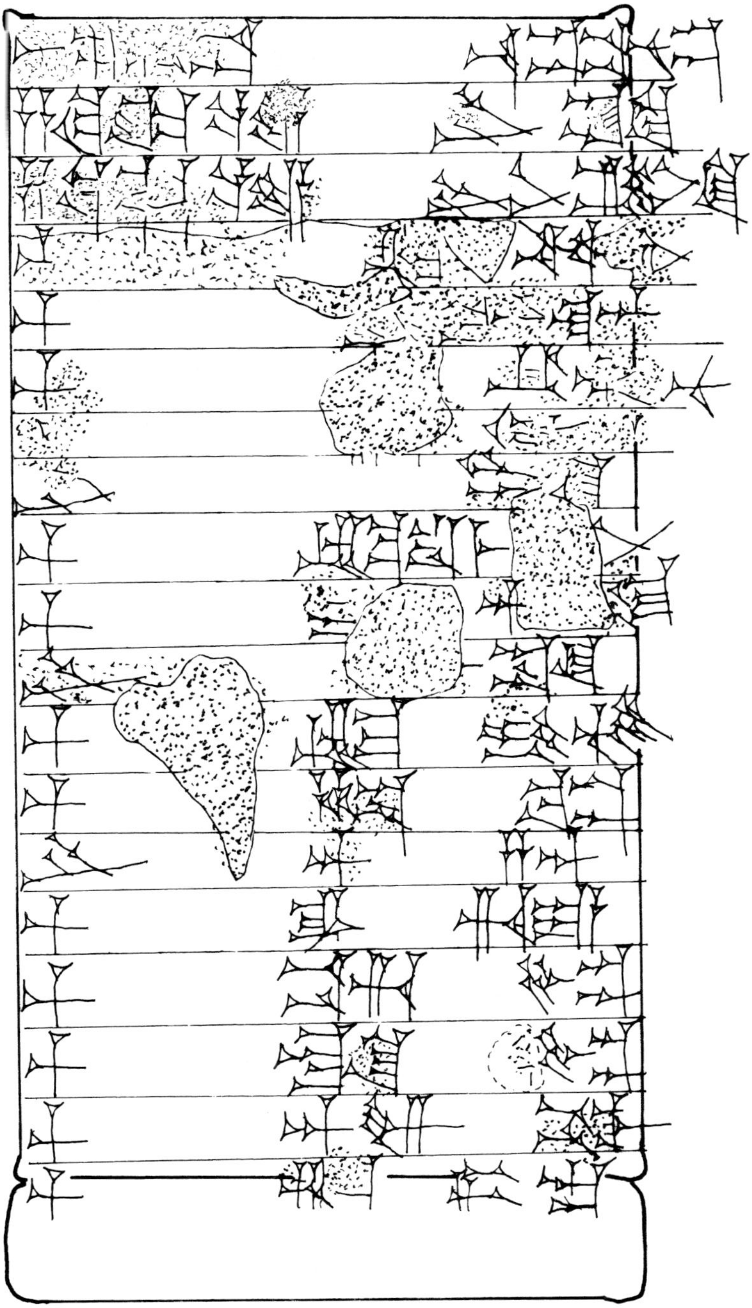

no. 5 obv.

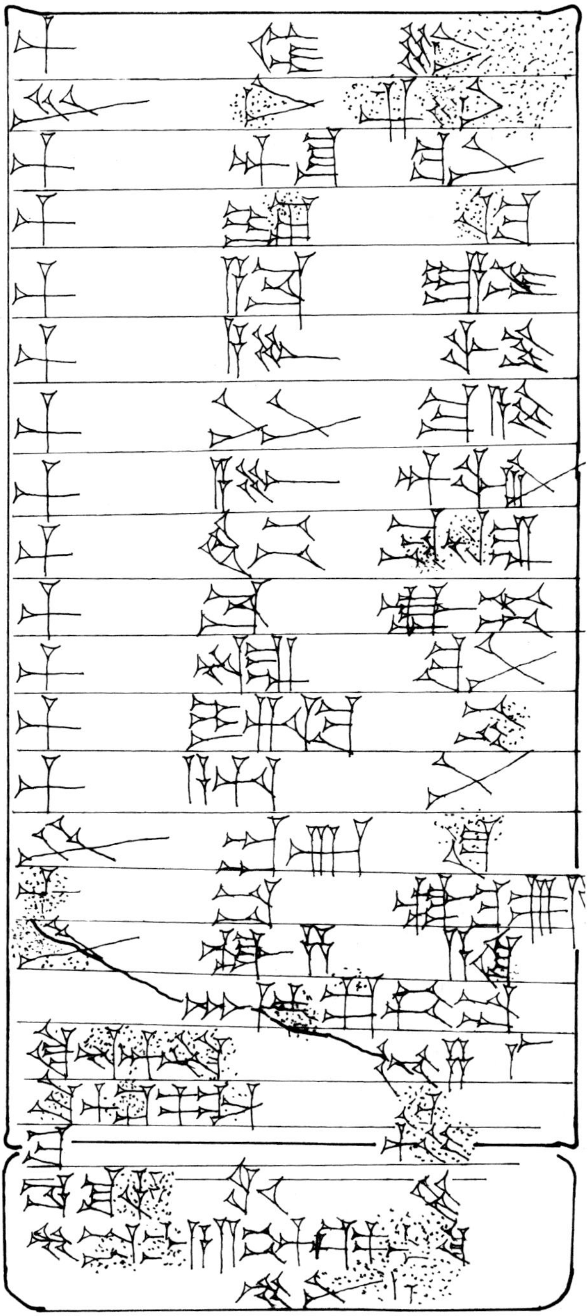

no. 5 rev.

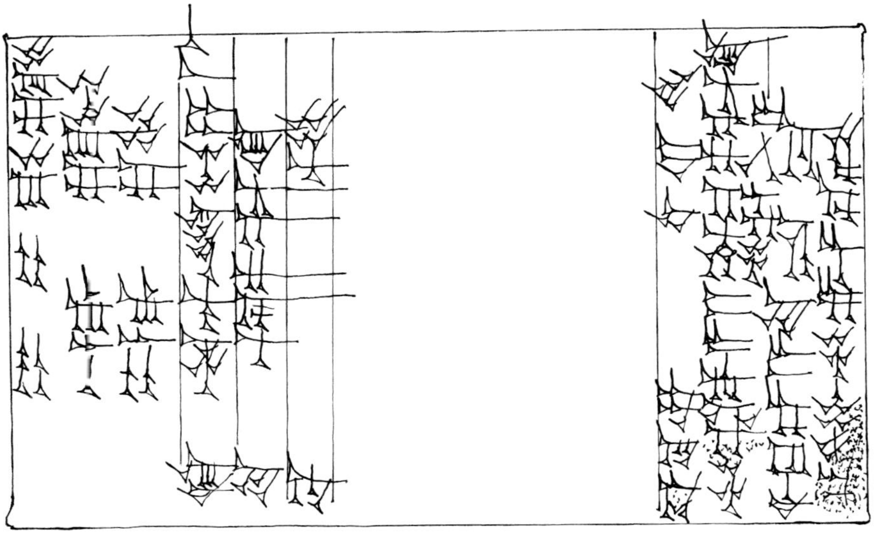

no. 6 rev.

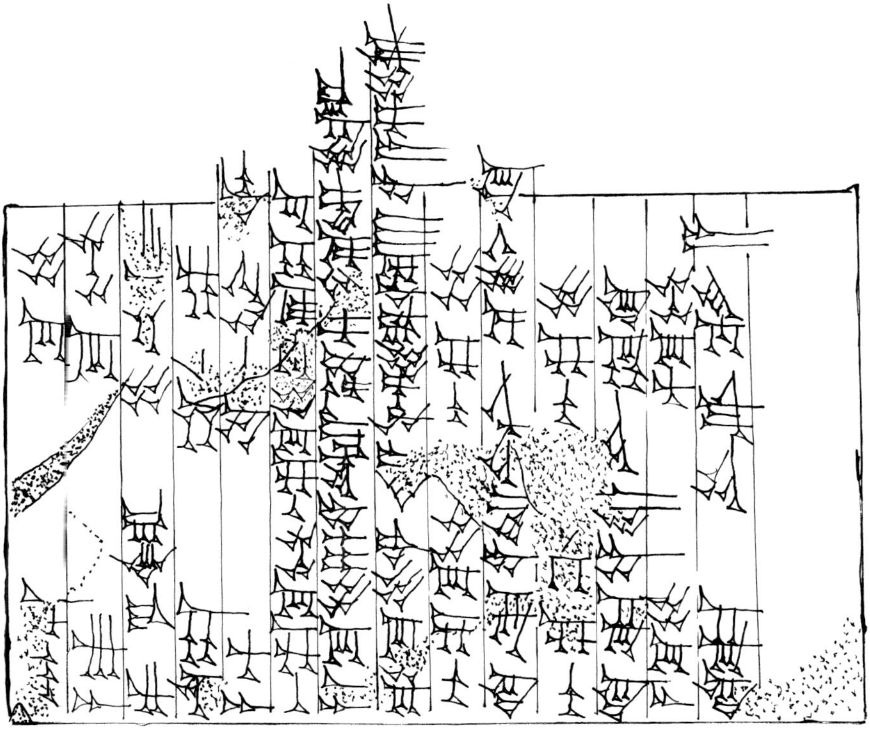

no. 6 obv.

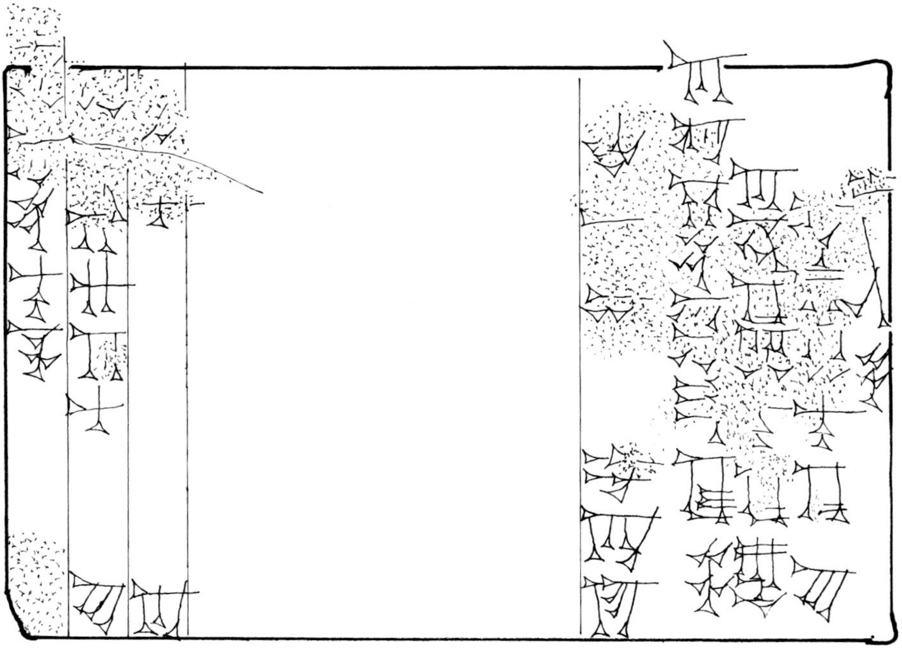
no. 7 rev.

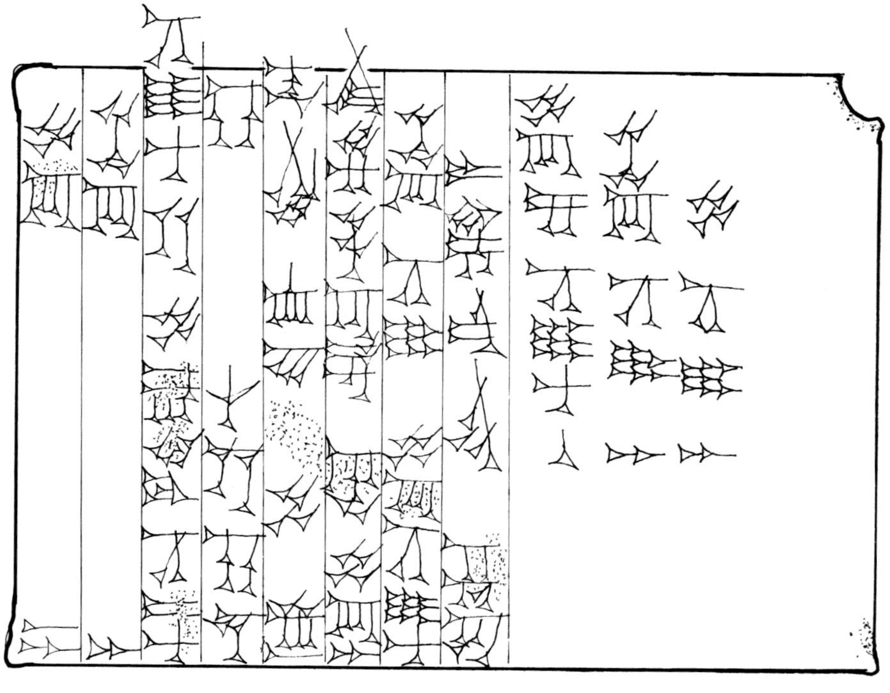
no. 7 obv.

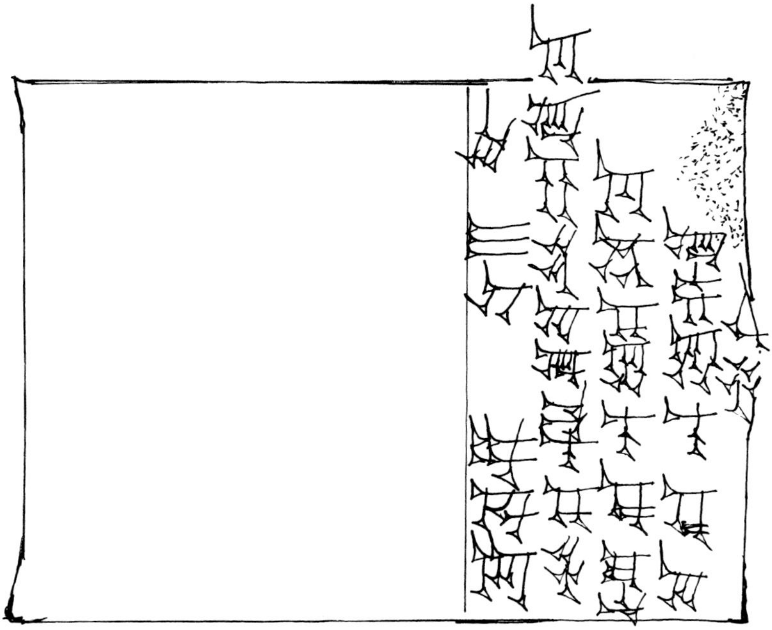

no. 8 rev.

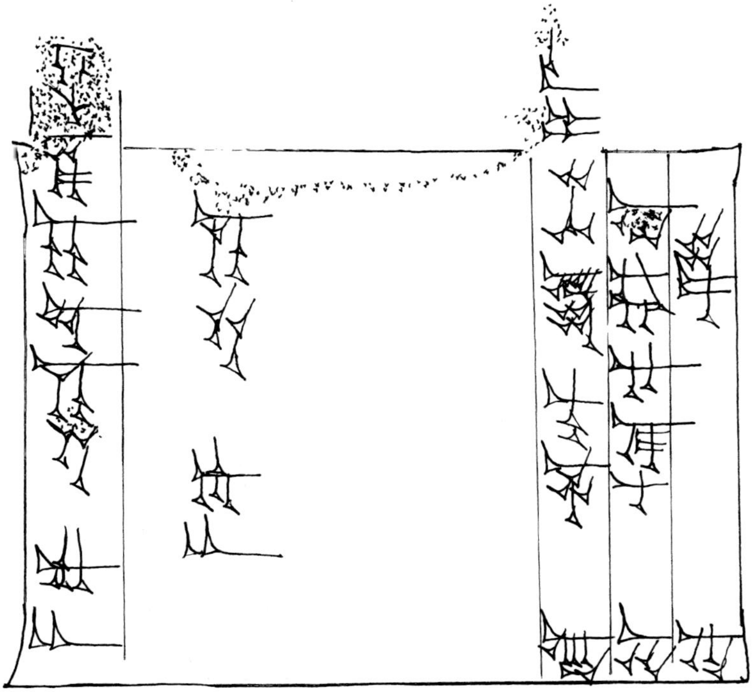

no. 8 obv.

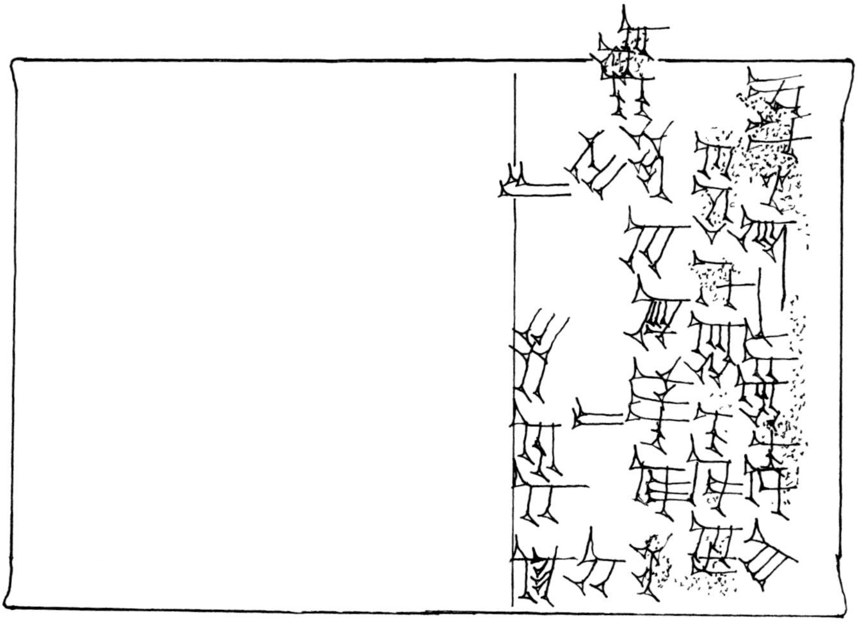

no. 9 rev.

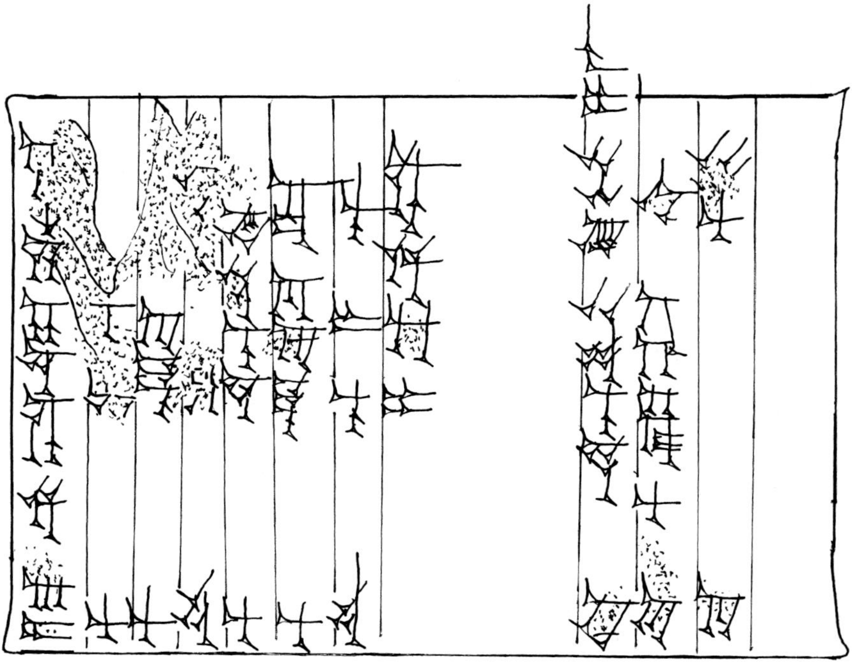

no. 9 obv.

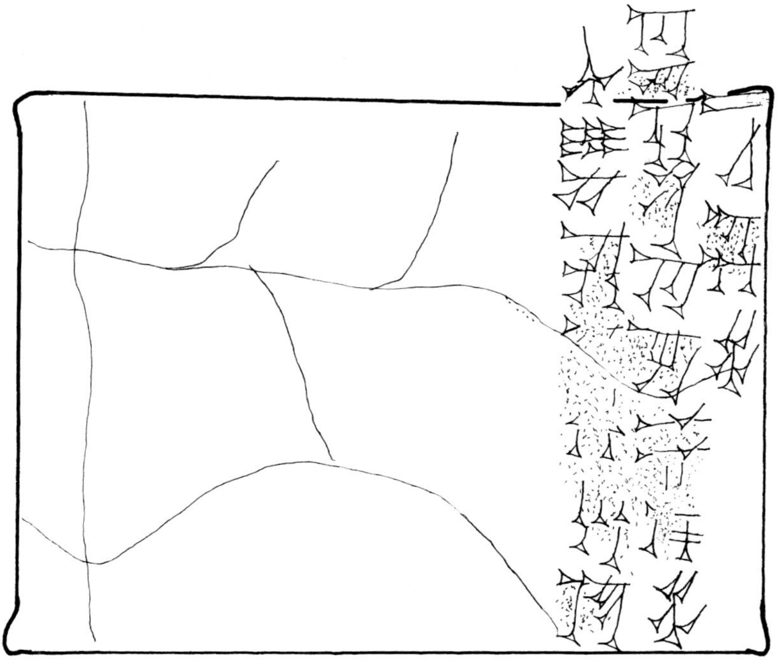

no. 10 rev.

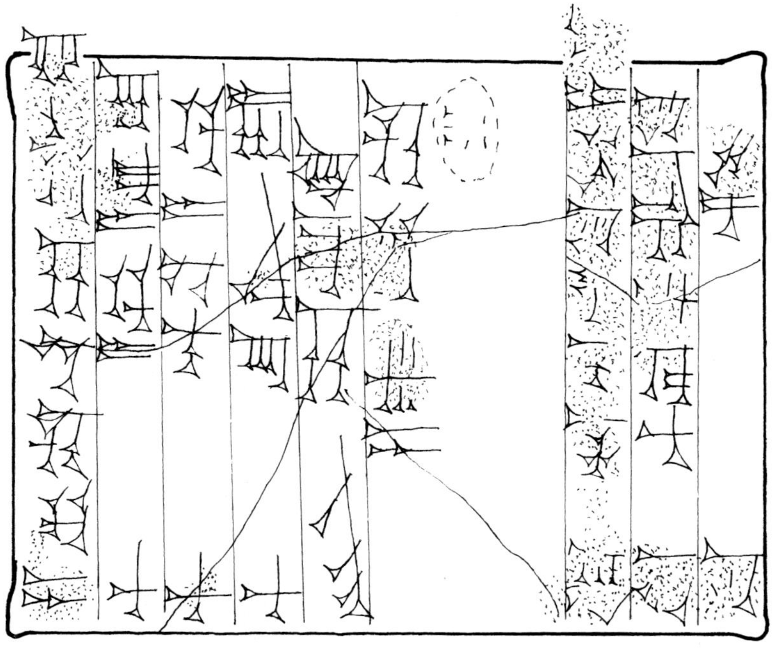

no. 10 obv.

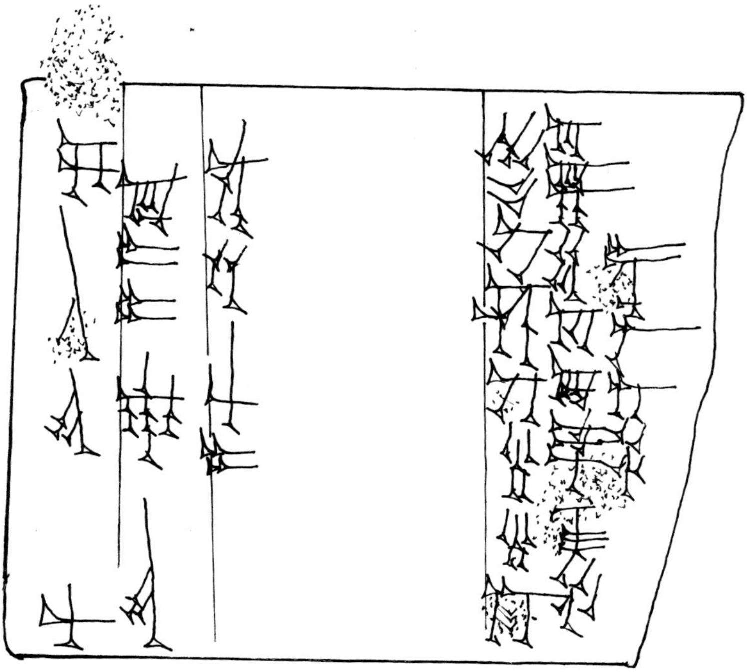

no. 11 rev.

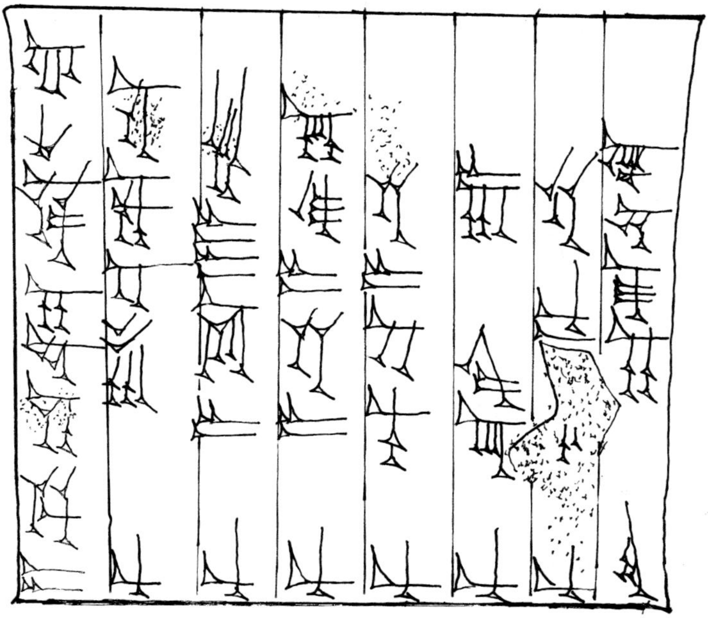

no. 11 obv.

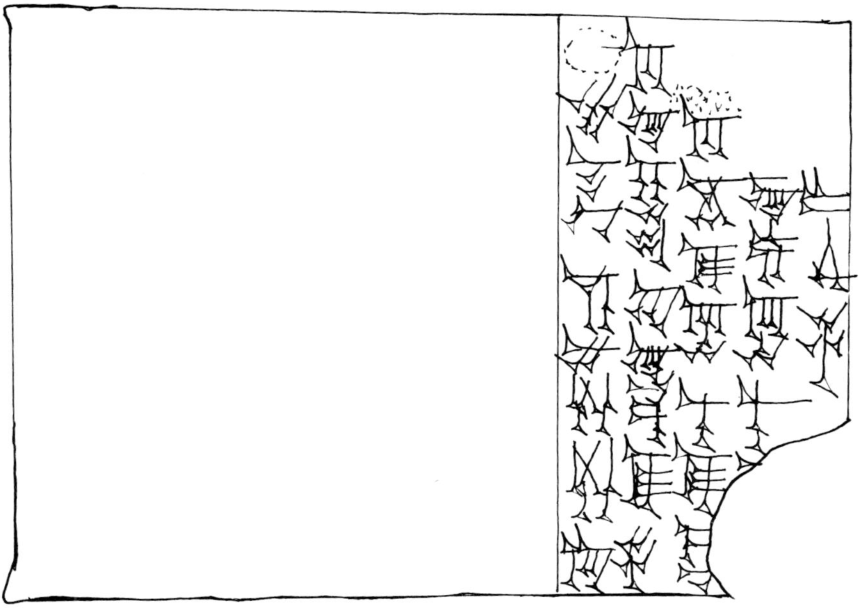

no. 12 rev.

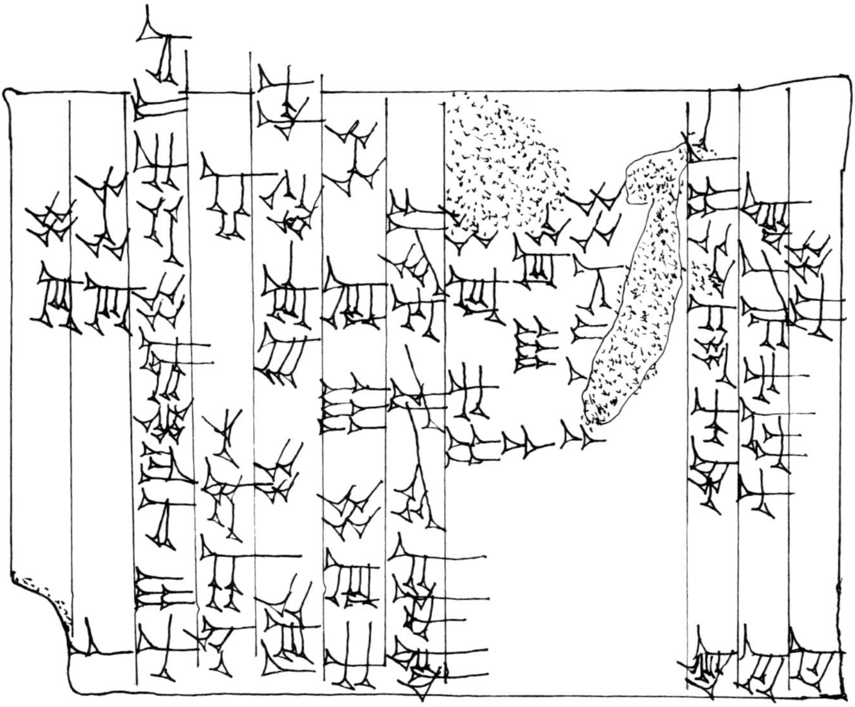

no. 12 obv.

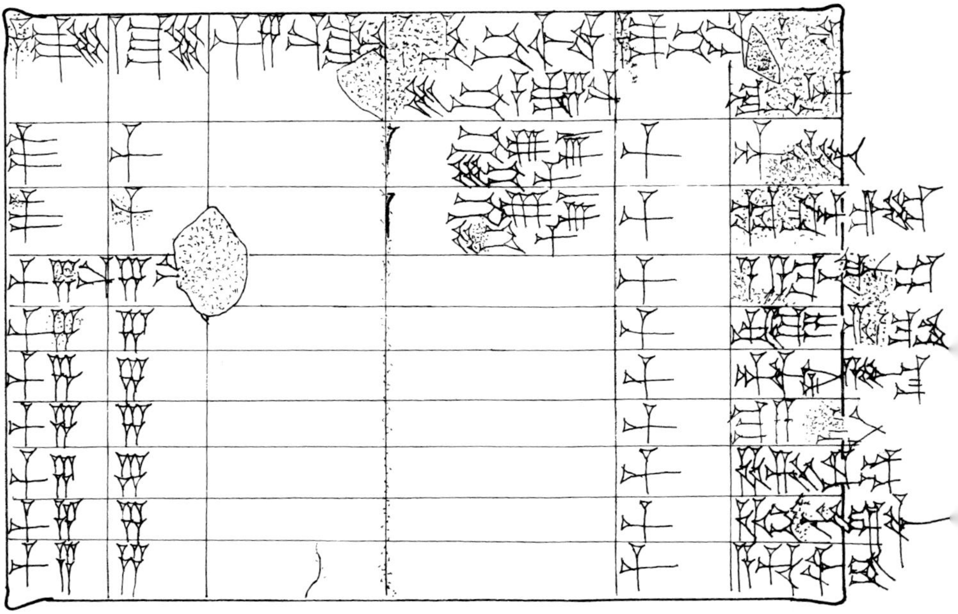

no. 13 obv.

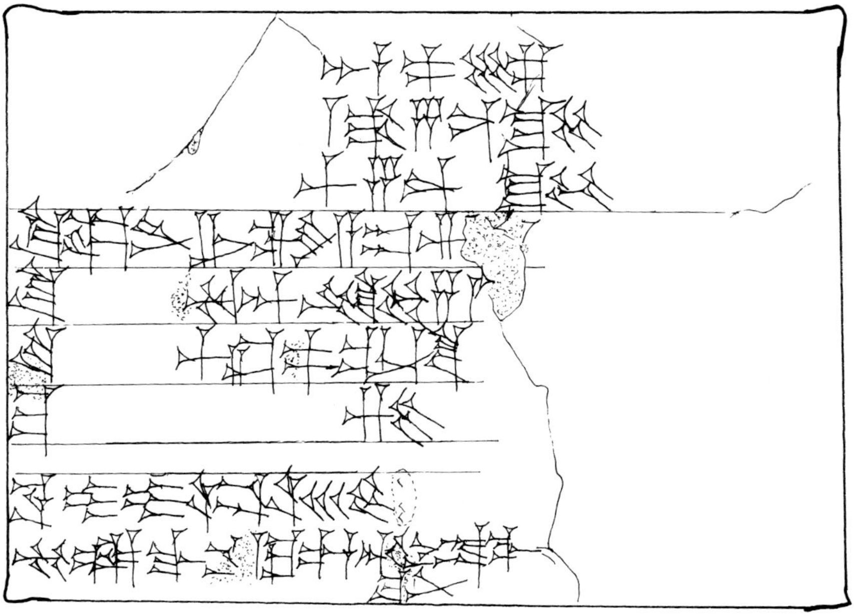

no. 13 rev.

NOTES D'ARCHÉOLOGIE LEVANTINE XXXIII
TÊTE D'UN DIGNITAIRE EN BASALTE DE TELL SAKKA[1]

Michel AL-MAQDISSI[1, 2] et Eva ISHAQ[1]
[1] DGAM - Damas
[2] USJ - Beyrouth

1. Introduction

Cette tête a été trouvée en 2001 par les membres de la mission syrienne au pied sud de Tell Sakka, à la surface d'un terrain aplatie par des travaux d'aménagement agricole[2].

Elle a été recueillie avec plusieurs objets de natures différentes dans un terrain qui a été vraisemblablement terrassé, ce qui a endommagé plusieurs structures dont plusieurs phases du IIème millénaire av. J.-C. et une nécropole caractérisée par des tombes individuelles, qui ont livré un matériel de la fin de l'âge du Fer[3].

Notons à cette occasion que la stratigraphie du site a surtout révélé un bâtiment[4] du IIe millénaire av. J.-C. qui pourrait abriter un petit palais en lien vraisemblablement avec le pays d'Apum (Damas du IIème millénaire av. J.-C.) [5].

2. Description

Il s'agit d'une tête en basalte soigneusement sculptée appartenant à une statue d'un haut dignitaire de grand module (Fig. 1).

Elle porte une barbe vraisemblablement lisse suivant la tradition amorite syrienne, et qui couvre une partie importante du visage. De même, elle est coiffée d'une calotte-turban lisse serrée par un bandeau mince du côté du front et plus large du côté de la nuque où il dégage les oreilles.

[1] Nos remerciements les plus sincères vont à Ahmad Taraqji, Dominique Parayre, Sa'ad Fansa et Mouhidin Hamoudé.

[2] Pour les travaux à Tell Sakka, cf. Al-Maqdissi 1988a, 1988b; Taraqji 1991, 1993, 1999, 2001. Par contre pour une synthèse sur Damas et sa région aux périodes anciennes, cf. particulièrement Pitard 1987.

[3] Cf. à ce propos, Bounni et Al-Maqdissi 2002: 8-10, fig. 1-3.

[4] Cf. principalement Taraqji 1999: 35-36, fig. 7 et Taraqji 2001: 33.

[5] Cf. à ce propos, Taraqji 2001.

Les yeux sont relativement larges et sculptés en relief et les sourcils, sommairement réalisés, dessinent une forme continue habituelle au-dessus du nez.

Le front masqué en partie par la calotte-turban assure une transition parfaite avec les sourcils et le départ du nez.

On observe sur la partie supérieure de la tête une cavité quadrangulaire assez profonde qui pourrait témoigner de la présence d'un élément qui y était enchâssé, mais dont nous ignorons cependant la nature.

Pierre basaltique d'une qualité moyenne avec des grains relativement fins.

Hauteur totale: 19 cm.

Largeur au niveau des oreilles: 15 cm.

Longueur moyenne des yeux: 3 cm.

Longueur moyenne des oreilles: 5,5 cm.

Largeur moyenne de la cavité: 12 cm.

Profondeur de la cavité: 8,4 cm.

3. Discussion

La présence de cette sculpture dans la région de Damas, dans le pays d'Apum, est un apport très important pour l'étude de ce type de production statuaire en Syrie du Sud. En effet, si nous essayons de comparer cette sculpture avec d'autres productions nous constatons des points de rencontre frappants avec la tête dite de Hammurabi découverte par la mission française à Suse et conservée au Musée du Louvre[6]. Les mêmes rapprochements peuvent être effectués avec la tête de la stèle dite du Code de Hammurabi, elle aussi conservée au Louvre[7]. Cependant si nous poussons plus en avant l'analyse nous trouvons dans la sculpture de Tell Sakka les traces d'une tradition syrienne marquée par les deux caractéristiques suivantes:

– la forme de la barbe (sans moustache) et sa nature lisse habituellement attestées dans les sculptures de la tradition amorite et cananéenne du

[6] Cf. à ce propos, Parrot 1960, 306-307, fig. 375 et André-Salvini 2008, 70-71. Parrot donne la description suivante: «Le sculpteur a fixé dans un bloc de stéatite bleu verdâtre, le masque fatigué, amaigri, sinon ravagé par la maladie, d'un Hammurabi vieilli. Les lèvres sont plissées par une sorte de rictus, les pommettes sont décharnées, les yeux sont moins grands ouverts qu'il n'est de règle».

[7] Cf. à ce propos, Parrot 1960, 305, fig. 373. Des comparaisons sont attestées dans la peinture de Tell Hariri-Mari, cf. Parrot 1958, 22, fig. 19, pl. VI, XI (tête de Zimri-Lim dans panneau central de la peinture de l'Investiture). En plus cf. récemment André-Salvini 2003.

Bronze moyen et du Bronze récent telles qu'à Tell Atchana-Alalakh[8], à Mishirfeh-Qatna (Al-Maqdissi, Morandi Bonacossi et Pfälzner 2009, 204) et à Ras Shamra-Ougarit[9].

– la forme lisse de la calotte-turban, serrée sur la tête, qui présente quant à elle des analogies frappantes avec plusieurs sculptures syriennes, et tout particulièrement avec la tête dite de Yarim Lim de Tell Atchana-Alalakh[10] et les deux statues des ancêtres de l'hypogée royal de Mishirfeh-Qatna (Al-Maqdissi, Morandi Bonacossi et Pfälzner 2009, 204).

L'ensemble des comparaisons proposées nous conduit à dater notre sculpture du Bronze moyen II, sans doute au XVIIIe siècle si le parallèle avec la tête dite de Hammurabi est pertinent [11]. Ceci est un élément relativement nouveau qui tend à confirmer l'importance de la production artistique de Damas et sa région à cette période.

D'une manière générale nous possédons très peu de documents pour confirmer la nature exacte de la production statuaire en Syrie[12], et les ateliers connus à Tell Mardikh-Ebla[13], à Tell Atchana-Alalakh (Spycket 1981, 264-265) ou à Ras Shamra-Ougarit (Yon 1991a et 1991b), apportent des éléments très précis sur la nature de la production, mais toujours liés à un style local[14].

Avant d'établir les caractéristiques exactes de cette production, nous devons attendre la découverte d'autres sculptures. Néanmoins, on peut d'ores et déjà avancer l'idée que dans la région de Damas il existe un type très différent de la production de l'Oronte, qui serait plutôt lié à la grande tradition babylonienne du Bronze moyen[15]. Cette proposition pourrait s'avérer cruciale, car si nous analysons les découvertes de la

[8] Cf. à ce propos, Woolley 1955, pl. XLII.

[9] Yon 1990; Yon 1991b, 347-348, fig. 2a; Yon 2004, 261, n° 304.

[10] Cf. à ce propos, Woolley 1955, pl. XLII.

[11] Cf. par exemple pour la même période la tête d'une peinture conservée au Musée d'Alep publiée dans Parrot 1960, 277.

[12] Cf. particulièrement Matthiae 1962 et Spycket 1981, 260-286.

[13] Cf. par exemple Matthiae et al. 1995, 390-398.

[14] Cf. particulièrement Spycket 1981, 257 où elle note «Le IIe millénaire est fortement marqué par les manifestations du Levant qui s'affirme face à la Mésopotamie. On ne peut parler d'unité sur l'ensemble des territoires qui vont de l'Asie Mineure à la Palestine, en incluant la Syrie et la Palestine».

[15] Notons que cette tradition babylonienne trouve ces origines au troisième millénaire av. J.-C. avec la production des deux périodes d'Ur III et des Shakkanakku, cf. particulièrement Spycket 1981, 184-223. Pour illustrer notre propos, nous proposons des exemples dans Parrot 1960, 208-209, 214, 228-229, 264-269.

mission syrienne de Tell Sakka nous pouvons attester une documentation picturale liée à une tradition mésopotamienne que l'on rencontre par exemple à Tell Hariri[16].

4. Conclusion

L'étude de cette sculpture révèle l'expression d'un visage grave et digne dont la vivacité du regard est rendue à la fois par la relation établie entre les yeux, le nez et la barbe, mais aussi et surtout par la position parfaite de la calotte-turban qui enserre une grande partie de la tête et confère à l'œuvre une grande cohérence. La sculpture de Tell Sakka s'inscrit parfaitement dans la tradition amorite du XVIIIe siècle, et les rapprochements avec la tête dite de Hammurabi du Louvre attestent que la région de Damas avait des relations directes avec la Babylonie, ce qui n'est pas étonnant puisqu'elle se trouvait sur l'axe de communication reliant la Palestine du Nord et la plaine de Houlé avec la Mésopotamie centrale[17].

Le site de Sakka n'a pas encore dévoilé tous ses secrets, et nous espérons que la poursuite de la fouille du bâtiment du Bronze moyen, qui a déjà livré deux tablettes cunéiformes (Abdallah 2009) et des peintures murales d'un style mixte égypto-mésopotamien, enrichira la documentation et complètera le dossier déjà fort important sur l'un des royaumes amorites de la Syrie du sud.

Bibliographie

Abréviations:

AJA = American Journal of Archaeology.
BAH = Bibliothèque Archéologique et Historique.
BSFE = Bulletin de la Société Française d'Egyptologie.
CAAS = Chronique des Activités Archéologiques Syriennes.
MAM = Mission Archéologique de Mari.
NCS = Note de Céramologie Syrienne.
RSOu = Ras Shamra-Ougarit.

ABDALLAH, F. 2009: «Découvertes d'une première tablette à Tell Sakka», *Berceau de la Civilisation*, 8-9, 178-181 (en arabe).
AL-MAQDISSI, M. 1988a: «Tell Sakka au sud-est de Damas, prospection en 1982», *NCS* III, Damas.

[16] Cf. Taraqji 1999, 37, fig. 9 et les comparaisons avec les peintures du palais royal de Mari, cf. Parrot 1958, 93, fig. 70, p. 97, fig. 74.
[17] Pratiquement *via* Tell Hariri-Mari et Khirbet ed-Diniyeh.

AL-MAQDISSI, M. 1988b: «Tell Sakka (région de Damas)», *Syria* LXV, 410, 413.

AL-MAQDISSI, M., D. MORANDI BONACOSSI et P. PFÄLZNER 2009: *Schätze des Alten Syrien, Die Entdeckung des königreichs Qatna*, Stuttgart.

ANDRÉ-SALVINI, B. 2003: *Le Code de Hammurabi*, Paris.

ANDRÉ-SALVINI 2008: B. Andrée-Salvini: «Babylon», *Beyond Babylon, Art, Trade, and Diplomacy in the Second Millennium B.C.*, éd. J. Aruz, K. Benzel et J. M. Evans, New York, pp. 18-26.

BOUNNI, A. et M. AL-MAQDISSI 2002: «Note sur une nécropole de la deuxième moitié du premier millénaire av. J.-C. à l'est de Damas», in L. Al Gailani Werr, J. Curtis, H. Martin, A. McMahon, J. Oates et J. Reade (éds.) *Of Pots and Plans, Papers on the Archaeological and History of Mesopotamia and Syria presented to David Oates in Honour of his 75th Birthday*, London, 7-10.

MATTHIAE, P. 1962: *Ars Syria, Contributi alla storia dell'arte figurativa siriana nelle età del Medio e Tardo Bronzo*, Rome.

MATTHIAE, P., F. PINNOCK et G. SCANDONE MATTHIAE (éds.) 1995: *Ebla, Alle origini della civiltà urbana*, Trent'anni di scavi in Siria dell'Università di Roma 'La Sapienza', Milan.

PARROT, A. 1958: *Le Palais*, peintures murales, Paris (= MAM II/2 et BAH LXIX).

— 1960: *Sumer*, Paris.

PITARD, W. T. 1987: *Ancient Damascus, A Historical Study of the Syrian City-State from Earliest Times until its Fall to the Assyrians in 732 B.C.E.*, Winona Lake-Indiana.

SPYCKET, A. 1981: *La statuaire du Proche Orient ancien*, Leyden-Cologne.

TARAQJI, A. 1991: «Sakka», *AJA*, 95, 727.

— 1993: «Tell Sakka», *Syria* LXX, 453-456 (= CAAS I).

— 1999: «Nouvelles découvertes sur les relations avec l'Egypte à Tel Sakka et à Keswé dans la région de Damas», *BSFE* 144, 27-43.

— 2001: «Eléments de rapprochement entre la Syrie Centrale et la Syrie du Sud au IIème millénaire av. J.-C.», *Etudes sur l'histoire de Restan et sa région*, Damas, 21-43-33 (en arabe).

YON, M. 1990: «El, père des dieux», *Mémoires et Monuments Piot* 71, 1-19.

— 1991a: «Stèles de pierre», in M. Yon (éd.) *Arts et industries de la pierre*, Paris, 273-344 (= RSOu VI).

— 1991b: «Note sur la sculpture de pierre», M. Yon (éd.) *Arts et industries de la pierre*, Paris, 345-352 (= RSOu VI).

— 2004: «Statue du dieu El», *Royaume d'Ougarit, aux origines de l'Alphabet*, Lyon, 361.

WOOLLEY, L. 1955: *Alalakh, An Account of the Excavations at Tell Atchana in the Hatay, 1937-1949*, Oxford.

Fig. 1. Tell Sakka, tête d'un dignitaire en basalte
(Sa'ad Fansa, DGAM - Damas).

THE BIRTH OF AN ERA

Tom Boiy
KU Leuven[1]

In colloquial language "era" is used for a long period of time with common characteristics. In chronography the era denotes a large time span during which years are numbered from a specific event, the epochal date. This special event that marked a drastic change in life and/or society was often recognized and designated as epochal date only much later.

World War II is without doubt the most important landmark for the twentieth century, but it is becoming more and more clear that the early nineties of the same century are also a serious candidate for the start of a new era: the fall of the Berlin wall, the reunification of Germany and the end of the Soviet era mark the end of the Cold War period that started after WW II and the invasion of Kuwait by Iraq that shifted most attention of the players on the international scene to the Middle East.

Also for me personally the year 1990 marks a special event. As a second year student of ancient history who was inundated with Hellenistic history[2] as a freshman, I decided in October 1990 to go and have a look one floor higher in the building of the Leuven Arts Faculty[3] to see what the section Ancient Near East had to offer. In the office of Karel Van Lerberghe I received a first glimpse of the world opened by the cuneiform

[1] All dates are BC, excepts those in the introduction referring to present-day events.

[2] This was actually something completely new to me. History courses in Belgian high schools focus on Egypt, Greece (the classical period and Alexander the Great) and Rome. Hellenistic rulers only appear when they oppose the Romans: Pyrrhus of Epirus, Philip V of Macedon, the Seleucid king Antiochus III, Attalus III of Pergamon, Mithradates VI of Pontus and, of course, the Ptolemaic queen Cleopatra VII. What had happened in the Eastern Mediterranean between the death of Alexander the Great and the reign of Antiochus III remained a big black hole, that was eagerly filled during my first year at University.

[3] The Arts Faculty in Leuven is housed in one building in the centre of Leuven, the so-called "Erasmushuis", and each department had one floor. The department of Classics was housed on the sixth floor and the department of Oriental and Slavonic Studies on the seventh. I was no exception. More students of Ancient History, Classical Philology and Archaeology found their way to the Ancient Near East either during or after their primary study. Since Archaeology was on the fourth floor all interested students had to go higher up and they all — or at least those I knew and/or told me so — considered climbing the stairs to the seventh floor indeed as a promotion.

sources and Karel convinced me that the information from the tablets was vital, also for someone studying the Hellenistic period. Although I probably did not realize it at that time, this decision did indeed change my view on Hellenistic and Seleucid history. My interest in chronology and chronography originates in the first place from my Ancient History studies, but as an appreciation for the role Karel played in the origin of an epochal date for my view on the Seleucid history I offer him here my study on the birth of the Seleucid era.

The Seleucid era is generally accepted as the first era system that was in practical use in daily life.[4] The Seleucid era has two epochal dates: 3 April 311 according to the Babylonian calendar and Autumn 312 according to the Macedonian calendar because the Babylonians celebrated New Year on the first new moon following the Spring equinox, whereas the Macedonian year started in Autumn, on the first new moon following the Autumn equinox. It is generally accepted (Samuel 1972, 245-246) that Seleucus returned to a dating system by the Argead king Alexander IV,[5] posthumous son of Alexander the Great, when he returned to Babylon in 311 after five years of absence because he had to flee Babylonia after his disagreements with Antigonus Monophthalmus. By doing so he abolished the revolutionary dating system introduced by his enemy Antigonus, who did not mention the name of the official Argead king anymore, but his own name and his title *rab uqu/a*.[6]

When Alexander IV was murdered soon afterwards in Macedonia[7] the Argead dynasty was extinct and, since no apparent heir was available, Seleucus and the other diadochi continued to date posthumously in the name of Alexander IV. After Antigonus Monophthalmus accepted the royal title for himself and his son Demetrius Poliorcetes after his son's victory over Ptolemy's navy at Salamis (Cyprus, June 306), the other

[4] There existed other era systems, the Olympiad reckoning e.g., but these dating systems were not used in daily life for official documents.

[5] Counting the regnal years of the king was the normal dating system in the Ancient Near East for already quite some time. It did not matter that Alexander IV was king of Alexander's Empire in name only and that the political power was in the hands of the generals.

[6] His title is only attested in the cuneiform documents (see Boiy 2002, 254-256); for the cuneiform tablets dated to Antigonus Monophthalmus, see Boiy (2007, 25). In the Aramaic ostraca from Idumaea dated to Antigonus Monophtalmus when he was *strategos* no title is mentioned (EN.56, EN.108, AL.50, AL.92, AL.93, AL.94, ISAP.212 and ISAP.2510; see Boiy 2007, 38). There are no Greek inscriptions dated in the name of *strategos* Antigonus Monophthalmus.

[7] Alexander IV was murdered in 310, but his death was kept secret at first.

diadochs followed suit and also Seleucus deleted the name of Alexander IV from the date formulas and started to date in his own name with the title king.[8] Seleucus did not start to count from his first year as Seleucid king, but he antedated his reign to the epochal dates in 312 and 311 by including — as generally accepted (Samuel 1972, 245) — his satrapal years starting from his return to Babylon after the five year absence. This method was not unusual since also Ptolemy continued to count his years in power in the Greek documents.[9] In 295 or 294 Seleucus appointed his son Antiochus I as coregent over the Seleucid empire, but the dating system remained unchanged.[10] When Seleucus was murdered in 281 by Ptolemy Keraunus, finally, Antiochus I decided not to start dating from year 1 onwards — probably because it was not his first year as Seleucid king because he was already coregent for quite some time — and he simply continued dating as his father had done. Since from this moment onwards there was no longer any link with the regnal period of

[8] CT 4 29d, the first document dated by king Seleucus, is dated 3 Nisannu 8 SE (16 April 304). Three literary tablets, the Babylon king list Iraq 16 pl. 53 (= BKL), the astronomical tablet AD 5 67 and the goal-year text AD 6 6 all identify Seleucus's first year as king with 7 SE:

BKL: obv. 6	mu-7-k[ám] *šá ši-i* mu-1-kám ^{m}*se-lu-ku* lugal
AD 5 67: 'flake' II' 12'	[m]u-7-kám ^{m}*se-lu-uk* lugal *šá ši-i* mu-1$^{?}$-kám
AD 6 6: obv.' 4	mu-1-kám ^{m}*se-lu-ku šá* IGI-*ta* mu-7

On the basis of the dating information in BKL I have argued that Seleucus adopted the royal title on 1 Nisannu 7 SE and that he deliberately made it coincide with Babylonian New Year (see Boiy 2011, 7-11).

[9] The earliest Greek papyrus P.Eleph. 1 is dated to the seventh year of Alexander IV and the fourteenth satrapal year of Ptolemy. After Ptolemy took the royal title for himself, the name of Alexander was removed and only the years of Ptolemy were left. The years of Ptolemy did not start all over again from the moment he adopted the royal title, his reign was antedated by including his satrapal years.

In the demotic documents, however, the count by king Alexander IV stopped and was replaced by the first year of king Ptolemy; see e.g. P.Ryl. 10, P.Phil.Dem. 2. and P.Brux. Dem. 2 2 (P.Brux. 8253).

Antigonus probably also continued counting his years as *strategos* when he took the royal title. Grzybek (1993) proposed to interpret the date of SEG 12 314, a Greek inscription from Beroia dated to the 27th year of king Demetrius, as 291/0 identifying the start of Demetrius's (virtual) rule with that of his father Antigonus Monophthalmus (for a full discussion of the inscription see Boiy 2009, 475-476). If this hypothesis is correct, this means that Demetrius's continued use of his father's years (as *strategos* and king) also qualifies as a chronological era and this "Antigonid era" is older than the Seleucid era.

[10] In Ptolemaic Egypt, Ptolemy I appointed his son Ptolemy II as coregent. The date formulas in the legal documents do not mention Ptolemy II and continue the counting of Ptolemy I. When Ptolemy I died in 282, Ptolemy II appears in the date formulas and that year was counted as his first year. Only later he antedated his reign from the moment he was appointed coregent by his father (see Pestman 1967, 14-19).

the ruling king(s),[11] a new dating system came into being and the Seleucid era was born. This means that Seleucus and Antiochus never planned to introduce the era as a new dating system, but that the introduction of a coregency led to a new system. Later Seleucid kings did not always appoint a coregent, but by that time the Seleucid era had become such a habit that they never started counting regnal years again.[12]

Let's return to the earlier events and the changed position of Seleucus. After the division of Triparadeisus (320[13]), Seleucus was awarded the satrapy of Babylon in recognition of his actions to remove Perdiccas from power. At the same conference Antigonus was confirmed as satrap of greater Phrygia and Lycia.[14] In addition, he was appointed as *strategos* over Asia[15] with the explicit order to fight Perdiccas's ally Eumenes in Asia Minor. After Antigonus had finally defeated Eumenes at Gabiene in the winter of 317/6,[16] he rearranged the Eastern satrapies.[17] Antigonus returned to Babylonia where he was welcomed by the satrap Seleucus who had supported him in his fights against Eumenes.[18] It did not take long before small incidents created a hostile climate between the *strategos* of Asia and the satrap of Babylonia. After Seleucus had punished an officer without asking the permission of Antigonus, Antigonus demanded account of the satrapy's finances. Seleucus refused and it was immediately clear to him that Antigonus considered this refusal as an infringement of his authority as *strategos* of Asia and that he would not leave

[11] Antiochus I immediately appointed his eldest son Seleucus as coregent. OECT 9 7, the oldest tablet without Seleucus I in the date formula already mentioned Antiochus I together with his son Seleucus (24.09.32 SE = 4.01.279).

[12] When Antiochus I died in 260, his son and coregent Antiochus II continued to rule as sole king. Antiochus II never appointed a coregent and his son Seleucus II only became king after his father's death in 246. Neither Seleucus II nor his son Seleucus III appointed a coregent. It was Antiochus III, the other son of Seleucus II, who reintroduced the system of a coregent in the Seleucid Empire.

[13] According to the low chronology. For the chronological problems of the Early Hellenistic period, see Boiy (2007).

[14] Diod. 18.39.6. See Klinkott (2000, 67-74).

[15] Diod. 18.39.7-40.1. Antipatros, who replaced Perdiccas as regent and guardian of the kings Philip Arrhidaeus and Alexander IV, was to take the kings to Europe and to reside there.

[16] According to the high chronology. For the so-called mixed chronology combining the low chronology for the first Diadoch War with the high chronology later on, see Boiy (2007, 120-124).

[17] Diod. 19.48.1-5. See Klinkott (2000, 75-76).

[18] When Eumenes arrived in Babylonia in 318 he tried to form an alliance with Seleucus and the Median satrap Peithon, but they both stayed loyal to Antigonus and tried to fight Eumenes although they were hopelessly outnumbered.

it at that. Seleucus saw the storm coming and preferred to flee the country. He was welcomed by Ptolemy in Egypt. In Babylonia Antigonus awarded the vacant satrapy to Peithon[19] son of Agenor, the former satrap of India.[20]

Seleucus helped his host by fighting Antigonus at sea and he never gave up hope to return to the satrapy he had received at Triparadeisus. In 312 the ideal moment had finally come: Antigonus was in Asia Minor and Syria was defended by his young son Demetrius. Seleucus convinced Ptolemy to attack over land and together they defeated the Antigonid army lead by Demetrius at Gaza. Seleucus received a small escort from Ptolemy and he immediately left for Babylonia. In Mesopotamia, he convinced Macedonian settlers to join him and also a district commander, Polyarchus, joined him with more than 1000 soldiers. When Seleucus arrived in Babylon in Spring 311 the Babylonian people welcomed him and those loyal to Antigonus fled to the citadel. Seleucus besieged the citadel and captured it. The military resistance in Babylonia probably was so minimal because its satrap Peithon had recently died during the battle at Gaza.[21]

Immediately upon his victory in Babylon Seleucus was thrown in the defensive. Nicanor, *strategos* over the upper satrapies,[22] gathered forces in Media, Persia and surrounding regions and marched against Babylonia. Seleucus ambushed him at night when he arrived at the river Tigris. Because most of the surviving soldiers were integrated into the army of Seleucus, he now had a large army force and he took advantage of the victorious momentum by going into the offensive himself. He marched east and took control over Susiane, Media and some of the surrounding regions.

When the news of Nicanor's defeat and Seleucus's subsequent campaign in the east arrived in Syria, Antigonus[23] ordered his son Demetrius

[19] Not the same Peithon as the satrap of Media mentioned above. On suspicion of treason Antigonus had this Peithon executed after the battles against Eumenes (Diod. 19.46.1-4).

[20] For a more detailed account of the events and the references to the classical sources, see Boiy (2004, 121-123).

[21] Diod. 19.85.2. Peithon was at that time probably also satrap of Mesopotamia (see Billows 1990, 415-416).

[22] Diod. 19.100.3; see Billows (1990, 409-410). Nicanor probably was also satrap of Media (App. *Syr.* 55; Bengtson 1964a:183). It is not known what happened to Orontobates who was appointed as satrap instead of the executed Peithon.

[23] After Seleucus had left for Babylonia, Demetrius returned to Syria and defeated Ptolemy's general Cilles. When Antigonus heard the news of Demetrius's victory he crossed the Taurus and joined his forces with Demetrius. Ptolemy retreated to Egypt and the Antigonids reconquered their Syrian territories. Before confronting Seleucus two unsuccessful expeditions against the Nabataeans, one by the general Athenaeus and one by Demetrius, were organized.

to reconquer Mesopotamia. With an army of 15.000 food soldiers and 4000 cavalrymen (Diod. 19.100.4) he met little resistance. Patrocles, who was put in charge over Babylonia by Seleucus before he left, decided it was unwise to resist this army and he advised the people of Babylon to evacuate the city and to take refuge in the desert behind the Euphrates or behind the Tigris. When Demetrius arrived in Babylon, the city was deserted and he besieged the city's citadels. One of the citadels was conquered immediately and plundered by Demetrius's soldiers (Diod. 19.100.7 and Plut. *Dem.* 7.2). After besieging the other citadel for a few days Demetrius appointed Archelaüs, one of his *philoi*, as *strategos* for the time of the siege. He left 5000 foot soldiers and 1000 cavalrymen[24] and he left for the west with the rest of his army (Diod. 19.100.7). The information on Babylonia in Diodorus breaks off here. From the Diadochi Chronicle (BCHP 3) it is clear that Antigonus himself returned the following year with an army and the hostilities between Antigonus and Seleucus in Babylonia continued in 310/09 and 309.[25] The same Archelaüs who was appointed by Demetrius as *strategos* for the siege of the second citadel in Babylon, is probably mentioned in BCHP 3: Rev. 28'[26] where he is appointed satrap of Babylonia (without doubt by Antigonus) in the month Addaru of Alexander's seventh year (310/09; Addaru is March-April 309).

It has always been assumed that when Seleucus returned to Babylonia, he regained his position as satrap of Babylonia and that he ruled as satrap until he took the royal title. The position of Patrocles, described as "*strategos* of Babylonia" by Diod. 19.100.5 was interpreted in the past as a temporary command over Babylonia because of the absence of its satrap Seleucus.[27] Van der Spek (2011) recently[28] proposed a new appealing theory: Seleucus took the title "*strategos* of Asia", the title

[24] According to Plut. *Dem.* 7.2 Demetrius left a garrison of 7000 soldiers in the conquered citadel.

[25] See BCHP 3: Rev. 15', 17', 21', 23', 25'-27', 37'-38' and L.E. 1'-2'; see also AD 1 -309: Obv.' 9 and 14.

[26] For this interpretation for ^{m}*a-ri-is-qí-la-mu*, see van der Spek (1992, 247-249). Geller (1990, 4 n. 19) identified ^{m}*a-ri-is-qí-la-mu* at first with Arkesilaüs. Since this person was satrap of Mesopotamia (not Babylonia) and nothing is heard of him anymore after 323, this proposal is less likely. In BCHP 3: L.E. 1' the same person appears together with the troops of Antigonus.

[27] See Bengtson (1964a, 190 and 1964b, 47) where he states that a normal satrapy at that time was ruled by a satrap, but temporarily Babylonia was ruled by a military commander by the appointment of Patrocles as *strategos*.

[28] He already mentioned Seleucus as *strategos* of Asia in 311 in an earlier article (van der Spek 1992, 247), but he did not elaborate the idea at that time.

of his mortal enemy Antigonus Monophthalmus, once he was back in power in the East and he gave the satrapy of Babylonia into the hands of Patrocles when he went to the East himself. Patrocles was given the title *strategos* of Babylonia (Diod. 19.100.5) and according to van der Spek this title was used because Seleucus did not want to give him the title of satrap of Babylonia, the office he had received after the division at Triparadeisus.[29] The absence of a satrap in Babylonia was no problem since Patrocles could rule as *strategos* and also Seleucus was as *strategos* of Asia fully competent to act in Babylonia. Confirmation of Seleucus as *strategos* of Asia can be found in the date formulas of the astronomical diaries AD 1 -308: 'Rev. 17' and U.E. 1 and probably also in the Diadochi Chronicle BCHP 3: Rev. 3'-4' where Seleucus appears as *strategos* (^{lú}gal eren$_2$.meš)[30] together with king Alexander IV.[31] The passage BCHP 3: Rev. 3'-4' is no date formula, but it probably is a description of the announcement that from that moment onwards, immediately

[29] Another possibility, that the title *strategos* was used to indicate the satrap of Babylonia, is not likely according to van der Spek.

According to Bickerman (1938, 198-200) the same function was sometimes described by different titles and a satrap could be called "*strategos*". This view would mean that Seleucus passed his title on to Patrocles when he became *strategos* of Asia himself. According to Bengtson (1964b, 47 and 90; see also Capdetrey 2007, 283-294) a Seleucid satrapy was ruled by a satrap, with the exception of Asia Minor where *strategoi* were appointed because of a reform there already during the reign of Antigonus Monophthalmus and temporarily in Babylonia in 311. It was not until the reign of Antiochus III (222-187) that also in the east of the Seleucid Empire *strategoi* were put in charge of the satrapies.

[30] Both ^{lú}gal eren$_2$.(meš) and ^{lú}gal *ú-qu/qa* were used to designate the title *strategos* (see Oelsner 1974, 130 and n. 5 and CAD U/W 203b-204a). Both designations were used for Antigonus Monophthalmus ^{lú}gal *ú-qu/qa* in the brewers' archive from Borsippa (see e.g. CT 49 35-41, 43-44 and 49) and ^{lú}gal eren$_2$ in other texts (AION Suppl. 77 81, Fs. Walker 122 (n° 9) and in the Babylon King List Iraq 16 pl. 53: Obv. 4). According to CAD U/W 203b CT 49 34: 24 combines both writings in ^{lú}gal eren$_2$-*qu*. However instead of ^{lú}gal eren$_2$-*qu* the reading ^{lú}gal eren$_2$ kur.kur is to be preferred (see also Stolper 1993, 53).

Also in the title *rab uqi ša ana muḫḫi 4 rab uqūti* ("the *strategos* who is in charge of the four *strategoi*"; CAD U/W 203b-204a) that appears in the historical notes of the astronomical diaries of the second half of the second century BC, the identification of ^{lú}gal eren$_2$.(meš) and ^{lú}gal *ú-qu/qa* is very clear: whereas the normal writing is ^{lú}gal eren$_2$.meš *šá ana muḫ-ḫi* 4 ^{lú}gal eren$_2$.meš (see e.g. AD 3 -155A: Rev. 13, AD 3 -136B: 'Rev.' 4' and AD 3 -118A: 'Rev. 21'), but also the writing *ana muḫ-ḫi* 4 ^{lú}gal *ú-qu-tú* (AD 3 -149B: 'Rev. 11') and *ana muḫ-ḫi* 4 ^{lú}gal *ú-qu-ú-tu* (AD 3 -140B: Rev.' 10) is attested. In AD 3 -140C: Obv. 37 and 'Rev. 31' a combination of both writings is found: ^{lú}gal eren$_2$.meš *šá ana muḫ-ḫi* 4 ^{lú}gal eren$_2$.meš *ú-qa*.

[31] The date formula of the astronomical diary AD 1 -309: 'Rev. 11' and U.E. 1 is not completely preserved, but it must most probably be restored in the same way as the date formula in AD 1 -308 (the name of Seleucus is partly visible in both 'Rev. 11 and U.E. 1).

following Seleucus's take-over of Babylon, "the seventh year of Antigonus Monophthalmus was to be counted as the sixth year of Alexander (IV), son of Alexander (III the Great) and Seleucus the *strategos*" (see van der Spek 1992, 245). The date formulas of the legal and administrative documents are dated in the traditional manner with the name and regnal year of the king Alexander IV only. This means that with taking Antigonus's title of *strategos* of Asia Seleucus did not continue Antigonus's innovation to date in his own name. Only in the Diadochi Chronicle and in the date formulas of the two astronomical diaries mentioned above his name and title (without year number) is added to the name and regnal year of king Alexander IV,[32] but in the other texts the date formulas are restored to the format they had before Antigonus's reform: name and regnal year of the king only.

What does this new view mean for Seleucus's dating methods and the birth of the Seleucid era? Until now it was thought that Seleucus started to think about a new dating method from the moment he accepted the royal title in 305 and that he antedated his regnal years at that time from the moment he returned to his satrapy Babylon in 311. For this reason no single text from the years 1 until 6 of Seleucus exists. Seleucus as *strategos* of Asia instead of Antigonus Monophthalmus as from 311 does not change this and it fits so much better in a logical flow of events.[33] Although Seleucus returned to the normal way of dating by naming the Argead king in the date formulas of the legal and administrative tablets, he did not abandon the innovation by Antigonus completely as can be seen in the announcement of change of dating system in BCHP 3: Rev. 3'-4' and in the date formulas of the astronomical diaries AD 1 -309 and -308 where his name and title *strategos* also appear without year number after the name and regnal year of king Alexander IV. It was, therefore, his taking the title of *strategos* of Asia and not his return to Babylonia as satrap[34]

[32] A similar dating method was followed by Ptolemy in Egypt in the Greek documents. P.Eleph. 1 is dated to the seventh year of Alexander IV and it also mentions the name of Ptolemy with his title satrap. In this case the satrapal year of Ptolemy (his fourteenth) is added.

[33] As soon as we accept Seleucus as *strategos* of Asia, the situation of Babylonia is for our chronographic purposes not of importance anymore: with a function for Seleucus on a central level, it did not matter anymore if there still was a satrap of Babylonia (either Seleucus, Patrocles or somebody else) or if Babylonia was ruled by Patrocles as military governor.

[34] If being satrap of Babylonia was the starting point for Seleucus's antedatation it would have been more logical to antedate to 320, the year when he became satrap of Babylonia after the Triparadeisus conference.

after five years of absence that prompted Seleucus to antedate his reign to 311 when he accepted the royal title in 305. This means that Seleucus post factum did count his years as *strategos* of Asia, just as Antigonus did when he was *strategos*. Also in combining his years as *strategos* of Asia with his rule as king Seleucus probably followed Antigonus's example (see above p. 45 n. 9). It was in 281 when Antiochus I continued the count of years of his father, first as *strategos* and later as king, that the Seleucid era was born.

In accordance with the preferred period of the honoree, I would like to venture a digression into the earlier history of Mesopotamia. During the Old Babylonian period, king Rīm-Sîn of Larsa (1822-1763)[35] ruled for sixty years and his conquest of the city of Isin in the middle of his reign gave rise to a chronological era according to modern scholars.[36] When Rīm-Sîn came to power Isin and Larsa had already a long history of rivalry and war for power in Mesopotamia. During that long period several other city states, especially in the north of Babylonia, had come to the foreground and it was clear that Isin's power was waning whereas Rīm-Sîn was becoming more powerful. After he annexed Uruk into his realm in 1803, he turned his full attention to Isin and in 1794 he was finally able to end the century long rivalry by conquering Isin. Rīm-Sîn took the title "king of Larsa, Uruk (and) Isin, king of Sumer and Akkad" and, as was the normal way of dating at that time, he called his 30th regnal year "the year Rīm-Sîn had Isin taken".[37] It is clear that the final victory of Larsa over Isin made quite an impression on Rīm-Sîn's contemporaries.[38] Also Rīm-Sîn was apparently very pleased by this victory and he named all

[35] Dates according to the traditional middle chronology. For other possibilities, see Gasche et al. (1998).

[36] See van de Mieroop (1993, 47). Robertson (1983, 150) calls it the "Isin era".

[37] For the full year-name see Sigrist (1990, 59-60).

[38] Not only Rīm-Sîn's contemporaries. Also modern scholars were impressed by this achievement and Rīm-Sîn's reign is often divided two periods, before and after the conquest of Isin, see van de Mieroop (1993, 49 and 55: "The early years", "The second half of Rim-Sin's reign") and Charpin et al. (2004, 119 and 124: 4.2. Les "trente glorieuses": la première moitié du règne de Rîm-Sîn [1822-1794]; 4.3 Le mystère de la seconde moitié du règne de Rîm-Sîn ([1793-1763]). It must be stressed, however, that this division is largely due to a problem of sources for the reconstruction of the second half of Rīm-Sîn's reign, underlined by both authors. Van de Mieroop deplores the decision to name every single year of Rīm-Sîn's reign after the fall of Isin to this event:

> "This decision turned out to be disastrous for the historian trying to reconstruct what happened in those years, as the list of yearly achievements disappeared." (van de Mieroop 1993, 55)

following years of his reign after this event, his 31st year being "the year following Rīm-Sîn had Isin taken", his 32nd "the second year following Rīm-Sîn had Isin taken" etc. It is this practice that has been interpreted as an era with the conquest of Isin as epochal date.

A year-name of the type "the year following <year-name of the previous year>" ("mu ús-sa" or "mu gibil") was not unknown in the date formulas of the Ur III, Isin/Larsa and Old Babylonian periods. It often concerned provisional year-names because no new year-name was promulgated yet or because the scribe did not yet know the new year-name and these provisional year-names were later replaced by an ordinary (and different) year-name. Since a new name was given to this year, the provisional name does not appear in the date lists that give a complete overview of all year-names of a certain period in chronological order.[39] In some cases, however, no new name was given to the year and the provisional name was used throughout the year and mentioned in the date lists. Even further years have been attested and these are best explained by the fact that the event referred to was so important or that hard times for the kingdom led to neglecting the promulgation of new year-names.[40] The conquest of Isin definitely falls into the first category, but the existence of other examples does indicate that we have to be careful with identifying it as an era.

The 30 years mentioning the conquest of Isin can be identified with an era in the colloquial sense of the word. There is no doubt that the conquest of Isin ended a long period of rivalry between Isin and Larsa and marked the beginning of a new political situation in the Isin/Larsa period. On the other hand, the mere appearance of 30 years during the reign of Rīm-Sîn after the event in the date formulas is in our view not enough to call it a chronological era: Rīm-Sîn was lucky enough to have a long reign and no other event in the second half of his reign, regardless whether his kingdom was on the decline or not, surpassed this legendary victory. The problem is also that Rīm-Sîn was not succeeded to the throne in a normal way, but that his realm was conquered by Hammurapi of Babylon and that it was integrated into the Old Babylonian kingdom.[41] If Rīm-Sîn had died a natural death or if he was at least succeeded by someone of his dynasty and if this new king had continued to date with

[39] Horsnell (1999, 139-142).

[40] Tammuz (1993, 60 n. 18) and Horsnell (1999, 140).

[41] The temporary fiction of a personal union between Babylon and Larsa with Hammurapi as king (see Charpin et al. 2004, 323) is of no importance here.

year-names that mentioned the conquest of Isin by his predecessor, there would be no issue and the "Isin era" would be a real chronological era.

A reference to another episode from the earlier history of Larsa casts doubt on the scenario sketched above: king Sumuel (1894-1866) called his 23rd year and all following years of his reign after the installation of the high-priestess of Nanna (Sigrist 1990, 20-21). It is exactly the same scenario as the so-called Isin era of Rīm-Sîn. The only difference is that Sumuel did not rule as long as Rīm-Sîn. He died in his 29th year (mu 7-kam en ^{d}Nanna ba-ḫun-gá; the sixth year following the year the high-priestess of Nanna was installed; Sigrist 1990, 21). The following year the era logic was broken and Sumuel's successor Nūr-Adad called his first full year, completely in accordance with the existing tradition in date formulas with year-names, "mu *nu-úr-*^{d}IM lugal" (Year Nūr-Adad became king; Sigrist 1990, 22).[42] This could have been the fate of the so-called Isin era too if a normal succession to the throne had taken place instead of the conquest by Hammurabi.[43] In addition, kings have a tendency of praising their own acts in year-names. It is therefore unlikely that any normal successor of Rīm-Sîn would continue to date with the formula "the xth year following *Rīm-Sîn* had Isin taken", however important the victory of his predecessor, renouncing the possibility to picture his own person in the date.

Another criterion is perhaps the formula used to indicate the year. As mentioned above this is fully consistent with the traditional way (provisional) year-names were written in the Isin/Larsa and Old Babylonian period, the only difference with the end of Sumuel's reign being that Rīm-Sîn reigned much longer and that he ended up with a much higher number. But also this method is not entirely watertight. If we take the Seleucid era, we see that also Antiochus I continued to use the traditional methods by mentioning the year number and the reigning king(s), the only difference being that the year number did not give the regnal years of the king(s) anymore.

A minimal requirement to speak of a real chronological era could be that it has to span at least more than one regnal period so as to make clear that the epochal date is important enough in the eyes of more than one king and that the succeeding king agreed to date after an event that

42 For the accession years, see also Horsnell (1999, 136-139).

43 The comparison is not completely without flaw, because also the succession Sumuel/Nūr-Adad was probably not a normal dynastic succession either: as usurper (Charpin et al. 2004, 101) Nūr-Adad had no profit in remembering an act by his predecessor and he had every reason to emphasize his own coming to the throne.

took place before the start of his own reign. If Larsa had not been conquered by Hammurapi of Babylon and a normal succession had taken place, it could have been the birth of an Isin era. Since a coregency, the reason why the Seleucid era came into existence by coincidence, did not exist in Larsa during the reign of Rīm-Sîn, it is however more likely that a new king would have emphasized his taking the throne by returning to the traditional method of calling his first full year "mu RN lugal". Since the course of history went as it did and Hammurapi defeated Rīm-Sîn of Larsa, we will never know for sure if the so-called Isin era could have come into being as a chronological era.

Another Old Babylon candidate for a chronological era recently came to light with the publication of Babylonian tablets from the first Sealand Dynasty in the Schøyen collection (Dalley 2009). King Pešgaldarameš and his successor Ayadaragalama are mentioned in the date formulas of these texts: year 27 and 29 for Pešgaldarameš and several year-names and year 7 and 8 for Ayadaragalama (Dalley 2009, 10-11). Dalley (2009, 10) follows the chronological data in the Babylonian King List giving Pešgaldarameš 50 regnal years and his successor Ayadaragalama 28 years. Because a gap of twenty years in the documentation is for prosopographical reasons very unlikely, Dalley concludes that — comparable to the so-called Isin era — as from his 22nd year Pešgaldarameš started to call all his regnal years after the same event as his 21st year. For his successor Ayadaragalama several regular year-names are preserved and year 7 and 8. If Dalley's theory concerning the reign of Pešgaldarameš is correct, the system changed to year-names again at the accession of the following king Ayadaragalama and — exactly like the so-called Isin era — we cannot call this dating system a chronological era. Van Koppen (2010, 456-457), on the other hand, concludes that the 50 years attributed to Pešgaldarameš by the Babylonian King List are erroneous and that his attested years 27 and 29 and the attested year 7 and 8 for king Ayadaragalama are simply counting their regnal years from the moment they ascended the throne. If van Koppen is correct, these date formulas simply give a year number as was customary later in Babylonia and since they started to count all over again at each accession, it is no chronological era either.

Finally, a so-called "Babylon era" has been proposed for the late Old Babylonian or early Kassite period. Economic texts found in the late Old Babylonian levels[44] of Tell Muḥammed, today enclosed by the modern

[44] Level I was attributed to the beginning of the Kassite period and levels II-VII to the Old Babylonian period (see Gasche et al. 1998, 83). The cuneiform documents were found in levels III and II.

city of Baghdad, have revealed date formulas with ordinary local year-names and date formulas that refer to the years 36-41 in connection with the city of Babylon (mu.x.kám.ma *ša* ká.dinger.ra^{ki} *uš-bu*). Three chronologically distinct groups of date formulas can be discerned:

1. date formulas with ordinary local year-names (from level III and II). In one text from level III a local king Ḫurbaḫ[45] is mentioned. In a text from level II the son of Ḫurbaḫ[46] initiating hostilities with the king is mentioned.
2. date formulas with a double date: a local year-name and a date of the type "mu.x.kám.ma *ša* ká.dinger.ra^{ki} *uš-bu*". The year numbers of the second type vary between 36 and 39. All texts were found in level II. In the year-name of the date formula dated to year 36 the killing of the son of Ḫurbaḫ is mentioned and in the following year a king named Šiptaulzi appears in the year-name.
3. date formulas of the type "mu.x.kám.ma *ša* ká.dinger.ra^{ki} *uš-bu*". All texts were found in level II and only year 41 is attested with certainty.

The formula "mu.x.kám.ma *ša* ká.dinger.ra^{ki} *uš-bu*" was at first translated as "year x that Babylon was resettled", linking it with Babylon's resettlement after the destruction by the Hittite king Mursili I and placing the texts in the early Kassite period (Gasche et al. 1998, 84). Sassmannshausen (1999, 414) preferred "the xth year after x sat down in Babylon" as translation and he interpreted the formula as referring to the installation of the Kassite dynasty in Babylonia, but he later accepted the earlier interpretation (Sassmanshausen 2004b, 64). Gentili (2002, 2003-04) interpreted the date formula as "the year x after Babylon was established (in the region)" and identified this event with the start of Babylon's control over Tell Muḥammed in the year 37 of king Hammurapi. Van Koppen (2010: 462), finally, stressed the late Old Babylonian characteristics of the legal formula and the stratified late Old Babylonian context of

45 IM 90602; in IM 90606_1 the same person appears but without royal title. Interpretation of the reading of the name by van Koppen (2010, 458). The name was originally read Ḫurduzum (Gasche et al. 1998, 86) and later interpreted as Ḫurbatum (Sassmannshausen 2004a, 302) and Ḫurbazum (Boese 2008, 204).

This king is identified with the seventh Kassite king of the Synchronistic King List (see van Koppen 2010, 459). Boese (2008, 204-205) also reads Ḫurbazum in the Synchronistic King List.

46 In this case this reading was already established by Gasche et al. (1998, 86). This king is identified as the eighth Kassite king of the Synchronistic King List (Boese 2008, 204-205; van Koppen 2010: 459).

level II where the tablets have been found.[47] He therefore dismissed the date proposed by Gentili as too early and that by Gasche et al. as too late. With a possible translation "the year that he/she/they sat down (in) Babylon" or "year that he (or they) took up residence in Babylon" he proposed a link with the moment a Kassite prince or garrison (the unmentioned subject in the date formula) had been awarded the privilege of guarding the capital city Babylon.

Only the name of king Šiptaulzi appears in the date formulas with reference to Babylon. To decide whether this so-called "Babylon era" meets the criteria for a real chronological era mentioned above, it is necessary to find out whether it was already in use before Šiptaulzi ascended to the throne. Sadly enough, we do not have any date formulas with a lower number than 36 and there is no other king mentioned in the preserved date formulas. In addition, the Synchronistic King List does not mention the number of Šiptaulzi's regnal years. The highest number of years associated with this formula (41) makes it plausible to presume that the event mentioned was before the start of Šiptaulzi's reign, but this is just a reasonable guess that is at present impossible to corroborate (especially in view of the long reign of our first example Rīm-Sîn of Larsa).

The "large time span during which years are numbered from a specific event, the epochal date" needed for a chronological era is here defined minimally as a period during which more than one king ruled. A dating system with regnal years or a year-names system referring to the same event for several years during the reign of one king does not qualify as a chronological era according to this criterion. The so-called "Isin era" and the dating systems by the Sealand kings Pešgaldarameš and Aya-daragalama were no chronological era's and it is impossible to say with certainty if the so-called "Babylon era" was a chronological era. After a long period of numbering regnal years in Babylonia from the middle of the thirteenth century until the beginning of the third century BC, Antiochus I continued the years of his father Seleucus and introduced the first chronological era in practical use in daily life. 1990 AD on the other hand, despite its importance for world history and my personal view on Seleucid history, is still far from becoming the epochal date of a chronological era.

[47] For the legal formula see also Gasche et al. (1998, 84 n. 340).

Bibliography

BENGTSON, H. 1964a: *Die Strategie in der hellenistischen Zeit. Ein Beitrag zum antiken Staatsrecht* (Münchener Beiträge zur Papyrusforschung und antiken Rechtsgeschichte 26), München.

— 1964b: *Die Strategie in der hellenistischen Zeit. Ein Beitrag zum antiken Staatsrecht* (Münchener Beiträge zur Papyrusforschung und antiken Rechtsgeschichte 32), München.

BICKERMAN, E. J. 1938: *Institutions des Séleucides* (BAH 26), Paris.

BILLOWS, R. A. 1990: *Antigonos the One-Eyed and the Creation of the Hellenistic State* (Hellenistic culture and society 4), Berkeley.

BOESE, J. 2008: "'Harbašipak', 'Tiptakzi' und die Chronologie der älteren Kassitenzeit", *ZA* 98, 201-210.

BOIY, T. 2002: "Royal Titulature in Hellenistic Babylonia", *ZA* 92, 241-257.

— 2004: *Late Achaemenid and Hellenistic Babylon* (OLA 136), Leuven.

— 2007: *Between High and Low. A Chronology of the Early Hellenistic Period* (Oikumene Studien zur antiken Weltgeschichte 5), Frankfurt am Main.

— 2009: "Date Formulas in Cuneiform Tablets and Antigonus Monophthalmus, Again", *JAOS* 129, 467-476.

— 2011: "The Reigns of the Seleucid Kings According to the Babylon King List", *JNES* 70, 1-12.

CAPDETREY, L. 2007: *Le pouvoir séleucide: territoire, administration, finances d'un royaume hellénistique (312-129 avant J.-C.)*, Rennes.

CHARPIN, D.O. EDZARD and M. STOL 2004: *Mesopotamien. Die altbabylonische Zeit* (OBO 160/4), Fribourg.

DALLEY, S. 2009: *Babylonian Tablets from the First Sealand Dynasty in the Schøyen Collection* (CUSAS 9), Bethesda.

GASCHE, H, J.A. ARMSTRONG, S.W. COLE and V.G. GURZADYAN (eds.) 1998: *Dating the Fall of Babylon. A Reappraisal of Second-Millennium Chronology* (MHEM 4), Gent-Chicago.

GELLER, M.J. 1990: "Babylonian Astronomical Diaries and Corrections of Diodorus", *BSOAS* 53, 1-7.

GENTILI, P. 2002: "The 'strange(r)' month names of Tell Muhammad and the Diyāla Calendars", *EVO* 25, 203-230.

— 2003-04: "Tell Muhammad... again!", *Sumer* 52, 34-38.

GRZYBEK, E. 1993: "Eine Inschrift aus Beroia und die Jahreszählweisen der Diadochen", in *Ancient Macedonia 5. Papers read at the Fifth International Symposium Held in Thessaloniki, 10-15 October 1989*, Thessaloniki, 521-527.

HORSNELL, M.J.A. 1999: *The Year-Names of the First Dynasty of Babylon*, Hamilton.

KLINKOTT, H. 2000: *Die Satrapienregister der Alexander- und Diadochenzeit* (Historia Einzelschriften 145), Stuttgart.

OELSNER, J. 1974: "Keilschriftliche Beiträge zur politischen Geschichte Babyloniens in den ersten Jahrzehnten der griechischen Herrschaft (331-305 v.u.Z.)", *AOF* 1, 129-151.

PESTMAN, P. W. 1967: *Chronologie égyptienne d'après les textes démotiques (332 av. J.-C.-453 ap. J.-C.)* (Papyrologica lugduno-batava 15), Leiden.

ROBERTSON, J.F. 1983: "An Unusual Dating System from Isin-Larsa Period Nippur: New Evidence", *ASJ* 5, 147-161.

SAMUEL, A.E. 1972: *Greek and Roman Chronology: Calendars and Years in Classical Antiquity* (Handbuch der Altertumswissenschaft 1.7), München.

SASSMANNSHAUSEN, L. 1999: "The Adaptation of the Kassites to the Babylonian Civilization", in K. Van Lerberghe and G. Voet (eds.), *Languages and Cultures in Contact at the Crossroads of Civilizations in the Syro-Mesopotamian Realm. Proceedings of the 42th RAI* (OLA 96), Leuven, 409-424.

— 2004a: "Kassite nomads: Fact or fiction", in C. Nicolle (ed.), *Nomades et sédentaires dans le Proche-Orient ancien. Compte rendu de la XLVIe Rencontre Assyriologique Internationale (Paris, 10-13 juillet 2000)* (Amurru 3), Paris, 287-305.

— 2004b: "Babylonian Chronology of the 2nd Half of the 2nd Millennium B.C.", in H. Hunger and R. Pruzsinszky (eds.), *Mesopotamian Dark Age Revisited. Proceedings of an International Conference of SCIEM 2000 (Vienna 8th-9th November 2000)* (Österreichische Akademie der Wissenschaften. Denkschriften der Gesamtakademie, Band XXXII), Wien, 61-70.

SIGRIST, M. 1990: *Larsa Year Names* (Institute of Archaeology Publications Assyriological Series 3), Berrien Springs, Michigan.

STOLPER, M.W. 1993: *Late Achaemenid, Early Macedonian and Early Seleucid Records of Deposit and Related Texts* (Istituto universitario orientale Napoli. Annali. Supplemento 77), Napoli.

TAMMUZ, O. 1993: *Archives from Lagaba* (PhD dissertation Yale University), New Haven.

VAN DE MIEROOP, M. 1993: "The Reign of Rim-Sin", *RA* 87, 47-69.

VAN DER SPEK, R.J. 1992: "Nippur, Sippar, and Larsa in the Hellenistic Period", in M. deJong Ellis (ed.), *Nippur at the Centennial: Papers Read at the 35e Rencontre Assyriologique Internationale, Philadelphia, 1988* (Occasional publications of the Samuel Noah Kramer Fund 14), Philadelphia, 235-260.

— 2011: "Seleukos, self-appointed General (strategos) of Asia (311-305 B.C.) and the Satrapy of Babylonia", in H. Hauben and A. Meeus (eds.), *The Age of the Successors (323-276 B.C.)* (Studia Hellenistica 53), Leuven (in print).

VAN KOPPEN, F. 2010: "The Old to Middle Babylonian Transition: History and Chronology of the Mesopotamian Dark Age", *Ägypten und Levante* 20, 453-463.

THE 'OCHRE' ROOM: SHEDDING SOME LIGHT ON A 'DARK' PERIOD OF TRANSITION TELL TWEINI IN THE EARLY IRON AGE

Joachim BRETSCHNEIDER, Greta JANS,
Anne-Sophie VAN VYVE and MICHEL DEBRUYNE
KU Leuven

For Karel, the laureate of this volume ...

From underneath the ever so charming 'Professor Zonnebloem'[1]-look a 'multi-disciplinary' person appears: exploratory (blowing ammonium chloride on tablets without any protection), critical (asking why you actually think you are reaching a floor level over and over again), determined (writing applications for yet another project), balanced (keeping a stable ratio between assyriology and archaeology), innovative (realizing the mini-dome for 3D reading of tablets), amiable (staying up late during excavations with a glass of beer or wine), funny (telling stories of past rencontres and excavations in Iraq and Syria), adventurous (riding the motor cycle through the Near East), ...

In working at the Near Eastern Department of the KU Leuven and while excavating in Tell Beydar and/or Tell Tweini, he influenced a great part of our lives and it has to be said: this actually was (and still is) a very nice part of our lives. And for that, we want to pass along an extremely warm thank you to Karel.

Introduction[2]

The ancient harbour town of Gibala, Tell Tweini (Syria), has been occupied from as early as the Early Bronze Age and flourished during the

[1] Professor Calculus or *Professeur Tournesol*.

[2] We are grateful to the following institutions which offered us financial assistance for the research in Syria: the Research Foundation Flanders (FWO), the Interuniversity Attraction Poles 6/34 and the *Onderzoeksfonds* KU Leuven.

It is our pleasure to thank the following people for assembling and analyzing specific parts of information: our square supervisors of this area — Elynn Gorris, Georg Neumann, Greta Jans and Ellen Van Belle —, our architects — Maarten Gernaey and Hendrik Hameeuw —, our ceramic specialists — Reinhard Jung, Karin Nys and Klaas Vansteenhuyse,

Middle and Late Bronze Age, ending in a collapse synchronous with the destruction of the Kingdom of Ugarit (Bretschneider and Van Lerberghe 2008, 44). Written sources mentioning the site of Gibala ceased to exist with the fall of Ugarit, but reappeared in the Iron Age II period, leaving a historical void of ca. 500 years. The transition from Bronze to Iron Age in the Eastern Mediterranean (1200-950 B.C.) is traditionally called the crisis years or Dark Age, and is characterized by destructions as well as the arrival of new population groups, such as the so-called 'Sea-People'.[3] Thus far these population groups have remained archaeologically discrete, but the ongoing excavations at Tell Tweini have revealed solid 12th to 10th century occupation.

Several clusters of Early Iron Age architecture including communal buildings and private habitations have been identified all through the area of Field A within the city walls. Throughout the period of assumed collapse (fire-destruction level 7A and reoccupation level 6GH), architectural features and ceramic evidence illustrate a slow transition and continuity, allowing the characterization of both social and urban changes. Subsequent occupation (level 6EF) at Tell Tweini during the 11th century is typified by amplified building activity and by the appearance of imported pottery and luxury items. This phase seems to end with a second conflagration identifiable through a thick layer of debris sealing off key loci holding intact primary contexts.

Especially striking in the material culture of Tell Tweini is the presence of a series of Aegean features including a type of public architecture (megaron-like buildings), early Mycenaean IIIC pottery, handmade burnished ware, loom weights and a figurine of the so-called 'Goddess with upraised hands'. These may be regarded as cultural markers of foreign settlers who can be identified as the 'Sea-People'[4] since they also show up in Philistine settlements in Israel.[5] A new indication of Sea People (Philistine) presence in the Northern Levant is offered by two monumental Hieroglyphic Luwian inscriptions mentioning the Land of Palistin, recently

and their team: Evy Cuypers, Elynn Gorris and Karolien Senica —, our archaeo-zoologists — Bea Decupere and Veerle Linseele —, our archaeo-botanists — Elena Marinova and Jan van der Valk, our palynologist — David Kanwieski —, and our logistic supervisor Wim Verhulst.

[3] Lehmann 2001; Dothan and Dothan 1992; Drews 1993; Gitin, Mazar and Stern 1998; Oren 2000.

[4] Karageorghis 2000; Barako 2000; Dickinson 2006.

[5] Dothan 1982; Deger-Jalkotzy and Bächle 2009; Hawkins 2011; Lehmann 2001; Gilboa 2005; Yasur-Landau 2010.

uncovered in the Temple of the Storm God in the Aleppo Citadel (Hawkins 2009, 164-173; 2011). They seem to confirm the formation of foreign policies centred around the site of Tell Tayinat, where Aegean influences also seem present in the material culture (Harrison 2009, 174-189).

One of the contexts linked to the new settlers is located on Field A and consists of an entire limited room, containing loom weights and well datable ceramics, producing excellent material for ^{14}C dating (Table 1). A detailed description, analyses and interpretation of this room can shed some light on a 'dark' period of transition.

Architecture and features

The different architectural phases attested for the transitional period at Tell Tweini can be summarized as follows: after the Late Bronze destruction (level 7A), the construction of new buildings indicate a reoccupation at the beginning of the Early Iron Age, level 6GH (Bretschneider et al. 2010) (Table 2). A second architectural phase is attested for the end of the Early Iron Age, level 6EF.

The Early Iron Age room 05873 is located to the south of the more recent Building A in Field A (Fig. 1 and 2). Enclosed by walls 05882 in the north, 06456 in the east, 06506 in the south (built on top of an older wall (6GH wall 06463) with a somewhat different orientation) and wall 06360 in the west, it has a long, rectangular shape of circa 7.5 m by 2.9 m. It seems as if the room was to be entered through a door in the northern part of wall 06360.

An issue that needs to be considered is the date of the room's construction. Throughout the Early Iron Age alterations have been made to different rooms in Field A. Room 05873 is no exception and most probably had a slightly different appearance during level 6GH than during level 6EF. It seems as if the room had an extension to the north, without wall 05882 and with wall 05584 as the northern limit. The western and eastern wall (06360 and 06456) belonged to the 6GH level. The ochre deposit however did not superimpose these latter walls, which is one of the reasons to conclude they were reused during the 6EF level. The 6GH wall 06463 in the south was covered with in situ 6EF ceramic material in the ochre layer and thus was not reused as an enclosing wall during 6EF. The southern wall 06506 is new to level 6EF and follows a different orientation than the 6GH wall 06463. The course of the street bordering the southern end of the room might be a motive for the slightly new direction of the southern wall. On top of the remains of the 6GH southern wall 06463 were eight in situ jars (Fig. 3). The demolished wall possibly served as the onset of the 6EF walking level.

So far there are no key loci with pure 6GH material. The second half of the Early Iron Age, 6EF, however is well represented by a large quantity of material located in the prominent yellow-ochre layer characterized by its loam chunks and sometimes black, burnt inclusions.[6] This layer covers the floor of the entire room and has a variable thickness ranging from 25 cm in the north to up to 50 cm in the central part of the room. The layer seems to slope or 'terrace' down from north to south, with a maximum difference in height of 30 cm. In the middle of the room there is a pit-shaped depression (underneath a 6AB-CD wall), possibly connected to the shattered installation 06409, which perhaps could be interpreted as remnants of an oven (Fig. 4). The bottom of this pit-shaped structure was covered with an ash layer (05872). Also in several other areas within the room, a thin black layer of ca. 5 cm thick (05877 and 05889) predates the ochre layer.

The ochre layer was filled with in situ ceramics, scattered around the room. Evidently these ceramics found on a certain level were resting on what is perceived as a floor level, in this case one of beaten earth, since no clear floor structure has been discerned so far.

Material Culture

The inventory of the ochre layer inside room 05873 comprises 100 objects, of which a substantial part can be described as clay loom weights (55) and jar stoppers (28), but also artefacts in bronze (9) and stone (8) can be assigned to this layer (Fig. 6).

The 55 unbaked or poorly fired[7] loom weights all have a fairly similar shape: they are either cylindrical or more spool shaped and imperforated (Fig. 7).[8] They measure between 8.70 and 13.20 cm in height and weigh between 300 and 580 grams. A fair amount of 34 weights was found in

[6] This layer is made up of different locus numbers: 05863, 05866, 05867, 05868, 05875, 05881, 5887, 06404, 06405, 06452 and 06454.

[7] Yasur-Landau (2010, 132) also mentions that this type of loom weights can be unbaked or poorly fired.

[8] Unbaked or poorly fired clay spools, either cylindrical or hourglass shaped are well known from Aegean and Philistine sites and are a common feature of LH IIIC/LM IIIC material culture assemblages (Yasur-Landau 2010, 841; Rahmstorf 2003). In the Northern Levant this Aegean type of loom weights appears after the Sea-People destructions at 12th and 11th century sites as Tell Taynat, Tell Afis and now also Tell Tweini.

assemblage to the west of installation 06409 (Fig. 5). All the loom weights (except for five exemplars) were retrieved from the north western quarter of the room.

Analogous with the loom weights, almost all 28 jar stoppers were found in the north western quarter of the room (Fig. 8).[9] The (fragmentary) jar stoppers come in different shapes but the technique of 'sealing' the jar seems to be alike for all the stoppers. The plane circular base was pressed on the rim with a strip of clay grasping over the outside of the rim; the upper part of the stopper was either conically shaped or more flat and rounded (Fig. 9). No impressions of textile, leather or string could be discerned. For the majority of the stoppers, the clay was rather coarse and the preservation state was poor, however some exemplars seem to have been made from a better quality of clay and they had a more smoothed surface. One jar stopper was discovered while still on top of the opening of a jar. Generally jar stoppers serve as a lid or covering of the contents of a container and the stopper can usually be removed without being broken and then replaced if required. The kind of jar stopper found at Tell Tweini appears to differ from this concept. In order to win access to the 'sealed' container, the jar stopper had to be — at least slightly — broken.

The nine bronze objects yielded from the ochre layer were recorded as three leaf-shaped arrowheads (Fig.10) — deposited together in the north western corner of the room —, one spear or javelin head, two simple pins, one rather large 'pair of tweezers' (33 cm high) and two unidentifiable fragments of bronze. One bronze artefact — a flat rectangular shape (3.5 cm high) with one of the small sides ending in a triangle — was stuck onto a loom weight.

Four of the stone objects can be classified as basalt pestles, one as a fragment of a basalt grinding stone, two probably as mortar bowls — low basalt bowls on three short feet, one circular in shape (20.9 cm diameter), the other rectangular with rounded edges (33 cm wide) (Fig. 11) — and one small vessel in greyish stone (with a diameter of 8.9 cm).

The ceramic inventory of the room consists of at least 35 large (storage) jars and several smaller fragmentarily preserved jars with one Cypriote White Painted I bowl (a two-handled deep bowl on a conical foot —

The proof of their use as loom weights comes from Ashkelon, where Lawrence Stager (1991, 14-15) discovered them in several instances in a row along the walls, together with linen fibres. For more information on textile industry in Northern Syria, see: Andersson et al. 2010, 159-176 and Cecchini 2000, 211-233.

[9] Five were excavated in the south western quarter of the room.

Nys and Middernacht 2011, 125). The greater part (31) of the storage jars was positioned in the southern half of the room with eight jars against the southern wall (Fig. 3), eleven in the south eastern part, four in the south western quarter and eight to the west of installation 06409.

The data on fauna and flora uncovered from the room lies within the expectations. It seems as if the species (for the fauna: sheep, goat, cattle, gastropod and for the flora: olive and wood) present are analogous to the information gathered from other parts of the tell.[10]

Interpretation and Conclusion

Based on the architectural structures and material culture of room 05873, it is clear that this area was highly significant during the period of transition from the Bronze to the Iron Age. The level 6GH traces have mostly survived in architectural and ceramological evidence. There are no visible traces of a destruction level ending level 6GH, nor are there visible, clearly distinguishable floor levels characterising this phase. The traces that survived may be the ones that were recycled during the following phase, 6EF.

Loom weights, implements related to grinding, numerous storage jars and jar stoppers, all of which were found in the ochre layer, show that certain domestic and storage activities took place inside this room. However there are no indications that the loom weights were in fact used in this room, apparently they were only stored here, possibly on a pile or a shelf against the northern part of the western wall.

The yellow colour present in the ochre layer is mostly explainable through the presence of loam and pieces of clay holding marks of braided hay, indicating the appearance of the room's masonry. The collapse of the walls of a higher floor or roof terrace cannot be excluded. The black layer underneath the ochre layer and the ochre layer itself seem to be part of the same 6EF level[11], thus at least a partial burning of the room can be inferred; according to the high quantity of in situ objects and ceramics, probably an intentional obliteration. So far no similar room contexts have been discerned throughout the rest of Field A, which seems to refute the idea that a general destruction took place during this time. Future research should provide more definitive answers on these issues.

[10] We thank Prof. Veerle Linseele (fauna) and Dr. Elena Marinova (flora) for this information.

[11] The black layer may indicate the use of a wooden floor.

Bibliography

AL-MAQDISSI, M., J. BRETSCHNEIDER, K. VAN LERBERGHE and M. BADAWI (eds.) 2011: *Tell Tweini. Onze Campagnes de Fouilles Syro-Belges (1999-2010)*, Damas (in print).

ANDERSSON, E., E. FELUCCA, M.-L. NOSCH and L. PEYRONEL 2010: "New Perspectives on the Bronze Age Textile Production in the Eastern Mediterranean. The First Results with Ebla as a Pilot Study", in P. Matthiae, F. Pinnock, L. Nigro and N. Marchetti (eds.) *Proceedings of the 6th International Congress on the Archaeology of the Ancient Near East, Rome 5-10 May 2008*, 159-176.

BRETSCHNEIDER, J. and K. VAN LERBERGHE (eds.) 2008: *In Search of Gibala* (Aula Orientalis Supplementa 24), Barcelona.

BRETSCHNEIDER, J., K. VAN LERBERGHE, K. VANSTEENHUYSE and M. MAQDISSI 2008: "The Late Bronze and Iron Age in the Jebleh Region: A View from Tell Tweini", in H. Kühne, R. Czichon and F. Kreppner (eds.) *Proceedings of the 4th International Congress on Archaeology of the Ancient Near East, 29 March — 3 April 2004, Berlin*, Vol. 2, 33-46.

BRETSCHNEIDER, J., G. JANS and A. VAN VYVE 2011: "Les Fouilles du Chantier A en 2009 et 2010. Une Analyse Préliminaire de la Transition du Bronze Récent et L'Age du Fer I", in M. Al-Maqdissi, J. Bretschneider, K. Van Lerberghe, M. Badawi (eds.), *Tell Tweini. Onze Campagnes de Fouilles Syro-Belges (1999-2010)*, Damas (in print).

CECCHINI, S. M. 2000: "The Textile Industry in Northern Syria during the Iron Age According to the evidence of the Tell Afis Excavations", *Ancient Near Eastern Studies Supplement* 7, 211-233.

DEGER-JAKOLTZY, S. and A. E. BÄCHLE 2009: *LH IIIC Chronology and Synchronisms III. LH III Late and the Transition to the Early Iron Age. Proceedings of the International Workshop held at the Austrian Academy of Sciences at Vienna, February 23rd and 24th, 2007.*

DREWS, R. 1993: *The End of the Bronze Age.*

DOTHAN, T. 1982: *The Philistines and their Material Culture.*

DOTHAN, T. and M. DOTHAN 1992: *People of the Sea: The Search for the Philistines*, New York.

GILBOA, A., 2005: "Sea People and Phoenicians along the Southern Phoenician Coast — A Reconciliation: An Interpretation of Sikila (SKL) Material Culture", *BASOR 337*, 1-32.

GITIN, S., A. MAZAR and E. STERN (eds.) 1998: *Mediterranean peoples in transition: Thirteenth to early tenth centuries BCE.*

HARRISON, T. P. 2009, "Neo-Hittites in the "Land of Palistin": Renewed Investigations at Tell Taʿyinat on the Plain of Antioch", *Near Eastern Archaeology* 72 (4), 174-189.

HAWKINS, J. D. 2009: "Cilicia, the Amuq, and Aleppo: New Light in a Dark Age", *Near Eastern Archaeology* 72 (4), 164-173.

— 2011: "The Inscriptions of the Aleppo Temple", *Anatolian Studies* 61, 35-54.

KANIEWSKI, D., E. PAULISSEN, E. VAN CAMPO, H. WEISS, T. OTTO, J. BRETSCHNEIDER and K. VAN LERBERGHE: Late Second — Early First Millennium BC Abrupt Climate Changes in Coastal Syria and their Possible Significance for the History of the Eastern Mediterranean, *Quaternary Research* 74, 2010, 207-215.

LEHMANN, G. 2001: "The "Sea-People Phenomenon", Migration and Transmission of Culture in the Levant at the End of the Late Bronze Age", in R. Eichmann and H. Parzinger (eds.) *Migration und Kulturtransfer*, 411-426.

OREN, D. (ed.) 2000: *The Sea Peoples and Their World: A Reassessment.*

NYS, K. and K. MIDDERNACHT 2011: "The Cypriot Pottery from Field A", in M. Al-Maqdissi, K. Van Lerberghe, J. Bretschneider and M. Badawi (eds.) *Tell Tweini. Onze Campagnes de Fouilles Syro-Belges (1999-2010)*, Damas, 123-30 (in print).

RAHMSTORF, L. 2003: "Clay Spools from Tiryns and Other Contemporary Sites: An Indication of Foreign Influence in LHIIIC?", in N. Kyparissi-Apostolika and M. Papakonstantinou (eds.) *Proceedings of the 2nd International Interdisciplinary Colloquium: The Periphery of the Mycenaean World, September 26-30, Lamia.*

RAHMSTORF, L. 2005: "Ethnicity and Changes in Weaving Technology in Cyprus and the Eastern Mediterranean in the 12th Century B.C.", in V. Karageorghis, H. Matthäus and S. Rogge (eds.) *Cyprus: Religion and Society: From the Late Bronze Age to the End of the Archaic Period: Proceedings of an International Symposium on Cypriote Archaeology, Erlangen, 23-24 July 2004*, Münster, 143-169.

STAGER, L. E. 1991: *Ashkelon Discovered: From Canaanites and Philistines to Romans and Moslems*, Washington D.C.

VANSTEENHUYSE, K. and J. BRETSCHNEIDER 2011: "Handmade cooking pots from the Early Iron Age in Tell Tweini (Syria)", in V. Karageorghis and O. Kouka (eds.) *On Cooking Pots, Drinking Cups, Loom Weights and Ethnicity in Bronze Age Cyprus and Neighbouring Regions*, 187-194.

Yasur-Landau, A. 2010: "Levant", in E. H. Cline (ed.) *The Oxford handbook of the Bronze Age Aegean*, Oxford.

Samples	**Layer (Field A)**	**Laboratory codes**	**Material**	**14C yr BP**	**2σ cal yr BP**	**1σ cal yr BP**	**Intercept cal yr BP**
TWE08 EP96	6E	Poz-26396	Charcoals	2780±35	2960–2790	2930–2845	2890
TWE08 EP148	6E	Poz-25442	Olive stones	2845±35	3070–2870	3000–2920	2960
TWE08 EP149	6E	Poz-25443	Charcoals	2880±35	3080–2920	3070–2960	3010

Table 1. Details of the 14C age determinations for the Level 6E. All ages have been calibrated with IntCal04-Calib Rev 5.0.1.

		PHASES OF TWEINI	FIELD A
1918 –	Modern	Tweini I B	Level 1
	Ottoman	Tweini I A (19^{e} c. AD)	Level 2
1516 –	Islamic		
636 –	Byzantine	Tweini II	
AD 395 –	Roman	Tweini III	Level 3
BC 64 –	Hellenistic	Tweini IV	
333 –	Iron Age III (Persian Achaemenid Period)	Tweini V A-B	Level 4 A-B
400 –			
500 –			
600 –	Iron Age III		Level 5 A-B
700 –	Iron Age II	Tweini VI A-B	Level 6 A-B
800 –			
900 –			Level 6 C-D
1000 –	Iron Age I	Tweini VII B	Level 6 E-F
1100 –		Tweini VII A	Level 6 G-H
1200 –	Late Bronze Age II B	Tweini VIII B	Level 7 A-B-C
1300 –	Late Bronze Age II A		
1400 –			
1500 –	Late Bronze Age I	Tweini VIII A	Level 7 D-E
1600 –	Middle Bronze Age II	Tweini IX B	Level 8 A-B
1700 –			
1800 –	Middle Bronze Age I	Tweini IX A	Level 8 C-D
1900 –			
2000 –	Early Bronze Age IVB	Tweini X B	Level 9 A-B
2100 –			
2200 –	Early Bronze Age IVA	Tweini X A	Level 10
2300 –			
2400 –	Early Bronze Age III	Tweini XI	Level 11?
2500 –			
2600 –			

Table 2. Tweini phases and levels.

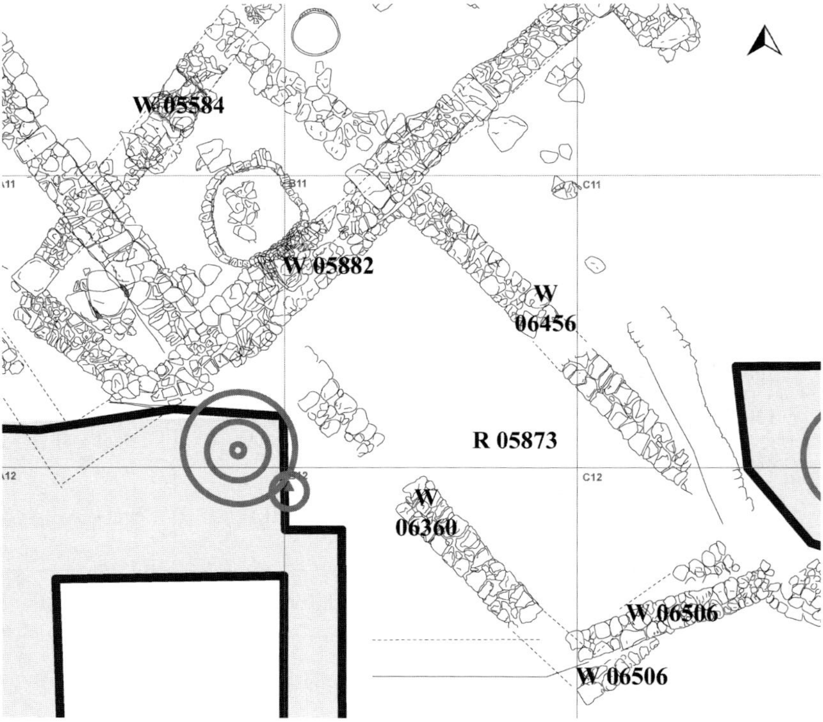

Fig. 1. Plan of room 05873
(excavated by E. Gorris, G. Jans, G. Neumann & E. Van Belle;
plan by M. Gernaey & H. Hameeuw).

Fig. 2. Room 05873 — View from the south.

Fig. 3. Eight jars positioned against wall 06506 — View from the west.

Fig. 4. Pit-shaped depression with ochre layer and ash layer in the centre of room 05873 — View from the south.

Fig. 5. Some loom weights in situ — View from the south.

Fig. 6. Part of the ochre layer with loom weights, jars and a basalt bowl in the northwestern part of room 05873.

Fig. 7. Spool shaped loom weights.

Fig. 8. Conically shaped jar stopper.

Fig. 9. An incomplete preserved jar stopper on a rim fragment.

Fig. 10. Three leaf-shaped arrowheads.

Fig. 11. Basalt bowl on three feet.

SEALING PRACTICES AT NEO-ASSYRIAN TIL BARSIB

CYLINDERS – STAMPS – *SISSIKTU* – SEAL BOX

Guy BUNNENS
Liège University

In the Neo-Assyrian period Tell Ahmar, the site of ancient Til Barsib on the left bank of the Syrian Euphrates, was the capital city of a province of the Assyrian empire. Excavations at the site have uncovered significant remains dating from that time, which shed a welcome light on life in an important centre of the empire. One aspect of life at Til Barsib, that is represented by few but surprisingly diverse examples, concerns sealing practices. It is hoped that Karel Van Lerberghe, who has promoted both philological and archaeological research, will find some interest in this study which stands on the border line between the study of material remains and that of written evidence. It must be said, from the very beginning, that all the objects that will be discussed below were found in a seventh century context, i.e. in remains roughly dating from the reigns of Esarhaddon and Ashurbanipal.

Nine, possibly ten, objects concerned sealing practices at Neo-Assyrian Til Barsib. All together, they bore twenty seal impressions. The surprise came from the small proportion of cylinder seal impressions — only two — found on these sealed documents compared with that of actual seals, which included nine cylinder seals and eight stamp seals. Less surprising was the observation that none of the actual seals was used to make any of the impressions found on various objects.

Among the tablets excavated in Room 12 and in the doorway between Rooms 11 and 12 of Building C1a, a few sealed documents were found.[1] A first group consisted of three contracts recording the sale of a slave. They were made in the standard format of Neo-Assyrian contracts. The tablets were higher than wide and the first lines gave the name of the seal's owner(s). Below these, one or more seal impressions were made, immediately above the text of the contract.

[1] The tablets were published by Dalley (1996-1997). On the archaeological context, see Guy Bunnens 1996-1997.

A blank seal?

One tablet, T13, which dated from the post-canonical eponymy of Shamash-da'inanni, bore two stamp seal impressions (Fig. 1).[2] The text above the impressions mentioned only one seal and specified that it belonged to one Tabaya, owner of the slave that was being sold. It can thus be assumed that the same seal was applied twice. Curiously enough, the sealings were perfectly flat (Fig. 2). The impression was clearly delimited by an oval depression, surely corresponding to the ring that was enclosing the seal, but no design was visible. As the seal has been impressed twice, the absence of decorative motive can hardly be accidental, as if, for instance, insufficient pressure had been exerted on the object. It must therefore be concluded that an undecorated ring was used, which had the same value as a seal that could be identified through its decoration. The symbolic meaning of the object, intimately associated with its owner, was probably more important than its function as an artefact.

Egyptianizing seals

A second contract — T8 (Fig. 3), the date of which was lost — had three impressions of the same stamp seal of which the owner's name was not preserved.[3] Its decoration consisted of Egyptian, or Egyptianizing, motifs (Fig. 4). Vanessa Boschloos (Belgian Royal Museum of Art and History) suggested to me a comparison with an 8th/7th century seal found at Carthage, which belongs to Feghali-Gorton's Type XI.[4] Seals of this group are split in three registers. Of the motifs usually combined to decorate these seals, tablet T8 includes, at the upper register, two antithetic falcons. The object between them is difficult to recognize. The middle register is usually decorated with divine figures and one could tentatively recognize a deity, or a deceased ancestor, on the left, and a worshiper or an attendant on the right. The middle figure remains enigmatic. The lower register should include a *neb* sign or an uraeus. The *neb* sign is clearly visible on T8.

[2] Dalley 1996-1997, 82-84, copy on plate 3, photograph on p. 98, fig. 6. Dimensions: 8.2 × 4.3 × 2.2 cm.

[3] Dalley 1996-1997, 76-77, copy on plate 2, photograph on p. 97, fig. 4. Dimensions: 8.9 × 5.0 × 2.2 cm.

[4] V. Boschloos, personal communication, with reference to Feghali-Gorton 1996, 32-33, Type XI, No.1, (= Vercoutter 1945, 157, No. 251, and plate VIII).

The third contract — tablet T9 (Fig. 5), a fragmentary record with no preserved date — also bore the impression of an Egyptian, or Egyptianizing, seal (Fig. 6).[5] The name of the owner was lost. Here again I have to thank Vanessa Boschloos for her suggestions concerning the interpretation of the seal. She proposes to reverse the impression, which has been made upside down with respect to the sense of writing, and to see, from left to right, the feather of Maat, a sun-disk, or the *khet* sign, above a sign that would be either the *neb* basket or the *t* sign, and a fourth motif which could be an uraeus. She suggests to read either *Neb-Maat-Re*, which was the praenomen of Amenhotep III, who was still revered a long time after his reign, or *khet-nebet-maat*, "everything just".[6] Vanessa Boschloos points to similar inscriptions on seals of Feghali-Gorton's Type XXII (Group A) that would have been made in Rhodes in the 8th/7th century (Feghali-Gorton 1996, 64-68).

It is quite remarkable that these Egyptian or Egyptianizing seals point to the Mediterranean and, more specifically, to the Phoenician world. They emphasize the cosmopolitan nature of the local culture.

A second group of texts included two tablets that were encased in a clay envelope. In both cases, the documents concerned a loan of silver and, in both cases, the seals — all stamp seals — were impressed on the envelope only.

Tablet T15 was fragmentary (Fig. 7), as was its envelope, but three seal impressions were still visible, two on one side and one on the other.[7] It is quite likely that there were originally four seal impressions, two on either side of the envelope. The three preserved impressions were made by three different seals. Only one of them, made on envelope fragment 1, was sufficiently detailed to recognize an animal moving to the left possibly in the posture of the so-called flying gallop (Fig. 8). The seal had been applied upside down with respect to the sense of writing. The two other seal impressions were difficult to interpret. The traces that were visible just allowed to recognize that they were made with two different seals.

The second silver loan deserves a special treatment.

[5] Dalley 1996-1997, copy on plate 2, photograph on p. 98, fig. 5. Dimensions: 7.2 × 2.7 × 1.1 cm.

[6] V. Boschloos, personal communication.

[7] Dalley 1996-1997, 85-86, copy on plate 4. Dimensions (without the envelope): 2.6 × 3.5 × 1.5 cm.

Sissiktu

Tablet T20 (Fig. 9) probably dated from the year after the eponymy of the last canonical eponym Bêl-harrân-shadûa, i.e. from 649, if Stephanie Dalley's restoration is correct.[8] Only the left half of the envelope, which was bearing the sealing, was preserved. There was thus room for at least one more sealing. However, the text written on the envelope mentions only one seal. The text on the tablet does not even refer to it. According to the first line of the envelope, it would be the impression of the seal of one Ishtar-dûri. However, the traces that are actually visible do not form the sort of device that was normally carved on a seal, but a kind of spiral with no figurative motif (Fig. 10). It could be the mark left by a shell,[9] as shells are known to have been used to seal documents (Homès-Frédéricq 1986, 111-118), but a closer look at the tablet in the Aleppo National Museum suggested another interpretation.[10] Twisted strands were clearly visible, indicating that a coiled string or cord had been impressed on the soft clay. The impression on the envelope of T20 must therefore have resulted either from the application of an independent cord — perhaps a cord that was holding a seal — or, more likely, from the impression of a thread belonging to the fringe of a garment. This would thus offer an example of the practice referred to as a mark of *sissiktu* in earlier periods.[11] This is quite unusual. In 1992 Suzanne Herbordt could still write "Beispiele von Abdrücken eines Gewandsaumes (*sissiktu*) sind in neuassyrischer Zeit nicht nachgewiesen" (Herbordt 1992, 41). And in 2007 Lionel Marti wrote "Cette pratique [the application of a garment hem or of a string on a tablet] est finalement documentée a Emar..., puis semble disparaître après cette époque" (Marti 2007). It must now be admitted that the practice lasted longer than it was formerly believed.

This practice was represented at Til Barsib by yet another example. On a "long" tablet (T14), found in the doorway between Rooms 11 and

[8] The envelope was published by Dalley 1996-1997, 89-90, copy on plate 5, photograph on p. 99, fig. 8. Dimensions: 3.5 × 3.9 × 2.5 cm. The tablet was published by Radner 2004, 25-27, No. 26, and 83, No. 82.

[9] As I suggested in a note inserted in Stephanie Dalley's publication of the tablet (Dalley 1996-1997, 85, n. 29).

[10] I thank Mr Nasser Sharaf, former keeper of pre-classical antiquities in the Aleppo National Museum, for his assistance in this matter.

[11] Durand 2000, 78, understands *sissiktu* as referring to the string that was holding the seal.

12, two different sealings were applied (Fig. 11).[12] The tablet reported instructions that were given to unnamed addressees not to talk to Hannî and Hashânu as long as a tablet had not arrived at the palace.[13] The text was dated to the eponymy of Sha-Nabû-shu (658). The names of the owners of the seals were preserved. The first named was Shulmu-ahhê, the "deputy" of Tarbusiba (the local form of the name Til Barsib), the second was Iqbi-Ashshur, the scribe. It may therefore be assumed that the seal on the left was that of the first named, Shulmu-ahhê, and the seal on the right the one of Iqbi-Ashshur.

The first seal, on the left, was an oval stamp seal turned on its side (Fig. 12). It was decorated with a crouching animal, a kind of wild goat, and a branch that extended over its head. The seal, probably a scaraboid, was of a type common in Iron Age Syria, although a close parallel is difficult to find.

Much more puzzling was the sealing on the right (Fig. 13). No obvious pattern nor shape were recognizable. The impression might have been made with another object than a seal, for instance a shell.[14] However, on closer examination of the tablet in the Aleppo National Museum, it became clear that some kind of fabric had been applied on the fresh clay. The traces of two thin cords ending in a fringe of tiny threads were recognizable. The cords were applied horizontally with their extremity towards the left. Such an impression cannot have been made but by the hem of a garment, which again recalls the Bronze Age practice of sealing documents with a *sissiktu*. The strange thing is that the text referred to it as a seal (^{na4}KIŠIB) and, still more surprising, that the "seal", in all likelihood, belonged to a scribe (^{lú}A.BA). It is hard to believe that Iqbi-Ashshur, who was involved in the highest level of local administration, did not have a seal of his own. Here again, the symbolic value of the object, a garment that may have been a status symbol, seems to have played a role in the selection of the sealing device.

It is thus clear that the practice of *sissiktu* sealings continued into the Neo-Assyrian period.

[12] Dalley 1996-1997, 84-85, copy on plate 3, photograph on p. 99, fig. 7. Dimensions: 3.1 × 5.5 × 2.0 cm.

[13] Dalley 1996-1997, 84, translates *ina* É.GAL on line 10 as "from(?) the palace", but it must be remembered that there was a palace at Til Barsib, which makes the translation "at the palace" more likely. The text may mean that, as long as the "sealed order" has not been received by the local administration, nobody can speak to Hannî and Hashânu.

[14] As suggested in my note to Dalley 1996-1997 (see above, n. 10).

A stamp-cylinder seal

It has been noted at the beginning that only two cylinder seals were used to seal documents at Til Barsib. One concerned a jar sealing found in Room 11 of Building C1a (Fig. 14).[15] The object presented itself as a lump of clay with a convex and smoothed surface on which the seal was applied. This surface was cut at almost right angle by an irregular surface on which imprints of a string and creases of a cloth were visible. It seems that the clay had been applied on the neck of a jar, the mouth of which was protected by some kind of fabric held by a string.

The cylinder seal was applied at the top of the preserved part of the object, but only its lower half was preserved, bordered by a straight groove that must be the imprint of its metal setting (Fig. 16). What remains is sufficient to see that the seal was carved in Neo-Assyrian style and represented at least three figures marching to the right, towards a standing figure facing left. The interesting thing is the presence, below and to the right of the cylinder seal impression, of five impressions of a round stamp seal, of which two were overlapping the cylinder impression. The decoration consisted of three elongated omega-like symbols and one small disk, possibly a stylized pomegranate (Fig. 15).

A question arises as to the relationship existing between the two seals. An answer would be that two persons, or authorities, sealed the jar with their own seal. It is strange, however, that the stamp seal was perfectly circular, with a diameter (c. 1.8 cm) close to that of a standard cylinder seal. It is quite possible, as was suggested by Madeleine Trokay, that they were one and the same seal, i.e. a cylinder seal within a setting the base of which was decorated and also used as a sealing device.[16] Such seals, which Dominique Collon calls stamp-cylinders, were already known in earlier periods (Collon 1987, 111-112). They would have reappeared towards the end of the seventh century as a compromise between the Assyrian tradition, which knew only cylinder seals, and the new developments that took place in the Iron Age, which witnessed the spread of the stamp seal (Collon 1987, 77, 111). We should not be surprised to find such an object, that is at the confluence of two cultural traditions, at a site like Til Barsib. Til Barsib was an Aramean settlement turned into an Assyrian centre as well as one of the most important stages on the road linking the core of the empire with its western provinces.

[15] TAH94 C895 O.1102. Dimensions: L. 8 cm, H. 4.5 cm, Th. 6 cm.

[16] Trokay 1995, 102-105 (with reference to the object under discussion here on p. 98, 105, and fig. 1, p. 99).

A sealed tag

A clay object in the shape of an irregular flat cone with a slighly concave side bore a stamp seal impression on its base (Fig. 17).[17] It was found in the fill of Room 9 of Building C2. At first sight one might think that it was a jar stopper, but no trace of contact with the regular shape of a jar opening was visible. It is therefore more likely that the object was not intended to be placed in or against another object. It might have been a kind of tag or bulla. As the point of the cone seems to have broken off, the object may have originally included a hole through which a string was inserted so that the sealing could be attached to whatever object.

The scene carved on the basis of the cone was Assyrian in style. It showed two figures facing each other, probably the king in front of a high official, the *turtânu* or the crown prince.

A door sealing

From area E, in the northern part of the lower town, comes a last sealing (Fig. 18), discovered in Stratum b, immediately underlying Building E1 where wall paintings were discovered.[18] It is convex on the outside and concave on the inside, and much thinner at the upper part than towards its bottom. It looks like a broken cone with a central perforation. Its base shows the marks of a string and traces of a ligneous object are visible in the round perforation. These are the typical features of a door sealing. A string, that was holding the door closed, was turned around a stick fixed either on the door itself or on the wall next to the door. The sealing consisted of a lump of clay applied against the string and the stick, and impressed with a seal.

The decoration of the seal — which was the second cylinder seal impression discovered at the site — figured a standing worshiper, to the left, in front of a storm-god holding thunderbolts in both hands. Between the two figures was an offering table below a winged disk. Behind the god was another standing figure, from which it was separated by a star, and, at the far right, a diamond-shaped symbol. Like *sissiktu*, door sealings do not seem to have been found in large numbers in Neo-Assyrian times.[19]

[17] TAH96 C92.23 O.92.5. Dimensions: 2.9 × 3.1 × 2.6 cm.

[18] TAH96 E15.26 O.15.13. Dimensions: H. 2, W. 2.5, Th. 1.3 cm. On the wall paintings, see Abbate 1994, 7-16; Bunnens 2006, 68-69 and fig. 55, p. 155.

[19] See the discussion by Herbordt 1992, 69-70.

An ivory seal box?

Another unicum may be represented by a small ivory head found in the debris filling Room 1 of Building C1a (Fig. 19).[20] It is a female figure in high relief, shown en face, with two locks of hair on either side of the head. A cavity has been cut on its back and a hole pierced from top to bottom through the head.

One might think that the cavity at the back was a mortise that would have fitted a tenon on an object of which the ivory head would have formed part of the decoration. However, the irregular shape of the cavity makes this explanation problematic. Also problematic is the vertical hole that goes through the head. It is hard to think of any function it might have served. However, a plausible hypothesis has been suggested to me by François Popelin. According to him, the ivory head would be an ancestor of the so-called seal boxes that were known in Roman times. A Roman seal box was a little bronze container with holes in its sides, that was attached to a fabric or leather container by cords passing through these holes and tied with a knot inside the box. The box was then filled with wax, so that the knot was no longer accessible, and a seal was applied on the wax. A lid protected the impression.[21] In the case of the Til Barsib ivory the vertical perforation would have served to let the cords enter the cavity and the knot would have been tied inside the cavity. This interpretation is extremely attractive, although the cavity in which the wax is supposed to have been laid is small compared with the average size of Iron Age seals. Besides this, there is no evidence that the ivory was equipped with a lid. Nonetheless, the hypothesis is plausible and, if correct, only a stamp seal could have been used.

Conclusion

The significance of the sealings discovered at Neo-Assyrian Til Barsib, all found in a 7th century context, is much greater than it could be expected from their comparatively small number. Firstly, they illustrate the spread of stamp seals into a Neo-Assyrian cultural environment. None of the six

[20] TAH91 C28.315 O.466. Dimensions: H. 2.5, W. 2.3, Th. 0.9 cm. Publication: Bunnens 1997, 438-439, No. 1.

[21] See Feugère and Abauzit 1995, 41-43 (previous research), 43-44 (typology); Derks and Roymans 2002, 89-93 (use and typo-chronology) and, most recently, Furger, Wartmann and Riha 2009.

sealed tablets discovered at the site were sealed with a cylinder. One of the seals — a stamp seal — seems even to have been blank, emphasizing the symbolic aspect of sealing practices. Another two seals had an Egyptian, or Egyptianizing, decoration which finds parallels in the Mediterranean and, more specifically, Phoenician world. A jar stopper bore the impression of what seems to have been a stamp-cylinder seal, i.e. a cylinder seal the setting of which had a round base carved with a decorative design, in an attempt to combine two cultural traditions with different sealing practices, sealings made with cylinders and sealings made with stamp seals. Two examples of sealings were made with the hem of a garment (*sissiktu*), probably giving the latest known examples of such sealings. In both cases, however, the text refers to them as "seals". Lastly, a small ivory head could give an early version of the seal boxes that became common in the Roman period.

Such a diversity gives a good illustration of the cosmopolitan nature of the Til Barsib culture under Neo-Assyrian rule.

Bibliography

ABBATE, L. 1994: "Wall-paintings from a Neo-Assyrian building at Til Barsib", *Abr-Nahrain* 32, 7-16.

BUNNENS, G. 1996-1997: "New texts from Til Barsib: The archaeological context", *Abr-Nahrain* 34, 61-65.

BUNNENS, G. 1997: "Carved ivories from Til Barsib", *American Journal of Archaeology* 101, 435-450.

BUNNENS, G. 2006: *A New Luwian Stele and the Cult of the Storm-God at Til Barsib-Masuwari*, with a chapter by J. D. Hawkins and a contribution by I. Leirens (Tell Ahmar II), Louvain.

COLLON, D. 1987: *First Impressions: Cylinder Seals in the Ancient Near East*, London.

DALLEY, S. 1996-1997: "Neo-Assyrian tablets from Til Barsib", *Abr-Nahrain* 34, 66-99.

DERKS, T. and N. ROYMANS 2002: "Seal-boxes and the spread of Latin literacy in the Rhine delta", in A. E. Cooley (ed.) *Becoming Roman, Writing Latin? Literacy and Epigraphy in the Roman West* (Journal of Roman Archaeology, Supplementary Series 48), Portsmouth, Rhode Island, 87-134.

DURAND, J.-M. 2000: *Documents épistolaires du palais de Mari*, III (Littératures anciennes du Proche-Orient 18), Paris.

FEGHALI-GORTON, A. 1996: *Egyptian and Egyptianizing scarabs: A Typology of Steatite, Faience and Paste Scarabs from Punic and other Mediterranean Sites* (Oxford Committee for Archaeology, Monograph 44), Oxford.

FEUGÈRE, M. and P. ABAUZIT 1995: "Les boîtes à sceau circulaires à décor zoomorphe riveté d'époque romaine", *Revue archéologique de l'Est* 46, 41-57.

FURGER, A. R., M. WARTMANN, and E. RIHA 2009: *Die römischen Siegelkapseln aus Augusta Raurica* (Forschungen in Augst 44), Augst: Römermuseum Augst.

HERBORDT, S. 1992: *Neuassyrische Glyptik des 8.-7. Jh. v. Chr.* (State Archive of Assyria Studies 1), Helsinki.

HOMÈS-FRÉDÉRICQ, D. 1986: "Coquillages et glyptique araméenne", in M. Kelly-Buccellati (ed.), *Insight Through Images: Studies in Honor of Edith Porada*, Malibu, 111-118.

MARTI, L. 2007: "Des *sissiktu* à Munbâqa", *NABU* 2007, No. 20, 20.

RADNER, K. 2004: "A Neo-Assyrian tablet from Til Barsib", *NABU* 2004, No. 26, 25-27 and No. 82, p. 83.

TROKAY, M. 1995: "Interconnections in glyptic art during the Neo-Assyrian period", *Abr-Nahrain* 33, 96-112.

VERCOUTTER, J. 1945: *Les objets égyptiens et égyptisants du mobilier funéraire carthaginois*, Paris.

Fig. 1. Tablet T13 (obverse).

Fig. 2. Impressions of a blank(?) seal on tablet T13.

Fig. 3. Tablet T8 (obverse).

Fig. 4. Impressions of an Egyptian, or Egyptianizing, seal on tablet T8.

Fig. 5. Tablet T9 (obverse).

Fig. 6. Impression of a seal with possible Egyptian hieroglyphs on tablet T9.

Fig. 7. Envelope of tablet T15.

Fig. 8. One of the seal impressions on tablet T15.

Fig. 9. Envelope of tablet T20.

Fig. 10. Imprint of a coiled cord on the envelope of tablet T20.

Fig. 11. Tablet T14 (obverse).

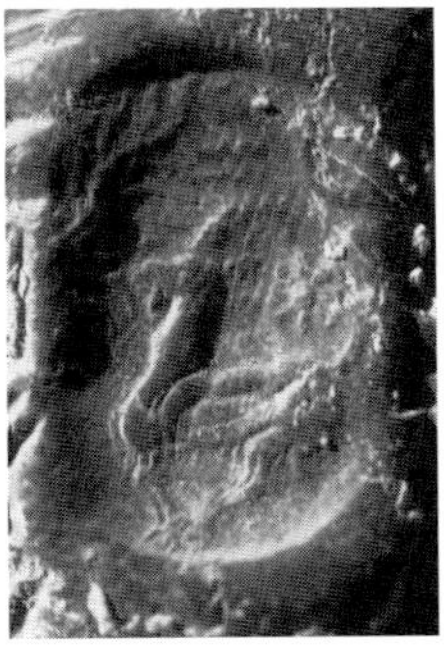

Fig. 12. Seal impression on tablet T14.

Fig. 13. Imprint of a cord or of a piece of fabric on tablet T14.

Fig. 14. Fragment of a jar stopper with seal impressions on its side (a) and imprint of a cord on its base (b).

Fig. 15. Impressions of a round seal on the jar stopper of Fig. 14.

Fig. 16. Impression of a cylinder seal on the jar stopper of Fig. 14.

a b

Fig. 17. Conical object (a) with a seal impression on its base (b).

b

a

Fig. 18. Impression of a cylinder seal on a door sealing (a) and marks of a cord on its base (b).

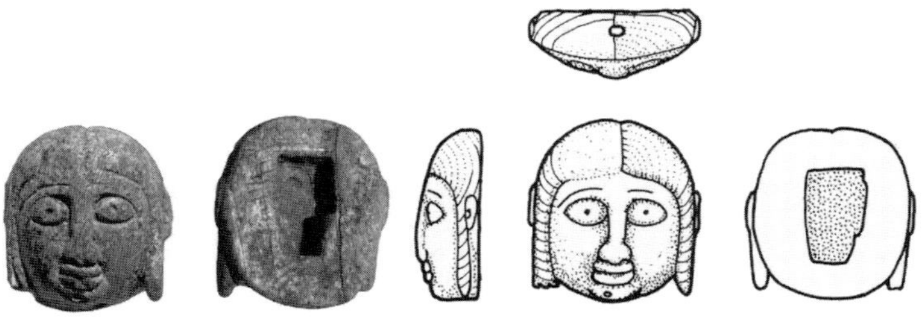

Fig. 19. Ivory head with a vertical perforation and a cavity at the back.

UNE LETTRE D'UN ROI INCONNU: NOUVELLES DONNÉES SUR LE DÉBUT DU RÈGNE DE ZIMRI-LIM*

Dominique Charpin
École pratique des Hautes Études
et UMR 7192 (CNRS), Paris

Le tout début du règne de Zimri-Lim reste une période encore mal connue, en dépit du progrès de nos connaissances ces dernières années. La chronologie a pu être affinée et ainsi la transition entre la fin du règne de Yasmah-Addu et le début de celui de Zimri-Lim mieux comprise (Charpin et Ziegler 2003, 170-184); de nouveaux documents ont été publiés (Guichard 2002a). On a également constaté que l'effondrement du royaume de Haute-Mésopotamie permit le retour chez elles de nombreuses personnes retenues ailleurs contre leur gré; plusieurs lettres ont également montré l'importance qu'avait eue dès ce moment le roi d'Andarig, Qarni-Lim (Guichard et Ziegler 2004).

La lettre ici éditée et commentée a déjà été signalée par M. Birot lorsqu'il rendit compte de nouvelles découvertes épigraphiques effectuées dans le palais de Mari (Birot 1973, 6[1]). On sait en effet que la deuxième

* Cette contribution a été préparée dans le cadre du projet «ARCHIBAB (Archives babyloniennes, XXe-XVIIe siècles)», dont la phase 2 est financée pour 2011-2014 par l'ANR (Agence Nationale de la Recherche) au titre des «programmes blancs». Je remercie la Direction des Antiquités et des Musées de Syrie ainsi que les directeurs du musée de Der ez-Zor, pour m'avoir permis de travailler sur cette tablette conservée avec l'ensemble des archives royales de Mari. Ma gratitude va également à J.-M. Durand pour ses suggestions dans la lecture du document ici publié, ainsi qu'à I. Arkhipov et M. Guichard pour leur relecture de mon manuscrit. Les circonstances ne m'ont pas permis de revoir une dernière fois l'original avant d'encrer la copie que j'avais préparée, de sorte que j'ai jugé préférable de reproduire celle-ci telle quelle.

[1] M. Birot avait ainsi résumé la lettre: «Un autre rapport sur le Šubartu [n. 6: N° 72-5] émane d'un nommé *Ḫa-ab-bu-u*[*m*] (?), un prince local qui se dit le «frère» du roi de Mari. Il y a là-bas des villes fortes occupées par des garnisons hanéennes et mariotes, mais il semble qu'elles y soient bloquées par les troubles qui ont agité le pays. Ḫabbum, qui avait fait, avec l'aide de *Šepraru* (autre dynaste nouveau pour nous), une première tentative infructueuse pour rétablir l'ordre, annonce qu'il part de nouveau avec Šepraru, qu'il fera sortir les garnisons et les ramènera. Il demande d'ores et déjà que Zimri-Lim lui envoie — apparemment en récompense de ses services — la belle-fille de Mubalšaga, un haut fonctionnaire bien connu de l'époque «assyrienne».» (Birot 1973, 6).

guerre mondiale avait empêché A. Parrot de parfaire l'exploration de la fameuse salle 115, où avait été retrouvée la plus grande part de la correspondance conservée dans le palais de Mari. C'est seulement au printemps 1972 que la mission reprit la fouille de ce locus, au moment où le dégagement du «palais présargonique» conduisait à faire disparaître ce qui subsistait des vestiges du palais, quarante ans après leur exhumation. Le long des murs et dans les deux niches des murs Est et Ouest de cette petite pièce, on découvrit alors une centaine de tablettes ou de fragments s'ajoutant aux quelque 10000 découverts en 1936 et 1937; la tablette TH 72.5 ici publiée en faisait partie[2].

Je suis heureux d'offrir l'édition de ce document à Karel Van Lerberghe, dont les travaux ont notablement contribué à faire progresser notre connaissance de l'époque paléo-babylonienne. Il s'est en particulier voué à l'étude de l'époque paléo-babylonienne tardive, depuis sa thèse sur les archives d'Ur-Utu (Van Lerberghe et Voet 1991), jusqu'au récent livre qu'il a consacré aux passionnantes archives de Dûr-Abi-ešuh (Van Lerberghe et Voet 2009). Je dois ajouter qu'il a été l'un des premiers assyriologues à contribuer au projet ARCHIBAB, en nous envoyant l'édition numérique de CUSAS 8, qui a alimenté notre base de données[3]. S'il n'a jamais publié d'étude portant sur Mari, on sait en revanche que la Syrie est une terre qui lui est chère: il a longtemps participé aux travaux de Tell Beydar et co-dirige depuis 1999 les fouilles de Tell Tweini près de Jablé, l'antique Gibala des archives d'Ugarit. J'espère donc qu'il trouvera plaisir à lire cette lettre, qui nous fait connaître un roi mystérieux...

1. Le texte (TH 72.5)

Cette lettre de Habbusum à Zimri-Lim peut être ainsi résumée. 1) H. est allé au pays de Šubartum, mais il n'est pas entré dans les villes qui avaient proposé leur ralliement. Il attend l'arrivée de Šepraru pour le faire et se propose alors de renvoyer à Z.-L. les Bédouins et les Mariotes retenus dans ces villes. 2) H. demande que Z.-L. lui envoie l'épouse de

[2] Cinq lettres découvertes lors de la campagne de 1972 ont déjà été publiées: TH 72.8+TH 72.39, TH 72.13, TH 72.15, TH 72.16 et TH 72.30, ainsi que l'étiquette de coffre à tablettes TH 72.128a. On trouvera la bibliographie afférente sur www.archibab.fr.

[3] Les transcriptions ont été intégrées à notre site Internet (www.archibab.fr) par les soins de B. Alexandrov, Maître de Conférences au Collège de France en 2010-2011, dont la collaboration au projet a été très fructueuse.

Mubalsaga. 3) Qarni-Lim a émis des prétentions infondées sur plusieurs villes. 4) H. souhaite que ses forces se joignent à celles de Z.-L. lorsque celui-ci ira «au cœur du pays», au moment que son correspondant choisira. 5) Formules de salutation finales.

a-[*na zi-im-ri-li-im*]
2 *qí-b*[*í-ma*]
um-ma ha-ab-bu-⸢*sú*⸣-[*um*]
4 *a-hu-ka-a-ma*
a-na ma-a-at šu-ba-ar-tim^{ki}
6 *a-na a-al da-an-na-tim ša a-di* u_4*-mi an-nu-ut-ti*-⸢*in*⸣
uk-ti-il-lu-ma la ìs-li-mu al-li-ik-ma
8 *ka-lu-šu a-na sa-li-mi-im*
qa-ba-a-šu id-<*di-nu*> *ù it-ti še-ep-ra-ru*
10 [*a*]*š-hu-ut-ma a-na a-al da-an-na-tim šu-nu-ti*
ú-ul e-ru-ub i-na-an-na ^{I}*še-ep-ra-ru*
12 *a-na a-al da-an-na-tim e-re-bi-im*
i-la-ak ù a-na-ku it-ti-šu-ma a-al-la-ak
14 HA.NA *ù* LÚ.MEŠ *ma-ra-yi*^{ki} *ša i-na a-al da-an-na-tim*
i-na šu-ba-ar-tim wa-aš-bu
16 *ú-še-ṣe-e-em-ma ú-ša-ar-ra-am*
⸢*ù* 1⸣*-te-en* LÚ.TUR-*ka ša it-ti-ia i-la-ku*
18 *ar-hi-iš ṭú-ur-dam*
ša-ni-tam ⸢^{munus}⸣[*k*]*a-al-la-at*
20 ^{I}MU.BAL.⸢SA$_6$⸣.GA
aš-ra-nu-um wa-aš-ba-at a-hi li-ša-re-eš-⸢*ši*⸣
22 *ù ki-ma* {x} *qar-ni-li-im*
T. ⸢*aš-šum a*⸣-[*lim*^{ki}] ⸢*sag*$^{?}$⸣-*ga-ra-tim*^{ki}
24 [...^{ki}]
R.26 *ù* [...]^{ki}
ú-ša-[*sú*$^{?}$]-*ú-ma*
28 *ù i-na la* [*ši-tu*]-*ul-tim*
iš-pu-⸢*ra*⸣-[*ak-kum*]
30 [*šu-um*] LÚ ÌR *a-bi*-⸢*šu ù-lu-ma ha-am-mi*⸣-*šu*
[*š*]*a aš-ra-nu-um ša i-na da-ri pa-nu-tim*
32 *li-iq-bé-e-ek-kum*
i-nu-ma a-na li-ib-bi ma-a-tim ta-al-la-kam-ma
34 *qa-qa-da-ti-ni*
nu-uš-te-em-me-du

36 *a-na* u_4*-mi-šu a-hi a-wa-as-sú li-iš-ku-un*
ša-al-ma-a-ku
38 [*šu*]*-lum a-hi-ia a-na ṣe-ri-ia*
lu-ú ka-ia-an
(reste anépigraphe)

[1-2]Dis à [Zimri-Lim]: [3-4]ainsi (parle) Habbusu[m], ton frère.

[5-7]Je suis allé au pays de Šubartum, vers les villes fortifiées qui jusqu'à ces derniers jours résistaient et n'avaient pas fait la paix: [8-9]toutes ont promis de faire la paix. [9-11]Mais par respect pour Šepraru, je ne suis pas entré dans ces villes fortifiées. [11-13]À présent, Šepraru va venir pour entrer dans ces villes fortifiées et moi, j'irai avec lui. [14-16]Je ferai sortir les Bédouins et les Mariotes qui demeurent dans les villes fortifiées dans le Šubartum et je les renverrai. [17-18]Envoie-moi rapidement un de tes serviteurs qui puisse aller avec moi!

[19-21]Autre chose. L'épouse de Mubalsaga demeure là-bas (= là où tu es): que mon frère me la fasse conduire!

[22-27]En outre, puisque Qarni-Lim a fait [*faire une proclamation* (?)] au sujet des villes de Saggaratum, [NG_2] et [NG_3] [28-29]et qu'il t'a écrit sans réfléchir, [30-32]qu'il te dise [le nom] du serviteur de son père ou de son grand-père qui s'y est trouvé lors des générations précédentes.

[33-36]Lorsque tu iras dans l'intérieur du pays et que nous réunirons nos forces, que mon frère place son affaire au jour qui lui convient!

[37-39]Je vais bien. Puissent de bonnes nouvelles de la santé de mon frère m'(arriver) constamment!

NOTES

On doit remarquer toute une série de particularités graphiques de cette tablette par rapport aux usages courants dans les archives de Mari:

- les signes BU et UL comportent un vertical, ce qui n'est pas fréquent;
- le signe ŠE est écrit avec deux fois trois clous;
- le trait de séparation des lignes est en retrait par rapport au premier signe (c'est surtout visible au revers).

1) La restitution s'appuie sur le parallèle de la lettre de Šepraru *ARM* 28 161, qui offre des caractéristiques analogues et qui est manifestement contemporaine (cf. §2.3).

3) La lecture du nom de l'expéditeur n'est pas totalement assurée. M. Birot avait lu *Ḫa-ab-bu-u*[*m*] (?) (Birot 1973, 6), mais le bas du dernier signe conservé ne saurait être celui d'un *um* et ressemble davantage à ⸢*su*⸣ ou ⸢*sú*⸣; en outre, vu l'alignement des signes de fin de ligne, il y a l. 3 la place pour un signe dans la cassure au dessus du *-ma* de la l. 4, d'où la lecture retenue: *ha-ab-bu-*⌜*sú*⌝-[*um*]. Je ne connais pas d'autre attestation de ce nom, ni dans les archives de Mari, ni ailleurs. Il pourrait s'agir d'un dérivé du verbe *habâṣum*, mais j'ai conventionnellement retenu la transcription Habbasum dans cette étude.

6) La nunation (*annûttin*) est un phénomène qui n'est pas rare dans les archives de Mari, mais qui n'a pas encore été systématiquement analysé (voir récemment *pa-nu-ut-ti-in* dans M.6242: 8' = Guichard 2002b, 111). Pour la nunation dans l'onomastique amorrite, voir Streck 2000, 260-261.

9) Il semble bien que le scribe ait omis deux signes, d'où la lecture proposée *id-*<*di-nu*>.

9-11) Lit. «j'ai eu peur de Šepraru et je ne suis pas entré dans ces villes». On relève une façon analogue de s'exprimer sous le calame de Mukannišum, non pas avec le verbe *šahâtum*, mais avec le synonyme *palâhum*[4]: «J'ai vu cette pièce, [elle était scel]lée au sceau de mon seigneur. Par respect pour mon seigneur, [je n'ai pas ouvert] cette pièce». On possède d'autres exemples avec *šahâtum*. Ainsi, Kibri-Dagan déclare[5]: «Par crainte de mon seigneur, je n'ai pas touché cet homme». Noter également la déclaration de Asqudum et Hali-hadun[6]: «Par crainte de notre seigneur, nous venons d'envoyer à présent ces hommes chez notre seigneur». Dans ces deux derniers cas, le contexte montre que la crainte du roi conduit à faire quelque chose contre son gré[7]. Le verbe *šahâtum* «craindre» régit le plus souvent un accusatif, mais des constructions indirectes (avec *ina* ou *ana*) sont attestées; je n'en ai pas trouvé avec *itti*. Étant donné l'omission de deux signes auparavant dans la même l. 9, on peut se demander si le scribe n'a pas commis ici une erreur. Une transcription *it-ti še-ep-ra-ru* [*a*]*š-hu-uṭ* avec une traduction «j'ai fait du pillage avec Šepraru» ne me semble pas à retenir d'après ce qui suit.

17) Le signe ⌜1⌝ se situe dans un passage endommagé, mais une lecture ⌜*iš*⌝*-te-en*, qui correspondrait à la façon habituelle d'écrire, est épigraphiquement peu probable. Noter que le signe *iš* l. 18 s'achève par deux verticaux qui vont jusqu'en bas: on devrait ici en voir la trace sous la cassure.

19) M. Birot avait parlé de «belle-fille de Mubalšaga», mais le sens de «épouse» pour *kallatum* a depuis été clairement établi (Ziegler 1999, 45-46).

4 Voir *ARM* 13 22 (= *LAPO* 16 262): (24) É *ša-a-tu a-mu-*[*ur*]*-ma* (25) *i-na ku-un-uk be-lí-*[*ia ka-ni-i*]*k** (26) *ap-la-ah-ma* É [*ku-nu-ki ú-ul ep-te*] aussi avec le verbe *adârum*: *ù a-na-ku ad-ra-ku-ma* dans A.175: 21 (Durand 2010, 112-113).

5 *ARM* 3 36 (= *LAPO* 17 704): (21) *be-lí aš-hu-ut-ma aš-šum ki-a-am* (22) LÚ *še-tu ú-ul* [*a*]*l-pu-ut*.

6 *ARM* 26/1 32: (14) *be-el-né ni*$_5$*-iš-hu-ut* (15) *i-na-an-na a-nu-um-ma*(16) [LÚ.M]EŠ *šu-nu-ti* (17) [*a-n*]*a ṣe-er be-lí-ne* (18) [*n*]*i-iṭ-ṭà-ar-dam*.

7 Dans A.1068: 16, l'expression *be-lí aš-hu-*UT est ambiguë (Guichard 2011, 73). M. Guichard avait lu (13) *i-na pa-ni-tim-*[*ma*](14) *i-ta-at* LÚ *ša-a-ti* (15) *as-hu-ur-ma a-na da-ki-š*[*u*] (16) *be-lí aš-hu-uṭ* et traduit: «Auparavant, j'avais menacé cet homme et j'avais (même) pressé mon Seigneur de le tuer». Mais il pense maintenant qu'on pourrait lire *be-lí aš-hu-ut* et traduire: «Auparavant, j'avais menacé cet homme, mais par respect pour mon Seigneur je ne l'avais pas tué» (lit.: j'ai eu (trop) peur de mon Seigneur pour le tuer»).

21 et 31) L. 21, *ašrânum* signifie clairement «là-bas = là où tu te trouves». En revanche, l. 31 *ašrânum* semble reprendre les noms des trois villes mentionnés l. 23-26.

22) Le signe effacé semble le *qar* de Qarni-Lim, dont le nom a finalement été écrit plus à droite par le scribe.

27) Vu le mouvement du texte, on s'attendrait à un sens comme «a émis des prétentions sur». M. Guichard me suggère de restituer une forme de *šasûm*, même si jusqu'à présent le système II n'est attesté qu'en MA (*CAD* Š/2, 166b).

28) Bien que l'expression *ina lâ šitûltim* ne soit pas attestée jusqu'à présent, la restitution ne me semble guère faire de doute.

30) La séquence *abum* / *hammum* confirme pour ce second terme le sens de «grand-père» proposé par J.-M. Durand (Durand 1992, 120 n. 174; le texte A.405 auquel il renvoie est cité dans Charpin et Ziegler 2003, 228 n. 531). Pour une attestation de *hammum* dans une lettre récemment publiée, voir *FM* 6 6: 8.

31) *dârum* est un mot aussi rare que célèbre, puisqu'il n'est autrement connu que par l'inscription de Samsi-Addu de Ninive: (14) *bi-tam ša iš-tu* (15) *šu-lum* A.GA.DÈ^{ki} (16) *a-di šar-ru-ti-ia* (17) *a-di ṣa-ba-at nu-ur-ru-gi*^{ki} (18) 7 *da-a-ru i-ti-qú-ma* (19) *i-na* LUGAL.MEŠ (20) *a-li-ku-ut pa-ni-*⸢*ia*⸣ (21) LUGAL *ma-an-na-ma* (22) *la i-pu-šu-*⸢*ma*⸣ «ce temple, qu'aucun des rois qui m'a précédé, depuis la chute d'Akkad jusqu'à mon règne, jusqu'à la prise de Nurrugum, sept générations ayant passé» (*RIME* 4, p. 53 n° 2). M. Streck n'a rien ajouté aux indications des dictionnaires, qui ont considéré le mot comme d'origine amorrite en le rapprochant de l'hébreu *dôrîm* «génération» (Streck 2000, 88). Le présent passage confirme cette étymologie.

37-39) On a ici un exemple supplémentaire de la formule par laquelle un correspondant déclare aller bien et souhaite recevoir des nouvelles de son interlocuteur (voir les références réunies dans Charpin 2008, 183b).

2. Commentaire

2.1. *L'auteur de la lettre*

La première ligne de la tablette a disparu, mais il ne fait à peu près aucun doute que cette lettre était adressée à Zimri-Lim[8]. Son correspondant se définit comme son «frère» (*ahuka* l. 4) et s'adresse à lui en écrivant «mon frère» (*ahî* l. 21 et 36), ce qui, selon les conventions de l'époque, signifie qu'il se jugeait son égal (Kupper 1991 et Lafont 2001, 232-237); il emploie tantôt la deuxième personne (l. 18, 32, 33) et tantôt la troisième (l. 21, 36).

[8] Certes, nous savons désormais qu'il faut prendre en compte l'existence de lettres interceptées (voir par exemple les deux lettres à Yanuh-Samar publiées dans Guichard et Ziegler 2004, avec commentaire p. 235-236). Mais en l'occurrence, on voit mal à quel autre roi que Zimri-Lim ce message pourrait avoir été adressé.

Le nom de ce Habbusum n'étant pas connu ailleurs dans les archives de Mari, l'identité de ce personnage nous échappe. On peut penser qu'il s'agit soit d'un roi ayant récupéré son trône à la chute du royaume de Haute-Mésopotamie, soit d'un important chef nomade. On a vu qu'il se considérait comme l'égal de Zimri-Lim[9]. En revanche, il semble se considérer comme inférieur à Šepraru. Cela ne nous aide guère à situer Habbusum, puisque Šepraru est pratiquement pour nous également un inconnu[10].

2.2. *La paix avec les villes du Šubartum*

Le contexte historique est clairement l'effondrement du royaume de Haute-Mésopotamie. Le «pays du Šubartum» dont il est question dans la lettre peut correspondre à une large partie de la Haute-Mésopotamie[11] et la lettre est trop allusive pour que nous sachions exactement quelles sont ces villes «qui résistaient». Le contexte donne l'impression que Šepraru et Habbusum étaient du même côté que Zimri-Lim, luttant contre les survivants du royaume de Haute-Mésopotamie. On sait en effet qu'après la chute de l'empire de Samsi-Addu, certains individus restés fidèles à Išme-Dagan, héritier du trône d'Ekallatum, s'enfermèrent dans des villes particulièrement fortes, comme Yarim-Addu à Kahat[12] ou Samiya à Šubat-Enlil[13]. On voit ici que Habbusum se montre très optimiste quant au fait que les villes auxquelles il fait allusion vont conclure la paix.

2.3. *Les échanges de personnes*

L'un des passages les plus intéressants de la lettre est la proposition de son expéditeur de renvoyer à Zimri-Lim les Bédouins et les Mariotes (l. 14: HA.NA[14] *ù* LÚ.MEŠ *ma-ra-yi*^{ki}) résidant dans les villes du Šubartum dans lesquelles il s'apprêtait à entrer. M. Birot avait compris la

[9] Ce que confirme la proposition de campagne commune des l. 33-35, avec l'expression bien connue *qaqqadâtini šutêmudum*.

[10] Voir ci-dessous §2.3. Il ne faut pas le confondre avec Šepratu, connu par les lettres de Shemsharra (Eidem et Laessøe 2001).

[11] Dans Charpin 1989, 39 j'ai défini le pays de Šubartum comme «la zone des affluents de rive droite du Tigre au nord du Sinjar», mais la définition est parfois plus large: voir Guichard 2002a, 134-137, qui distingue une acception géographique et une acception politique.

[12] Voir Charpin et Ziegler 2003, 186.

[13] Voir Charpin et Ziegler 2003, 167 et 192.

[14] Pour l'étymologie de *Hanû*, voir Durand 2000, 417-418 et pour la justification de la traduction de *Hanû* par «Bédouins», voir en dernier lieu Charpin 2005/6, 284b.

situation ainsi: «Il y a là-bas [= dans le Šubartum] des villes fortes occupées par des garnisons hanéennes et mariotes, mais il semble qu'elles y soient bloquées par les troubles qui ont agité le pays.» (Birot 1973, 6). À vrai dire, une telle interprétation ne s'impose pas: le texte ne parle pas explicitement de *garnisons*. Il me semble plus vraisemblable qu'il s'agit de Mariotes qui avaient été obligés par le pouvoir de Samsi-Addu de quitter leur royaume d'origine et qui souhaitaient rentrer chez eux.

Cette interprétation repose notamment sur la demande de Habbusum qui suit: il souhaite que l'épouse de Mubalsaga quitte Mari et lui soit envoyée. On ignore dans quelles circonstances elle arriva dans la capitale du Moyen-Euphrate. Cette demande doit être mise en rapport avec la lettre A.3356 (Guichard et Ziegler 2004, 230-231): Zakura-abum y indique qu'une fois arrivé à Mari, manifestement avant l'arrivée même de Zimri-Lim, il en a fait sortir tous les Ekallatéens qui s'y trouvaient. On voit donc qu'après la chute du royaume de Haute-Mésopotamie, de nombreux déplacements de personnes eurent lieu: les ressortissants du royaume d'Ekallatum purent rentrer chez eux, de même qu'en sens inverse ceux du royaume de Mari[15]. On ne sait à quel titre Habbusum souhaite que l'épouse de Mubalsaga lui soit envoyée. Il pourrait intervenir en faveur de Mubalsaga, pour que ce dernier retrouve sa femme[16]. Mais certains souverains, au même moment, semblent avoir essayé d'accroître leur harem en y faisant entrer des femmes capturées à l'étranger; cela semble être le cas de Qarni-Lim, qui fit de le sœur de Yanuh-Samar une de ses concubines (Guichard et Ziegler 2004, 238 et 241).

C'est dans le même contexte qu'il faut situer la lettre manifestement contemporaine qu'écrivit Šepraru à Zimri-Lim[17]:

[15] M. Guichard me signale une lettre acéphale, mais sûrement attribuable à Zakura-abum, dans laquelle celui-ci déclare: «Mon seigneur Zimri-Lim m'a écrit de faire sortir les déportés mariotes. Je veux m'approcher pour faire sortir les déportés». Inédit M.9093: (27') … *be-lí zi-im-ri-li-im* (28') *a-na šu-ṣú na-sí-hi* LÚ.MEŠ *ma-ra-i* (29') *iš-pu-ra-am lu-uṭ-hi* LÚ.MEŠ *na-sí-hi* (30') *lu-še-ṣé-em*. Il y eut manifestement de très nombreux mouvements de ce genre. M. Guichard me rappelle également la façon dont Zimri-Lim, après la prise de Kahat, renvoya chez eux les habitants de Rapiqum qui avaient été déportés dans cette ville par Samsi-Addu (M.6242, publiée dans Guichard 2002b, 109-116; pour la déportation des habitants de Rapiqum, voir Charpin et Ziegler 2003, 85 n. 75).

[16] Pour la carrière de Mubalsaga, voir Villard 2001, 102-105 et 111.

[17] J.-R. Kupper avait indiqué: «La lettre de Šepraru à Zimri-Lim (n° **161**) traite d'une affaire privée et ne contient aucun indice chronologique ou géographique. On relèvera le ton bref de l'adresse et l'emploi de l'impératif» (Kupper 1998, 233). Le parallèle avec TH 72.5 permet désormais d'aller plus loin dans l'interprétation de ce document. Pour un commentaire de *ARM* 28 161 et du problème général du sort des femmes en période de guerre et à l'issue des conflits, voir Ziegler sp.

> «Dis à Zimri-Lim: ainsi (parle) Šepraru. Une fillette dont le nom est Šawan-nikizi(?) demeure dans la maison d'Aham-nuta, le marchand. Or cette fillette est ma parente. Pour une mine d'argent, fais-la sortir de la maison du marchand et fais-la conduire chez moi. De la même façon que moi-même je vais libérer des citoyens mariotes, dix ou cinq hommes, (toi) à présent, fais sortir cette fillette de la maison du marchand et fais-la amener chez moi.»

Šepraru réclame donc à Zimri-Lim qu'il rachète auprès d'un marchand mariote une femme de sa famille et il s'engage en contrepartie à libérer de cinq à dix hommes originaires de Mari. Cette dernière opération semble être identique à celle qu'évoque Habbusum dans TH 72.5: 14-16, puisque l'entrée de Habbusum dans les villes où se trouvent les Mariotes à libérer doit se faire conjointement avec Šepraru (l. 11-13).

2.4. *Le différend avec Qarni-Lim*

Habbusum poursuit sa lettre avec un autre sujet: le différend qui oppose Zimri-Lim et Qarni-Lim. Nous en ignorions tout jusqu'à présent. On savait seulement que Qarni-Lim avait pu récupérer le trône d'Andarig avant que Zimri-Lim n'entre à Mari (Charpin et Ziegler 2003, 189 n. 146) et qu'il avait joué un rôle important dans les semaines ou les mois qui suivirent l'écroulement du royaume de Haute-Mésopotamie (Guichard et Ziegler 2004, 238-240). Dans la redistribution des cartes qui eut lieu à ce moment, Qarni-Lim aurait manifesté un appétit peu apprécié de certains autres prétendants au trône. Malheureusement, le passage l. 22-27 est endommagé mais il semble bien que Qarni-Lim revendiquait trois villes ayant appartenu au royaume de Mari, dont Saggaratum. Habbusum semble prendre le parti de Zimri-Lim, en disant que cette lettre de Qarni-Lim a été envoyée «sans réflexion» (*i-na la* [*ši-tu*]-*ul-tim*, l. 28). Il conseille au roi de Mari de rappeler à Qarni-Lim quelle avait été la situation antérieure: l'appel au souvenir du passé est un des éléments clés des négociations diplomatiques de cette époque[18]. Qarni-Lim doit être sommé de donner le nom de serviteurs de son père ou de son grand-père qui auraient été en poste dans ces trois villes. Le principal intérêt du passage est de nous montrer que Qarni-Lim appartenait à une famille royale implantée à Andarig depuis plusieurs générations: son père et son grand-père sont

[18] Voir Charpin 1998. Noter en particulier A.1289 (*LAPO* 16 281), où Ibal-pi-El II d'Ešnunna, qui revendiquait la possession de Harradum, écrivit à Zimri-Lim: «Interroge tes serviteurs âgés et ils t'apprendront que (etc.)».

en effet clairement présentés comme ayant occupé le même trône avant lui. On retrouve le même nombre de générations qu'à Mari (Yagid-Lim, Yahdun-Lim et Zimri-Lim).

2.5. *Une campagne espérée*

La lettre se poursuit avec l'offre, par Habbusum, de joindre ses forces à celles de Zimri-Lim lorsque celui-ci se rendra dans la région. Malheureusement, l'expression *ina libbi mâtim* (l. 33) est trop vague dans ce contexte pour qu'on sache dans quelle région pourrait avoir lieu cette opération militaire commune qu'envisage Habbusum. Cependant, d'autres correspondants expriment à peu près au même moment le désir général que Zimri-Lim «vienne». Zakura-abum se fait ainsi l'écho de ce souhait[19]: «Toutes les forteresses ne cessent de m'écrire: 'Que notre seigneur, le roi Zimri-Lim, vienne! Assurément, nous (lui) ouvrirons (nos portes)!'.» De même, Yaqbi-Addu, le nouveau roi d'Ašnakkum, écrivit à Zimri-Lim[20]: «Arrive vite afin que nous expulsions ces hommes!».

Conclusion

On ne doit pas s'étonner outre mesure de n'avoir pas d'autres attestations de Habbusum, l'expéditeur de la lettre ici publiée. Il n'est en effet pas seul dans son cas: d'autres monarques, ou candidats au trône, connus au tout début du règne de Zimri-Lim, disparaissent ensuite complètement de notre documentation. Tel est le cas, par exemple, de Abi-Samar et de Ikšud-la-šemišu: Zimri-Lim leur adressa une de ses premières lettres[21], mais on ne sait pas ce qu'ils devinrent par la suite. On peut penser que certains trouvèrent la mort dans les soubresauts qui suivirent l'écroulement du royaume de Haute-Mésopotamie, avant que les pouvoirs ne finissent par trouver un nouvel équilibre, tout relatif d'ailleurs.

Bibliographie

BIROT, M. 1973: «Nouvelles découvertes épigraphiques au palais royal de Mari (salle 115)», *Syria* 50, 1-11.

[19] *FM* 6 5: (7) … *da-na-tum ka-lu-ši-na* (8) [*i*]*š-ta-na-pa-ra-nim um-ma-mi be-el-ni* (9) [LU]GAL *zi-im-ri-li-im li-il-li-kam-ma i ni-ip-te*.

[20] *FM* 6 6: (19') … *ar-hi-iš k*[*u*]*-uš-dam ù* [LÚ.MEŠ] (20') *an-nu-tim i nu-še-*[*ṣí*]. Selon M. Guichard, «ces hommes» sont Adalšenni et les Turukkéens.

[21] *ARM* 28 148.

CHARPIN, D. 1989: «L'akkadien des lettres d'Ilân-ṣurâ», dans M. Lebeau et P. Talon (éd.), *Reflets des deux fleuves, volume de mélanges offerts à André Finet*, Akkadica Supplementum 6, Louvain, 31-40.

— 1998: «L'évocation du passé dans les lettres de Mari», dans J. Prosecky (éd.), *Intellectual Life of the Ancient Near East. Papers Presented at the 43rd Rencontre assyriologique internationale Prague, July 1-5, 1996*, Prague, 91-110.

— 2005/6: «compte rendu de M. Streck, *Das Amurritische Onomastikon der altbabylonischen Zeit. Band 1*», *AfO* 51, 282-292.

— 2008: «compte rendu de: P. Marrassini et al. (éd.), *Semitic and Assyriological Studies presented to Pelio Fronzaroli by Pupils and Colleagues*», *RA* 102, 183-184.

CHARPIN, D. et N. ZIEGLER 2003: *Florilegium marianum V. Mari et le Proche-Orient à l'époque amorrite: essai d'histoire politique*, Mémoires de NABU 6, Paris.

DURAND, J.-M. 1992: «Unité et diversités au Proche-Orient à l'époque amorrite», dans D. Charpin et F. Joannès (éd.), *La circulation des biens, des personnes et des idées dans le Proche-Orient ancien, Actes de la XXXVIII*[e] *Rencontre Assyriologique Internationale (Paris, 8-10 juillet 1991)*, Paris, 97-128.

— 2000: *Les Documents épistolaires du palais de Mari*, tome III (LAPO 18), Paris.

— 2010: «Un centre benjaminite aux portes de Mari: Réflexions sur le caractère mixte de la population de Mari», dans S. Dönmez (éd.), *Veysel Donbaz'a Sunulan Yazılar DUB.SAR É.DUB.BA.A. Studies Presented in Honour of Veysel Donbaz*, Istanbul, 109-114.

EIDEM, J. et J. LÆSSØE 2001: *The Shemshara Archives Vol. 1 The Letters* (Historisk-filosofiske Skrifter 23), Copenhague.

GUICHARD, M. 2002a: «Le Šubartum occidental à l'avènement de Zimrî-Lîm», dans D. Charpin et J.-M. Durand (éd.), *Recueil d'études à la mémoire d'André Parrot, Florilegium marianum VI* (Mémoires de NABU 7), Paris, 119-168.

— 2002b: «Les relations diplomatiques entre Ibal-pi-El II et Zimri-Lim: deux étapes vers la discorde», *RA* 96, 109-142.

— 2011: «Un David raté ou une histoire de habiru à l'époque amorrite. Vie et mort de Samsī-Ērah, chef de guerre et homme du peuple», dans J.-M. Durand, Th. Römer et M. Langlois (éd.), *Le jeune éhros. Recherches sur la formation et la diffusion d'un thème littéraire au Proche-Orient ancien*, OBO 250, Fribourg/Göttingen, 29-93.

GUICHARD, M. et N. ZIEGLER 2004: «Yanûh-Samar et les Ekallatéens en détresse», in J. G. Dercksen (éd.), *Assyria and Beyond. Studies Presented to Mogens Trolle Larsen* (PIHANS 100), Leyde, 229-247.

KUPPER, J.-R. 1991: «Zimri-Lim et ses vassaux», in D. Charpin et F. Joannès (éd.), *Marchands, diplomates et empereurs. Études sur la civilisation mésopotamienne offertes à Paul Garelli*, Paris, 179-184.

— 1998: *Lettres royales du temps de Zimri-Lim* (Archives royales de Mari 28), Paris.

LAFONT, B. 2001: «Relations internationales, alliances et diplomatie au temps des royaumes amorrites», in J.-M. Durand et D. Charpin (éd.), *Mari, Ébla et les Hourrites: dix ans de travaux. Actes du colloque international (Paris, mai 1993). Deuxième partie* (Amurru 2), Paris 213-328.

STRECK, M. P. 2000: *Das Amurritische Onomastikon der altbabylonischer Zeit. Band 1: Die Amurriter. Die onomastische Forschung. Orthographie und Phonologie. Nominalmorphologie* (Alter Orient und Altes Testament 271/1), Münster.

VAN LERBERGHE, K. et G. VOET 1991: *Sippar-Amnānum. The Ur-Utu Archive. Volume 1* (Mesopotamian History and Environment Texts 1/1), Gand.

— 2009: *A Late Old Babylonian Temple Archive from Dūr-Abiešuḫ* (Cornell University Studies in Assyriology and Sumerology 8), Bethesda.

VILLARD, P. 2001: «Les administrateurs de l'époque de Yasmah-Addu», dans J.-M. Durand et D. Charpin (éd.), *Mari, Ébla et les Hourrites: dix ans de travaux. Actes du colloque international (Paris, mai 1993). Deuxième partie* (Amurru 2), Paris, 9-140.

ZIEGLER, N. 1999: *Florilegium marianum IV. Le Harem de Zimrî-Lîm. La population féminine des palais d'après les archives royales de Mari* (Mémoires de NABU 5), Paris.

— sp: «Kriege und ihre Folgen: Frauenschicksale anhand der Archive aus Mari», dans H. Neumann et al. (éd.), *Krieg und Frieden im Alten Vorderasien* (SANTAG), Wiesbaden.

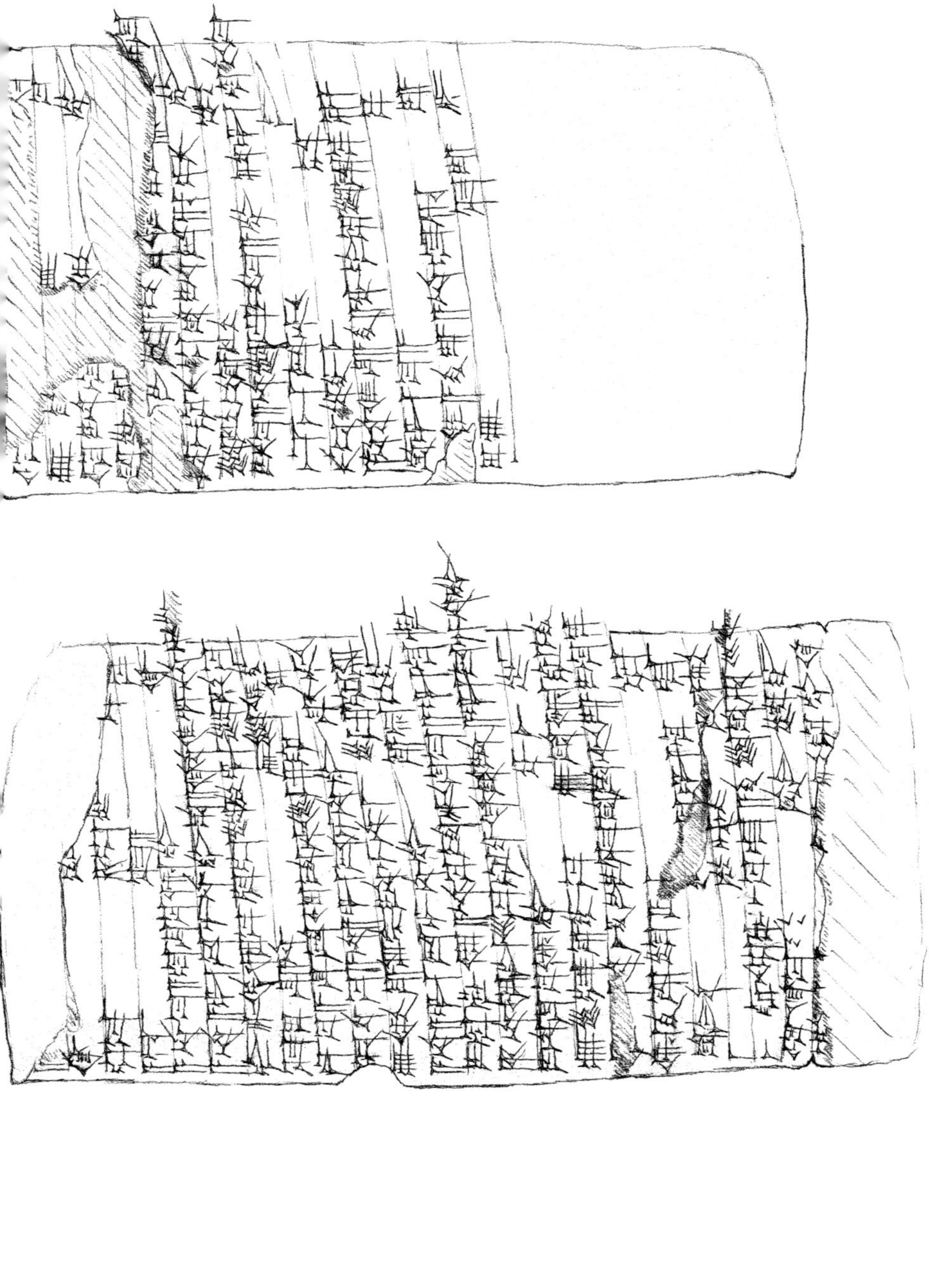

Fig. 1.

URUK *MATER URBIUM*: THE SIGN URU IN PROTO-CUNEIFORM WRITING

Petr CHARVÁT
University of West Bohemia, Plzeň

This paper represents continuation of a project that I initiated at the beginning of the 90's of the last century. Having received a DAAD fellowship to study the earliest Sumerian texts in Berlin, I was fortunate enough to meet there Robert K. Englund, who was working on their publication. I acknowledge here my deep thankfulness to him for his friendly help throughout my Berlin days, but especially for his having placed at my disposal the transcriptions of the up to that time unpublished proto-cuneiform texts which he had prepared, and which constitute the base of this undertaking.

The major research result that has come out of my Berlin endeavour is a book that I published in 1997(Charvát 1997). At that time, my plans surpassed reality, and I realized that I will not be able to submit all the research results that I have gathered in Berlin. Therefore, I render account of a part of the work done, but hitherto unpublished, here. In my Prague book I analyze seven key terms for the social composition of early Sumerian society: AB, E_2, EN, LU_2, LUGAL, $MURUB_2$ and NIN. Here I proceed to add the evidence for another term of crucial importance, URU, which later came to mean "city, municipality"[1].

An early and most interesting, completely preserved tablet[2] features what can apparently be interpreted as three components of the Adab "settlement nucleus" — the religious centre (ADAB), the nearby "civil-service focus" (URU) and the watermeadow area (RAD), constituting the closest-proximity segment of the city's economic hinterland.

The "municipal community" received comestibles, presumably grain, from the ZATU 651+GAR in the form of UR_2 URU_{a1} U_{2a}, and also from

[1] ZATU No. 597 p. 306. On the earliest cities of SW and S Asia see Aruz-Wallenfels 2003, on the most recent archaeological evidence for early Mesopotamian cities see the contributions published in Margueron et al. 2007, especially Connan and Deschesne 2007, Emery-Barbier 2007, Fenollós 2007, Nicolini 2007 and Spycket 2007.

[2] ATU 1, 7 = W 9312 h (my No. 1).

the GA_a+ZATU 753[3]. A link between field produce and the URU may be surmised in one text[4], while a reference to APIN in another[5] may, in fact, actually pertain to plows employed in the fields.

Together with other specialized groups(?), the URU handled livestock (bulls? oxen?)[6]. Wool[7] and potted goods[8] are mentioned together with this entity. In one instance[9], AN's beer is dispensed in NE DUG URU ŠEŠ, which might possibly be a "new pot (= hollow measure?) of the ŠEŠ of URU"[10]. The URU may also deal in fish[11] and is referred to in connection with craft activities[12].

On the other hand, a "city architect" (ŠIDIM URU) boasted precious materials, silver and "beads" (NUNUZ), presumably sent from abroad[13].

Let us now see how the URU fitted into heavenly and earthly hierarchies. Also, items dedicated to An(?) left the ZATU-686 URU and were recorded as EN_a X GU_7[14]. Another text[15] refers to an URU_c, the superior instance of which was apparently AN, and beer of AN[16] was measured out in pots of the ŠEŠ of URU[17]. We even find a direct link between URU and AN[18].

As to the earthbound dignitaries, an EN was recorded in connection with URU IB, presumably as its overlord[19]. Deliveries to ZATU 752 EN passed through URU+KALAM[20]. The URU might also have received rations on the occasion of MAGUR EN[21], and an URU+NIMGIR is known to us[22].

[3] Texts W 20552, 8[+] (my No. 33) and W 20274, 5 (my No. 30).

[4] Text W 17729, GG (my No. 27).

[5] Text W 22101, 6 (my No. 37).

[6] The URU disposed over cows and bulls in text ATU 1, 339 = W 7227 a (my No. 15).

[7] Text ATU 1, 159 = W 9656, cu (my No. 7).

[8] Text ATU 1, 109 = W 9656, hd (my No. 5).

[9] Text W 19408, 25 (my No. 28).

[10] See the Jemdet Nasr find of a storage-jar rim fragment with inscription EN NE DUG KAŠ, MSVO 1 No. 244 p. 83.

[11] Texts W 20500 a (my No. 31) and W 24008.19 (my No. 38).

[12] $UMUN_2$ PAP_a: text ATU 1, 342 = W 9656 es (my No. 16).

[13] Text W 14263 (my No. 20). See the seal impression of this text, featuring a "foreign" motif with animals springing up hillocks: ATU 6 pp. 12, 13.

[14] Text W 15833, A2 = IM 23440 (my No. 22).

[15] Text ATU 1, 209 = W 9656, ga (my No. 10).

[16] Is this history's first recorded publicity, with a beer denomination translated possibly as "celestial beverage"?

[17] Text W 19408, 25 (my No. 28).

[18] Text W 21060, 12 (my No. 36).

[19] Text W 20776 (my No. 34).

[20] Text ATU 1, 98 = W 9579 e (my No. 4).

[21] Text ATU 1, 203 = W 9655, s (my No. 9).

[22] Text ATU 1, 74 = W 9579, cb (my No. 2).

What of the denizens of early Sumerian URU? SAL find mention as inhabitants (or labour hands?) of URU[23]. The same, however, goes for UŠ[24]. A SAG received rations (?, BA) for his or her URU[25]. Hither belong also the SAL ERIN, serving probably the $BARA_2$ of URU+NIMGIR[26]. Surprisingly enough, the URU seems to have played the role of (or merely contained?) a cattle pen or cattle corral[27].

Finds of proto-cuneiform texts from sites other than Uruk[28] contribute but little. Connections with various offices(?) find illumination in the ME (išib?) URU of text MSVO 4, 33, and the EN URU of text MSVO 4, 36. Text MSVO 4, 36 lists possibly "rations of river fish to E_2" (BA KU_6 A E_2). Text MSVO 4, 57 records a distribution of "large field surfaces associated with named individuals or institutions"[29], and names, as a novelty, ŠITA and AN $ŠU_2$+EN as officials connected with URU.

Texts dating to the final phase of the proto-cuneiform age and found at Jemdet Nasr[30] add some information that could help us along. First and foremost, some of these texts bear seal impressions, and thus indicate that dispositions concerning the URU required authorization of a seal-bearing office[31]. The character of the art motifs used does indicate that the seals represent creations of the foremost centres of this period of time, and imply thus that the texts may have been sealed outside Jemdet Nasr itself and brought there as instructions or orders.

A number of these texts refer to grain deliveries[32]. Text MSVO 1, 191 reiterates the traditional connection between URU and EN.

A novelty as against the earlier situation is represented by the closer connection of URU with the E_2. In text MSVO 1, 75, the closing formula "rations for the E_2 BU" obviously includes those issued to URU BU+DU_6. Text MSVO 1, 128 denotes in its closing formula the PA URU E_2 GAL, an office finding a parallel in text MSVO 1, 197 with its PA URU E_2 BU. Another PA linked with URU appears in text MSVO 1, 204, with its PA UDU URU.

[23] Texts ATU 1, 74 = W 9579, cb (my No. 2) and W 15892 P^+ = IM 23446 (my No. 24). On servile personnel in proto-cuneiform texts see most recently Englund 2009.
[24] Text ATU 1, 98 = W 9579 e (my No. 4)
[25] Text ATU 1, 227 = W 9579 cd (my No. 11).
[26] Text ATU 1, 74 = W 9579, cb (my No. 2).
[27] Text ATU 1, 550 = W 9656 f (my No. 19).
[28] Listed in MSVO 4 on p. 85.
[29] MSVO 4, p. 26 sub No. MSVO 4, 57
[30] Listed in MSVO 1, on p. 161. On MSVO 1 see also Neumann 1996.
[31] This pertains to MSVO-1 texts 28, 61, 63, 75, and 197.
[32] MSVO-1 texts 28, 61, 75.

Female labourers serving in the SAR URU turn up in texts MSVO 1, 212 and 213. Finally, text MSVO 1, 224, found immured in the Kish palace, shows the subordination of URU to a PA E_2 and/or to a SAG GIR_3.

We may thus subsume our findings by the conclusion that the earliest version of the lexeme, which later evolved into a designation of a city or municipal community, is likely to have denoted "civil-service settlements" built to support the activities of temple centres of the Late Uruk-Jemdet Nasr age, and making up, together with these centres and their agricultural hinterland, tripartite settlement units. The URU units indulged in agriculture and craft production and (some of them) obviously engaged in trade. Their population showed obvious social differentiation, from low-status labourers up to fairly wealthy citizens who proudly displayed luxury goods including those of foreign origin.

The sign URU in proto-cuneiform texts

Serial No. and citation	Summary of item	Notes
1. ATU 1, 7 = W 9312 h	Tablet, Qa XVI, 2 Qa XVI, 3, below the levelling of level III	ADAB URU_{a2}+1 N_{58} RAD_b
2. ATU 1, 74 = W 9579, cb	Tablet, Qa XVI, 2 below the levelling of level III	O0101: 1 N_2; URU_{a1}+NIMGIR $BARA_{2b}$ SAL $ERIM_a$
3. ATU 1, 88 = W 6748, a	Tablet, Pd XVI, 3, in the layer of sherds against the niched wall belonging to level IV	O0101: 1 N_{14}; $ERIM_{b2}$ AMA_a. O0102: 1 N_{14};ZATU 752 $SILA_{4c}$ EN_b. O0201: URU_{a3}+$KALAM_a$
4. ATU 1, 98 = W 9579 e	Tablet, Qa XVI, 2 below the levelling of level III; ATU 5 p. 44 s. No. W 9579 e: "this text belongs to a group of Uruk IV period accounts recording in succession numbers of objects designated BA, followed by an entry consisting as a rule of the sign combination GU_4 DUB+$DIŠ_{a/b}$ and including an entry of n x N_2".	O0201: 6 N_2; UR_a TE NUN_a URU_{a1} $UŠ_a$
5. ATU 1, 109 = W 9656, hd	Fragment, Qa XVI, 2 below the levelling of level III	3 N_1 [ ]; DUG_b+HI.$GUNU_a$ URU_c [ ]

Serial No. and citation	Summary of item	Notes
6. ATU 1, 148 = W 9579, de	Complete tablet, Qa XVI, 2 below the levelling of level III; fingerprints on tablet surface	1 N_{34}; NAM_2 URU_{b2}
7. ATU 1, 159 = W 9656, cu	Tablet, Qa XVI, 2 below the levelling of level III	1 N 5 N [ ] SIG_{2a3} URU_{a1}
8. ATU 1, 176 = W 9656, am	Tablet, Qa XVI, 2 below the levelling of level III	2 N_{14}; 3 N_{58} URU_{b2} NAM_2 $GURUŠDA_a$ GAR_3
9. ATU 1, 203 = W 9655, s	Tablet, Qa XVI, 2 below the levelling of level III	O0101: 1 N_1; KUR_a $URUDU_a$ $ERIM_a$. O0102: 1 N_1 SAL SU_a. O0201: RAD_b. R0101: 1 N_1; URU_{a2} BA EN_b $MAGUR_a$
10. ATU 1, 209 = W 9656, ga	List of quantified items (heads of cattle?), NUN, URU, UŠ AN; col. ii contains a lonely AN sign; GU_4 UŠ GEŠTU, AB_2 KAB, DUG+ AB_2 UZ, AB_2 BAEN TUR_3; Qa XVI, 2 below the levelling of level III	O0102: 2 N_1; URU_c
11. ATU 1, 227 = W 9579, cd	Tablet, Qa XVI, 2 below the levelling of level III; ATU 5 p. 46 s. No. W 9579 cd: "numerical notations in the EN system together with use of an accounting(?) line on corner of reverse"[33].	Obv.: 2 N_{7a} 1 N_9; SAG URU_{b1} BA NAM_2 KAB?, rev.: numerals only.
12. ATU 1, 252 = W 9655 f	Assignment of bulls (?, GU_4) to EN, SAL X, LAGAR, SUHUR and URU, Qa XVI, 2 below the levelling of level III	O0105: 1 N_1; URU_{b2}
13. ATU 1, 288 = W 9656 ar	Tablet, Qa XVI, 2 below the levelling of level III; ATU 5 p. 50 s. No. W 9656 ar: "possibly an exercise tablet; note the correspondence of the	O0101: 1 N_1 URU_{a1}

[33] ATU 5, p. 20: "EN system — system attested to only in the Uruk IV period with uncertain application; possibly used to note weight measures"

Serial No. and citation	Summary of item	Notes
	ideograms representing professions in this text with the first entries of the lexical list Lú A". Numeral N_1 followed by URU, ERIN, DI NAM_2, ŠE+NAM_2, ZATU 753 PAP	
14. ATU 1, 333 = W 9656 a1	Tablet, Qa XVI, 2 below the levelling of level III; ATU 5 p. 49 s. No. W 9656 a1: "note the correspondence of the ideograms representing professions in this text with the first entries of the lexical list Lú A". List of quantitied items, $MUŠ_3$, KAB, URU, MAŠ ERIN, NAM_2, IŠ, ZATU 758 (only sign in col. iii); rev. col. ii ZATU 758	O0104: 6 N_1; URU_{a2}
15. ATU 1, 339 = W 7227 a	ATU 5, p. 37 s. No. W 7227 a: "the account includes the largest number of large cattle attested in the Uruk IV text corpus". ATU 5, p. 38 s. No. W 9123 b: "account of cows". UŠ, UŠ RU, EN, DUB, KAŠ, PA, $UMUN_2$ SANGA, GA GAL, SUG_5 SANGA, NIR, NAM_2, UMBIN, IŠ, NIM, ŠITA,URU, PAP, UB. Rev. 5 N_{14} 4 N_1; GU_4 AB_2. Qa XVI, 2 in Pe XVI, 3, in the layer of sherds NE of the niched wall belonging to the level IV.	O0503: 1 N_1; URU_{b2}
16. ATU 1, 342 = W 9656 es	List of offices, communities and singular humans, unknown quantified commodity in connection with a particular storage facility (GA_{2a4}); $UMUN_2$ PAP_a = seed for/of coppersmith(s)? Or is PAP_a a toponym?	O0102: $5N_1$ [ ] URU_{a2}+ $1N_{58}$

Serial No. and citation	Summary of item	Notes
17. ATU 1, 409 = W 9656 be	Fragment, Qa XVI, 2 below the levelling of level III;	O0101: 3 N_1 NAM_2 DI GI_{4b}. O0102: 1 N_1; URU_{b1} GI_{4b} [ ]; col. ii: numerals only.
18. ATU 1, 501 = W 9123 l	Tablet, Qa XVI, 2 "Qa XVI, 3, below the levelling of level III, 1.5 m above the height of the base of the Limestone Temple, 4.5 m SW of the preserved corner"; list of quantified items, KISAL NUN, PA, SUKKAL, BALAG, URU, KISAL	R0202: 1 N_1; URU $_{a1}$+?
19. ATU 1, 550 = W 9656 f	Tablet, Qa XVI, 2 below the levelling of level III; list of quantified items; GU_4 APIN, UŠ+UŠ UNUG, APIN UŠ UŠ $MUŠ_3$, URU+AMAR, GI IŠ, EŠDA $NINDA_2$ BU APIN, UŠ+UŠ, $NINDA_2$ MU, 1 N_{14} URU+AMAR; "grand total" seems to be O0203: URU+AMAR	O0203: [ ]; URU_{a1}+AMAR [ ]; R0204: 1 N_{14} URU_{a1}+AMAR
20. W 14263 = VAT 21304, publ. ATU 6, p. 44	Tablet, Qa XVI, 2 PbXVII, 3, "im Schutt über Riemchen unter neubabylonischen Häusern"; sealed, seal No. 12 (ATU 6 p. 12, 13): "Berge hinaufspringende Steinböcke mit Löwen — ähnliches bietet die Abrollung Nr. 12".	ZATU 777 KU_{3a} $NUNUZ_{a2}$ URU_{a1} ŠIDIM(?)
21. W 14804, a+, published in ATU 6 p. 54-55	Oe XVI, 3, +19.50 m; list of quantified items, subscript: EN_a TUR	O0803: $UŠ_a$ URU_{a1}
22. W 15833, A2 = IM 23440	Fragment; [ ]; AN RU_a MAR_b? URU_{a1} ZATU 686_a. MUŠEN ZATU 686_a, rev.: [ ] EN_a X GU_7	O0101: AN RU_a MAR_b? URU_{a1} ZATU 686_a
23. W 15892 K = IM 23446	Fragment	[ ]; URU_{a1} X [ ]. [ ]; X SAG [ ]

Serial No. and citation	Summary of item	Notes
24. W 15892 P+ = IM 23446	List of offices and structured(?) human groups (AB E_2 SUKKAL, NIN SIG_7, UNUG) pertaining to grain ($ŠE_a$ NIM_{b1})[34], issue list from a storeroom (00305: GU_7 ZATU 651+GAR)?	00203: $1N_1$ DUG_{c1} LAL_{3a} SAL URUa1 [ ]
25. W 15895 BL = VAT 17766, d, published ATU 6	Fragment, Qa XVI, 2 "Oe XVII, 1, unter den neubabylonischen Häusern am Suchgraben"; "wohl lexikalisch"	[ ]; URU_{a1}+1 N_{57} [ ]
26. W 16750 = VAT 21322	Fragmentary; 2 columns on obverse, 2 columns on reverse	The only legible sign of the text is R0201: URU_{a1}
27. W 17729, GG	List of quantified items; IŠ SAR PAP, SI URU, ZATU 694 MAR, GAN_2, DUB 3-N_{57} U_4	O0101: 1 N_{50} [ ]; X $IŠ_a$? SAR_a PAP_a? [ ], SI URU_{a1}
28. W 19408, 25	List of quantified items, KAŠ AN, NE DUG URU ŠEŠ	5 N_2; $KAŠ_{c1}$ X AN. 5 N_1; NE_a DUG_{c1} URU_{a1} $ŠEŠ_a$
29. W 19408, 69	Fragment	[ ]; X [ ]. [ ]; NE_a. [ ]; X URU_{a1}?
30. W 20274, 5	A list of expenditures(?) in potted fish (EN_a AB_b DUG_a ZATU 686_a) consumed by offices, communities and humans; rev.: i. a. GU_7; GA_a+ZATU 753	O0301: $5N_1$; GA_{2a1}+ U_4 1 N_4 PAP_a URU_{a1} $ŠAH_{2a}$?
31. W 20500 a	List of quantified items; DU SANGA, UTUL, $SILA_3$+1 N_{57}, SANGA, URU, rev.: IB, SUHUR HI	O0301: URU_{a1} [ ]
32. W 20522.6	Fragment	ii: [ ]; X GI_6 URU_{a1} PAP_a [ ] iii: 2 N [ ]; [ ]
33. W 20552, 8+	List of arable plots and distribution of harvest?; 00201: 4 N_{14} [ ]; $UŠ_a$ $ŠE_a$ GI [ ]' total: MEN_a DU_7?[35] ŠU PAP_a $SANGA_a$ DUR_2? [ ]	O0203: 2 N_{14} [ ]; UR_2 URU_{a1} U_{2a}

[34] See ePSD s. v. še-nim: LEX/unknown/unknown [še] nim SLT 018 r iii 3' = high barley.

[35] DU_7 = (to be) fitting, suitable, see ePSD s. v. du_7.

Serial No. and citation	Summary of item	Notes
34. W 20776	List of rations (?, BA) issued to various agencies of an EN; rev. 00101 BA, rev. 00102 GI — balanced account?	Rev. O0201: 8 N_{34} 2 N_{14}; [ ] SU_a EN_a URU_{a1} IB_a
35. W 20994, 1	Tablet	2 N_1; URU_{a1}
36. W 21060, 12	Fragment	i: [ ]; X [ ]. [ ] 1 N_1; U_4 X [ ]. ii: [ ]; ADAB PA_a $NUNUZ_{a1}$? [ ]. 1 N_{14}; AN URU_{a1} [ ]
37. W 22101, 6	List of quantified items; APIN EZEN DU, APIN SAG, ZATU 714, APIN NAM URU	R0101: [ ]; X $APIN_a$ NAM_2 URU_{a1}
38. W 24008.19	List of quantified items; KU_6, ZATU 759+KU_6, SUHUR URU ZAG DU, $ŠE_3$	O0103: $SUHUR_a$ URU_{a1} ZAG_a DU [ ]

Bibliography

ATU 1 see Falkenstein 1936
ATU 5 see Englund and Boehmer 1994
ATU 6 see Englund, Nissen and Boehmer 2005
ePSD see Philadelphia Sumerian Dictionary (Electronic resources)
MSVO 1 see Englund, Grégoire and Matthews 1991
MSVO 2 see Englund and Matthews 1996
ZATU see Green and Nissen 1987

ARUZ, J. and R. WALLENFELS (eds.) 2003: *Art of the First Cities – The Third Millennium B.C. from the Mediterranean to the Indus*, New York - New Haven - London.

CHARVÁT, P. 1997: *On people, signs and states – Spotlights on Sumerian society, c. 3500-2500 B. C.*, Prague.

CONNAN, J. and O. DESCHESNE 2007: "Le bitume à Mari", in J.-C. Margueron, O. Rouault and P. Lombard (eds.) *Akh Purattim 1*, Lyon, 165-206.

EMERY-BARBIER, A. 2007: "Les restes végétaux à Mari", in J.-C. Margueron, O. Rouault and P. Lombard (eds.) *Akh Purattim 1*, Lyon, 207-213.

ENGLUND, R. K. 2009: "The Smell of the Cage", *Cuneiform Digital Library Journal* 2009:4, 1-27.

ENGLUND, R. K., J.-P. GRÉGOIRE and R. J. MATTHEWS 1991: *The Proto-Cuneiform Texts from Jemdet Nasr I: Copies, Transliterations and Glossary* (Materialien zu den frühen Schriftzeugnissen des Vorderen Orients 1), Berlin

ENGLUND, R. K. and R. M. BOEHMER 1994: *Archaic administrative texts from Uruk – The early campaigns* (Archaische Texte aus Uruk 5), Berlin.
ENGLUND, R. K. and R. J. MATTHEWS 1996: *Proto-Cuneiform Texts from Diverse Collections* (Materialien zu den frühen Schriftzeugnissen des Vorderen Orients 4), Berlin.
ENGLUND, R. K., H. J. NISSEN, R. M. BOEHMER 2005: *Archaische Verwaltungstexte aus Uruk, Vorderasiatisches Museum II* (Archaische Texte aus Uruk 6), Berlin.
FALKENSTEIN, A, 1936: *Archaische Texte aus Uruk*, Berlin - Leipzig.
FENOLLÓS, J. L. M. 2007: "Le travail du cuivre et du bronze à Mari, Un projet archéo-métallurgique", in J.-C. Margueron, O. Rouault and P. Lombard (eds.) *Akh Purattim 1*, Lyon, 215-219.
GREEN, M. and H. J. NISSEN 1987: *Zeichenliste der Archaischen Texte aus Uruk* (Archaische Texte aus Uruk 2), Berlin.
MARGUERON, J.-C., O. ROUAULT and P. LOMBARD (eds.) 2007: *Akh Purattim 1*, Lyon.
NEUMANN, H. 1996: "Review of MSVO 1", *Orientalische Literaturzeitung* 91/1, 22-27.
NICOLINI, G. 2007: "Les ors de Mari, état de la recherche en juin 1997", in J.-C. Margueron, O. Rouault and P. Lombard (eds.) *Akh Purattim 1*, Lyon, 221-228.
SPYCKET, A. 2007: "La statuaire de Mari", in J.-C. Margueron, O. Rouault and P. Lombard (eds.) *Akh Purattim 1*, Lyon, 261-268.

Electronic sources

Philadelphia Sumerian Dictionary (ePSD), http://psd.museum.upenn.edu/epsd/nepsd-frame.html, cited June 29, 2009.
Cuneiform Digital Library Initiative (CDLI), http://cdli.ucla.edu/, cited June 4, 2009.

BEROSSOS' *BABYLONIACA*: PURPOSES AND INTERPRETATIONS

Geert DE BREUCKER
Rijksuniversiteit Groningen

When I moved from Classics to Ancient Near Eastern Studies, it was Karel Van Lerberghe, who introduced me in the fascinating world of cuneiform script and Mesopotamian archaeology. I vividly remember how he commented on Akkadian texts by telling heroic stories about famous Assyriologists. Being an expert in the Old Babylonian period, he was not very happy when I announced that I wanted to write my MA thesis on the Seleucids. Nobody could foretell, except perhaps some *bārû* ("diviner"), that a footnote in that thesis would become the subject of my PhD: Berossos. It is with gratitude that I dedicate this contribution on the Babylonian historian to Van Lerberghe, who is now a famous Assyriologist himself.

The *Babyloniaca* of Berossos has a unique place in Babylonian historiography; obviously because it is written in Greek, shaped as a Greek ethnographical history and accommodated to Greek concepts and tastes. Apart from this, it is also the only written narrative overview of Babylonian history (from creation to Alexander the Great), composed by a Babylonian scholar, who used and interpreted cuneiform sources and native traditions[1]. This makes the *Babyloniaca* a truly product of Babylonian historiography. In this contribution I would like to discuss the aims Berossos had in mind for composing his work. I especially want to focus on his political motives and the problems thereby involved. For this discussion it is important to recall that Berossos dedicated his work to Antiochus I (BNJ 680 T 2)[2], which provides a rough date for its composition.

[1] For an analysis of Berossos' sources, see De Breucker 2010a, 2010b and 2011, 643-647. The *Dynastic Chronicle* (Glassner 2004, no. 5) gives an overview of Babylonian history from creation to somewhere in the period between the middle of the 8th and the middle of the 7th c. BC, but this text is mainly an enumeration of "dynasties", kings and years. The composition was very likely an important source for Berossos.

[2] BNJ: *Brill's New Jacoby*, at this moment only available online. It is an update and expansion of F. Jacoby's monumental work, *Die Fragmente der griechischen Historiker*.

It is generally assumed that Berossos composed and dedicated his work, when Antiochus I was king of the Seleucid Empire, i.e. in the period 281-261 BC (e.g. Schwartz 1897, 309; Schnabel 1923, 8-10; Burstein 1978, 4 and 34). There is, however, no reason to exclude the possibility that the Babylonian scholar made the dedication, when Antiochus was co-regent with his father Seleucus I (from 295-294 BC; see Boiy 2004, 138-139). Lehmann-Haupt (1938, 2) objects that it is impossible that Berossos would not have addressed the reigning monarch, but this is not a convincing argument. Dedications to royal princes instead of the king are not uncommon in Antiquity[3]. Moreover, Antiohus' co-regency provided a good occasion for dedicating to him a work on Babylonia. As co-ruler Antiochus had the supervision over the Upper Satrapies, to which Babylonia belonged. It is known that during this period, somewhere in the years 291/0-283/2, Antiochus was in Babylonia and visited Babylon, as is recorded in a Babylonian chronicle[4]. The fairly broken text notes that "Antiochus the crown prince" visited two temples of the moon god Sîn in Babylon and brought sacrifices[5]. It is even possible that during his co-regency Babylon was one of Antiochus' residence cities until the newly founded city of Seleucia on the Tigris was firmly settled[6].

In BNJ 680 T 2, an important testimony of the Christian apologist Tatian, Antiochus is specified as the third successor "after him" (i.e. Alexander the Great), which must refer to Antiochus I. In his version of Tatian's testimony Eusebius of Caesarea reads "after Seleucus (I)" (*Praep.Ev.*, 10.11.8). In that case Antiochus II (261-246) is meant. Glassner (2004, 28 n. 3) dates Berossos around 250 BC, without explaining this unconventional date. Perhaps he used Eusebius' statement. Since Berossos was born under or a contemporary of Alexander the Great — the Greek sources are ambiguous on this point — this later date is unlikely.

[3] I give two examples: Pliny the Elder dedicated his *Naturalis Historia* to the son of the reigning monarch, his co-ruler Titus. The polymath Juba II of Mauretania dedicated his work on Arabia to a grandson of Augustus, Gaius Caesar, who undertook an expedition in the East (BNJ 275 F 1).

[4] BCHP (= *Babylonian Chronicles of the Hellenistic Period*) 5. The only year number that has been preserved in the text is damaged (BCHP 5 obv. 1). According to Van der Spek 2006a two signs denoting the number '10' can be discerned, followed by some traces of wedges. It means that a year number '20 + x' of the Seleucid Era was written. The entry describing Antiochus' visit to Babylon deals with a subsequent year (obv. 6).

[5] Another chronicle, BCHP 6, describes that the "son of the king" was in the Esagila, the main temple complex of Babylon. He made sacrifices and deployed his army and elephants in order to remove the debris of the temple. Van der Spek 2006b suggests that this prince is also Antiochus I, but this is far from certain.

[6] According to the interpretation of Van der Spek 2006a, a broken passage in the aforementioned chronicle BCHP 5 (see n. 4) notes that Antiochus settled all Macedonians from Babylon to Seleucia on the Tigris, meaning that he populated the new city (BCHP 5 rev. 7'-9'). The restoration of the passage is, however, rather speculative.

Let us now turn to the purposes Berossos aimed at by composing a Greek work and dedicating it to Antiochus. His first aim was obviously to present to a Greek speaking audience an apparently objective and reliable history of Babylonia. Since the Babylonian scholar addressed Antiochus, he especially aimed to reach the new ruling elite in Mesopotamia and beyond. In the eyes of this Greek audience Berossos had the right qualifications for composing a native history — and he was well aware of that: he was a native priest, for Greeks the bearers of oriental autochthonous culture, and had access to local sources, which, as he states in his prologue, had been preserved with great care in Babylon (BNJ 680 F 1a-b).

Berossos gives a glorifying image of Babylonia. The country has an extremely long history that in length surpassed all other cultures: by assigning to the antediluvian period 432,000 years Berossos sets the start of Babylonian history much earlier than that of other countries. The first kings of Babylonia were autochthonous and since autochthony of a people and its rulers was highly regarded in the Greek world, this contributed to the glory of Babylonia. Moreover, the country was the "cradle" of civilisation: in the beginning of its long history, in the first year when kingship was introduced, Oannes — Uan(na) in Mesopotamian texts — civilised humankind. He taught "everything that is connected with a civilised life" (BNJ 680 F 1b) and nothing else had been invented from that time. It should be noted that Berossos did not create this glorious past himself, he could draw on his Babylonian sources. Berossos was not an exception in glorifying his own country. His "Egyptian counterpart" and contemporary, the native priest Manetho (BNJ 609) stresses the long history of Egypt[7]. The Greek authors Hecataeus of Abdera (BNJ 264) and Megasthenes (BNJ 715) idealised in their historical ethnographies the country they treated, Egypt and India respectively[8].

[7] The chronological relationship between Berossos and Manetho is unclear, as the latter is linked by ancient sources with Ptolemy I (323-283) as well as with Ptolemy II (285-246). The Byzantine chronographer Syncellus states that Manetho imitated Berossos (BNJ 680 T 10 and BNJ 609 T 11b). His dating of Manetho is very likely based on the fact that he accepts that the Egyptian priest dedicated a work called the *Book of Sothis* to Ptolemy II. Since this book is a forgery, the dedication can not be used to date Manetho and, as a consequence, Syncellus' statements about the interdependency between Berossos and Manetho can not be trusted, see also Verbrugghe and Wickersham 1996, 97.

[8] Both works, respectively entitled *Aegyptiaca* and *Indica*, have been only preserved in fragments. Hecataeus, who was connected to the Ptolemaic court, probably composed his work in the early reign of Ptolemy I; Megasthenes probably wrote his work somewhere in the period 310-290 BC. Berossos may have known both works and be inspired by them.

Berossos very likely also aimed to counterbalance the Greek works on Babylonia-Assyria[9], like those of Herodotus and Ctesias (BNJ 688), and to correct their errors. Josephus remarks in his apologetic work *Contra Apionem* after his citation from Berossos on Nebuchadnezzar II (604-561) that the author censured those Greek historians who wrongly ascribed the foundation of Babylon and the erection of its magnificent buildings to the Assyrian queen Semiramis (BNJ 680 F 8a)[10]. Berossos implicitly attacks Ctesias, who extensively wrote on Semiramis' foundation of Babylon (see Diodorus Siculus 2.7.2-9.9). Criticising other historians was a *topos* in Greek historiography; historians even criticised predecessors and at the same time used their works. Greek historians wrote in a competitive environment and had to attract the attention of an audience. In the case of Berossos his attack was justified and, therefore, more than a generic topic, but at the same time he aimed to show the unreliability of Greek historians.

Berossos' enterprise to write a history of his nation must be seen in the broader cultural context of his time: faced with the new order of the Hellenistic world he wanted to redefine Babylonian culture and to position it against the dominant Hellenic culture. As far as we can judge from the remaining fragments, Berossos did not seek to link Babylonian history with that of the Greeks. Another non-Greek historian, Xanthus the Lydian, who composed a history of Lydia in the first half of the 5th c. BC, tried to place his country in the panhellenic framework by connecting Greek mythological and legendary characters with Lydia[11]. Xanthus wanted to demonstrate that Lydia was part of Greek history. Berossos, on the other hand, sets Babylonia apart from that broad panhellenic framework. He mentions a victory of Sennacherib (704-681) in Cilicia against Greeks (BNJ 680 F 7c and BNJ 685 F 5), but there is no parallel story among the Greeks[12]. The only synchronism with Greek

[9] Classical literature often made no difference between Assyria and Babylonia and used "Assyria" as a synonym of Mesopotamia (thus including Babylonia).

[10] Josephus had a strong interest in stressing that Greek historians were not reliable because they did not support the antiquity of the Jewish people, which Josephus had set out in his *Jewish Antiquities*. This does not, however, undermine the credibility of Berossos' attack of Greek historians.

[11] BNJ 765 F 14, 20a-b, 21 and 22. Xanthus links two heroes of the Trojan War with Lydia. For Greeks the Trojan War was the oldest "historical" event of their past and a landmark in their history.

[12] In the aftermath of this victory Sennacherib built Tarsus. Berossos aimed to correct the Greek story that it was the Assyrian king Sardanapallos who founded that city (Burstein 1978, 24 n. 80).

history we find in the excerpts is the statement that the famous Greek philosopher Pythagoras was a mercenary in the time of Esarhaddon [680-669] (BNJ 680 F 7c and BNJ 685 F 5). This remark is, however, very likely a later interpolation.

Berossos was not alone in feeling the urge to redefine his native history in the new context of the Hellenistic world. Other non-Greek authors, like Manetho and the Judean Eupolemus (BNJ 723), who probably lived around 150 BC, did the same. Sterling (1992, 17) labels these non-Greek historians as "apologetic historians": they told the story of their own group by reshaping local traditions into a Hellenic model in an effort to give a self-definition of their group and to establish its identity within the larger world. This is certainly a correct analysis, but the approach of these native authors is not essentially different from that of Greek local historians in the Hellenistic period: these authors too intended to redefine the identity of their city and to place it in the new setting of the Hellenistic world (Schepens 2001, 14; Clarke 2008, 194). Like the "barbarian" histories, their works also have a flavour of local pride and chauvinism. Both groups of local historians actually reacted in a similar way to the same cultural phenomenon.

In Babylonia this local pride and glorification of the past can also be found in cuneiform texts from the late period. Grayson (1980, 192-193) suggests that the Babylonians had a pronounced interest in their past in the Hellenistic period. Ruled by Greeks they attempted to preserve their declining traditional culture and to promote a sense of pride. In my view, this interest already started in the Achaemenid period, as there is an increase of historical texts from that time on. The problem with such an interpretation is that we never can be sure whether this increase is purely coincidental, simply because more texts of the later period have survived, or that it indeed is an indication of a greater interest in history and historiography. In any way, there is a larger corpus of historical narratives (epics) and (fictitious) royal letters dating from the Late Babylonian period[13]. Most of these texts treat Babylonian kings who had liberated Babylonia from foreign domination, as Nebuchadnezzar I (1125-1104), Adad-šuma-usur (1216-1187) and Nabopolassar (625-605). The first king defeated Elam and brought back the statue of Marduk to Babylon; the others expulsed the Assyrians from Babylonia. The interest in these kings can be interpreted as an expression of nostalgia or pride in a glorious

[13] For an overview of historical epics, see Grayson 1975; for the letters, see Frahm 2005.

past. It is too speculative to suggest that it also reflects political hopes in regaining independence.

These cuneiform texts and Berossos' *Babyloniaca* are both part of the process of dealing with the new political situation. Berossos, however, addressed a non-Babylonian audience in the first place. Is it possible that he also wanted to address his fellow Babylonians? Oelsner (1978, 114) sees in the *Babyloniaca* a reaction against the penetration of Greek culture in Babylonia. As Kuhrt (1987, 53) reformulates his view, Berossos wanted to remind those of his countrymen who were eager to adopt Greek culture of the great history of their nation and their cultural identity. As Kuhrt rightly opposes, there is no evidence for a cultural confrontation and deliberate policy of Hellenisation in Babylonia. As the case of Ptolemaic Egypt shows, "Hellenised" Babylonians, just as Berossos himself, were very probably embedded in two cultures — Greek and Babylonian — and had a "double" cultural identity. Dillery (2007, 229), too, believes that Berossos also wrote for Babylonians. In his view Berossos' favouring of Babylon over other Babylonian cities is only meaningful for his countrymen. This is not a compelling argument, as it is also possible to argue that Berossos, being an inhabitant of Babylon, intended to convince his Greek audience of the glorious past of his city. And as we shall see below, there might have been political motives for this glorification.

Notwithstanding these objections, it is quite possible that Babylonians who knew Greek were anxious to read what a fellow countryman had written on their history. It may have influenced their view of their past. We have, however, no firm indications that Berossos' *Babyloniaca* had an impact on the way in which Babylonians looked at their history. As I observed elsewhere (De Breucker 2011, 652), the tradition of the antediluvian sages (*apkallū*) and the first of them, Uan(na)/Oannes, flourished in the late period. The fish-*apkallu* was a popular motive on seals. The Bit-Resh, the main temple of Hellenistic Uruk, traced back its foundation to the time of Uan. This was obviously a forgery since the temple had been founded in the late period. It is, however, impossible to say whether Berossos' portrait of the *apkallū* and Oannes, the inventor of civilisation, enhanced the popularity of the tradition of the antediluvian sages.

So far we have presented Berossos' "cultural motives": informing, promoting and redefining Babylonian identity — which, of course, can also have political implications. The question arises whether Berossos had a clearly political message. Dillery (2007, 228) regards the *Babyloniaca* as a kind of *Fürstenspiegel*. In the words of the author, Berossos intended "to model for the new rulers successful strategies for governance as well as to present the required ideology for becoming truly legitimate kings". And, Dillery adds, to warn them implicitly not to undertake actions that would make their rule illegitimate in the eyes of the native population. In Babylonian ideology a good king had to take care of the country and its people and to honour the gods. The latter implied executing the appropriate rites, e.g. during the New Year's Festival, and building and restoring temples. In historical cuneiform texts from the first millennium — epics and fictitious royal letters — we find what we can call the "Marduk ideology": the king who neglects the god, his temple Esagila and his city Babylon, will be severely punished; the ruler who honours them, will enjoy prosperity. In the extant fragments of the *Babyloniaca* we have no concrete indications for this "Marduk ideology". It is true that Berossos states that Nebuchadnezzar II lavishly decorated the temples of Bel and the other gods (BNJ 680 F 8a), which is confirmed by the king's inscriptions[14]. At the same time, however, Berossos notes that Artaxerxes II (423/2-405) introduced the cult of a non-Babylonian goddess in Babylon, Anaïtis (BNJ 680 F 11), obviously an example not to be followed by the Seleucids. But we must be aware that we do not know the context in which Berossos mentioned this religious innovation.

We may assume that Berossos hoped to reach more than gaining respect and admiration for his native culture. He very likely attempted to encourage the Greco-Macedonian ruling elite to foster and support that culture. Perhaps his *Babyloniaca* was an appeal to the Seleucids to pursue a pro-Babylonian policy. Schnabel (1923, 8) thinks that the *Babyloniaca* was a "thank-offering" to Antiochus because of his pro-Babylonian policy. This is rather unlikely; if so, Berossos undoubtedly aimed to encourage the king to continue this policy. Burstein (1978, 5-6) supposes that Berossos specifically attempted to convince Antiochus I to reverse the policy of his father Seleucus I to degrade Babylon by Seleucia on the Tigris. When he failed in doing so, he disappointedly migrated to the island of Cos, which was controlled by the rivalling dynasty of the Ptolemies. This conclusion is very speculative — and the authenticity of Berossos' migration to Cos is even very doubtful (Schwartz 1897, 316; Kuhrt 1987, 43; De Breucker 2010a). But are there arguments for Burstein's assumption that Berossos aimed to prevent the development of the newly founded city of Seleucia?

[14] See e.g. Neumann 2000, 323, no. 1, col. ii, ll. 1-10.

Cuneiform sources provide no information on the attitude of the Babylonians toward the "royal city" of Seleucia. Classical sources describe its foundation as a deliberate act of Seleucus I to diminish Babylon and the "Chaldaeans" attempted to prevent it[15]. It is certain that Seleucus did not deliberately envisage to ruin Babylon. As Sherwin-White (1987, 18-20) and Boiy (2004, 136) point out, economic and military reasons were far more important to found a new city on that particular spot, at the confluence of the Tigris and the King's Canal. But it is possible that the Babylonians themselves considered the foundation as a degradation of their own city. The loss of Babylon's royal status — the city considered to be the centre of the world[16] — may have had ideological implications.

Despite of the fragmentary character of the *Babyloniaca*, it is clear from the extant fragments that Berossos centred his history on Babylon, his hometown and the most important city of Babylonia. It was the first antediluvian city (BNJ 680 F 3a-b) and its walls were built by Bel-Marduk himself (BNJ 685 F 1a-b). Since Babylonian history surpassed all other countries in time, Babylon was simply the oldest city of the world. Nebuchadnezzar II, according to Berossos the greatest Babylonian king, splendidly renovated the city (BNJ 680 F 8a). The great fame of this king even found its way to Greek literature, as Megasthenes, who lived with Seleucus I, ranks him among the greatest barbarian world-conquerors (BNJ 715 F 11a; see also F 1a-b). One could speculate that Berossos made an appeal to Antiochus to follow the example of his famous predecessor and to renovate Babylon.

It is possible that Berossos implicitly warned Antiochus not to continue the building of Seleucia on the Tigris. A passage in the fragments could be interpreted in this way. After his Cilician campaign Sennacherib built Tarsus after the image of Babylon (BNJ 680 F 7c). The parallel version of Abydenus explains what this likeness entailed: just like the Euphrates flows through Babylon, so the Cydnus flows through Tarsus (BNJ 685 F 5). This signifies that the two cities were built on both sides of the river — an unusual feature for Greek cities (Dalley 1999, 76). This explanation is very likely a later gloss and does not go back to Berossos himself. In some cuneiform texts building a city as a copy of Babylon is considered as a taboo. In the *Chronicle of Ancient Kings*, known from a copy of the Late Babylonian period, it is said that Sargon of Akkad built

[15] Appian, *Syr.* 58.300-308; Strabo 16.1.5; Pliny, *HN* 6.122 and Pasuanias 1.16.3.

[16] See the *Babylonian Map of the World*, known from a copy of the Late Babylonian period, see Horowitz 1998, 20-42.

a copy of Babylon near Agade and was therefore punished by Marduk: the god diminished his people by famine, they revolted against him and he himself was afflicted with restlessness[17]. In the *Weidner Chronicle* — in fact a fictitious literary letter — Sargon built a city facing Agade and called it "Babylon"[18]. As in the former text, a revolt and restlessness were Marduk's punishment. Furthermore, one of the crimes of king Nabonidus (555-539) might have been that he built a palace in Tayma (in Arabia), where he dwelled for ten years instead of in Babylon, "like that of Babylon"[19]. Sennacherib himself was killed by his own son. This was easily interpreted as a punishment of the gods because of Sennacherib's sins against Babylon, in the first place his destruction of the city and abduction of Marduk's statue in 689 BC. It is tempting to connect the passage from Berossos with the taboo and to give it an actual political interpretation: Seleucus I had founded his new "Babylon", Seleucia on the Tigris, and was murdered on his way to his homeland Macedonia. In other words, we could interpret the passage as an implicit warning to Antiochus not to complete the building of Seleucia and to keep Babylon as regional royal capital. This interpretation is, of course, mere speculation.

Equally speculative is the "political interpretation" of another passage. Berossos relates that in the interregnum between the death of Nabopolassar and the accession of Nebuchadnezzar II the Chaldaeans administered the affairs and maintained the kingdom for the latter (BNJ 680 F 8a). It is unclear whether with the "Chaldaeans" the inhabitants of Babylonia or the "Chaldaean priests" are meant. The latter seems the most likely. It is possible that Berossos aimed to demonstrate to Antiochus that the Babylonian clergy was loyal to the legitimate ruler and could be entrusted with administrative duties.

[17] Glassner 2004, no. 39, ll. 18-23.

[18] Glassner 2004, no. 38, ll. 60-61. The oldest attested version of this text dates from the Neo-Assyrian period; see also the parallel passage in a historical omen dating from the Neo-Assyrian period (King 1907, no. 3, obv., §III, 10). Van de Mieroop (1999, 335; see also Glassner 2004, 291 n. 10) assumes that the copyist made an error, when he wrote down that Sargon founded Babylon because that city had already been mentioned in the *Weidner Chronicle* before. I think that it is possible to retain the text as it is transmitted: Sargon founded a new city and by calling it "Babylon", he in fact created a second Babylon, a copy as is noted in the *Chronicle of Ancient Kings*. Van de Mieroop (1999, 335-339) connects this evidence of the taboo to the fate of Sargon II of Assyria: he founded a new royal city, Dur-Sharrukin, and died an ominous death: he perished on the battlefield and his corpse remained unburied.

[19] *Verse Account of Nabonidus*, col. ii, ll. 28'-31'; see Schaudig 2001, 575. The *Verse Account* describes the "crimes" committed by Nabonidus and aims to portray him as a bad ruler.

These interpretations are no more than speculations and confront us with a fundamental problem: interpreting an ancient work that only has been preserved in fragments will always remain hazardous. Features that can be clearly discerned in the remaining fragments may not be representative for the original composition in its entirety. Wordings preserved in the text may go back to later excerptors and, as a consequence, do not reflect the attitude of the author himself. Moreover, similarities between ancient texts can be mere coincidence, being not the result of interdependency or deliberate allusions. I give two examples to illustrate this.

Berossos narrates that when Nebuchadnezzar II was informed in Syria on the death of his father, he crossed the desert with a few companions in order to ascend the throne in Babylon (BNJ 680 F 8a). At face value there is a striking similarity with the way in which Seleucus started the recapture of his satrapy, which was occupied by Antigonus the "One-eyed": after the battle of Gaza in 312 BC Seleucus rushed with a small contingent through the desert to Babylonia[20]. It is tempting to connect both stories with each other, as Eddy (1961, 125-126) did. He even interprets Berossos' story as an expression of anti-Hellenic sentiments: the Babylonian would have used the story of Nebuchadnezzar II in order to belittle Seleucus. Unlike him, Nebuchadnezzar reached Babylonia without any difficulty and with fewer soldiers and he could immediately take power. Eddy's interpretation is not convincing. Berossos' story is probably heavily shortened and less specific. Moreover, Diodorus of Sicily (19.91.1-2) states that on his return to Babylonia Seleucus was warmly welcomed by the local population. More basically, the correspondences between both stories are very likely purely factual and not created by purpose: the route through the Syrian-Arabian desert was the shortest way to Babylon and taking an entire army with oneself was time-consuming.

Berossos continues that on arrival in Babylon Nebuchadnezzar gained possession of his father's "entire" (ὁλοκλήρου) realm (BNJ 680 F 8a). The mention of "entire" is remarkable. Did Berossos use this adjective by purpose? The historian Memnon of Heraclea on the Pontus (1st c. BC) remarks that Antiochus had recovered his father's kingdom with much difficulty and even so not completely (BNJ 434 F 1). This sharply contrasts Nebuchadnezzar's easy and complete take over of his father's empire. It would, however, be too far-fetched to connect both texts with each other, especially because it would be very strange that Berossos

[20] Diodorus Siculus 19.90.1-91.5; Appian, *Syr.* 54.273-274; see also Libanius, *Or.* 11.82.

implicitly criticised Antiochus, the addressee of his work, for having failed in recovering the entire realm of Seleucus I. These interpretations demonstrate that if one is convinced of an interpretation, arguments in favour are easily found. An ancient fragmentary text is a nice playground for modern creative minds indulging in sophisticated interpretations.

In modern scholarship a firmly established interpretation of the *Babyloniaca* is that Berossos aimed to provide with it support of the Seleucid dynasty. Kuhrt, in her fundamental article on the Babylonian historian (1987, 55-56), e.g. assumes that Berossos wished to help in creating an ideological foundation of Seleucid rule. His *Babyloniaca* was a tool in the war of propaganda against the rivalling Ptolemaic dynasty. In particular, it could be considered as the Babylonian/Seleucid response to that idealising work on Egypt, the *Aegyptiaca* of the Ptolemaic courtier Hecataeus of Abdera. The main reason for this interpretation is apparently Berossos' dedication to Antiochus I. Modern scholars take it as proof that Berossos wrote his work under the patronage of or even by the request of the Seleucids (e.g. Lehmann-Haupt 1938, 3; Tarn 1985, 41; Kuhrt 1987, 55; Verbrugghe and Wickersham 1996, 14). These scholars consider the Babylonian scholar as being connected to the court or as a "court historian"[21]. This interpretation fits our view of Hellenistic monarchy and court-life. There is, however, no other evidence corroborating that Berossos dwelled in the entourage of Antiochus. The simple fact of his dedication to the Seleucid does not necessarily mean that he was working for the Seleucid court. Other motives for the dedication can easily be found: begging for a position at court, hoping to be engaged by the rulers or aiming to influence the policies of the new ruling dynasty and its entourage by addressing and sending the work to Antiochus.

As a priest of Bel-Marduk Berossos was connected to the Esagila in Babylon and thus belonged to the local urban elite. Members of this group had close contacts with the Seleucid administration, for which the Esagila and the other temples in Babylonia were important local institutions. The latter's administrators represented the autochthonous population in the Seleucid administration (Boiy 2004, 194-204). The Seleucids supervised the temples, directly by appointing their own royal representatives; indirectly since the local families that administered the temple were ultimately dependent on the good-will of the Seleucids. It is in this

[21] Burstein (1978, 5) assumes that Berossos was perhaps one of the Chaldaean astrologers who, according to classical authors, were consulted by Seleucus and his predecessors. There is no evidence for this.

framework of contacts and relations that I situate Berossos' dedication to the Seleucid ruler. Not the royal court, but the city and temple were Berossos' environment.

But are there any pro-Seleucid tendencies to be discerned in the extant fragments of the *Babyloniaca*? Kuhrt (1987, 56; see also Dillery 2007, 224) assumes that Berossos' description of Nabopolassar and his son Nebuchadnezzar II prefigures the reigns of Seleucus I and Antiochus I. In both cases, father and son cooperated and the father founded an empire, whereas the son consolidated it. In this way Berossos would have represented Seleucus and Antiochus as the legitimate heirs of these famous Babylonian kings. Berossos' account of the reigns of Nabopolassar and his son is in general lines historically correct: Nabopolassar revolted against Assyria and became king of Babylonia. Nebuchadnezzar II expanded the realm by annexing the territories that had been under Assyrian control. The son helped his father, as e.g. in 605 BC, when Nabopolassar — probably due to his poor condition, as Berossos notes — sent his son to Syria in order to fight against the Egyptians. It is, therefore, not impossible that the resemblances between both pairs of rulers are merely coincidental.

According to Burstein (1978, 24 n. 93 and 26 n. 102), Berossos' use of the term "Coele Syria" proves that he supported the Seleucid claims on that region, which was then occupied by the Ptolemies. "Coele Syria" is, however, in the first place a neutral geographical term designating the region between Cilicia and Egypt west of the Syrian-Arabian desert, in which Phoenicia was mostly not included. It is, therefore, very speculative to attribute to the use of the term political or propagandistic significance. The Ptolemaic administration itself called the province "Syria and Phoenicia" (Bagnall 1976, 15).

In the remaining fragments two campaigns against Coele Syria and Egypt are mentioned. Axerdis, i.e. Esarhaddon conquered Coele Syria and Egypt (BNJ 685 F 5). Nebuchadnezzar II defeated the satrap of Coele Syria, Phoenicia and Egypt, who had become rebellious, and brought these regions again under Babylonian rule (BNJ 680 F 8a)[22]. This could

[22] This episode is in many ways unhistorical. The historical core of the story is the battle of Carcemish in 605, when Nebuchadnezzar defeated an Egyptian army and broke Egyptian supremacy in the Levant. The rebellious satrap must refer to the Egyptian pharaoh Necho II. Coele Syria, Phoenicia and Egypt were not a province of Nabopolassar's realm, but previously belonged to the Assyrian empire (in the case of Egypt, only short-living). After Carcemish Nebuchadnezzar II had to launch much more campaigns to Syria and Phoenicia in order to consolidate Babylonian rule. He could never conquer Egypt, but an Old Testament tradition states the opposite; see *Jeremiah* 43.8-13; *Ezekiel* 29.19 and 30.20-26 and Josephus, *AJ* 10.182.

suggest that Berossos wanted to stress that the contested regions of Coele Syria and Phoenicia and even the heartland of the rivalling dynasty, Egypt itself, historically belonged to the Seleucid empire. We should, however, be aware that Syria-Phoenicia and Egypt were of great interest for the Jewish and Christian excerptors of Berossos' work — our main sources, as these regions were the geographical settings of Biblical episodes. For example, Nebuchadnezzar's victory over the rebellious satrap historically refers to the battle of Carcemish, which is also described in the Old Testament tradition[23]. It is very likely that Berossos treated much more campaigns of Babylonian kings than now have been preserved. Since the regions involved, as e.g. Elam, had no particular interest for later excerptors, these campaigns were left out. As a consequence, we may lay too much emphasis on the campaigns in Coele Syria and Egypt than Berossos himself intended.

These critical remarks are not intended to discard completely the pro-Seleucid view. My aim is to show that it is no more than a possible interpretation. It is also conceivable that the supposed pro-Seleucid tendencies are a side effect of Berossos' pro-Babylonian agenda or that both converged. The Babylonian made his new rulers clear that they ruled over an ancient and superior culture with the purpose of gaining respect and support of it. At the same time the Seleucids could use this image in their imperial ideology — and Berossos may have hoped that his country benefitted from this use. He demonstrated that the Seleucids were the heirs of a great empire and showed at the same time that the capital of this empire was Babylon. His work could have been the Babylonian response to the *Aegyptiaca* of Hecataeus of Abdera in a double way: not only did he want to glorify his culture vis-à-vis Egypt, but the antiquity and greatness of his country could also be politically and ideologically capitalised by the Seleucid rulers in their war of propaganda against the Ptolemies.

Interpreting a fragmentary ancient text and searching for the author's aims and purposes is always a very tricky enterprise. We must take into account that we only have a partial and often biased view of the composition. The extant fragments may not reflect the author's original intentions. In the case of Berossos' *Babyloniaca* it is clear that his aim was to provide a reliable "standard work" on the history of Babylonia, which presented a positive, even glorifying image of Babylonian culture. Berossos undoubtedly wanted to impress his Greek audience and the Greco-Macedonian ruling elite in particular. He very probably hoped to influence their attitude

[23] *Jeremiah* 46.2-12; LXX *Jerermiah* 26.2; see also Josephus, *AJ* 10.84-86.

towards his country. It is possible that Berossos had also political motives, whether it was encouraging the Seleucids to pursue a pro-Babylonian policy or/and contributing to the development of a Seleucid imperial ideology. But in the end these interpretations must remain speculative.

Bibliography

BAGNALL, R. S. 1976: *The Administration of the Ptolemaic Possessions outside Egypt* (Columbia Studies in the Classical Tradition 4), Leiden.

BOIY, T. 2004: *Late Achaemenid and Hellenistic Babylon* (Orientalia Lovaniensia Analecta 136), Leuven.

BURSTEIN, S. M. 1978: *The Babyloniaca of Berossus* (Sources from the Ancient Near East 1/5), Malibu CA.

CLARKE, K. 2008: *Making Time for the Past. Local History and the Polis*, Oxford and New York.

DALLEY, S. 1999: "Sennacherib and Tarsus", *Anatolian Studies* 49, 73-80.

DE BREUCKER G. 2010a: "Berossos (680)", *Brill's New Jacoby Online.*

— 2010b: "Abydenos (685)", *Brill's New Jacoby Online.*

— 2011: "Berossos between tradition and innovation", in Radner, K. and E. Robson (eds.), *The Oxford Handbook of Cuneiform Culture*, Oxford, 637-657.

DILLERY, J. 2007: "Greek Historians of the Near East: Clio's "Other" Sons", in J. Marincola (ed.), *A Companion to Greek and Roman Historiography*, Oxford, 221-230.

EDDY S. K. 1961: *The King is dead. Studies in the Near Eastern Resistance to Hellenism, 334-1 B.C.*, Lincoln.

FRAHM, E. 2005: "On Some Recently Published Late Babylonian Copies of Royal Letters.", *N.A.B.U.*, no. 43.

GLASSNER, J.-J. 2004: *Mesopotamian Chronicles* (Writings from the Ancient World 19), Atlanta GA.

GRAYSON, A.K. 1975: *Babylonian Historical-Literary Texts* (Toronto Semitic Texts and Studies 3), Toronto and Buffalo.

— 1980: "Histories and Historians of the Ancient Near East: Assyria and Babylonia", *Orientalia*, NS 49, 140-194.

HOROWITZ, W. 1998: *Mesopotamian Cosmic Geography* (Mesopotamian Civilizations 8), Winona Lake IL.

KING, L. W. 1907: *Chronicles concerning Early Babylonian Kings Including Records of the Early History of the Kassites and the Country of the Sea*, London.

KUHRT, A. 1987: "Berossus' *Babyloniaka* and Seleucid Rule in Babylonia", in A. Kuhrt and S. Sherwin-White (eds.), *Hellenism in the East. The interaction of Greek and non-Greek civilisation from Syria to Central Asia after Alexander*, London.

LEHMANN-HAUPT, C. F. 1938: "Berossos", *RlA* 2, 1-17.

NEUMANN, H. 2000: "Historische Keilschrifttexte im Kestner-Museum Hannover, II. Nebuchadnezar II.", in J. Marzahn and H. Neumann (eds.), *Assyriologica et Semitica. Festschrift für Joachim Oelsner anläßlich seines*

65. Geburtstages am 18. Februar 1997 (Alter Orient und Altes Testament 252), Münster, 319-330.

OELSNER, J. 1978: "Kontinuität und Wandel in Gesellschaft und Kultur Babyloniens in hellenistischer Zeit", *Klio* 60, 101-116.

SCHAUDIG, H. 2001: *Die Inschriften Nabonids von Babylon und Kyros' des Großen samt den in ihrem Umfeld entstandenen Tendenzschriften* (Alter Orient und Altes Testament 256), Münster.

SCHEPENS, G. 2001: "Ancient Greek city histories. Self-definition through history writing", in Demoen, K. (ed.), *The Greek city from Antiquity to present. Historical reality, ideological construction, literary representation*, Leuven and Paris, 3-25.

SCHNABEL, P. 1923: *Berossos und die babylonisch-hellenistische Literatur*, Leipzig and Berlin.

SCHWARTZ, E. 1897: "Berossos 4)", *RE* 3.1, 309-316.

SHERWIN-WHITE, S. 1987: "Seleucid Babylonia: a case study for the installation and development of Greek rule", in A. Kuhrt and S. Sherwin-White (eds.), *Hellenism in the East. The interaction of Greek and non-Greek civilisations from Syria to Central Asia after Alexander*, London, 1-31.

STERLING, G. E. 1992: *Historiography and Self-Definition: Josephos, Luke-Acts and Apologetic Historiography* (Novum Testamentum Supplement 64), Leiden.

TARN, W. W. 1985: *The Greeks in Bactria and India*, 3rd ed., Chicago.

VAN DE MIEROOP, M. 1999: "Literature and political discourse in Ancient Mesopotamia: Sargon II of Assyria and Sargon of Agade", in B. Böck, E. C. Cancik-Kirschbaum and T. Richter (eds.), *Munuscula Mesopotamica. Festschrift für Johannes Renger* (Alter Orient und Altes Testament 267), Münster, 327-339.

VAN DER SPEK, R. J. 2006a: "Chronicle concerning Antiochus and the Sin temple (BCHP 5)", last modified August 9, 2006, accessed October 10, 2011. http://www.livius.org/cg-cm/chronicles/bchp-antiochus_sin/antiochus_sin_01.html.

— 2006b: "Ruin of Esagila chronicle (BCHP 6)", last modified August 9, 2006, accessed October 10, 2011. http://www.livius.org/cg-cm/chronicles/bchp-ruin_esagila/ruin_esagila_01.html.

VERBRUGGHE, G. P. and J. M. WICKERSHAM 1996: *Berossos and Manetho. Introduced and Translated. Native Traditions in Ancient Mesopotamia and Egypt*, Ann Arbor MI.

LEAD ISOTOPIC ANALYSIS OF COPPER ALLOY ARTIFACTS FROM TELL TWEINI

CHANGING ORE SOURCES FROM THE EARLY BRONZE AGE TO THE IRON AGE?

Patrick DEGRYSE[1], Hamdy EL-DESOUKY[1], Joachim BRETSCHNEIDER[1], Greta JANS[1], Frank VANHAECKE[2], Philippe MUCHEZ[1]

[1] KU Leuven
[2] Ghent University

Introduction

Identifying the geological provenance of an artifact, i.e. the origin of the ores used to produce a metal, provides important information on ancient relationships and connections, trade, and the movement of raw materials and/or objects. The initial approach to this provenance question applied elemental chemical analysis of artifacts and their proposed ore sources, but soon proved to be ineffective due to chemical heterogeneities in ore deposits and variable fractionations of many elements between ore, slag and metal during the smelting processes (Biswas and Davenport 1980; Gale and Stos-Gale 1982, 2000; Stos-Gale and Gale 2009). Contrary to element concentrations, it has been proven that lead isotope ratios of ore minerals and the metal smelted from them, are not modified by weathering, smelting, or other pyrotechnical processes (Barnes et al. 1978; Begemann et al. 1989; Gale 1989; Stos-Gale and Gale 2009). Therefore, lead isotopes have been intensively used for metal provenancing since the 1960s (Stos-Gale and Gale 2009). The technique of Pb isotope provenancing is based on comparing the Pb isotopic signatures of archaeological materials with the Pb isotopic fingerprints of the ore deposits that might have been exploited in ancient times (Stos-Gale and Gale 2009). For proper comparisons, Pb isotope ratios of ancient ore deposits are often collected in large Pb isotope databases (e.g. Stos-Gale and Gale 2009; Cattin et al. 2009).

Materials

A reconnaissance study of the lead isotopic composition of a number of copper alloy artifacts from the site of Tell Tweini was performed. Tell

Tweini is located in the Syrian coastal plain, approximately 1.5 km east of modern-day Jebleh and 40 km south of Ras Shamra-Ugarit, capital of the ancient Kingdom of Ugarit. Since 1999, the site of ca. 12 hectares is under excavation by the Syro-Belgian team headed by Dr. Al-Maqdissi, Dr. Badawi (Department of Antiquities, Damascus) Prof. Karel Van Lerberghe and Prof. Bretschneider (Catholic University Leuven). Work has been concentrated in three areas on the summit of the tell (Fields A, B and C). Especially Field A (central part of the tell) has produced a full, uninterrupted archaeological sequence, mainly spanning from the Early Bronze Age IV (ca. 2400 B.C.) up to the Iron III period (ca. 500 B.C.). The most intensive occupation occurred during the Late Bronze Age and Iron Age period, when a fortified city occupied the site.

Copper alloy artifacts in the form of tools, weapons and jewellery are frequently attested in all occupation levels of the site. All samples were obtained from objects discovered in the A Field. The majority of these objects originate from filling layers, but two of them derive from tomb contexts.[1] A Middle Bronze I corbelled-vault tomb (00954) contained the body of a young man[2] lying on his back with the legs pulled up. The inventory consisted of a bag-shaped juglet[3], a bronze pin and a bronze ring, which was still around a finger of the left hand.[4] The sample was taken from the ring. In the profile of a small sounding, a Middle Bronze Age II jar burial (02542) was located some 60 to 70 cm below a plaster floor. The human remains in the jar — most likely of three different persons — were mixed and disturbed. Two intact red burnished dipper juglets, fragments of two small black slipped juglets and a bronze bracelet were found inside the jar.

Methods

All samples were weighed into pre-cleaned Teflon screw-top beakers and decomposed in *aqua regia* (1:3 mixture of 14 M HNO_3 and 12 M HCl) on a hotplate at ca. 110 °C. After complete digestion, the solutions were

[1] This information was extracted from: Hameeuw and Jans 2008, 75-86.

[2] The anthro-biological examinations on the human remains found at Tell Tweini were conducted by F.-X. Ricaut during the 2006-2007 seasons.

[3] The juglet is the main chronological reference for the tomb; a parallel was found at Doumet-Serhal 2004, Table 7, fig. 14, S/1803.

[4] Finger rings are not often attested at the beginning of the second millennium in the Levant and Mesopotamia (see: Hausleitner 2006, 413-14). A similar context, but with three scarabs adorning the fingers of the deceased, is attested in a Middle Bronze Age tomb (burial 12) in Sidon (Doumet-Serhal 2004, 114, fig. 14.).

evaporated to dryness and taken up in 1 M HNO_3. Part of this solution was used for elemental analysis, a second part was used for Pb isolation (De Muynck et al. 2008) and subsequent isotopic analysis. Semi-quantitative analysis of Pb was performed using MC-ICP-MS. Quantitative determination of Pb concentrations was performed only on a selection of samples for which enough unweathered metal was preserved, using a Varian 730-ES inductively coupled plasma optical emission spectroscopy (ICP–OES) instrument. The operating conditions were adjusted according to the operating parameters described in Calderon (2006). Lead isotopic analyses were performed using a Thermo Electron Neptune multi-collector inductively coupled plasma — mass spectrometer (MC-ICP-MS) at the Department of Analytical Chemistry, Ghent University (Belgium). For Pb isotopic analyses, lead was separated and purified from the sample matrix by extraction chromatography using the Pb spec™ crown ether-based resin. Samples were loaded in 1 M HNO_3, matrix elements were removed with 0.1 M HNO_3, and the purified Pb fractions were collected with 0.05 M ammonium oxalate ($(NH_4)_2C_2O_4$), following the procedure described in detail in De Muynck et al. (2008). The advantage of this isolation protocol is its quantitative Pb recovery and pure Pb fraction. The purified Pb fractions were evaporated to dryness, treated with *aqua regia* to remove the ammonium oxalate, re-evaporated to dryness, and finally taken up in 1% HNO_3 for Pb isotope ratio measurements (De Muynck, 2008).

The Pb concentrations in the purified fractions were determined using a PerkinElmer SCIEX Elan 5000 quadrupole-based ICP-MS instrument using Tl as internal standard. Samples and NIST SRM 981 standard solutions were prepared at a Pb concentration of 300 μg/L. To correct for instrumental mass bias, thallium (NIST SRM 997 isotopic standard) was added at a concentration of 30 μg/L to achieve a Pb/Tl ratio of about 10. All isotope ratio measurements were carried out by static multi-collection with Faraday cups. The detectors Low 3, Low 2, Low 1, Central, High 1, High 2, and High 3 were used to record the ion intensities of ^{202}Hg, ^{203}Tl, ^{204}Pb, ^{205}Tl, ^{206}Pb, ^{207}Pb, and ^{208}Pb, respectively. The intensity at m/z = 204 was corrected for ^{204}Hg interference using a ^{204}Hg/^{202}Hg ratio of 0.229. However, the ^{204}Hg/^{204}Pb ratio turned out to be negligible. The samples were measured using both sample-standard bracketing with a solution of NIST SRM 981 Common Lead as isotopic standard, and Tl external normalization. Mass discrimination correction was performed via Russell's exponential law as described by White et al. (2000). Russell's equation was used to calculate the mass discrimination factors β_{Tl} (using the certified NIST SRM 997 $^{205}Tl/^{203}Tl$ ratio of 2.38714) and β_{Pb} (using the accepted values for NIST SRM 981 as given by Galer and Abouchami 1998; $^{208}Pb/^{206}Pb$=2.16771) for the standards. Blank Pb signals were negligible compared to the Pb signals encountered for samples and standards. The average Pb isotope ratios obtained for NIST SRM 981 over the duration of this study matched the accepted values of Galer and Abouchami (1998). Pb isotope ratios were calculated from the average of two measurement runs. The isotope ratios of the samples were plotted against a Pb isotope database of ore sources in Cyprus, Turkey and Jordan (Gale et al. 1997; Hamelin et al. 1988; Hauptmann 2007; Seeliger et al. 1985; Wagner et al. 1985, 1986;Yener et al. 1991).

Results

The results of the semi-quantitative analysis of Pb concentrations performed on all samples and the quantitative analysis on a selection of samples are given in Table 1. The samples studied, all copper alloys, are characterized by a highly varying Pb content that ranges from less than ~10 μg/g to ~15% Pb. For the artifacts with low Pb content (<1%), this lead is likely inherited from the Cu ore source used to produce the Cu alloy. Hence, their Pb isotopic composition likely reflects Cu ore minerals and the Pb isotope ratio data of the artifacts should only be compared to those of Cu ores. Artifacts with a much higher Pb content (here ~15% Pb) can obtain such a high Pb content through the use of polysulphide ores (having both high Pb and Cu contents) or through the mixing/recycling of lead ores/artifacts with copper ores in the production process. In this case, the Pb isotopic composition of the artifact should be compared to a database of lead or polysulphide ore deposits to identify the source of the lead end member. In case of the use of polysulphide ores (e.g. Cu-Pb-Zn deposits), it will be likely to also see high Zn contents in the artifacts. The Pb isotopic composition of the samples is most diverse, showing (a) linear (mixing?) trend(s) between highly radiogenic and much less radiogenic Pb sources (Fig. 1).

Discussion

The apparent mixing line of Pb isotopic compositions for a first selection of Tweini artifacts analyzed, remains valid, independent of lead content and age of the samples. This indicates that the source material of the artifacts was likely obtained from ore minerals from different sources, or from already recycled material.

The sample that shows the highest lead content is plotting away from the other samples, indicating a source material of the lead added to the (recycled) Cu alloy that is quite different in its Pb isotopic composition than the copper ore source(s). This ore is very radiogenic and may originate from Sardinia.

The Pb isotopic composition of the low-Pb artifacts, which should be compared with the Pb isotope database of Cu ore deposits to identify the Cu end member, is overlapping with ore deposits from Turkey, Jordan and/or Cyprus. It is remarkable that there is a good correspondence between the isotopic composition of a few of the Tweini artifacts and the Cu ore deposits of the Faynan region in Jordan (Hauptmann 2007). According to Hauptmann, the Faynan Cu ore deposits are characterized by variable Pb isotopic signatures and variable Pb contents ranging from ~0.04 to 20%. Most samples however, show a correspondence with the Turkish Taurus (Seeliger et al. 1985; Wagner et al. 1985, 1986; Yener et al. 1991) and the Cypriote (Hamelin et al. 1988; Gale et al. 1997) ore fields.

When chronology is taken into account (Fig. 1), it is noteworthy that the artifacts older than the Late Bronze Age IIB (older than 1200 B.C.) show a likely correspondence with Cypriote, as well as with Faynan and/or Turkish ores, while the younger (post 1200 B.C.) samples no longer show no correspondence with Cypriote ore sources (when all four isotopes are taken into account), but seem to have at least two ore sources, in the Taurus and in Faynan.

Conclusion

It is remarkable that the lead isotopic composition of the Cu alloy artifacts from Tell Tweini is clearly different as a whole before and after 1200 B.C., respectively. A difference in material culture pre and post this time has been observed before at the site, and has been linked to Sea People incursions in the area. A set of ^{14}C dates (Kaniewski et al. 2010) and sporadic finds of locally produced Late Helladic IIIC early ceramics date the fall of the Late Bronze Age city of Gibala (Jung 2011), probably caused by the Sea People, around the first quarter of the 12th century B.C., simultaneously with the fall of the capital Ugarit. Contrary to Ugarit, Tweini was immediately resettled by "newcomers" after a fire-destruction, visible in the archaeological record as an ash layer, labeled level 7A. The ceramological material displays a continuation of the local material into the Iron Age without the common imported Late Bronze Age wares from Cyprus or the Aegean world.

Aside from the change in the isotopic composition of the Cu alloy artifacts, other alterations in the material culture of the household are also documented, such as the much-discussed appearance of handmade cooking pots (Vansteenhuyse & Bretschneider 2011) and the appearance of the spherical loom weight (Rahmstorf 2005; Bretschneider et al. in this volume). An additional apparent change is the swift decrease of imports from the Aegean world. It is clear that further archaeometrical study of the Tell Tweini Cu alloy artifacts may provide a more profound insight on Bronze Age to Iron Age contacts and metal movements in the eastern Mediterranean.

Acknowledgements

The authors wish to sincerely thank Karel Van Lerberghe for his dedication to interdisciplinary archaeology, as one of the first promoters of the Centre for Archaeological Sciences at the KU Leuven. Kris Latruwe is thanked for analytical support.

Bibliography

BARNES, I. L., J. W. GRAMLICH, M. G. DIAZ, R. H. BRILL 1978: "The possible change of Lead isotope ratios in the manufacture of pigments", in G. F. Charter (ed.), *Archaeological Chemistry* II, The American Chemical Society, 273-279.

BEGEMANN, F., S. SCHMITT-STRECKER, E. PERNICKA 1989: "Isotopic composition of lead in early metal artifacts", in A. Hauptmann, E. Pernicka and G. A. Wagner (eds.) *Old World Archaeometallurgy* (Der Anschnitt, Suppl. 7), Deutsches Bergbaumuseum Bochum, 269-278.

BISWAS, A. K. and W. G. DAVENPORT 1980: *Extractive Metallurgy of Copper*, 2nd ed., Pergamon Press, Oxford.

CATTIN, F., B. GUÉNETTE-BECK, M. BESSE, V. SERNEELS 2009: "Lead isotopes and archaeometallurgy", *Archaeological and Anthropological Sciences* 1, 137-148.

CALDERON, V. 2006: "Rapid measurement of major, minor and trace levels in soils using the Varian 730-ES", *ICP-OES Application Note Number* 35.

DE MUYNCK, D. 2008: *Development of separation methods and measurement protocols for Sr and Pb isotopic analysis of archaeological artifacts by means of single-collector and multi-collector ICP-mass spectrometry. Ph.D. thesis*, Department of Analytical chemistry Ghent University, Belgium (http://dx.doi.org/1854/11739).

DE MUYNCK, D., C. CLOQUET, E. SMITS, A. F. DE WOLFF, G. QUITTÉ, L. MOENS and F. VANHAECKE 2008, "Lead isotopic analysis of infant bone tissue dating from the Roman era via multicollector ICP–mass spectrometry", *Analytical and Bioanalytical Chemistry* 390, 477-486.

DOUMET-SERHAL, C. 2004: "Excavating Sidon", in C. Doumet-Serhal (ed.) *A Decade of Archaeology and History in the Lebanon*, Beirut 2004, 102-123.

GALE, N. 1989: "Studies of Late Bronze age ox-hide ingots from the Mediterranean region", in A. Hauptmann, E. Pernicka, G. A. Wagner (eds.), *Old World Archaeometallurgy* (Der Anschnitt, Suppl. 7), Deutsches Bergbau-museum Bochum, 247-268.

GALE, N. H. and Z. A. STOS-GALE 1982: "Bronze Age copper sources in the Mediterranean: A new approach", *Science Vol.* 216, 11-19.

GALE, N. H. and Z. A. STOS-GALE 2000: "Lead isotope analyses applied to provenance studies", in E. Ciliberto and G. Spoto (eds.) *Modern analytical methods in art and Archaeology*, Wiley, New York, 503-584.

GALE, N. H., Z. STOS-GALE, J. HOUGHTON and R. SPEAKMAN 1997: "Lead isotope data from the Isotrace Laboratory, Oxford", *Archaeometry data base 4, ores from Cyprus*, (Archaeometry 39), 237-246.

GALER, S. J. G. and W. ABOUCHAMI 1998: "Practical application of lead triple spiking for correction of instrumental mass discrimination", *Mineralogical Magazin* 62A, 491-492.

HAMEEUW, H. and G. JANS 2008: "Burial Customs at Tell Tweini — Field A", in J. Bretschneider & K. Van Lerberghe (eds.) *In Search of Gibala. An Archaeological and Historical Study Based on Eight Seasons of Excavations at Tell Tweini (Syria) in the A and C Fields (1999-2007)* (Aula Orientalis Supplementa 24), 75-86.

HAMELIN, B., B. DUPRE, O. BREVART and C. J. ALLEGRE 1988: "Metallogenesis at Paleo-spreading centers: Lead isotopes in sulfides, rocks and sediments from the Troodos ophiolite (Cyprus)", *Chemical Geology* 68, 229-238.

HAUPTMANN, A. 2007: *The Archaeometallurgy of Copper: Evidence from Faynan, Jordan,* Springer, Heidelberg, Berlin, New York.

HAUSLEITNER, A. 2006: "Ring", *RlA* 11, 413-14.

JUNG, R. 2011: "La céramique de typologie Mycénienne", in M. Al-Maqdissi, K. Van Lerberghe, J. Bretschneider and M. Badawi (eds.), *Tell Tweini, The Syro-Belgian Excavations, Les fouilles Syro-Belges, De Syro-Belgische opgravingen* (Documents d'Archologie Syrienne X), Damascus, 115-23.

KANIEWSKI, D., E. PAULISSEN, E. VAN CAMPO, H. WEISS, T. OTTO, J. BRETSCHNEIDER and K. VAN LERBERGHE 2010: "Late Second-Early First Millennium B.C. Abrupt Climate Changes in Coastal Syria and their Possible Significance for the History of the Eastern Mediterranean", *Quaternary Research* 74, 207-215.

RAHMSTORF, L. 2005: "Ethnicity and changes in weaving technology in Cyprus and the eastern Mediterranean in the 12th century BC", in V. Karageorghis, H. Matthäus and S. Rogge (eds.) *Cyprus: Religion and Society from the Late Bronze Age to the End of the Archaic Period*, Bibliopolis, Möhnesee, 143-69.

SEELIGER, T. C., E. PERNICKA, G. A. WAGNER, F. BEGEMANN, S. SCHMITT-STRECKER, C. EIBNER, O. OZTUNALI and I. BARANYI 1985: *Archaometallurgische Untersuchungen in Nord- und Ostanatolien* (Jahrbuch des Romisch-Germanisches Zentralmuseums Mainz 32), 597-659.

STOS-GALE, Z. A. and N. H. GALE 2009: "Metal provenancing using isotopes and the Oxford archaeological lead isotope database (OXALID)", *Archaeological and Anthropological Sciences* 1, 195-213.

VANSTEENHUYSE, K. and J. BRETSCHNEIDER 2011: "Handmade cooking pots from the Early Iron Age in Tell Tweini (Syria)", in *Proceedings of the International Archaeological Symposium: On Cooking Pots, Drinking Cups, Loom Weights and Ethnicity in Bronze Age Cyprus and Neighbouring Regions, Nicosia 6-7 November 2010*, 2011, 187-194.

WAGNER, G. A., E. PERNICKA, T. C. SEELIGER, O. OZTUNALI, I. BARANYI, F. BEGEMANN and S. SCHMITT-STRECKER 1985: "Geologische Untersuchungen zur frühen Metallurgie in NW-Anatolien", *Bulletin of the Mineral and Exploration Institute of Turkey* 100-101, 45-81.

WAGNER, G. A., E. PERNICKA, T. C. SEELIGER, I. B. LORENZ, F. BEGEMANN, S. SCHMITT-STRECKER, C. EIBNER and O. OZTUNALI 1986: "Geochemische und isotopische Charakteristika früher Rohstoffquellen fur Kupfer, Blei, Silber und Gold in der Türkei", *Jahrbuch des Romisch-Germanisches Zentralmuseums Mainz* 33, 723-752.

WHITE, W. M., F. ALBARÈDE and P. TÉLOUK 2000: "High-precision analysis of Pb isotope ratios by multicollector ICP-MS", *Chemical Geology* 167, 257-270.

YENER, K. A., E. V. SAYRE, E. C. JOEL, H. OZBAL, I. L. BARNES and R. H. BRILL 1991: "Stable lead isotope studies of Central Taurus Ore sources and related artifacts from Eastern Mediterranean Chalcolithic and Bronze Age sites", *Journal of Archaeological Science* 18, 541-577.

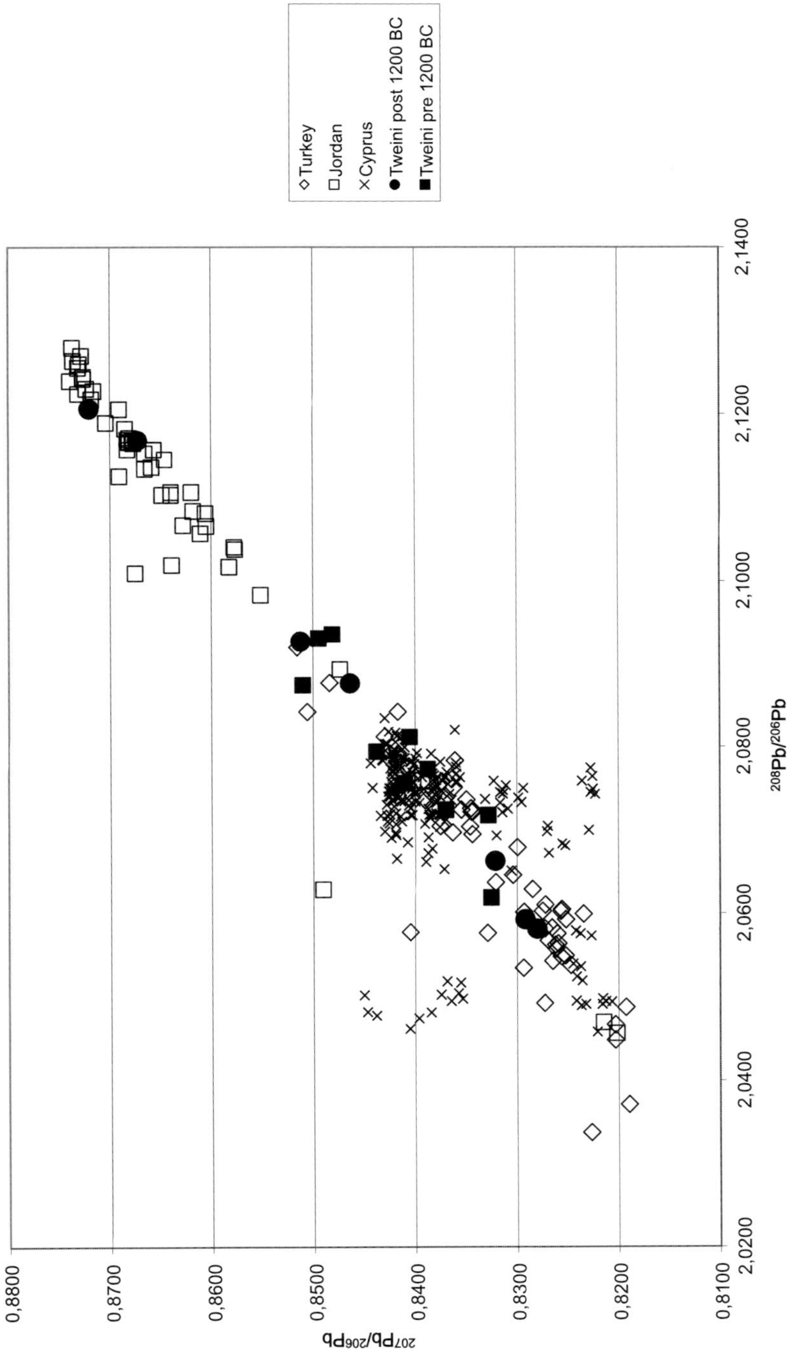

Fig. 1. $^{207}Pb/^{206}Pb$ versus $^{208}Pb/^{206}Pb$ isotope ratios of the copper alloy artifacts from Tell Tweini compared with the corresponding Pb isotope ratios of copper ores from Turkey, Jordan and Cyprus. The isotopic data for Turkey, Jordan and Cyprus are compiled from Gale et al. (1997), Hamelin et al. (1988), Hauptmann (2007), Seeliger et al. (1985), Wagner et al. (1985, 1986) and Yener et al. (1991).

Original sample ID	Context	Pb (%) MS	Pb (%) OES	Stratigraphy — Chronology
TWE-08-A-06405-M001	Layer	0.300	0.285	LEVEL 5-6 — IRON AGE III-I
TWE-08-A-05814-M003	Layer	0.747	–	LEVEL 6-7 — IRON AGE — LATE BRONZE AGE
TWE-08-A-07103-M003	Layer	0.053	0.050	LEVEL 6?-7 — IRON AGE?-LATE BRONZE AGE
TWE-05-A-01716-M001	Layer	–	–	LEVEL 6A — IRON AGE II
TWE-05-A-02522-M001	Layer	14.884	–	LEVEL 7B — LATE BRONZE AGE II
TWE-05-A-00185-M003	Layer	0.254	–	LEVEL 7B — LATE BRONZE AGE II
TWE-05-A-01513-M002	Layer	0.323	–	LEVEL 7B — LATE BRONZE AGE II
TWE-05-A-01950-M002	Layer	0.035	–	LEVEL 7B — LATE BRONZE AGE II
TWE-A-08-06053-M001	Layer	0.008	0.011	LEVEL 7 — LATE BRONZE AGE
TWE-05-A-00551-M001	?	0.170	0.157	LEVEL? — LATE BRONZE AGE?
TWE-05-A-00945-M002	Layer	0.327	–	LEVEL 7D — LATE BRONZE AGE I
TWE-08-A-06049-M003	Layer	0.001	–	LEVEL 6-7 — IRON AGE — LATE BRONZE AGE
TWE-05-A-00945-M003	Layer	0.046	–	LEVEL 7D — LATE BRONZE AGE I
TWE-08-A-05817-M002	Layer	0.026	–	LEVEL 7B-C — LATE BRONZE AGE II
TWE-05-A-02542-M001	Grave	0.033	0.036	LEVEL 8B — MIDDLE BRONZE AGE II
TWE-05-A-01055-M001	Layer	0.688	–	LEVEL8 (9?) — MIDDLE BRONZE AGE (EARLY BRONZE AGE)
TWE-05-A-00923-M001	Layer	0.307	–	LEVEL 8B — MIDDLE BRONZE AGE II
TWE-05-A-00954-M002	Grave	1.331	–	LEVEL 8D — MIDDLE BRONZE AGE I
TWE-05-A-00942-M001	Layer	0.063	0.064	LEVEL 9 — EARLY BRONZE AGE IVB

	^{204}Pb		^{204}Pb		^{204}Pb		Pb		Pb		Source	
TWE-08-A-06405-M001	18,04556	0,00356	15,65103	0,00321	38,19985	0,00752	0,86731	0,00005	2,11686	0,00013	Faynan	
TWE-08-A-05814-M003	18,40439	0,00334	15,66681	0,00286	38,51459	0,00696	0,85125	0,00007	2,09269	0,00012	Turkey	
TWE-08-A-07103-M003	18,97656	0,00885	15,71308	0,00754	39,05705	0,01859	0,82803	0,00009	2,05817	0,00022	Turkey (or possibly Cyprus)	**• Group 2 (younger than 1200 BC): copper is mainly obtained from (1) new ores from Faynan and Turkey <u>or</u> (2) new ores from Faynan and recycling of Turkey/ Cyprus-related artifacts**
TWE-05-A-01716-M001	18,87993	0,28412	16,09215	0,24084	39,51630	0,00865	–	–	–	–	lead content not measured	
TWE-05-A-02522-M001	17,95755	0,00251	15,65995	0,00235	38,08222	0,00571	0,87205	0,00005	2,12068	0,00011	lead content high, Sardinia?	
TWE-05-A-00185-M003	18,87960	0,00379	15,71057	0,00315	39,01091	0,00811	0,83215	0,00005	2,06630	0,00012	Turkey (or possibly Cyprus)	
TWE-05-A-01513-M002	18,53667	0,00414	15,68982	0,00367	38,69731	0,00865	0,84642	0,00005	2,08761	0,00011	Faynan	
TWE-05-A-01950-M002	18,97363	0,01856	15,73336	0,01541	39,07248	0,03798	0,82922	0,00013	2,05930	0,00028	Turkey	
TWE-08-A-06053-M001	18,86002	0,03830	15,70174	0,03212	38,88752	0,07915	0,83254	0,00023	2,06190	0,00039	Turkey	
TWE-05-A-00551-M001	18,58352	0,00478	15,68090	0,00420	38,64256	0,01049	0,84381	0,00006	2,07940	0,00013	Cyprus/Faynan	
TWE-05-A-00945-M002	18,47148	0,00373	15,66652	0,00334	38,67164	0,00754	0,84815	0,00006	2,09359	0,00011	Faynan/Turkey	
TWE-08-A-06049-M003	18,77031	0,10536	15,72897	0,08766	38,69307	0,00946	–	–	–	–	too low lead concentration	
TWE-05-A-00945-M003	18,77172	0,01320	15,71122	0,01102	38,90329	0,02734	0,83696	0,00011	2,07244	0,00022	Turkey/Cyprus	**• Group 1 (~2000 to ~1200 BC): Cu is mainly obtained from new ores from Cyprus and Turkey**
TWE-08-A-05817 -M002	18,58570	0,02086	15,63164	0,01749	38,57623	0,04316	0,84106	0,00016	2,07559	0,00031	Cyprus (or possibly Turkey)	
TWE-05-A-02542-M001	18,62769	0,02323	15,65724	0,01940	38,76684	0,04857	0,84054	0,00016	2,08114	0,00033	Cyprus (or possibly Turkey)	
TWE-05-A-01055-M001	18,36710	0,00492	15,63124	0,00366	38,34010	0,00944	0,85105	0,00011	2,08743	0,00018	Faynan/Turkey	
TWE-05-A-00923-M001	18,72471	0,00602	15,70556	0,00341	38,89630	0,00947	0,83876	0,00019	2,07727	0,00026	Faynan	
TWE-05-A-00954-M002	18,44393	0,00374	15,66799	0,00277	38,60496	0,00737	0,84949	0,00012	2,09310	0,00014	Faynan/Turkey	
TWE-05-A-00942-M001	18,82234	0,01198	15,67529	0,00974	38,99575	0,02516	0,83280	0,00015	2,07178	0,00022	Cyprus (or possibly Turkey)	

Table 1. Chronology and compositional information on the samples studied: Pb concentration in wt % based on ICP-OES measurements and semi-quantitative MC-ICP-MS measurements, next to the lead isotopic composition of the artifacts and their most likely ore source.

THE AMARNA LETTERS FROM ḪATTI
A PALAEOGRAPHIC ANALYSIS

Elena DEVECCHI
Ludwig-Maximilians-Universität, München

This contribution is devoted to a question which has been intriguing me for years, and still does: who was in charge of drawing up Akkadian texts at the Hittite court? Hittite scribes trained to write Akkadian? Or rather foreign scribes whose mother tongue was Akkadian, stemming perhaps from Syria? Or both?

The analysis of the language and script of the Akkadian texts from Boğazköy is the starting point for trying to answer these questions. However, one is often hampered in this task not only by the lack of suitable tools, but also by the fact that the relevant texts are archival copies, and thus could have gone through several stages of copying, so that their linguistic and palaeographic features might contain a sort of "stratification" resulting from the intervention of the hands of several scribes at different times.[1] This is true not only in the case of texts that are usually preserved in several duplicates (e.g. historical, religious and mythological composition, but also international treaties), but also in the case of letters, which belong to the group of documents mainly attested as *unica*.[2] In fact, these *unica* can be the result of a redactional history as much as any other text, and each stage of the process which shaped the tablet that has reached us might have left a mark on it and influenced its final features. We struggle with similar issues even when we have — as in the case of the Amarna correspondence — the final document that was actually sent to its destination, since one can imagine that also in this case that letter may be the result of some redactional process. In fact, the composition of the final document was very likely preceded by at least the drafting of a rough copy, as the presence in the Ḫattuša archives of mainly Hittite, but in some cases also Akkadian,

[1] See Devecchi 2012 for an overview on the difficulties linked to the study of Akkadian texts from Boğazköy.

[2] See van den Hout 2002, 864-876 for a discussion of the two text groups in the Ḫattuša archives.

drafts of letters belonging to the Hittite-Egyptian and Hittite-Assyrian correspondence from the 13th century[3] suggests.

These difficulties should not prevent us from at least trying to address the issues at hand, and it seems appropriate to add a piece to the puzzle by providing a palaeographic analysis of the letters sent from Ḫatti to the Pharaoh(s) and found in the Amarna archive (EA 41, 42, 43 and 44):[4] this dossier offers the valuable opportunity of studying a group of Akkadian texts surely dated to a relatively short time period (the reign of Šuppiluliuma I)[5] and stemming from a phase when the ductus used for the Hittite texts was still clearly distinct from the non-Hittite ductus used e.g. in Syria and northern Mesopotamia, which makes it easier than in other cases to distinguish between Hittite and non-Hittite sign forms.[6]

The analysis has been carried out on a limited group of signs (see Table 1), selected either because they are the relevant ones for dating the Hittite ductus or because they show peculiar variants which can be traced back to specific traditions.

In order to "classify" and interpret the sign-forms occurring in EA 41-44 they have been compared with those from contemporary Hittite texts as well as from material of other contemporary scribal traditions. As for the Hittite texts I used mainly KUB 19.20++, a Hittite letter which has been interpreted as the draft of a message from Šuppiluliuma I to the Pharaoh, recovered at Ḫattuša.[7] As reference points for the contemporary

[3] See Edel 1994, 208-231 and Mora and Giorgieri 2004, 23-24 tables 3-4 and 43 ff. Their nature as drafts is indicated by the absence of the greeting formulas.

[4] EA 41 is kept in the Egyptian Museum in Cairo (CG 4747), EA 42 and 44 in the Vorderasiatisches Museum in Berlin (VAT 1655 and VAT 1656, respectively), EA 43 in the Ashmolean Museum in Oxford (AN1893.1-41 (408)).

[5] Ideally one would have included in this study also the letter RS 17.132 (CTH 45), sent by Šuppiluliuma I to Niqmaddu II of Ugarit and recovered in the archives of the Syrian town, but I did not have access to the tablet or to pictures of it, and a palaeographic analysis based only on the cuneiform copy would not have provided reliable results. However, based on an examination of the copy alone, I am inclined to regard its ductus as non-Hittite (see also below, fn. 24).

[6] Later, during the 13th century, the Hittite script starts showing features that largely correspond to those typical of the (Assyro-)Mittanian ductus: this can make it difficult to decide whether some sign forms attested in 13th-century Akkadian texts from Ḫattuša should be interpreted as late Hittite or non-Hittite (Devecchi 2012).

[7] Van den Hout 1994. It has been suggested that KBo 49.13 would be an indirect join to the reverse of KUB 19.20+KBo 12.23, but if the second paragraph line indicated in the cuneiform copy is correct, it seems unlikely that the fragment should be placed as indicated in http://www.hethport.uni-wuerzburg.de/hetskiz/sk.php?f=154/s or anywhere else in the reverse: in fact, the reverse of KUB 19.20+KBo 12.23 preserves no paragraphs of only four lines that could correspond to the four-line paragraph of KBo 49.13 7'-9'.

non-Hittite traditions I used the sign lists of Schroeder (1915) for the other Amarna dossiers, Schwemer (1998) for the Mittanian, Assyro-Mittanian and early middle Assyrian ductus, and van Soldt (1977) for the Ugarit texts.[8]

The tablets have been collated on photographs,[9] which also served as the basis for tracing the signs included in Table 1. It goes without saying that the exactness of such a study depends to a large degree on the quality of the photographs, and therefore one can only hope that in the coming years valuable tools such as the Portable Light Dome developed by Prof. Van Lerberghe and his team[10] will be employed more and more often in order to make available high resolution images of cuneiform texts.

EA 41 — From Šuppiluliuma I to Ḫuriya.

This rather well preserved tablet is historically the most important letter of the dossier, because the identification of the addressee with one or the other Pharaohs who reigned during the Amarna Age is one of the cruxes for the reconstruction of ancient Near Eastern chronology.[11]

Beckman regarded this document as an example of the "chancellery script", namely that type of ductus which, according to Beckman, was first used at the Hittite court for drafting Akkadian-language diplomatic material and later adopted also for Hittite-language texts: the "chancellery script" would therefore correspond to the late Hittite script (Beckman 1983, 98-100 and fn. 13). Beckman's theory has been rejected by some (Klinger 2003, 239), and in any case the sign inventory of EA 41 was not a good example of the "chancellery script" because it shows a number of sign variants that did not belong to the late Hittite ductus, such as IT, KÙ, RU, ŠA and UM.

Among the analysed sign forms, some can be regarded generally as non-Hittite (AK, KU, KI, LA, LI, NI and RU), while others are rather indicative of precise traditions:

8 In the sign analysis the generic label "non-Hittite" will be used when a sign form is attested in all these traditions.

9 I was able to collate EA 41 on pictures generously made available to me by Dr. Jana Mynářová, whom I would like to thank for her kindness. Pictures of EA 42 and 44 were taken by myself, but see also the website http://amarna.ieiop.csic.es/. Pictures of EA 43 were provided by the Ashmolean Museum.

10 http://www2.arts.kuleuven.be/info/ONO/Meso/digitalisatie.

11 See Miller 2007 for a recent discussion of the different hypotheses.

- AL occurs in a variant which at this time can be either Hittite or south-Syrian (Phoenician coast and Amurru).
- The forms used for EN, KÙ and ḪA can be either Babylonian or Hittite.
- IT occurs in the Babylonian form.
- The form of ŠA is Syrian, Mittanian, Assyro-Mittanian and early middle Assyrian but not Babylonian.
- UM occurs in the Syrian, Mittanian and Babylonian form, which is different than the Assyro-Mittanian and early middle Assyrian ones.

How should one interpret this rather mixed picture? One might start with reference to two interesting features in the structure and formulary of EA 41. First, it has been pointed that the heading *umma* PN_1 *ana* PN_2 *qibīma* is unique among the Akkadian letters of the Amarna correspondence:[12] this can be explained by the origin of EA 41, since this is the typical opening formula of the Hittite royal correspondence, used by the Hittite kings for messages to other Great Kings as well as for messages to their subjects.[13] Second, Mynářová has shown that the greeting formula is the one typically used in the letters sent from Mittani,[14] and this could be linked with the predominantly non-Hittite palaeographical features of the letter and suggest that the author of the letter came from Mittani or from the Mittani-controlled territories in North-Syria. One could object that a scribe accustomed to the Mittanian tradition would have used not only the typical Mittanian greetings, but also the typical Mittanian heading (*ana* PN_1 *qibīma umma* PN_2(*ma*)),[15] but this is not necessarily the case: in fact, considering that drafts of letters usually do not contain the

[12] Moran 1992, xxii; Mynářová 2007, 102.

[13] Hagenbuchner 1989a, 40, 44-45 and recently Mora and Giorgieri 2004, 45-47. As examples of the usage of this formula in letters to other Great Powers, see e.g. KBo 1.10+ (Ḫattušili III to Kadašman-Enlil), IM 50966 (a Hittite King to a Babylonian Queen), KUB 3.41 (Ḫattušili III to Ramses II) and the evidence from the Hittite-Assyrian correspondence listed by Mora and Giorgieri 2004, 41-42. Interestingly enough, an archival copy of a letter in Hittite addressed by Amenophis III to Tarḫunta-radu of Arzawa (EA 31) actually provides another attestation of this opening formula from the Amarna corpus: apparently the Egyptian chancellery was aware of this Anatolian epistolary custom and adopted it when corresponding with Anatolian rulers.

[14] Mynářová 2007, 112-113, 120. EA 41 obv. 4-6: "[For me all goes w]ell. For you may all go wel[l. For yo]ur [wives], your sons, your household, your troops, your chario[ts, and i]n your country, may all go very well" (after Moran 1992, 114). The same formula is attested also in some of the Alašiya letters, but Mynářová stresses that here it is only one of the greeting formulas used by the Alašiyan king, while it is the only type used in the Mittanian royal correspondence.

[15] See "Type 2" in Mynářová's (2007, 117-118) classification.

salutation formulas,[16] one can imagine that the scribe of EA 41 kept the Hittite heading he found in the draft he was copying/translating from and introduced the greeting formula he was most familiar with (i.e. the Mittanian one).

To sum up, the presence of the typical Hittite heading witnesses the intervention of a Hittite "hand" at some stage of the composition of the letter, most likely in the composition of a rough draft, while the Mittanian salutations would have been inserted in a second phase, perhaps when the final document was prepared. This could also explain the occurrence in EA 41 of some sign forms that can be traced back to the Hittite contemporary tradition (AL, EN, KÙ and ḪA) next to a majority of non-Hittite forms. One can therefore conclude that both the ductus and the formulary of EA 41 are a mix of the Hittite and Mittanian/North-Syrian traditions, the first probably going back to the draft-stage of the letter, the second having exerted its influence mainly in the final redactional stage.

EA 42 — From Šuppiluliuma I (?) to the Pharaoh.

The Hittite origin of this letter, already assumed on the basis of its content and formal similarities with EA 41, has been confirmed by the results of optical mineralogy and petrographic analysis, which revealed that the clay of EA 42 shows the features of the Ḫattuša clay fabric (Goren et al. 2004, 31-32; Goren et al. 2011, 692). The heading is missing, but the attribution to Šuppiluliuma I is suggested by the use of expressions such as ŠEŠ-*ia* "my brother" which indicates that the two correspondents were of equal rank.

Knudtzon (1915, 1093-1094) noted that the signs of this tablet are very similar to those of EA 41, but also pointed out that the ductus shows "mancherlei Abweichungen so bei la, li, ru, höchstwahrscheinlich auch bei uš und amêlu, teilweise auch bei aḫu." Indeed, while in EA 41 the signs LA, LI, RU and ŠEŠ occur in non-Hittite variants, in EA 42 the picture is somewhat more complicated: LA, LI and ŠEŠ are attested in both the Hittite (LA: Obv.12, LI: Obv. 16; ŠEŠ: Obv. 19) and non-Hittite forms (LA: Obv. 26, Rev. 28; LI: Obv. 14; ŠEŠ: Obv. 8), while RU shows only the contemporary Hittite variant. Another sign which occurs only in the contemporary Hittite form is AL. Only non-Hittite forms are

[16] Mora and Giorgieri 2004, 43 with previous literature.

attested for IT, KI, LÚ, NI and ŠA, to which one can add also ŠAR (Obv. 23 and Rev. 27) and DUB (Obv. 15 and Rev. 27). Once again these results can be interpreted as the features of a mixed ductus.

EA 43 — From Šuppiluliuma I (?) to the Pharaoh.

This rather poorly preserved tablet was first attributed to the Hittite dossier (Knudtzon 1902, 331-334), then tentatively regarded as a message of some north-Syrian king (Knudtzon 1907, 305; 1915, 1094-1095),[17] then finally recognized again as another letter from Ḫatti (Artzi 1993 and Na'aman 1995). Data from optical mineralogy and petrographic analysis are not available, but it should be recalled that according to Knudzon (1915, 1094) the clay of this tablet looked identical to that of EA 41, 42 and 44. Unlike the other letters, though, EA 43 shows lines on the obverse which are very much slanted upward to the right.

Artzi's (1993, 7 n. 1) statement that "almost all the signs-shapes belong to the late, 'Chancellery' stage of the Hittite foreign-language service (= 'Empire')" must be revised.[18] In fact, comparison between the signs of EA 43 and those of KUB 19.20++ demonstrates that the two tablets use the same sign-shapes, which can be regarded as the typical Hittite sign inventory of the time of Šuppiluliuma I. EA 43 was therefore very likely drafted by a Hittite scribe, a result which confirms the supposed Hittite origin of the text.

EA 44 — From Zida to the Pharaoh.

The Hittite origin of this letter is based on the identification of its sender with the homonymous Hittite prince, brother of Šuppiluliuma I, and on the results of the optical mineralogy and petrographic analysis carried out on the tablet, whose clay shows a characteristic Ḫattuša fabric (see Goren et al. 2004, 31-32; Goren et al. 2011, 692).[19] The tablet shows several traces of erasures and corrections especially on the reverse, which leads to significant variation in the size and depth of several signs.

[17] This was mainly due to the consideration that EA 43 showed more similarities to EA 44, which at that time was regarded as a north-Syrian letter, than to EA 41 and 42 (Knudtzon 1902, 334; 1915, 1094-1095).

[18] On the "chancellery script", a label coined by Beckman 1983, see above the remarks on EA 41.

[19] This renders obsolete Moran's remark that "the writer seems not to have been in the Hittite capital at the time of writing" (Moran 1992, 117).

As for the ductus, two opposite opinions have been expressed: Moran (1992, 117) believes that the scribe of EA 44 "was either trained there (i.e. in Ḫattuša) or under its influence", while more recently it has been proposed that this document does not show "the normal sign forms typical for texts in the Hittite archives of this period" (Goren et al. 2011, 692). Both statements are partially correct: in fact, it is true that the forms of LUGAL, ŠA, DUMU and KI would be very unusual in contemporary Hittite texts, but AK, KU, LA, NI, RU and UM occur in variants which are typical of the contemporary Hittite texts, while not attested in the contemporary non-Hittite traditions. Thus, also some features of its script agree with the Hittite origin of EA 44, which can be regarded as another example of mixed ductus.

To conclude, palaeographic analysis shows that three of the examined texts attest a mixed ductus (EA 41, 42 and 44), while one has a completely Hittite ductus (EA 43), i.e. contrary to the *communis opinio* (Goren et al. 2011, 692) none of the Amarna letters from Ḫatti shows an entirely non-Hittite ductus. The appearance of the mixed ductus remains somewhat difficult to explain, since it lends itself to different interpretations.[20] However, at least in the case of EA 41 I am inclined to suggest that the features of a Hittite rough draft might have influenced those of the final document, probably drafted by a Mittanian/North-Syrian scribe.

The fact that at least one of the letters was written in the Hittite ductus is particularly interesting, because it indicates that the Ḫattuša chancellery did not always felt the need to use a special script for Akkadian texts, even when those documents were destined to be sent abroad rather than kept in the Hittite archives. It should be stressed, in fact, that the other Akkadian-language texts whose ductus has been so far interpreted as Hittite are archival copies,[21] and that they thus had a different purpose and addressee than documents such as the letters found in Amarna. Notably, EA 43 stands out not only from the other Amarna letters, but in general

[20] It could be hypothesized, e.g., that it is the result of several stages of copying by the hands of scribes who belonged to different scribal traditions (e.g. one Hittite and one Akkadian), or that some Hittite scribes were trained to write Akkadian with a ductus different than the Hittite one and would sometimes "mix" the two scripts (see Devecchi 2012).

[21] See e.g. KBo 1.5 (CTH 41.I.A, treaty between Tutḫaliya I/II and Sunassura of Kizzuwatna), KUB 3.7+ (CTH 49.I.A, treaty between Šuppiluliuma I and Aziru of Amurru), KUB 48.72 (CTH 75.E, Muwattalli's official copy of the treaty between Muršili II and Talmi-Šarruma of Aleppo) and the relevant remarks in Klinger and Neu 1990, 154; Klinger 2003, 242; Schwemer 2004, 76.

from the corpus of Akkadian-language texts (letters, edicts, verdicts) whose official copies have been recovered abroad, which generally show a non-Hittite ductus.[22]

Table 1.[23]

	EA 41	**EA 42**	**EA 43**	**EA 44**	**KUB 19.20++**
EN (40)	 Obv. 25	——	——	——	 Obv. 5 passim
RU (43)	 Rev. ⸢7⸣, 14[24]	 Obv. 23	 Obv. 4’	 Obv. 10	 Rev. 8’
KÙ (69)	 Obv. 25  Rev. 14	——	——	 Rev. 26	——
NI (72)	 Obv. 9 passim	 Obv. 9, ⸢13⸣	 Obv. 2’, 5’	 Obv. 1, Rev. 24, 27[25]	 Obv. 4’ passim
LÚ (78)	⸢Obv. 7⸣[26]	 Rev. 27	 Obv. 4’	 Rev. 23	 Obv. 6
ŠEŠ (79)	 Obv. ⸢16⸣, 21, 28	 Obv. 8  Obv. 19	 Rev. 29’	——	 Rev. [3]1’, 33’

[22] This is the result of a preliminary survey of the cuneiform copies of Akkadian documents of Hittite origin discovered in the Ugarit archives, which represent the bulk of Akkadian texts from Ḫatti recovered abroad. On the palaeographic features of some of these documents see also Klinger 2003, 239-240 and Devecchi in print. The courtesy letter IM 50966 sent from a Hittite king to a Babylonian queen discovered in Dūr-Kurigalzu (Baqir 1946, 89-90 and fig. 13 and Hagenbuchner 1989b, 300-301) does not show enough relevant signs to allow a decisive palaeographic assessment: one can note the NI with two inscribed verticals (obv. 2) and perhaps also the LUGAL with one inscribed vertical (obv. 1 and 2), but these two variants alone cannot be taken as sure evidence of a non-Hittite ductus, especially when attested in Akkadian texts of the 13th century, as is the case with this letter (cf. Devecchi 2012).

[23] The signs, listed according to the numbering in HZl, are all reproduced at a scale of 3:2.

[24] According to the copy, the RU signs at Obv. 7, Rev. 11 and 12 have this shape too, but I was not able to collate them, since they are on the edge and not visible on the photos available to me.

AK (81)	 Obv. 21 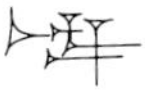 Rev. 10	—	 Obv. 10’	 Obv. 11, Rev. 28	 Obv. 17’, 21’, Rev. 21’
LA (95)	 Obv. 13 passim	 Obv. 12  Obv. 26  Rev. 28	 Obv. 15’, 16’, 17’	 Rev. 26	 Obv. 8’, Rev. 13’
UM (98)	 Rev. 8, 11	—	—	 Obv. 4, Rev. 27[27]	—
LUGAL (115)	Obv. ⸢1, 9, 11⸣[28]	—	—	 Obv. 1, 3	 Obv. 9’  Rev. 17’
ŠA (158)	 Obv. 6  Obv. 26[29]	 Obv. 15	 Obv. 3’, 5’, 13’, 14’, ⸢Rev. 29⸣	 Obv. 11	 Obv. 2’ passim
AL (183)	 Obv. 24, 25	 Obv. 14[30]	—	—	 Obv. 3’
KU (206)	 Obv. 19[31]  Rev. 10	—	 Obv. 6’	 Obv. 9, 10, Rev. 20, 24, 25, 29	 Obv. 17’ passim

25 Contrary to what is indicated in the copy, collation on photos shows that the NI does not have the two inscribed verticals.

26 According to the copy and to Knudtzon 1907, 298 fn. c, LÚ occurs in the form with several inscribed verticals, but I was not able to collate it on the pictures at my disposal.

27 Collation on photos could not confirm the presence of the inscribed verticals hinted at in the copy.

28 All the LUGAL signs are badly preserved and impossible to collate on the pictures at my disposal. Note, however, that according to Knudtzon 1907, 298 fn. c all the LUGAL signs seem to be lacking the inscribed verticals that are found in the ŠEŠ and LÚ signs.

29 Collation on photos shows that there are two inscribed *Winkelhaken* rather than only one as indicated in the copy.

30 Collation on photos could not confirm the presence of the inscribed *Winkelhaken* indicated in the copy.

31 According to the copy, also the KU in Obv. 17 and Rev. 15 begin with a vertical, but I was not able to collate them.

DA (214)	Obv. 20 (?)[32]	 Obv. 17	——	 Rev. 28[33]	 Obv. 6' passim
IT (215)	 Obv. 13, Rev. 4	 Obv. 25	 Obv. 5', 10'	 Obv. 9, 10	 Obv. 17 passim
DUMU (237)	——	——	 Obv. 12'	 Obv. 3, 4, 8, Rev. 21	
KI (313)	 Obv. 17  Rev. 14, 15	 Obv. 8, 19	 Obv. 8', 9', 14'	 Obv. 2  Obv. 9	 Obv. 14', Rev. 15', 19'  Obv. 19', Rev. 11', 19'
LI (343)	 Obv. 26, Rev. 4[34]	 Obv. 14  Obv. 16	——	——	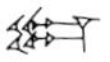 Rev. 9', 35'
ḪA (367)	 Obv. 18 passim	 Obv. 22	 Rev. 29	 Obv. 8 passim	 Obv. 2' passim

Bibliography

ARTZI, P. 1993: "EA 43, An (Almost) Forgotten Amarna Letter", in A. F. Rainey (ed.) *kinattūtu ša dārâti. Raphael Kutscher Memorial Volume*, Tel Aviv, 7-10, Plate I.

BAQIR, T. 1946: "Iraq Government Excavations at 'Aqar Qūf. Third Interim Report, 1944-5", *Iraq* 8, 73-93.

BECKMAN, G. M. 1983: "Mesopotamians and Mesopotamian Learning at Ḫattuša", *JCS* 35, 97-114.

DEVECCHI, E. 2012: "The So-called "Mixed Ductus" in the Akkadian Texts from Boğazköy", in E. Devecchi (ed.), *Palaeography and Scribal Practices in Syro-Palestine and Anatolia in the Late Bronze Age* (PIHANS 119), Leiden, 47-63.

[32] The sign reproduced in the copy as a DA (DA-*a-pa-a-nu*) looks on the photographs more like a ŠA: 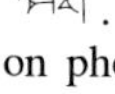.

[33] Collation on photos does not confirm the presence of the *gebrochene* horizontal indicated in the copy.

[34] According to the copy, also the LI at Obv. 1 has this shape, but I was not able to collate it.

— in print: "Treaties and Edicts in the Hittite World", in G. Wilhelm (ed.) *Acts of the 54th RAI*, Winona Lake.

EDEL, E. 1994: *Die ägyptisch-hethitische Korrespondenz aus Boghazköi in babylonischer und hethitischer Sprache*, Opladen.

GOREN, Y., I. FINKELSTEIN and N. NA'AMAN 2004: *Inscribed in Clay. Provenance Study of the Amarna Tablets and Other Ancient Near Eastern Texts*, Tel Aviv.

GOREN, Y., H. MOMMSEN and J. KLINGER 2011: "Non-destructive provenance study of cuneiform tablets using portable X-ray fluorescence (pXRF)", *Journal of Archaeological Science* 38, 684-696.

HAGENBUCHNER, A. 1989a: *Die Korrespondenz der Hethitern I. Teil* (THeth 15), Heidelberg.

— 1989b: *Die Korrespondenz der Hethitern II. Teil* (THeth 16), Heidelberg.

KLINGER, J. 2003: "Zur Paläographie akkadischsprachiger Texte aus Ḫattuša", in G. Beckman et al. (eds.) *Hittite Studies in Honor of Harry A. Hoffner Jr. on the Occasion of His 65th Birthday*, Winona Lake, 237-248.

KLINGER, J. and E. NEU 1990: "War die erste Computer-Analyse des Hethitischen verfehlt?", *Hethitica* 10, 135-160.

KNUDTZON, J. A. 1902: "Weitere Studien zu den El-Amarna-Tafeln", in F. Delitzsch and P. Haupt (eds.) *Beiträge zur Assyriologie und semitischen Sprachwissenschaft* (BA 4), Leipzig, 279-337.

— 1907: *Die El-Amarna-Tafeln*, Leipzig.

— 1915: *Die El-Amarna-Tafeln. Zweiter Teil: Anmerkungen und Register* (VAB 2.2), Leipzig.

MILLER, J. L. 2007: "Amarna Age Chronology and the Identity of Nibḫururiya in the Light of a Newly Reconstructed Hittite Text", *AoF* 34, 252-293.

MORA, C. and M. GIORGIERI 2004: *Le lettere tra i re ittiti e i re assiri ritrovate a Ḫattuša* (HANE/M 7), Padova.

MORAN, W. L. 1992: *The Amarna Letters*, Baltimore - London.

MYNÁŘOVÁ, J. 2007: *Language of Amarna — Language of Diplomacy: Perspectives on the Amarna Letters*, Prague.

NA'AMAN, N. 1995: "Tushratta's Murder in Shuppiluliuma's Letter to Akhenaten (EA 43)", *Abr-Nahrain* 33, 116-118.

SCHROEDER, O. 1915: *Die Tontafeln von Tell el-Amarna* (VS 12), Leipzig.

SCHWEMER, D. 1998: *Akkadische Rituale aus Ḫattuša. Die Sammeltafel KBo XXXVI 29 und verwandte Fragmente* (THeth 23), Heidelberg.

— 2004: "Ein akkadischer Liebeszauber aus Ḫattuša", *ZA* 94, 59-79.

VAN DEN HOUT, T. 1994: "Der Falke und das Küchen: der neue Pharao und der hethitische Prinz?", *ZA* 84, 60-88.

— 2002: "Another View of Hittite Literature", in F. Pecchioli Daddi and S. De Martino (eds.) *Anatolia antica. Studi in memoria di Fiorella Imparati* (Eothen 11), Firenze, 857-878.

VAN SOLDT, W. H. 1977: *Het Akkadisch van Ugarit* (MA Thesis).

REMARKS ON EQUATIVE AND COMPARATIVE DEGREE IN HITTITE AND AKKADIAN

An De Vos
Bayerische Julius-Maximilians-Universität, Würzburg

1. Comparative and Superlative Degree in Hittite (*Status Quaestionis*)[1]

Unlike in other Indo-European languages such as Greek, Latin or English, in Hittite the comparative and superlative degrees of adjectives are expressed syntactically rather than by suffixes (Hoffner and Melchert 2008, 273 §1.12-17.20)[2]. The only Indo-European languages without morphologically constructed comparative adjectives are Armenian, Tocharian and Hittite; for Tocharian and Hittite it remains unclear whether suffixes for the comparative degree were secondarily lost or have not been inherited; for Armenian it has been shown that the suffix for the comparative degree disappeared according to phonetic rules (Zeilfelder 1998, 475-482). It is *communis opinio* that the Hittite comparative degree is expressed by three elements: the compared item (also called tenor[3]), the predicative adjective specifying the *tertium comparationis* and the object of comparison (also called vehicle) in dative-locative (resp. following the Akkadian preposition *ANA*). This can be seen e.g. in *namma=kan anzel* TI-*anni [UL Š]A BĒLU*<<MEŠ>>=*NI* TI-*tar nakki* (KUB 31.42 ii 18-19), translated by Hoffner and Melchert 2008, 273 as "if the life of our lord (i.e., the king) (*ŠA BELU-NI* TI-*tar*) is not dearer (to us) (*UL* + *nakkī*) than our own life (*anzel* TI-*anni*)". Zeilfelder notices that the well-documented use of the dative-locative cannot have belonged to the proto-language since in the Indo-European languages the ablative, the instrumental or the successive casus of the respective language are used for expressing

[1] Abbreviations follow those of CAD and http://www.hethport.uni-wuerzburg.de/hetkonk/hetkonkabkrz.html. I would like to thank Dr. Alfredo Rizza for his stimulating remarks.

[2] On the comparative and superlative degree in Hittite see Friedrich 1926, 185-186; Friedrich 1940, 25 §94-96, 71-72 §232-234; Friedrich 1960, 61 §93-95, 127 §221-223; Puhvel 1973, 146-147; Hoffner 1993, 50; Zeilfelder 1998, 475-482; Cotticelli Kurras 2000, 33-45; Hoffner and Melchert 2008, 273-276 §17.12-17.20.

[3] For the terminology tenor, vehicle, *tertium comparationis* and simile-marker see Wasserman 2003, 99. See also Streck 1999, 31.

the object of reference (Zeilfelder 1998, 479). She assumes that in Hittite the case for the comparative degree probably has been changed analogously to the dative rection of the verb *dakk-* "to be like" (Zeilfelder 1998, 479; see also Cotticelli Kurras 2000, 37-38, 43; Hoffner and Melchert 2008, 275 §17.16).

As for the superlative degree, apart from the expression by lexical means it is constructed syntactically in two different ways in Hittite texts (which all stem from the post-Old-Hittite period): The compared item and the adjective specifying the *tertium comparationis* are combined with a plural form in *-aš* which can be either a dative-locative plural or a genitive plural (Hoffner and Melchert 2008, 275-276 § 17.17-20; Cotticelli Kurras 2000, 40-41). The object of comparison can be strengthened by the adjective *ḫumant-* "all". Repetition of the adjective, as can be seen e.g. in KUB 31.141 l. 3 *šallayaš=kan* DINGIR.MEŠ-*aš kuiš šalliš* "he who among the great gods is the great(est)" (translation by Hoffner and Melchert 2008, 275), can also indicate superlative meaning (Cotticelli Kurras 2000, 41). Occasionally, forms in dative-locative plural are constructed with *ištarna* "in the midst of", whereas if the adjective is not a predicate, the objects with which comparison is made stand in the genitive (Hoffner and Melchert 2008, 275). As an example of the syntactic construction with dative-locative plural and *ištarna*, Hoffner and Melchert 2008, 275 cite [DIN]GIR-*LUM* DINGIR.MEŠ-*aš ištarna tarḫuilešzi* "the god is the bravest among the gods" (KUB 36.55 ii 31)[4]. For the syntactic construction with the object of comparison in the genitive plural they cite — assuming that *ḫantezziyaš* is not substantivized here, in which case it would not be a superlative — *daššuš=a=šši Anuš* DINGIR.MEŠ-*aš ḫantezziyaš=šmiš peran=še[t] arta* "mighty Anu, foremost of the gods, stands before him" (KUB 33.120 i 9-10).

2. Aim of this paper

In what follows we will study the question whether there has been Akkadian influence on the Hittite way of expressing comparison. We will focus on the constructions generally considered as modes for expressing the comparative degree in Hittite and Akkadian, discuss how equative comparisons (like "A is as ADJECTIVE as B") can be expressed in Akkadian and Hittite and ask whether there are criteria to differentiate

[4] See also Archi 2002, 8 ("[']will [this g]od become mighty among the gods…?").

between equative degree, comparative degree and other kinds of comparison. Whereas comparative and superlative degrees are categories of their own in languages which express them by morphological means, differentiation between them is not always unequivocal when they are expressed syntactically (for Hittite see e.g. Zeilfelder 1998, 478; for Akkadian see e.g. Kouwenberg 1997, 405 n. 29). The observation that Akkadian influence on the Hittite language cannot *a priori* be excluded stems also from the hypothesis of Popko (2007, 575-581) and (independently) van den Hout (2009, 33) that in the Hittite kingdom before about 1500 B.C. only Akkadian may have been written. There are some references in secondary literature to possible influences of Akkadian on the Hittite language[5].

3. Comparative and Superlative Degree in Akkadian (*Status Quaestionis*)

Just as Hittite, Akkadian does not dispose of special forms for expressing the comparative and superlative degrees (GAG §68)[6]. In Akkadian the comparative degree is expressed by the preposition *eli* "above, towards, against, more than" which governs (as is the rule for Akkadian prepositions) the genitive. This can be seen e.g. in ZA 49 170 iv 12: *eli kakkabī šamê mādā* "they are more numerous than the stars of heaven" (see AHw 201a).

Apart from the expression by lexical means (by D- or Š-stem verbal adjectives[7]), the Akkadian superlative degree can be expressed by a combination of *status-constructus* and genitive case or by a combination with the preposition *ina* "in the midst of". An example for the construction with *ina* could be En. El. iv l. 3: *attāma kabtāta ina ilī rabûti* "you are the most important among the great gods" (Talon 2005, 15 and 51 line 3).

[5] For a discussion of the lexical and semantical relations between Hittite and Akkadian see Schwemer 2005-06, 220-234. Concerning Akkadian influence on the Hittite iterative in *-šk* see von Soden 1973, 311-319 (see also Edzard 1996, 11 note 10 and Streck 1998, 193). Akkadian influence on the Hittite free-standing genitive is discussed e.g. in Sommer 1947, 82; Kronasser 1966, 331-334; Kammenhuber 1969, 203; Watkins 1970, 351-352 n. 20; Yoshida 1987, 1-2 and Hoffner and Melchert 2008, 256 § 16.63.

[6] For the comparative and superlative degree in Akkadian see AHw 201a; CAD E 89; GAG §68; Rosenberg n.d., 23 Nr. 22; Ungnad 1906, 29; Schott 1926, 33-35; Mercer 1961, 50; Ryckmans 1938, 99; Finet 1956, 88; De Meyer 1962, 79; Ungnad-Matouš 1969, 58; Giacumakis 1970, 39; Riemschneider 1978, 163; Buccellati 1996, 443; Huehnergard 1997, 302; Kouwenberg 1997, 397, 405 n. 29; Wasserman 2003, 151.

[7] See GAG §68b for the noun construction patterns *purrus* and *šuprus*, more often with an elative meaning.

A superlative expressed by a *status-constructus*-construction can be found in RA 22 170, 172, 174 l. 4b (*Ištar*) *rabīt Igigi* "(Ištar) the greatest of the Igigi-gods" [8]. Repetition of the adjective occurs in the example KAR 158 vi 7 given by GAG §68b *emuqti emqēti* "the wisest of the wise ones". Comparisons with *eli* can also express superlative connotation, as can be seen e.g. in VS 10.214 vi 22 *qardat el kala ilātim* "she is the most warlike of all the gods" (Buccellati 1996, 443 n. 14) [9].

4. Similarities and differences between the Hittite and the Akkadian way of expressing comparison

Looking at the above discussion, one notices the striking fact that Hittite and Akkadian use the same three ways of expressing the superlative degree. Both languages can express the superlative degree by lexical means[10]. In Akkadian just as in Hittite constructions of the superlative degree the object of comparison can stand in genitive plural (in Akkadian as part of a *status-constructus*-construction). Repetition of the adjective to indicate superlative meaning can be found both in Hittite and Akkadian. Just as in Hittite the postposition *ištarna* can be connected to the object of comparison, in Akkadian the preposition *ina* "in the midst of" can. It is difficult to establish whether the different constructions are used in similar ways in Hittite and Akkadian because in post-Old-Hittite texts the ending *-aš* can stand both for the genitive and for the dative-locative-plural so that it often remains unclear which construction is used. Interestingly Hoffner and Melchert 2008, 275 § 17.19 mention: "When the adjective is not a predicate, the objects with which comparison is made

[8] Although Huehnergard 1997, 302 translates the phrase *Ištar rabīt ilātim* as "Ištar is the greatest of the goddesses", the predicative use of the adjective would require an Akkadian stative (Huehnergard 1997, 219-223; GAG § 77). Since in Akkadian a verbal adjective is used, an interpretation as attribute adjective is more correct.

[9] Kouwenberg 1997, 405 n. 29 notices "Since Akkadian does not have a grammatical category for the grades of comparison (...) *gašrat eli* should be translated 'the most powerful of' or 'more powerful than', depending on whether we regard the subject as being one of the set of entities with which it is compared, or as being placed outside this set".

[10] In Hittite there are the adjectives with superlative and/or comparative meaning *ḫantezzi(ya)-* "first, front, foremost", *a(p)pezzi(ya)-* "last", "lowest", *šaraz(z)i(ya)-* "upper", "superior" and *katter(r)a-* "lower", "inferior" (see e.g. CHD Š 247-249; HED A 92-93; HED Ḫ 108-112; HED K 131-133; HEG A 46-47; HEG Š 882-886; HW^2 A 185-192; HW^2 Ḫ 174-182; Friedrich 1960, 61; Zeilfelder 1998, 477; Cotticelli Kurras 2000, 33-35 with further references). In Akkadian there are adjectives like *panû* "first", "front", "former", *(w)arkû* "rear", "hindmost", "later", *elû* "upper" and *šaplû* "lower" (see e.g. CAD A/2, 286-290; CAD E 111-114; CAD P 96-98; CAD Š/1, 473-477; Mercer 1961, 50 and further entries in the dictionaries).

stand not in the dative-locative but in the genitive". In Akkadian too, if the adjective is not a predicate, a *status-constructus*-construction with genitive can be used, whereas if the adjective is a predicate, a stative (and not a *status-constructus*-construction) is used (see note 8).

In contrast to the situation for the superlative degree, the way of expressing the comparative degree — such as it is commonly understood — differs in Akkadian and in Hittite in important aspects. Whereas in Akkadian the preposition *eli* is used in front of the object of comparison, in Hittite the preposition *ANA* or the dative-locative is used. Since the Akkadian preposition *eli* is otherwise equated with the Hittite postposition *šer/šara* (Friedrich 1991, 307a) and since the spectrum of meanings of the Akkadian preposition *eli* does not correspond to the known usages of the dative-locative-case in Hittite, it is unlikely that these are comparable constructions. In Akkadian texts from Boğazköy in expressions of the comparative degree the object of comparison follows *eli* (for examples see Labat 1932, 120).

There are (a few) Hittite clauses containing the verb *dakk-* "to be like/similar" with the object of comparison in dative-locative resp. following the Akkadian preposition *ANA*[11]. In Akkadian in combination with the verb *mašālu* "to be similar", the object of comparison follows in many cases the preposition *ana* (as is the case in examples from Boğazköy — see AHw 623a), but the object of comparison can also be expressed by the terminative-adverbial-ending *-iš* (in later texts) or by a dative (see AHw 623-624)[12].

Considering the similarities and differences in constructing the superlative resp. comparative degree in Hittite and Akkadian it can be remarked that whereas the positive, comparative and superlative degree of adjectives are all discussed and documented in Hittite and Akkadian studies, the equative degree ("A is as ADJECTIVE as B") is not. In the following we will search for modes to express the equative in Akkadian and Hittite[13].

[11] See also HEG D 31-32; Zeilfelder 1998, 479; Cotticelli Kurras 2000, 37, 38; Hoffner and Melchert 2008, 275.

[12] See also CAD M/1, 355-358; Schott 1926, 9-10; Wasserman 2003, 131.

[13] We cannot discuss all the modes of expressing comparison in Akkadian and Hittite here; for this see the article on *iwar* "like" by Hoffner (1993, 39-51), the studies on comparison in Akkadian by Schott (1926, 8-68), Streck (1999, 34-42), Wasserman (2003, 99-156). As in the rest of this paper, the content of the similes, the figurative language itself will not be investigated (for this see e.g. Streck 1999 and Wasserman 2003, 135-156 with further references), but only the formal realisation will be discussed.

Both Hittite and Akkadian dispose of an unequivocal way to express the equative degree in comparisons of measurement. Under the entry of the adjective *mašiwant-* "equal in size or amount to, as much/little as, as big/small as" in CHD M 208b-209 the text passage KUB 21.27 iii 39 is mentioned among others. There we read *nu uwami ANA* ^d*Liliwani* GAŠAN-*IA* ALAM KÙ.BABBAR *ŠA* ^I*Ḫattušili* ^I*Ḫattušiliš mašiwanza* SAG.DU-*SU* ŠU.M[EŠ-*Š*]*U* GÌR.MEŠ-*ŠU ŠA* KÙ.GI *iyami* "I will come, make for Liliwani, my lady, a silver statue of Ḫattušili — (it will be) as big as Ḫattušili, its head, hands, and feet of gold" (KUB 21.27 iii 39-41). In CHD M 208 under the entry of the adverb *mašiwan* "as much as, as many as"[14] there is a reference to KBo 13.49 obv. 9-11, where one reads: *mašiwan ḫikkirmaḫiya pankur labar*[*ni* LUGAL]/ ^MUNUS*tawannanni* MUNUS.LUGAL DUMU.MEŠ-*ŠU ḫaššeš* [ ] / [*ḫ*]*anzaššeš* MU.KAM. ḪI.A-ŠU *ašandu* "may Labarna's (and) Tawannannas's offspring and years be as numerous as a clan in a ḫ. (is)"[15]. In Akkadian the equative degree of measurement can be expressed by the preposition *mala*, "to the same amount", "according to", "as large as" (CAD M/1, 147b; Streck 1999, 36)[16]. This can be seen e.g. in the SB Etana-Text SAACT 2 tablet 3 l. 37 *u tâmtu rapaštu mala buginni* — in the translation of CAD M/1, 148b "the wide sea is as (large as) a basket"[17]. The Hittite construction of the adjective *mašiwant-*, agreeing with the object of comparison in case, numerus and genus, does not have parallels in the Akkadian material where either comparative sentences introduced by *mala* (as conjunction/ relative pronoun) or expressions with the preposition *mala* are used.

Although the Hittite postpositions *iwar* "in the manner of, as", *mān* "like, as" and *maḫḫan* "like, as" are all used to express comparisons with the object of comparison being a noun or a pronoun and although they are sometimes used in much the same way (Hoffner 1993, 49 and *passim*), there are differences in the syntactical constructions[18]. Hoffner 1993, 49 and Hoffner and Melchert 2008, 301 §20.31 mention the following differences: Whereas *iwar* governs the genitive, the object of comparison referred to by the postpositions[19] *mān*/ *maḫḫan* "like, as"

[14] See for *mašiwan, mašiwant-, mašiyan* and related forms CHD M 206-208; HED M 94-97; HEG 158-159, 160; Hoffner 1993, 49.

[15] See also CHD P 93b; HW² Ḫ 398b (*pankur* translated as "Tierhaar"), 581b.

[16] See also AHw 591-592; CAD M/1, 147-149.

[17] See also CAD B 306b ("and the wide sea is like a trough"); CAD T 151b.

[18] See for *mān*, *maḫḫan* and *iwar* also CHD M 100-102, 144-146; HED I 499-502; HED M 39-43; HEG I 452-454; HEG M 86-88, 116-117; Hoffner 1993, 39-51.

[19] One could wonder whether *mān* and *maḫḫan* are to be labeled not as postpositions but rather as particles of comparison, since by Bußman (ed.) 2002, 734 the latter do not

governs the case which corresponds to the case of the object which is being compared. Unlike *iwar,* neither *mān* nor *maḫḫan* are used after non-clitic pronouns, neither of them is able to govern proper names, and neither of them is used with negated substantives. Whereas *maḫḫan* can be construed with a preceding interrogative pronoun, *iwar* never is. In Akkadian the prepositions *kīma* (*kī+ma*) and *kī* are used to express comparisons with the object of comparison being a noun or a pronoun[20]. Although we cannot discuss similarities and differences in detail here, it is interesting to notice that all syntactical elements in which *iwar* differs from *mān* and *maḫḫan* are also known for *kīma*: Like Akkadian prepositions, *iwar* governs the genitive — also in later periods, when other Hittite postpositions govern the dative-locative. Just as *iwar* can govern proper names, Akkadian *kīma* can (see e.g. Wasserman 2003, 115 item 105). Just as *iwar* is used with negated substantives, *kīma* also is (e.g. Wasserman 2003, 149-150). But whereas the negation with *iwar* is indicated with *UL* (Hoffner 1993, 49) or Hittite *natta*, in Akkadian individual words are negated by *lā* (GAG § 122a). Just as *iwar* is not attested together with a preceding interrogative pronoun, there is no attestation for *kīma* with preceding interrogative pronoun among the examples in Wasserman 2003, 104-130, CAD and AHw under *kīma*, *mannum* and *mīnum*. Just as *iwar* is attested with independent pronouns, *kīma* is (see e.g. GAG § 114g the Old-Assyrian example *ša kīma jâti*). Finally, those syntactical constructions for *iwar* — apposition to the subject, the object, free-standing genitive and modification of the verb — which are shown by Hoffner (1993, 40-46) are also known for *kīma* (see e.g. Wasserman 2003, 104-130). Since there is no secured Indo-European etymology for *iwar*, considering the similarities with Akkadian *kīma* it cannot be excluded *a priori* that the syntactical construction patterns of the Akkadian preposition *kīma* influenced those for Hittite *iwar*. If this is accepted, has the prepositional use of *iwar* from the time of Ḫattušili III onwards (Hoffner 1993, 47) also been influenced by Akkadian constructions? And was the "conjunctive" use of *iwar* where the case of the compared noun agrees with the case of the comparing noun (Hoffner 1993, 46) influenced by the Hittite (and Indo-European) construction with *mān* and *maḫḫan*?

have a rection, i.e. they are not relevant for the case of the object of comparison: "Das zweite Vergleichsglied steht jeweils im gleichen Kasus wie das erste" — just as is the case with *mān* and *maḫḫan*.

[20] See for *kī* and *kīma* also AHw 468-469, 476-477; CAD K 322-325, 367-370; Wasserman 2003, 103-135. For other ways of expressing comparison in Akkadian see e.g. Streck 1999, 90-96.

It is to be remarked, that whereas *iwar* is uncommon in Old Hittite texts and not attested in texts with Old Hittite script, *mān* and *maḫḫan* are.

It remains to be asked whether the Hittite *iwar*, *maḫḫan* and/or *mān* and/or Akkadian *kīma/kī* are used in equative expressions. Among all the attestations for *iwar* presented by Hoffner 1993 there is none with a construction "A is as ADJECTIVE as (*iwar*) B". Although Hoffner 1993, 51 construed the sentence *šiwatteš=teš=wa=tta nepišaš ḫaštereš mān maggāeš ašandu* "may your days be as numerous as the stars of heaven" there are no attestations for the construction "A is as ADJECTIVE as B" with "as" expressed by the postposition *mān* or *maḫḫan* among the examples cited in CHD 101-102, 145-146 under *maḫḫan* and *mān*. All constructions of comparison with *maḫḫan/mān* and the *tertium comparationis* being expressed by an adjective are translated as "A is ADJECTIVE like B". For example, KUB 24.7 ii 18 ANŠE-*ašmaza* GIM-*an puntarriyališ z[ik]* is translated in CHD M 102a as "Like an ass you are stubborn". In the same way CAD K *sub kīma* does not mention an attestation of a construction "A is as ADJECTIVE as B" with the object of comparison following *kīma* and the *tertium comparationis* being expressed by an adjective. Although in other places the construction *ma'id mimmūšu kīma ajāb* in EA 89 l. 46 is translated as "his property is as great as the sea" (CAD M/1, 25)[21], considering the above it cannot be excluded that the translation "his property is great like the sea" would be more appropriate[22].

Both Hittite and Akkadian can express comparisons by so-called partial-sentence similes, i.e. "similes whose *tertium comparationis* is repeated twice and common to both the vehicle and the tenor: 'A is X, just as B is X'" (Wasserman 2003, 147). Whereas the *tertium comparationis* can be expressed in different ways, in the following only a Hittite and an Akkadian example of a partial-sentence simile expressing the *tertium comparationis* by means of a copular verb with adjective will be given. As a Hittite example[23] with the comparative sentence containing *maḫḫan* one could cite e.g. KBo 15.10 ii 5.6 *ki* ^{NA4}*peru maḫḫan ukturi BĒLU U*

[21] See also Knudtzon 1915, 425 (otherwise understood); Albright and Moran 1950, 164; Moran 1992, 162.

[22] See also Cavigneaux and Al-Rawi 1994, 88 *kīma šeršerrim lē[ssa...] warqat* in the translation of Wasserman 2003, 113 "[Her (Lamaštu's) j]aw is as *pale* as š-paste" vs. in the translation of Cavigneaux and Al-Rawi 1994, 88 "la joue verdâtre comme l'enduit *šeršerru*".

[23] For other examples of Hittite comparative clauses containing *maḫḫan* or *mān* see CHD M *maḫḫan* 2., 103a-105a; CHD M *mān* 2., 146b-147a. Comparative clauses are not further discussed in Hoffner and Melchert 2008.

DAM-*SU* DUM[U.MEŠ-*Š*]*U QĀTAMMA uktureš ašandu* "just as this boulder is everlasting so let the lord (the king) and his wife and his children be everlasting" (CHD M 103a). As an Akkadian example[24] GAG § 178f mentions VAB 2/1 8 (= EA 8) l. 11-12 from an Amarna letter sent by Burnaburriaš to Amenhotep IV: *kī abbū-ni itti aḫāmiš ṭābū nīnu lū ṭābānu* "just as our fathers were friendly with each other, so let us be friendly". Since the meaning of these partial-sentence similes (which stress the likeness of a feature) is not exactly the same as the meaning of comparisons expressed by the equative degree (which stresses that the feature is equivalent) it will not be discussed further here.

5. Questions and Consequences for the Interpretation of the Akkadian Text Passages

Whereas the above-mentioned way of expressing the Akkadian comparative degree with the object of comparison following the preposition *eli* is listed in the grammars, a look at Akkadian dictionaries and translations reveals that there are other constructions translated and interpreted as comparative degrees. In what follows only a sample of text passages in which the object of comparison is following the preposition *ana* will be presented. CAD M/1, 27a translates the text passage *ana gipiš tâmāti panūka mādū* (Ebeling 1953, 90 l. 3) from an Akkadian "Handerhebung"-prayer as "your (Marduk's) face is bigger than the expanse of the sea"[25]. Whereas Lambert 1959, 131 translates the passage *aṣaḫḫir ana ṣiḫirūti* [*ana š*]*aplûti assipili* (STT 65 l. 15) in a Neo-Assyrian prayer as "I am smaller than the small, I have become lower [than] the low" [26], CAD Ṣ 122 translates this line as "I have become as lowly as servants, as humble as those of low status".

Since none of the grammars and the dictionaries mentions the use of *ana* to introduce the object of comparison in modes of expressing the comparative degree, we cannot exclude that the interpretation of the above cited sentence STT 65 l. 15 by CAD Ṣ 122 with an equative degree is more appropriate. In this case it remains to be asked whether also other comparative constructions with an adjectival verb and the object of comparison following *ana* should better be interpreted as indicating the

[24] For comparative clauses in Akkadian see GAG §178.

[25] See also CAD G 85a (*ana gi-piš tâmati panūka ma'du* [*šaknu*] "you set out many times for the expanse of the sea"); Ebeling 1953, 91.

[26] See also CAD Š/1, 424a.

equative degree of gradable adjectives. On the basis of the context neither of the two options is to be favored or excluded. Considering however that the basic meaning of *eli* is "over" (i.e. passing over) whereas the basic meaning of *ana* is "to, towards" (i.e. not passing over), it seems reasonable to differentiate as proposed above between the two constructions. If this hypothesis is accepted, other examples could also document differences in meaning between comparisons with the object of comparison *ana* vs. *eli*: Do constructions like X *eli miniātīšu irabbi*/*irrik* etc. with adjectival verbs (for examples see CAD M/2, 86-87) mean "X is greater/longer than his normal size", whereas constructions like X *ana miniātīšu irabbi*/*irrik* etc. (for examples see CAD M/2, 86-87) mean "X is as big/long as his normal size"? Are the cases where *watārum* is construed with *eli* as e.g. in En. El. i 12 *Anšar u Kišar ibbanûma elīšunu atrū* "Anšar and Kišar were created exceeding those (before them)" (CAD A/2, 498b) to be interpreted as comparative degrees? And are cases where *watārum* is construed with *ana* as e.g. in CT 27 42 Obv.[!] 18 *mārūšu kussâ iṣabbat ana abīšu uwattar* "his son will ascend the throne and become as important as his father"[27] to be interpreted as equative degree?

6. Questions and Consequences for the Interpretation of the Hittite Text Passages

If we accept significant parallels between the Hittite and the Akkadian ways of expressing comparison, the different way of constructing the comparative degree in the two languages is remarkable. Can we explain why in the Hittite construction for the comparative degree the object of comparison is expressed — as is generally assumed — in dative-locative or with the Akkadian preposition *ANA*, whereas in Akkadian the object of comparison is combined with the preposition *eli*? Or should we think that, just as argued above for Akkadian, also in Hittite there was a difference between the Hittite equivalent to the Akkadian constructions with the object of comparison following the preposition *eli*, expressing the comparative degree, and constructions with the object of comparison in dative-locative or following the (Akkadian) preposition *ANA*, expressing the equative degree? Let us have a look at the Hittite examples.

The example *nu=wa=kan ANA* ÉRIN.MEŠ-*KA* ÉRIN.MEŠ-*YA mekki ANA* ANŠE.KUR.RA.MEŠ=*ma=wa=tta* ANŠE.KUR.RA.MEŠ-*YA mekki*

[27] For other translations see e.g. CAD A/2, 490b.

(KUB 19.29 iv 18-19) from the extensive annals of Muršili II is in the available editions interpreted as expressing a comparative degree — in the translation of Hoffner and Melchert 2008, 273: "My troops are more numerous than your troops, my horses are more numerous than your horses"[28]. In the context of this sentence in the Muršili Annals the speaker mentions that Muršili is only a child, that his country is not in good condition and that his troops and charioteers are few. Considering that the speaker presumably would have had less troops than Muršili, the declaration that his troops are as numerous as those of Muršili would be almost as effective as the declaration that his troops are more numerous than those of Muršili. So the context does not exclude the interpretation "as numerous as...".

All the available translations for the passage *ANA* LUGAL KUR URUU-*tašša=kan* 1-*aš* LÚ*tuḫukantiš šalliš ešdu namma=ma=šši=kan lē kuiški šalliš* from the bronze tablet column ii lines 80-81 (dating to the reign of Tutḫaliya IV) prefer an interpretation with a comparative degree — like e.g. in Hoffner and Melchert 2008, 273 "Only the crown prince (*tūḫukantiš*) shall be greater than the King of Tarḫuntašša; let no one else be greater"[29]. To my opinion, however, the interpretation "Only the crown prince shall be as great as the King of Tarḫuntašša; let no one else be as great" cannot be ruled out, even seems more plausible: assuming that the paragraph concerns the situation in the land Tarḫuntašša the statement that (in Tarḫuntašša) apart from the crown prince nobody shall be *greater* than the King of Tarḫuntašša would not rule out the possibility that other persons could *of the same greatness* as the king of Tarḫuntašša, which certainly is not intended.

The following text passage from a ritual, KUB 43.53 i 19-23, has also been interpreted unanimously with a comparative degree: *eššari=šett=a eššari* GAL-*li* SAG.DU=*SÚ ANA* SAG.DU=*Š[U* GAL-*li*] [K]IR$_{14}$=*ŠU ANA* KIR$_{14}$=*ŠU* GAL-*li* IGI.ḪI.A=*ŠU ANA* IGI.ḪI.A GAL-*li* [*a*]*īš=šet=a iššī* GAL-*li* EME=*ŠU ANA* EME=*ŠU* GAL-*li* [*kap*]*ru=šet=ašta kapruaz* GAL-*li mieli=ššet=a* [*mi*]*eliaš* GAL-*li iški*<*š*>=*šet=ašta iškiši* GAL-*li*.

[28] See also CHD M 246b-247a; HED M 120; Friedrich 1926, 185; Goetze 1933 (reprint 1967), 19; Friedrich 1940, 71; Hoffner 1993, 48; Zeilfelder 1998, 477-478: Cotticelli Kurras 2000, 36-37. Hoffner and Melchert 2008, 273 n. 6 mention that whereas ÉRIN.MEŠ and ANŠE.KUR.RA.MEŠ are common gender-nouns, "mekki may be construed as a collective noun 'a large amount' serving as the predicate". "As a noun and not an adjective, it need not show agreement" (see also CHD M 246-247 and Cotticelli Kurras 2000, 37).

[29] See also HEG Š 768; HEG T 410; Otten 1988, 19; Beckman 1999, 118; Hoffner 2003, 103b; Klinger 2005, 134.

Hoffner and Melchert 2008, 274 translate this passage as follows: "this one's (lit., his) stature is greater than that one's (lit., his) stature; his head is greater than his head; his nose is greater than his nose; his eyes..., his mouth..., his tongue..., his *mieli*... his back is greater than his back"[30]. The passage continues with further comparisons and then breaks off. The ablative of comparison (*kapruaz*) for which there are no other examples in Hittite texts is considered "secondary at best" by Hoffner and Melchert 2008, 274; but see e.g. Cotticelli Kurras 2000, 38 for the *ablativus comparationis* in other Indo-European languages. Again it can be asked whether an interpretation with equatives "this one's (lit., his) stature is as great as that one's (lit., his) stature; his head is as great as his head" etc. would not be more fitting. At the beginning of the (preserved part of the) ritual the text specifies how the substitute corresponds with the patient (the king): his head corresponds with the head (of the patient), his nose, his eyes and so on. Why should the body parts of the substitute be described as being bigger than those of the patient if at the beginning everything is done to demonstrate that the substitute really substitutes the patient and corresponds to him? Goedegebuure (2003, 70-71) argues that "the practitioner is trying to convince the deity that the substitute is even better than the king" so that as the logical conclusion the deity should take the substitute instead of the king. She also refers to the text of a prayer to Gaššulawiya, KBo 4.6 obv. 12' with the statement *n=aš=kan ammuk kattan* SIG_5-*anza* about the substitute, translated by Goedegebuure 2003, 71 as "She is better than me"[31]. But is it not possible that in KUB 43.53 the practitioner reinforces the value of the substitute by repeating that it really corresponds to the patient rather than contradicting his own statement about the substitute? And does the passage of the prayer to Gaššulawiya (one remarks the postposition *kattan*) not state that the substitute is as good as the speaker? Interestingly Goedegebuure (2003, 61-73) proposes a new lemma (LÚ) *ānt-* "equal" which refers to the substitute.

[30] See also CHD M 250a; CHD P 80a; HED E 314; HED I 424 ("His back [is] big [in relation] to the [other's] back"); HED K 66; HED M 124-125; HEG K 494; HEG P 401 (reference without translation); HW^2 A 49a; HW^2 E 125a; Sommer and Falkenstein 1938, 219-220; Haas 1971, 417; Neu 1980, 26; Haas 1987, 233-234; Giorgieri 1992, 64-69; Zeilfelder 1998, 479; Cotticelli Kurras 2000, 36-37.

[31] See also Lebrun 1980, 251 ("A côté de moi, elle est bonne"); Tischler 1981, 13 ("und es (nimmt sich) neben mir ausgezeichnet (aus)"); Singer 2002, 72 ("Compared to me she is excellent").

The last passage currently interpreted as expressing the comparative degree is KUB 31.42 ii 18-19 (from instructions for dignitaries, given by Arnuwanda I and Ašmunikkal). The passage reads *namma=kan anzel* TI-*anni* [(*UL Š*)]*A BĒLU*<<MEŠ>>=*NI* TI-*tar nakki*, in the translation of Hoffner and Melchert 2008, 273 "(if) the life of our lord is not dearer (to us) than our own life" (KUB 31.42 ii 18-19 // KUB 31.44 16-17)[32]. On the basis of the context both the interpretation given above and the interpretation with an equative degree "(if) the life of our lord is not as dear (to us) as our own life" are possible. It could be remarked that an Akkadian text passage from Shemshāra reads *ša...šâtu bēlšu kīma napištīšu irammušu*, in the translation of CAD N/2, 297 "whom his master loves as his own life" (Læssœ 1959: 81 Nr. 812 l. 57). Although the Akkadian passage expresses a comparison by *kīma* (and not a comparative or equative degree of gradable adjectives) and although the Akkadian passage concerns the lord loving a subordinate (and not, as in the Hittite passage, subordinates who need to love their superior), the interpretation "(if) the life of our lord is not as dear (to us) as our own life" could perhaps be favored on the basis of the Shemshāra parallel.

Of course, as long as we do not have examples for the construction of the comparative degree in Hittite with the Akkadian preposition *ELI* or with a similar Hittite construction, it is difficult to prove the above hypothesis; but there are arguments to question whether the interpretation of the given examples as a comparative degree is the only possible one.

7. Selective Bibliography

ALBRIGHT, W. F. and MORAN, W. L. 1950: "Rib-Adda of Byblos and the Affairs of Tyre (EA 89)", *JCS* 4, 163-168.

ARCHI, A. 2002: "Ea and the Beast. A Song related to the Kumarpi Cycle", in P. Taracha (ed.) *Silva Anatolica. Fs. Popko*, Warsaw, 1-10.

BECKMAN, G. 1999: *Hittite Diplomatic Texts.* 2nd ed., Atlanta (Georgia).

BUCCELLATI, G. 1996: *A Structural Grammar of Babylonian*, Wiesbaden.

BUSSMAN, H. (ed.) 2002: *Lexikon der Sprachwissenschaft*, Stuttgart.

CAVIGNEAUX, A. and AL-RAWI, F. N. H. 1994: "Charmes de Sippar et de Nippur", in H. Gasche, M. Tanret, C. Janssen and A. Degraeve (eds.), *Cinquante-deux réflexions sur le proche-orient ancien offerts en hommage à Léon De Meyer* (MHE Occasional Publications 2), Leuven, 73-89.

[32] See also CHD N 365a; HED N 44; HW^{2} Ḫ 665b (as question); Friedrich 1940, 71-72; von Schuler 1956, 230 and 233; Houwink ten Cate 1983, 169; Zeilfelder 1998, 478; Giorgieri n.d., 225.

COTTICELLI KURRAS, P. 2000: "Zum hethitischen Komparativ", in M. Ofitsch and Ch. Zinko (eds.), *125 Jahre Indogermanistik in Graz*, Graz, 33-45.
DE MEYER, L. 1962: *L'Accadien des contrats de Suse*, Leiden.
EBELING, E. 1953: *Die Akkadische Gebetsserie "Handerhebung"*, Berlin.
EDZARD, D. O. 1996: *Die Iterativstämme beim akkadischen Verbum. Die Frage ihrer Entstehung, ihre Funktion, ihre Verbreitung*, München.
FINET, A. 1956: *L'Akkadien des Lettres de Mari*, Brussel.
FRIEDRICH, J. 1926: "Der Ausdruck der Komparation beim hethitischen Adjektiv", *AfO* 3, 185-186.
— 1940: *Hethitisches Elementarbuch. 1. Teil. Kurzgefasste Grammatik*, Heidelberg.
— 1960: *Hethitisches Elementarbuch. 1.Teil. Kurzgefasste Grammatik*, 2nd ed., Heidelberg.
— 1991: *Kurzgefaßtes Hethitisches Wörterbuch* (Unveränderter Nachdruck der Ausgabe 1952-1966), Heidelberg.
GIACUMAKIS, G. 1970: *The Akkadian of Alalaḫ*, The Hague – Paris.
GIORGIERI, M. n.d.: *I testi ittiti di giuramento*, diss., Firenze.
— 1992: "Un rituale di Scongiuro antico ittita per Labarna-Ḫattušili", *SMEA* 29, 47-98.
GOEDEGEBUURE, P. M. 2003: „KBo 17.17+: Remarks on an Old Hittite Royal Substitution Ritual", *Journal of Ancient Near Eastern Religions* 2, 61-73.
GÖTZE, A. 1933: *Die Annalen des Muršiliš* (MVAG 38), Darmstadt.
HAAS, V. 1971: "Ein hethitisches Beschwörungsmotiv aus Kizzuwatna, seine Herkunft und Wanderung", *Or.* 41, 410-430.
— 1987: "Magie und Zauberei. B.", *RlA* 7, 234-255.
HOFFNER, H. A. Junior 1993: "Hittite *iwar* and Related Modes of Expressing Comparison", *Istanbuler Mitteilungen* 43 (Festschrift Neve), 39-51.
— 2003: "The Treaty of Tudḫaliya IV with Kurunta of Tarḫuntašša on the Bronze Tablet Found in Ḫattuša", in W. E. W. Hallo (ed.), *The Context of Scripture* 2, Leiden – Boston – Köln, 100-106.
HOFFNER, H. A. JUNIOR and MELCHERT, H. C. 2008: *A Grammar of the Hittite Language*, Winona Lake (Indiana).
HOUWINK TEN CATE, Ph. H. J. 1983: "Instructies voor hittitische functionarissen", in K. R. Veenhof (ed.) *Schrijvend verleden. Documenten uit het Oude Nabije Oosten vertaald en toegelicht*, Leiden, 160-181.
HUEHNERGARD, J. 1997: *A Grammar of Akkadian*, Atlanta (Georgia).
KAMMENHUBER, A. 1969: "Hethitisch, Palaisch, Luwisch und Hieroglyphenluwisch", in B. Spuler (ed.), *Altkleinasiatische Sprachen* (HdO 1/2/1-2/2), Leiden – Köln, 119-357.
KLINGER, J. 2005: "Der Vertrag Tutḫalijas von Ḫatti mit Kurunta von Tarḫuntašša", in B. Janowski and G. Wilhelm (eds.), *Texte aus der Umwelt des Alten Testaments. Neue Folge* 2, Gütersloh, 130-138.
KNUDTZON, J. A. 1915: *Die El-Amarna-Tafeln* (VAB 2), Leipzig.
KOUWENBERG, N. J. C. 1997: *Gemination in the Akkadian Verb* (Studia Semitica Neerlandica 32), Assen.
KRONASSER, H. 1966: *Etymologie der hethitischen Sprache* I, Wiesbaden.
LABAT, R. 1932: *L'Akkadien de Boghaz-köi. Étude sur la Langue des Lettres, Traités et Vocabulaires Akkadiens trouvés à Boghaz-Köi*, Bordeaux.

LÆSSØE, J. 1959: *The Shemshāra Tablets. A Preliminary Report*, Kopenhagen.
LAMBERT, W. G. 1959: "The Sultantepe Tablets: A Review Article", *RA* 53, 119-138.
LEBRUN, R. 1980: *Hymnes et prières hittites*, Louvain-la-Neuve.
MERCER, S. A. B. 1961: *Assyrian Grammar with Chrestomathy and Glossary*, New York.
MORAN, W. L. 1992: *The Amarna Letters*, Baltimore and London.
NEU, E. 1980: *Althethitische Ritualtexte in Umschrift* (StBoT 25), Wiesbaden.
OTTEN, H. 1988: *Die Bronzetafel aus Boğazköy. Ein Staatsvertrag Tutḫalijas IV.* (StBoT Beiheft 1), Wiesbaden.
POPKO, M. 2007: "Althethitisch? Zu den Datierungsfragen in der Hethitologie", in D. Groddek and M. Zorman (eds.), *Tabularia Hethaeorum. Hethitologische Beiträge Silvin Košak zum 65. Geburtstag* (Dresdner Beitäge zur Hethitologie 25), 575-581.
PUHVEL, J. 1973: "Nature and Means of Comparison in Proto-Indo-European Grammar", *JIES* 1, 145-154.
RIEMSCHNEIDER, K. K. 1978: *An Akkadian Grammar*, translated by Th. A. Caldwell, J. N. Oswalt and J. F. X. Sheehan, S. J., Milwaukee (Wisconsin).
ROSENBERG, J. n.d.: *Assyrische Sprachlehre und Keilschriftkunde für das Selbststudium*, Leipzig.
RYCKMANS, G. 1938: *Grammaire accadienne* (Bibliothèque du Muséon 6), Louvain.
SCHOTT, A. 1926: *Die Vergleiche in den akkadischen Königsinschriften* (MVAG 30), Leipzig.
SCHWEMER, D. 2005-06: "Lehnbeziehungen zwischen dem Hethitischen und dem Akkadischen", *AfO* 51, 220-234.
SINGER, I. 2002: *Hittite Prayers*, Leiden – Boston – Köln.
SOMMER, F. 1947: *Hethiter und Hethitisch*, Stuttgart.
SOMMER, F. and FALKENSTEIN, A. 1938: *Die hethitisch-akkadische Bilingue des Ḫattušili I. (Labarna II.)*, München.
STRECK, M. P. 1998: "The Tense System in the Sumerian-Akkadian Linguistic Area", *Acta Sumerologica Japan* 20, 181-199.
— 1999: *Die Bildersprache der akkadischen Epik* (AOAT 264), Münster.
TALON, Ph. 2005: *The Standard Babylonian Creation Myth Enūma Eliš* (SAACT 4), Helsinki.
TISCHLER, J. 1981: *Das hethitische Gebet der Gassulijawija*, Innsbruck.
UNGNAD, A. 1906: *Babylonisch-Assyrische Grammatik mit Übungsbuch*, München.
UNGNAD, A. and MATOUŠ, L. 1969: *Grammatik des Akkadischen*, München.
VAN DEN HOUT, Th. 2009: "A Century of Hittite Text Dating and the Origins of the Hittite Cuneiform Script", *Incontri Linguistici* 32, 11-35.
VON SCHULER, E. 1956: "Die Würdenträgereide des Arnuwanda", *Or.* 25, 209-240.
VON SODEN, W. 1973: "Iterativa im Akkadischen und Hethitischen", in E. Neu and Ch. Rüster (eds.), *Festschrift Heinrich Otten*, Wiesbaden, 311-319.
— 1995: *Grundriss der akkadischen Grammatik.* 3., ergänzte Auflage unter Mitarbeit von W. R. Mayer, Roma.
WASSERMAN, N. 2003: *Style and Form in Old-Babylonian Literary Texts* (Cuneiform Monographs 27), Leiden – Boston.

WATKINS, C. 1970: "Studies in Indo-European Legal Language, Institutions, and Mythologie", in G. Cardona (ed.), *Indo-European and Indo-Europeans. Papers presented at the third Indo-European conference at the Univ. of Pennsylvania*, Philadelphia, 321-354.

YOSHIDA, D. 1987: *Die Syntax des althethitischen substantivischen Genitivs* (Texte der Hethiter 13), Heidelberg.

ZEILFELDER, S. 1998: "Steigern und Vergleichen im Hethitischen", in J. Prosecký (ed.), *Intellectual Life of the Ancient Near East. Papers Presented at the 43rd Rencontre assyriologique internationale Prague*, Prague, 475-482.

THE CHALDEANS THE LEADING PEOPLE IN BABYLONIAN HISTORY AND HISTORIOGRAPHY DURING THE FIRST HALF OF THE FIRST MILLENNIUM BCE[1]

Manfried DIETRICH
Westfälische Wilhelms-Universität, Münster

List of Contents

1. Introductory Remarks

Whenever the gentilic "Chaldeans" is mentioned, then we immediately think of the following two groups of people from ancient Babylonia: on the one hand, the rulers of the Neo-Babylonian kingdom (626-539 BCE) as the last indigenous dynasty of Mesopotamia, and on the other, in a figurative sense, the Babylonian scribes and priests of this period, who because of their outstanding expertise in magic, soothsaying and astrology,[2] acquired lasting fame.[3] In this paper I will attempt to trace the path taken

[1] An earlier draft of this study was read as a paper on January 24, 2011, during the 14th Annual Meeting of THE ISRAEL SOCIETY FOR ASSYRIOLOGY AND ANCIENT NEAR EASTERN STUDIES at the University of Haifa, Israel, under the auspices of Professor GERSHON GALIL. The topic of the 14th Annual Meeting was "History and Historiography in the Ancient Near East."

I extend my cordial thanks to my highly esteemed colleague and friend WILFRED G.E. WATSON (Northumberland) for his translation from German "Die Kaldäer — das führende Volk in der Geschichte und Geschichtsschreibung Babyloniens in der ersten Hälfte des ersten Jahrtausends v. Chr." and for his valuable comments.

[2] Edzard 1964, 1124:37-38; Edzard 1976-1980, 296-297: "hervorragende Kenntnisse in Magie, Wahrsagekunst, Astrologie und Astronomie".

[3] There is an erroneous reference in *Wikipedia* (*sub voce*) to the allegedly similarly pronounced name of the god *Haldu*, the god of the Urartian kingdom on Lake Van, the initial velar fricative /ḫ/ of which was represented by classical Greek writers also with a X ('Chi': "Chaldoi") like the voiced velar plosive at the beginning of Kaldu.

by the "Kaldu" tribe and its members the "Kaldāyū, Chaldeans", whom the Greek call Chaldaioi. This tribe gained during the first half of the first millennium BCE its well-known great cultural, economic and political importance. Once the Chaldeans had come to power, they became dominant over Babylonia and were able to transfer their name to those scholars and priests who, alongside the "*magi, magoi*", belonged to the most famous in the religious world of the ancient Near East.

As the Chaldeans were a significant factor of the history and supporters of the Mesopotamian culture in the first half of the first millennium BCE, it seems advisable to devote a fresh study to their gaining power and to their contribution to history and the writing down of history. Such a study is overdue, because in the course of the last decades the understanding of well-known texts and the publication of numerous new ones have promoted our insights in many ways into the importance of the Babylonian Chaldeans in their heyday.

I dedicate this study to my colleague and friend KAREL VAN LERBERGHE and hope, that he will find some of it's passages noteworthy.

In my exposition I intend to concentrate on the following topics:

- *The name, settlement area and ethnic classification of the Chaldeans* (point 2)
- *The Chaldeans in the period of the Neo-Assyrian Empire (9th-7th centuries BCE)* (point 3)
- *The "Chaldean Dynasty" and the Neo-Babylonian Empire (626-539 BCE)* (point 4) and
- *Outline of the essentials of Chaldean Religion and Culture* (point 5).

The paper then closes with thoughts on *The Chaldeans in History and Historiography* (point 6).

2. The name, settlement area and ethnic classification of the Chaldeans

2.1. *Name and ethnic classification*

To represent the name "Kaldu," the cuneiform texts without exception start from the sequence *kald-* — similarly they name the inhabitants of the settlement area, "Chaldeans":[4] using *māt*/KUR.*Kal-du*/*dù*/*di* (Kaldu),

[4] The basic forms such as *kašdu* (HAL 477b / HALOT 502a, see Koehler and Baumgartner 2004; Ges.[18] 576a — a hypothetically reconstructed form, based on the assumption

māt/KUR.*Ka-al-du* for the settlement area,[5] LÚ.*Kal-du*/*di* or LÚ.*Kal-da*/*dà-a-a* (Kaldayā) and LÚ.*Kal-da-nu*/*ni* (Kaldānu/i)[6] for the gentilic and ^{m}*Kal-da-a-a* (Kaldayā) for names of individuals from Kaldu.[7]

The base *kald-* is also presupposed by most of the later traditions: by the Greeks and Romans (for example, Herodotus, Hesychius, Berossus, Pliny[8]), and by Syrians, Babylonian Jews, Mandaeans, Palestinian Christians and Palmyrenes, with only few exceptions, whenever they mention "Babylonians" in general or members of a priestly class.[9]

This standardised tradition is in contrast to the gentilic *kaśdîm* (< **kesed*) in the Old Testament, which has the equivalent *Chaldaioi* in the Septuagint,[10] as well as South Arabian *kśdyyhn* (Ḥadramaut) and mediaeval Arabic *kasdaniyyun* — where the form *kaldaniyyun* also occurs.[11] This tradition indicates a basic form **kaś*/*sd-*, which could be connected with the root *KŚD "to reach, attack, conquer"[12] and could give the primarily geographically attested name possibly a concrete meaning: "raider".[13]

The co-existence of both the basic forms **kald-* and **kaś*/*sd-* suggests that the *l*/*ś*/*s-* interchange goes back to an attempt at representing the lateral fricative (ll^{s}l) of Proto-Semitic, as in "Arabic or at least one Arabic dialect",[14] for example. This in turn would allow us to consider how the root **kal*/*ś*/*sd-* fits into known Semitic languages and in addition to speculate about the original homeland of the Chaldeans.[15] Considerations of this kind must now be supplemented by also taking into account the original homeland of the Chaldeans as mentioned in relevant texts.

that the phoneme sequence *-ld-* could go back to a *-šd-* —; Google Wikipedia) or *Ḫal-du* (Saggs 2006, 157, 180) do not occur in the cuneiform texts (e.g. see Parpola 1970, 203 and 142-143; Zadok 1985a, 198-199 and 147; cf. Edzard 1976-1980, 296a).

5 Parpola 1970, 188-190; Zadok 1985a, 191-192; for its location see Parpola and Porter 2001, 10, 16 — cf. also the place-name URU.*Kal-di*: Zadok 1985a, 192.

6 Parpola 1970, 198-190; Zadok 1985a, 192.

7 Berlejung 2000, 599a.

8 See e.g. Edzard 1964, col. 1124; Edzard 1976-1980, 296-297 (with additional literature).

9 See e.g. Steiner 1977, 137; HAL 477b / HALOT 502a; Ges.^{18} 576a.

10 HAL 477-478 / HALOT 502a; Ges.^{18} 576.

11 See e.g. Brinkman 1968, 265; Steiner 1977, 137-138; Zadok 1985b, 49; on South Arabian *ks^{2}dyyhn* cf. also Keetman 2009, 373-374.

12 Akk. *kašādu* "erreichen, ankommen, erobern", AHw. 459-461 ["to reach, arrive; accomplish, conquer", CDA, 152a]; CAD K 271-284: "1. to reach, to arrive (said of a moment in time), to reach and equal in value.., 2. to conquer a country, a city, to defeat an enemy, to arrest a fugitive, a criminal, to surprise (in the act), so seize (said of diseases, evil spirits, misfortunes, etc.), to obtain a wish…"

13 Cf. Zadok 1985b, 49; Lipiński 2000, 418-419.

14 Keetman 2007, 372: "das Arabische oder zumindest ein arabischer Dialekt."

15 Steiner 1977, 137-143; Keetman 2007, 370-372.

The cuneiform texts prove that, at the beginning of the 9th century BCE, the area where the Chaldeans settled in this early time was in southeastern Mesopotamia.[16] From there they could have extended their sphere of influence towards the northwest, the Central and Northwestern parts of Babylonia. In the view of several scholars, this would fit considerations about the original language of the name **kal/ś/sd-* and indicate the original homeland of those bearing this name to be in the Arabian peninsula to the southeast of Mesopotamia as far as for instance Oman or the Yemen. Accordingly, the Chaldeans would have originated in Arabia and migrated from the southeast towards Mesopotamia.[17]

However, that would contradict the prevailing view that, before the end of the second millennium BCE, the Chaldeans were a branch of Aramaeans from Syria in the west who came to Mesopotamia. This is supported, on the one hand, by the fact that all the waves of immigration known from historical sources came from the northwest into southeastern Mesopotamia,[18] and on the other hand, that the linguistic elements of Chaldean personal names, the geographical names compounded with *bīt-*"House" and the words and grammatical constructions associated with them are close to Western Aramaic.[19]

Recently J. Keetman[20] has attempted to invalidate the "Arabia hypothesis", which depends not only on an early settlement area of the Chaldeans in southeastern Mesopotamia, but also on the existence of a lateral fricative (|l^{s}|), by proving that this lateral fricative, which presupposes the sound change *št* > *lt* in Babylonian — as is well known, this does not apply to Assyrian — can also be shown to exist in the northwest and can even be proved for the texts of Ebla at the end of the 3rd Millennium BCE. By migrating into Babylonian Mesopotamia, the Chaldeans themselves could have assisted a rapid spread of the sound change dependent on a lateral fricative, from the middle of the second millennium BCE, especially as this particular sound also occurs in their own name.[21]

With this hypothesis, in combination with other arguments in favor of the Chaldeans being more probably a branch of the Aramaeans of Syria

[16] See e.g. Brinkman 1968, 261-265; Lipiński 2000, 415, 421; Veenhof 2001, 209-211.

[17] Cf. Steiner 1977, 137-143, with previous literature; Saggs 2005, 157-158.

[18] Keetman 2007, 374: "Kanaanäer, Aramäer und Araber sind über Syrien nach Mesopotamien gekommen."

[19] Cf. e.g. Zadok 1985b, 53-54; Lipiński 2000, 418-419.

[20] Keetman 2007, especially 374-375; Keetman 2009, 461-464.

[21] The question as to whether or not the name *Kal/ś/sdu* has a specific meaning remains open.

— irrespective of whether in "secondary" or "primary" position[22] — than a branch of the Arabs, J. Keetman seems to have solved one of the most important problems of Mesopotamian history linguistically. For now there is no longer anything to make us deny that the Chaldeans, as generally accepted by ancient writers and scholars, had belonged to the northwest-semitic Aramaeans and reached Mesopotamia at the head of the only hazily tangible Aramaic wave of migration[23] — it is not possible to determine an exact date for their migration, but it must have taken place shortly after the middle of the second millennium BCE, at the latest, however, in the "crisis period of the 11th and 10th centuries BCE,"[24] i.e., several centuries before the first ever mention of "Arabs".

2.2. *Region of settlement*

As already pointed out, the first mention of the Chaldeans by the Assyrians can be dated to the year 878 BCE and goes back to the Annals of Assurnaṣirpal II (883-859). The reference informs about the "country Kaldu" (*māt*/KUR.*Kal-du*) and indicates that, in his time, the Chaldeans were already an established economic and political entity in southern Mesopotamia and that they lived, at least partly organized by *bīt*-Houses, in fortified towns.[25] The question as to why these Chaldean structures occur in the southeast and not, for instance, in central Babylonia or in areas lying even further to the west, which would reflect their migration route more faithfully, is easily answered: in the marshlands of the Tigris and Euphrates and on the almost inaccessible banks of the Great Lagoon (*māt Tâmti* "Sealand"), the newcomers were able to consolidate and to spread themselves out undisturbed. This was because, from the perspective of the Assyrian administration, they were located at the "end of the world." In addition, here the rough marshy landscape offered them natural protection — somehow comparable to Venitia — and in case of need their Elamite neighbors could give them political and military security also.

Over the centuries, the Chaldeans, while largely retaining tribal structures, had to a large extent adopted traditional urban Babylonian elements from the centers of culture with which they co-existed in direct contact.

[22] See Zadok 1985b, 54.
[23] Cf. Dietrich 1970, 5; Berger 1973, 1; Brinkman 1984, 12-13; Albertz 2001, 48.
[24] Veenhof 2001, 211: "Krisenzeit des 11. und 10. Jahrhunderts v. Chr."
[25] Zadok 1985b, 49-63: list of villages of the "chaldäischen Territorien [Chaldean territories]."

This also meant that soon they appeared to be quite strongly "Babylonized": they readily adopted Babylonian names, fostered Babylonian language and culture, set up territories using Babylonian models of administration and authority — and devoted themselves to long-distance trade, agriculture and livestock farming.[26] In this way though, they had acquired a lifestyle that was clearly different from that of their fellow tribesmen on the land, so that a clear co-existence of "Chaldeans" and "Aramaeans" had developed.[27] In addition, this has meant that, according to the relevant sources from the time of the closing stages of the Neo-Assyrian Empire, the concept "Aramaeans" (LÚ.*A-ra-mu*) had exchanged its primarily ethnic connotation for one that is social.[28]

3. The Chaldeans in the Neo-Assyrian Empire period (9th-7th centuries BCE)

J.A. Brinkman divides the Chaldeans living in southern Mesopotamia into tribes, each named after a tribal ancestor. They lived in districts and were assigned a leader who had his own governor's residence:[29]

> "*Each Chaldean tribe is referred to as the 'House of PN' (Bīt-PN), with the PN standing for the name of the eponymous ancestor; and each tribe seems to have been governed by a single ruler. For members of the tribe, tribal affiliation was usually indicated in the form PN 'son' of* PN_2*, with* PN_2 *standing for the eponymous tribal ancestor rather than the person's real father.*"

For the period of the Neo-Assyrian Empire, the following five Chaldean tribal districts can be named, which were probably the largest and most important — from north to south:

- Bīt-Dakūri in central Babylonia with the governor's residence in Borsippa;
- Bīt-Šīlāni and Bīt-Ša'alli in central Babylonia;
- Bīt-Aw/mukāni in south Babylonia with the governor's residences in Uruk, Šapīya and Šamēlē;
- Bīt-Jakīni, also called *māt Tâmti* "Sealand", in south Babylonia on the Great Lagoon, with the governor's residences in Ur and Nagītu.[30]

[26] E.g. Brinkman 1968, 260-261; Brinkman 1984, 15; Frame 1992, 36-38; Veenhof 2001, 211-212.

[27] Cf. Brinkman 1977, 306; Frame 1992, 45; Lipiński 2000, 414-416.

[28] See e.g. Zadok 1985a, 27; Lipiński 2000, 417-418; Albertz 2001, 48; cf. Dion 1995, 1286.

[29] Brinkman 1977, 306; cf. Dion 1995, 1286.

[30] See e.g. Dietrich 1970, 5, on its location: folding map; Edzard 1976-80, 293; Brinkman 1977, 306; Brinkman 1984, 14-15; Zadok 1985b, 49-63, with details of the fortified towns; Lipiński 2000, 419.

The Houses of this region were independent and together with their hinterland were able to become an increasingly significant economic, political and military power.

On the one hand, the Chaldean leaders (*ra'šānu* "leader, headman") often directed their attention to fighting each other and on the other hand, kept an eye on the Assyrian central power when it was forced to ignore Babylonia due to other problems. To enhance their fighting ability, the Chaldeans then formed anti-Assyrian alliances, which never enjoyed a sustained success. Copious examples of this could be given from the reigns of the Sargonid kings Esarhaddon and Assurbanipal, the most important of which are the following three:

1. In the battle of Ḫalulê in 693, Nabûšumiškun, a son of the Jakīnite Merodachbaladan II (721-710, 703), led a coalition of Babylonians, Chaldeans, Aramaeans and Elamites against Sennacherib. The Assyrian king was able to decide on the outcome of the conflict.[31]
2. A conspiracy in central and southern Babylonia, mounted by Ṣillāya during the turmoil over the succession after the murder of Sennacherib in 680, which Esarhaddon was only able to put down with difficulty in 675.[32]
3. A conspiracy by Sāsî of Ḫarrān in ca. 671, which must have been connected with the conspiracy by Ṣillāya and was part of the inner-political turmoil that Esarhaddon had provoked by naming Assurbanipal as crown prince.[33]

Anti-Assyrian activities, like the ones mentioned, frequently originated from Bīt-Jakīni/*māt Tâmti*,[34] as here the conspirators were backed by Elam and the Assyrians only rarely penetrated so far to the southeast.

When the opportunity arose, the Chaldean leaders also sided with a ruler residing in Babylon and together with him — possibly with additional allies from east of the Tigris and from Elam — formed a coalition. Examples of this are the battle of Dūr-Papsukkal against Šamšī-Adad V (823-810) in 814,[35] the battle of Halulê against Sennacherib

[31] See Dietrich 1970, 11-12; Brinkman 1977, 316 (with a misunderstanding); cf. Brinkman 1984, 63; Frame 1992, 61-62; Mayer 1995, 370-372; for an indirect reference to the battle see also Parpola 2002, 571-576.

[32] See Dietrich 1970, 39-49; cf. Frame 1992, 84-90; Brinkman 1984, 20.

[33] Dietrich 1970, 50-57; Frame 1992, 86. 99. 101; Nissinen 1998, 135-151; cf. Frahm 2010, 125-126.

[34] Cf. Brinkman 1984, 23-25.

[35] See e.g. Brinkman 1968, 207-210; Edzard 1976-80, 294-295.

(704-681) in 691, already mentioned, or the so-called fratricidal war between Assurbanipal (668-627) and Šamaššumukīn (668-648) in 652-648[36] — a war in which the Chaldean leader Nabû-bēl-šumāti, a son of Merodachbaladan II (721-710, 703), was the most important ally of Šamaššumukīn and so also a forerunner of the later Neo-Babylonian empire.

From time to time, the leaders of Chaldean Houses were able to combine so much power that they even set themselves up as "Kings of Babylonia" against the Assyrians — the most important were: Marduk-apla-uṣur (?-774),[37] Erība-Marduk (ca. 773-761),[38] Marduk-apla-iddina (Merodachbaladan) II (721-710, 703) from Bīt-Jakīni,[39] Nabû-šum-iškun (ca. 760-748)[40] and Mušēzib-Marduk (692-689) from Bīt-Dakūri[41] and (Nabû-)Mukīn-zēri (731-729) from Bīt-Aw/mukāni.[42]

4. The "Chaldean-Dynasty" and the Neo-Babylonian Empire (626-539)

The power of Assyria faded away during the reign of Assurbanipal (668-ca. 627) and left the way open to their increasingly powerful neighbors in the east (Medes, Persians) and southeast. Here, after their leader Nabû-bēl-šumāti clashed with Assurbanipal and his army, the Chaldeans from the House of Bīt-Jakīni and the *māt Tâmti* "Sealand" no longer wished to loose their influence over events in Babylonia: in 626, the army commander Nabopolassar from the same House, probably a descendant of Merodachbaladan II,[43] after initial difficulties, ascended the throne of Babylon and founded the "Neo-Babylonian Empire". This was also simplified to the "Chaldee-Empire", after the tribal affiliation of the ruler:[44] Nabopolassar (Nabû-apla-uṣur: 626-605) was followed by Nebuchadnezzar

[36] See e.g. Dietrich 1970, 78-119; Edzard 1976-80, 294-295; Brinkman 1984, 93-104; Frame 1992, 131-190; Mayer 1995, 405-407; Veenhof 2001, 273-274.

[37] Brinkman 1968, 215; Brinkman 1989, 37; Edzard 1976-80, 294-295.

[38] Brinkman 1968, 220-224; Brinkman 1989, 37-38 (44-46: the ethnic classification of named persons on the basis of their names is more than problematic); Edzard 1976-80, 294-295; Lipiński 2000, 422.

[39] Brinkman 1964; Dietrich 1970, 10-11; Edzard 1976-80, 294-295; Mayer 1995, 321-341; Lipiński 2000, 422; Veenhof 2001, 212.

[40] Brinkman 1968, 224-226; Edzard 1976-80, 294-295; Lipiński 2000, 422.

[41] Dietrich 1970, 12; Edzard 1976-80, 294-295; Lipiński 2000, 422.

[42] Brinkman 1968, 235-240; Brinkman 1984, 22-23; Lipiński 2000, 422.

[43] Mayer 1995, 413.

[44] According to Beaulieu 1995, 969, this period is better called the "Neo-Babylonian Dynasty or Empire" than the "Chaldean Dynasty". For "*this label is derived from a misunderstanding of classical authors, who used it as a synonym for 'Babylonian'*" — on

(Nabû-kudurrī-uṣur II: 605-562), Amēl-Marduk (562-560), Neriglissar (Nergal-šarra-uṣur: 559-556), Lābāši-Marduk (556) and Nabonidus (Nabû-na'id: 556-539).[45]

Essentially, the Chaldean leaders could fall back on two inherited elements for the construction of the "Neo-Babylonian Empire": on the one hand, an efficient administration and the battle-tried army of Assyria and on the other, a thousand-year-old Babylonian culture. The first was gifted to them by the shared victory over Assyria, when they employed the experienced Assyrian government officials and commanding officers. With their help they were able to extend and stabilize their empire in a few years from the *māt Tâmti* "Sealand" as far as the Nile delta.[46] The rulers of the Neo-Babylonian Empire took over the legacy of Sumero-Babylonian culture (language and literature) and continued the promotion of the Babylonian educational centers that had grown over numerous generations.

Here it must be stressed that the take-over of Sumero-Babylonian culture is not to be connected only with the start of the reign of the first Chaldean king Nabopolassar. Rather, it had already begun quite a few centuries earlier, when for example the Chaldeans Marduk-apla-uṣur or Erība-Marduk at the beginning of the 8th century BCE for a short time held the Babylonian throne. It is important to keep this in mind in order to answer numerous questions on the religious and cultural effect of Babylonia on the Chaldeans.

5. Outline of the Essentials of Chaldean Religion and Culture

After their migration to southern Mesopotamia, the more the Chaldeans, identified themselves with the culture of their new surroundings and settled down in the traditional centers there, the more difficult it is for us modern onlookers, by examining the macro-syntax, to describe what may be typical of Chaldean religion, its gods and its culture. The following facts provide examples of the readiness of the Chaldeans to adjust to the Babylonian world: The ascent to the throne of both rulers Marduk-apla-uṣur and Erība-Marduk, who ruled briefly in the 8th century BCE, must be considered as the result of a long process of integration which it seems

this cf. also Da Riva 2008, 1-2. As yet, not a single instance has been found where, Nabopolassar, for example, is called a "Chaldean".

45 See e.g. Sack 1972, 2-23 (with a list of classical, mediaeval and Hebrew sources); Sack 1994, 1-22; Brinkman 1998, 15; Da Riva 2008, 2-18.

46 See e.g. Veenhof 2001, 278-280; Mayer 1995, 417.

must have begun already before the end of the second millennium BCE. For it cannot be proved that they were usurpers.[47]

In the Sargonid century (end of the 8th to the end of the 7th century BCE) the Chaldeans were so closely connected with the ancient and venerable Sumero-Babylonian culture, that today it is scarcely possible to recognize whether the tradition of the formative centers and the teaching and god-lists transmitted in the theological schools from that period, originated with the old established "Babylonians" or already with the "Chaldeans".[48] Perhaps, from many aspects it would be better to stop differentiating elements of religion and culture of the 8th/7th centuries BCE into "Babylonian" and "Chaldean" and use instead the dual concept of "Babylo-Chaldean". In the process, the emphasis would be on the descriptive adjective "Babylo", i.e. "Babylonian", representing traditional Sumero-Babylonian culture. The co-ordinate adjective "Chaldean" would then be secondary, especially in scholarly discussion today where, unlike making outlines of lexical, grammatical and stylistic "Aramaisms," understanding Aramaic religious and cultural ideas is strongly neglected. But even in respect of philological "Aramaisms," it would be important to speak here of "Chaldo-Aramaisms," since most so-called "Aramaisms" are clearly "Chaldaisms."

In respect of West-Aramaic influences on language,[49] to be found not only in the texts of daily life, in letters and documents, but also in hymns and epic literature, no less important questions also arise about the poem *Enūma elîš*,[50] e.g.: when was it composed and what was its spiritual home?[51] In spite of the steadily increasing influence of Aramaic,[52] even at the time of Nabonidus (556-539), — the last ruler of the "Chaldean Dynasty" — and of Cyrus II (ca. 559-530) — the first ruler of the Achaemenids — the literati of Babylonia were quite able to put together and compose a work such as *Enūma elîš* based on a reliably transmitted tradition.[53]

[47] Brinkman 1968, 220-224.

[48] Cf. e.g. Brinkman 1968, 265-266; Dietrich 1970, 5; also 2.2. above.

[49] Cf. Beaulieu 1995, 969: "Chaldean West-Semitic-speaking tribe".

[50] New comprehensive edition: Kämmerer and Metzler 2012.

[51] Dietrich 2006, 160-161, where reasons are given for the thesis that *Enūma elîš* can be considered as a work of the court theologians of Merodachbaladan II on the occasion of his enthronement in Babylon.

[52] See e.g. von Soden 1995: §2h: "babylonisch-aramäische Mischsprache"; Streck 1995, XXIV; Da Riva 2008, 89-91.

[53] Cf. Schaudig 2001, 315-317.

It is almost impossibly difficult for research scholars to make an outline of the Chaldo-Aramaic religious concepts[54] in the Sumero-Akkadian literature from the extensive libraries of Mesopotamia in the first millennium BCE because of the macro syntactic facts. This because the adoption of traditional Sumero-Babylonian language and literature in the course of the first half of the first millennium BCE has overlaid a genuine Chaldean understanding of religion and cult so intensively that only weak traces of it are available. As an example, one can refer to the fact that Nabonidus devoted himself to the cult of the god Sîn of Ḫarrān, which is to be linked with a thousand-year-old ancient cult of the moon of the Arameans. [55]

The points set out above make it clear why traditional Sumero-Babylonian culture and their scholarly works on language and literature, astronomy, mathematics, science and religion could be labeled "Chaldean" by posterity.

6. The Chaldeans in History and Historiography

The aim of the first three topics of the foregoing considerations — "*The Name, settlement area and ethnic classification of the Chaldeans*", "*The Chaldeans in the period of the Neo-Assyrian Empire (9th-7th centuries BCE)*" and "*The 'Chaldean-Dynasty' and the Neo-Babylonian Empire (626-539 BCE)*" — was to show the rise of the West-Aramaic Chaldeans from a shadowy existence during the period of the Neo-Assyrian Empire (beginning of the 9th to the end of 7th century BCE) to their seizure and display of power in the Neo-Babylonian Empire (end of the 7th to the mid-6th century BCE).

In the next section — "*Outline of the Essentials of Chaldean Religion and Culture*" — it should be imagined that after their migration to south and southeast Babylonia, the Chaldeans were so closely connected with the indigenous Sumero-Babylonian culture there, that today it is hardly possible to determine whether the numerous literary works composed during the Neo-Babylonian Empire from the knowledge acquired by traditional Babylonian centers of education and by scholars,[56] were written

[54] Cf. e.g. Lipiński 2000, 599-640.

[55] Cf. Lipiński 2000, 620-623; also Mayer 1998, 257-261.

[56] See the collections and monographs: for works from the period of the Neo-Assyrian empire e.g. Frame 1995 — for works from the Neo-Babylonian empire, for example, Grayson 1975, Borger 1984, Sack 1972, Sack 1994, Millard 1997, Schaudig 2001 and Weippert 2010; here the survey in Da Riva 2008 is particularly informative.

by established "Babylonians," or whether they are the products of a symbiosis of Babylonian and Chaldean ("Babylo-Chaldean") scholars. Unlike research into philological questions, research into macro-syntax from the aspect of literature is still at a very early stage.

From all this, it should now be clear that in the first half of the first millennium BCE, the Chaldeans in conjunction with the Babylonians were a significant factor for the development of the history and culture of Babylonia. At all times, their rulers were very interested in promoting the writing down of history. In this way, court theologians and historians could justify their masters' right to rule in the sight of their contemporaries and at the same time, more or less intentionally, create for themselves a lasting name in the afterworld.

Bibliography

ALBERTZ, R. 2001: *Die Exilszeit 6. Jahrhundert v. Chr.* (Biblische Enzyklopädie 7), Stuttgart.

BEAULIEU, P.-A. 1995: "King Nabonidus and the Babylonian Empire", in J. M. Sasson (ed.) *Civilizations of the Ancient Near East I-II*, Peabody MA, 969-979.

BERGER, P.-R. 1973: *Die neubabylonischen Königsinschriften. Königsinschriften des ausgehenden babylonischen Reiches (626-539 a. Chr.)* (AOAT 4/1), Kevelaer – Neukirchen-Vluyn.

BERLEJUNG, A. 2000: "Kaldāiu ('Chaldean')", in S. Parpola (ed.) *The Prosopography of the Neo-Assyrian Empire. Vol. 2/1*, Helsinki, 599.

BORGER, R. 1984: "Historische Texte in akkadischer Sprache aus Babylonien und Assyrien", in O. Kaiser (ed.) *Historisch-chronologische Texte I.* (Texte aus der Umwelt des Alten Testaments I/4), Gütersloh, 354-409.

BRINKMAN, J. A. 1964: "Merodach-Baladan II", in *Studies Presented to A. Leo Oppenheim*, Chicago, 6-53.

— 1968: *A Political History of Post-Kassite Babylonia 1158-722 B.C.* (AnOr 43), Roma.

— 1977: "Notes an Arameans and Chaldeans in Southern Babylonia in the Early Seventh Century B.C.", *Or.* 46, Roma, 304-325.

— 1984: *Prelude to Empire. Babylonian Society and Politics, 747-626 B.C.* (Occasional Publications of the Babylonian Fund 7), Philadelphia.

— 1989: "A Legal Text from the Reign of Erība-Marduk (c. 755 B.C.)", in H. Behrens et al. (eds.) *DUMU-E$_2$-DUB-BA-A. Studies in Honor of Åke W. Sjöberg* (Occasional Publications of the Samuel Noah Kramer Fund 11), Philadelphia, 37-47.

— 1998: "Nabopolassar", *RlA* 9, 12-16.

DA RIVA, R. 2008: *The Neo-Babylonian Royal Inscriptions. An Introduction* (Guides to the Mesopotamian Textual Record 4), Münster.

DIETRICH, M. 1970: *Die Aramäer Südbabyloniens in der Sargonidenzeit (700-648)* (AOAT 7), Kevelaer – Neukirchen-Vluyn.

— 2006: "Das *Enūma eliš* als mythologischer Grundtext für die Identität der Marduk-Religion Babyloniens", in M. Dietrich and T. Kulmar (eds.) *The Significance of Base Texts for the Religious Identity* (Forschungen zur Anthropologie und Religionsgeschichte 40), Münster, 135-163.

DION, P.E. 1995: "Aramaean Tribes and Nations of First-Millennium Western Asia", in J. M. Sasson (ed.) *Civilizations of the Ancient Near East I-II*, Peabody MA, 1281-1294.

EDZARD, D.O. 1964: "Chaldaia, -oi", *Der Kleine Pauly. Lexikon der Antike* 1, 1123-1124.

— 1976-1980: "Kaldu (Chaldäer)", *RlA* 5, 291-297.

FRAHM, E. 2010: "Hochverrat in Assur", in S. M. Maul and N. P. Heeßel (eds.) *Assur-Forschungen. Arbeiten aus der Forschungsstelle »Edition literarischer Keilschrifttexte aus Assur« der Heidelberger Akademie der Wissenschaften*, Wiesbaden, 89-137.

FRAME, G. 1992: *Babylonia 689-627 B.C. A Political History* (Publications de l'Institut historique-archéologique néerlandais de Stamboul 69), Leiden.

— 1995: *Rulers of Babylonia From the Second Dynasty of Isin to the End of Assyrian Domination (1157-612 BC)* (RIMB 2), Toronto.

GRAYSON, A. K. 1975: *Assyrian and Babylonian Chronicles* (TCS 5), Glückstadt – Locust Valley NY.

KÄMMERER, Th. R. and K. A. Metzler 2012: *Das babylonische Weltschöpfungsepos Enūma elîš* (AOAT 375), Münster.

KEETMAN, J. 2007: "Wann und warum sprach man im Akkadischen einen Lateralfrikativ?", *UF* 38, 363-378.

— 2009: "Die Triade der Laterale und ihre Veränderungen in den älteren semitischen Sprachen", *UF* 41, 449-469.

KOEHLER, L. and W. BAUMGARTNER 2004^3: *Hebräisches und aramäisches Lexikon zum Alten Testament* (HALOT), Leiden – Boston.

LIPIŃSKI, E. 2000: *The Arameans. Their Ancient History, Culture, Religion* (OLA 100), Leuven.

MAYER, W. 1995: *Politik und Kriegskunst der Assyrer* (Abhandlungen zur Literatur Alt-Syrien-Palästinas und Mesopotamiens 9), Münster.

— 1998: "Nabonids Herkunft", in M. Dietrich and O. Loretz (eds.) *dubsar anta-men. Studien zur Altorientalistik. Festschrift für Willem H.Ph. Römer* (AOAT 253), Münster, 245-261.

MILLARD, A. 1997: "Historiography", in Hallo, W. W. (ed.) *The Context of Scripture. Vol. I. Canonical Compositions from the Biblical World*, Leiden – et al.

NISSINEN, M. 1998: *References to Prophecy in Neo-Assyrian Sources* (SAAS 7), Helsinki.

PARPOLA, S. 1970: *Neo-Assyrian Toponyms* (AOAT 6), Kevelaer – Neukirchen-Vluyn.

— 2002: "A Letter to Sennacherib Referring to the Conquest of Bit-Ha'iri and Other Events of the Year 693", in O. Loretz et al. (eds.) *Ex Mesopotamia et Syria Lux. Festschrift für Manfried Dietrich* (AOAT 281), Münster, 559-580.

PARPOLA, S. and M. PORTER 2001: *The Helsinki Atlas of the Near East in the Neo-Assyrian Period*, Helsinki.

SACK, R. H. 1972: *Amēl-Marduk 562-560 B.C. A Study based on Cuneiform, Old Testament, Greek, Latin and Rabbinical Sources. With Plates* (Orient und Altes Testament. Sonderreihe 4), Kevelaer – Neukirchen-Vluyn.

— 1994: *Neriglissar—King of Babylon* (AOAT 236), Kevelaer – Neukirchen-Vluyn.

SAGGS, H. W. F. 2005: *Völker im Lande Babylon*, Stuttgart.

SCHAUDIG, H. 2001: *Die Inschriften Nabonids von Babylon und Kyros' des Großen samt den in ihrem Umfeld entstandenen Tendenzschriften. Textausgabe und Grammatik* (AOAT 256), Münster.

STEINER, R.C. 1977: *The Case for Fricative-Laterals in Proto-Semitic* (AOS 59), New Haven CO.

STRECK, M.P. 1995: *Zahl und Zeit. Grammatik der Numeralia und des Verbalsystems im Spätbabylonischen* (Cuneiform Monographs 5), Groningen.

VEENHOF, K. R. 2001: *Geschichte des Alten Orients bis zur Zeit Alexanders des Großen* (Das Alte Testament Deutsch, Ergänzungsreihe 11), Göttingen.

VON SODEN, W. 1995[3]: *Grundriss der akkadischen Grammatik* (AnOr 33), Roma.

WEIPPERT, M. 2010: *Historisches Textbuch zum Alten Testament* (Grundrisse zum Alten Testament Das Alte Testament Deutsch, Ergänzungsreihe 10), Göttingen.

ZADOK, R. 1985a: *Geographical Names According to New- and Late-Babylonian Texts* (Répertoire géographique des textes cunéiformes 8), Wiesbaden.

— 1985b: "Zur Geographie Babyloniens während des sargonidischen, chaldäischen, achämenidischen und hellenistischen Zeitalters", *WO* 16, 19-79.

VENGEANCE D'UN EXILÉ[*]

Jean-Marie DURAND
Collège de France et École Pratique des Hautes-Études, Paris

La tablette M.11495 se présente banalement comme le fragment bas d'une tablette, assez bien conservé mais pour lequel aucun joint n'a encore été réalisé. Il appartenait vraisemblablement à une lettre envoyée depuis Babylone au roi de Mari par un de ses envoyés, militaire, diplomate ou missionnaire épisodique qui avait été en contact direct avec le roi Hammu-rabi de Babylone. Il est possible que l'auteur en ait été Ibâl-pî-El, si à la l. 11' il faut lire *a-tù-ra-am* et non *a-du-ra-am* (*âduram*) (et *ri-iš*$_{15}$*-dú-um* et non *re-eš-tu-um* à la l. 16') car l'interversion de notation des sourdes et des sonores est une des caractéristiques les plus marquées de ce personnage[1] et l'emploi du verbe *târum* est ici attendu.

Le texte a pu être revu au musée de Dêr ez-Zôr et de bonnes photographies (cf. illustration jointe) en être prises en septembre 2009.

Tel quel le document, malgré son état fragmentaire, suffit pour nous renseigner sur beaucoup d'aspects de cette société de l'époque amorrite, sa mobilité et le jeu des grandes puissances de l'époque. J'espère que sa publication dans les présents *Mélanges* serviront à honorer un savant dont les recherches se sont déroulées sur un territoire à proximité immédiate de celui où l'inconnu guti avait trouvé refuge.

M.11495

(…)
[*i-n*]*a-an-na a-wa-tum ši-i a-he-*⸢*et*⸣
2' ^{I}*ha-am-mu-ra-bi ki-a-am iq-bé um-ma-a-mi*
1 lú gal mar-tu *ša* lugal *qú-ti-im*^{ki}
4' *ša i-na ba-ma-at* èš-nun-na^{ki} *ma-as-sú*
ša-ak-na-at iš-tu mu 3-kam

* Merci à Michaël Guichard, Dominique Charpin et Lionel Marti pour leur relecture de cet article.

[1] D. Charpin qui doit donner une édition des lettres d'Ibâl-pî-El en mission à Babylone, me signale d'autre part le texte inédit de Mari A.192 où Ibâl-pî-El parle de «l'entrée de 3 rois des Gutis à Ešnunna», ce qui montrerait une situation analogue à celle de notre document concernant les rapports entre Ešnunna et le Gutium.

6' *a-na* èš-nun-na^{ki} *ha-pí-ir*
i-na-an- *na*
8' *a-na* sukkal elam-ma *a-wa-tim*
uš-te-pí-iš-ma um-ma-a-mi lu-ul-li-ik
10' *ù ki-a-am lu-uq-bi um-ma a-na-ku-ma*
be-lí ù ma-a-ti ah-sú-ús-ma a-tù-ra-[*am*]
12' *an-ni-tam lu-uq-bi ù iš-te*$_9$*-et lu-pu-úš*
an-ni-tam uš-te-pí-iš-ma lú *šu-ú a-na ma-ti-šu*
14' *it-ta-la-ak i-na a-lim*^{ki} *ša ik-šu-du* lugal *ul* [*w*]*a-*[*ši-i*]*b*
[*b*]*e-el-šu ú-ul wa-ši-ib i-mu-ur-ma ki-ma be-*⸢*el*⸣*-šu*
16' [*ú-u*]*l*° *wa-aš-bu a-na ṣa-bi-im* elam-ma *ša* ⸢*ri*⸣*-iš*$_{15}$*-dú-u*[*m*]
[*qé-er-bu i*]*š*[2]*-pu-ur-ma* 3 *a-la-*[*ni iš-l*]*u-ul-*⸢*ma*⸣
18' [*ù ša-al-l*]*a*$^{?}$*-tu-um ša qú-*[*ti-im*^{ki} *ša i-tab-l*]*am*$^{?}$
[…… *a-n*]*a pa-ni-š*[*u*…
(…)

«(…) Maintenant cette affaire est vraiment étrange.»
Hammu-rabi a dit ceci: «1 général du roi du Gutium dont le 'pays' s'était installé dans la plaine d'Ešnunna, se trouvait émigré (*hapir*) depuis 3 ans à Ešnunna. Or voici qu'il a adressé un discours artificieux à l'Empereur d'Élam en lui disant: 'Je vais aller en tenant ce discours: 'J'ai repensé à mon seigneur et à mon pays mais je reviendrai (*aturram*).' Voilà ce que je vais dire. En fait, je veux tenter un coup!»
Ayant tenu ce discours artificieux, cet homme est parti pour son pays. Le roi ne se trouvait pas dans la ville qu'il atteignit; son seigneur ne s'y trouvait pas. Il vit que son seigneur était absent. Il envoya un message(r) à des soldats élamites dont *un établissement*[3] *était proche*; il a pillé 3 villages. Alors, le butin sur le Gutium qu'il avait emporté, ... par devers lui...[4]

Lorsque le texte commence quelqu'un, sans doute l'expéditeur de la lettre, termine un discours par une phrase difficile à situer: soit Hammu-rabi fournit un exemple de ce qui vient de lui être dit au moyen de l'anecdote qu'il rapporte, soit il donne des précisions à sa disposition au sujet de ce qui vient de lui être raconté.

[2] On ne voit pas les deux perpendiculaires caractéristiques du IŠ, mais [...*š*]*u-pu-ur* serait difficile à utiliser et pour ce qui est d'un IŠ il est vraisemblable que la surface n'a pas été suffisamment nettoyée.

[3] La lecture matérielle semble assez sûre mais il est difficile de faire quelque chose de /reštum/ ou /reštûm/. J'ai donc postulé que l'on ait ici un terme, inattesté il est vrai, de **rišdum*, à partir de RŠD, et qui désignerait un établissement (militaire en l'occurrence) pérenne ou au moins fortifié fortement.

[4] La fin de l'histoire se devine plus qu'elle ne se laisse restaurer sûrement paléographiquement. Il est vraisemblable que la découverte du joint donnera la version définitive.

Le Gutium, soit la région du Zagros, était un endroit avec lequel les grandes monarchies de la plaine avaient des liens relativement étroits: tant Ekallâtum que Babylone ont contracté des alliances matrimoniales avec ses rois, et il est vraisemblable qu'elles avaient des apparentements avec eux[5].

Le présent texte montre un «général», gal mar.tu, du Gutium venir s'installer dans les «plaines d'Ešnunna». Il est dommage que nous ne connaissions pas mieux la situation historique du document parce que ce *bamât Išnunak* pourrait désigner l'état d'abandon du royaume d'Ešnunna tel qu'il est détruit lorsque les Élamites l'évacuèrent. On nous parle effectivement alors du grand nombre de villes détruites de ce royaume[6], au moins pour sa partie orientale, limitrophe de l'Élam, et ce «vide» pouvait inciter d'autres à venir s'y établir. C'est, semble-t-il, ce qui s'est passé pour la partie Nord, en ce qui concerne les Bédouins mâr sim'al de Haute-Djéziré, les Yabasa, qui ont poussé de plus en plus vers l'Est jusqu'à occuper la région du Zâb et couper les relations entre Babylone et le Zagros, ce qui n'a pas dû que peu contribuer à l'attaque de Babylone contre Mari[7].

Il est, en effet, étonnant de voir dans ce texte l'absence complète de mention d'un pouvoir ešnunnéen, alors que la seule référence politique semble y être celle de l'Élam. Ce serait donc une anecdote qui nous renseignerait sur les menées élamites sur sa frontière occidentale dans une région au delà des perspectives mariotes, notre seule véritable source de renseignements pour l'époque.

Le «pays» du gal mar-tu se trouve «installé» (*šaknat*). Il s'agit de gens sédentarisés et à demeure. M. Guichard me suggère de comprendre que l'exilé vient en fait rejoindre des contribules (*mâtum*) car les *hapirum* ne s'exilent pas n'importe où, donnant la préférence aux endroits où se trouve de la famille à eux. On le voit bien par l'exemple d'Idrimi dont les frères rejoignent la fratrie[8], puis qui se dirige vers une ville où se trouvent plusieurs réfugiés du royaume d'Alep[9]. Le *mâtum* en question serait donc antérieur à l'établissement du chef guti en exil.

Le verbe employé est en effet *šakânum* qui indique l'installation durable, à l'opposition de *sakânum* réservé aux installations temporaires, comme celles des nomades ou des troupeaux. Un tel terme est, dans ce

5 Cf. Durand à venir.
6 *ARM* XXVI/2 373: 23.
7 Pour cette reconstruction historique, cf. Durand 2004, 144-145.
8 Pour le sens à attribuer à *ahhatum* dans ce texte, cf. Durand 2010, 114.
9 Cf. *ibid.*, p. 116.

contexte, très intéressant. Hammu-rabi, roi de Babylone, emploie un mot akkadien qui correspond à ce qui se dirait *lîmum* (*li'mum*) ou, en l'occurrence, *gâyum* à Mari et qui unit les notions de peuplement et de conscription, *nîšûtum* ou *bîtum* étant en revanche des termes réservés pour de simples individus. On voit bien par Mari que la conscription des Bédouins ou des populations mal ou récemment sédentarisées comme les Mâr sim'al *yabasa* ou *ašarugâyu* s'opère avec leurs autorités tribales pour les encadrer. De la même façon, lorsqu'un chef va s'installer comme roi, il amène avec lui tout un ensemble humain qui est, en revanche, susceptible de s'en aller avec lui lorsqu'il renonce à son établissement[10]. Ici, quelque soit le nombre de ceux que le général a entraînés avec lui, il faut supposer que des «colonies gutis», ou au moins des communautés de cette ethnie, préexistaient à son exil au royaume d'Ešnunna. On n'en connaît pas l'ancienneté: elles peuvent dater de l'époque où la population du royaume se raréfiait.

En l'occurrence le chef militaire du Guti'um se voit qualifié de *hapirum*. Il faut dès lors comprendre que son départ de chez lui a eu des raisons politiques, trois ans avant l'événement relaté. La documentation de Mari montre en abondance que la notion de *hapirum* est d'abord politique[11]. Que cet individu ait été chassé avec son clan entre encore dans la thématique mariote. Il faut ajouter que, les «généraux» appartenant volontiers à la famille royale, on ne peut exclure qu'il y ait eu localement une lutte pour le pouvoir qui ait mal tourné pour l'exilé. Il n'a cependant pas le titre de *mâdarum*, ce qui serait le cas s'il se posait en challenger d'un roi. Rien ne nous dit ce qui a pu se passer puisque tous les protagonistes sont anonymes mais on connaissait déjà l'existence de *hapirum* originaires du Zagros par *ARM* XXII **153+170** et plusieurs de ces *hapirum* possèdent d'ailleurs une onomastique non-sémitique, voire franchement hourritophone[12]. Il a dû y avoir dans le Zagros de grands troubles locaux qui se sont réglés de la même façon que dans la Haute-Djéziré au sujet de laquelle nous sommes bien mieux informés.

Le rêve de tous les *hapirum* a été de revenir chez soi en triomphateurs. On a l'exemple cependant d'Idrimi qui, en exil à Emar, revient dans son pays pour y fonder une principauté dans la partie occidentale de l'ancien

[10] Cf. la relecture de A.751 dans Marti 2002, 541-543.

[11] Cf. Durand 2004-2005, 563-584.

[12] = *ARM* XXX, 301. Il s'agit de 7 Turukkéens, qualifiés de *hapirum*. Des NP comme Parhen-adal, Pardip-šarri, Arip-Pizaiš peuvent avoir été des hourritophones, mais des gens comme Ibâl-Samsî ou Šamaš-rabi doivent avoir été des sémitophones. Ils forment pourtant les uns et les autres un groupe unitaire.

royaume du Yamhad autour d'Alalah[13]. Dans le cas présent, le retour du général est sous le signe de la vengeance pure. Il est d'ailleurs taxé de roublardise (*šûtepušum*) dès l'abord par Hammu-rabi de Babylone qui, il est vrai, n'avait nul intérêt à ménager ni l'Élam ni les transfuges du Guti'um. Il profite de l'absence du roi local, sans doute parce que ce dernier était parti en expédition militaire quelque part avec troupes et compagnons faire du pillage, pour réussir un coup de main avec l'aide des Élamites et piller «trois villes», sans doute de simples villages, la «ville» royale elle-même semblant avoir été à l'abri, sans doute, de ses murailles.

Ce qui semble-t-il est un motif tenu pour plausible à l'époque de «retour chez soi», c'est l'ennui où l'on serait de sa patrie, propos singulier mais qui a son écho dans d'autres prétextes, comme d'accomplir les rites funéraires familiaux ou de vénérer ses dieux, thèmes bien représentés dans les textes de Mari pour légitimer un retour (temporaire) d'une princesse mariée au loin dans son lieu d'origine.

Bibliographie

DURAND, J.-M. 2004: «Peuplement et sociétés à l'époque amorrite», dans Nicolle, Chr. (ed.), *Nomades et sédentaires dans le Proche-Orient ancien. Compte rendu du 46e Rencontre assyriologique internationale, (Paris, 10.07.2000-13.07.2000)* (Amurru 3), 111-198.

— 2004-2005: «Assyriologie», *Annuaire du Collège de France* 104, 817-859.

— 2010: «La fondation d'une lignée royale syrienne...», dans J.-M. Durand et Th. Römer (éd.), *Le Jeune héros, Actes du colloque du Collège de France, avril 2008* (OBO 250), 94-50.

— à venir: «Le *kispum* paléo-babylonien», dans J.-M. Durand, Th. Römer et J. Hutzli (éd.), *Les Vivants et leurs morts*, Actes du Colloque du Collège de France, avril 2009, *OBO* à venir.

MARTI, L. 2002: «Notes sur l'histoire d'Išme-Dagan», dans D. Charpin et J.-M. Durand (éd.), *Recueil d'études à la mémoire d'André Parrot* (Florilegium Marianum VI), Paris, 541-544.

[13] Cf. Durand 2010, 94-134.

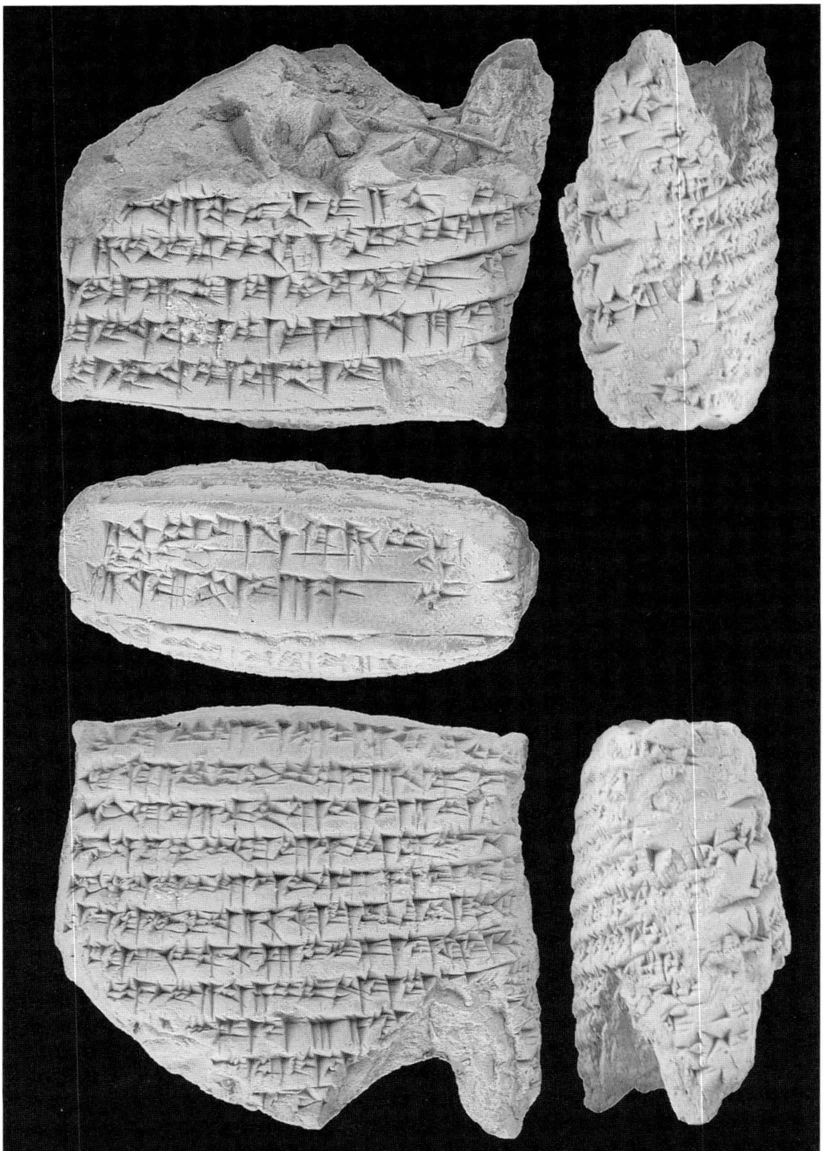

THE "GIBSON COLLECTION" AT THE ORIENTAL INSTITUTE, CHICAGO

Gertrud and Walter FARBER
The Oriental Institute, Chicago

The seven tablets to be published here were recently donated to the Oriental Institute by Greg Gibson, on behalf of the heirs of Joseph W. Gibson, in the latter's memory. The tablets are part of a group of texts that originally were purchased from Edgar J. Banks in the early 20th century. We still have a list of the assemblage (or more likely the original sales offer?), signed by Banks, and describing 15 tablets with individual prices between $ 2.00 and $ 10.00. Of these, only seven have survived in the Gibson family, six of which can be tentatively identified with tablets mentioned in Banks' list. One of the tablets (Gibson 2) does not seem to correspond to any of the tablets described by Banks, and the whereabouts of the remaining nine[1] is presently unknown. The seven tablets that were donated still bear pencil numbers 2, 3, 3a, 4, 6, 10 and 11, which only partially coincide with Banks' numbering. Those same numbers are used in a 1983 correspondence between J. W. Gibson and J. Carswell, then curator of the Oriental Institute Museum, when a donation to the O.I. was first considered but did not come to fruition. At that time, only these seven tablets were mentioned. It remains unclear whether any more than these ever were purchased from Banks, but the non-sequential pencil numbers seem to speak in favor of this. We refer to them by these numbers.

Although the group of tablets, like most Banks acquisitions, is not of coherent contents, nor do the individual texts belong to a single site or archive, we have decided to publish them together as a group, as originally envisaged by the Gibson heirs. We want to take this opportunity to thank them again for their generosity in donating the documents to the Tablet Collection of the Oriental Institute, Chicago.

[1] In addition to the inevitable Sîn-kāšid cone and five unidentified Ur-III tablets from Drehem and Jokha, the list also mentions three NB tablets "from Babylon," the first supposedly a letter dated to Nebuchadnezzar, the second "a very unusual late Babylonian tablet with a business contract, dating from about 600 B.C.," and the last one a contract dated to "month ASH, the day 30, the year 2 of Nabonidus, King of Babylon" (30.XI.Nbn2 = 7./8.III.553 B.C.).

We have split the edition of these tablets between us as follows: copies and editions of the three Ur III texts and the OB tabular account, Gibson nos. 2, 3a, 4, 6 (now A 161000, A 160994, A 160995, A 160996 respectively) were prepared by G. Farber, those of the three OB contracts from Larsa, Gibson nos. 3, 10, 11 (now A 160999, A 160997, A 160998) were edited by W. Farber.

It is with great pleasure that we present this article to our friend and colleague Karel Van Lerberghe on the occasion of his retirement, and we wish him many years of healthy, unstressed joy and fruitful research to come!

Three Ur III Texts

The following three small tablets from Drehem and Umma bearing the Gibson pencil numbers 3a, 4, and 6 correspond to numbers 3, 4, and 6 or 7 on Banks' list respectively.

Gibson 3a, now A 160994:
Ur III, Drehem
Withdrawal of small cattle
– / VI-X / Š 48

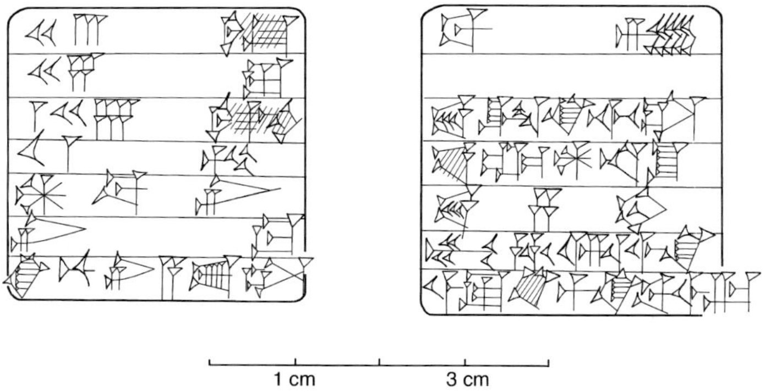

obv. 1) 23 kir_{11}
25 udu
87 ^{munus}áš-gàr
11 máš
5) DINGIR-*ba-ni*
ì-dab_5
ki *be-lí*-A.ZU-ta

rev. ba-zi
(blank)
iti á-ki-ti-ta
iti ezen-an-na-šè
iti 4-kam
mu ḫa-ar-ši^{ki}
ù ki-maš^{ki} ba-ḫul

Comments:

7: Š 48 is *be-lí*-A.ZU's first year in office, see Sigrist 1992, 320.

Gibson 4, now A 160995:
Ur III, Drehem
Receipt for dead animals
28 / V / AS 8

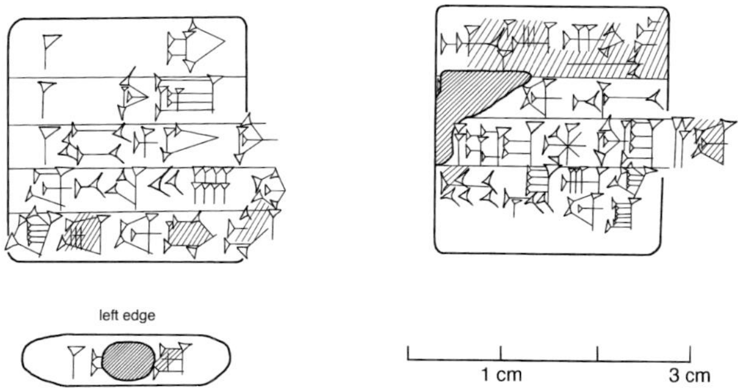

obv. 1 gu$_4$
1 kir$_{11}$
1 amar máš-dà munus
ba-ug$_5$ u$_4$ 28-kam
ki zu-ba-ga-ta
rev. ^{d}šul-gi-⸢iri-g̃u$_{10}$⸣
š[u] ba-ti
[it]i ezen-^{d}nin-⸢a⸣-zu
mu en eridu^{ki}
ba-ḫug̃
l.e. 1 g[u$_4$ 2] udu

Comments:

5: For zu-ba-ga who was in office V/AS 8 - XII/AS 9 see Hilgert 2003, 359-370.

l. e.: In summations máš-dà "gazelles" seem to have been counted under udu "sheep," see also Hilgert 2003 no. 243.

Gibson 6, now A 160996:
Ur III, Umma
Delivery of onion sets to the palace for planting
– / IV / AS 4
The entire text has been sealed over.

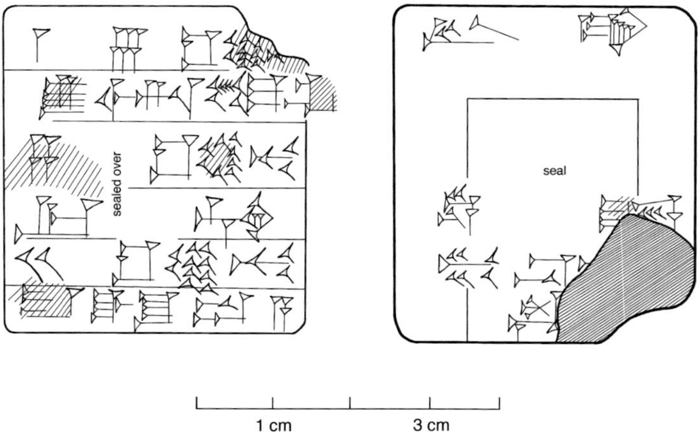

obv. 1) 66 kilib sum-nu[mun]
ú-ar-dú-um
240 (or 4) kilib sum-numun
ur-kun
5) 20 kilib sum-numun
˹é˺-gal-šè DU-a
rev. lú-ga
(seal)
iti nesag̃
mu-ús-s[a $^{(d)}$gu-za]
^{d}e[n-líl-lá ba-dím]
Seal: ur-˹^{d}šul-pa˺-[è]
dub-˹sar˺
dumu lugal-[kù-ga-ni]

seal on reverse of Gibson 6 (= A 160996)

Comments:

2: For the PN *ú-ar-dú(-um)* see Hilgert 2002, 338.

Date: Since the month nesag̃ is known from the Umma calendar only, our text must come from Umma, as also suggested by the owner of the seal.

During the tenure of ur-^{d}šul-pa-è[2] only the year names AS 3, ŠS 2, 6, and 8 and their ús-sa years contain the name of ^{d}en-líl or ^{d}en-ki. The seal used on this tablet is no. 878.3 in Mayr 1997, 481. Since ur-^{d}šul-pa-è used this seal from only Š 46 - AS 9, the date of our text must be restored as AS 4.

Four OB Tablets from Larsa ("Found at Senkereh")

Three of these tablets, pencil numbers 3, 10, and 11, seem to correspond to numbers 10-12 in Banks' list, but individual identifications are impossible due to Banks' insufficient descriptions. He gives Senkereh as their place of origin. The tabular account Gibson 2 cannot be identified on

[2] ur-^{d}šul-pa-è comes from a family of scribes and is one of eight brothers, all known as scribes.

Attestations are taken from the website Molina 2010 and from the catalogue in Mayr 1997, 180-491:

lugal-é-maḫ-e, 342 times attested on seals, Š 31-ŠS5
lugal-^{giš}kiri$_{6}$, three times attested on seals, Š 31- Š 39
ur-^{d}en-líl-lá, 20 times attested on seals, Š 41-ŠS 1
ur-^{d}šul-pa-è, now 159 times attested on seals, Š 42- ŠS 9
lú-^{d}sukkal-an-ka, seven times attested on seals, Š 44-ŠS 2
lugal-á-zi-da, five times attested on seals, Š 46 and AS 2
ur-é-maḫ, 13 times attested on seals, AS 7-IS 3
^{d}šára-ḫé-g̃ál, twice attested on seals, ŠS 5 and 8.

Banks' sales list, but undoubtedly comes from Larsa as well; tablets from Larsa with exactly parallel contents were also sold by Banks to George A. Plimpton, see below.

Gibson 2, now A 161000:
OB, Larsa
Tabular account of supplies for oxen.
27 / VII-3 / RS 31

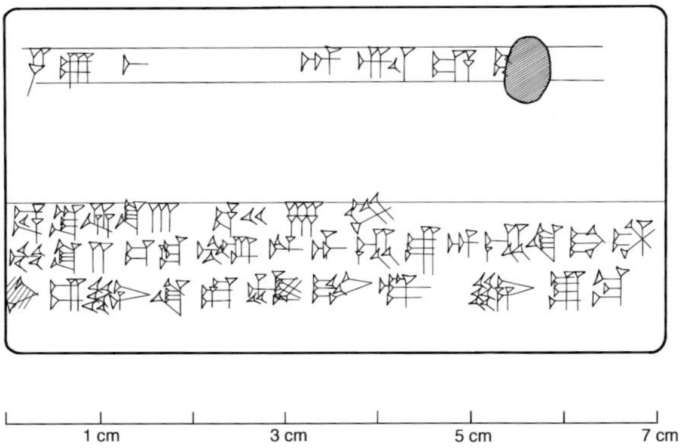

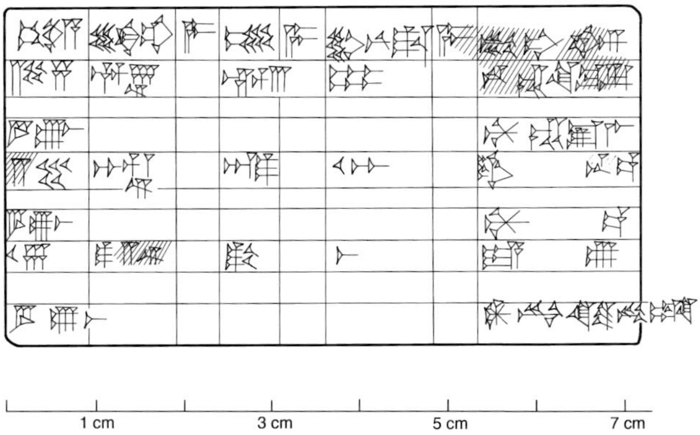

The individual columns of this account list supplies delivered for oxen: še mur-gu$_4$ "fodder," duḫ "bran," and in-nu-da "straw." After each of these items there is space which is left empty to enter any deficit (lál). In the last column the responsible herdsmen are listed.

Each transaction belongs to a different temple administration (níĝ-ú-rum), and all are summarized as níĝ-ú-rum diĝir-re-e-ne.

obverse:

gu$_4$$^{\text{ḫi-a}}$	še mur-gu$_4$	lál	duḫ	lál	in-nu-da	lál	mu-bi-im
164	1.2.1.7 ⅓ (gur)		1.3.1.3 (gur)		6 (gur)		^{d}EN.KI-*ma-lik*
		(ruled blank line)					
níĝ-ú-rum							^{d}en-líl-lá
170$^{?}$	2.0.1.1 ⅓ (gur)		2.1.3 (gur)		12 (gur)		⸢*i*$^{!}$⸣-*din*-^{d}UTU
		(ruled blank line)					
níĝ-ú-rum							^{d}utu
16	0.0.3.2$^{?}$ ⅓ (gur)		0.0.5 (gur)		1 (gur)		*ia-ú*
		(ruled blank line)					
níĝ-ú-rum							^{d}nanna šà urí^{ki}

reverse:

(blank space)	
níĝ-ú-rum	diĝir-re-e-⸢ne⸣
(blank space)	
iti du$_6$-kù ki-3 u$_4$ 27-kam mu ki-2 ^{ĝiš}tukul-maḫ an$^{!}$ ^{d}en-líl ^{d}en-ki-ga-ta ì-si-in^{ki} iri nam-lugal-la in-dab$^{\text{(sic)}}$-ba	

Comments:

This text belongs with a group of 12 unpublished Larsa texts, all tabular accounts, that Banks sold to George A. Plimpton in 1923 for $ 100, as described by E. Robson (2002, 256-257). Eleven of these texts deal with supplies for oxen, as does Gibson 2, and are from RS 31 as well, dating from 23 VII-1 to 16 VII-4. These eleven Plimpton texts are now nos. 286-294, 314, and 324 of the Plimpton Collection at Columbia University, New York. They will be published by E. Robson, who has graciously made them available to me in transliteration.

For the strange month notations during the years after the conquest of Isin, i. e. after Rīm-Sîn 30, where some months occur in sets of several months numbered "ki-n", thus creating years with more months than twelve, see Kraus 1959, 136-167; also Robertson 1983, 148-161; and Hüttner and

Oelsner 1990. While the more common notation in Nippur is "iti ki-n monthname," the notation in Larsa (see Kraus 1959, 156-158) is "iti monthname ki-n."

Gibson 3, now A 160999:
OB, Larsa
Loan contract
– / XIIa / RS 7
The entire tablet has been sealed over.

obv.

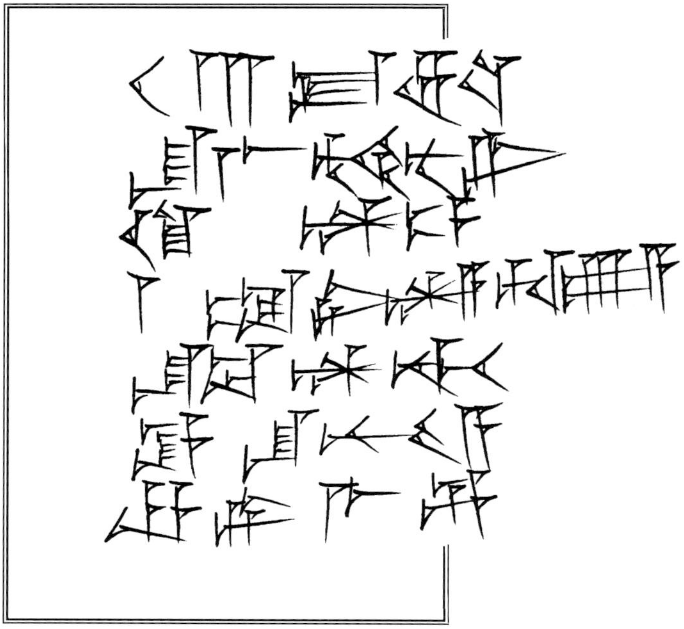

(scale 1:1.5)

obv. 1) 13 gín kù.babbar
šu.lá máš nu.tuku
ki ^{d}utu
^{m}*ṣi-lí-*^{d}*a-ḫu-ú-a*
5) šu ba.an.ti
^{iti}šu.numun.a
kù ì.lá.e

rev. igi *ša*-DINGIR-*a-mur*
igi *ip-qú-*^{d}*li*$_{9}$*-si*$_{4}$

igi ^{d}EN.ZU-*pu-uṭ-ra-am*
igi ÌR-^{d}*ki-it-tum*
igi ^{d}nanna-ì.zu
igi *ra-bu-ut*-^{d}EN.ZU
kišib lú.inim.ma.ab.bi.meš
^{iti}diri še.gur$_{10}$.ku$_{5}$
mu ká.A 2.a.bi
šà maš-kán-šabra^{ki}
l. e. mu.un.dù.a
ù e a.šà šà.túm.ma
4 danna^{na} mu.un.si.{ig.}ga

rev.

l.e.

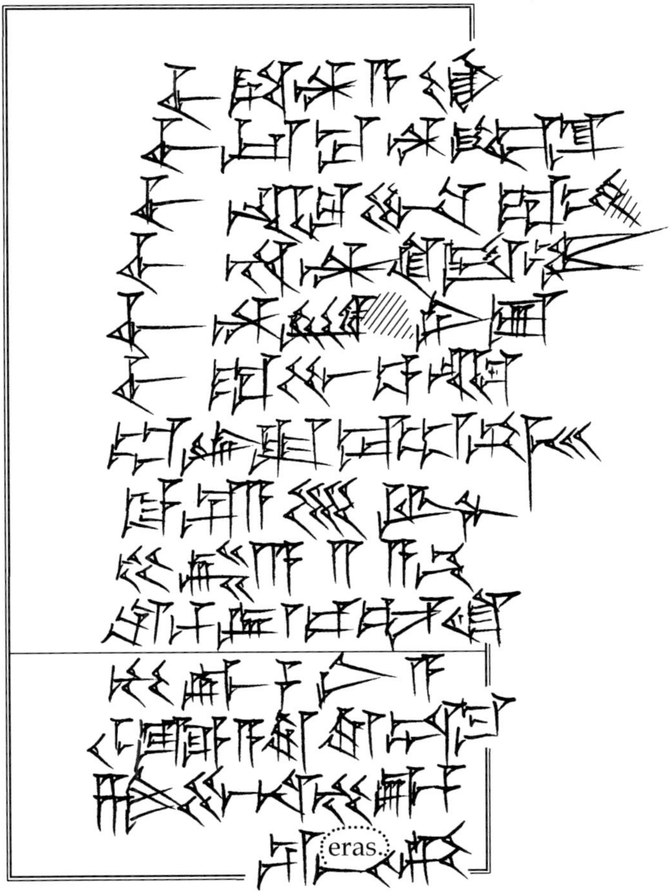

(scale 1:1.5)

Seal: Only one sign each from the middle of what are probably the second and third lines of the seal inscription can be read: AN and A respectively.

1) 13 shekels of silver,
a short-term loan without interest,
from (the temple of) Šamaš,
Ṣilli-Aḫū'a
5) has received.
In the month Dumuzi (=IV)
he shall pay (back) the silver.

8-13) (Names of 6 witnesses)

Seal(s) of the witnesses.

15) Month: intercalary Addar (=XIIa).
16-20) Year: "The two city gates," *etc.* (Rīm-Sîn 7)

Comments:

The tablet is probably a *Hüllentafel*, although this cannot be proven at this moment. The Oriental Institute now follows a policy by which we do no longer attempt to open enveloped tablets, in the expectation that in a few years technical methods will have been developed to read the inside tablet without physical damage to the envelope. Significant results have been made in this direction by several teams of scientists, but unfortunately, none have yet been found to be practically usable on a larger scale.

The tablet is sealed around the four edges, and on the uninscribed left margins of both the obverse and the reverse. This was (deliberately?) done in such a way that mainly the representations of the seal(s) are visible. Only at the top of the left edge can one see traces of the inscription (see above), but not enough to identify the owner with any degree of certainty.

4: For the rare DN *Aḫū'a* in OB PNs see Stamm 1939, 56-57.

8: With this unusual name, cf. the MB PN *Ammar-ša-Adad* "I will see the (deeds/character) of Adad," and the discussion of *Danknamen* of the type *xx-ilim-āmur/ātamar* in Stamm 1939, 86-87.

11: "Divine Justice" (^{d}*kittum*) is not otherwise known to me as an element of OB PNs, but the deity is mentioned in the letter LIH 30, ll. 6 and 10. Without the determinative, but as *mārat* ^{d}*Šamaš* obviously also of divine nature, we encounter her in the extispicy prayer RA 38, 86 rev. 22 (for these OB references, see CAD K 471a). Whether the unique

Gibson 3 (= A 160999) obverse

Gibson 3 (= A 160999), left edge

Gibson 3 (= A 160999), lower edge

spelling in JCS 34, 161 no. 12: 2 GIŠ.BÁN AN *ki-it-tum* for *sūt kittim* "correct *sūtu* measure" (see CAD K 471b) is actually to be connected with this deity (thus Richter 1999, 298, reading ^{d}*ki-it-tum*), or should rather be seen as a clumsy spelling GIŠ.BÁN^{an} *ki-it-tum* (for *-tim*), I do not know. A deity of this name, usually understood as the son (or daughter) of Šamaš, is much better known from later sources, see CAD K 471a.

14ff.: The scribe's insufficient familiarity with Sumerian is visible here twice, first in the addition of an uncalled-for sign -ab- in *inim-ma-bi, and then in two mistakes in the date formula (A for ká, and the mistaken addition of -ig- in the final verbal form, which he, however, noticed and erased himself).

Gibson 10, now A 160997:
OB, Larsa
Purchase of a slave girl
– / VII /?

obv. igi ^{d}iškur-*še-mi* kù.dí[m]
igi ^{d}utu-*ga-mi-il* lú.ugula[.x$^{?}$]
igi *ga-mi-ìl* šu.ḫa
igi ^{d}EN.ZU-*na-ṣi-ir*
igi ^{d}EN.ZU-*a-bu-šu*
igi *i-šar-ku-bi*
igi *im-lik$^{?}$-èr-ra* dam.gàr
lú(.)pú$^{?}$(.)^{d}en.líl.lá
igi *sí-na-tum* dub.sar

lú.inim.ma.bi.meš
ša i-na ma-aḫ-ri-šu-nu
a-na 17 gín kù.babbar
rev. 1 sag.géme *taš-me-*[*ḫ*]*a$^{?}$-ià$^{?}$* mu.ni.im
ki *nu-úr-ku-bi* dumu *wa-*[*r*]*a$^{?}$-a-a*
ù š[*a$^{?}$-a*]*t$^{?}$-ì-lí-a* ama.a.ni
^{m}[*ṣ*]*i$^{?}$-x*[*x*]-^{d}*ba-ba$_{6}$*
in.š[i].sa$_{10}$

^{iti}du$_{6}$.kù u$_{4}$.11.kam
mu 15$^{?}$ x[x … … … … x]x
é ^{d}x[x … … … … …]
u. e. ki$^{?}$ ^{d}utu ⸢ì$^{?}$⸣.[ba]l$^{?}$

1-9) (Names and professions of 7 witnesses and the scribe).

10) (Those are) the witnesses

11) before whom
16) Ṣixxx-Baba
17) bought
12) for 17 shekels of silver
13) one slave girl named Tašme-Ḫaja?
14) from Nūr-Kubi son of Waraja?
15) and his/her mother Šāt-ilija.

18) Month: Tašrīt (=VII), day: 11.
19-21) Year: (unclear year name, king unknown)

Comments:

7: The reading *lik* is not absolutely certain. The sign on the tablet is obviously incorrect, and probably the result of one sign written over another without first erasing the former. The two best possibilities that seem to remain for a PN starting with *im*-would thus be *gur* or *lik*, the latter fitting slightly better to the wedges on the clay. Neither **Imlik-Erra* nor **Imgur-Erra* are common names, and without extensive prosopographical files, I was unable to find either name for a *tamkārum*.

8: I am not able to make good sense of this line. The identification of the second sign is not absolutely certain, since it seems to be missing the first vertical wedge, but no better reading than PÚ came to mind. It then could either be a GN ("Enlil's Well") specifying the origin of the person in line 7 ("PN the merchant, the man from GN"), but unfortunately no GN *Pu-Enlila is known to me. The other possibility would be a second PN, qualifying the first PN as belonging to, or acting on behalf of this person ("PN_1 the man of PN_2") but again, no fitting Sumerian personal names are known to me, and I was unable to find other evidence for a merchant being described as "the man of" (i.e., somehow dependent on) another person of at best equal rank.

15: Unfortunately, the person of reference for the Sumerian suffix /ani/ remains unclear. Šāt-ilija thus could be either the mother of Nūr-Kūbi from l. 14, or of the slave girl herself. Either interpretation would lead to several possible scenarios explaining the joint ownership of the slave girl, but without external evidence for the people involved, I am unable to propose a solution or even express a preference for "his" or "her."

18ff.: It is somewhat frustrating not to be able to identify this year name, with a number of signs fully or partially preserved. Nevertheless, I had to give up and wish someone else (what about the dedicatee of this Festschrift?) better luck, or deeper knowledge than mine.

obv.

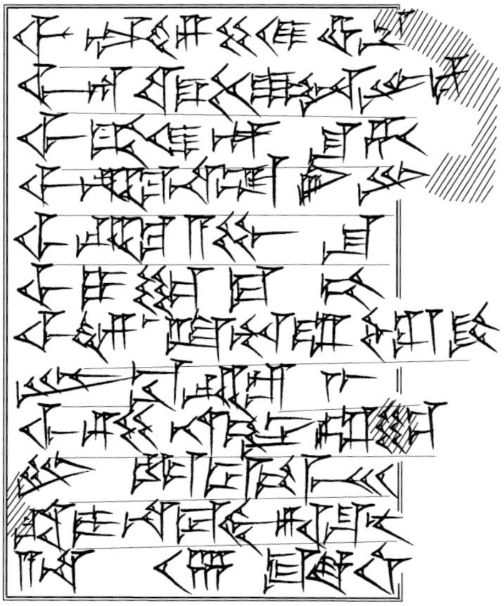

rev.

u.e.

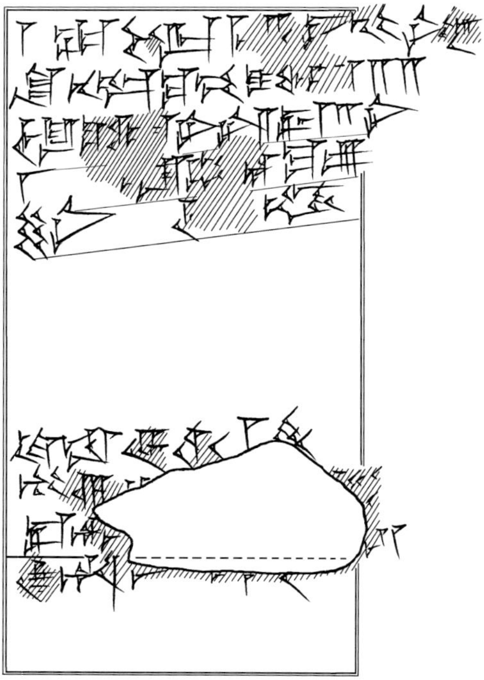

(scale 1:1.5)

Gibson 11, now A 160998:
OB, Larsa
Receipt for barley
10 / VII / RS 49
sealed by *ḫa-z*[*i*]-*ra*?-*n*[*um*?]

obv.

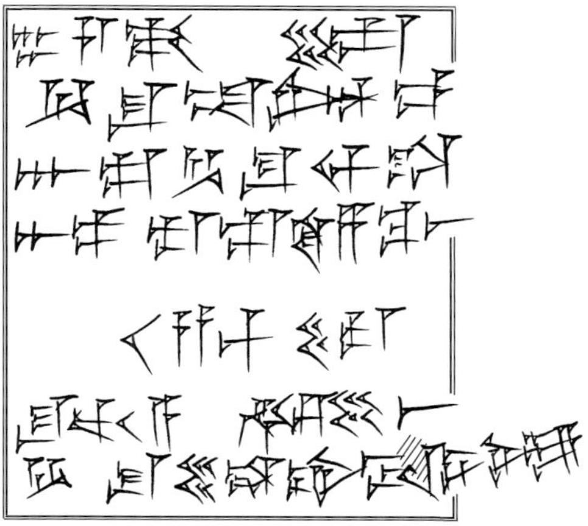

rev.

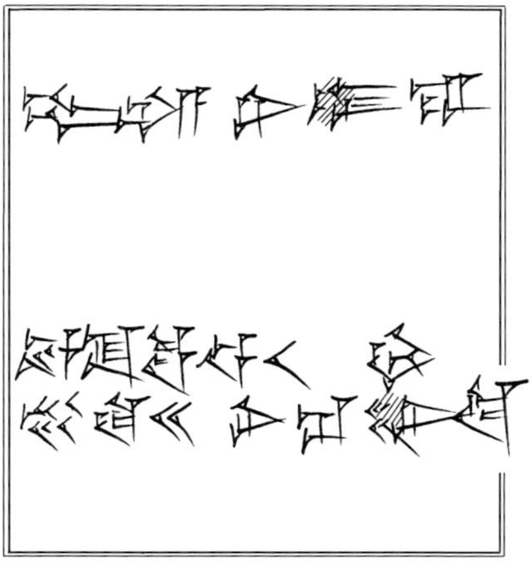

seal

(scale 1:1.5)

obv. 1) 5.3.5 še.gur
níg.šu *ṣi-lí*-^{d}utu
3.0.0 gur níg.šu *u-bar-ša*
2.0.2 gur uru^{ki} *za-ku-rum*

5) 10.4.1 še.gur

šu ti.a *ḫa-zi-rum*
níg.šu *li-pí-it-ì-lí-ia*

rev. íb$^{?}$.bi.a.ni íb.ra

^{iti}du$_{6}$.kù u$_{4}$.10.kam
10) mu ki.20 ì-si-in^{ki}

Seal: *ḫa-z*[*i*]-*ra*$^{?}$-*n*[*um*$^{?}$]
dumu *ḫa-aB-x*[*x*]
ìr ^{d}utu

1) 5.3.5 kor of barley,
responsible: Ṣilli-Šamaš,
3 kor of barley, responsible: Ubarša,
2.0.2 kor of barley (from) the town of Zakkurum,

5) (altogether) 10.4.1 kor of barley,

received by Ḫāzirum,
responsible: Lipit-ilija.

Sealed with his *seal*(!?).

Month: Tašrīt (=VII), day: 10.
10) Year 20 (of the) Isin (era) (= Rīm-Sîn 49)

Comments:

The tablet is sealed with one single seal on the upper, left, and lower edges and in all blank spaces, with the copy of the seal reconstructed from several partial impressions. The seal is always impressed in a way that shows only the inscription, never any part of a pictorial scene.

4: The GN Zak(k)urum has, according to RGTC 3 (Groneberg 1980) 258, only been known from one text of unknown provenance, but which has been shown to most probably have been written in Ur (YOS 8, 98: 9 and 42; for the provenience, see most recently W. Farber 2007, 75). If the tablet is correctly identified as one of nos. 10-12 in Banks' list (see above), and Banks' statement "Found at Senkereh" is correct, this would provide further evidence for the possible location of Zak(k)urum.

6: Note the similarity of the name of the recipient, Ḫāzirum, to that of the owner of the seal on this tablet, Ḫāzirān[um]?. Could this be a scribal mistake, or possibly reflect a family naming tradition in an inherited seal? For the name Ḫāzirum see Gelb 1980, 586 and, in the context of all names containing the root ᶜḎR, Gelb 1980, 259-260; see also Streck 2000, 329 §5.24 (in the index p. 406b s.v. *ᶜāḏir* wrongly quoted as §3.24). Note that none of these sources contains any references to the name Ḫāzirānum.

8: The signs on the tablet make no sense. I assume that ÍB.BI is simply a mistake for *kišib.ba, maybe partly due to the rhyming sound pattern of the first sign in each group, or, more likely, as an anticipatory mistake from the following *íb.ra. Note also that the scribe wrote two different sign forms for the two ÍB signs, the first one being quite defective. Why he then continued with an "incorrect" spelling bi(.a) instead of the conventional ba(.a), I do not know.

Seal: See above, commentary to l. 6. For names beginning with the signs *ḫa-aB-*, see Gelb (1980, 580-581). The faint traces of the seal impression do not allow me to propose a probable reading for the final sign(s); although D[U] looks like a good candidate, there does not seem to be enough space for the additional signs needed to yield a viable PN. Another possibility would be *ḫa-ab-d*[*a*?*-an*?], which at least seems compatible with the space available.

Bibliography

Farber, W. 2007: "Imgur-Sîn und seine beiden Söhne: Eine (nicht ganz) neue altbabylonische Erbteilungsurkunde aus Ur, gefunden wahrscheinlich in Larsa", in M. T. Roth et al. (eds.) *Studies Presented to Robert D. Biggs, June 4 2004* (From the Workshop of the Chicago Assyrian Dictionary 2), Chicago, 65-79.

Gelb, I. J. 1980: *Computer-Aided Analysis of Amorite* (Assyriological Studies 21), Chicago.

Groneberg, B. 1980: *Die Orts- und Gewässernamen der altbabylonischen Zeit* (Répertoire Géographique des Textes Cunéiformes 3), Wiesbaden.

Hilgert, M. 2002: *Akkadisch in der Ur III-Zeit* (Imgula 5), Münster.

— 2003: *Drehem Adminstrative Documents from the Reign of Amar-Suena* (Cuneiform Texts from the Ur III Period in the Oriental Institue 2, OIP 121), Chicago.

HÜTTNER, K. and J. OELSNER 1990: "Verwaltungsurkunden aus der Zeit Rīm-Sins von Larsa in der Hilprechtsammlung Vorderasiatischer Altertümer der Friedrich-Schiller-Universität Jena", *AoF* 17, 355-359.

KRAUS, F. R. 1959: "Ungewöhnliche Datierungen aus der Zeit des Königs Rīm-Sin von Larsa," *ZA* 53, 136-167.

MAYR, R. H. 1997: *The Seal Impressions of Ur III Umma* (unpublished dissertation), Leiden.

MOLINA, M. et al. 2010: "Database of Neo-Sumerian Texts (BDTNS)", last modified July 2010, accessed March 2011. http://bdtns.filol.csic.es/index.php?reg=si

RICHTER, Th. 1999: *Untersuchungen zu den lokalen Panthea Süd- und Mittelbabyloniens in altbabylonischer Zeit* (AOAT 257), Münster.

ROBERTSON, J. F. 1983: "An Unusual Dating System from Isin-Larsa Period Nippur: New Evidence", *ASJ* 5, 148-161.

ROBSON, E. 2002: "Guaranteed Genuine Originals: The Plimpton Collection and the Early History of Mathematical Assyriology", in C. Wunsch (ed.) *Mining the Archives, Festschrift for Christopher Walker on the Occasion of his 60th Birthday*, Dresden, 231-278.

SIGRIST, M. 1992: *Drehem*, Bethesda, MD.

STAMM, J. J. 1939: *Die Akkadische Namengebung* (MVAG 44), Leipzig.

STRECK, M. P. 2000: *Das amurritische Onomastikon der altbabylonischen Zeit, Band 1: Die Amurriter, Die onomastische Forschung, Orthographie und Philologie, Normalmorphologie* (AOAT 271/1), Münster.

UNFULFILLED DESTINIES
YET AGAIN ON THE OLD BABYLONIAN SUMERIAN SCRIBAL CURRICULUM

Alhena Gadotti and Alexandra Kleinerman
Towson University, Towson MD and Cornell University, Ithaca NY

JON 16 is a small, well preserved tablet, measuring 48*54*24 mm (photo below). The obverse is inscribed, whereas the reverse is blank with the exception of a few signs, possibly random numerical notations, or doodling. The paleography suggests an Old Babylonian date, and the provenance is unknown. We dedicate the study of this tablet to Karel Van Lerberghe, our colleague and friend, in the hope that he will enjoy this as much as we enjoyed his company during his stays at Cornell.[1]

At first glance, the text appeared to be a list of incipits. The obverse contains six lines of seemingly disjointed sentences. The final line is separated from the colophon by a single horizontal line.

JON 16

1. ^{d}en-ki en zag-dib an ki-a nam-⌜ma⌝-[ni] ⌜zag⌝ nu-sá
2. lú ^{na4}kinkin gul-gul-dè
3. ú-sal ì-ru-ú
4. ní-zu é bùru-dè ì-DU
5. *ma-ti aš-ru-ú* ì$^{!}$-ib-du$_7$
6. á<-áĝ>-ĝá á-áĝ-ĝá um-mi-a-ak

[1] We wish to thank David I. Owen and the anonymous owners of the tablet for providing us with the opportunity to study it. This article is published with the memory of the owners' son Jonathan ז"ל in mind. Many thanks also to Laura Johnson-Kelly, Rosen Foundation Conservator and Photographer in the Jonathan and Jeannette Rosen Ancient Near Eastern Studies Seminar at Cornell University, for her beautiful photographs of the tablet. We are very grateful to Bendt Alster for taking the time to look at several drafts of our manuscript and providing many helpful suggestions. Finally, we would like to thank Miguel Civil, Andrew George, David I. Owen and Gonzalo Rubio for their comments.

7. i_6-lí-ip-pa-al-sà-am

1. Enki, magnificent lord of heaven and earth, [his] decisions are unparalleled.
2.-3. The man, who should recondition the millstone, hides (in) the meadow (instead).
4.-5. The thief, who goes in order to break into the house, pushes into the ground (instead).
6. The instructions of the master.

Colophon: Ili-ippalsam

Commentary

1. The restoration is based on Old Babylonian parallels, e.g. Anam A l. 30[2] and Sin-iddinam E4.2.9.15 l. 32[3]. The role of Enki as the determiner of destinies is well established in Sumerian and Akkadian literature, e.g. the composition Enki and Ninmah.

2. For ^{na4}kinkin gul-gul see Civil 2006, 123.

3. Although ú-sal is attested primarily with the locative marker, it does occur without it (Warad-Sin E4.2.13.24 l. 14[4]). ru is fairly common in Old Babylonian Sumerian literature as a variant for ri, especially in royal hymns (e.g. Šulgi B 11[5], Išme-Dagan A+V 43[6]). The meaning of ru/ri is "to lay down", but the implication here is that the man is hiding in the meadow in order to avoid his work.

4. For ní-zu as a variant of ní-zuh see Alster 1997, 265 col. vi l. 4 and comm. p. 446. The imagery of a thief breaking into a house is fairly well attested in Sumerian literature, for which see the references in Sjöberg 1973, 134. Although one might expect ĝen-na, we opted to translate with a relative pronoun in English to maintain the parallelism between ll. 2-3 and 4-5.

[2] Falkenstein 1963.
[3] Frayne 1990, 178.
[4] Frayne 1990, 248.
[5] Castellino 1972, 27-69.
[6] Ludwig 1990, 161-225.

5. The interpretation of this line is problematic. du_7/*nakāpu* is not typically used to describe such mundane human action. Although kalam and ki are attested in hendiadys, the Akkadian *mātu* and *ašru* are not. Indeed, the grammatical relationship between the words is unclear. Finally, it is uncertain why the scribe switches to Akkadian, especially given that these are elementary terms. We are at present unaware of any other examples of Sumerian proverbs or other short didactic compositions in which the scribe abruptly changes languages. As such, we recognize the tentative nature of our interpretation; however, this solution fits well within the context of ll. 2-3.

6. An alternative translation, without restoration, would read "Under my control (are) the instructions of the master."

Colophon. According to Civil (personal communication) the name must be Ili-ippalsam, although the reading of i_6 for KU is attested only in Ea 1: 149 (MSL 14, 184). The name itself does occur in the Old Babylonian period, see CAD P s.v. *palāsum*.

Discussion

Upon further examination, it emerged that JON 16 was not a list of incipits but a coherent narrative. Although unparalleled, we propose that the lexicon, grammar, and structure of the text indicate that it is a Sumerian proverb.[7] The final line suggests that it is a scribal exercise completed by one Ili-ippalsam.[8]

The text first introduces Enki, who is the lord of heaven and earth, but, more importantly here, the one whose decisions establish the destinies for all of humanity. However, despite Enki's best intentions, humans still cannot manage to fulfill even the most menial and debased of their destinies.[9] So, the stone cutter is too lazy to cut stone and the thief too incompetent to break into the house.

In the final line the student acknowledges that he has completed his assignment. This is not a common practice in the Old Babylonian school material. However, this deviation should not come as a surprise. It is now well established that the majority of Sumerian scribal exercises published to date derive from the Nippur schools and so reflect only the Nippur

[7] We use the term here in the most loose sense. For a review of the problematic definition of this term in regard to the Sumerian corpus see Taylor 2005.

[8] For the use of á-áĝ-ĝá as a task or assignment, see Eduba C ll. 4, 13, 14, 15.

[9] Thanks to Bendt Alster (personal communication) for this suggestion.

tradition and curriculum. There is compelling evidence that even the Ur material is very different.[10]

Additional support that this text falls outside of the Nippur tradition comes from the use of the lexicon. For instance, we would expect ú-sal nú where we have ú-sal ru. Indeed, almost every line has an instance idiosyncratic usage, so that l. 4 uses ní-zu in place of ní-zuh and l. 5 employs du_7 in a context outside the normal semantic range of the verb. Another example is á-áĝ-ĝá in l. 6, which, at least in one Eduba text (Eduba R),[11] indicates the rules of the school as opposed to the assignments.

When considered in its entirety, JON 16 provides yet another piece of evidence that the Old Babylonian school system was varied and multifaceted, and operated on a local, rather than regional, level.[12] As new documents emerge it continues to become clear that the educational system reconstructed for Nippur[13] is not immediately applicable to southern Babylonia at large. Further discoveries and studies on this type of documentation will certainly enhance our understanding of the Old Babylonian Sumerian scribal school curriculum.

Bibliography

ALSTER, B. 1997: *Proverbs of Ancient Sume*r, Bethesda, Md.

ALSTER, B. 2005: "Groats dropping on the Widow: HS 1461. Studies in Bilingual Proverbs 1", *Kaskal* 2, 91-95.

ALSTER, B. and T. OSHIMA 2006: "A Sumerian Proverb Tablet in Geneva with Some Thoughts on the Sumerian Proverb Collections," *OrNS* 75, 31-72.

CASTELLINO, G. 1972: *Two Shulgi Hymns (B, C)* (Studi semitici 42), Rome.

CIVIL, M. 2006: "The Song of the Millstone", in G. Del Olmo Lete, L. Feliu, and A. Mille Albà (eds.) *Šapal tibnim mû illakū. Studies Presented to Joaquín San Martín on the Occasion of his 65th Birthday*, Barcelona, 121-138.

DELNERO, P. 2006: *Variation in Sumerian Literary Compositions. A Case Study Based on the Decad*, Ph.D. dissertation, University of Pennsylvania.

FALKENSTEIN, A. 1963: "Zu den Inschriftenfund der Grabung in Uruk-Warka 1960-1961", *Baghdader Mitteilungen* 2, 1-82.

FRAYNE, D.R. 1990: *Old Babylonian Period (2003-1595 BC)* (RIME 4), Toronto.

[10] For examples from other corpora see Kleinerman 2011.

[11] Gadotti and Kleinerman In Preparation.

[12] That being said, there was certainly an overarching tradition from which school teachers drew when determining their curriculum. For further discussion see Kleinerman 2011 and Gadotti and Kleinerman 2011.

[13] E.g. Delnero 2006, Robson 2001, Veldhuis 1997, 2004.

GADOTTI, A. and A. KLEINERMAN 2011: "'Here is what I have. Send me what I am missing.'Exchange of Syllabi in Ancient Mesopotamia", *ZA* 101, 72-77.

GADOTTI, A. and A. KLEINERMAN In Preparation: "The Rules of the School: A New Sumerian Literary Composition."

KLEINERMAN, A. 2011: *Education in Early 2nd Millennium BC Babylonia: The Sumerian Epistolary Miscellany* (Cuneiform Monographs 42), Leiden.

LUDWIG, M-C. 1990: *Untersuchungen zu den Hymnen des Išme-Dagan von Isin* (SANTAG 2), Wiesbaden.

ROBSON, E. 2001: "The Tablet House: A Scribal School in Old Babylonian Nippur," *RA* 95, 39-66.

SJÖBERG, Å. 1973: "Der Vater und sein missratener Sohn," *JCS* 25, 105-169.

TAYLOR, J. 2005: "The Sumerian Proverb Collections," *RA* 99, 13-38.

VELDHUIS, N. 1997: *Elementary Education at Nippur. The Lists of Trees and Wooden Objects*. Groningen.

VELDHUIS, N. 2004: *Religion, Literature and Scholarship: the Sumerian Composition of Nanše and the Birds* (Cuneiform Monographs 22), Leiden.

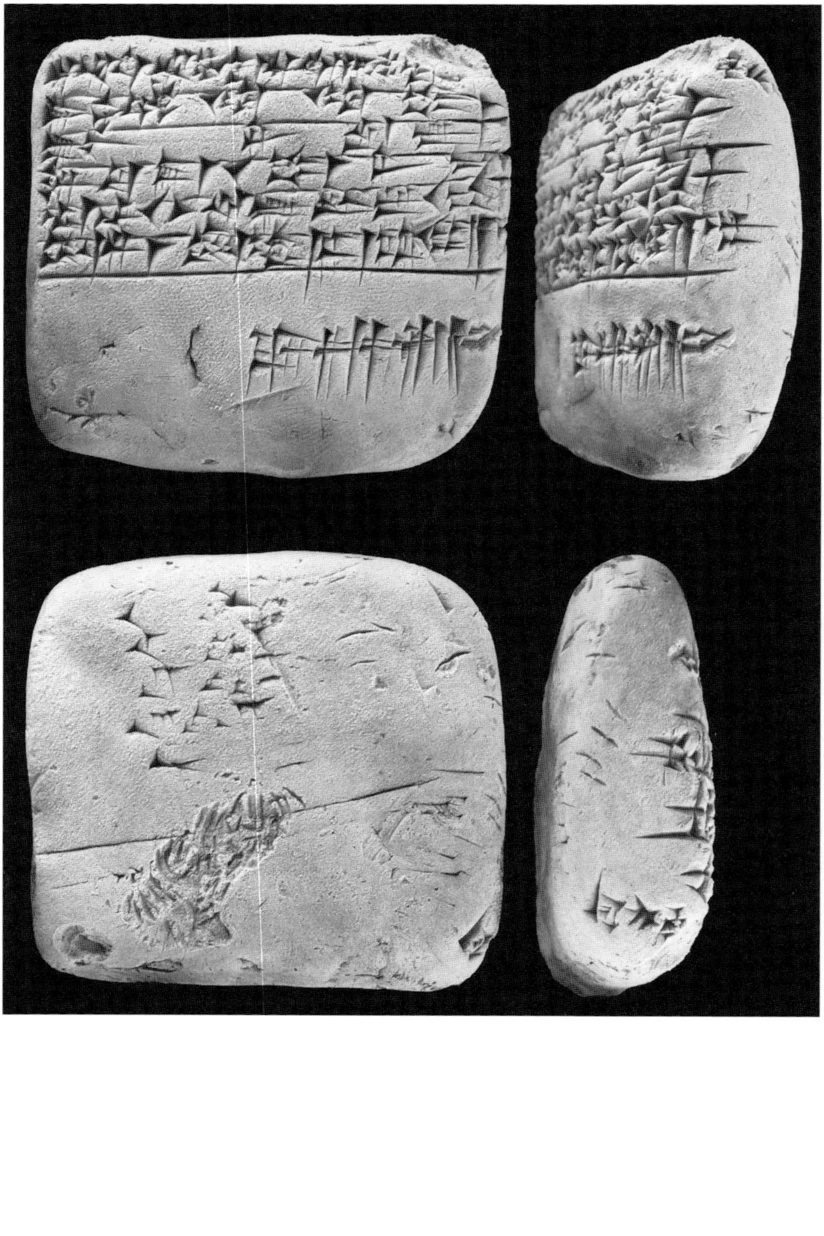

SEALING IN OLD BABYLONIAN NIPPUR

Anne GODDEERIS
KU Leuven

In the course of his investigations into the Dūr-Abi-ešuḫ tablets, the honoree asked me for background information about the sealing practices on the Old Babylonian documents from Nippur, which I was investigating in the context of the DFG project "Altbabylonische Wirtschaftstexte Jena".[1] Having provided him a short answer in an e-mail, I am happy to take this opportunity to give him a more complete answer.

Karel and Bieke have always taken special interest in sealing practices. Their monographs (Van Lerberghe 1986, Van Lerberghe and Voet 1991, 2009) stand out for their detailed description and discussions of the sealings on the cuneiform tablets. Moreover, they have investigated the functional aspects of sealings on Old Babylonian contracts in several essays.[2] For the largest part, they have investigated the sealing practices in Sippar, but since the last decade, they also look for continuity and change in the traditions in Nippur and Dur-Abi-ešuḫ.

Already in 1907, Poebel described how the sealing practices in Nippur differed from those used in Sippar, the only site from which a representative number of Old Babylonian sealed documents was published at that time. He observed that the seals do not include any iconography and the legends are often incised in a sloppy and coarse way. Moreover, the inscription often mentions two or more contractants. We can add that, in Nippur, the contracts are sealed by the party who relinquished a right in the transaction or who assumed an obligation. In northern Babylonia, on the other hand, the witnesses enroll their personal seal on the contracts. Also, the whole surface of both tablet and case is covered with seal impressions in Nippur, whereas only the edges and empty spaces on the case bear seal impressions in contracts from Sippar.

These seals enrolled on the contracts from Nippur are now generally labeled "burgul seals", a term referring to the Sumerian word bur-gul,

[1] I want to thank Manfred Krebernik, curator of the Hilprecht-Sammlung, for providing me with the opportunity to study the Old Babylonian tablets.

[2] Especially Van Lerberghe and Voet 1989, 1991, 1993 and 1997.

the seal cutter, who often witnesses the documents sealed with these seals and who manufactured the seals on the occasion of the contract. In antiquity, they were referred to as "kišib mu-sar-ra-a-ni", seal with his name written (Charpin 1980, 15). Several seals of that type have been recovered in excavations[3], and they appear to be small cylinders made out of clay or limestone.

However, not all the contracts from Nippur are sealed with "burgul-seals", personal seals[4] occur on loans, leases, and on other types of contracts. In the following paragraphs, the factors governing the use of seal types on contracts from Nippur will be investigated. First, a description of the Nippur material will be given. Then follows a survey of the sealing practices in other Old Babylonian towns. In this way, the practices in Nippur will be analyzed against this background and the underlying principles will be exposed.

A. Sealing contracts in Old Babylonian Nippur

In Nippur, the case as well as the tablet of a contract is sealed. The use of the Portable Light Dome system has allowed me to identify seal impressions on the written surface of some of the contracts in the Hilprecht-Sammlung, impressed before the tablet was inscribed and hardly visible because of the writing (TMH 9 19, Fig. 1). Thus, the seals are impressed on all the edges of the tablet, and sometimes also on the surface before it is being written on. The case, as well, seems to be sealed before it was written on (TMH 9 50b, Fig. 2). However, the lay-out of the text is taken into account already, since clear and complete impressions of the seal legends are situated on the empty space to the left of the writing and between the witnesses and the date.

If the seal bears a legend, this part of the seal is enrolled fully, whereas the possible iconographic part (only on personal seals) is considered less relevant. Personal seals without legend sometimes are identified with a by-script.

Only in exceptional cases (e.g. TMH 9 25 and TMH 9 34), the contracts contain a clause concerning the sealing of the document. Both these texts will be looked at more thoroughly below.

[3] AS 17 (1969) n° 13 and n° 53; UE X, n° 446-458, plate 30. UE X n° 451 even contains the names of two contractors.

[4] Stone (1987, 215-221) uses the term "stone seal" to make a distinction between both types, but this is not entirely correct, since burgul-seals may be manufactured out of soft stone. Therefore, I adopt the terms "personal seal" versus "burgul" or "temporary seal" here.

The following overview gives a typology of the contracts occurring in the Nippur corpus, while investigating the occurrence of burgul seals versus that of personal seals. All the tablets from the Hilprecht-Sammlung, and most of the published tablets, are taken into account. Since cylinder seal impressions may look like burgul seals if only two lines of the legend are enrolled, doubtful cases have not been taken into account. Also, some publications do not give all the details concerning the sealings on the tablet (e.g. PBS 8/2).

1. *Contracts serving as title deeds*

These documents serve as proof for the possession of property and, therefore, have a permanent character. They may be kept in an archive for more than 200 years. In Nippur, they always contain an oath formula, in which the party giving up his rights on the property swears that, in future, he, nor any of his heirs, will claim the property. The burgul seals impressed on the documents bear the name(s) of this party. The document is kept by the other party, who may use it as proof for ownership. When documents are sealed by two (or more) different parties, duplicates of the contract are drafted, to be kept by the different parties. Title deeds may take the form of different types of contracts:

– In Nippur, **sale documents** are always sealed with a burgul seal mentioning the seller(s), the party who renounces his claims on the object sold. No duplicates of sale documents have been recovered.

BE 6/2 18 (Ha 41) and TMH 9 34 (Ha 42) are the only unambiguous exceptions to this rule. The personal seal on the first text belongs to the seller, and those on the second one to the father of the sellers of the unbuilt plot (identical to the seller in BE 6/2 18) and to one of the sellers. The reason why these texts are sealed with a personal seal remains obscure. However, this phenomenon is restricted to one single file.

In TMH 9 57, a temple office sale sealed by the buyer and his two associates, actually does not record the sale. The contract is drafted twenty years later and settles the division of the income derived from the temple office. Thus, this text does not form an exception to the rule.

– **Exchange documents** and **bequests** are sealed along the same principles. In the first case, both parties seal with a burgul seal, the second type is sealed by the giver.

– **Transactions relating to family law** involving the transfer of property, such as adoption and marriage contracts, serve as title deeds as well.

Although, generally, only one party gives up his rights on the property, the burgul seal(s) may refer to both parties.

- **Marriage contracts** are sealed with a burgul seal mentioning both husband and wife, also if only one party brings in property (a dowry in the case of the wife, a marital gift in the case of the husband). The sample contains only one exception, TMH 9 5, which is sealed by the husband and by the sons of the wife from an earlier marriage. This inconsistency is easily explained because these sons were adopted by the new husband. This type of marriage/adoption contract is attested only in Nippur, and more than 70% of the marriage contracts from Nippur contain clauses pertaining to the adoption of children from an earlier marriage (Goddeeris in print). Unfortunately, the details concerning the seals remain unpublished for several of these marriage contracts (PBS 8/2 107 and PBS 8/2 155). However, SAOC 44 1, ARN 37, BE 6/2 48[5], TMH 9 1 and TMH 9 2 are all sealed by husband and wife. The burgul seal enrolled on MesCiv 3 27 bears the names of the wife, identified with her patronymic, the husband, identified as "her husband", and the four adopted sons, identified as "heirs of the husband". Thus it appears that these contracts are concluded between husband and wife, but that the children of the wife may take over the position of the wife in the transaction. One marriage contract (TMH 9 1) is preserved in two copies, one for the wife and one for the husband.
- The situation is slightly different for real **adoption contracts** (Stone and Owen 1991). These may be sealed (always with burgul seals) by the adoptive parent(s), or by both the adoptive parent(s) and the adoptive child(ren).
  (1) Adoption contracts sealed **by the adoptive parent(s) only** (ARN 45, BE 6/2 24, BE 6/2 57, BE 6/2 28, OECT 8 20, OECT 8 21, TIM 4 13, TMH 9 6 and TMH 9 7) are kept by the adoptive son, who can use it as proof to enforce his claims on (part of) the property (Charpin 1994, 95). Apparently, the obligations to be met by the adoptive children speak for themselves here. Only TMH 9 6 can be situated in an archival context. This context illustrates that a tight bond between both families existed already prior to the adoption (Goddeeris in print).

[5] In the catalogue of ARN, Kraus (Cig, Kizilyay and Kraus 1952) also discusses the tablets published in BE 6/2 and now located in Istanbul, and recapitulates the details concerning the seal impressions on these tablets, which Poebel could not complete due to (a) lack of time (1909, 54).

(2) **When the adoptive child seals as well** (ARN 65, ARN 100, SAOC 44 30, TMH 9 8, TMH 9 9 and TMH 9 10), the document also serves as insurance for the adoptive parents that the adoptive children will meet their obligations. The contracts are too isolated and concise to understand the exact reasons for the extra seal. However, some factors playing a role in this process could be identified.

- In TMH 9 9 (Si 23), two brothers are adopted by a man who is presumably the brother of their deceased father. They bring their father's share in the paternal estate into the household of their uncle, and will be entitled to the share of the eldest brother and a normal share when the inheritance of their adoptive father/uncle is divided. Thus, this text records a transfer of property in two directions. Not only will the adoptive sons inherit from their adoptive father, also, they bring their biological father's share into the household of their adoptive father. Here, the double sealing speaks for itself. The copies for both parties have been preserved.
- The adoption recorded in TMH 9 8 (case BE 6/2 46, Si 15) involves the transfer of an exceptionally large amount of real estate to the adoptive daughter. One of the houses transferred appears to belong to Šamaš-liwwir, the brother of the adoptive mother, a *nadītum* priestess of Ninurta, rather than to herself (BE 6/2 12, cf. Goddeeris in print). The adoption is cancelled nine years later by Šamaš-liwwir, who thus redeems the family properties. In order to achieve this, he has to reimburse all the expenses for the sustenance. Apparently, Šamaš-liwwir was unable to support his sister during the economic crisis in the middle of the reign of Samsuiluna, and had to yield family properties to a party unrelated to the family. This lack of family relation may explain why the sustenance is not self-evident in this case, and why the adoptive daughter had to apply her burgul seal as well.
- The adoption recorded in TMH 9 10 (Si 28) may have been concluded in involuntary circumstances as well. Why else would a heiress give her rights on the *nešakkum* office of Enlil, rather than passing them on to her sons? However, the exact circumstances remain obscure. The profession of the adoptive son, a royal scribe, leads one to suspect that he moved in circles different from those of his adoptive mother. Thus, the social distance between the two parties may necessitate the drafting of a two-way contract.

- ARN 65 (Ha 30) is an amendment of ARN 45 (RS 56), where three brothers are adopted by a father. They will inherit his possessions. The earlier contract is sealed by the father, and serves as a title deed for the sons. The penalty in case of renouncement is heavier for the father than for the sons. In ARN 65, drafted some years later, on the other hand, the adopted sons face slavery if they break the contract. The reasons behind this amendment remain obscure, but the penalty clause implies a change in the position of the sons, which entitles the father to sell his sons if they do not live up to the unwritten part of the agreement. In these circumstances, the father would keep a sealed copy of the contract as well.
- ARN 100 (Si 16) and SAOC 44 30 (Si [ ]) are fragmentary. On SAOC 44 30, only the seal of the adoptive son is preserved, but only a fragment of the contract is preserved. It must be noted that the adopted child in SAOC 44 30 will be sold into slavery if he breaks the contract. However, the threat of slavery does not necessitate the presence of the seal of the son, as shown by BE 6/2 57.

(3) Four adoption contracts do not fit into the scheme, and are sealed by others than the adoptive parents and the adoptive children. All these exceptions can be explained.

- The burgul seal enrolled on SAOC 44 15 (Si 16) contains the names of the adopted son and of the natural son of the adoptive parents (Charpin 1994, 95 and Van de Mieroop 1991-1993, 126). This document thus serves to proof that both sons will receive their shares in the inheritance.
- BE 6/2 57 also resolves around the future division of the estate between the natural son and the adopted son, but the adopted son has a lower status here (will be sold into slavery if he renounces the contract).
- TIM 4 14 (RS 32) is sealed by the adoptive son and by a third party. The legend of this seal cannot be read, but is certainly not the name of the adoptive father. It may be one of the other parties mentioned in atypical clauses of the contract, a certain Aḫassunu, who becomes the daughter of the adoptive son, or a certain Lulīja, who receives sustenance.
- The sealings on BE 6/2 4 (RS 6) are easily explained; they mention the adoptive mother and the natural parents of the girl (who give up the rights on their daughter in return for a sum of silver as "upbringing payment").

– In Nippur, **divisions of inheritance** usually open with a description of the extra share of the eldest brother, and then list the shares of all the heirs (Klima 1940, 20-21). Each heir receives a duplicate, which can serve as title deed for his share. The tablets are sealed with burgul seals — either with a single seal enumerating all heirs before giving the patronymic, or with a separate seal for each heir. The only exception to this rule is formed by the eldest (undated but earlier than the reign of Sumu-el) and most extensive division of inheritance, TMH 9 13, which is preserved in two duplicates. One duplicate is too damaged to identify any seal impressions, the other copy consists of three fragments, located in three different museums. The edge of the fragment preserved in Istanbul, published previously as ARN 20, displays impressions of two different burgul seals belonging to two of the four heirs. The largest fragment, now kept in the Hilprecht-Sammlung in Jena, bears an impression of the cylinder seal of the eldest son, on which he is described as $gudu_4$ ^{d}Nin-líl-lá, an office he inherits as his extra share in the text.

– Finally, the possession of property may be established by **judicial documents** assigning the property to one of the parties and confirming the decision by an oath in which the party giving up his rights on the property swears that, in future, he, nor any of his heirs, will claim the property. Since some of the judicial documents bear personal seal impressions, and others burgul seal impressions, they are discussed more thoroughly below.

2. *Contracts securing future obligations*

PBS 8/2 116 (RS 50) and TMH 9 11 (Si 4) are atypical contracts, recording the obligation of a number of brothers to **support** their sister, who is a *nadītum* priestess of Ninurta in both cases. I do not know of any other contracts concerned only with future obligations. Contrary to the transactions related to family law discussed in the above section, which also include the conclusion of future obligations, the "obligation contract" TMH 9 11 is sealed with a personal seal.[6] Unfortunately, the owner of the seal cannot be identified. The publication of PBS 8/2 116, concerning the support of the aunt of the *nadītum* sustained in TMH 9 11, contains no details concerning its sealings.

The application of a personal seal here confirms that the **marriage and adoption contracts** are title deeds in the first place, and that the

[6] The details concerning the sealing of PBS 8/2 116 are not published.

sustenance clauses in these contracts are self-evident, that they do not need to be secured by a sealed contract, a hypothesis put forward already above, in the discussion of the party mentioned on the burgul seal in adoption contracts.

Besides adoption and marriage contracts, **bequests** are a third type of text which include future obligations (Stol 1998). Although TIM 4 27 (Enlil-bani d), sealed with burgul seals of three brothers, opens with a support clause for their mother, it also records how the sons give her a slave girl in order to provide in this support. Thus, this contract must be considered as a title deed of the slave girl. This assumption is confirmed by PBS 8/1 1 (Bur-Sîn a), a contract consisting of a bequest and a support clause as well. Here, a mother assigns all her possessions (a house and a slave girl) to her daughter in return for sustenance. The contract is sealed by the mother only. A last bequest document, ARN 29 (RS 24), records how a father, Enlil-rabi, and a brother, Iddin-Šamaš, give two fields and a slave girl to Bēltani, a *nadītum* priestess of Ninurta, and how Iddin-Šamaš, along with his other brothers, declares that he will provide for her. The document is sealed with a burgul seal mentioning Enlil-rabi, the father. Again, the sealing does not concern the sustenance. Together with his now named brothers and sister, Iddin-Šamaš repeats his declaration concerning the sustenance 26 years later in PBS 8/2 116 (cf. above).

PBS 8/1 16 (Damiq-ilīšu 13), a division of inheritance drafted during the father's lifetime, includes a support clause as well, but is sealed with burgul seals belonging to the two heirs.

These obligations to support wife and children, to support parents in their old age, and to support unmarried sisters, are based on long term traditions, rooted in a patrilocal and patrilineal society. Therefore, there is little need to draft a sealed contract for this aspect of the family transactions.

3. *Short term obligations*

Loans and leases are concluded for a much shorter period, mostly a year or less. After the fulfillment of the obligation, the written contract is usually destroyed. Therefore, we do not have all the loans and leases concluded in the archives at our disposal. However, the sample is large enough to allow conclusions concerning the sealing habits. Loans and leases are sealed with personal seals, sometimes belonging to the lessee or debtor, sometimes to one or several of the witnesses, sometimes to both.

Rarely, the owner of the seal can be identified on the basis of the seal legend. Occasionally, the impression comes with a by-script mentioning the owner. Often, though, the owner of the seal cannot be identified at all.

4. *Judicial documents*

Witnessed documents related to lawsuits may be sealed with personal seals or with burgul seals in Nippur. This provides us with an ideal test case to investigate the factors determining the choice of seal.

First a chronological overview of the judicial documents sealed with burgul seals is given:

- PBS 8/1 2 + ARN 4 (Bur-Sîn 4): Fragments of a lawsuit concerning a division of inheritance. The tablet is sealed with the burgul seals of the heirs.
- SAOC 44 36 (Lipit-Enlil c): Three individuals (brothers?) make a claim concerning a built plot belonging to a fourth individual. They receive 1 šekel of silver (the final payment for the plot sold earlier), swear by the king that they will not make claims in future and seal with a burgul seal.
- ARN 11 (Enlil-bani o): Ilšu-muballiṭ and KA-kugani make a claim concerning a field lease. The accused, Lu-tilimuzu, Miršaganan and Lu-Bau swear a no-claim oath and seal the tablet with burgul seals.
- ARN 12 + OIMA I 6 (Iter-pîša a): Dispute between KA-kugani, brother of Ilšu-muballiṭ, and Sal-kala, wife of Ilšu-muballit, concerning a share of the inheritance of Ilšu-muballiṭ. Sal-kala gives KA-kugani and his mother a built plot. In return, KA-kugani swears a no-claim oath and seals the tablet with a burgul seal.
- Belleten 26 2 (Damiq-ilīšu 6): Nanna-adaḫ makes a claim against Ḫunabatum concerning a house that Ḫunabatum bought from Geme-Nanna, sister of Nanna-adaḫ, two years earlier. Ḫunabatum gives an amount of silver to Nanna-adah. Nanna-adaḫ and Geme-Nanna swear a no-claim oath and seal the document with burgul seals.
- ARN 38 (RS 42 [+x]): Sîn-remenni disinherits his son Mannum-kīma-Adad. Mannum-kīma-Adad swears a no-claim oath and seals with a burgul seal.
- ARN 36 (RS 48): Nannatum disinherits his son Rīm-Adad. Rīm-Adad swears a no-claim oath and seals with a burgul seal.
- BE 6/2 10 (Ha 33): Mar-erṣetim and Mutum-ilī, heirs of Adad-rabi, make a claim concerning a field, which Ududu, brother of Adad-rabi,

had given to Adad-rabi as equivalent for a temple office which he inherited. The court ordered the heirs of Ududu to give a built plot, the equivalent of the field. Iškur-gira and Ipqatum, heirs of Ududu, swear a no-claim oath and seal with burgul seals.

- ARN 59 (Ha [ ]): Fragment of a lawsuit concerning the adoption of a slave girl (?). Sealed with a burgul seal belonging to Niši-inišu, daughter of Taribum, who apparently gives up her claims on the girl.
- PBS 8/2 129 (Si 5): a large piece of unbuilt property, acquired by Imšiši and KA-Damu through inheritance and purchase, but left undivided, is divided between the heirs of Imšiši and KA-Damu, several generations later. The heirs of Imšiši and KA-Damu swear a no-claim oath and seal with burgul seals.
- OECT 8 11 (Si 11): Ninurta-muštal, Namaršu-lumur and Munawwirum give a term in a temple office to Mannum-mešu-liṣṣur, to compensate for the expenses incurred for their father. Ninurta-muštal, Namaršu-lumur and Munawwirum swear a no-claim oath and seal the document with burgul seals.
- BE 6/2 49 (Si 19): Šumum-libši makes a claim concerning a field once inherited by Apil-ilīšu and since transferred to other parties. One of the accused has given Šumum-libši an amount of silver. Šumum-libši swears a no-claim oath and seals the tablet with a burgul seal.
- ARN 16 (—): An amount of silver belongs to Ku-Amurrum. His heart is satisfied. Enlil-sipa and Ilšu-muballiṭ swear a no-claim oath and seal with a burgul seal.
- SAOC 44 24 ([ ]): Concerning the adoption of Ili-u-Šamaš by Amurrum-šemi from Marti-erṣetim (biological mother of Ili-u-Šamaš). [ ]. The judges decide to dissolve the adoption and to draft a no-claim tablet. The tablet is ratified by a no-claim oath sworn by Ili-u-Šamaš and by the application of his burgul seal.
- ARN 59 ([ ]): Fragment of a judicial document. Although this badly preserved judicial document does not contain a no-claim oath, but rather concludes with a statement giving the authorities and the location of the trial, it is sealed with a burgul seal.

Here follows a list of judicial documents sealed with personal seals belonging to one of the parties or to one or several of the witnesses.

- TMH 9 101 (RS 37) describes the proceedings of a case initiated by Ipqatum and Mār-erṣetim against Ṣilli-Ninurta concerning the ownership of a slave-girl. The judges decide that the slave girl and her infant belong to Rubatum, sister of Ṣilli-Ninurta, and that the daughter of the slave girl will be set free and ordained as a *nadītum* priestess of Numušda. The no-claim clause is included in the sentence of the judges, not in an oath by the king.

- PBS 8/1 81 (Ha 31 / VI): In the temple of Amurrum, Lugal-zimu and Ur-Pabilsaĝa settle their accounts in front of witnesses. They swear a no-claim oath, and the tablet is sealed by one of the witnesses (identified in a by-script).
- PBS 8/1 82 (Ha 31 / VII): Lugal-zimu swears an oath concerning the sustenance of his sister in the temple of Amurrum in front of witnesses. Sealed by one of the witnesses.[7]
- PBS 8/2 125 (Ha 31 / IX): Lawsuit resulting in the repayment of a loan. Sîn-iqīšam, the creditor, (?) swears a no-claim oath. Sealed with two personal seals, one belonging to a witness and one belonging to a father of a witness.
- BE 6/2 14 (Ha 37): Concerning a division wall, Mar-erṣetim has satisfied his neighbor with an amount of silver. Sealed by several witnesses.
- In very different terms, the tablet and the case of TMH 9 103 (Ha 41) state how Zikir-ilīšu has set free Naramtum and her sons (and has married Naramtum). Šamaš-bani (brother of Zikir-ilišu), Bēlānum and his brother, do not have any claim of Naramtum and her sons and on Zikir-ilīšu's properties. The tablet does not include a no-claim clause.
- BE 6/2 62 (Si 1): Concerning Bēlī-iddinam and his sons, whom Ilima-AN had seized. His family established that he was a native of Nippur. Ilima-AN swears a no-claim oath and seals with his personal seal. Three other personal seals, belonging to three of the witnesses (two can be identified on the basis of their legend, one bears a caption) are enrolled as well.
- In TMH 9 104 (Si 2), Damiq-ilīšu brings charges against his second wife (cf. TMH 9 3) in front of witnesses. The document relates how the case is settled, but does not contain a no-claim clause.
- ARN 82 (Si 7): Fragment of a judicial document. Opens with a list of witnesses. Sealed with personal seals of four witnesses, identified by captions.
- BE 6/2 30 (Si 11): In front of witnesses, Mar-erṣetim, Mutum-ilī and Ipqatum swear that if they reopen the judicial case concerning the exchange, the judges may inflict a penalty (they probably refer to the lawsuit concluded about 20 years earlier in BE 6/2 10, cf. above). The

[7] Identified in a caption. The witness, Nanna-zimu uses the seal of a certain Warad-ilīšu, according to the legend.

text describes the swearing of a no-claim oath, but does not actually record it. Moreover it opens with the witnesses. The owner of the personal seal cannot be identified.

- ARN 98 (Si 13): Concerning the barley that Narubtum has lent from [ ]unzitum, She will give the daily bread offerings during four months. Sealed with an unidentified personal seal.
- ARN 101 (Si 22): Ṭab-ṣillašu has provided for Lamassum for a long time. Šamaš-liwwir, brother of Lamassum made a claim against Ṭab-ṣillašu concerning his parental estate. He (Ṭab-ṣillašu?) set a term of 5 months for the return of the estate and the sustenance. If Šamaš-liwwir does not bring his son and his brother (as pledges), he will compensate Ṭab-ṣillašu for the expenses and the sustenance. The owner of the personal seal enrolled on the tablet cannot be identified. The silver paid for these expenses and the sustenance is calculated in TMH 9 105 (Goddeeris in print). This confirms that the case is not settled when ARN 101 is drafted.
- BE 6/2 58 (Si 23): Lawsuit concerning an unexecuted marriage agreement. The tablet does not mention a no-claim oath. The owner of the personal seal cannot be identified.
- ARN 77 ([ ]): fragment of a judicial document, sealed with a personal seal.

Some judicial documents, such as ARN 57 and 58, TMH 9 105, SAOC 44 4 and BE 6/2 52-54 are unsealed. Probably, these are not official documents, but drafts to investigate the evidence for a case.

Two features catch the eye in the enumeration above. On the one hand, the documents starting with a list of the witnesses (PBS 8/1 81, ARN 82 and TMH 1 104) are always sealed with personal seals. Here, the emphasis lays on what happened in front of these witnesses, the court proceedings, and the witnesses play an essential role, therefore, they seal. On the other hand, except for the fragment ARN 59, all the judicial documents sealed with a burgul seal conclude with a no-claim oath, whereas only three of the thirteen documents sealed with personal seals contain this clause. The no-claim oath is sworn only in title deeds and does not occur in loans, leases and sustenance contracts. It displays more or less the same distribution as the burgul seal. The judicial documents sealed with a burgul seal and containing a no-claim oath must therefore be considered as title deeds. The case is settled in a definitive way, and the ultimate ownership is assigned. The three documents containing a no-claim oath but sealed with personal seals are situated on the border between title deeds and court proceedings. PBS 8/1 81 describes how the ownership is assigned, but is not a title deed since the object of the judicial procedure is not thoroughly described. Although PBS 8/2 125 and BE 6/2 62 describe the object of the lawsuit, they concentrate on the proceedings of the lawsuit, opening with *aššum*. However, BE 6/2 49 opens with *aššum* as well, and is sealed with a burgul seal. Thus, not all the factors determining what type of seal must be used can be explained, but the above comparison has clearly established the function of the two types of seals used in Nippur.

5. *Some atypical documents*

Several one-of-a-kind documents cannot be fitted in the typology described above. The bequest of a field located on palace land recorded in TMH 9 25 (Si 12) seems a sale document in disguise. Enlil-nīšu gives his share in the field belonging to his father to his brother, in return for an amount of silver qualified as "expenses". However, it is sealed with the personal seal of the scribe. This ambiguity is related to the restrictions on the alienation of palace land. TMH 9 91 (Si 24) is an atypical contract regulating the arrangement of the performance of a temple office and is sealed with a personal seal.

B. Sealing contracts in other Old Babylonian towns

Sealing practices in other Babylonian towns were different from those described above. The most recent overview was given by Leemans (1982, 226-236). Here follows an updated summary of his outline.

Southern Babylonia

In **Larsa**, title deeds are sealed by the witnesses with their personal seal. At the end of the list of witnesses, the documents contain the phrase "kišib (lú)-inim-ma-bi-meš íb-ra", the witnesses enroll their seal. Other contracts, in which a party is entering into an obligation, such as loans, rental contracts, leases and herding contracts, may not contain witnesses and are sealed in those cases with the personal seal of the party taking on a commitment. When witnesses are present on these documents, they may seal as well, in which case the phrase "kišib lú-inim-ma-bi-meš" reappears (Leemans 1982, 228-229).

The earlier sealing practices in **Ur** were comparable to those known from Nippur and described in depth above. Title deeds are generally sealed with burgul seals mentioning the party giving up the right on the property. Divisions of inheritance were sealed by all the heirs, on a single seal or on different seals. Rental contracts, loans and receipts on the other hand were sealed with personal seals. In those cases where the owner of the seal can be identified, it belongs to the lessee, the debtor or the beneficiary (Charpin 1980, 11-17; Leemans 1982, 226-227). In the course of the reign of Rīm-Sîn of Larsa, the sealing customs of Larsa are taken over in Ur; all title deeds are sealed with the personal seals of witnesses and a lease is sealed with a personal seal belonging to the farmer.

The small town **Kutalla**, located in the proximity of Larsa, holds the same practices as Larsa. However, under the reign of the kings of Babylon, some title deeds are sealed with the personal seals of the seller as well as those of the witnesses (Leemans 1982, 230), a practice assumed from Babylon.

Central Babylonia

The sealing practices in use in **Nippur** have been described thoroughly above.

The sealings on the early contracts from **Isin** display the same characteristics as those from Nippur and Ur. However, towards the end of the reign of Rīm-Sîn of Larsa, the system used in Larsa and Kutalla is adopted, yet, without adding the phrase "kišib lú-inim-ma-bi-meš (íb-ra)". Under the reign of Samsuiluna, the traditions of Babylon are adopted, and the seller seals alongside the witnesses in Isin.

In Kisurra, the contracts, all dating to the early Isin-Larsa period, are sealed by the party giving up rights or assuming obligations (seller, debtor, lessee). Contrary to Kienasts' (1978, 51) observations, permanent seals are not attested. In Kisurra, debtors and lessees seal with a burgul seal as well (Goddeeris 2009).

Northern Babylonia

The early Old Babylonian contracts from **Marad**, the **Mananaia dynasty** and **Kiš** adopt the same system as the one observed in Kisurra, bearing impressions of the burgul seal of the seller, debtor or lessee. The contracts from Kiš dating to the later Old Babylonian period, when Kiš is part of the core of the Babylonian empire, on the other hand, bear impressions of personal seals belonging to the seller and the witnesses, corresponding to the traditions from Babylon. Above, we have observed that these practices are gradually adopted in Isin and Kutalla as well.

In the core area of the Babylonian empire, north of Marad and Kiš, a tradition very different from that of Nippur and Ur can be observed. In **Sippar**, the cases of the sale contracts are sealed by some of the witnesses and sometimes also by the seller. If the seller seals, his seal appears first, on the upper edge or the top of the left margin. The witnesses seal on the left margin of the case in a random order (Tanret 2010, 223). Again, contracts without no-claim oath are sealed according to different rules. Most often, they did not have a case; the tablet is sealed by the farmer, the tenant or the debtor, sometimes also by a witness.

The sealing practices in **Babylon** are the same as those known from Sippar (Klengel-Brandt 1983, 102-103; 1989, 353). Personal seals belonging to witnesses — and rarely to debtor, seller, farmer or tenant — are enrolled on the cases of the contracts. From the reign of Samsuiluna onwards, they increasingly figure on the tablets.

The earliest Old Babylonian contracts from **Dilbat** reveal inconsistent sealing practices. Some tablets give the impression that the seller has to seal, whereas others are sealed with the personal seals of some of the witnesses (Leemans 1982, 235-236). However, the later tablets are all sealed according to the practices known from Sippar and Babylon.

The Diyala region

The sites from the Diyala region have mainly yielded documents originating from temple or palace archives. The contracts that have been recovered cannot be placed in the context of a family archive. Unfortunately, the text publications contain only limited details concerning the sealings. In **Ešnunna** (Whiting 1977), all real estate sales bear impressions of both a burgul and a personal seal. The personal seal belongs to the official who has measured the plot sold (*šassukkum* or *kakikkum*). The seller always seals the document with a burgul seal. It is remarkable that these documents contain no oath. The reason may be that the records were kept in a central archive in the palace (Reichel 2001, 129). As far as the findings from **Nerebtum** allows any conclusions, personal seals seem to occur on different types of documents (Greengus 1986). Loans seem to remain unsealed (Greengus 1979). On some of the contracts from **Šaduppum**, which originate from private archives, personal seals of the witnesses are enrolled as well (Simmons 1959-1961; Ellis 1971, 1988).

Conclusion

The Ur III period witnesses the appearance of sealed contracts. The party who undertakes an obligation (seller, debtor, etc.) enrolls his personal seal on the (envelope of the) contract. Also, the document may be sealed by a family member of this party or by an official (Steinkeller 1977). With the upsurge of written contracts around 1900 BC, sealing practices further develop. The political fragmentation of the area brings about a clear-cut variation in sealing practices. Three major traditions of sealing contracts are attested in the Old Babylonian.

(1) In Babylon, Sippar, Larsa, Kutalla, Nerebtum and Šaduppum, witnesses usually enroll their seal on the title deeds, occasionally alongside the sellers. Debtors, lessees and other parties giving up their rights or taking up an obligation may enroll their seal as well. The use of burgul seals is not attested in these towns.
(2) In Marad, Kisurra, Mananaia and Kiš, the party giving up his rights on property or taking on a future obligation, confirms this by a burgul seal.
(3) The title deeds from Nippur, Ur and Isin are impressed with burgul seals belonging to the party giving up its rights, which are then kept in the archives of the new owner. On contracts recording obligations, the personal seals of witnesses and/or the party assuming an obligation are enrolled in these cities.

The real estate sales from Ešnunna form a singular case. Not containing an oath, and kept in the central palatial archive, they cannot be considered as normal title deeds. The burgul seal of the seller is reminiscent of the title deed aspect of the documents, whereas the personal seal of the official emphasizes their administrative side.

Parallel to the territorial unification of Babylonia, the sealing practices assimilate, until the use of the burgul seal completely disappears after the reign of Samsuiluna. Under the successors of Sumu-la-el of Babylon, the contracts from Kiš assume the procedures from Babylon. Marad, Kisurra and Mananaia do not have any documentation more recent than the reign of Sabium. Ur and Isin take over the tradition known from Larsa and Babylon in the course of Rīm-Sîn's reign. Nippur holds on to its own system until the written documentation from the city ceases in the 30th year of Samsuiluna.

In the subsequent Middle Babylonian period, the sealing tradition introduced in southern Babylonia by the dynasty of Babylon is carried on in a slightly altered way. Personal seals of the party undertaking an obligation (and of the witnesses) are enrolled on the contract (Renger 1977, 77-78).

The unambiguous alternation that can be observed in the distribution of burgul seals and personal seals on the contracts from Nippur demonstrates how important it is to distinguish title deeds from other contracts in Babylonian archive-keeping. Our traditional classification, opposing contracts to judicial documents, and associating adoption and marriage contracts with sustenance contracts under the heading "family law" versus "real estate documents" comprising sales and leases, appears to be an artificial construction.

Bibliography

BIGGS, R. D. and McG. GIBSON (eds.) 1977: *Seals and Sealing in the Ancient Near East* (BiMes 6), Malibu.

CIĞ, M., H. KIZILYAY and F. R. KRAUS 1952: *Eski Babil zamanina ait Nippur hukukî vesikalari / Altbabylonische Rechtsurkunden aus Nippur*, Istanbul.

CHARPIN, D. 1980: *Archives familiales et propriété privée en Babylonie ancienne: Étude des documents de "Tell Sifr"*, Genève.

— 1994: "Review: E. C. Stone and D. I. Owen, *Adoption in Old Babylonian Nippur and the Archive of Mannum-mešu-liṣṣur*", *JAOS 114*, 94-96.

— 1998: "Noms de personnes et légendes des sceaux en Babylonie ancienne", in A.-M. Christin (ed.), *L'écriture du nom propre*, Paris, 43-55.

ELLIS, M. deJ. 1971: "Old Babylonian Economic Texts and Letters from Harmal", *JCS 24*, 1-62.

— 1988: "Old Babylonian Texts from Harmal — and Elsewhere?", in M. deJ. Ellis, P. Gerardi and E. Leichty (eds.), *A Scientific Humanist: Studies in the Memory of Abraham Sachs*, 119-141.

GODDEERIS, A. 2009: *Tablets from Kisurra in the collections of the British Museum.* (SANTAG 9), Wiesbaden.

— in print: "The Adoption of Women in Old Babylonian Nippur", in G. Suurmeyer (ed.), *Adoption in the Old Babylonian period.*

GREENGUS, S. 1979: *Old Babylonian Tablets from Ishchali and Vicinity*, Istanbul.

— 1986: *Studies in Ishchali Documents* (BiMes 19), Malibu.

KIENAST, B. 1978: *Die altbabylonischen Briefe und Urkunden aus Kisurra* (FAOS 2), Freiburg.

KLENGEL-BRANDT, E. 1983: "Siegelabrollungen auf altbabylonischen Tontafeln aus Babylon", *AoF 10*, 65-106.

— 1989: "Altbabylonische Siegelabrollungen (VS VII-IX)", *AoF 16*, 253-356.

KLIMA, J. 1940: *Untersuchungen zum altbabylonischen Erbrecht*, Prague.

LEEMANS, W. F. 1982: "La fonction des sceaux, apposés à des contrats vieux-babyloniens", in G. van Driel, Th. J. H. Krispijn, M. Stol and K. R. Veenhof (eds.), *Zikir šumim. Assyriological Studies presented to F.R. Kraus on the Occasion of his Seventieth Birthday*, Leiden, 219-244.

POEBEL 1907: "Der bur-gul als Notar in Nippur", *OLZ 10*, 175-181.

— 1909: *Legal and Business Documents from the time of the First Dynasty of Babylon chiefly from Nippur* (BE 6/2), Philadelphia.

REICHEL, C. D. 2001: "Seals and Sealings at Tell Asmar: A new Look at an Ur III to Early Old Babylonian Palace", in W. W. Hallo and I. J. Winter (eds.), *Proceedings of the XLV^{e}Rencontre Assyriologique Internationale Part II, Yale University: Seals and Seal Impressions*, Bethesda, 101-131.

RENGER, J. 1977: "Legal Aspects of Sealing in Ancient Mesopotamia", in R. D. Biggs and McG. Gibson 1977, 75-88.

SIMMONS, S. D. 1959-1961: "Early Old Babylonian Documents from Harmal and Elsewhere", *JCS 13*, 71-93 and 105-119, *JCS 14*, 23-32 and 75-87, *JCS 15*, 49-58 and 81-83.

STEINKELLER, P. 1977: "Seal Practice in the Ur III Period" in R.D. Biggs and McG. Gibson (eds.), *Seals and Sealing in the Ancient Near East* (BiMes 6), Malibu, 41-53.

STOL, M. 1998: "The Care of the Elderly in Mesopotamia in the Old Babylonian Period", in M. Stol and S.P. Vleeming (eds.), *The Care of the Elderly in the Ancient Near East* (SHCAN 14), Leiden, 59-117.

STONE, E. 1987: *Nippur Neighborhoods* (SOAC 44), Chicago.

TANRET, M. 2009: *The Seal of the Sanga. On the Old Babylonian Sangas of Šamaš of Sippar-Jahrūrum and Sippar-Amnanum* (Cuneiform Monographs 40), Leiden-Boston.

VAN DE MIEROOP, M. 1991-1993: "Review: E. C. Stone and D. I. Owen, *Adoption in Old Babylonian Nippur and the Archive of Mannum-mešu-liṣṣur*", *JCS 43-45*, 124-130.

VAN LERBERGHE, K. 1986: *Old Babylonian Legal and Administrative Texts from Philadelphia* (OLA 21), Leuven.

VAN LERBERGHE, K. and G. VOET 1989: "A Long Lasting Life", in H. Behrens, D. Loding and M. Roth (eds.), DUMU-E2-DUB-BA-A, Studies in Honor of Å. W. Sjöberg, Philadelphia, 525-538.

— 1991: "On "Quasi-Hüllentafeln"", *Northern Akkad Project Reports,* 6, 3-8.

— 1993, "Sealing in Philadelphia and Elsewhere", *Acta Archaeologica Lovaniensia 32*, 43-58.

— 2009: *A Late Old Babylonian Temple Archive from Dur-Abieshuh* (Cornell University Studies in Assyriology and Sumerology 8), Bethesda.

WHITING, R. M. 1977, "Sealing Practices on House and Land Sale documents at Eshnunna in the Isin-Larsa Period", in R. D. Biggs and McG. Gibson 1977, 67-74.

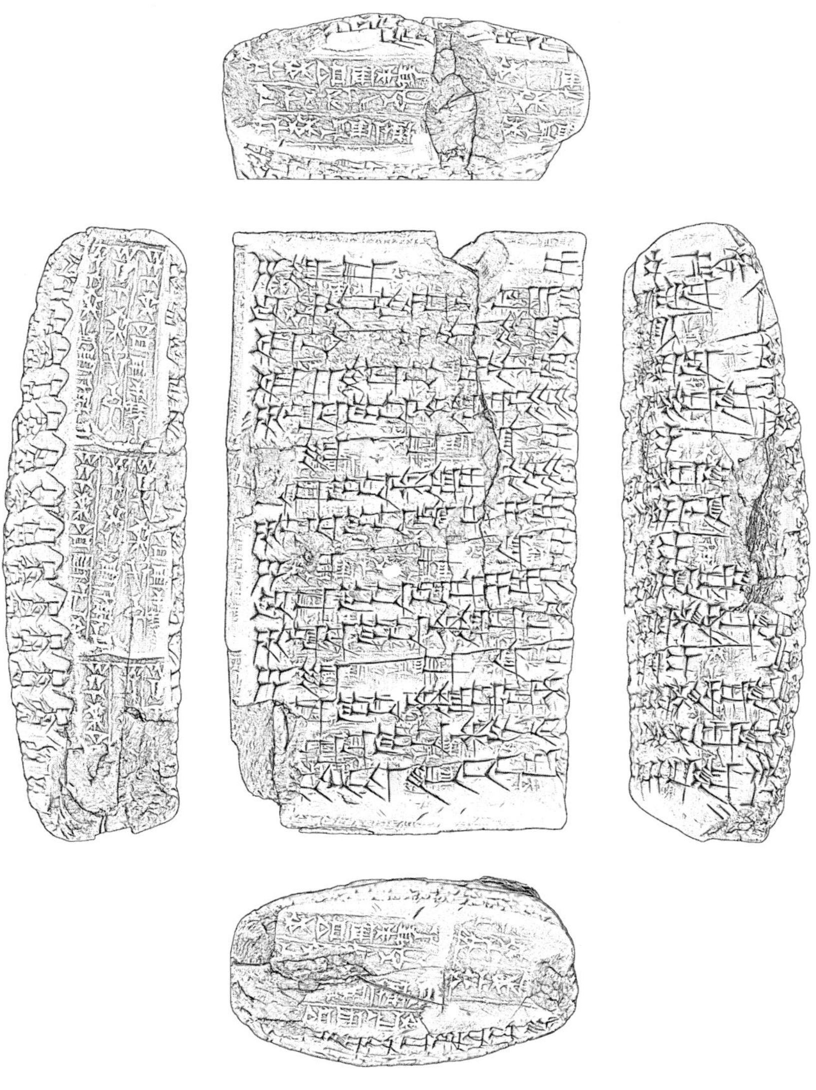

Fig. 1. TMH 9 19 obverse.

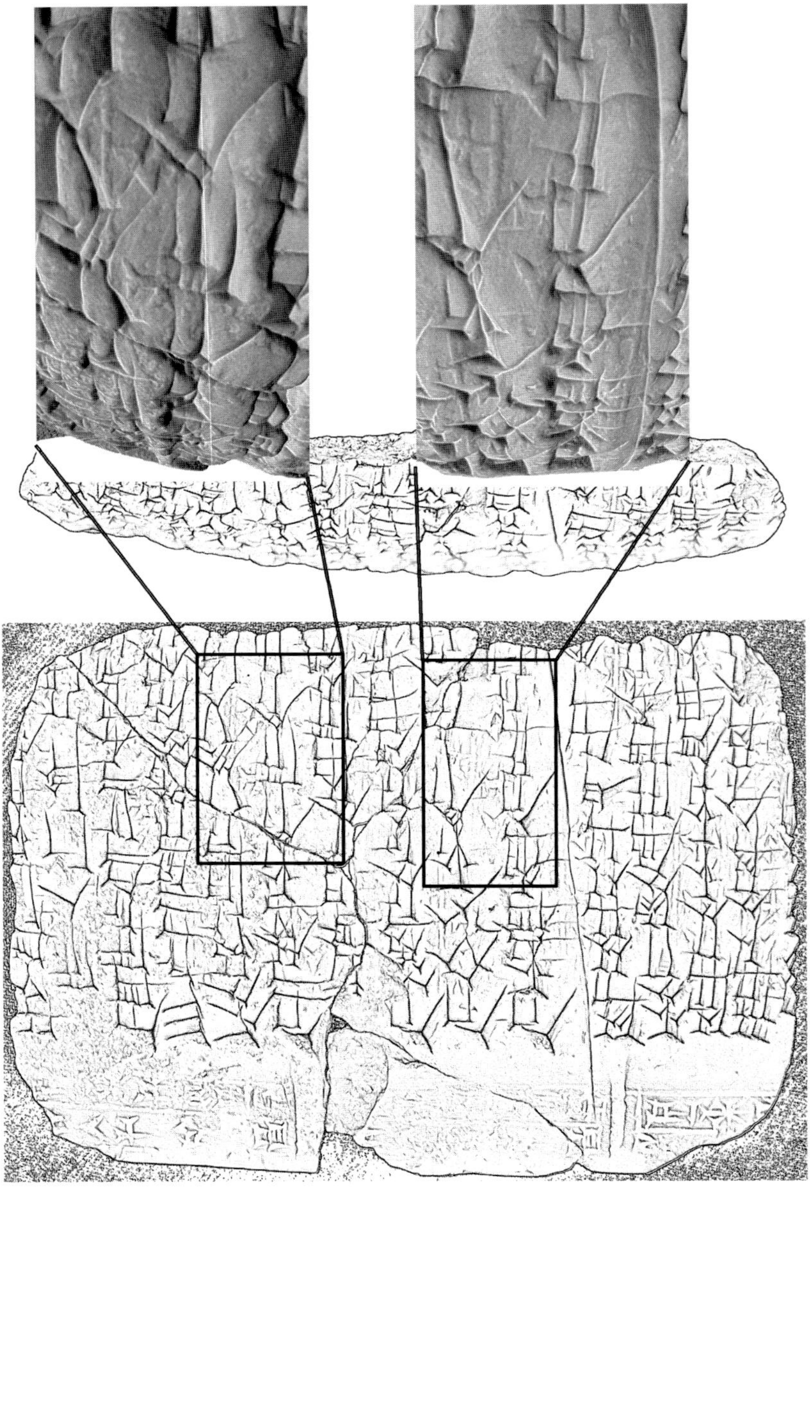

Fig. 2. TMH 9 50b obverse.

THE CLAY RATTLES FROM TELL TWEINI (SYRIA) AND THEIR CONTRIBUTION TO THE MUSICAL TRADITION OF THE ANCIENT NEAR EAST

Elynn GORRIS*
Université catholique de Louvain

Archaeological sites in the Levant and Mesopotamia have revealed numerous examples of musical instruments such as cymbals, bone whistles, bells, clay rattles and conch trumpets. Other instruments like the lyre, lute, double pipe and round-frame drum are generally known from representations on reliefs and statuettes (Braun 2002, table 1).

Recent excavations at the site of the coastal harbor town Tell Tweini, in North West Syria, have unearthed several musical instruments, including two conch trumpets (Gorris-Verhulst forth., 21-28) and three clay rattles from the Iron Age. Tell Tweini or ancient Gibala is a peer-shaped mound, located c. 1,5 kilometers land inwards from the Mediterranean Sea nearby the modern town of Jebleh (fig. 1). This village is occupied since the early Bronze Age and was presumably the southernmost harbor of the Ugaritic kingdom during the Late Bronze Age. After the collapse of the Ugaritic Kingdom (c. 1200 B.C.), Gibala extended its maritime trade under Phoenician and Neo-Assyrian domination.

It is a pleasure to present this article on the Tell Tweini clay rattles to my dear professor of Ancient Near Eastern languages & archaeology K. Van Lerberghe, who headed the Tell Tweini excavation project for ten years (1999-2008).

1. The Clay Rattle as Musical Instrument

The clay rattle is one of the earliest and most basic shaken musical instruments recovered in representative numbers in the Ancient Near East (Haifa Music Museum 1971, *Intro*) and appeared in all kinds of shapes (Savariego 2010), such as spools, pie-crusts, jugs, animals, with or without

* I am grateful to W. Verhulst and S. Willaert of the Musical Instruments Museum (Brussels) for sharing their musical insights on the matter. Tell Tweini is excavated by a Syro-Belgian team under the direction of Prof. M. Al-Maqdissi (Department of Antiquities, Syria) and Prof. J. Bretschneider (Catholic University of Leuven). I thank them for giving me the opportunity to work on the material of the Tweini mission.

a handle. In the classification of musical instruments, made by E. M. von Hornbostel and C. Sachs (1914; 1961, category 112.13), these clay rattles are categorized as "indirectly struck idiophones", since *the sound is produced by the body of the instrument* and *the percussion results indirectly through another movement by the player*. More specifically, the clay rattle belongs to the subclass of the "vessel rattles", because *the rattling objects enclosed in a vessel strike against each other or against the walls of the vessel, or usually against both.*

Thus, the sound volume of the clay rattle largely depends on the rattling objects enclosed and the perforations in the body. Most clay rattles have a number of clay pellets sealed inside, although the earliest Ancient Near Eastern examples (until the 4th millennium B.C.) might have been filled with dried fruit seeds or small pebbles instead of clay pellets. These fruit seeds did not survive the ravages of time, resulting in hollow clay rattle bodies. The number of clay pellets varies from one larger clay pellet to about twelve small pellets, depending on the shape and size of the body. The clay rattle with one clay pellet produces a muffled sound, while the rattle with the multiple pellets sounds louder and sharper, since the pellets bounce against each other as well as against the body. Also the perforations in the body, varying in number, contribute to the acoustic effect of the rattle by letting the vibrations escape (Piamenta 2007, 77). Late Bronze Age rattles are often lacking these perforations, which leads to the sound being muffled.

Most Ancient Near Eastern rattles are manufactured in baked clay, although other materials such as bronze were not excluded. In Ebla (Tell el-Mardikh) in North East Syria, four bronze rattles (2000-1800 B.C.) with an elongated body were discovered inside tombs (Pinnock 1979, 185-190; Matthiae 1995, 423 n° 292). The bronze rattles flourished especially in Western Iran during the early first millennium B.C. A large collection of these West Iranian bronze rattles is exhibited in the Metropolitan Museum, New York (1987.514. 3, 4, 12-19, 22, 24, 36, 37). Generally, bronze rattles have only one bronze pellet sealed inside. The stylistic tradition of the bronze rattles is different from that of the clay rattle and does therefore not fall within the scope of this article.

According to B. A. Rodgers, clay objects belong to the most durable and long lasting objects made by man. The artifact itself may be broken, but the component from which it is constructed is almost indestructible (Rodgers 2004, 141). The clay rattle is especially well preserved at Mesopotamian archeological sites of Middle Bronze Age (2000-1600 B.C.). S. A. Rachid (1984, 98-101) counted more than a hundred clay rattles in Mesopotamia, while eighty-four clay rattles between the Stone Age and the Iron Age have been uncovered so far in the Southern Levant (Braun 2007, 22). An in-depth research of the clay rattles in the Northern Levant is still missing, because not much is published on musical traditions of the region in general. This article wants to add new information on Northern Levantine musical traditions through discussion of the style, function and manufacturing methods of the three Tell Tweini clay rattles and through comparison with the Southern Levantine and Mesopotamian exemplars.

2. The Tell Tweini Clay Rattles

a. *Description*

During the archaeological campaigns of 2000, 2002 and 2008 three spool-shaped clay rattles were excavated in the Iron Age II layers (900-700 B.C.), at the centre of Tell Tweini. The first complete clay rattle (TWE-A-08-6351-M001) measures 10,0 cm in length by 9,0 cm at its widest point (fig. 3). The narrowest point in the middle has a width of 5,4 cm. The clay rattle is perforated twice, at the top and at the bottom, with small holes of about 8 mm to increase the sound. Inside the slightly damaged clay rattle, twelve clay pellets were enclosed. These pellets have an average diameter of 1,1 cm. The rattle contains no traces of decoration, incisions or paint.

The second complete Tell Tweini clay rattle (TWE-A-02-222-M003), was found in a heavily eroded condition. This instrument is slightly larger than the first rattle and measures 11,1 cm in length by 8,3 cm at its widest point (fig. 4). The narrowest point in the middle has a diameter of 5,9 cm. This rattle too is perforated twice at the top and at the bottom of the body and has no traces of paint or incised decoration. Its shape suggests that the second spool-shaped rattle too contained clay pellets, now lost.

The third Tell Tweini clay rattle (TWE-A-00-501-C038) is only partially preserved. Archaeologists found an undecorated sherd from the spool-shaped upper body, which had identical dimensions as the upper body (9,0 cm wide) of the first Tell Tweini clay rattle (fig. 5), but were unable to recover the clay pellets.

All three Tell Tweini rattles were made out of the same clay, which is pinkish grey on the outside and greyish on the inside. The clay of these rattles is identical to the Tell Tweini F4 storage jars (Vansteenhuyse 2008, 120) which were, as established through petrographic research, locally manufactured during the Iron Age at Tell Tweini.

b. *Archaeological Context*

During the early Iron Age II, a new economic impulse under Assyrian domination stimulated the redevelopment of the city centre at Tell Tweini (Bretschneider-Van Lerberghe 2008, 43). The reorientation of the city centre appeared mainly in the architecture of public buildings (buildings A, B and C), storage rooms, workshops and dwellings. The public area of the town was located between the south and central street of the A-field (fig. 2). The first clay rattle (TWE-A-08-6351) was found in a layer (locus 6351) at the northern edge of the south street which ran from the northwest to the southeast. Along the street, workshops and store-rooms have been excavated; they contained a large amount of storage jars (Bretschneider et al. in this volume 63-64). To the north of those workshops, two large buildings A and B appear, revealing architectural similarities of a double temple (Bretschneider-Van Lerberghe 2008, 44).

A more residential area with space for craftsmanship and commercial activities was located in the north of the A-field. In this area, some large olive presses (Iron Age II/III) and basins have been excavated. The second rattle (TWE-A-02-222) was found in a layer nearby a basin (locus 223) in the southeast corner of a room. In the neighboring room (locus 422), connected by a joined wall 401, one of the Tell Tweini conch trumpets was discovered. The third rattle (TWE-A-00-501) was unearthed in a similar context in a room, located northeast of the second clay rattle. The spool-shaped sherd was found in a layer (locus 501) right beneath the surface layer.

3. The Clay Rattle in the Ancient Near East

a. *Chronological Classification*

Ancient Near Eastern rattles appear in all kinds of shapes since the early third millennium B.C. Although no strict classification of clay rattles is associated with a specific historical period, one can make a certain distinction. The earliest examples of mass-produced clay rattles were fabricated during the late Early Bronze Age (2300-2000 B.C.) and were found in Northern Mesopotamia as well as in the Levant. These clay rattles have generally a zoomorphic or a fructiform design. The thin, long handle (av. diameter 2 cm, 6-8 cm in length) of the fructiform rattle (*Kugel-rasseln*) is easy to hold, while the round body (av. diameter 6-8 cm) is characterized by the many decorative perforations to enhance the sound.

Examples of this type of rattle have been discovered in great number in the Northern Levant at Çatal Höyük in the Amuq plain (Pruβ 2010, 322 n° 567), Jerablus-Tahtani (Peltenburg 1996, 9), Halawa and Tell Chuera (Pruβ 1999, 56-61). A variation on the fructiform rattles were the zoomorphic rattles in the shape of a bird, uncovered at sites as Ur (Dumbrill 2009, 27), Assur, Nippur (Rachid 1984, 98), Tell Brak, Tell Chuera and Halawa (Pruβ 1999, 70-72).

During the Middle Bronze Age (c. 2000-1550 B.C.), the most common design for the clay rattle becomes the pie-crust shape (*Kapselrasseln*: av. diameter 6-8 cm), although the fructiform rattle, represented by the Qatna examples (Gubel 2007, Ratel), remained popular until the early Middle Bronze Age (2000-1800 B.C.). The earliest pie-crust rattles in the Levant were found in Mari (Parrot 1956, 206), but most of them were produced at the Southern Mesopotamian sites: at Ur (Dumbrill 2009, 7-27), Nippur, Tello, Kish and Larsa (Rashid 1984, 100-101). Zoomorphic rattles such as pigs, boars, fish, and sheep appear simultaneously with the pie-crust rattles at the same Mesopotamian archaeological sites. The pie-crust rattles as well as the zoomorphic rattles were provided with incised decorations.

The most significant characteristic of Late Bronze Age (1550-1200 B.C.) clay rattles is the handle on the top or along the body to insert a finger. In some cases, the clay rattles had an eyelet on one end to hang the instrument in some manner (Braun 2002, 100). During the early Late Bronze Age, clay rattles have a more elongated body (Piamenta 2007, 77-78), like the one of Tell el-Far'ah (McDonald 1932, pl. 47) in the Southern Levant. The elongated bodies are often decorated with paint or modeled in animal shapes. In this tradition, four Cypriot elongated owl-shaped rattles, classified under the white painted ware, make their appearance in the Levantine collection. One was found at Ugarit (Matoïan 2003, 105-110), at the Northern Levant, the others at Tell el-Hesi (Piamenta 2007, 78), Gezer and Lachish (Tufnell 1958, 90 n° 24) in the Southern Levant. In the Late Bronze II Age, the body of the rattles becomes more round, like a ball (Haifa Music Museum 1971, n° 51-54). These idiophones have almost no perforations in the body. At the end of the Late Bronze Age, some jug-shaped rattles with a handle from the top to the bottom are introduced, like the Gezer rattle (Seger 1988, 77; Piamenta 2007, 49). Except for the Cypriot rattles, only few of the Late Bronze Age rattles were decorated.

During the Bronze to Iron Age transition rattles lose their handle and a new type of rattle is developed; the spool-shaped rattle (6-11 cm in length, av. diameter 4-7 cm). In the Iron Age II period (c. 900-700 B.C.), this rattle becomes the most common type. Usually, the spool-shaped rattle is perforated at the top and the bottom. The middle of the body is reduced in size to give the musician a firmer grip, making a handle redundant. The spool-shaped rattles were sometimes decorated with paint or incisions. The two Hazor rattles have red horizontal painted stripes (Yadin 1960, 49, 56), while the Sarepta rattle, with its small decorative perforations and incisions (Pritchard 1975, 46), is a more sophisticated, embellished version of the spool-shape rattle.

By the late Iron Age (Persian period), the quantity of clay rattles had diminished and a new idiophone — the iron bell – gradually replaced the clay rattles (Braun 2007, 19). Nevertheless, the popularity of the clay rattle during Iron Age II is remarkable, the more since in this period a large variety of instruments is available, such as sistrums and cymbals, producing almost the same rhythmic sound as the rattle (Haifa Music Museum, *Intro*).

b. *Manufacturing Methods*

The wide variety of shapes implies several manufacturing methods and distinct levels of craftsmanship. The fructiform clay rattles or *kugelrasseln* were likely manufactured in two separate parts (Pruβ 1999, 57-58). First, the lower part of ball-shaped body was formed together with the pillar-shaped handle. Then, the pellets were added and the upper body was attached by hand. Before the rattle was baked, multiple perforations were made into the body.

The pie-crust clay rattles were probably fabricated in moulds or in preshaped domes. Several moulds were found during the Ur excavations at an industrial area (Woolley-Mallowan 1976, 125-8). These moulds indicate a standardized mass production of the clay rattles as early as the late third millennium B.C. However, none of the British Museum pie-crust rattles show traces of joints. Therefore, R. Dumbrill (2009, 23) suggests a production method in which the clay was molded around a core of wax. The clay pellets were placed in the wax that melted away when the clay rattles were baked. The large inclusions and the structure of the clay imply that the pie-crust rattles were sun dried or baked on a low temperature.

The animal-shaped clay rattles were produced with two different methods, depending on the animal depicted. Birds (e.g. chickens, goose) were modelled in an upper and lower part similar to the method of the fructiform rattles (Pruβ 1999, 57-58). The two legs of the bird-shaped rattles were stretched to be used as a handle. The upper part, bearing the representation of the bird, was made by hand. Animals with four legs or no legs at all like pigs, boars, sheep, bears and fish were probably fabricated in one piece, as the pie-crust rattles were. Unlike the pie-crust rattles, no pre-shaped moulds existed, since no two animal-shaped rattles look the same. Designing an animal-shaped rattle required more craftsmanship than a pie-crust or a fructiform rattle and was probably made by professionals.

Since the Late Bronze Age, most clay rattles show traces of spinning marks, indicating the fabrication on a potter's wheel. The designs were simplified to elongated shapes, balls and jugs, generally without any decoration, that could be produced in a workshop as well as in a domestic sphere. The handle was manually attached to the body in a second phase.

The Iron Age spool-shaped rattle was manufactured in two or three parts. First, the spool-shaped body was made on a potter's wheel, sometimes with the bottom already attached, sometimes with the bottom added later together with the top after the insertion of the pellets (Albright 1943, 141-2; Pritchard 1975, 46). The easy design of the spool-shaped rattle allowed people to construct this rattle at home or to mass-produce it on a potter's wheel, making it also available to a large part of the population (Braun 2002, 100).

The raw material of the rattle, being clay, was naturally present in the Levant and Mesopotamia and freely accessible to all the inhabitants of these regions. This easily modifying material did not need highly skilled labor to manufacture relatively solid objects. Therefore, it comes as no surprise that almost every Ancient Near Eastern rattle was made out of local clay regardless the design or the historical period in which it was produced. Only in the Late Bronze Age, some Cypriot intrusions appear at the coastal Levant. The "white painted" clay rattle of Ugarit was probably imported from Cyprus (Matoïan 2003, 105-110), while the others were likely local imitations of the Cypriot white painted ware (Piamenta 2007, 78).

c. *The Use of the Clay Rattle in the Ancient Near East*

The various archaeological contexts, in which Ancient Near Eastern clay rattles were discovered, may provide some indications on the use of clay rattles. They were found in considerable quantities in cultic contexts;

inside tombs or temples. At several archaeological sites such as Tell Gezer (Seger 1988, 77), Tell el-Hesi, Tell Zecharia, Samaria, Tell el-Farah (McDonald 1932, 25 pl. 47) and Tepe Gawra (Tobler 1950, 165) clay rattles appear in the vicinity of graves or inside tombs. In Lachish, more than ten clay rattles in various shapes were discovered amongst the grave goods of Late Bonze Age and Iron Age tombs (Tufnell 1958, 90 pl. 28: 24-26; 1953, 187 pl. 27-28, 374).

Less numerous are the clay rattles in sanctuaries. In Hazor, a bell-shaped rattle was found in the vicinity of a Late Bonze Age sanctuary (Yadin 1961, pl. CCCVIII: 26, CCLXXVI: 24, Yadin 1958, 256), while another one was located near an altar (Yadin 1960, pl. CXLVI). The most interesting example however was the Iron Age clay rattle, uncovered in the sanctuary of Horvat Qitmit (late 7th century B.C.). Here, a statue of a goddess with a spool-shaped rattle on her head was found just outside the inner enclosure of an Edomite shrine (Beit-Arieh 1995, 78-80).

Clay rattles were also found in a domestic sphere, where they were possibly applied in apotropaic rituals or as child toys. Most Early and Middle Bronze Age rattles were excavated in private houses at sites such as Tell Chuera and Halawa (Pruβ 1999, 66). The Late Bronze Age rattle of Ugarit was discovered in the southeast corner of the *Prêtre-magicien* house at a domestic area, south of the Acropole (Matoïan 2003, 107). In Hazor, two spool-shaped rattles were found in the corner of the yard, connected to a house (Yadin 1960, 49, 56). The yard was probably used for the local production of ceramics and textile, because the floor was covered with a thick layer of shattered vessels and loom weights.

Some clay rattles were found in pottery workshops. In the *diqdiqqah* area of Ur, located on the canal banks, several pie-crust and animal-shaped rattles were excavated together with moulds (Dumbrill 2009, 7; Woolley-Mallowan 1976, 125-8). The clay was cultivated in this canal area and therefore associated with the local pottery industry in the late third and early second millennium B.C. The Iron Age rattle of Sarepta was found in an industrial area of pottery workshops as well (Pritchard 1975, 46).

Apparently, Ancient Near Eastern clay rattles were mainly used in religious and cultic context. The rattles found in graves were probably applied during funerals. The abundance of the clay rattles in the Levant during the Iron Age (Braun 2002, 106) can be explained by the fact that the clay rattle as musical instrument played an important role in the religious practices of the Kingdom of Israel and the Kingdom of Judah during the

First Temple period (10-8th century B.C.). In Mesopotamia, temple priests may have used the rattle during apotropaic rituals. The rhythmic noise produced by the rattle helped the priest to expel demons (Rachid 1984, 100). The large amount of excavated rattles, however, betrays a more common use. Clay rattles were most likely also played during processions, dances and at home. The location of several clay rattles in the vicinity of workshops or store rooms seems obvious, since ceramic instruments were also fabricated in workshops where they were probably stored like the finished jars.

A. Kilmer (2002, 791) suggests that the clay rattle may have been used as a child toy, but this seems only possible for a limited amount of shapes. The pie-crust models, designed to be tied up at some sort of string, might have hang above the baby's cradle. The fructiform clay rattles with their thin handles could be held by a child, but would have been broken easily when falling on the ground. The Late Bronze and Iron Age clay rattles are too heavy and too large for small children to play with. The average diameter of a spool-shaped rattle at its narrowest point is 5 cm (Haifa Music Museum 1971, n° 57, 59); only the hand of an adult is large enough to hold it firmly.

But what about the use of the Tell Tweini spool-shaped rattles? A burial context for these rattles can be ruled out, since the only Iron Age tomb of Tell Tweini, found underneath a beaten floor of a house (Hameeuw-Jans 2008, 83-84), was not located in the direct vicinity of the clay rattles.

The first Tell Tweini rattle (TWE-A-08-6351) was uncovered in the street not far from building A and B, which is currently identified as a double temple. The context of the street adds a new location to the already numerous find spots of clay rattles. Being found in a filling layer of the street, the rattle was already put out of its original context in ancient times. Since the street runs in the direction of a public square in front of the building A, B and C (fig. 2), the use of the rattle could be connected to certain rituals in the temple building. This situation is comparable to the rattle found near the Edomite sanctuary in Horvat Qitmit (Beit-Arieh 1995, 78-80). Or the rattle was related to the workshops and store rooms along the street (Bretschneider et al. in this volume), as is the case in Sarepta (Pritchard 1975, 46).

The two other Tell Tweini rattles were located in a more residential area of Gibala nearby basins, olive presses, workshops and store rooms. Interestingly, three musical instruments (two rattles and one conch trumpet) were uncovered in three neighbouring rooms. The section in which the second rattle (TWE-A-02-222) was found might have been a domestic atelier, revealing besides the rattle, storage jars, lamps, a stamp seal, and a basin. The third rattle was found in a similar situation at a room north-east of the second rattle, comparable to the archaeological context of the spool-shaped Hazor rattles (Yadin 1960, 49, 56).

4. Conclusion

Since prehistoric times, Ancient Near Eastern clay rattles were geographically spread from Anatolia, the Levant and Mesopotamia to Persia until these instruments were gradually replaced by iron bells in the late Iron Age. Despite large scale presence of these idiophones, no export pattern can be established between the several Ancient Near Eastern regions, except for a few Late Bronze Cypriot white painted clay rattles found in the Levant. For centuries, these rattles were manufactured in local clay to provide the population with musical instruments.

Although the production of clay rattles remained within the local community, the innovations in design spread rapidly through the Ancient Near East. In about two millennia (3rd millennium B.C. – 1st millennium B.C.), the design of the clay rattle made a remarkable development, which allows to classify these instruments in a rough chronological way. Early Bronze Age clay rattles are characterized by their perforated body, while Middle Bronze Age clay rattles generally have a pie-crust or animal shape. Late Bronze Age clay rattles are provided with a handle or in some cases with an eyelet, while most Iron Age clay rattles have a spool-shaped body. The spool-shaped rattle was in large amounts present in the Southern Levantine sites during the Iron Age, while this tradition seems to be nearly absent in the Northern Levant and Mesopotamia. The three Tell Tweini (North Syria) clay rattles together with the Çatal Höyük (South Turkey; Pruβ 2010, 322) clay rattle are rare examples of this type of instrument in the Northern Levant. Most likely, new archaeological excavations will reveal more evidence on these idiophones in the Northern Levant to confirm the chronological innovations. Modifications to this chronology, such as the fructiform rattle in the Late Bronze Age layers of Bab-e Dhra (Piamenta 2007, 77) or the bird-shaped rattles in the Late Bronze Age layers of Tell Fray and Munbaqa (Pruβ 1999, 60) are not exceptional, although most variations on this chronological pattern fit into periods of transition.

The Ancient Near Eastern clay rattles were found in various archaeological contexts; in tombs, sanctuaries, workshops, houses, yards and streets.

The overwhelming majority of clay rattles was discovered in funerary and religious contexts, which clearly favours the clay rattle as a ritual instrument, whether these were apotropaic rituals in a domestic context or funerary and temple practices within a larger community. The archaeological context of the Tell Tweini clay rattles cannot provide a definite answer for the use of these idiophones during the Iron Age, but a funerary context is excluded for them. The spool-shaped rattles were most likely found in the area in which they were manufactured. One Tell Tweini rattle (TWE-A-08-6351) may even be related to the temple building.

Bibliography

ALBRIGHT, W. F. 1943: *The Excavation of Tell Beit Mirsim III: The Iron Age* (AASOR 21-22), New Haven.

BEIT-ARIEH, I. and P. BECK 1995: *Horvat Qimit. An Edomite Shrine in the Biblical Negev*, Tel Aviv.

BRAUN, J. 2002: *Music in Ancient Israel/Palestine. Archaeological, Written and Comparative Sources*, Cambridge.

BRAUN, J. 2007: "Music in the Ancient Land of Israel: Archaeological and Written Sources", in J. G. Westenholz (ed.) *Sounds of Ancient Music*, Jerusalem, 11-23.

BRETSCHNEIDER, J. and K. VAN LERBERGHE 2008: "Tell Tweini, ancient Gibala, between 2600 B.C.E. and 333 B.C.E.", in J. Bretschneider and K. Van Lerberghe (eds.) *In Search of Gibala. An Archaeological and Historical Study based on eight Seasons of Excavations at Tell Tweini (Syria) in the A and C fields (1999-2007)* (Aula Orientalis-Supplementa 24), Barcelona, 11-68.

DUMBRILL, R. J. 2010: *Idiophones of the Ancient Near East in the Collections of the British Museum*, London.

GORRIS, E. and W. VERHULST forth.: "Summon the Gods and the People by the Sound of the Conch", in R. J. Dumbrill (ed.) *ICONEA 2009-2010*, 21-28.

GUBEL, E. 2007: "Ratels", in E. Gubel and B. Overlaet (eds.) *Van Gilgamesh tot Zenobia. Kunstschatten uit het Oude Nabije Oosten en Iran* (Koninklijke Musea voor Kunst en Geschiedenis), Brussel.

HAIFA MUSIC MUSEUM AND AMLI LIBRARY 1971: *Music in the Ancient World. Exhibition at the Haifa Music Museum*, Haifa.

HAMEEUW H. and G. JANS 2008: "Burial Customs at Tell Tweini – Field A", in J. Bretschneider and K. Van Lerberghe (eds.) *In Search of Gibala. An Archaeological and Historical Study based on eight Seasons of Excavations at Tell Tweini (Syria) in the A and C fields (1999-2007)* (Aula Orientalis-Supplementa 24), Barcelona, 103-140.

VON HORNBOSTEL, E. M. and C. SACHS 1914: "Systematik der Musikinstrumente. Ein Versuch", *Zeistschrift für Ethnologie* 46, 553-590.

— 1961: "Classification of Musical Instruments: Translated from the Original German by A. Baines and P. Wachsmann", *The Galpin Society Journal* 14, 3-29.

KILMER, A. D. 2002: "On Drums and Strings and Trumpet Blasts", *JAOS* 122/4, 788-796.

MATOÏAN, V. 2003: "Un hochet chypriote White Painted à Ougarit (Syrie)", *Report of Department of Antiquities of Cyprus*, 105-112.

MATTHAIE, P., F. PINNOCK and G. SCANDONE-MATTHIAE, 1995: *Ebla. Alle Origini della civiltà urbana*, Milano.

MCDONALD, E. and L. HARDING 1932: *Beth Pelet II* (British School of Archaeology in Egypt and Egyptian Research Account 52), London.

PARROT, A. 1956: *Mission Archéologique de Mari 1: Le temple d'Ishtar* (Bibliothèque archéologique et historique de l'Institut français d'archéologie du Proche-Orient: Beyrouth-Damas-Amman 65), Paris.

PELTENBURG, E., D. BOLGER, S. CAMPBELL, M. A. MURRAY and R. TIPPING 1996: Jerablus-Tahtani, Syria, 1995: Preliminary Report, *Levant* 28, 1-25.

PIAMENTA, M. 2007: "Rattle", in G.J. Westenholz, *Sounds of Ancient Music*, Jerusalem, pl. 2, 34, 35.

PINNOCK, F. 1979: "Nota sui 'sonagli' della Tomba del Signore dei Capridi", *Studi Eblaiti* 1, 185-190.

PRITCHARD, J. B. and W. P. ANDERSON 1975: *Sarepta. A Preliminary Report on the Iron Age* (Excavations of the University Museum of the University of Pennsylvania, 1970-72), Philadelphia.

PRUSS, A. 1999: "Glöckchen, Rasseln, Pfeifen: Musikinstrumente aus Ton", in M. Mode (ed.), *Zwischen Nil und Hindukusch* (Hallesche Beiträge zur Orientwissenschaft 28), Halle, 56-87.

— 2010: *Die Amuq-Terrakotten. Untersuchungen zu den Terrakotta-Figuren des 2. und 1. Jahrtausends v. Chr. aus den Grabungen des Oriental Institute Chicago in der Amuq-Ebene* (Subartu 26), Turnhout, 322.

RASHID, S. A. 1984: "Mesopotamien", in W. Bachmann (ed.), *Musikgeschichte in Bildern. II. Musik des Altertums*, Leipzig, 98-101.

RODGERS, B. A. 2004: *The Archaeologist's Manual for Conservation. A Guide to Non-Toxic, Minimal Intervention Artifact Stabilization*, New York.

SAVARIEGO, A. 2010: "Masks Rattles and Purim Customs", http://www.antiquities.org.il/article_Item_eng.asp?sec_id=17&sub_subj_id=535#MMMas.

SEGER, J. D. and H. D. LANCE 1988: *Gezer V: the Field I Caves* (Nelson Glueck School of Biblical Archaeology 5), Jerusalem.

TOBLER, A. J. 1950: *Excavations at Tepe Gawra II* (University of Pennsylvania Museum of Archaeology and Anthropology), Pennsylavania.

TUFNELL, O., 1953: *Lachish III. The Iron Age* (The Wellcome-Marston Archaeological Research Expedition to the Near East Publications 3), London.

— 1958: *Lachish IV (Tell ed-Duweir). The Bronze Age* (The Wellcome-Marston Archaeological Research Expedition to the Near East Publications 4), London.

VANSTEENHUYSE, K. 2008: "The Ceramic Material from Tell Tweini – Field A" in J. Bretschneider and K. Van Lerberghe (eds.); *In Search of Gibala. An*

Archaeological and Historical Study based on eight Seasons of Excavations at Tell Tweini (Syria) in the A and C fields (1999-2007) (Aula Orientalis-Supplementa 24), Barcelona, 103-140.

WOOLLEY, L. and M. E. L. MALLOWAN 1976: *The Old Babylonian Period* (Ur Excavations 7), London.

YADIN, Y., Y. AHARONI, R. AMIRAN, T. DOTHAN, I. DUNAYEVSKY and J. PERROT (eds.) 1958: *Hazor I. An Account of the First Season of Excavations, 1955* (The James A. de Rothschild Expedition at Hazor), Jerusalem.

— 1960: *Hazor II. An Account of the Second Season of Excavations, 1956* (The James A. de Rothschild Expedition at Hazor), Jerusalem.

YADIN, Y., Y. AHARONI, R. AMIRAN, A. BEN-TOR, M. DOTHAN, T. DOTHAN, I. DUNAYEVSKY, S. GEVA, E. STERN and J. PERROT (eds.) 1961: *Hazor III-IV. An Account of the Third and Fourth Seasons of Excavations, 1957-1958* (The James A. de Rothschild Expedition at Hazor), Jerusalem.

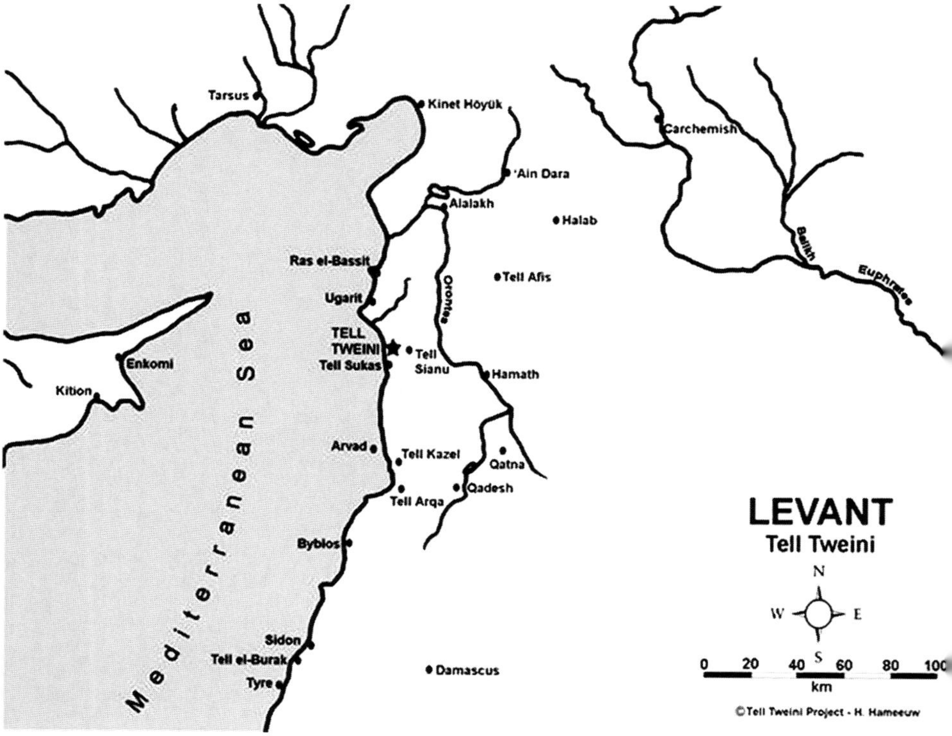

Fig. 1. Tell Tweini and the Northern Levant.

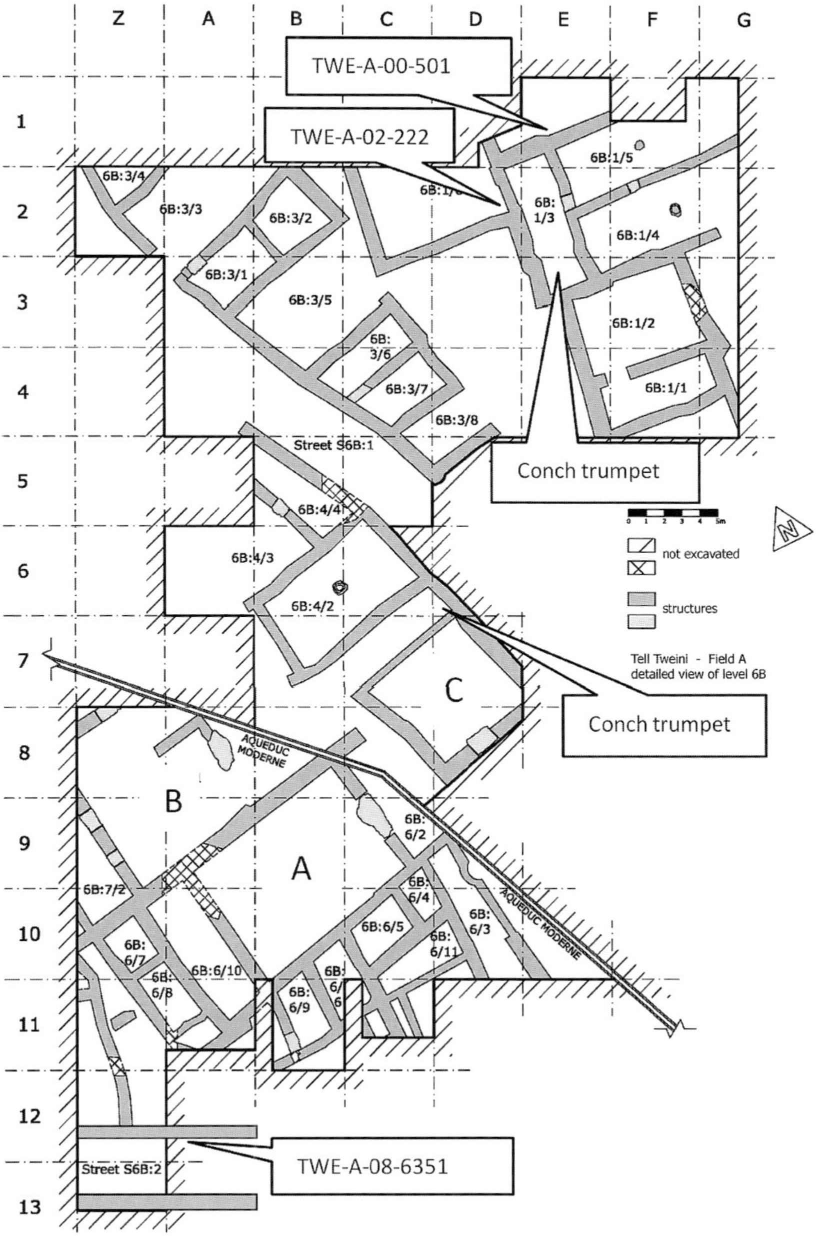

Fig. 2. Tell Tweini clay rattles at the A-field.

Fig. 3. Tell Tweini clay rattle (TWE-A-08-6351-M001).

Fig. 4. Tell Tweini clay rattle (TWE-A-02-0222-M003).

Fig. 5. Tell Tweini clay rattle (TWE-A-00-0501-C038).

EPISÈME DE BOUCLIER OU ÉGIDE (ŚAM'ALITE?) À INSCRIPTION OUEST SÉMITIQUE

Eric GUBEL
Université Libre de Bruxelles et Musées Royaux d'Art et d'Histoire, Bruxelles

1. Introduction

La section Proche-Orient & Iran des Musées Royaux d'Art et d'Histoire de Bruxelles a pu récemment acquérir un disque de protection en bronze provenant de la collection de feu A. Guttmann[1] (Fig. 1: a-b). Cet objet est important à plus d'un titre. Il s'agit en effet d'un témoignage de l'art de la Syrie du Nord remontant à l'époque de l'apogée des états (louvito-) araméens, à la veille de la conquête néo-assyrienne. Datant du dernier tiers du IXe siècle av. n.è. l'inscription nous renseigne sur l'organisation palatiale de l'un de ces états, probablement celui du royaume de *Yu'addī / Bīt-Gabbar, dont la capitale Śam'al est située à l'emplacement de l'actuel Zincirli Höyük, entre les crêtes de l'Amanus à l'Ouest et celles du Kurd Dağ à l'Est (Fig. 2; également la référence pour les toponymes cités ci-dessous, §2)[2].

2. L'inscription (Fig. 1)

2.1. *Paléographie*

Dans l'*editio princeps*, Manfred Krebernik avançait des arguments d'ordre paléographique et lexicaux, selon lesquels l'inscription sur le support en

[1] Axel Guttmann (° 1944 Krems, Autriche – † Berlin 2001) était un collectionneur passionné et avisé dont les intérêts touchaient aussi bien les domaines de la peinture, du mobilier, des grands crus, de la porcelaine Meisen que celui de l'histoire militaire antique et médiévale. Mécène des musées berlinois et de leurs projets scientifiques, Guttmann se faisait un point d'honneur d'investir sans cesse dans la restauration et la conservation de sa collection qu'il mettait à la disposition des chercheurs de façon exemplaire jusqu'à son décès prématuré en 2001, à la suite duquel nombre de ses pièces les plus remarquable passèrent aux enchères: *The art of Warfare. The Axel Guttmann Collection* I, Christie's South Kensington, 06/11/2002, II, 28/04/2004.

[2] Pour le contexte historique de la formation des états araméens de la Syrie, cfr. Sader 1987; Lemaire 1991,133-146; Lipiński 1995, 44-46; Dion 1997; Lipiński 2000; Sader 2000; Hawkins 1995.

bronze fut rédigée à l'aide de caractères phéniciens identiques à ceux employés par le roi Kilamuwa de Śam'al (c. 840-810 av. n.è.) dans sa célèbre inscription monumentale de Zincirli[3]. Kilamuwa disposait vraisemblablement des services d'un scribe phénicien, comme jadis son confrère Abdélim, au service de Kapara, roi de Gōzān (Tell Halaf) au royaume de Bīt-Bahiāni à la fin du Xe s. av. n.è.[4] et gouverné plus tard, en 656 av. n.è., par un gouverneur portant le nom phénicien de Milkiramu[5]. A peine une génération après les règnes de Kilamuwa et de Kapara, le régent Yariris, de Karkemish sur l'Euphrate, se vantera lui aussi de maîtriser «l'écriture tyrienne»[6]. D'autres indices de la présence phénicienne dans la région et de la propagation de leur culture sont vraisemblablement déjà fournis par le nom phénicien de Gēri-Dadi, roitelet du pays de Aššа, entre Hilvan et Siverek, durant le deuxième quart du IXe s. av. n.è. (Lipiński 2000, 137 n.21; Lipiński 1992), tandis qu'une inscription phénicienne de Çatal Hüyük sur l'Afrin, passée sous silence depuis son édition, remonterait au VIIIe siècle av. n.è., quand l'état d'Unqi/Pattina auquel ce site vraisemblablement appartenait, était passé sous l'égide du royaume d'Arpad/Bēt-Gūš/(A)gūsi (Gevirtz 1967, 13-16). C'est à Brēdj, non loin de là, que son roi Bar-Hadad dédia une stèle représentant l'image de Melqart, grand dieu de Tyr aux alentours de 800 av. n.è. (Briquel-Chatonnet 1992, 94-100; Lipiński 2000, 214-216). Toujours dans le même contexte, rappelons la découverte d'inscriptions phéniciennes lapidaires[7] et sigillaires en Cilicie (l'ancien royaume de

[3] Krebernik et Seidl 1997, 101-111, cfr. depuis Lemaire 2001, 187-188 et Lipiński 2000, 511. Pour Kilamuwa, voir Donner et Röllig 2002, 24. A noter qu'il s'agit, comme dans le cas des inscriptions de ses successeurs Panamuwa I (c. 790-750 av. n.è.), Panamuwa II (c. 740-733 av. n.è.) et de Bar-Rakāb (c. 733-713/1 av. n.è.), d'inscriptions en *champlevé*, ce qui suggérerait que les Phéniciens de Śam'al seraient plus spécifiquement d'origine gyblite, seule région de la côte phénicienne ayant livrée un prototype (du IXe s. av. n.è.) de cette technique rarement attestée en épigraphie ouest sémitique: Bordreuil 1977. Pour un autre lien avec Byblos, cfr. déjà Galling 1950; ajoutons que ce sarcophage représente le roi (défunt) avec une fleur, voire un sceptre floral, dans la main, détail qui sera également repris dans la sculpture de Śam'al ainsi que sur les ivoires trouvées *in situ*: Winter1973, 201 et 283 resp.

[4] Lipiński 1994, 25. Situé ici cependant d'après la haute datation récemment proposée par Cholidis et Martin 2010, 50-52.

[5] Barnett 1957, 48; quant au nom, cfr. Lemaire 1976, 83-93 et Lipiński 1991.

[6] Lipiński 2000, 242 et 117 respectivement et, pour la date, Hawkins 2010, 848-717. Pour une inscription phénicienne d'époque plus tardive de ce site, voir *infra*, note 15.

[7] Notamment la bilingue d'Azitawadda de Karatepe: Bron 1979; Çambel, Röllig et Hawkins 1999. Concernant l'influence de l'art phénicien sur l'iconographie des orthostates, cfr. Winter 1979, 120-125, 136-140; Akurgal 1981, 131-141; Gubel 1987, 120-123, 254-255; Gubel 1996, 15-151; Çambel et Özyar 2003, 61-63, 84-89, 100-104.

Qué/Qawa, dont l'une au nom «du Tyrien») de la fin du VIIIe s. av. n.è.[8]. Les bilingues louvito-phéniciennes de Çineköy, de Hassan-Beyli et de Cebelireis Daği corroborent également l'importance du phénicien comme une langue officielle dans le royaume de Qué aux VIIIe-VIIe siècles (Tekoğlu et Lemaire 2000, 961-1006, Lipiński 2004, 119-130), tandis que la bilingue d'Ivriz suggère qu'il était aussi censée être compris dans les régions limitrophes[9]. Enfin, plusieurs sites de la Cilicie ont livré de la céramique phénicienne, présente aussi dans les centres majeurs de la Syrie du Nord et jusqu'en Anatolie (Manuelli 2010, 78-81).

Pour en revenir à Śam'al, remarquons que l'un des ministres du roi Bar-Sūr (c. 750-745 av. n.è.) était sans doute d'origine phénicienne, comme en témoigne son nom ('Azzi-Baal) (Lipiński 2000, 243; Deutsch et Lemaire 2000, 112 n° 105). Sauf si elles résultent d'une importation par de tierces personnes, certaines plaquettes d'ivoire trouvées à Zincirli/Śam'al ont pu être gravées *in situ* par des artistes familiers avec le style phénicien, tandis que la teinture de la laine, déjà attestée sous Kilamuwa (c. 840-810 av. n.è.), pourrait fort bien représenter un produit d'*Ersatz* inspiré de l'industrie phénicienne du pourpre[10]. Une pierre de touche destinée à vérifier l'aloi de métaux précieux et inscrite au nom d'un Phénicien actif autour de 750 av. n.è. explique sans doute une autre facette de l'intérêt que portaient les marchands de la côte centrale du Levant à cette région proche de l'Amanus[11]. Le fait qu'au moins un Phénicien attesté dans la littérature était arrivé à participer activement à l'administration locale d'un peuple à deux composantes (les *mškbm* et les *b'rrm*, semi-nomades et sédentaires de souche louvite: Lipiński 2000, 236) n'est peut-être pas étrangère à l'iconographie de la stèle qu'Assarhaddon (681-669 av. n.è.) fit ériger plus tard à Śam'al (ainsi qu'à Til Barsip: Nevling Porter 2000, 143-176). Avec Nevling Porter, nous pouvons conclure que la défaite du roi tyrien Abdi-Milkutti (680-677 av. n.è.) et de son allié égyptien servait parfaitement la cause de la propagande assyrienne, c.-à-d. servir d'exemple pour ceux qui comploteraient contre leur autorité. Cependant, dans le cas spécifique de Śam'al, nous pourrions y voir

[8] Dupont-Sommer 1950-51, 43-45; Lemaire 1977, 29-40, pl. VI; Lipiński 1983, 133-139; Bordreuil 1986, 42-43 n° 38 (considéré comme suspect); Avigad et Sass 1997, 314 n° 840, 528; Lemaire 1997, 123–126; Lipiński 2004, 121, 130-133 qui préfère lire «l'Égyptien» au lieu du «Tyrien». Pour un sommaire récent, cfr. Novák 2010.

[9] Lemaire 2007, 210; Lipiński 2004, 133-135 qui la date entre 738 et 732 av. n.è.

[10] von Luschan, 1943, pls 65: l-n, 66-67: a-f, i, 68: i; et, pour l'industrie de teinture, Lipiński 2000, 541.

[11] Bordreuil 1986, 72-2 n° 4, qui compare l'iconographie de ce sceau (étendard de Sin) avec des détails iconographiques de l'inscription de Bar-rakāb de Śam'al.

aussi une référence indirecte à une tradition de relations amicales avec les sujets des villes marchandes de la Phénicie, dont l'extension et l'intensification du réseau commercial est signalé par la diffusion de l'alphabet phénicien esquissée ci-dessus[12]. Comme on l'a vu, l'emploi du phénicien sur la stèle de Kilamuwa n'est pas unique dans la région[13]. Cette *lingua franca* du commerce figure en effet en deuxième rang après le louvite dans l'inscription bilingue de Karatepe (Azatiwataya) au NO de Zincirli (Çambel, Röllig et Hawkins 1999). À treize km à l'Ouest de cette dernière ville, Hassan Beyli, dans le royaume voisin de Qué, a livré une stèle dont l'inscription remonte aux alentours de 715 av. n.è., sinon même plus tôt[14]. Enfin, une série d'inscriptions comme celle d'époque achéménide d'une certaine «Milkat-Ba'al, veuve de Sidiqmilk, fils de 'Abd['e]l[im]» sur une brique émaillée de Karkemish, celle d'un 'Ešel sur un conoïde néo-babylonien du même site ou, encore, celle d'un «Hur (fils de) Nmq» d'Ougarit, mériteraient d'être réexaminées, même si elles sont de date plus récente[15].

Dans une étude récente, A. Lemaire réfute cependant l'identification de l'inscription du bouclier comme phénicienne à l'aide d'une argumentation quelque peu circulaire «Malheureusement l'inscription ne comporte aucun mot typique du phénicien, du sam'alien ou de l'araméen d'empire; tout au plus peut-on proposer de la dater paléographiquement de la deuxième moitié du VIIIe s. ce qui ferait plutôt pencher la balance en faveur du sam'alien ou de l'araméen d'empire» (Lemaire 2001, 185-193, esp. 188). Mais pourquoi descendre la date de cette inscription d'un siècle alors que l'inscription phénicienne de Kilamuwa fournit précisément les parallèles les plus proches sur le plan paléographique, à l'encontre d'inscriptions plus tardives qui elles seules, si elles existaient, justifieraient une attribution à l'écriture śam'alienne ou araméenne d'empire? En outre, chercher une origine non phénicienne de l'inscription serait en flagrant conflit avec l'article terminant sur *t* dans le terme *mšmʿt* (*infra*), là où l'on s'attendrait, comme l'a souligné M. Krebernik, à un *h* dans l'écriture sam'alienne ou araméenne[16]. Somme toute, il nous semble plus prudent

[12] Et Lipiński 2004, 135-143 sur le commerce.

[13] Pour la présence phénicienne dans la région, cfr. Lipiński 1985, 81-84; Lebrun 1987, 23-27; Lipiński 1992a, 29; Lipiński 2004, 110-143.

[14] Lemaire 1983, 17-19. Lipiński 2004, 117-119 toutefois, préfère une date autour de 765 av. n.è. si le texte comporte effectivement le nom d'Ashurdan III.

[15] Woolley et Barnett 1952, 280: A.33n (avec pl. A.33n), A.33o (avec fig. 15, p. 183); Lipiński 2004, 116; Segert 2001, 231-234.

[16] Krebernik et Seidl 1997, 105: «Ein Artikel (**hmšmʿt*) ode reine Emphaticus-Endung (**mšmʿt'*) ist nicht vorhanden. Scheidet man Hebräisch bzw. Moabitisch aufgrund der

de s'en tenir à la proposition d'origine, qui n'enlève rien, voire ajoute même du poids à la thèse perspicace d'A. Lemaire selon laquelle «l'abandon du phénicien et l'adoption du sam'alien comme langue écrite du royaume de Sam'al semblent traduire dans la culture écrite un changement d'orientation politique: au lieu d'être soumis au royaume de Qué, Kilamuwa préfère désormais se rallier à Assur et lui payer tribut tout en essayant d'affirmer son indépendance culturelle en donnant au dialecte araméen local ('sam'alien) le rang de langue officielle» (Lemaire 2001, 189).

2.2. *Onomastique*

L'inscription, probablement précédée du *lamed* d'appartenance, effacé depuis par la corrosion du métal, nous a conservé le nom du propriétaire de l'objet, suivi de son titre *rb mšmʿt*, «chef/commandant/préposé des gardes de corps» (*infra*). La lecture du nom du propriétaire (⌈*k*⌉ ?)*rkdy* proposée par M. Krebernik (et Seidl, 1997, 103-104), fut restituée de façon indépendante endéans les trois années suite à l'*editio princeps* comme ⌈*t*⌉)*rkdy* par A. Lemaire (2001, 187-8) et E. Lipiński (2000, 511 n.155), nouvelle lecture qui offre l'avantage que le nom *Tarko(n)day* est en effet attesté en milieu louvite (cfr. *Tarhunazi*, roi de Milid/Malatay, ? – 712 av. n.è.) sous la forme Ταρκονδαιος[17]. L'élément théophore du nom *trk*, enfin, représente la transcription araméenne du nom du dieu louvite des orages, à savoir Tarhunt/*Trkmnh*/Τρογομωνης. D'après l'analyse onomastique, il semblerait donc que le propriétaire de l'objet inscrit relevait de la classe des *b'rrm*, sédentaires de souche louvite représentant la classe supérieure dans la hiérarchie sociale au royaume de Śam'al — comme on pouvait s'y attendre au vu de ses responsabilités.

2.3. *Vocabulaire*

Le nom du propriétaire de l'objet est suivi du titre *rb mšmʿt*, «chef», «commandant des gardes du corps». Amplement attesté dans les milieux

Paläographie aus, so würde die als *–t*, nicht *–h* notierte Femininendung — unter der Voraussetzung, dass der Singular vorliegt — auf das Phönizische weisen, da man im Sam'alischen wie im Aramaïschen (ausser bei nominae tertiae infirmae) *–h* (fûr/ -ah/ > /-ā) erwarten würde).»

[17] En ce qui concerne l'absence du n, cfr. Lipiński 2000, 511 n. 155: «Vor einem Konsonant ist der Nasal nicht besonderes fest»: citant Zgusta 1964, 488 n. 42. Sur le dieu louvite Tarhunt, voir maintenant Craig Melchert 2003, 220-224.

phénico-puniques, le titre *rb* doit représenter un emprunt au phénicien[18]. Pour *mšmʿt*, attesté en moabite (stèle de Mešaʿ) comme en hébreu, M. Krebernik compare le terme avec la désignation des gardes du corps de Saul et de David (I Sam. 22, 14; II Sam. 23, 23; I Chron. 11, 25), ajoutant que le titre apparaît ici pour la première fois (dans un milieu araméen)[19]. Ajoutons toutefois que la fonction à laquelle ce titre renvoie devrait déjà être connue au Bronze récent dans le grand port de la Syrie du Nord, à Ougarit. Une lettre des archives d'Ourtenou, adressée au roi Ammourapi, révèle en effet les origines de *B3j*/Beya, trésorier syrien du pharaon Siptah[20] dont la faiblesse lui permettait d'assumer le pouvoir en Egypte. Dans le texte akkadien précédant ces évènements, Beya se nomme en effet «chef des gardes du Pharaon» (Yon 1997,136-137 n° 4).

3. Iconographie

Dans l'*editio princeps*, notre collègue Ursula Seidl a mis l'image de la tête de taureau associé à une série de globes/rosaces en rapport avec des représentations semblables dans d'autres média de l'art louvito-araméen. Elle en conclut que le bucrane représenterait le symbole du dieu de l'orage, qui occupait une place prépondérante dans le panthéon de Śam'al (Krebernik et Seidl 1997, 106-11). Dans leur étude consécutive couvrant un cadre géographique bien plus vaste, Monika Bernett et Othmar Keel (1998, 32-41) ont pu retracer la même image, identifiée par les auteurs comme symbole de la lune, à partir de l'époque sumérienne jusqu'à l'iconographie palmyrénienne du dieu lunaire au nom significatif d'ʿAglibol — «taureau du Seigneur». À ces documents, il convient d'ajouter plusieurs cylindres associant la tête de taureau, voire le bucrane, à d'autres corps du ciel nocturne, dont ceux de «Baraq serviteur d'Atarshamin» et d'«Elamar» (Fig. 3) de la fin du IXe s. (Bordreuil 1993,77-79 n° 6). Sur un cachet araméen (Qué ou Śam'al?), doté postérieurement d'une inscription phénicienne par un propriétaire qui ne se rendait apparemment pas compte de sa signification, la tête du bovidé est flanquée de

[18] La traduction de *rb* en araméen dans le sens de «commandant» se justifie par analogie avec les titres *rbhyl'* (commandant de garnison) et *rb m't'* (commandant de compagnie) dans les papyri araméens d'Eléphantine: Muffs et Levine 2003, 231 *s.v.*

[19] Krebernik et Seidl, 1997, 104; cependant, cfr. Lipiński 2000, 511-512 qui suspecte une translittération de l'araméen *rab heylā* dans la désignation du commandeur en Chef de l'armée de Hadadezer de Damas (II Sam. 10, 16.18; I Chron. 11, 25).

[20] Helck 1958, 355 mais surtout Bierbrier 2011; Dodson 2011 pour une récente remise en question.

«deux séries de Shibitu représentant les sept étoiles»[21]. Les Pléiades (ar. *SBT*) et la tête de taureau se retrouvent également sur une coupe araméenne datée des environs de 750 av. n.è., jadis dans la collection Foroughi à Téhéran et passée récemment dans celle de S. Mussaïef à Londres (Fig. 4: Barnett 1966, 269-276, pl. XXIV; Bernett et Keel 1998, 39-40, fig. 64). André Lemaire propose de lire l'inscription au-dessus de la tête du bovidé *R'Š.ŠR'*– «(la?) tête de/du taureau», renvoi direct à la constellation homonyme (Lemaire 1999, 200-201).

L'implantation des oreilles par rapport aux cornes, telle qu'elle figure sur le bronze des Musées royaux d'Art et d'Histoire, n'est pas sans rappeler un trait similaire sur des têtes de taureau ornant les chaudrons de bronze de Kourion et de Salamine (Chypre) (Amandry 1938, 73-80, pl. V g-i, VI: a-b), d'Olympie, de Delphes et de Samos[22], importés du monde louvito-araméen vers la fin du VIIIe siècle av. n.è. Le chaudron de la tombe royale de Salamine se distingue de ce groupe comme le plus intéressant pour notre propos, puisque la paire des trois protomes de taureaux fixée sur le rebord sous les anses est montée sur une plaquette décorée d'une tête hathorique entre deux ombelles de papyrus. Il s'agit là d'un motif phénicien, comme une comparaison avec des images sigillaires l'indique[23]. Tout comme le chaudron à protomes de griffons à côté duquel il a été retrouvé (identifié comme étant une interprétation chypro-phénicienne des trépieds du groupe de Praenestre: Herrmann 1966, 146), celui-ci doit représenter l'interprétation d'un type de chaudron louvito-araméen, vraisemblablement exécuté par un artiste phénicien actif en Syrie du Nord.

[21] Bordreuil 1986, 27 n° 13. Ce sceau ainsi qu'un autre où on retrouve la rosace et les oiseaux flanquant l'arbre sacré (Buchanan et Moorey 1988, pl. X: 289) partagent des particularités avec les sceaux phénicien de la Cilicie (Bordreuil 1993, 42-43 n° 38) de par la présence des compartiments en «L» dans le registre supérieur préfiguré sur des scarabées Hyksos (Culican 1986, 533, pl. III: c; Lemaire1977, 19-40).

[22] Herrmann 1966, 114-130. Les attaches en forme de tête de taureau des chaudrons ourartéens également présent en occident, se distinguent par des oreilles collées aux flancs.

[23] Boardman 2003, 31 n°s 6/4, 6/5, pl. 4. Il s'agit ici apparemment d'une réduction de l'image de la déesse nue de face entre deux éléments végétaux, préfigurée par une production phénicienne de plaquettes en or (éléments de *polos*) représentée à Chypre: Laffineur 1986, 15 n° 5. Dans cette série où des éléments phéniciens et araméens (habit sacerdotal, chariot, Laffineur 1986, n° 6) s'entremêlent, l'image de la déesse est en effet réduite à un buste (Laffineur 1986, n° 8), selon le même procédé de la «partie pour le tout» préfiguré en Syrie (Ougarit, Tell Kazel) par le transfert du motif de la déesse nue sur des plaquettes en terre cuite à la représentation de son buste sur des pendentifs en or: Barrelet 1958, 34-36.

4. Typologie: bouclier ou élément de cuirasse?

Des traces autour du trou central de l'objet étudié ici suggèrent la présence d'une applique à cet endroit «über dessen Form und Material die Spuren nichts aussagen» (Krebernik et Seidl 1997, 101). Or, il ne peut s'agir ici que d'un élément de taille assez discrète de façon à ne pas obscurcir l'épisème en forme de bucrane, ce qui exclut la restitution d'un clou du type de ceux des boucliers phéniciens (Barnett 1977, 157-169, spéc. 163). En fait, mieux vaut se tourner de nouveau vers Zincirli (Śam'al), où des appliques de casques trouvées *in situ* pourraient aider à sa reconstitution (von Luschan 1943, 76 figs. 86-87).

Le long de son pourtour, l'applique métallique est perforée de 126 trous à distances régulières. Leur diamètre s'avère toutefois trop important que pour penser à un système d'attachement à l'aide d'un fil[24]. Aussi, et comme les traces de corrosion autour de certains trous nous invitent à le faire, il faut donc imaginer une fixation sur une âme rigide (bois?) assurée par des clous métalliques à tête hémisphérique formant ainsi une frise de perles, comme on le verra apparaître sur des boucliers syriens[25], dédaliques et assyriens[26]. Ces parallèles indiquent en outre qu'une frise perlée concentrique de clous identiques pouvait doubler celle du support sur lequel l'applique de bronze était fixée comme une sorte d'*umbo* et qui était vraisemblablement «fait de bois ou de joncs tressés, recouvert de cuir, frotté d'huile» à en croire la tradition biblique[27].

Une série de coupes (syro-) phéniciennes nous permet de poursuivre cette analyse des frises perlées concentriques dans la toreutique levantine. On la retrouve en effet sur la coupe de Delphes (Fig. 5), sur laquelle l'artiste a représenté l'Astarté guerrière munie d'un arc et de flèches, brandissant une massue au-dessus de sa tête et portant une cuirasse protégeant sa poitrine, dont la forme ainsi que le décor géométrique rappellent de près notre applique[28]. Ce document nous fournirait donc une interprétation alternative pour la fonction de l'applique en question, à savoir celle d'un

[24] Les frises en zigzag décorant l'intérieur des boucliers sargonides pourraient illustrer un système de ce genre pour attacher le bronze sur un fond de cuir, cf. les exemples dans Hrouda 1965, pl. 23: 25-26.

[25] Une pyxide du type de Tell Halaf montre la frise perlée à l'intérieur d'un bouclier de grande taille: Barnett 1957, pl. XXVII: S 12a-d).

[26] Krebernik et Seidl 1997, 101-102, n.2. Le cœur des rosettes et d'autres éléments de frises végétales décorant le type de bouclier en vogue sous Sargon II pourraient en fait représenter un écho d'un dispositif analogue (Hrouda, 1965, 90-91, pl. 23: 21, 27, 28).

[27] Citation d'après Lemaire 1987, 218 («bouclier», -hb. *māgēn*) avec références à 2S 1,21; Is 21,5).

[28] Childs 1978, 57 avec bibliographie antérieure et, dernièrement, Hermary 1986, 177-194, spéc. 189-190.

précurseur de l'égide d'Athèna, ou plutôt des *cardiophylakes* italiques du VIIIe siècle av. n.è, portées sur la poitrine ainsi que dans le dos[29]. Sans rejeter cette thèse, il serait cependant tout aussi logique d'assumer qu'il ne s'agit ici que d'une convention artistique bien attestée dans l'art oriental et exprimant le désir de représenter les divinités avec leurs multitude d'attributs, certains «flottant» de façon bien peu réaliste sur ou autour de leurs corps. La coupe en question appartient à la classe des patères à médaillon en «rosebud / boutons de rose», attribuée à un centre de production de la Syrie du Nord du IXe s. av. n.è. et représenté, outre à Delphes, à Olympie, dans la grotte du Mont Ida (Crète) ainsi qu'à Nimrud et en Iran (Barnett 1974, 18-20). Le mélange d'éléments phéniciens et araméens s'expliquerait parfaitement si on les considère comme les témoins matériels de la présence phénicienne en Syrie du Nord dont les témoignages épigraphiques ont été discutés plus haut. Comme nous l'avions proposé précédemment dans une étude confrontant un détail iconographique de l'une de ces coupes et la composition d'un cachet phénicien inscrit, on pourrait même penser plus spécifiquement, dans au moins l'un de ces cas, à l'œuvre d'un artiste itinérant ou expatrié d'origine tyrienne (Gubel 1983, 39, figs. 12-13). Toujours est-il qu'en Crète, plusieurs boucliers importés de la Syrie du Nord et leurs adaptations dédaliques représentent des variantes richement historiées du type du bouclier à frises perlées (Kuenze 1931, pls 10-21; Markoe 1985, 168-169, pl. CR 13). On retrouve ce dernier sur la coupe, de souche purement phénicienne, d'Amathonte datant du début du VIIe siècle av. n.è. et qui reprend le thème de la coupe de Delphes d'une ville assiégée cette fois par des Ioniens ou Cariens[30]. Enfin, les coupes phéniciennes de Caere / Cerveteri témoignent de la transmission du type à l'Étrurie par l'intermédiaire des éléments orientaux actifs dans la pénétration phénicienne du bassin méditerranéen[31]. La comparaison entre des *umbos* de ce même site et de bien d'autres centres italiques avec les boucliers d'époque néo-assyrienne vers la fin du VIIIe siècle av. n.è. démontre d'ailleurs bien leur impact sur la production indigène[32].

[29] Pour ce type, voir Chamay 1994, 140 n° 50 avec bibliographie.

[30] *Pace* A. Hermary 1986, 177-194; Barnett 1957; pour des raisons qui seront discutées en détail ailleurs, je crois que la scène du patère d'Amathonte garde le souvenir des attaques de pirates grecs contre les villes côtières, auxquelles Sargon II mit à fin à l'aide de la flottille de Tyr (là-dessus, Katzenstein 1973, 238-243).

[31] G. Markoe 1985, pl. E8 cf. E 11 pour des représentations similaires sur une coupe d'origine inconnue.

[32] À noter que les *umbos* italiques remplacent souvent les perforations par des bossettes ou des boutons saillants exécutés au repoussé: Chamay 1994, 140 n° 50 avec bibliographie et 141 n° 51 pour un élément de cuirasse équestre picénien et Tomedi 2000; Naso 2003,

C'est un véritable plaisir de saisir cette opportunité pour offrir ces quelques réflexions à Karel et son épouse Bieke, dont la chaleureuse amitié et collégialité ont agrémenté tant d'activités scientifiques, que ce soit ici au Musée ou ailleurs en Belgique, à Damas ou sur la côte syrienne. Je remercie les éditeurs du présent volume de m'en avoir donné l'occasion.

Bibliographie

AKURGAL, E. 1981: «Aramaean and Phoenician Stylistic and Iconographical Elements in Neo-Hittite Art», in A. Biran (éd.), *Temples and High Places in Biblical Times, Jerusalem*, 131-141.

AMANDRY, P. 1938: «Objets orientaux en Grèce et en Italie aux VIIIe et VIIe siècles avant J.-C. », *Syria* 35, 73-80.

AVIGAD, N. et B. SASS 1997, *Corpus of West Semitic Stamp Seals,* Jerusalem.

BARNETT, R. D. 1966: «Homme masqué ou dieu ibex?», *Syria* 43, 269-276.

— 1957: *A Catalogue of the Nimrud Ivories in The British Museum*, Londres.

— 1974: «The Nimrud Bowls in the British Museum», *RSF* II, 11-33.

— 1977: «The Amathus Shield-Boss Rediscovered and the Amathus Bowl Reconsidered», *RDAC*, 157-169.

BARRELET, M.-Th. 1958: «Deux déesses syro-phéniciennes sur un bronze du Louvre», *Syria* 35, 27-44.

BERNETT, M. et O KEEL 1998: *Mond, Stier und Kult am Stadttor. Die Stele von Betsaida (et-Tell)* (Orbis Biblicus et Orientalis 161), Freiburg – Göttingen.

BIERBRIER, M. 2011: «Bye-Bye Bay », in M. Collier et S. Snape (éds.), *Ramesside Studies in Honour of K.A. Kitchen*, Bolton, 19-22.

BOARDMAN, J. 2003: *Classical Phoenician Scarabs. A Catalogue and Study*, Oxford.

BORDREUIL, P. 1977: «Une inscription phénicienne champlevée des environs de Byblos», *Semitica* XXVII, 23-27.

— 1986: *Catalogue des sceaux ouest-sémitiques inscrits de la Bibliothèque Nationale, du Musée du Louvre et du Musée biblique de Bible et Terre Sainte*, Paris.

— 1993: «Le répertoire archéologique des sceaux araméens et leur évolution », *Die Ikonographie des norwestsemitischen Namenssiegel (Orbis Biblicus et Orientalis),* Freiburg – Göttingen, 74-100.

BRIQUEL-CHATONNET, F. 1992: *Les relations entre les cités de la côte phénicienne et les royaumes d'Israël et de Juda* (Orientalia Lovaniensia Analecta 46 / Studia Phoenicia 12), Leuven.

BRON, F. 1979: «*Recherches sur les inscriptions phéniciennes de Karatepe*», Genève – Paris.

160-166. Pour l'inspiration étrangère, voir déjà de Meester de Ravestein 1880, 178 (R 961) à propos de l'*umbo* d'un bouclier samnite: «L'on voit donc que ceux qui travaillaient le bronze, avant le temps des Étrusques, avaient différents procédés et une grande habilité, qui devaient nécessairement leur être venus par leurs relations avec l'Asie».

BUCHANAN, B., P. R. S. MOOREY 1988: «*Catalogue of ancient Near Eastern Seals in the Ashmolean Museum» III, The Iron Age Stamp Seals*, Oxford.
ÇAMBEL, H., W. RÖLLIG et J. D. HAWKINS 1999: *Corpus of Hieroglyphic Luwian Inscriptions II. Karatepe – Arslantaş*, Berlin – New York.
ÇAMBEL, H. et A. ÖZYAR 2003: *Karatepe – Arslantaş*, Azatiwataya. *Die Bildwerke*, Mayence sur Rhin.
CHAMAY, J. 1994²: L'art des peuples italiques: 3000 à 300 avant J.-C., Genève.
CHILDS, W. A. P. 1978: *The City-Reliefs of Lycia*, New Jersey.
CHOLIDIS N. et L. MARTIN 2010: *Tell Halaf. Im Krieg zerstörte Denkmäler und ihre Restaurierung* (Tell Halaf V), Berlin – New York.
CRAIG MELCHERT, H. 2003: *The Luwians*, Leiden – Boston.
CULICAN, W. 1986: *Opera Selecta*, Göteborg.
DE MEESTER DE RAVESTEIN, E. 1880: *Musée de Ravestein. Notice*, Bruxelles.
DEUTSCH, R. A. LEMAIRE 2000: *Biblical Period Personal Seals in the Shlomo Moussaieff Collection*, Tel Aviv.
DION, P.-E. 1997: *Les Araméens à l'âge du Fer: Histoire politique et structures sociales* (Etudes bibliques 34), Paris.
DODSON, A. 2011: « Fade to Grey: The Chancellor Bay, Éminence Grise of the Late Nineteenth Dynasty», in M. Collier et S. Snape (éds.), *Ramesside Studies in Honour of K. A. Kitchen*, Bolton, 145-158.
DONNER, H. et W. RÖLLIG 2002: *Kanaanäische und Aramäische Inschriften²*, Wiesbaden.
DUPONT-SOMMER, A. 1950-51: «Deux nouvelles inscriptions sémitiques trouvées en Cilicie», *Jahrbuch für Kleinasiatischen Studien* 1, 43-47.
GALLING, K. 1950: «Die Achiram-Inschrift im Lichte der Karatepe-Texte», *WO* I, 421-425.
GEVIRTZ, S. 1967: «A Spindle whorl with Phoenician Inscription», *JNES* 26, 13-16.
GUBEL, E. 1983: «Art in Tyre during the Early First Millennium B.C. A Preliminary Survey», *Studia Phoenicia* I, 23-52.
— 1987: *Phoenician Furniture* (Studia Phoenicia 7), Leuven.
— 1996: «Between Egypt and the Near East: New light on Phoenician furniture», in G. Herrmann (éd.), *Western Asiatic Furniture, ancient and traditional*, Mainz/Rhein, 139-15.
HAWKINS, J. D. 1995: «The Political Geography of North-Syria and South-East Anatolia in the Neo-Assyrian Period», in M. Liverani (éd.), *Neo-Assyrian Geography*, Rome, 87-101.
— 2010: «*Corpus of Hieroglyphic Luwian Inscriptions, I, Inscriptions of the Iron Age*», 1, Berlin 2001.
HELCK, W. 1958: «*Zur Verwaltung des Mittleren und Neuen Reiches*», Leiden – Köln.
HERMARY, A. 1986: «La coupe en argent du British Museim («the Amathous bowl»)», in R. Laffineur, A. Forgeau, A. Hermary (éds.), *Amathonte III. Testimonia 3, L'orfèvrerie* (= *Etudes Chypriotes* VII), Paris, 177-194.
HERRMANN, H.-V. 1966: *Die Kessel der orientalisierenden Zeit*, I (Olympische Forschungen VI), Berlin, 114-130.
HROUDA, B. 1965: *Die Kulturgeschichte des assyrischen Flachbildes*, Bonn.
KATZENSTEIN, J. 1973: *The History of Tyre*, Jerusalem.

KREBERNIK, M. et U. SEIDL 1997: «Ein Schildbeschlag mit Bukranion und alphabetischer Inschrift», *ZA* 87, 101-111.

KUENZE, E. 1931: *Kretische Bronzereliefs*, Stuttgart.

LAFFINEUR, R. e.a. 1986: *Amathonte III, Testimonia 3*, Paris.

LEBRUN, R. 1987: «L'Anatolie et le monde phénicien du Xe au IVe siècle av. J.-C.», in *Studia Phoenicia* V, Leuven, 23-27.

LEMAIRE, A. 1976: «Milkiram, nouveau roi phénicien de Tyr? », *Syria* 53, 83-93.

— 1977: «Essai sur cinq sceaux phéniciens», *Semitica* XXVII, 29-40.

— 1983: «L'inscription phénicienne de Hassan Beyli reconsidérée», *RSF* 11, 9-19.

— 1987: «Bouclier», *Dictionnaire encyclopédique de la Bible*, Turnhout, 218.

— 1991: «L'écriture phénicienne en Cilicie et la diffusion des écritures alphabétiques», in Cl. Baurain, C. Bonnet et V. Krings (éds.), *Phoinikeia grammata* (Studia Phoinikia 6), Liège-Namur, 133-146.

— 1997: «Sceau phénicien de la région de Karaman (Turquie)», *Epigr. Anat* 29, 123-126.

— 1999: «Coupe astrale inscrite et astronomie araméenne», in Y. Avishur et R. Deutsch (éds.), *Michael. Historical, Epigraphical and biblical Studies in Honour of Prof. Michael Heltzer*, Tel Aviv – Jaffa, 195-211.

— 2001: «Les langues du royaume de Sam'al aux IXe-VIIIe s. av. J.C. et leurs relations avec le royaume de Qué », in E. Jean, A. M. Dinçol et S. Durugönül (éds.), *La Cilicie: espaces et pouvoirs locaux (2e millénaire av. J.C. – 4e siècle ap. J.C.), Actes de la Table Ronde internationale d'Istanbul, 2-5 novembre 1999*, Paris, 185-193.

— 2007: «La diffusion de l'alphabet dans le bassin méditerranéen», in R. Viers (éd.), *Langues et écritures de la Méditerranée (Actes du Forum des 9, 10 et 11 mars 2001, Maison du Séminaire, Nice),* Paris, 210.

LIPIŃSKI, E. 1983: «Notes d'épigraphie phénicienne et punique», *OLP* 14, 133-139.

— 1985: «Phoenicians in Anatolia and Assyria 9th – 6th centuries B.C.», *OLP* 16, 81-84.

— 1991: «Phéniciens en Assyrie: L'éponyme Milkiram et la surintendante Amat-Ashtart», Atti del II congresso internazionale di studi fenici e punici I, Roma, 151-154.

— 1992: «Gérdādi », *Dictionnaire de la civilisation phénicienne et punique*, Turnhout – Paris, 187.

— 1992a: «Anatolie», *Dictionnaire de la civilisation phénicienne et punique*, Turnhout – Paris, 29.

— 1994: *Studies in Aramaic Inscriptions and Onomastics* II (Orientalia Lovaniensia Analecta 57), Leuven.

— 1995: *Dieux et déesses de l'univers phénicien et punique* (Orientalia Lovaniensia Analecta 64), Leuven.

— 2000: *The Aramaeans. Their ancient History, Culture, Religion* (Orientalia Lovaniensia Analecta 100), Leuven – Paris – Sterling.

— 2004: *Itineraria Phoenicia* (Orientalia Lovaniensia 127/Studia Phoenicia XVIII), Leuven – Paris – Dudley, MA.

MANUELLI, F. 2010: «Foreign influences and local tradition in the Iron Age pottery production from Arslatepe: evidence from the new excavations of neo-Hittite levels», *Mesopotamia* XLV, 71-84.

MARKOE, G. 1985: *Phoenician Bronze and Silver Bowls from Cyprus and the Mediterranean*, Berkeley – Los Angeles – London.

MUFFS Y. et B. A. LEVINE 2003: *Studies in the Aramaic Legal Papyri from Elephantine*, Leiden – Boston, 231.

NASO, A. 2003: «*I bronzi etruschi e italici del Römisch-Germanisches Zentral-museum*», Mayence sur Rhin.

NEVLING PORTER, B. 2000: «Assyrian Propaganda for the West. Esarhaddon's stelae for Til Barsip and Sam'al», in G. Bunnens (éd.), *Essays on Syria in the Iron Age*, Louvain – Paris – Sterling, 143-176.

NOVÁK, M. 2010: «Kizzuwatna – Hiyawa – Quwe. Ein Abriss der Kulturgeschichte des Ebenen Kilikien», J. Becker, R. Hempelmann et E. Rehm (éds), *Kulturlandschaft Syrien. Zentrum und Peripherie. Festschrift für Jan-Waalke Meyer* (AOAT 371), Münster, 397-425.

SADER, H. 1987: *Les Etats araméens de Syrie depuis leur fondation jusqu'à leur transformation en province assyriennes*, Beirut.

— 2000: «The Aramaean Kingdoms of Syria. Origin and Formation Processes» in G. Bunnens (éd.), *Essays on Syria in the Iron Age*, Louvain – Paris – Sterling, 61-67.

SEGERT, S. 2001: «Une inscription phénicienne trouvée à Ras Shamra (fouille 1963)» in M. Yon et D. Arnaud (éds), *Études ougaritiques I. Travaux 1985-1995*, Paris 2001, 231-234.

TEKOĞLU, R. et A. Lemaire 2000: «La bilingue royale louvito-phénicienne de Çineköy», *Craibl* 144:3, 961-1006.

TOMEDI, G. 2000: *Italische Panzerplatten und Pantzerscheiben*, Stuttgart.

VON LUSCHAN, F. 1943: *Die Kleinfunde von Sendschirli*, Berlin.

WINTER, I. J. 1973: *North Syria in the Early First Millennium B.C., with Special Reference to Ivory Carving*, Ann – Arbor.

— 1979: «On the Problems of Karatepe: The Reliefs and their Context», *AnSt* 29, 115-151.

WOOLLEY L. et R. D. BARNETT, 1952: *Carchemish. Report on the Excavations of Jerablus on Behalf of the British Museum, III, The Excavations in the Inner Town*, Londres.

YON, M. 1997: «*La cité d'Ougarit sur le tell de Ras Shamra*», Paris.

ZGUSTA, L. 1964: «*Kleinasiatische Personennamen*», Prag.

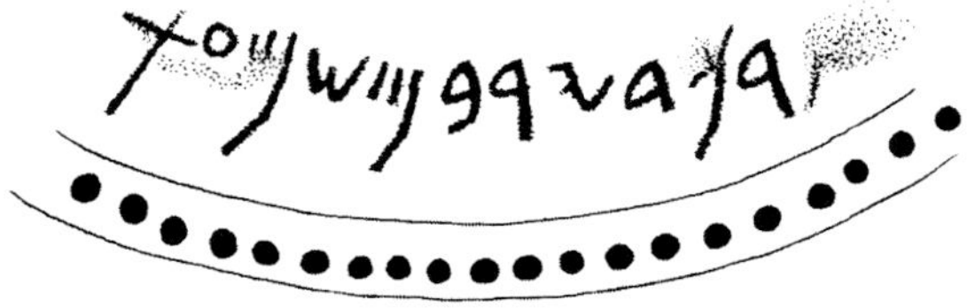

Fig. 1. Umbo de bouclier ou égide, bronze, diam. 25,4 cms, Bruxelles, MRAH O.4794 (d'après E. Gubel – B. Overlaet (éd.), *De Gilgamesh à Zénobie*, Bruxelles 2007 – Paris 2008, p. 220 n° 468).
© MRAH

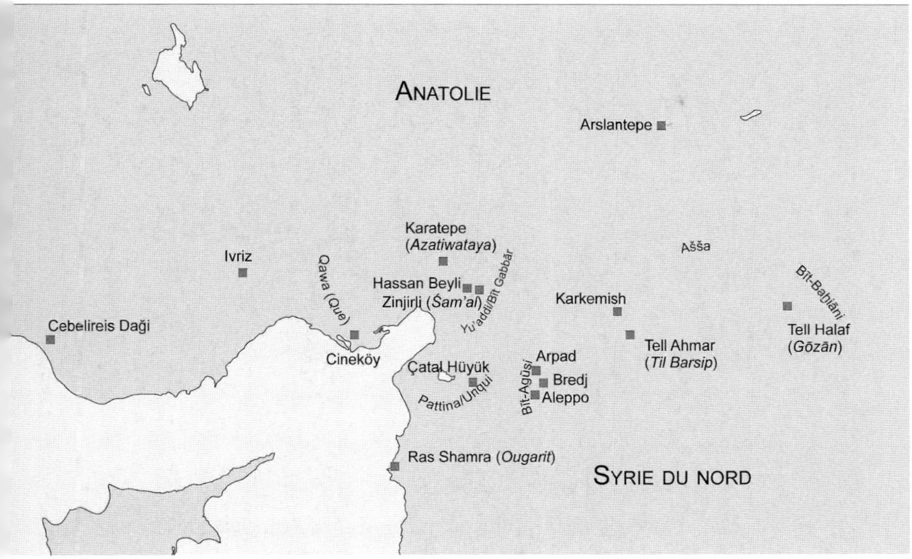

Fig. 2. Principaux sites de la Syrie du Nord et de la Cilicie mentionnés dans le texte (noms antiques en italiques, royaumes en oblique recourbé). © MRAH (I. Hodiaumont)

Fig. 3. Cylindre d'El'amar (ex coll. Marcopoli, Alep) (d'après Bordreuil 1993, fig. 6).

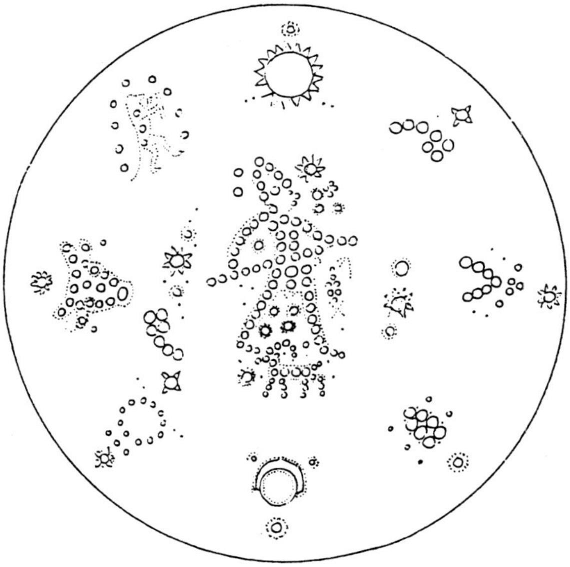

Fig. 4. Coupe à inscriptions araméennes, ex coll. Foroughi, Téhéran, coll. S. Moussaïef, Londres (d'après Bernett – Keel 1998, fig. 64).

Fig. 5. Détail de la coupe en bronze phénicienne de Delphes, (d'après Childs 1978, fig. 28).

1947: TWO TABLETS AS A CHRISTMAS GIFT TO A LEUVEN ASSYRIOLOGIST

Hendrik HAMEEUW
KU Leuven

With gratitude towards Karel Van Lerberghe, my mentor in the field of Assyriology, I present this contribution in celebration of his long commitment to ancient Near Eastern studies. His enthusiastic teaching and stories gave me insight into the history of Mesopotamia as well as the world of those who made it their life task to study it; the latter has truly proven bottomless. As a colleague he granted full freedom in all my endeavors and was never scarce with advice. For this and other reasons I am much indebted to Karel and wish him many more years in the company of cuneiform tablets.

After my formal studies in 2003, Karel gave me the opportunity and confidence to participate in a newly established interdisciplinary project on the development and use of technology to digitize and facilitate the study of cuneiform tablets, and archaeological objects in general, the outcome of which we called the 'minidome' or Portable Light Dome system (Willems et al., 2005; Hameeuw and Willems, 2011). During the testing phase several series of recordings were completed. One of these initial test subjects were the cuneiform tablets of the collection of the KU Leuven. These include two unpublished texts that drew my attention, and now form the subject of this contribution.

Introduction

Most of the cuneiform texts in the collection of Leuven were published by Leuven scholars in the past. The vast majority — those of Neo-Sumerian origin — by text copy in MVN II (Sauren, 1974) and by transcription and translation in OLP 4 (Naster and Sauren, 1973). Later, two small Old Babylonian texts were published in OLP 18 (Vandendriessche, 1987).

It was the collecting efforts by Leuven scholars in the Near East around 1911, plus gifts and bequests of a later date (Naster and Sauren, 1973, 17-19, 70; Naster, 1978, 15; Baudot 1987-1988, 113-114), which settled the total number of tablets in the Leuven Collection. The oldest part of the collection has a museum accession number beginning with "MB", indicating they are the texts formerly kept at the *Musée Biblique* in Leuven. In addition to these, the collection's corpus includes forty-four tablets gathered in Beirut by Paul Naster, a former professor of Assyriology at Leuven; they received the accession prefix "NP" — *Naster Paul* — and together with the MB tablets dating to the Neo-Sumerian period are as thus part of the publications of Naster and Sauren mentioned above.[1] Since the division of the university in 1970, the MB collection is kept at the Katholieke Universiteit Leuven (KU Leuven) and the Université catholique de Louvain (UCL). The NP tablets are all preserved at the KU Leuven. In the OLP 4 publication with the Neo-Sumerian material by Naster and Sauren, the authors promised a later publication of tablets more recent in date, but that study, which most probably intended to include the two texts presented in this contribution, never saw publication. The only non-Neo-Sumerian tablets of the Leuven collection to be published are the two Old Babylonian texts in OLP 18 by Mia Vandendriessche (1987).[2]

In Naster and Sauren's publication of the Neo-Sumerian tablets, the corpus of the forty-four NP texts are mentioned and labeled as *almost* all the tablets belonging to Naster (Naster and Sauren, 1973, 18)[3]. The two tablets discussed below are most probably among those not listed by Naster on that occasion. Today all of them form part of the Leuven collection and include even a few other tablets, assumed to be collected by Naster as well. For the sake of completeness they are listed here:

NP 46	Letter	Middle Assyrian	this publication
NP 47	Delivery	Neo-Sumerian	this publication
NP 48	Messenger Text	Neo-Sumerian	unpublished
NP 49	Letter	Old Assyrian	unpublished
NP 50	List	Neo-Sumerian	unpublished

In addition to these tablets listed with a NP-number, the Leuven collection also contains six fragments of cuneiform tablets. Presumably they were collected by Paul Naster as well, but never received a collection number. Today they are labeled as NP 51 to NP 56.

[1] In the OLP 4 publication the NP-tablets are listed as belonging to Naster; today they are all part of the Leuven Collection.

[2] Spaey 1989-1990 includes the publication of three sealed dockets from the Musée Biblique.

[3] That are NP 1-11 and 13-45; there is no NP 12.

The Christmas gift

The two texts treated in this contribution were to my knowledge not studied or published in the past. They are discussed together as apparently they found their way to the Leuven Collection together. In terms of both in time and probably provenance, there is no relation between the two tablets. However, the texts are accompanied with a similar label handwritten by Paul Naster connecting the texts with Susa.

Both clay tablets appear to be a gift of Roman Ghirshman, director of the French excavations at Susa from 1946 to 1967, to Paul Naster. The two labels in the boxes wherein the tablets are kept mention this transaction, saying: "at/from Susa given (to Paul Naster) by R. Ghirshman, director of the (French) excavations on 24 December 1947" (see labels below). These gifts are dated to 24 December 1947, the day before Christmas; perhaps a present on Christmas Eve?

Paul Naster traveled throughout the Near East on several occasions, mostly accompanied by his wife, Lydie. The label from NP 46 suggest Naster received these tablets at Susa itself, implying he visited the site in the winter of 1947-48. When inspecting the *Journal de fouilles* of Ghirshman, his entry on 23 December 1947 mentions "visite de P. Naster de Bruxelles"[4]. This accords perfectly with the location and time of the gifts as mentioned on Naster's labels in the Leuven Collection.

The main question in regard to this gift is where did these texts originate. When inspecting the work conducted by Ghirshman and his team since his fist campaign from 4 December 1946 until 23 April1947, and his second campaign which started on 21 November 1947, he had not yet excavated the site extensively by the time of Naster's visit on 23/24 December 1947 (Steve et al., 1980, 107-108). In fact, during the first years of Ghirshmans work at Susa, no mention is made of tablets being discovered. In addition, both texts have by their contents and paleography seemingly no relation to the ancient city of Susa. A Susa provenance, or finding place can therefore be doubted; establishing their place of origin is even harder. When R. Ghirshman started his series of excavation seasons at Susa he inherited the work of J. de Morgan and R. De Mecquenem. It could be suggested the two texts formed part of unspecified archaeological objects of the old excavations left in the cellars of the *château*, which turned up when they were cleaned by

[4] Personal communication from Hermann Gasche; Dr. Gasche does bring up Ghirshmans journal does not state Naster spent the night at Susa. Normally, Ghirshman noted this type of information in his journal.

Ghirshman in 1946-47. Still, in that case, it is questionable why well-preserved tablets would not have been registered by the previous directors of the French excavations at Susa; and in fact, it is known what was left by the previous excavation teams, was no more than fragments of archaeological objects, and by no means well-preserved clay tablets. In addition and of significance, why would R. Ghirshman present cuneiform texts to a visitor as Paul Naster? Ghirshman was not the person to disperse antiquities dug up during excavations.

The texts, based on their contents and paleography, most probably do not originate in Susa and secondly it is very implausible Ghirshman presented objects excavated at Susa to visitors. So how do the labels accompanying both tablets in the Leuven Collection and written by Paul Naster explain themselves? A solution can only be argued on uncertain grounds as no records with evidence or a hint concerning this issue have survived. Most probably the tablets were attained via one of the many antiquity dealers active all over the Near East at that time.[5] The tablets seem to have a different place of origin, NP 46 somewhere in northeastern Syria and NP 47 in the Lagash region. Thus, they might have been acquired during more than one occasion at two geographically distinct locations. With caution, it can be suggested they were acquired during the trip towards Susa.

Texts

In 2010 both texts were digitally recorded with the Portable Light Dome system. Based on this recorded data, a 'discolored/shaded image', a '3D-image' and an objective 'line drawing' have been extracted (see illustrations); here presented together with a transliterations, translations and commentary. These recordings can be consulted on-line, together with all the tablets of the Leuven Cuneiform Collection via the website of the ancient Near East unit of the KU Leuven.[6]

[5] Interestingly, Hermann Gasche noted to the author of this contribution such antique dealers were even active at the small city of Shūsh, beside the tell of Susa. If the tablets were acquired at Shūsh, it can even be suggested Paul Naster bought the tablets himself. Of course, that idea would imply Naster wrote a false label, obscuring his purchase. That again would be surprising as Naster made no secret of for example the acquisition of tablets he made on the antiquities markets of Beirut (Naster and Sauren, 1973, 18).

[6] I thank sincerely the appreciated input by Katrien De Graef, Stefan Jakob and David Owen for their suggestions in regard to the dating or correct interpretation of the texts contents.

NP 46

Date: Middle Assyrian (13th century)
Provenance: Susa?/unknown
Origin: Northeast Syria
Dimensions: 5.9 × 5.3 × 2.3 cm
Label by Naster:

te <u>Susa</u>	at <u>Susa</u>,
aan P.N. 24 dec. 1947	to P[aul] N[aster], 24 Dec[ember] 1947
geschonken door	given by
Ghirshman, dir$^{\underline{r}}$ der[7]	Ghirshman, dir[ecto]r of the
Franse opgravingen	French excavations

OBVERSE

1.	*a-na* ^{Id}iškur-en-dingir^{meš}	To Adad-bēl-ilāni
2.	*qí-bi-ma*	speak,
3.	*um-ma* ^{I}*sa-mi-du-ma*	thus: Sāmidu.
4.	*a-na ku-a-ša* é-*ka*	May you and your house
5.	*lu-ú šul-mu*	be well.
6.	*pa-ni-ma iš-*⸢*tu*⸣ *a-*⸢*ḫa*⸣*-iš*	Previously together
7.	*ni-id-du-bu-ub*	we have spoken,
8.	*ta-at-ta-at-la-ak*	you left,
9.	⸢*la-a*⸣ *ta-tu-ra*	you did not return.
10.	[...]⸢u$_4$$^{?}$⸣*-ma* ⸢*ar*⸣*-ḫi-iš*	... today at once
11.	[...] ⸢2⸣ anše.nigida [še$^{?}$] ⸢SIG$_5$⸣.meš	... 2 *emār* 6 *sūt* of good barley$^{?}$

LOWER EDGE

12.	*le-*⸢*qe*⸣*-a*	take
13.	*ar-ḫi-iš*	at once

REVERSE

14.	*a-*⸢*di us*⸣*-ba-ku-ni*	till I remain
15.	*a-na* ^{URU}*ta-*⸢*i*⸣*-di*	to Ta'idu
16.	*al-ka* še-*am*	come! The barley

[7] The now-obsolete Dutch plural genitive "*der*" < "*van de*" (= "of the").

17.	*la-a ad-di-na-ak-ku*	I did not give to you
18.	*a-di ia-*⌜x-*ša*⌝*-am-ma*	till…
19.	*la-a ni-lu-ku-né*	we do not come
20.	še-*am la-a ad-di-na-ku*	the barley I will not give to you.
21.	u_4-26-kam	Day 26.

Light brown-orange, almost squared, tablet with some damage and cracks on its surface. The letter is of the typical Middle Assyrian squared-shape type. While the label written by P. Naster accompanying the tablet in the Leuven Collection mentions he received the tablet from R. Ghirshman at Susa, it does not suggest its provenance was Susa itself, in contrast to the label of NP 47. Based on the *ductus* and contents — the city of Ta'idu is mentioned in line 15 — a northeastern Syrian origin and date in the late 13th century BCE for the tablet is likely.

Concerning the appearance of Ta'idu in the letter, the exact location of this city is still debated; a number of settlements are in the balance (Wäfler, 1994; Szuchman, 2007, 4-5, 47-50 & 75-78). Several texts title the city as a Mittanian and Middle Assyrian capital. Based on the archaeological evidence and in relation to the textual evidence in the Dur-Katlimmu texts (Röllig, 1983), Ta'idu corresponds best with modern Tell Hamidiye in the Upper Khabur (Eichler et al., 1985, 53-76; Wäfler, 2003). Other settlements in the northern Assyrian provinces, i.e. the region around Mardin and in between Cizre and Diyarbakir, have also been suggested for Ta'idu's location. Kessler considered on well-examined grounds (Kessler, 1980, 95-109) the tell next to the modern Turkish village of Üçtepe to be the ancient city. When he wrote that argumentation, Kessler had no knowledge of the Dur-Katlimmu texts who suggest Tell Hamidiye as Ta'idu and recently, he argued in favor of Tell al-Hamidiye.[8] An alternative proposition for the northern location is Tell Ermen in the centre of the modern Turkish city of Kiziltepe, south of Mardin (Lipiński, 2000, 142-144). As a consequence, it is put forward there may have been two settlements called Ta'idu in the region, although that possibility is contested as well (Szuchman, 2007, 49-50).

The text is a letter order with a standard address formula and *šulmu*-well being formula[9]. The letter deals with a transaction of barley. While

[8] During the *Rencontre Assyriologique Internationale* at Paris in 2009 he presented a small archive found at Tell Hamidiye as Ta'idian.

[9] On this formula see Cancik-Kirschbaum (1996, 59-60).

line 18 is difficult to understand and the passage of lines 10-11 is partly damaged, it seems that it was previously agreed that barley would be brought by Sāmidu to Adad-bēl-ilāni when he came to Ta'idu, but that did not occur and therefore the letter informs Adad-bēl-ilāni the barley is not yet given.

NP 47

Date: Ibbi-Sîn 2
Provenance: Susa?/unknown
Origin: Central Sumer — Lagash
Dimensions: 7.2 × 4.7 × 2.2 cm
Label by P. Naster:

van <u>Susa</u>	from <u>Susa</u>
gegeven door	given by
R Ghirshman, dir$^{\underline{r}}$	R. Ghirshman, dir[ecto]r
v. de opgravingen	o[f] the excavations
24 dec. 1947	24 Dec[ember] 1947

OBVERSE

1	5.0.0.0 še.gur	5 *gur* barley
2	kìšib lú-^{d}nin.gír.su	received by Lu-Ningirsu
3	dub.sar edin	the '*edin*-scribe'[10],
4	6.1.0.0 gur[11] še kù.ga	6 *gur* and 1 (*pi*) barley (in?) silver,
5	1.2.0.0 gìri ur.mes É.ŠU	1 (*gur*) and 2 (*pi* of barley) *via* Urmes ...,
6	1.0.0.0 ur.^{d}ba.ba$_6$	1 (*gur* of barley) Ur-Baba
7	dumu ur.sa$_6$.sa$_6$.ga	son of Ur-Sasaga,
8	0.1.0.0 nu.za.ba nar	1 (*pi* of barley) Nuzaba the singer,
9	0.2.0.0 géme.^{d}šul.pa.è	2 (*pi* of barley) Geme-Šul-pa'e
10	gìri lugal.ezem	*via* Lugal-ezem,
11	0.1.0.0 ur.^{d}ig.alim	1 (*pi* of barley) Ur-Igalim
12	lú.laḫtan$_4$	the LU-LAḪTAN[12],

[10] Same title at MVN 22, 84:3.
[11] Above erasure of še?
[12] Schneider 1935: 614, 616 or REC 286; see also HSS 04, 049: lu$_2$-lahtan$_4$-me", Hussey 1915, text 49: rev. II 10.

REVERSE

13. šu.nigin 10+4.2.0.0 gur	a total of 14 *gur* and 2 *pi* (barley)
14. ki nimgir.ra.kam.ta	from Nimgirra-kam[13]
15. mu.túm	delivery.
16. mu en.^{d}innana	The year the *en*-priest of Inanna
17. maš.e ì.pàd	by means of the omens was chosen.

Light brown rectangular plano-convex shaped tablet. Its top left corner is broken off — most probably modern damage — and repaired. The label accompanying NP 47 in the Leuven Cuneiform Collection says: "from Susa", in contrast to the label of NP 46 that mentions Naster received the tablet "at Susa". This small difference in notation by Naster, if it was intended, suggests NP 46 tablet was only given "at" Susa but was not found at Susa, whereas NP 47 does reveals the provenance by writing "from". The date on the tablet, Ibbi-Sîn 2, allows this provenance; it is generally accepted the rule of the Ur III dynasty at Susa only faded away by the beginning of the Ibbi-Sîn 3 (Jacobsen, 1970; Potts, 1999, 142). Nevertheless, the language, paleography and prosopography do not argue for a Susian origin for the tablet, but rather a Southern Mesopotamian — Central Sumer one. The official Nimgirra-kam (l. 14) is uniquely known from Girsu; it is therefore in the Lagash region the origin of this tablet most probably has to be found.

The contents of the document is a typical Neo-Sumerian delivery-document, wherein varying amounts of barley are allocated to different persons.

Bibliography

BAUDOT, M. P. 1987-88: "The Ancient Near Eastern Seals and Gems in the Biblical Museum at the Catholic University of Leuven", *Acta Archaeologica Lovaniensia* 26-27, 113-130.

CANCIK-KIRSCHBAUM, E. C. 1996: *Die mittelassyrischen Briefe aus Tall Šēḫ Ḥamad* (BATSH 4/1), Berlin.

EICHLER, S., V. HAAS, D. STEUDLER, M. WÄFLER and D. WARBURTON 1985: *Tall al-Hamidiya 1, Vorbericht 1984* (OBO, Series Archaeologica 4), Freiburg – Göttingen.

[13] Nimgirra-kam is known from Nebrask 65 (Ibbi-Sîn 4 – provenance unclear); STA 25 (Šulgi 46 – Girsu); TCTI 2: 4195 (Šu-Sîn 7 – Girsu); Zinbun 21, pl. 1: 37 (Amar-Sîn 2 – Girsu); BPOA 1: 155 + seal (Šulgi 45 – Girsu); RA 10, p.66: 104 (no date – Girsu); MVN 9:151 (no data – Girsu); a time span of Šulgi 46 to Ibbi-Sîn 4, some 25 years.

HAMEEUW, H. and G. WILLEMS 2011: "New Visualization Techniques for Cuneiform Texts and Sealings", *Akkadica* 132/2, 163-178.

HUSSEY, M. I. 1915: *Sumerian Tablets in the Harvard Semitic Museum, Part II*, Cambridge (Harvard).

JACOBSEN, T. 1970: "The Reign of Ibbi-Suen", in W. L. Morgan (ed.) *Toward the Image of Tammuz and Other Essays on Mesopotamian History and Culture*, Cambridge (Harvard), 173-186.

KESSLER, K. 1980: *Untersuchungen zur historischen Topographie Nordmesopotamiens nach keilschriftlichen Quellen des 1. Jahrtausends v. Chr.* (TAVO B 26), Wiesbaden.

LIPIŃSKI, E. 2000: *The Aramaeans: Their Ancient History, Culture, Religion* (OLA 100), Leuven.

NASTER, P. 1978: "De assyriologie aan de universiteit Leuven", *Akkadica* 6, 8-16.

NASTER, P. and H. SAUREN 1973: "Textes cunéiformes conservés à Louvain", *OLP* 4, 17-70.

POTTS, D. T. 1999: *The Archaeology of Elam: Formation and Transformation of an Ancient Iranian State* (Cambridge World Archaeology), Cambridge.

RÖLLIG, W. 1983: "Ein Itinerar aus Dur-Katlimmu", *Damaszener Mitteilungen* 1, 279–284.

SAUREN, H. 1974: *Wirtschaftsurkunden aus der Zeit der III Dynastie von Ur im Besitz des Musée d'art et d'histoire in Genf und kleinerer Sammlungen* (Materiali per il Vocabolario Neosumerico 2), Rome.

SCHNEIDER, N. 1935: *Die Keilschriftzeichen der Wirtschaftsurkunden von Ur III nebst ihren Charakteristischsten Schreibvarianten systematisch zusammengestellt* (Keilschrift-Paläographie 2), Rome.

SPAEY, J. 1989-1990: "The Inscribed Seals and Sealings at Leuven", *Acta Archaeologica Lovaniensia* 28-29, 1-2.

STEVE, M.-J., H. GASCHE and L. DE MEYER 1980: "La Susiane au deuxième millénaire: à propos d'une interprétation des fouilles de Suse", *Iranica antiqua* 15, 49-154.

SZUCHMAN, J. J. 2007: *Prelude to Empire: Middle Assyrian Hanigalbat and the Rise of the Aramaeans*, Los Angeles. (PhD dissertation, UCLA)

VANDENDRIESSCHE, M. 1987, "Two Old Babylonian Tablets in the Collection at Leuven", *OLP* 18, 61-66.

WÄFLER, M. 1994: "Taddum, Tîdu und Ta'idu(m)/Tâdum", in P. Calmeyer, K. Hecker, L. Jakob-Rost and C. B. F. Walker (eds.) *Beiträge zur altorientalischen Archäologie und Altertumskunde: Festschrift für Barthel Hrouda zum 65. Geburtstag*, Wiesbaden, 293–302.

WÄFLER, M. 2003: *Tall al-Hamidiya 4: Vorbericht 1988–2001* (OBO, Series Archaeologica 23), Freiburg — Göttingen.

WILLEMS, G., F. VERBIEST, W. MOREAU, H. HAMEEUW, K. VAN LERBERGHE and L. VAN GOOL 2005: "Easy and Cost-effective Cuneiform Digitizing", in M. Mudge, N. Ryan and R. Scopigno (eds.) *The 6th International Symposium on Virtual Reality, Archaeology and Cultural Heritage (VAST 2005)*, Pisa, 73-80.

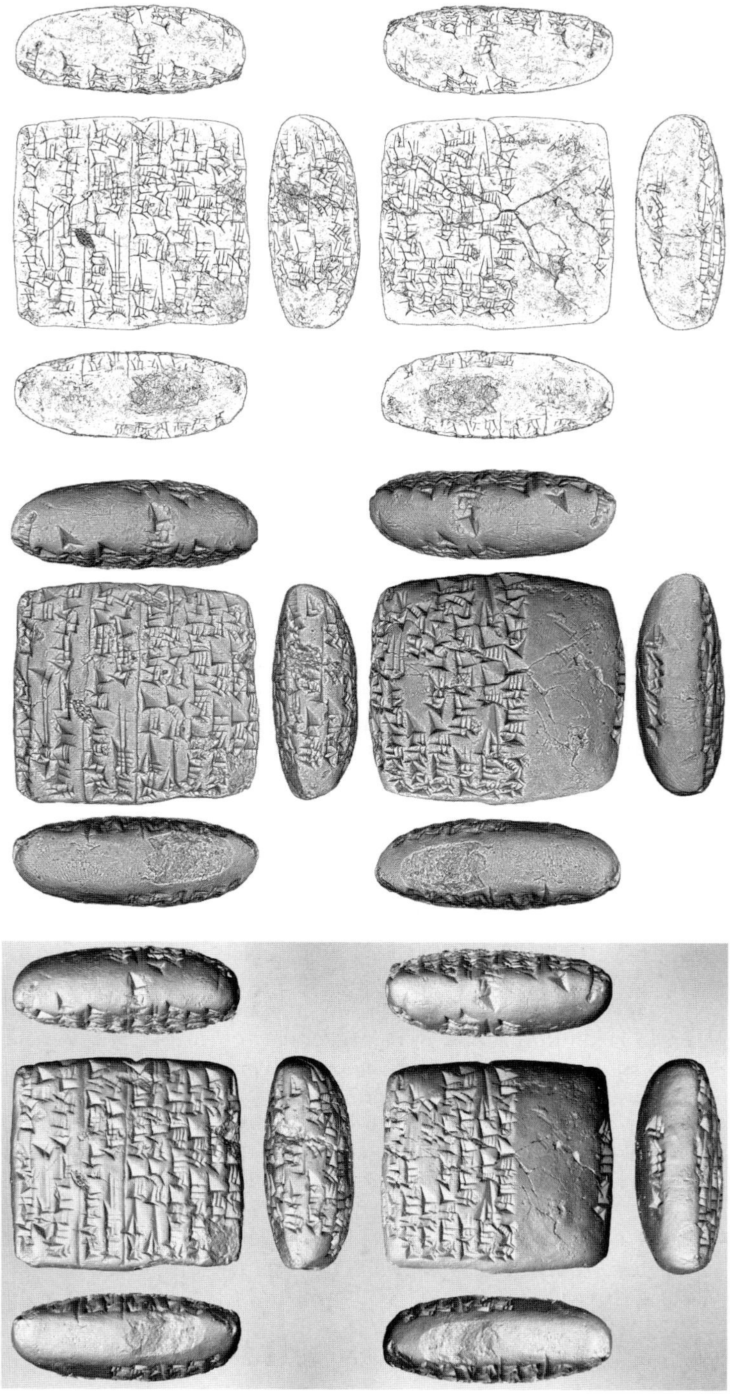

Computer-generated images based on the recording of tablet NP 46 with the Portable Light Dome system

Shaded filter (PLD viewer)

3D images with radiance scaling filter (Meshlab v1.3.0 viewer)

Line drawing (PLD viewer)

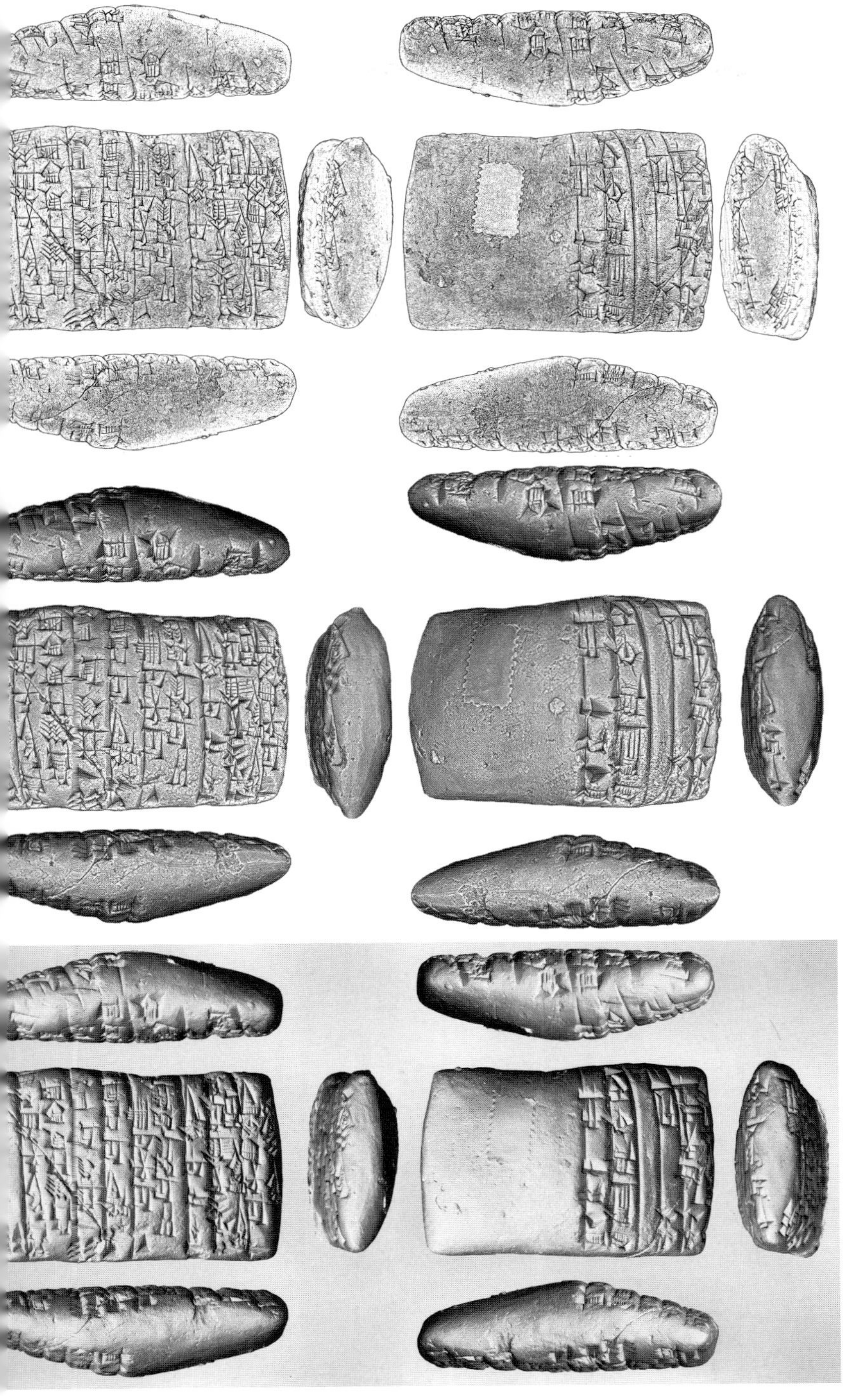

Computer-generated images based on the recording of tablet NP 47 with the Portable Light Dome system

Line drawing (PLD viewer)

3D images with radiance scaling filter (Meshlab v1.3.0 viewer)

Shaded filter (PLD viewer)

THE GUARD WHO MOLESTED GENTLEMEN …
A LETTER *ANA AWĪLĒ*, FROM THE UR-UTU ARCHIVE

Caroline JANSSEN
Ghent University

I was a beginning Assyriologist and standing a few meters from Ur-Utu's house when Karel Van Lerberghe said "they always write the same." As a sign of my appreciation for my colleague, I looked for a letter which was a little bit out of the ordinary.

Di 1285 is a letter 'ana awīlē', in plural, about a man who hit gentlemen with a mud brick.

In this contribution I will first give a brief explanation about the context in which the letter was found and the question of the addressees of the letters from the Ur-Utu archive. I will then analyze the letter and try to answer the question why this letter was sent to Ur-Utu.

1. The context of Ur-Utu's letters

Ur-Utu's archive is a late Old Babylonian private archive from Sippar-Amnānum. Its owner held the function of *gala.maḫ* (chief dirge singer) of Annunītum, as did his father Inanna-mansum. During its excavation meticulous notes were taken allowing us to know where exactly his tablets — over 2000 — were found. It was clear from the outset that this archive had been abandoned in the face of an imminent threat, and that it was nearly complete.[1]

Indeed, it seemed an ideal 'closed context': an archive that had been left intact when its owner abandoned the house, an event that could be narrowed down to the end of the summer of Ammi-ṣaduqa 18. But there is a difference between an ideal and a real archive, as we would gradually discover.

A group of texts found in the courtyard (group O) gave us a hint that Ur-Utu or people from his entourage had attempted to save the most vital documents.[2] Our study on the chains of transmission of real estate

[1] Gasche 1989 provides the basic data concerning the excavation of the house and its archive, see in particular pp. 9-44 and pl. 2-4.

[2] Gasche 1989, 29.

documents gave us a first estimate of the extent of what had been carried out of the house.[3]

Ur-Utu's archive contains a number of tablets which had been drawn up for his father, as he lived (for the latter part of his life, from Ad 28 onward) in the same house.[4] There were also some older pieces, recording events linked to their ancestors. Michel Tanret suggested that these documents had lost their original value but were kept for emotional reasons.[5] He also observed that the archive contains further surprises: tablets that so far cannot be linked to the Ur-Utu family in any way. In the case of real estate documents, their presence can be easily explained. They are pieces connected to the history of the property, not to that of the family.[6] For other pieces such an explanation is absent so far, so that the author comes to the conclusion that some smaller groups of tablets had probably been entrusted to Ur-Utu by other people.[7]

The house was renovated by Ur-Utu shortly before it burnt down (Aṣ 17-18).[8] His archive was in the process of reorganization when fate struck.[9] Some older pieces had been discarded; there was an old archive room which still contained the majority of the texts lying about in heaps (room 22), and a newly built archive room, to which documents had been transferred and in which new documents were kept (room 17). The arrangement of tablets in room 22 (one group blocking the passage through the doorway) shows that the reorganization was in full process.[10]

[3] Tanret and Janssen (in preparation) were able to reconstruct coherent dossiers. It was possible to determine that some pieces found in group O belonged to larger dossiers whose other pieces are not among the tablets found. As group O landed on the floor by accident, when somebody stumbled on his way out, it seems logical to assume that the related pieces were successfully removed.

[4] Gasche 1989 gives the history of the house; the chronology of the house's occupation is further elaborated in Janssen, Gasche and Tanret 1994, which ends in a table where archaeological and textual data are placed in a timeline. Tanret 2008 addresses the question of what tablets Inanna-mansum brought with him when he moved to his new house.

[5] Tanret 2008.

[6] The practice of transferring real estate tablets was first described by Charpin 1986. His hypothesis was confirmed and further developed by Tanret and Janssen (in preparation). The framework of this system is explained in Janssen 1996.

[7] The 'nomad tablets' and the archive composition are discussed in Tanret 2004.

[8] Gasche 1989, 28-29.

[9] Early attempts to find the key to the archive's organizational principles failed; Tanret and Janssen (in preparation) provides more insights in the state and causes of (dis)organization, as for the first time it was possible to group texts into meaningful and coherent dossiers — groups of tablets one would expect to find together, in an organized household.

[10] Gasche 1989, 29 n. 93.

While the majority of texts belong to the later occupational level IIIb, some texts were found in the lower layer IIId, or in the *remblai* of the renovation works (IIIc).

The old archive room was left undisturbed in the final hours of the house's occupation; the new archive room was completely turned upside down, because an attempt was made to bring important documents into safety. In the process many letters were dropped on the floor, while other more important pieces were put in baskets and removed.

The archive underwent some minor disturbances in later times, when tombs were built on its site. Some texts from Ur-Utu's archive ended up as *remblai* of these tombs.[11]

2. The letters from the Ur-Utu archive

Ur-Utu's archive contained some 200 letters. L. De Meyer witnessed that some were very fragile, and that letters were particularly prone to disintegration at the time of their excavation.

The majority of the letters were found in his new archive room; the older archive room still contained 35 letters. While most letters were found in the most recent level of occupation (IIIb, Aṣ 17-18), a few were found in the *remblai* originating from the reconstruction works (IIIc: Di 743), or in later tombs (T256:Di 175; T326:Di 2223 and Di 2224). The latter belong to the Ur-Utu archive, but their context was disturbed. A few letters were found in the older level of occupation (end Ammiditana-Aṣ 17), IIId[12] (Di 2201, Di 2202, Di 2233).[13]

3. Forms of address in the letters from the Ur-Utu archive

In none of the letters Ur-Utu is addressed by his name. One letter is addressed to the '*gala.maḫ* of Annunītum', i.e. by function (Di 1353).[14] It is a royal letter issued by Ammiditana, which means that its addressee is Inanna-mansum.

[11] Gasche, 1989, 28-33 and pl. 2-4.

[12] Janssen, Gasche and Tanret 1994, 121-2. Inanna-mansum bought the house in Ammiditana 28 and renovated it (purchase of wood beams in Ad 29).

[13] The major part of Ur-Utu's letters are transcribed, translated and interpreted in Janssen, unpublished PhD. Some have been published by Van Lerberghe 1991, De Meyer 1982 and 1989, and Janssen 1992.

[14] Maybe there was a second letter, Di 1542, sent by Ammi-... (no greeting formulae), but in this case the first line is lost.

All the other letters use honorific titles in the address, or are without address. It is remarkable how many different forms of address are used for (what we suppose is) the same person: apart from the aforementioned *ana gala.maḫ annunītum* we encounter *ana awīlim, ana abīya, ana aḫīya, ana bēlīya, ana šāpirīya*; or no address at all, as is the case in most of the *zeḫpum*-type letters.

Most of the letters have the standard greetings from the late Old Babylonian period, some mention the king's name; more unusual religious formulae are seen in a fairly large percentage of this corpus of letters. Some have brief formulae, or no greetings at all. This variety can be attributed to the background of the sender, and the relationship between sender and addressee. There are many different correspondents, and even if the same sender occurs, there may be some variation in the use of greeting formulae, depending on the occasion.[15]

4. Unexpected finds

While we can reasonably assume that most of the letters were sent to Ur-Utu, or possibly his father Inanna-mansum (something especially to be considered for letters from Room 22), some do not fit our initial expectation.

These include:

1. Letters whose *sender* is Ur-Utu[16]
2. A letter written to a female addressee
3. Letters written to persons mentioned by names other than Ur-Utu/ Inanna-mansum
4. A letter *ana awīlē* (discussed below)

For the first group, we found indications (form[17] and contents[18]) that some were not original letters, but copies of letters sent by the chief dirge singer (Di 167 and Di 1194; *MHET* I, 68-69, and probably the very damaged letter Di 371), or perhaps we should say 'extracts' (where the beginning is preserved it is clear that we only have the body of the text, not the address or greeting formulae).

[15] Janssen, unpublished PhD. For more observations on this subject see Sallaberger 1999, 30ff.

[16] Charpin 2010, 129-130 deals with the fact that an archive contains passive correspondence, and that usually no copies were made.

[17] The shape of the tablet, lining, the lack of address and greeting formulae.

[18] Published and discussed in Janssen, 1992.

More enigmatic is *MHET* I, 70, a letter without address which bears Ur-Utu's seal, which proves that it is a real letter, meant to be sent; K. Van Lerberghe suggests that for some reason this never happened; one could suggest the same for a partially destroyed letter *'ana abīya'* by Ur-Utu (Di 229).[19]

Di 377 written by Ur-Utu, 'your slave' *'ana bēlīya'* may be seen as a letter to his father during an absence (see note 19 for the address). It must then have been sent in the short time span after Ur-Utu had assumed his religious name, and succeeded his father as *gala.maḫ,* and before Inanna-mansum died. In this damaged letter, a conflict between the town of Kirraya and the temple of Annunītum is described, concerning baskets of gold, silver and stones of Šamaš of the Edikudkalamma. The letter seems to be a report of events or rumors, and Ur-Utu seems to be excited about it (*ša ašmu šemi*!, 'hear what I have heard!'). A letter from Ur-Utu to a deity is a curiosity.[20]

There is one letter in which female imperatives allow us to conclude that it was written to a woman close to the chief dirge singer (the address is broken, one might think of Rā'imtum). In it, she is asked to intervene with the *gala.maḫ* concerning the *muqabbirūtum* rites (Di 372).

As for the letters addressed to people other than the *gala.maḫ*, we can be short. They are few and some are badly damaged (even the names of the addressees). Two of these letters were found in the lower level of occupation (IIId); they probably belonged to Inanna-mansum's archive, for some reason, but they were not transferred as part of the living archive (Di 2202, Di 2233). Furthermore, there is one royal letter by Ammiditana concerning the temple of Annunītum, to Awīl-Nabium and Sin-tayyār (Di 1736), who are known to have held the position of *gal.ukkin.na.* Probably the *gala.maḫ* received or made a copy of this letter, which must be dated in the first decade of Ammiditana's reign.[21]

At the end of this list, there is Di 1285, the letter *ana awīlē*, exceptionally in plural, which is the object of this investigation. Who sends this letter, and why? Why does Ur-Utu receive this letter? Is he one of the *awīlū*? And who are the others?

[19] In spite of the fact that at first sight this may be considered as a letter from Ur-Utu to his father Inanna-mansum (during an absence), I doubt whether that is the case, because there is also a letter from Ur-Utu which is addressed *ana bēlīya*. As that is the address other relatives use for Ur-Utu, I wonder whether he would address his father as '*abī*' if he wrote a letter to him.

If the name Ur-Utu were not so exceptional, I would assume that it had been written by a person of the same name (note that Inanna-mansum has a namesake who is a *gala*).

[20] De Meyer 1989.

[21] *BDHP* 50; *OLA* 21, 22.

5. Di 1285

The letter is given in transliteration and translation, and divided in segments, to facilitate its discussion.[22]

a. *The address and greeting formulae*

(obv.) [1] [a-na a]-wi-le-e [2] [qí]-bí-ma [3] um-ma ⌜ib-ni⌝-^{d}⌜EN⌝.ZU [4] ù ⌜ip⌝-[qú-^{d}] na-bi-um [5] ⌜^{d}utu ù ^{d}marduk da-ri-iš⌝ u$_4$-mi [6] li-ba-al-li-ṭú-ku-nu-ti [7] lu ša-al-ma-⌜tu⌝-nu ⌜lu ba⌝-al-ṭa-tu-nu [8] dingir na-ṣi-ir-ku-⌜nu re⌝-eš-ku-⌜nu⌝ a-na da-mi-iq-⌜tim⌝ [9] li-ki-il [10] a-na šu-ul-mi-ku-nu aš-⌜pu-ra-am⌝ [11] šu-lum-ku-nu ma-ḫar ^{d}utu ù ⌜^{d}marduk⌝ [12] lu da-ri

Tell the gentlemen; thus Ibni-Sin and Ipqu-Nabium. Šamaš and Marduk may keep you forever in good health! May you be well, may you be healthy! May your protective deity be favorably disposed to you! I am writing to (inquire about) your well-being. May your well-being last forever before Šamaš and Marduk!

The senders are Ibni-Sin and Ipqu-Nabium. Although, as usual, there is no patronymic, I think they can be identified because they appear combined. Ibni-Sin is a *gal.ukkin.na* (*mu'errum*), who is attested in dated texts from Aṣ 9 and 12,[23] and Ipqu-Nabium a *šu.i* (*gallābum*), attested from Aṣ 5 to Aṣ 11,[24] which gives us an idea about the time this letter was written (somewhere in the early years of Ur-Utu's *gala.maḫ*-ship, which starts at the end of Aṣ 4). The identification of these persons is supported by the contents of the letter.

The *gal.ukkin.na* and the *šu.i* often occur together, in juridical contexts.[25] The *gal.ukkin.na* is, as the word says, the head of the assembly (*puḫrum*); he leads it and sees to it that its decisions are executed.[26] It is a popular abbreviation for the longer title *gal.ukkin.na ša erín ká é.gal*, 'the *mu'errum* of the people of the Palace Gate',[27] which, in this case, is

[22] I express my gratitude towards M. Stol, whom I consulted for a few questions and who gave me a number of valuable observations and remarks.

[23] *TCL* I, 164 = Aṣ 9/5/9 and *BE* 6/1, 99 = Aṣ 12/4/4.

[24] *CT* 8, 19a = Aṣ 5/5/18; *CT* 8, 11b = Aṣ 5/9/10; *TCL* I, 164 = Aṣ 9/5/9; *CT* 8, 19b = Aṣ 11/10/5; *MHET* Vol. II Part 4 no. 521 = Aṣ 11/[...]. Ibni-Sin and Ipqu-Nabium also appear in letters from and outside the Ur-Utu archive.

[25] There is a clear connection, as Els Woestenburg observed in her unpublished thesis (based on evidence from AbB 12). I came to the same conclusion based on the materials from the Ur-Utu archive. We find these functions listed in Dombradi 1996, *Halbband* II, 29;36.

[26] Charpin 1980, 462-463, contra Yoffee.

[27] Charpin 1980, 464a.

situated in Sippar-Amnānum. Ibni-Sin is a local official, as D. Charpin has argued;[28] note that in our text the accused (see below) is a guard of this palace gate.

The greeting formulae are the standard late Old Babylonian ABC_2D_2,[29] the most frequent pattern in the letters from the Ur-Utu's archive,[30] with, in this case, plural addressees.

The letter was found in the older archive room 22 in group I, which contained 5 letters, among which two royal ones. They all seem important letters about legal and official matters. Di 1285 has probably arrived in Ur-Utu's house in the first years of his *gala.maḫ*-ship (date based on the identification of the senders as the *gal.ukkin.na* and the *šu.i*). He kept the letter, and had he had the time, he would probably have transferred it to his new archive room; but the house burnt down while the archive was still in a state of disorganization.

b. *The account*

> 13 ^{p}a-ḫa-am-nir-ši ša ⸢i-na⸣ é.gal ud.kib.nun^{ki} am-na-nim 14 i-na mu-uḫ-ḫi ma-aṣ-ṣa-ar-ti 15 wa-aš-bu 16 a-wi-le-e ša u_4-mu-šu-nu i-ta-ar-ku 17 pa-qí-dam la i-šu-ú 18 qá-as-sú ú-še-še-er-ma (lo.e.) 19 a-wi-le-e ub-ta-az-zi-⸢ma⸣ (rev.) 20 ù i-na li-bi-it-ti 21 a-wi-le-e ú-ma-aḫ-ḫi-iṣ 22 da-ba-ba-am šu-a-ti 23 ú-ub-⸢lu⸣-ni-a-ši-im-ma
>
> *Aḫam-nirši who is serving in the palace of Sippar-Amnānum at the head of the guard, exploited(?) gentlemen whose days had lasted long and who had nobody to take care of them, and pressed them for money; furthermore, he repeatedly beat gentlemen, with a mud brick.*
>
> *This report they transmitted to us,*

The general outline of the text is self-explanatory, yet there are difficulties in the interpretation. There has been a complaint that the guard Aḫam-nirši abused his power vis-à-vis gentlemen: they were elderly and not being taken care of by anyone.[31] In other words their position in society was

28 Ibni-Sin the gal.ukkin.na is linked to the palace of Sippar-Amnānum, see Charpin 1980, 466b, who refers to *BE* 6/1; 99:13.

29 Sallaberger 1999, 75-76 and Janssen, unpublished PhD.

30 Janssen, unpublished PhD.

31 The expression 'whose days have become long' needs explanation. I initially interpreted these words intuitively. Having taken into consideration what was in the CAD and the discussion on '*râqum*' by Veenhof, in *AbB* 14 p.215, I still adhere to the idea that the expression refers to age. In order to substantiate this, I compare "*umūšunu itarku*" with the phrases given under *arāku* c.1.2' (p. 224) ('with words of life, reign: to last long'). 'Their days' would then be a metaphor for their life. Similarly, in the Š-stem, we find 'to

weak, these people were vulnerable. He pressed them for money (or services) and (when they failed to comply?) beat them with a mud brick.

Note the repetition of the word *awīlē* (16;19;21) and the syntax in *ina libitti awīlē umaḫḫīṣ*.[32] The threefold use of *awīlē* and the remarkable syntax stress the status of the victims – in spite of their weak position they belonged to the class of respected citizens – and it expresses the senders' indignation.

The expression *qāssu ušēšer* is unclear and the translation is tentative. A first difficulty is that the expression *qāssu (<qātum) šūšurum* is attested in (much later) texts as a ritual act: a king who prepares his hand ('himself') for a sacrifice, or a diviner who prepares himself.[33] Our text is much earlier, so that caution is advised; but it must be some kind of gesture with possibly symbolic connotations; or maybe it is simply an idiomatic expression. The second difficulty for interpreting the phrase is the fact that both *awīlē* and *qāssu* seem to be objects of *šūšurum*. A third problem is that the connotations of the verb *šūšurum* are mostly positive. It seems to me that maybe there is some kind of irony involved (he did something!) or that it is an expression which means something like 'to exploit, to abuse' ('to make his hand go straight to ...'). The translation reflects this interpretation, which is speculative. Without further attestations this expression will remain clouded. One element is interesting though: whatever his hand did, it is not an autonomous part of the crime; the phrase does not reoccur in lines 26-29, in the investigators' conclusion.

c. *Checking the facts*

> ^{24} a-na é.gal e-ru-ub ša-ap-ti-šu-nu ^{25} ni-iš-mé-e-ma ^{26} ⸢i⸣-na a-wi-le-e bu-uz-zu-i ^{27}ù li-bi-it-ta i-na mu-úḫ-ḫi-šu-nu ^{28} pu-us-su-si ^{29} uk-ti-in-nu-šu ^{30} ^{p}a-ḫa-am-nir-ši šu-ú $^{31\text{pd}}$iškur-ma.an.sum tap-pa-šu ^{32} id-du-uk-ma ṣú-ba-as-sú ^{33} ù ^{túg}bar.⸢si.gá-šu⸣ ^{34} ⸢xx⸣ [...]⸢x⸣-sú ^{35} i-na x⸢x⸣ [...]⸢xx⸣ ub-lu-ni-a-ši-im ^{36}wa-ar-⸢ka-sú⸣ ša ka?- ⸢lu⸣-ú ^{37}⸢ni⸣-ip-ru-ús-ma ^{38} [mu]-úḫ-ḫu-sú a-an-nam ú-ša-⸢pi-lu⸣
>
> *and I entered the palace. We heard their account ('lips'), and they established that he has pressed the gentlemen for money and had beaten them*

attain length of life'. Under *ūmum* 1d (CAD U/W, 150-53) we find 'days' as 'span of life, lifetime', and examples which make the association between 'long days' and 'long life'.

32 A parallel can be found in *AbB* 12 65:29 for the D-stem of *maḫāṣum*, which W. Van Soldt translates as 'to beat repeatedly' (i.e., as an intensive).

33 CAD E, 358 (*ešērum* 7b).

repeatedly with a mud brick on their heads. This Aḫam-nirši has also beaten[34] *his comrade Iškur-mansum, then …*[35] *his garment and his sash from him. In … they brought us … and we investigated his case ….*

Having heard about the abuse, the *gal.ukkin.na* — note the shift to the singular- entered the palace (of Sippar-Amnānum) to hear at first hand what had happened.[36] There, together with the *šu.i* Ipqu-Nabium or other witnesses (the text goes back to the first person plural), he listened to witnesses. Not only did he learn that what had been told was true, he also found out that this same Aḫam-nirši had beaten up a comrade (and robbed him of his cloths?). The text is damaged on this point, and although the traces on the following lines seem rather clear, I have some difficulties in interpreting them. They must have brought in tablets (*ṭuppē?*) or witnesses as evidence. I have no convincing suggestion how to understand *warkassu ša? ka?-lu-ú*.[37]

d. *The confession'*

38 [mu]-úḫ-ḫu-sú a-an-nam ú-ša-⌜pi-lu⌝

They made him admit the fact of his beating.

Aḫam-nirši is confronted with the facts and the investigators 'make him admit'[38] his beating.

e. *The purpose of the letter*

39 a-na šu-di-ku-nu ni-iš-pu-ra-am

We wrote to you in order to inform you.

The purpose of the letter is stated explicitly at the end of the text: it is written so that the gentlemen be informed. If we look at the references for *idûm*, Š, we see that the notification in some of the parallel texts have

34 The verb is usually understood as 'to kill' but can also refer to 'beating', which seems to be a better choice in this letter (see CUSAS 10 130:29, a reference I owe to M. Stol).

35 Somehow "stolen, removed". The verb could not be identified because the traces are unclear.

36 *Erub* must refer to the first of the two senders. The syntax without *–ma* seems abrupt.

37 I am not entirely sure how to read the signs, and hope to solve this before the final edition of the Ur-Utu letters.

38 'To make say yes' can mean 'to make admit', see CAD A/2, 165. It can also mean 'to make somebody say 'yes', agree', as is the case in *AbB* 8, 141:17.

an official character (cf. the announcement to the owner of a dog with rabies by the *bābtum*).[39] This is also the case here, the *gal.ukkin.na* and *šu.i* write an official letter, as the principal investigators of this case of abuse.

6. Tell the gentlemen ...

The end is interesting, in fact. The notification is the confirmation that Aḫam-nirši had been found guilty, the circumstance that he had committed another crime as well, and that he had confessed the maltreatment of the elderly gentlemen. This is what the letter announced to the *awīlū*. But an intriguing question is also why it does not tell us more after that.

What happened to the perpetrator after he confessed? Had he been sentenced, or would he be sentenced, and if so, where and how? We learn nothing about the consequences of the findings.

Why are the gentlemen (just) informed? Is it obvious to them how this will end? Or — a more daring interpretation — are they perhaps involved in this decision? Are they part of the judiciary?

This idea may seem far-fetched at first sight. The senders do not ask the addressees for a written answer or a judgment; it is as if the gentlemen to whom the letter was sent were totally passive and had no role to play other than to be informed.

The problem with the interpretation of letters however is that there are previous encounters, agreements, relations between people, customs, expectations, ... many things that are obvious to the sender and the addressee, and need not be explained. We need knowledge and empathy, for which we have to rely on emotional intelligence and imagination. Meanwhile we have to keep this precarious balance between *interpretieren* and *hineininterpretieren*.

Why do a *gal.ukkin.na* and a *šu.i* officially inform an undefined group of gentlemen among whom, we know, a *gala.maḫ*, about a guard's evil deeds? Are they involved in the process of dealing with crime, on some level?

There is in fact some support to be found in favor of this hypothesis, which arose from the question why the gentlemen were informed of the crimes and the confession, but not of the outcome of the process.

[39] CAD I/J, 33 (*idû* 6).

E. Dombradi lists '*awīlū*' under the 'Organe der Rechtsprechung/ Körperschaften'.[40] She summarizes various hypotheses about the status of the *bābtum* and the *awīlū* (which she groups together), referring to theories put forward by Driver and Miles, E. Stone and others.[41] The following picture emerges from the data she presents. A group of respectable citizens (*awīlū*) can gather and act, on a local level, as '*Spruchkörper*', which means that they are involved in making a verdict. They are people from the neighborhood (a unit smaller than the *šibūt ālim*, it seems), who know what neigbors know, and thus best placed to judge in certain cases, it seems. [42]

How exactly it works is a grey zone for me, and evidence is scanty, but the whole point is, I think, that they know the accused and are the people best placed to influence his behavior through social control. It seems that the respectable citizens from the neighborhood are responsibilized to address this kind of situation.

Aḫam-nirši's guilt has already been officially established and the official investigators have made him confess. The one question that remains is what to do with this man. [43] Is there need for information from citizens from the neighborhood, are they better placed, as they have known Aḫam-nirši and his family since a long time, to pass a sentence? Maybe we should consider this thought. This is an isolated case of misbehavior, on a personal level, which has become a social problem. Social control and condemnation by the immediate environment might be a good tool to control people like our guard Aḫam-nirši.

If so, this letter '*ana awīlē*' would be comparable to other letters to collective groups, such as the ones directed to the *kārum* or the *šibūt ālim*.[44]

7. The private and professional

This brings us to our next question. If the *awīlū* are indeed the respected citizens of the neigborhood, and represent a more or less formal gathering, what is Ur-Utu's role in this? Is he the only one to receive this letter, and does he have to spread the word, or did several copies exist? Is he the main addressee, or not?

[40] Dombradi, 1996: Halbband II, 18.

[41] Dombradi, 1996: Halbband I, §320, p. 245; II §§1414-1422, p.197f.

[42] See VS 7 16, ll. 16-18, cited in Dombradi, 1996: Halbband II §1419, p. 197f.

[43] It is interesting to compare this with P. Dresch's observations on tribal authority in Yemen.

[44] Sallaberger 1999, 30; 39.

Why is he involved? What is the link between him and this case?

There is no link between Ur-Utu's function, as *gala.maḫ*, and the case about which he is informed, it seems, apart from the social status he derives from being a chief dirge singer. He is not addressed in person, or as part of the religious elite, but merely as one of the *awīlū*.

If the hypothesis about the function of the *awīlū* is correct, Ur-Utu is living in the right neigborhood to be knowledgeable about the case. He may have been the most important representative (if only one copy of this letter existed), or just one of them (in the case of multiple copies). He has prestige and is considered as a powerful person.

We also know that Ur-Utu knew the perpetrator personally. His archive contains a letter from Aḫam-nirši (who writes together with a person called Rīš-Šamaš) (Di 636). This letter opens with the phrase that 'the guard is well' (*maṣṣartum šalmat*), which makes it very likely that it is the same person, even if we have no patronymic to confirm the identification.

As for the formal aspects of their letter, it is written '*ana bēlī-nī*'; Aḫam-nirši and Rīš-Šamaš call themselves the addressee's 'slaves'. There are no greeting formulae, and the text opens, as said, with a line that all (*in casu* the guard) goes well.[45] These features are found in a number of other letters in the Ur-Utu archive: Ur-Utu's brothers (Kubburum, Ilī-iqīšām, Ḫuzalum) and his wife (Rā'imtum) use this format. There are a few more senders in this group, whose affiliation is not clear; but from the contents of their letters it is obvious that they are close to Ur-Utu. This means that there is evidence pointing to the fact that there was a close personal link between Ur-Utu and the man who hit the gentlemen.

How close are they? Could Aḫam-nirši be a member of the family?

A dive in the archive gave us some hope to answer this question. There is an Aḫam-nirši whose father is Ḫuzalum (Di 2130, Ammiditana, year broken). He is a witness on a real estate document of a purchase by Inanna-mansum, Ur-Utu's father.[46] Inanna-mansum has a son who is

[45] The letter is badly damaged so that little can be said about its contents.

[46] The identification is impossible, if M. Tanret's hypothesis about Ur-Utu's age is correct (Tanret 2011). The young age he attributes to Inanna-mansum's eldest(?) son is based on the school texts found in Ur-Utu's house. When we discussed the case he mentioned that he had earlier considered the possibility that Ur-Utu was born under Abi-ešuḫ's reign. In that case we must understand that the school texts that were found in Ur-Utu's house were not written by a young Ur-Utu but by the children of his household. I personally think that Ur-Utu was already born when Inanna-mansum became *gala.maḫ*, as Di 720 mentions the (unnamed) children of the *gala.maḫ*, next to his wife and brothers (and a large number of other people). I would assume that Ur-Utu was one of these children. In this case his brother Ḫuzālum can have an adolescent son who acts as a witness in an Ammiditana text.

called Ḫuzalum, who is Ur-Utu's brother, and lives in the same street as his father and brother.

If Aḫam-nirši of Di 1285, Di 636 and Di 2130 is the same person, he is Ur-Utu's nephew. Are we lucky, or are we merely tricked into believing that these people are the same?

Ur-Utu would be an ideal mediator to represent the *awīlū* of this area, as the perpetrator's uncle and honorable citizen of his neigborhood. It would be a logical choice to send the letter *ana awilē* to him. But for the moment this is as far as we can go in our interpretation. We have already ventured on thin ice.

Cuneiform texts sometimes seem to play a game of hide and seek in their elusive archives, especially when for one time they do not write 'the same'.

Bibliography

CHARPIN, D. 1980: "Remarques sur l'administration Paléobabylonienne sous les successeurs d'Hammurapi", = review of: N. Yoffee, *The Economic Role of the Crown in the Old Babylonian Period, JAOS* 100, 461-471.

— 1986: "Transmission des titres de propriété et constitution des archives privées en Babylonie Ancienne", in K.R. Veenhof (ed.), *Cuneiform Archives and Libraries* (= *CRRAI* 30), Leiden, 121-140.

— 2010: *Reading and Writing in Babylon*, Cambridge MA and London.

DEKIERE, L. 1995: *Old Babylonian Real Estate Documents. Part 4: Post-Samsu-iluna documents* (= *MHET* II/4), Ghent.

DE MEYER, L. 1982: "Mubabbilūtum dans une lettre paléo-babylonienne tardive", in J. Quaegebeur (ed.), *Studia Paulo Naster Oblata II, Orientalia Antiqua* (= OLA 13), 31-36.

— 1989: "Une lettre d'Ur-Utu gala.maḫ à une divinité", in M. Lebeau and Ph. Talon (eds.) *Akkadica Supplementum* VI, 41-43.

DOMBRADI, E. 1996: *Die Darstellung des Rechtsaustrags in den altbabylonischen Prozessurkunden* (= *FAOS* 20), Stuttgart.

DRESCH, P. 1989: *Tribes, Government and History in Yemen*, Oxford.

GASCHE, H. 1989: *La Babylonie au 17e siècle avant notre ère: approche archéologique, problèmes et perspectives (= MHEM II),* Ghent.

Janssen, C. 1992: "Inanna-mansum et ses fils: relation d'une succession turbulente", *RA* 86, 19-52.

— 1996: "When the house is on fire and the children are gone", in K. Veenhof (ed.) *Houses and Households in Ancient Mesopotamia. Papers read at the 40th Rencontre Assyriologique Internationale, Leiden, July 5-8, 1993*, Leiden, 237-46.

JANSSEN, C., H. Gasche and M. Tanret, 2004: "Du chantier à la tablette. Ur-Utu et l'histoire de sa maison à Sippar-Amnānum", in H. Gasche et al. (eds.), *Cinquante-deux reflexions sur le Proche-Orient ancien offertes en hommage à Léon De Meyer (= MHEO II)*, Leuven, 91-123.

SALLABERGER, W. 1999: *"Wenn Du mein Bruder bist, ..." Interaktion und Textgestaltung in altbabylonischen Alltagsbriefen*, Groningen.

TANRET, M., 2004: "Verba volant, scripta non manent. Tablettes nomades dans les archives des gala.mah à Sippar-Amnānum", in *Nomades et sédentaires dans le Proche-Orient ancien. Actes de la XLVIe Rencontre assyriologique internationale (Paris, 10-13 juillet 2000)* (= *Amurru* 3), Paris, 249-270.

— 2008: "Open the tablet box. New aspects of archive keeping in Old Babylonian Sippar", in R.J. Van der Spek, *Studies in Near Eastern World View and Society presented to Marten Stol on the occasion of his 65th birthday, 10 November 2005, and his retirement from the Vrije Universiteit Amsterdam*, Bethesda, 131-147.

— 2011: "Learned, rich, famous and unhappy: the life of the Chief Dirge Singer Ur-Utu in Old Babylonian Sippar", in K. Radner and E. Robson, *The Oxford Handbook of Cuneiform Culture*, Oxford, 270-289.

TANRET, M. and C. JANSSEN in preparation: *Chains of Transmission.*

VAN LERBERGHE, K. and G. Voet 1991: *Sippar-Amnānum: the Ur-Utu archive, Vol. I* (= MHET I/1), Ghent.

Fig. 1. Di 1285 Obverse.

Fig. 2. Di 1285 Reverse.

AN OLD-BABYLONIAN VERSION OF THE TRIBUTE LIST

Theo J. H. KRISPIJN
Leiden University*

Introduction

In spring 2001 Mark J. Geller showed me his handcopy of a prism from the Old-Babylonian period, which he had seen at an antiquities dealer. He had to make the copy within a short time because the prism was about to be sold. Unfortunately he had no photographs at his disposal, so that I could check only the copy. But since Mark is well known for his accurate copies of cuneiform texts, I can work well with his copy. Mark gave me permission to publish this text. It became clear that this prism was an Old-Babylonian version of a lexical text known from copies from the Uruk III (± 3000 B.C.) till the Old-Babylonian period. After this identification I postponed any publication of the 'Geller Prism', and considerable time passed while I was waiting for more versions to be published that could help to interpret the complicated text. Civil's recent publication (2010, 215-228) in which he used some entries of the Geller Prism, was for me the stimulus to present here Mark's copy with a transliteration and supplementary notes.

I am pleased to dedicate this article to my colleague and friend Karel Van Lerberghe, who together with his wife Bieke became dear friends for me so many years ago in his Leiden period as assistant of F.R. Kraus.

Research on the 'Tribute List'.

The publication of the Archaic Lexical lists from Uruk in ATU 3 (Englund and Nissen 1993) formed a milestone in the research of the lexical tradition of the third millennium B.C. For the first time an almost complete survey of reconstructed lexical series of the Uruk-period was given. It became much easier to relate the early Uruk versions to the

* I am much indebted to Mervyn E. Richardson for improving the English of this paper and for some valuable suggestions concerning the paper itself.

later versions from Ur, Fara, Abu Salabikh and Ebla and to follow the lexical tradition through a period of ± 1200 years. Englund paid more attention to one of the lexical lists, which he called the Tribute List, than to other lexical lists in the introduction to ATU 3 (Englund and Nissen 1993, 25-29) and in his article on the Uruk period (Englund 1998, 99-102). Other scholars designate the text as the Early Dynastic Wordlist C (Pettinato 1981; Civil 2010).

The reason for this special attention was his assumption that it is the earliest known piece of Mesopotamian literature. Some entries of the list seemed to be literary phrases. Englund gave also a clear survey of the sections of the list, some of which are repeated in the texts. Joan G. Westenholz elaborated this assumption in her paper at the Prague RAI (Westenholz 1998), seeing in the first entries indications that the text contains secret lore. Niek Veldhuis (2006) made a thorough analysis of the structure of the list on the basis of Englund's analysis, criticizing the suggestion that the text should be considered as the earliest known literary text or as secret lore. The apparent character of the text as an early lexical list, with many links to other lexical material, justifies the classification of the list as lexical. In his last impressive publication M. Civil discussed the tribute list and presented in score format the versions known to us together with photographs of the texts in the Schøyen-collection (Civil 2010, 215-228). In his table of texts Civil refers to the Geller Prism as X_4, but he uses the prism only occasionally.

General remarks

The Geller Prism contains the complete text of the Tribute List in six columns. On the upper edge of the prism a hardly readable colophon is written. In the following transliteration of the text I give the column lines of the Geller prism in the first column, followed by the line numbering of Miguel Civil (2010, 216-226) in the second column.

I 1	1	AD:GI$_4$:
I 2	2	KI:SAG
I 3	3	AD:HAL
I 4	4	ME:[N]UN:DU (= ABRIG?)
I 5	5	GIŠxMIN (=MUNU$_3$!)
I 6	6	GIŠxAŠ$_2$ (=GAZI)

I 7	7	GA$_2$xHA! (*incomplete*?)
I 8	8	ŠE+HU! (=UZ) (*archaic*) AMA (?)
I 9	9	MAŠ$_2$ (*incomplete*) SI$_4$!
I 10	10	T[U] (*incomplete*?)
I 11	11	[K]UNGAL
I 12-13	12	AB$_2$:GA (*incomplete*):RI / A
I 14-15	13	AMAR:GA:KA (=NAG) (*incomplete*) / A
I 16	14	EŠ$_2$:SUHUR
I 17	15	ZIZ$_2$:GANA$_2$
I 18	16	LAK 171 (=KAD$_4$!)
I 19-20	17	GA / BAD (= U?) (*erroneus split*?) = U+GA (LAK 384)
II 1	18	GIRI$_2$:AN
II 2-3	19	ANŠE:DA / TA:DU (?)
II 4	20	G[A] (?)
II 5	21	GA-*gunû* (?)
II 6	22	AB$_2$
II 7	23	NIN[DA$_2$ (?)]
II 8	24	U$_8$ (?)
II 9	25	UTUA (*incomplete*?)
II 10	26	UD$_5$ (*incomplete*)
II 11	27	MAŠ$_2$
II 12-13	28	NUNUZ:LAK 173 (= KAD$_5$) / ^{mušen} (*archaic*)
II 14	29	IŠ
II 15	30	L[UL]
II 16	31	GAR (*incomplete*)
II 17-18	32	URI:IŠ / ŠA$_3$ (!) NAM:<GU$_2$>:SUM (?)
III 1	33	[GIŠxMIN (=*MUNU$_3$)]
III 2	34	GA$_2$xAŠ$_2$ (=GAZI)
III 3	35	GA$_2$xHA (*incomplete?*)
III 4	36	[Š]E+HU (*archaic*) AMA
III 5	37	MAŠ$_2$:(*incomplete*) SI$_4$
III 6	38	<u>TU</u>
III 7	39	[GU]KKAL

III 8-9	40	[A]B$_2$:GA:RI (?) /A
III 10-11	41	[AMA]R:GA:NAG / A
III 12	42	E[Š$_2$] (?)+SUHUR
III 13	43	ZIZ$_2$:[GAN]A$_2$
III 14	44	LAK 171 (=KAD$_4$!)
III 15	45	U+GA (=LAK 384)
III 16	46	GIRI$_2$:A[N]
III 17-18	47	ANŠE:D[A]:/ T[A:x]
III 19	48	GA (!)
III 20	49	GARA$_2$
IV 1	50	AB$_2$
IV 2	51	NINDA$_2$
IV 3	52	U$_8$
IV 4	53	UTUA (*incomplete*?)
IV 5	54	UD$_5$
IV 6	55	MAŠ$_2$
IV 7	56	NUNUZ:LAK 173 (= KAD$_5$) / $^{\text{[m]ušen}}$ (*archaic*)
IV 8	57	[IŠ]
IV 9	58	N[A]R
IV 10	59	GAR
IV 11-12	60	[URI:I]Š / ŠA$_3$ (!) N[AM:<GU$_2$>] SUM (!)
IV 13	61	ŠAR$_2$:KI
IV 14	62	ŠAR$_2$:ŠA$_3$ (?)
IV 15	63	GIR$_2$ (= GIR$_2$-*gunû*/ KISIK?)
IV 16	64	ŠENNUR
V 1	65	[GIŠ:BI]
V 2	66	[GI:BI]
V 3	67	[ZI/ZI]+EŠ$_2$ (?)
V 4	68	[[ZI/Z]I+EŠ$_2$ (?)
V 5	69-70	[E$_2$:PI]RIG:BAD! (=UG$_7$?) / [N]IN[DA$_2$] (?) TAR ME:KARA$_2$
V 6	71	EN:ME:KARA$_2$
V 7	72	[E]N:ZI:ME / KARA$_2$
V 8-9	73	[D]AM:URUM$_2$ (=URUxAŠ?):A

V 10	74	AL:MA:TAR
V 11	75	AL:TAR:RA (?)
V 12	76	$ŠA_3$:GU_2:BI (!) NAM / GI_4
V 13-14	77	PA_5!:BI
V 15	78	PA_5-*gunû*(?) ZU+ZU:S[AR] (?)
V 16	79	GIŠ:BI
V 17	80	^{ĝiš}APIN:$ERIN_2$ / A:NI
V 18	81	GI:BI
VI 1	82	GI:DUR_2:K[U_5?]
VI 2	83	ZI+ZI:$EŠ_2$:BI
VI 3	84	ZI+ZI:$EŠ_2$:GIŠ:$ŠU_2$!:NI:EŠ
VI 4	85	ZI+ZI:LAGAB:BI
VI 5-6	86	ZI+ZI:LAGAB:DUR (!):TAR:A:/ NI
VI 7-8	87	ENx$GANA_2$:AD: ME / $KARA_2$
VI 9	88	SANGA
VI 10	89	KI:AN
VI 11	90	ŠE:GIN_2:A
VI 12	91	ZA:GIN_3
VI 13	92	SAL+ME:TUR_3
VI 14	93	UR:UR
VI 15	94	U_2:A:HI
VI 16	95	BA:BA:$ŠE_3$
VI 17		$BAHAR_2$+$SILA_3$ (= $BAHAR_x$)
Colophon	1	[^{d}]nisaba za_3(!).[mi_2]
	2	*traces*
	3	[Š]A_3(!) [NAM]. / GU_2 B[I] [G]I_4 (?)
	4	[60] +30+3 (?) ŠU.$NIGIN_2$ (?) [ ]
	5	[x] KAM 60 [?] 30 [?]
	6	[x] KAM 7 / X [GIŠ.T]UG_2.PI.RU (?) 14 (?)
	7	[DU]B.SAR.MAH (?)
	8	UR.[ ].MAH (?)
	9	[ ] X

Paleography and writing style:

Since we have no photograph at our disposal, it is difficult to give an exact dating of the script, but at first sight, according to Mark's copy, it could have been written either in the Ur III or in the Old-Babylonian period. The signs that help to arrive at a date paleographically are:

- ANŠE (II 9) Schn. N° 461 (Ur III) <-> Mit. N° 292 (Old-Babylonian).[1] The PA-shaped part of ANŠE is attested from the Ur III period on (KWU 461).[2]
- IŠ (II 14) Schn. N° 278 <-> Mittermayer N° 162. The 4 horizontals of the sign are more frequently attested in the Ur III than in the Old-Babylonian period.
- NAM (II 18) Schn. N° 121 <-> Mit. N° 042. The tiny 'winkelhaken' before the third horizontal fits the early Old-Babylonian (Lipit-Ištar) shape of the sign better than the Ur III shape.
- TAR (V 11) Schn. N° 340 <-> Mit. N° 231. This sign is typically Old-Babylonian in shape.
- ZI/ZI.LAGAB (VII 4-5) Schneider N° 128 <-> Mittermayer N° 149. This sign is closer to the Old-Babylonian than to the Ur III shape.

Therefore, from a paleographic viewpoint, dating it to the Early Old Babylonian period seems most probable. The clumsily written colophon seems to confirm this. Nevertheless, elsewhere signs are written in an archaic pre-Ur III way: ŠE+HU! (I 8 // III 4), MUŠEN (II 13 // IV 7).

Often signs are written incompletely: GA_2xHA (I 7), $MAŠ_2$ (I 9 // III 5), GA (I 12), KA (=NAG) (I 14), UD_5 (II 10), GAR (II 16).

Another striking feature of the text is the lack of numbers, which are so prominent in other versions of the list.

Conclusion:

The Geller prism is an extraordinary text. The mixture of Early Old Babylonian, archaic, incomplete signs, and erroneous splits gives the impression that the Tribute List was copied from an older pre-Ur III version by a scribe who was not very advanced. Whenever he recognized signs he replaced them with Early Old Babylonian counterparts; whenever he did not, he tried to copy the original archaic form as well as he could.

[1] Schn. = Schneider 1935, Mit. = Mittermayer 2006.

[2] Cf. also Mittermayer 2005, 116-117.

Nevertheless, the effort this apprentice scribe made to copy the Tribute List underlines the prestige of the text, as was assumed by Veldhuis (2006).

Much work has still to be done on the interpretation of the Tribute List, but I hope this publication of the Geller Prism will contribute something to our understanding of this intriguing text. [3]

Bibliography:

Civil, M. 2010: *The Lexical Texts in the Schøyen Collection* (CUSAS 12), Bethesda.

Englund, R.K. and H.J. Nissen 1993: *Die lexikalische Listen der archaischen Texte aus Uruk* (Archaische Texte aus Uruk 3), Berlin.

Englund, R.K. 1998: "Texts from the Late Uruk Period", in P. Attinger and M. Wäfler, *Mesopotamien* (OBO 160/1), Freiburg, 13-233.

Mittermayer, C. 2005: *Die Entwicklung der Tierkopfzeichen: Eine Studie zur syro-mesopotamischen Keilschriftpaläographie des 3. und frühen 2. Jahrtausends v. Chr.* (AOAT 319), Münster.

— 2006: *Altbabylonische Zeichenliste der sumerisch-literarischen Texte*, Fribourg.

Pettinato, G. 1981: *Testi lessicali monolingui della biblioteca L. 2769* (MEE 3), Napoli.

Schneider, N. 1935: *Keilschrift-Paläographie Heft 2: Die Keilschriftzeichen der Wirtschaftsurkunden von Ur III nebst ihren charakteristischen Schreibvarianten systematisch zusammengestellt*, Rome.

Veldhuis, N. 2006: "How did they learn Cuneiform? Tribute/Word List C as an elementary Exercise", in P. Michalowski and N. Veldhuis (eds.) *Approaches to Sumerian Literature Studies in Honour of Stip (H.L.J. Vanstiphout)* (CM 35), Leiden and Boston, 181-200.

Westenholz, J. G. 1998: "Thoughts on Esoteric Knowledge and Secret Lore", in J. Prosecký (ed.), *Intellectual Life of the Ancient Near East* (CRRAI 43 Prague, July 1-5, 1996), Prague, 451-462.

[3] I hope to continue the research on the text in the near future myself, being intrigued by signs such as UB // URI (II 17 // IV 11) = "Akkad" (?) and IŠ (II 17 // IV 11) = *iš* (?), the early Akkadian preposition in Pre-Sargonic Mari and Nabada/Tell Beydar.

Fig. 1. Prism (copy by Markham J. Geller).

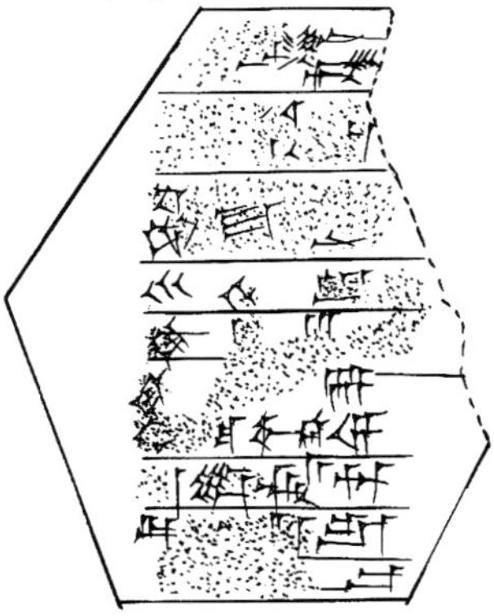

Fig. 2. Prism Colophon
(copy by Markham J. Geller).

THE RESTORATION OF TEMPLE D AT TELL BEYDAR/NABADA (FIELD N, SEASONS 2004 AND 2005)

Marc Lebeau and Marie-Eve Sténuit
ECUMS, Brussels

From the start of the Tell Beydar archaeological mission in 1992, the University of Leuven (KU Leuven) was a constant and faithful partner under the responsibility of Karel Van Lerberghe. This long-term collaboration continued for a decade and ended in 2002. Many students and young scholars from this university took part to the excavations, acquiring more and more experience and responsibilities in the course of time. Karel van Lerberghe, together with Philippe Talon (University of Brussels, ULB) were the first to study and copy the 3rd Millennium tablets discovered under the floor of a modest building in Field B in 1993 and 1994. They were later assisted by Farouk Ismail and Walther Sallaberger (Ismail, Sallaberger, Talon & Van Lerberghe 1996). This long-term collaboration resulted in the development of a very wide environmental and technical program, initiated and developed by Karel Van Lerberghe and Gabriella Voet (Van Lerberghe & Voet 2000).

This short contribution is dedicated to the friend and scholar without whom the Beydar mission would never have been able to reach its level of success.

The KU Leuven staff took part in the excavation of many areas at Beydar that included fields A, E, F1 and K. The last field dug under the responsibility of the KU Leuven team was Area N, where a temple — Temple D — was identified. This excavation was supervised by Michel Debruyne and Kurt Bertrem. Like Temples B and C of Tell Beydar/Nabada, Temple D is located on the intermediate terrace of the acropolis of the city but on the other side, i.e. east, of *Main Street*, the official, main access with stairs to the Upper Palace. It belongs to the same complex and shares the same architectural characteristics as the other temples.[1] Its primary function in the Early Jezirah IIIb period (c. 2450-2340 BC) — a temple — changed later (in the Early Jezirah IVa), and the former temple probably became the residence of a local ruler.

[1] See architectural description in Lebeau 2006, 107-113.

Temple D was first excavated by a team of the KU Leuven in the years 2001 and 2002 (Debruyne & Jans 2007, 76-81), then, in 2004, by the ECUMS team (Sténuit 2011a, 93-100).

It was the ninth building to be restored at Tell Beydar. The restoration work was started in spring 2004 (Sténuit 2007, 264), during the second restoration campaign, and was concluded after the completed excavation of the building, in 2005 (Fig. 1).[2] At that time KU Leuven no longer participated in the Tell Beydar project, but Karel Van Lerberghe continued to provide financial support for the restoration work. We remain grateful for his generous support.

The state of preservation at the time of the discovery

Generally speaking, Temple D was one of the most damaged buildings of Tell Beydar. This situation was mostly due to historical factors. First, the existence of an EJ IV phase of occupation above the EJ IIIb level, which modified the plan of the central part of the building and second, the digging of deep, large pits from the Hellenistic period, through the ruins of the two earlier archaeological layers (Fig. 8a).

However, after the EJ IV level had been dismantled and the bottom of the pits reached, the EJ IIIb walls were sufficiently preserved to allow a clear reconstruction of the plan. This was also facilitated by the presence of a well preserved baked brick courtyard in the central part of the building (room 14047) (Fig. 2, 3, 9), by the preservation of the thresholds and doorways (the most damaged one was the entrance to room 14084, of which only the northern frame was still in place, but the threshold was still apparent) (Fig. 5), of large areas of floor plaster (room 14063) (Fig. 2) and, for the most disturbed rooms, of floor fragments in the corners (14226, 14080, 14084). In the entrance room (14041) (Fig. 4, 6, 7), the presence of a canalisation and the top of the entrance staircase clearly indicated the level of the EJ IIIb floor.

Some installations were also still identifiable: a toilet-like installation (14058) in room 14063 (a plastered, pierced low bench with vertical drain), a low bench with traces of bitumen and a smaller one in room 14071 (Fig. 9), additionally to a door socket, another low podium in room 14080, and, in the ceremonial room 14226, the edges of a low bench with buttressed façade (Fig. 5, 9).

[2] For the completion of the restoration work in Temple D, see Sténuit 2011b, 268.

The chosen phase

In accordance with the general restoration programme of the site, it was decided, as was the case for the other 3rd Millennium buildings, to concentrate the restoration work on the EJ IIIb phase in order to illustrate as faithfully as possible the original plan of the city at that time.

The techniques used

The techniques used and the general strategy of restoration at Tell Beydar were described already and explained elsewhere (Sténuit 2007, 255-309) and will not be detailed here.

In summary, the techniques chosen included the following:

- For the walls: mud bricks of the same shape and dimensions as the original ones were made and placed, then covered with an earth plaster; the top of the walls slightly bulging, in order to avoid water infiltration; the height of the restored and/or reconstructed walls, which had been much damaged both by the implantation of the later EJ IV building and by the digging of Hellenistic pits, was arbitrarily limited to c. 1m; the base of the walls was protected from undermining by the application of a 50cm high white *juss* band.
- For the floors: it was decided to keep the same material as found in the excavation, i.e. baked bricks for the courtyard (with grey *juss* in the lacunae) and white *juss* for the inner floors.
- For the drainages: the canalisations were repaired with the original baked bricks that constituted these installations; the inner part of the drainages was cleaned in order to allow water circulation.
- For the installations: the walls, thresholds, toilets, benches and other installations were restored with mud bricks similar to the original ones and *juss* was applied when appropriate.
- Roofing: since no information about the roofing of that building was found during the excavation, no restoration was attempted.

A specific problem encountered: the southern façade of Temple D (wall 14222) (Fig. 8-9)

The restoration of the southern façade of Temple D was more problematic. At first sight, it appeared to have been completely destroyed by the large pits that also punctured the floors of rooms 14226 and 14084. The southern limit of the temple was however clear thanks to the survival of a small part of the south-west corner of room 14226, which had been spared by pit 14008. A new wall was thus reconstructed in order to close the building and complete its restoration. The orientation of that wall followed the axis provided by the preserved angle.

However, in later years, when excavation expanded in Area S, south of Temple D — the large courtyard 14112 nicknamed "Southern Square" — this wall appeared to assume a double function. On the one hand, the upper part (the part we had reconstructed, starting from the level of the floor of the southern wing of Temple D) constituted, as already known, the southern wall of the building, but, on the other hand, the lower part happened to be also the northern wall of courtyard 14112 located around 3,50m lower than the base of Temple D, on the next terrace. This meant that wall 14222 also functioned as a terrace wall, counterbalancing the pressure of the terrace on which Temple D was built.[3]

Indeed, in the course of the excavation of "Southern Square", the lower section of that wall was revealed. It was preserved at different heights but on its entire length (16,45m) under the bottom of the pits. Once it was completely exposed and the floor of the courtyard reached, a slight discrepancy between the axis of the reconstructed upper part of the wall and the position of the lower part was observed. The upper part had been reconstructed following a straight line along the axis provided by the preserved corner of room 14226. However this wall, at the time, was not built exactly straight but was slightly curved, following the curve of the upper terrace. The reconstructed southern wall of Temple D is consequently protruding c. 5cm to the south. Fortunately, the wall is wide (1,30m) and this small projection seems to have little effect on the stability of the terrace since, after six years of restoration, that high buttressed wall is still standing and still assuming its function as a retaining wall.

Moreover, since the excavation work was completed in "Southern Square" and the space completely opened, and since restoration work was completed in that area (restoration of the baked brick pavement of the courtyard and main drainage again being operational), the base of wall 14222 is now secure from being undermined during the rainy season.

It is however the goal of ECUMS to restore this most important terrace wall to match its original, exact axis and to ensure the security of circulation in that area. Because aged bricks are notably weaker than new ones due to the degradation of the straw within their core, a complete

[3] This terrace wall is described in detail in Dezzi Bardeschi and Sténuit 2011, 209-253.

reconstruction of wall 14222 is being considered (as was done for Temples B and C) (Sténuit 2007, 262-263) and is part of a restoration programme that was submitted to the DGAM. As soon as an agreement is concluded about this particular wall, the restoration will be started.

In the meantime, maintenance, as well as timely consolidation work is performed regularly, where and when necessary.

Bibliography

DEBRUYNE, M. and G. JANS 2007: "The South-Eastern Area of the "Palatial Complex" of Tell Beydar: The EJ III/ED III Main Entrance, Monumental Stairway and Temple D", in M. Lebeau & A. Suleiman (eds.), *Tell Beydar, Rapport préliminaire sur les campagnes de fouilles 2000-2002 et les campagnes de restauration architecturale 2003-2004* (= *Subartu* XV), Brepols, Turnhout, 75-84.

DEZZI BARDESCHI, Ch. and M.-E. STÉNUIT 2011: "Chantier S: Le "Parvis Sud" (Southern Square). Campagnes 2004-2009", in M. Lebeau & A. Suleiman (eds.), *Tell Beydar, The 2004/2-2009 Seasons of Excavations, The 2004/2-2006 Seasons of Architectural Restoration. A Preliminary Report* (= *Subartu* XXIX), Brepols, Turnhout, 209-253.

ISMAIL, F., W. SALLABERGER, Ph. TALON and K. VAN LERBERGHE 1996: *Administrative Documents from Tell Beydar (Seasons 1993 – 1995)* (= *Subartu* II), Brepols, Turnhout.

LEBEAU M. 2006: "Les Temples de Tell Beydar et leur environnement immédiat à l'époque Early Jezirah IIIb", in Butterlin, Lebeau, Monchambert, Montero Fenollós & Muller (eds.), *Les espaces syro-mésopotamiens. Dimensions de l'expérience humaine au Proche-Orient ancient* (= *Subartu* XVII), Brepols, Turnhout, 101-140.

STÉNUIT M.-E. 2007: "Deux campagnes de restauration architecturale à Tell Beydar/Nabada (automne 2003 – printemps 2004)", in M. Lebeau & A. Suleiman (eds.), *Tell Beydar, Rapport préliminaire sur les campagnes de fouilles 2000-2002 et les campagnes de restauration architecturale 2003-2004* (= *Subartu* XV), Brepols, Turnhout, 255-309.

— 2011a: "La fouille du chantier N (Temple D) – Campagnes 2004-2005", in M. Lebeau & A. Suleiman (eds.), *Tell Beydar, The 2004/2-2009 Seasons of Excavations, The 2004/2-2006 Seasons of Architectural Restoration. A Preliminary Report* (= *Subartu* XXIX), Brepols, Turnhout, 93-100.

— 2011b: "Cinq campagnes de restauration architecturale à Tell Beydar/Nabada (troisième à septième campagnes: 2004/2, 2005, 2006, 2008, 2009)", in M. Lebeau & A. Suleiman (eds.), *Tell Beydar, The 2004/2-2009 Seasons of Excavations, The 2004/2-2006 Seasons of Architectural Restoration. A Preliminary Report* (= *Subartu* XXIX), Brepols, Turnhout, 267-278.

VAN LERBERGHE K. & G. VOET (eds.) 2000: *Tell Beydar. Environmental and Technical Studies* (= *Subartu* VI), Brepols, Turnhout.

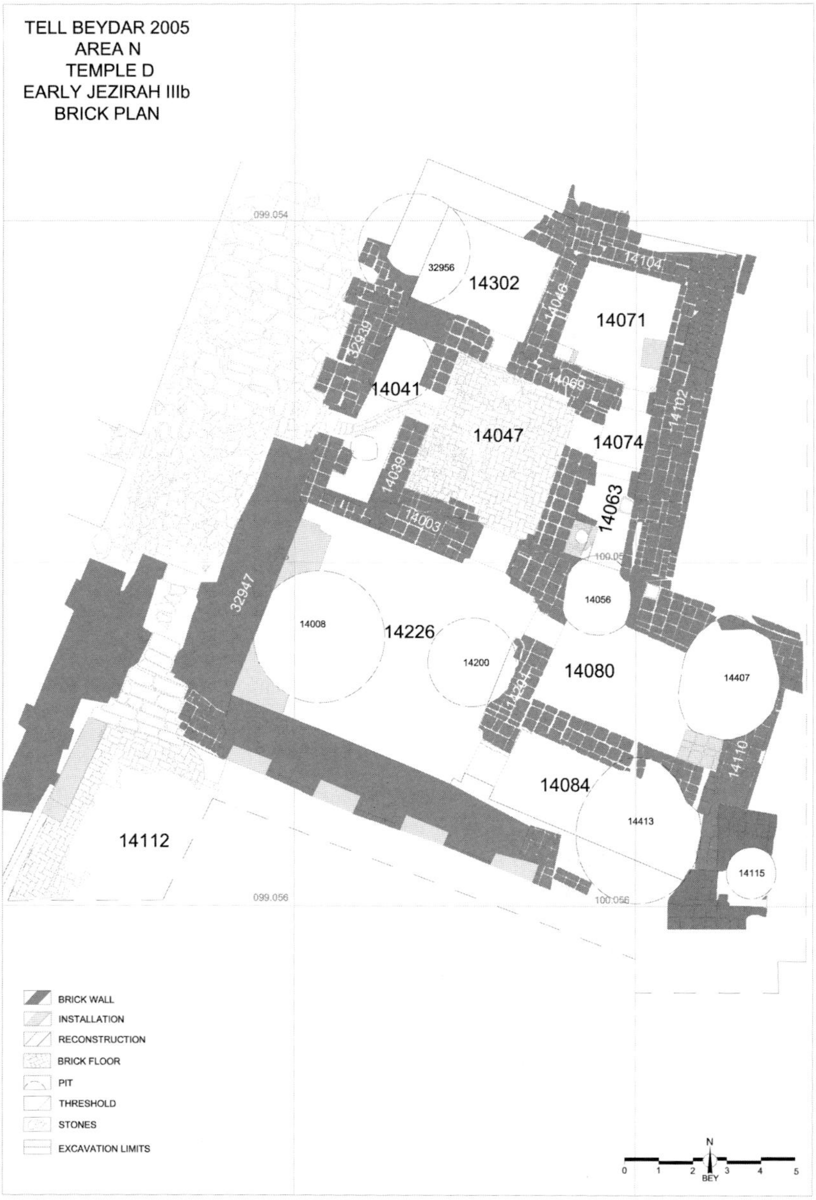

Fig. 1. Tell Beydar, brick plan of Temple D: the restored EJ IIIb level.

Fig. 2 a-b. Tell Beydar, Temple D before and after restoration
Left: plastered rooms 14074 and 14063.
Right: paved courtyard 14047 (from north to south).

Fig. 3 a-b. Tell Beydar, Temple D before and after restoration
Foreground: courtyard 14047.
Background: ceremonial room 14226 (from north to south).

Fig. 4 a-b. Tell Beydar, Temple D before and after restoration.
Canalisation of entrance room 14041 (from east to west).

Fig. 5 a-b. Tell Beydar, Temple D before and after restoration.
Room 14226 and its installations (from east to west).
Foreground: entrance to room 14084.

Fig. 6 a-b. Tell Beydar, Temple D before and after restoration.
Staircase to entrance room 14041 (from west to east).

Fig. 7 a-b. Tell Beydar, Temple D before and after restoration.
Entrance and western façade on "Main Street" (from west to east).

Fig. 8 a-b. Tell Beydar, Temple D before and after restoration.
General view (from south to north).

Fig. 9. Tell Beydar, Temple D. General view after restoration (from north to south).

DEUX OBJETS INSCRITS DE TELL TWEINI

René LEBRUN et Jan TAVERNIER
Université catholique de Louvain

Les fouilles syro-belges de Tell Tweini (fig. 1), l'ancienne Gibala, conduites depuis 1999 par la Direction Générale des Antiquités et des Musées de Syrie et la KU Leuven de Belgique ont déjà livré beaucoup d'informations sur l'histoire et l'archéologie de la région littorale du nord de la Syrie. Les parties du tell déjà fouillées ont fourni la preuve d'une habitation continue sur le site à partir de l'Age du Bronze Ancien jusqu'à l'Age du Fer.

Nous avons l'honneur et le plaisir de présenter à notre cher collègue Karel Van Lerberghe, qui a été le directeur des fouilles de Tell Tweini de 1999 à 2008, la publication de deux objets inscrits découverts lors des fouilles.

Les deux objets furent trouvés dans le chantier A, où se situait l'ancien centre de la ville (fig. 1). Ils datent de la période durant laquelle l'empire hittite exerçait le contrôle sur le royaume d'Ougarit, auquel Gibala appartenait selon un édit de Mursili II (c. 1321-1295 av. J.-C.) réglant la sécession de Siyannu (RS 17.335+379+381+235:19 [PRU 4 72]).

Objet No.1 (TWE004-00838-M003; fig. 2)

Il s'agit d'un sceau biconvexe de pierre, qui était porté en sautoir comme une sorte de pendentif autour du cou et qui servait à sceller/authentifier des documents écrits. Le sceau fut découvert en 2004 dans le coin nord-ouest d'une place située dans le nord-est du chantier A (fig. 4). Il date probablement d'env. 1250-1200 av. J.-C., c'est-à-dire de la période tardive de l'empire hittite. Il a un diamètre de 2,5 cm et une épaisseur de 1,4 cm.

Comme souvent, il porte une inscription en écriture hiéroglyphique louvite. Cette inscription consiste en un nom personnel et un titre. Le nom a été lu Sakapiya (Bretschneider et Van Lerberghe 2008, 33), mais de nouvelles recherches ont donné une autre lecture.

Face A: au centre l'anthroponyme Sà-us-ga-pi-ya (L104-L421-L434-L66-L209), avec à droite VIR$_2$ PASTOR (L386 L438). A gauche se trouve une étoile décorative.

Face B: Sà-us-ga-pi-ya VIR$_2$ PASTOR VIR$_2$ PASTOR (L104+L421-L434-L66-L209 L370 L386 L438).

L'anthroponyme est un théophore de Šauška, une épithète de facture hourrite de la déesse mésopotamienne Ištar[1] (Trémouille 2000, 124-126). Il est un composé en *-piya-* «don», de même structure donc qu'un autre théophore bien connu: Arma-piya- «don du dieu Lune». Le nom est donc à traduire «don de Šauška».

Le nom Šauška signifie probablement «La (très) grande» (Wegner 1995; Sharlach 2002, 105). Il est dérivé du hourrite *šavoši* «grand» (le sens de ce mot étant assuré par la bilingue hourrito-hittite de Boğazköy, où l'équivalent hittite est *salli* «grand»)[2], suivi d'un suffixe honorifique *k* et un *a* final, lettre qui se trouve souvent à la fin des noms divins (Trémouille 2000, 125). Le nom original Šauša, comme attesté dans les périodes d'Ur III et paléo-babyloniennes (ex. Ša-ú-úš-a-an dans un texte hourrite de Mari [RA 36 2 no.1:17]), fut plus tard élargi par un suffixe *-k-*, comme vu dans les orthographies plus récentes (cf. Wegner 1988, 149; Trémouille 2009, 99).

La déesse Šauška fut particulièrement populaire en Anatolie (Hattusa) et Syrie (Alalaḫ, Emar, Ougarit). Toutefois, ses premières attestations datent de la période d'Ur III (ex. ^{d}Ša-ù-ša dans Nik 2 316: Vo 7 [Umma]; ^{d}Ša-u$_{18}$-ša dans ARRIM 1 25 H36c: Ro 15 [Drehem, date inconnue]; BIN 3 382:8 [Drehem; Amar-Suen 9], Kang 1972 no. 172:15 [Drehem; Šu-Suen 1], MVN 11 157 Ro 1 [probablement de Lagash; date inconnuee], OIP 121 576:7 [Drehem; restored; Amar-Suen 9] et SAT 3 1402:5 [Umma; Šu-Suen 4]). Son culte persiste dans la période paléo-babylonienne, bien que la déesse soit seulement attestée deux fois. Clairement, la documentation mésopotamienne reste maigre comparée aux sources anatoliennes et syriennes.

[1] L'identification entre Šauška et Ištar est aussi attestée dans les textes de Hattusa, plus précisément par les orthographies ^{d}*Eš$_4$-*DAR*-pu-uš-ga* (KUB 27.1 ii 44) et ^{d}*Ša-wu$_u$-uš-ga* (KUB 27.29 iv 15) (Brandenstein 1934, III; Gelb 1943, 252).

[2] D'autres théories moins convaincantes sont celles de Laroche (1948, 119; dérivation participiale de *šau-* «armer», donnant «la déesse armée»), Landsberger (1954, 124; *šau-* «armer», suivi par *-ška*, un suffixe diminutif anatolien), D'jakonov (1971, 74 n.74, qui ne donne pas une nouvelle solution, mais qui dénonce l'idée de Laroche) et Wegner (1981, 24-25; dérivation de *šaw-* «compléter»).

Dans l'empire hittite, le culte de Šauška connut un succès grandissant avec le règne du Grand roi hittite Hattusili III (c. 1267-1237 av. J.-C.) et de son épouse Puduhépa, qui était la fille d'un prêtre de cette déesse. Hattusili III avait d'ailleurs fait de la Šauška de Samuha sa divinité personnelle (Lebrun 1976, 56-65; Wegner 1981, 16-19). Šauška figure surtout dans des textes hourrites de Hattusa, mais il y a aussi des attestations hittites et une attestation dans un texte louvite (^{d}*Ša-uš-qa-a* dans KUB 35.82:7). Les orthographies syllabiques sont ^{d}*Ša-a-u-uš-ga*, ^{d}*Ša-a-uš-ka*, ^{d}*Ša-uš-ga*, ^{d}*Ša-uš-ga-a*, ^{d}*Ša-uš-ka*, ^{d}*Ša-uš-qa*, ^{d}*Ša-u-uš-ga*, ^{d}*Ša-u-uš-kán*, ^{d}*Ša-pu-uš-ga*, ^{d}*Ša-wu*$_{u}$*-uš-ga* et ^{d}*Ša-wu*$_{ú}$*-uš-ga*. Ses logogrammes sont ^{d}GAŠAN, ^{d}*IŠTAR* et ^{d}LIŠ[3], parfois pourvus des suppléments phonétiques: ^{d}GAŠAN-*ga*, ^{d}GAŠAN-*uš-ga*, ^{d}*IŠTAR-bu-uš-ga*, ^{d}*IŠTAR-ga*[4], ^{d}*IŠTAR-ka*, ^{d}*IŠTAR-uš-ga* et ^{d}LIŠ-*ga* (cf. Wegner 1981, 21-23 et van Gessel 1998, 385-394).

La popularité de la déesse s'est probablement affaiblie avec l'effondrement de l'empire hittite: il n'y a que deux références datant du premier millénaire: une sur l'orthostate Malatya 6 (Sà-us-ka dans CHLI I 307-308 [début du 1e millénaire av. J.-C.]) et une sur un cylindre de Sargon II.

Une épithète importante de cette déesse est la ville de Ninive[5]. Parfois, dans la Mésopotamie ainsi que dans l'Anatolie, Šauška est appelée «de Ninive». En outre, plusieurs villes anatoliennes célébraient une fête de Šauška de Ninive (Wegner 1981, 11).

(1) Ur III: ^{d}Ša-u$_{18}$-ša Ni-nu-a-kam[6] (Drehem; AnOr 7 79:5-7).
(2) Paléo-babylonien: ^{d}INANNA Ni-nu-a, probablement à lire Šauša (Richter 1999, 246-247).
(3) Bronze tardif (Mitanni): le roi du Mitanni envoie au pharaon Amenophis III une statue de la déesse, comme son père Šuttarna II l'avait déjà fait (EA 23:13,26,31). Bien que le nom de la déesse soit écrit logographiquement (^{d}INANNA), on peut sûrement accepter une lecture Šauška. Dans sa lettre hourrite au pharaon le nom de la même déesse est écrit ^{d}*Ša-uš-kaš* (ergatif; EA 24 i 76) et ^{uru}*Ni-nu-a-a-we*

[3] Cet idéogramme n'est pas connu en Mésopotamie comme équivalent pour Šauška (Laroche 1952, 117n.26a; Wegner 1981, 22n.79).

[4] Aussi dans KBo 40.92:2, 52.209:5' (-g[a]).

[5] Durant la période d'Ur III la ville de Ninive fut probablement contrôlée par les Hourrites. Un texte datant de la troisième année de Šu-Sin (JCS 28 173-174) nomme Tiš-atal, le roi d'Urkeš, ville hourrite par excellence, en tant que «homme de Ninive» (LÚ Ni-nu-a^{ki}). Alors, pour les Mésopotamiens, Ninive fut une ville hourrite, ce qui rend logique la connexion avec la déesse hourrite Šauška.

[6] Probablement une erreur pour Ni-nu-a^{ki}.

^{d}*Ša-uš-ka-a-wa* (datif; EA 24 iii 98). Ceci implique que dans la lettre EA 20:25 (de nouveau une lettre de Tušratta) le nom est aussi à lire Šauška.

(4) Bronze tardif (Anatolie): ^{uru}*Ni-nu-wa-ḫi-ni-eš-ša* ^{d}*Ša-wu*$_{ú}$*-uš-ga-wa*$_{a}$ (KUB 45.60 vo ii 12'), ^{uru}*Ni-nu-wa-wa*$_{a}$ ^{d}*Ša-uš-ga* (KUB 47.17:3), ^{uru}*Ni-nu-wa-a-we*$_{e}$ ^{d}*Ša-uš-[ga]* (KBo 27.217 vo 17), ^{uru}*Ni-i-nu-we*$_{e}$ ^{d}*Ša-uš-g[a]* (KBo 27.217 i 35), etc.[7]

(5) Néo-assyrien: ^{d}*Ša-uš-ga ra-ši-bat* ABxḪA^{ki} (Sargon Zyl.:54). Trémouille (2009, 101) lit *a*$^{!}$*-ši-bat* «L'habitante». Fuchs (1994, 41) suit la copie de Lyon (1883, no. 9:54) en lisant *ra-ši-bat* «La terrifiante».

Son importance est aussi visible par l'usage de son nom dans des anthroponymes. Bien que de tels noms ne soient pas attestés fréquemment, ils couvrent une période chronologique étendue (de la période d'Ur III jusqu'à l'âge du Bronze tardif). De plus, la zone géographique dans laquelle ces noms sont attestés, est assez large: la Mésopotamie, la Syrie et l'Anatolie. Les noms attestés sont:

1 Période Ur III (env. 2100-2000 av. J.-C.)[8]

1.1 Drehem: Ur-Šauša:

- (1) Ur-^{d}Ša-ù-ša: BIN 3 355:4 (Šulgi 37).
- (2) Ur-^{d}Ša-u$_{18}$-ša: AASF 92 503:3, Env.4 (Šulgi 40); PDT 1 503 Ro 4, env 4, sceau 1 (Šulgi 39).

1.2 Gu'aba(?)

1.2.1 Ur-Šauša:

- (1) Ur-^{d}Ša-u$_{18}$-ša: SANTAG 6 139 Ro i 19 (Amar-Suen 5).

1.3 Girsu

1.3.1 Géme-Šauša: ARRIM 7 13-17 no.10: Vo vii 6 (Amar-Suen 5).

- (1) Géme-^{d}Ša-u$_{18}$-ša: ASJ 18 88 24 Ro iii 5 (Šulgi 46); CTNMC 54 Vo ii 33, iii 2 ([Géme]-; Amar-Suen 4); HSS 4 49 Vo i 21 (u18-[sha]) (Amar-Suen 1); ITT 3 6518 Ro 7 (Girsu, Amar-Suen 7), 6520 Ro 2,9 (date inconnuee), 6543 Ro i 7 (Amar-Suen 7); MVN 2 175 Vo ii 8 (Girsu, Šulgi 46); MVN 17 54 Ro iv 24 (Girsu; Šulgi 48); RTC 400 Ro ii 12, iii 16,18, Vo ii 11 (date inconnue); SAT 1 435 Ro ii 24, Vo i 16 (date inconnue); STA 10 Vo iii 34 (date inconnue); TUT 154 Ro iv 15 (Amar-Suen 2), 158 Ro i 11 (date inconnue).

[7] En toute probabilité les attestations d'Ištar de Ninive font référence à Šauška. Pour des exemples, voir van Gessel (1998, 923-949, surtout 941)

[8] Les trois noms attestés sont donc Geme-Šauša, Lu-Šauša et Ur-Šauša (Wilcke 1988, 21; Trémouille 2009, 102).

(2) Géme-^{d}Ša-u-u_{18}-ša: RTC 399 ii 28 (Géme-^{d}Ša-u-u_{18}-<ša>), v 23 (Ibbi-Sin 3).

1.3.2 Lú-Šauša:

(1) Lú-^{d}Ša-u_{18}-ša: ITT 3 5263 Ro 12 (-[^{d}Ša]-) (Šu-Suen 8); MVN 6 240 Ro 12 (date inconnue); TUT 154 Ro i 10 (Amar-Suen 2).

1.3.3 Ur-Šauša:

(1) Ur-^{d}Ša-u_{18}-ša: ASJ 18 88 24 Ro vi 10 (Girsu, Šulgi 46); AulOr 17-18 220 no. 8 Ro 4,5 (date inconnue); CT 5 44 - BM 18358 ii 5 (Šulgi 45); CT 10 28 Ro ii 16 (Amar-Suen 2); CUSAS 16 15:20 (Šulgi 39); HLC 21 Vo ii 11 (Šulgi 37); HSS 4 7 Vo ii 18 (Šulgi 48); ITT 3 6512 Ro 2 (-[ša-u_{18}]-; Šu-Suen 7), 6535 Ro 4 (-[u_{18}-ša]; date inconnue); MVN 6 307 Ro 2,8 (Šulgi 38); MVN 12 30 Ro 1 (Šulgi 46), 117 Vo i 10 (Šulgi 46), 297 Ro i 15 (Šulgi 48); SAT 1 376 Ro 3 (date inconnue), 435 Ro i 5 (date inconnue); SNAT 216 Ro 8 (date inconnue); ZA 55 68 Ro 3 (date inconnue).

(2) Ur-$^{d}U_{18}$-ša-u_{18}: HLC 19 Vo i 4 (Amar-Suen 9), 51 Vo i 12 (Amar-Suen 9), 70 Vo i 5 (Amar-Suen 9), 375 Vo i 6 (Amar-Suen 9).

1.4 Nippur

1.4.1 Ur-Šauša:

(1) Ur-^{d}Ša-u_{18}-ša: NATN 4 Ro 4 (Nippur; Šu-Suen 2).

1.5 Umma

1.5.1 Ur-Šauša:

(1) Ur-^{d}Ša-u_{18}-ša: SANTAG 6 139 Ro i 19 (Amar-Suen 5).

1.6 Ur

1.6.1 Géme-Šauša:

(1) Géme-^{d}Ša-u_{18}-ša: UET 3 1034 Vo i 12 (Ibbi-Suen 6), 1415 Ro 4 (Ibbi-Suen 6).

1.6.2 Ur-Šauša:

(1) Ur-^{d}Ša-u_{18}-ša: UET 3 970 sceau 3 (Ur: Ibbi-Suen 6), 1351 Ro ii 9 (Ur; date inconnue), 1359 sceau 3 ([Ur]-) (Ur; Šu-Suen 6); UET 9 21 Ro 4 (Ur; Ibbi-Suen 6)[9].

1.7 Origine inconnue

1.7.1 Ur-Šauša:

(1) Ur-^{d}Ša-u_{18}-ša: BCT 2 47 Ro 7 (date inconnue).

[9] Pas Ur-^{d}Ša-é-ša, comme le lisait Loding (1976, 71).

2 Période du Bronze tardif (env. 1500-1000 av. J.-C.)

2.1 Alalaḫ (noms hourrites dans des textes akkadiens)[10]

2.1.1 Arib-Šauška[11] «Šauška a donné» (cf. Laroche 1980, 52-53)

(1) A-ri-[i]b-ša-aš-šu-ka$_4$: AlT 182:39[12].

(2) A-ri-ib-ša-uš-ga: AlT 21:16 (-r[i-ib-ša-uš-ga]), 22:16.

(3) A-ri-ib-ša-uš-ka: AlT 20:13, 26:Vo 7 (-r[i-i]b-), 203:21, 373:4, 378:6.

2.1.2 Wandi-Šauška[13] «Šauška (est) droite» (cf. Laroche 1980, 293-294)

(1) Wa-an-di-ša-uš-ka: AlT 206:7, 257:16.

2.2 Nuzi

2.2.1 Akap-Šauška «Šauška a amené» (cf. Laroche 1980, 36)

(1) ^{f}A-kap-šu-uš-qa[14]: HSS 5 95:23[15].

2.2.2 Ar-Šauška «Šauška a donné» (cf. NPN 202-203).

(1) Ar-ša-mu-uš-qa: JEN 76:25 (-[qa]), 412:8.

(2) Ar-ša-wu-uš-ga: JENu 968.

(3) Ar-ša-wu-uš-qa: JEN 242:20; 267:26; JENu 958.

2.3 Ougarit

2.3.1 Šauškamuwa «force-vitalité de Šauška», roi d'Amurru (cf. van den Hout 1995, 112-115)

Le nom du roi d'Amurru, Šauškamuwa, est toujours écrit ^{d}*IŠTAR-mu-wa* (AnOr 48 11-12:4,9,14,17,21; PRU 3 41-44:1,28,35,40; PRU 4 128:1; PRU 4 137-138:1; PRU 4 139-141: Ro 1,

[10] Un autre nom construit avec Šauška pourrait être Šaušatti (AlT 161 rev. i 11'; AlT 215:4). Dans le texte AlT 161, Wiseman (1953, 146) lit Ša-uš-ša-at-[tar] et compare ce nom avec Šauštatar, le roi mitannien (c. 1440-1410 av. J.-C.). Bien qu'un nom Šaušatti soit confirmé par le texte AlT 215 et que ce nom puisse être considéré comme variante archaïque (Šauša > Šauška) ou assimilée (Šauška > Šaušša), on doit tenir compte que ce serait l'unique fois où le nom de la déesse serait archaïsé ou assimilé dans les textes du Bronze tardif.

Notons aussi le nom Šauška-madi «Sagesse de Šauška» (^{fd}INNIN-ma-ti$_4$) dans AlT 298 iii 6.s

[11] Ce nom est d'habitude écrit logographiquement: ^{m}A-ri-ip-^{d}INNIN, ^{m}A-ri-ip-^{d}Iš$_8$-DAR. Notons aussi la variante Ari-Šauška, uniquement écrit logographiquement (^{m}A-ri-^{d}INNIN et ^{m}A-ri-^{d}Iš$_8$-DAR; cf. von Dassow 2008, 421-422).

[12] Dans sa translittération de cette tablette, Wiseman (1953, 72) lit A-ri-ib-^{d}*IŠTAR*. Toutefois, Draffkorn (1959, 24) et von Dassow (2008, 422) préfèrent la lecture mentionnée ici.

[13] Ce nom est généralement écrit logographiquement (^{m}ZAG-^{d}INNIN; von Dassow 2008, 493).

[14] Cette orthographie de Šauška est aussi attestée dans les textes de Kültepe: ^{f}Šu-uš-kà et ^{m}Šu-uš-kà-na (cf. Landsberger 1954, 124 et n.288).

[15] Ecrit logographiquement ^{m}A-kap-^{d}INNIN dans un texte d'Alalaḫ (AlT 195:41).

Vo 5',11',13'; PRU 4 141-143:16,21,35,41; PRU 4 144-146: Vo 18',33'; PRU 4 147-148:8,14).

Par contre, il est écrit syllabiquement sur les sceaux en louvite hiéroglyphique: Sà-us-ka-BOS (Ugaritica 3 31 figs. 38-40) et Sà-us-ka-[BOS] (Ugaritica 3 33 figs. 41-42).

2.3.2 Šaušku(ru)wa (?)

Dans un texte akkadien d'Ougarit un nom peu lisible apparaît deux fois (PRU 4 182-184:4,15): ^{m}Ša-uš-ku-[ ] et ^{m}Ša-uš-ku-[ù/ru]-wa. Nougayrol (1956, 183; aussi Laroche 1956, 133) lit Šauškuwa, tandis que Laroche (1966, 161), plus tard, préfère Šauškuruwa. Dans les deux cas, le sens du nom reste trouble. Laroche (1966, 293) se demande si le nom ne serait pas un composé de Šauška et *uruwa*. D'un autre côté, on pourrait également penser à un nom Šauška pourvu d'un suffixe *-wa* (comme attesté dans Kukku — Kukkuwa, Lullu — Lulluwa, etc.; cf. Laroche 1966, 245).

2.4 Hattusa[16]

2.4.1 Šauškakuruntiya- (cf. Laroche 1966, 161 no. 1144)

Dans les textes cunéiformes ce nom est écrit ^{d}*IŠTAR*-^{d}LAMMA (VS 28 125 Ro 4'; cf. Groddek 1999, 194 pour la lecture) ou ^{d}LIŠ-^{d}LAMMA (IBoT 1.32:11,17; KUB 40.88 iii 18), tandis que les versions hiéroglyphiques ont Sà-us-ka-CERVUS-ti (OIP 45 Pl.63:3; SBo 2.8, 2.30, 2.67).

2.4.2 Šauškamuwa «Force vitale de Šauška» (cf. Laroche 1966, 161 no. 1141; Singer 2009)

La plupart des notations cunéiformes de cette personne sont écrites logographiquement (^{md}*IŠTAR-mu-u-wa*, ^{md}*IŠTAR-mu-wa*, ^{md}*IŠTAR*-A.A). Un fragment contient une notation syllabique: ^{m}Ša-uš-ga-mu-u-wa (Bo 86/299 iv 32).

Par contre, les sceaux en écriture louvite hiéroglyphique sont inscrits syllabiquement: Sà-us-ka-BOS (BoHa 19 365-371; SBo 2.79), Sà-us-ka-BOS$_{2}$ (BoHa 19 372).

2.4.3 Šauškapiya «Don de Šauška» (cf. Laroche 1981, 39)

Comme l'on peut s'y attendre, ce nom est écrit logographiquement (^{d}LIŠ-SUM) dans un texte cunéiforme[17] et partiellement

[16] Dans les textes de Hattusa, les noms avec l'akkadogramme Ištar sont tous attestés dans les textes cunéiformes, tandis que les noms syllabiques apparaissent sur les sceaux en écriture hiéroglyphique louvite.

[17] KUB 40.86 Ro 5; KUB 40.88 iv 19.

syllabiquement en écriture hiéroglyphique sur une empreinte de cachet sur une jarre (Sà-<us>-ka-pi [WVDOG 88 29 A79]; cf. Laroche 1973, 121). Dès lors, notre nom n'est pas un nouveau nom.

2.4.4 Šauškaruntiya
Personne seulement attestée sur les sceaux de Hattusa, en écriture louvite hiéroglyphique: Sà-us-ka-CERVUS$_3$-ti (BoHa 19 373-381). Le nom est probablement une abréviation de Šauška-Kuruntiya-.

2.4.5 Šauškatti, nom en *-atti* (cf. Laroche 1966, 161 no. 1142 et 332)
Le seul nom féminin dans le corpus.
- ^{f}Ša-uš-ga-at-ti: KUB 34.45+KBo 16.63:7,8 (-[uš]-)[18].

2.4.6 Šauškawalwi «Lion de Šauška»
Cette personne est attestée une fois en hittite hiéroglyphique: Sà-<us>-ka-LEO$_2$ (BoHa 19 382). La lecture est assurée par Hawkins (apud Herbordt 2005, 271).

2.4.7 Šauškaziti «Homme de Šauška» (cf. Laroche 1966, 161 no. 1143)
Nom attesté surtout dans sa forme logographique (^{md}*IŠTAR*-LÚ) dans les textes cunéiformes[19] et dans sa forme syllabique (Sà-us-ga-VIR-zi) sur deux sceaux en louvite hiéroglyphique, datant de l'époque hittite tardive (JEA 8 Pl.25 no.20; cf. Hogarth 1922: 217; JNES 32 138 no.4). Ici le signe ZI fonctionne comme indicateur de lecture du logogramme.

2.4.8 Šauš[ka]
Dans KBo 16.27 iii 14' une personne apparaît avec un nom cassé: ^{m}Ša-a-uš-[ga-]

Evidemment, ces noms sont tous des hybrides hourrites-anatoliens et surtout louvites (Laroche 1966, 293; Trémouille 2009, 102) À ce jour, 7 noms tels (y inclus Šauškapiya) sont attestés à Hattusa[20].

Šauškapiya fut un *vir*, c.à.d. un citoyen jouissant de la plénitude de ses droits et il occupait la fonction de PASTOR «berger». Que recouvrait exactement cette fonction? Il s'agit probablement de la désignation d'un fonctionnaire chargé de la gestion de pâturages/de terrains royaux et de l'entretien des troupeaux appartenant au palais ou à différents temples (Herbordt 2005, 102-103).

[18] Cf. Werner (1967, 50-51). Le même nom est d'habitude écrit ^{fd}*IŠTAR*-at-ti: KBo 2.6 ii 37,38,43,50, etc.; KBo 41.179 Ro 6',14' (-[ti]); KUB 8.27 Vo 8; KUB 16.69 Ro 4; RA 43 57 i 13 (^{fd}*IŠ*[*TAR*-at-ti-iš]), 62 iv 8 (cf. Laroche 1966: 161 no.1142). KUB 50.87:4

[19] KBo 10.10 iv 6; KBo 13.35 iii 42; KBo 15.29 i 4,5; KUB 40.80:3,5,7,27; KUB 54.1 i 37,55,56,63, ii 8, iv 19.

[20] Un autre nom contenant l'akkadogramme *IŠTAR* pourrait être lu avec l'élément Šauška: ^{m}GAL-^{d}*IŠTAR* (KBo 47.11 Ro 7,10).

Objet No.2 (fig. 4)

L'objet discuté ici est un sceau-bague en bronze et fut aussi trouvé dans le chantier A, plus précisément dans le coin sud-est d'une chambre au nord-est du chantier (fig. 3). Comme l'autre objet, ce sceau-bague date probablement du Bronze tardif.

Le sceau-bague porte le nom du propriétaire gravé à l'aide de signes se définissant comme étant de l'écriture hiéroglyphique hittite-louvite assez cursive, qui peuvent être comparés avec les formes des hiéroglyphes sur les empreintes d'autres sceaux trouvés en Syrie.

Le nom se lit Tu-ra/i-zi et est probablement une abréviation de Tūri-ziti «homme au sceptre; homme à la lance» avec les composants *tūri-* «lance» (akk. *šukuru* ; cf. Tischler 1994, 455-457, Kloekhorst 2008, 899-900 et Brosch 2010, 282) et le louvite *ziti-* «homme». Une lecture *tūri-* est préférée ici à cause de l'accusatif en *-i*, ce qui implique que le nominatif appartient également au thème en *-i* et que le substantif est neutre.

L'élément onomastique *tūri-* «lance» n'est pas seulement attesté sur le sceau discuté ici. D'autres exemples sont Tūri-Dagan (Tu-ra/i-tà-ka; Beyer 2001, 83 no. A60 = Gonnet 1991 no. 23b), Tūri (Tu-ra/i; Beyer 2001, 128 no. B22 = Gonnet 1991 no. 24b) et Tūriya (Tu-ra/i-ia; Beyer 2001, 132 no. B35 = Gonnet 1991 no. 88b) à Hattusa.

À ce moment, les deux objets étudiés ici sont les seuls objets inscrits trouvés sur le site de Tell Tweini. Il n'est pas étonnant qu'il s'agisse de deux sceaux en écriture louvite hiéroglyphique, l'écriture par excellence pour les sceaux des hauts fonctionnaires. De pareils sceaux ont été trouvées dans toute la région (cf. Gonnet 1991, 198-214; Beyer 2001, 19-164). De même, il est assez logique que les objets furent découverts dans le chantier A, qui est situé au milieu de la ville et dans lequel se trouvait le centre administratif de la ville. Šauškapiya fut peut-être un des administrateurs de la ville, tandis que Turaziti était un fonctionnaire subordonné à Šauškapiya, mais ceci est provisoirement hypothétique et ne peut qu'être confirmé ou affaibli par la trouvaille de nouveaux documents textuels dans la région.

Bibliographie

Beyer, D. 2001: *Emar IV: Les sceaux* (OBO 20), Mainz.

Bretschneider, J. et K. Van Lerberghe 2008: «Tell Tweini, ancient Gibala, between 2600 and 333 B.C.E.», dans J. Bretschneider et K. Van Lerberghe (éd.), *In Search of Gibala: An archaeological and historical study based on eight seasons of excavations at Tell Tweini (Syria) in the A and C fields (1999-2007)* (AuOr Suppl. 24), Barcelona, 11-68.

BROSCH, C. 2010: «Nominalkomposita und komponierende Ableitungen im Hethitischen», *AoF* 37, 263-301.

D'JAKONOV, I.M. 1971: *Hurrisch und Urartäisch* (MSS. Beih. 6), München.

DRAFFKORN, A.E. 1959: *Hurrians and Hurrian at Alalaḫ*, Ann Arbor.

FUCHS, A. 1994: *Die Inschriften Sargons II. aus Khorsabad*, Göttingen.

GELB, I.J. 1943: *Nuzi Personal Names* (OIP 57), Chicago.

GONNET, H. 1991: «Sceaux hiéroglyphiques anatoliens de Syrie», dans D. Arnaud, *Textes syriens de l'âge de bronze récent* (AuOr. Suppl. 1), Barcelona, 198-214.

GRODDEK, D. 1999: «compte-rendu de L. Jakob-Rost, *Keilschrifttexte aus Boghazköy im Vorderasiatischen Museum* (VS 28), Mainz, 1996», *OLZ* 94, 193-200.

HERBORDT, S. 2005: *Die Prinzen- und Beamtensiegel der hethitischen Grossreichszeit auf Tonbullen aus dem Nişantepe-Archiv in Hattusa* (BoHa 19), Mainz.

HOGARTH, D.G. 1922: «Engraved Hittite Objects», *JEA* 8, 211-218.

KANG, Sh. T. 1972: *Sumerian Economic Texts from the Drehem Archive* (Sumerian and Akkadian Cuneiform Texts in the Collection of the World Heritage Museum of the University of Illinois 1), Urbana.

KLOEKHORST, A. 2008: *Etymological Dictionary of the Hittite Inherited Lexicon* (Leiden Indo-European Etymological Dictionary Series 5), Leiden.

LANDSBERGER, B. 1954: «Assyrische Königsliste und 'Dunkles Zeitalter'», *JCS* 8, 106-133.

LAROCHE, E. 1948: «Teššub, Hebat et leur cour», *JCS* 2, 113-134.

— 1952: «Le panthéon de Yazilikaya», *JCS* 6, 115-123.

— 1956: «Documents hiéroglyphiques hittites provenant du palais d'Ugarit», *Ugaritica* 3, 97-160.

— 1966: *Les Noms des Hittites* (Etudes Linguistiques 4), Paris.

— 1973: «Ouvrages reçus», *RHA* 31, 115-121.

— 1980: *Glossaire de la langue hourrite* (Etudes et commentaires 93), Paris.

— 1981: «Les noms des Hittites: Supplément», *Hethitica* 4, 3-58.

LEBRUN, R. 1976: *Samuha: Foyer religieux de l'empire hittite* (PIOL 11), Louvain-la-Neuve.

LODING, D. 1976: *Economic Texts from the Third Dynasty* (UET 9), Philadelphia.

LYON, G. 1883: *Keilschrifttexte Sargon's Königs von Assyrien (722-705 v. Chr.)* (Assyriologische Bibliothek 5), Leipzig.

NOUGAYROL, J. 1956: *Textes accadiens des archives sud* (PRU 4), Paris.

RICHTER, T. 1999: *Untersuchungen zu den lokalen Panthea Süd- und Mittelbabyloniens in altbabylonischer Zeit* (AOAT 257), Münster.

SHARLACH, T. 2002: «Foreign Influences on the Religion of the Ur III Court», dans D. I. Owen et G. Wilhelm (éd.), *General Studies and Excavations at Nuzi* 10/3 (SCCNH 12), Bethesda, 92-114.

SINGER, I. 2009: «Šaušgamuwa», *RlA* 12, 96-99.

TISCHLER, J. 1994: *Hethitisches Etymologisches Glossar III/10*, Innsbruck.

TRÉMOUILLE, M.-C. 2000: «La religione dei Hurriti», *La Parola del Passato* 55, 114-170.

— 2009: «Šawuška, Šauška. A. Philologisch», *RlA* 12, 99-103.

VAN DEN HOUT, Th. 1995: *Der Ulmitešub-Vertrag: Eine prosopographische Untersuchung* (StBoT 38), Wiesbaden.

VAN GESSEL, B. H. L. 1998: *Onomasticon of the Hittite Pantheon* (HdO 1/33), Leiden.

VON BRANDENSTEIN, C.-G. 1934: *Kultische Texte in hethitischer und hurritischer Sprache* (KUB 27), Berlin.

VON DASSOW, E. 2008: *State and Society in the Late Bronze Age: Alalaḫ under the Mittani Empire* (SCCNH 17), Bethesda.

WEGNER, I. 1981: *Gestalt und Kult der Ištar-Šawuška in Kleinasien* (AOAT 36), Neukirchen-Vluyn.

— 1988: «Grammatikalische und lexikalische Untersuchungen hurritischer Beschwörungsformeln aus Boğazköy», dans V. Haas (éd.), *Hurriter und Hurritisch* (Xenia 21), Konstanz, 145-155.

— 1995: «Der Name der Ša(w)uška», dans D. I. Owen et G. Wilhelm (éd.), *Edith Porada Memorial Volume* (SCCNH 7), Bethesda, 117-120.

WERNER, R. 1967: *Hethitische Gerichtsprotokolle* (StBoT 4), Wiesbaden.

WILCKE, K. 1988: «Ти'амат-Башти и богиня Ша(в)уш(к)а Ниневийская», *Drevnej Vostok — Hin Arevelk* 5, 21-26.

WISEMAN, D. J. 1953: *The Alalakh Tablets* (Occasional Publications of the British Institute of Archaeology at Ankara 2), London.

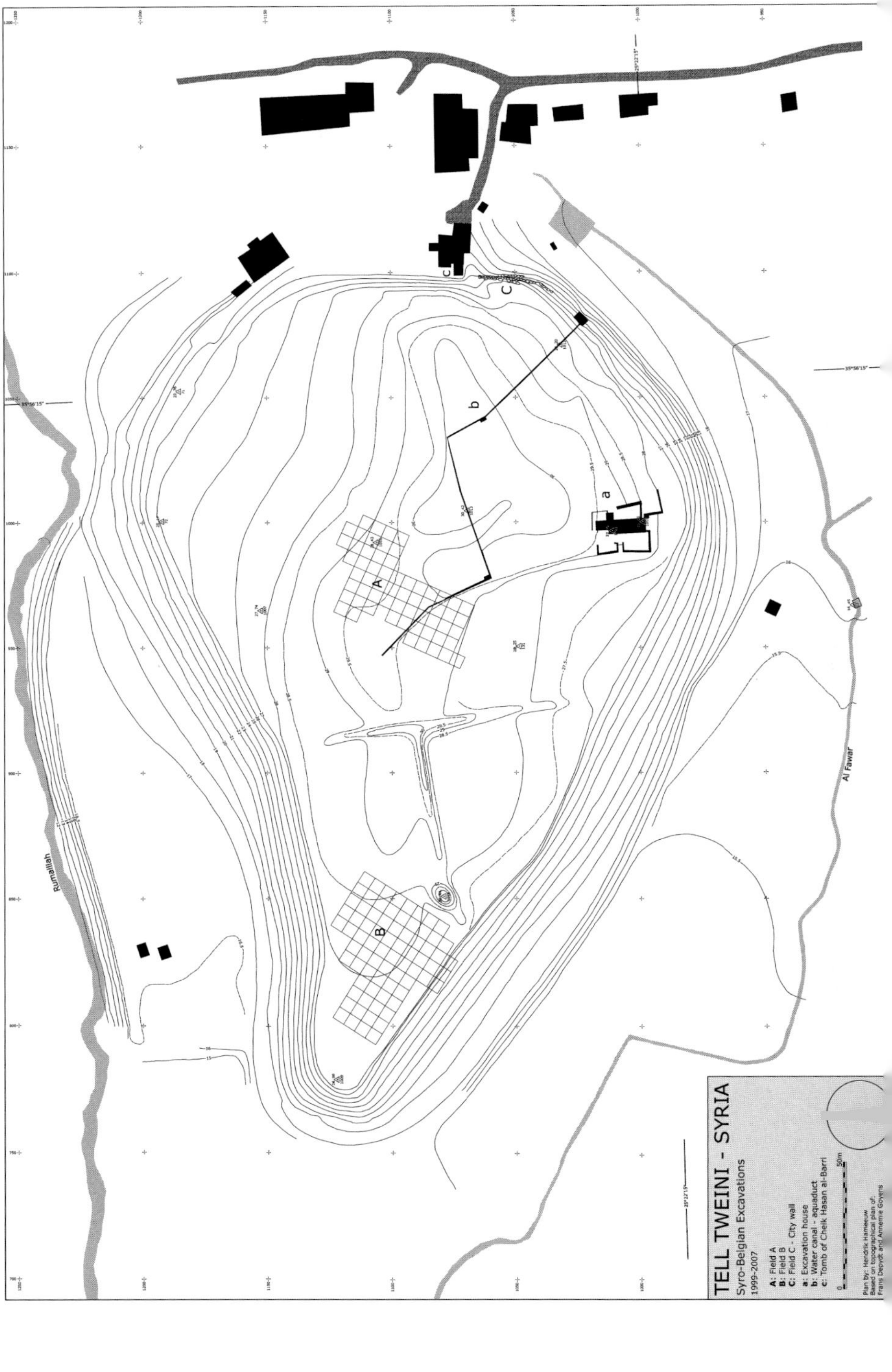
TELL TWEINI - SYRIA
Syro-Belgian Excavations
1999-2007
A: Field A
B: Field B
C: Field C - City wall
a: Excavation house
b: Water canal - aquaduct
c: Tomb of Cheik Hasan al-Barri
0
50m
Plan by: Hendrik Hameeuw
Based on topographical plan of:
Frans Depydt and Annemie Goyens
Rumaillah
Al Fawar

Fig. 2. Objet no.1.

Face A Face B

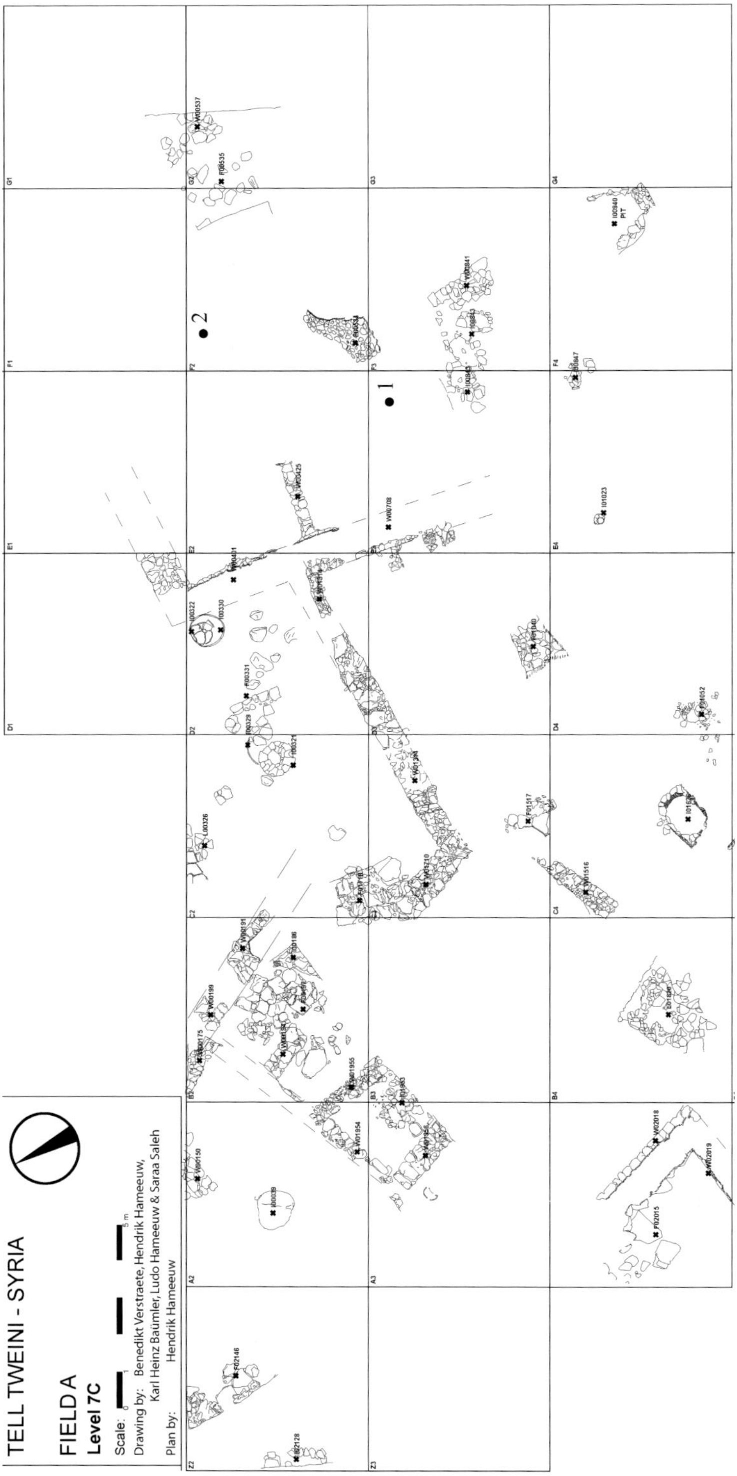

Fig. 3. Lieux de trouvailles des objets 1 et 2.

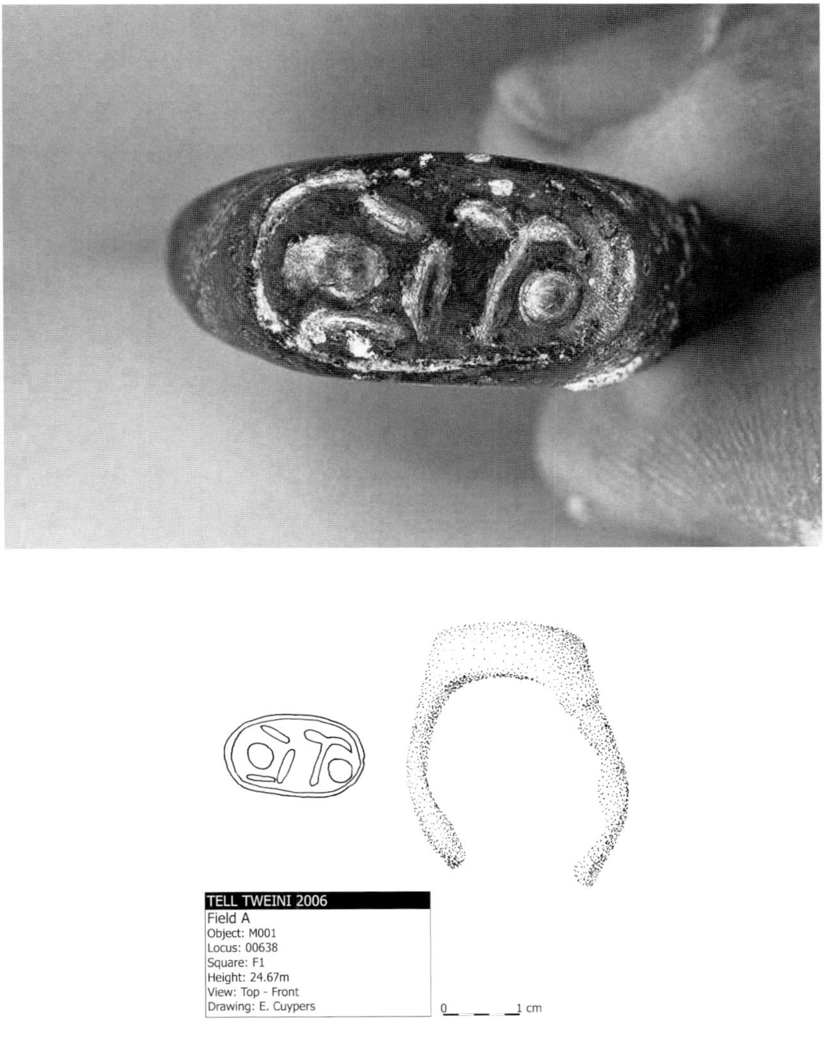

Fig. 4. Objet no. 2.

DAGĀN, THE MASTER OF PLOUGHING

Edward LIPIŃSKI
KU Leuven

The Amorite noun *pagrā'um* of the Mari texts is clearly distinguished in CAD from *pagru(m)*, "body, corpse", but an etymological connection seems to be assumed in AHw. Both dictionaries translate it by "offering" or "sacrifice", although its use in *nīq pagrā'im* rather points at a qualification of sacrifices, comparable for instance to *nīq warḫim* (ARM 5, 65, 30), "the offering of the (New) Moon". The nominal pattern *fa'lā'u* is used in West Semitic languages, especially in Arabic, to form verbal substantives, substantivized adjectives or derivatives expressing an abstract notion, e.g. *rahbā'u*, "fear, fright", *ḥasnā'u*, "a beauty", *'aḏrā'u*, "virgin, Virgo" (astron.), *ḥamrā'u*, "rusting, rust" (disease affecting cereals), *fayfā'u*, "desert". It can be compared to Babylonian *pursā'u* < *purussā'u* (GAG § 56, 34; cf. MAD 2[2], 155). Considering the phrase *Dagān bēl pagrê* in ARM 10, 63, 15 and the relation of Dagān to the *pagrā'um* sacrifices in other texts, especially in *nīq Dagān ša p*[*a*]*gr*[*ā'im*] *i*[*qqi*] (FlM 7, 51, 24-25), "offer a sacrifice to Dagān of *Pagrā'um*", one should examine the use of the verbal root *pgr*, Arabic *fǧr*, in other available sources.

Now, the basic meaning of *pgr* seems to be "to cleave, break up, dig up" the ground[1], hence the Sabaic connotation "to furrow" or the like. In an inscription from Haram we thus read: *w-'l hwfyhmw f-fgr s²rghmw b-ḏt'n w-ḫrfn mn mwm qllm w-bllm* (CIH 547, 8-11), "and God saved them and furrowed their dry land[2] in spring and autumn with[3] little or much water". This use of the verb *fgr* is close to the meaning of Stem II in Classical and Literary Arabic with *faǧǧara* signifying "to create a passage for water" or "to let water flow, pour forth". A verbal substantive derived from this root should thus mean "digging, furrowing". When

[1] Lane 1863-93, 2359: "he made an opening or intervening space".

[2] The noun *s²rg* does not mean "watercourse" but "dry land", like Egyptian Arabic *šarāqī*, which designates not-irrigated land, not reached by the Nile floods. Ancient *gāf* may be found today as *qāf*.

[3] The preposition *mn* in lieu of *bn* occurs only in inscriptions from Haram and its neighbourhood.

it is related to Dagān, whose name means "corn, grain, seed" in Ugaritic and in Hebrew, the connotation "furrowing, ploughing" seems to be quite obvious, eventually "tilling" in a more general sense. This understanding of Dagān's function, related to his role at Ugarit as the father of the storm-god Baal, is confirmed in the Euphrates valley by the Old Babylonian proper name *Iz-ra-aḫ-*[d]*Da-gan* occurring on a tablet from Terqa (TCL 1, 238, 33 and seal), the main centre of Dagān's cult in this region. The name means "Dagān has sown", clearly revealing a conception of the deity, which remained unchanged for ages.

In fact, Dagān was identified in the Late Bronze Age with Hurrian Kumarbi, regarded as a god of agriculture and the counterpart of Hittite Ḫalki, "Grain", and of Hattian Kait, also "Grain". The same conception of Dagān reappears in Hellenistic times, in the *Phoenician History* of Philo of Byblos, quoted by Eusebius of Caesarea in his *Praeparatio evangelica* I, 10, 25. According to Philo, "Dagon, since he had invented the corn and the plough, was called Zeus the Plougher", Ζεὺς 'Αρότριος. Philo also knew that Dagon's name meant "corn", Σίτων (I, 10, 16). In consequence, *pagrā'um* in relation to Dagān can only mean "ploughing" or the like.

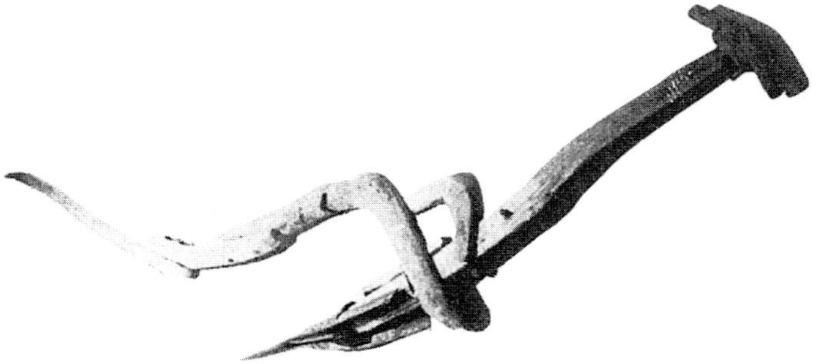

The plough invented by Dagān

Ploughing is also implied by the Ugaritic month name *yrḫ pgrm* in KTU 4.172, 2; 4.182, 40; 4.193, 1-2.6-7; 4.266, 2. *Waraḫ pagri* occurs already at Alalakh in several texts of Level VII: AlT 35, 7; 37, 10; 44, 7; 252, 21; 254, 28; 269, 17.25. In AlT 252, it follows *waraḫ attanati*, which must be the seventh month, like at Nuzi, and thus correspond to September/October. *Waraḫ pagri* is then the eighth month, October/November, indicated by the logogram ITI.APIN, i.e. "month of the plough". At Mari, it is called "month of Dagān". In fact, ploughing and sowing began in

November after the early rains. It is likely therefore that *pgr* was an ancient name of the plough[4], derived from the same root *pgr*, thus "month of the plough(s)". The month name occurs also at Terqa, but *waraḫ pagrē* is written there with an initial BA: ITI *pá-ag-re-e* (BiMes 16, 6, 49). Its relation to Dagān, "the inventor of the plough", was probably felt better at Terqa, since this was one of the main centres of the Dagān cult. The proper name *pa-gi-rum*, attested at Terqa (Podany 2002, 244), is probably an old noun meaning "ploughman".

A different connotation of *fağara*, "break up", is attested in Arabic by the noun *fağr*, "daybreak", used also in Ethio-Semitic (Harari, Tigre, Gurage). The same meaning should very likely be attributed to Ugaritic *špš pgr*, "the Sun of the daybreak", as seen half a century ago by J. Aistleitner (1963, 253, No. 2189). This is a divine name occurring in sequences of theonyms: KTU 1.39, 12.17; 1.102, 12. *Špš-pgr*, whose name is written as one word in KTU 1.39, 12, was possibly identified with the Sun-goddess of Arinna, as a Hittite hymn might suggest. It apparently addresses the goddess as the Sun-deity of the dawn: "For you they open the door of heaven; you are allowed to pass through the gate of heaven". However, Telepinus can be addressed in the same way in a parallel version of the hymn (ANET 397). Considering the alternations *b/p* and *g/q* in Semitic languages, the question must of course be raised whether Hebrew *boqer*, "daybreak", and *ba-qí-ra-am*, "at dawn", in Mari texts (ARM 1, 70, 5; A 1153, 18), do not go back to the same root. The answer should probably be positive, since the basic meaning of the Hebrew verb *bqr* is practically the same as that of Arabic *fağara*.

Another Arabic verb, *faqara*, means "to pierce, bore"; it must go back to a dialectal variant of *pgr* with *g* pharyngealized in the vicinity of *r*. Besides, the Qatabanic verb *bqr*, "dig up, level" fields, is very likely an offshoot of the same basic root. We have probably to do here with a dialectal voicing of *p* next to the voiced consonant of *pgr*. This could have happened in an early period, before the South-Arabian and Arabic change *p* > *f* in *fağara* and *faqara*. It has been argued that *bqr*, "bovines, large cattle", initially designated beasts for ploughing, a possibility that cannot be excluded. The verb *bqr* occurs, for instance, in the sequence *ṣyr w-bqr w-grb w-bql w-s¹qḥ kl 's¹rrs¹* of a Qatabanic inscription from Wadi Ḍurra (RÉS 3856, 1): "he set to work, tilled, terraced, planted, and put all his cultivated land in order". All the attestations of Amorite *pagrā'um* could be transliterated and transcribed *paqrā'um*, and this

[4] Perhaps the ᵍⁱˢb a - g u r₄ of MSL 5, 153, 42.

would have prevented not only the confusion of two different roots and of two different nominal patterns, viz. *fa'lu* and *fa'lā'u*, but also the speculations on Dagān's relation to funeral sacrifices or to offerings of carcases[5].

The noun *pagru*, "body", hence "corpse" or "carcase" of animal, belongs to another root the first phoneme of which in some West-Semitic languages is a voiced consonant. In Arabic, the elative adjective *abǧar* means "corpulent", and Argobba, an Ethio-Semitic language related closely to Amharic, preserves the noun *bägära*, "buttocks", a fleshy part of the body. Differences between voiced and voiceless consonants occur often in Semitic languages, especially between East-Semitic and West-Semitic, but Ugaritic, Canaanite, and Aramaic *pagru / peger / pagrā*, "body", stands in this particular case on the side of East-Semitic or Akkadian. However, one should notice the spelling *ba-ag-ru*, "carcase" of sheep, at Mari in the so-called period of the *šakkanakku* (ARM 19, 303, 3). It would seem therefore that the Amorite noun for "body" was pronounced *bagru* in the early second millennium B.C.[6]

A less frequent connotation of *pgr*, "body", is indeed "statue" or more likely "embodiment", like an aniconic stele symbolizing the presence of a deity and possibly adorned in a convenient way. This connotation is prepared by the use of *pagrum* in the sense of "representative" in Old Babylonian letters. The writer of a letter thus informs the addressee: *kīma pagrija awīlam aṭrud* (ARMT 26, 21, 20), "I sent a gentleman as my representative". Another Mari letter records that "the Amorite chief of the land of Ṣubat-Ištar is like the representative of his lord", *rabbi Amurrim ša māt Ṣubat-Ištar* [*ša*] *kīma pagar bēlišu* (ARMT 27, 72 bis, 36'-37'; cf. ARMT 28, 115, 34-35). The addressee of a further letter is reminded of his high position: *kīma pagrija ina muḫḫi ṣābija wašbāti*, "You stand on top of my troops as my representative".

The use of *pagru* in the sense "statue" is attested in Old Babylonian, for instance in TCL 11, 245, 33 (cf. 27), and in the Assyrian ritual *Bît rimki* (Laessøe 1955, 37, 7; cf. Seux 1976, 388), where a figurine is said

[5] Two quotations will suffice here, viz. Bodi 1991, 100. "Il ressort de l'analyse des textes de Mari que le terme *pagrû* représente le cadavre de l'animal sacrifié au dieu Dagān"; Durand 2008, 343: "le rituel aux morts offert à Dagan (*pagrâ'u*) se faisait au moyen d'animaux morts et l'on recourait alors à l'usage du terme de 'carcasse' (*pagrum*): l'idée est que l'on offre le mort aux Morts".

[6] This is perhaps confirmed for an earlier period by Eblaic NE:SAG = *ba-ga-lu-um* (VE 243) and NE.SAG-*il* (TM.75.G.1871, obv. III, 4), i.e. *Bagar-il*, "God's image", to be compared to *Ṣalam-ili* (TMH 2, 19, 12).

to be identical to a sorceress' body: *šuklulti pagri ana šuklulti pagri maškil*, "the entirety of the figurine is identical to the entirety of the body". This meaning of *pagru* occurs also at Ugarit, in KTU 6.13, 2 and 6. 14, 1, and in Hebrew, in Lev. 26, 30 and Ez. 43, 7.9[7]. The Ugaritic texts were often discussed and *pgr* was then related to Mari *pagrā'um* despite the different nominal patterns. The reason was simple: the Ugarit steles in question were dedicated to Dagān, closely related at Mari to the *pagrā'um*. However, a simple comparison of the inscriptions shows that *pgr* is a synonym of *skn*, used in KTU 6.13, 1, with a slight insistency of *pgr* on the function of the stele as "embodiment" of the deity. This connotation appears also in the listed biblical passages, where the usual translations "carcases of idols" and "corpses of kings" make little sense: the texts refer to steles dressed in open-air hill-shrines or recording passed kings in the temple precinct, like the Assur steles. In other words, *pagrā'um* does not occur either at Ugarit or in the Bible.

Ploughing or tilling was one of the crucial activities of rural societies. The Mishnah, containing legal comments on immemorial practices, seems to allude to four yearly ploughings, which correspond more or less to the four *Pagrā'um* celebrations mentioned in Mari texts, viz. in month II (April/May), in month VIII or month of Dagān (October/November), in month X (December/January), and in month XII (February/March). The first ploughing took place after the harvest, with broad lines or plots far apart (Kilaim 2, 6). It was preceded at Mari by the *Pagrā'um* of month II (ARM 21, 62). The second ploughing took place in autumn, after the first rains, and then, too, the furrows were not too close to one another. In Palestine, spaces were left intentionally between the furrows to prevent torrential rains from eroding the soil (Kilaim 2, 3). In this way, each field would consist of alternate furrows and ridges. This work was preceded at Mari by the *Pagrā'um* of month VIII (ARM 21, 70; 21, 147; 26, 25; M 18087)[8]. Due to the lunar calendar, ill-adapted to agriculture even if used with some intercalation, possibly due also to early rains and an earlier ploughing season, the *Pagrā'um* could sometimes be celebrated towards the end of month VII (M 13377, 5-8). The deep ploughing followed soon with the furrows close to one another, making the soil ready for sowing (Kilaim 2, 3). This was done from November/December to

[7] This was shown already by Neiman 1948, 58, followed by de Vaux 1960, 112, by Vink 1962, 96 for Lev. 26, 30, Zimmerli 1969, 1070 and 1082-1083 for Ez. 43, 7.9, and by Lipiński 1973, 201, n. 69, for KTU 6.13 and 6.14.

[8] References to inedited tablets M are based on information published by J.-M. Durand.

January/February and was followed by the fourth ploughing to cover the seed (Tosefta, Kilaim 1, 15). This period would correspond to the *Pagrā'um* of month X (M 18088; M 18153). Millet and chickpeas were sown later, in March/April, and the preceding ploughing would seem to fit the *Pagrā'um* of month XII (ARM 21, 76; M 18014; M 18075).

Ploughing was undoubtedly placed under the protection of the appropriate deity each time it was performed. Sacrifices had to be offered and their purpose or occasion, i.e. "ploughing", mentioned in the records. This ritual and popular celebration was most likely called in the same way. Since ploughing is generally regarded as the basic tillage practice, we may call it "Ploughing-feast" or "Ploughing-party".

Ploughing in modern times

There is no problem in such an understanding of the phrase *nīq pagrā'i*, "the sacrifice of the Ploughing-feast", which occurs in several Mari texts. One of them provides interesting information. It is a letter sent to king Zimri-Lîm by Yaqqim-Addu, the governor of Sagaratum. The *muškēnū* of the province have prepared their sacrifices for the *Pagrā'um*-feast they wanted to celebrate on the eighth day of the coming month. The governor thus asks the king for authorization, most likely because this festival implied an interruption in some urgent works at the Habur dam. The request of the *muškēnū* is reported in ARM 14, 12, rev. 3'-6': *muškēnū niqê*[*tiš*]*unu ša pagrā'i uštēršûma, umma šunuma niqêtuni ersête*: *warḫam erībam ūmam samnam nippeš*, "The commoners have prepared their sacrifices for the Ploughing-feast; they said : 'Our sacrifices are ready. We shall do it in the coming month, on the eighth day'". The Ploughing-feast appears as a festival of the *muškēnū* and, no doubt, of the country people in general. Its date was not fixed by the calendar, since they chose the eighth day of the coming month, but they needed an authorization. Unfortunately, the name of the month is not specified, but the approximate date of the festival was well known. A king's order issued by letter thus states that, in the given eventuality, "this gentleman should stay with you until the Ploughing-feast", *awīlum šû adi pagrā'i maḫrīka līšibma* (FlM 3, 138, rev. 5'-6'; cf. FlM 2, 55, 19-20 and 56, 19-20). At any rate, the festival had no link with the *kispu* ritual for dead kings, which never mentions the *pagrā'um*.

The *kispu* ritual was known in the Mari kingdom and, when a writer was referring to it, he used the appropriate term. This appears clearly from a letter sent to king Zimri-Lîm by Kibri-Dagān, governor of Terqa (ARM 3, 40, 7-23). He thus writes: "Besides, the day I sent this tablet of mine to my lord, [a pro]phet of Dagān came and addressed me as follows: 'The god sent [me]. Hurry, write to the ki[ng] that they are to perform the mortuary ritual for the sha[de] of Yaḫdun-Lîm', *kispī ana iṭemmim ša Iaḫdun-Lîm likrubû*. This is what this prophet said to me, and I have therefore written to my lord. Let my lord do what pleases him" (cf. ANET 624). It is worth-while stressing here the radical difference in the aim of the performed celebrations: *kispī* ***ana*** *iṭemmim* versus *pagrā'um* ***ana*** *Dagān* (ARMT 26, 233, 51).

In another letter, ARM 2, 90, 18-23, Kibri-Dagān transmits a further divine message to king Zimri-Lîm: "[The day I sent th]is tablet of mine [to] my lord, [... the prophet[9] o]f Dagān ad[dressed me] as follows: *aššum nīq* [*pagrā'i*] *epēšim Dagān išpu*[*ranni*], *ana bēlika šupurma: warḫam erībam ina ūmim erbēšerîm nīq pagrā'i linnepeš, mimma nīqam šetu lā ušeteqū*, 'Dagān se[nt me] concerning the performance of the sacrifice [of the Ploughing-feast]. Write to your lord that in the coming month, on the fourteenth day, the sacrifice of the Ploughing-feast is to be performed. On no account are they to omit this sacrifice'. This is what this man said to me. I now hereby write to my lord. May my lord do what in accordance with his deliberation pleases him" (cf. ANET 624).

Another case is probably referred to in ARM 2, 137, 43-46, where the writer records a grievance of Yašūb-Dagān, who complains that the useless presence of a 'mayor' (*ḫazannum*) hinders him from organizing sacrifices requested by the god Dagān: *Dagān neqêtim* [*ša pagrā'*]*i ītenerrišanni* [*u m*]*atima inūma ḫazannum ibaššû nadān neqêtim ul elê*, "Dagān keeps asking me offerings [for the Ploughing-feas]t, but I have never been able to give offerings when the 'mayor' is present".

[9] There are two possibilities: *muḫḫûm* or *āpilum* / *aplûm*.

These messages show that the authorities did not always agree to the celebration of the Ploughing-feast at a given date. Their refusal probably explains the mention of god's discontent in ARM 18, 38, 5-7, where the verb *nadānum* seems to be used in the sense of "permitting", a connotation occurring in several Mari letters (ARM 2, 37, 10; 2, 50, 11'; 3, 58, 15; etc.): *ilum aššum pagrêm nadānim īgumanni*, "the god is angry at me because of the matter of agreeing to the Ploughing-feast"[10]. Instead, the celebration of the *Pagrā'um* is taken into due account in the letter ARMT 26, 233. The writer of this letter to king Zimri-Lîm is Itūr-Asdu, known both as the governor of Nahur, on the upper Habur, and as an official at the court of Mari. It is in the latter capacity that he seems to have sent this message to the king, who must therefore have been absent from Mari (ANET 623). Hence the tablet has been brought back to Mari, as seems to have been done quite often. The letter reports the dream of a certain Malik-Dagān, a man from Shakka in the district of Sagaratum, who had got a revelation in the temple of Dagān at Terqa. He was not sent on to the king, because he was to "give a *Pagrā'um* for Dagān", *pagrâm ana Dagān inaddin* (ARMT 26, 233, 51-52), obviously a cultic celebration with sacrifices.

In another letter, Zakira-Ḫammu, governor of Qaṭṭunân, writes to the king to let him know that he intends to come to Mari for a sacrifice of the *Pagrā'um*: *aššum ana nīq pagrêm alākija*, "regarding my coming for the sacrifice of the Ploughing-feast" (ARMT 27, 59, 5-6). Instead, Asqudum is invited by king Zimri-Lîm to the sacrifice of *Pagrā'um* and to the sacrifice to Ištar: *ana nīq pagrā'i ša Dagān u nīqi ša Ištar qerêta* (ARMT 26, 25, 38-39), "You are invited to the sacrifice of the Ploughing-feast for Dagān and to the sacrifice for Ištar". This letter associates Ištar to Dagān because the feast of the goddess was celebrated in the beginning of month IX, while the Ploughing-feast in question was planned for the end of month VIII, as appears from ARM 26, 25, 4-7. Both celebrations are associated also in M 17009.

Another temporal connection of two celebrations appears in FlM 7, 45, 3-4, where more deities are mentioned. This letter was sent by the ambassadors of Mari in Aleppo, where they have assisted in the palace at a ritual in memory of Sumu-epuḫ, the deceased founder of the dynasty.

[10] The passage could also be understood in a different way, assuming that *pa-ag-ri-im* is the genitive of *pagrum*, "body". The text should then be translated as follows: "the god is angry at me because of the matter of giving a carcase", obviously to a temple for a festival.

The text distinguishes this ceremony, performed in the inner circle of the family, from the Ploughing-feast, celebrated by commoners outside the palace. A correct translation of the passage reads as follows: "At the time of the Ploughing-feast of Dagān, Šalaš, and Hepat, we were sitting in the palace at the great lamentation for Sumu-epuḫ, and Hammurapi has arranged the meal in front of the gods", [*inū*]*ma pagrā'im* (*pa-ag-ri-a-im*) *ša Dagān, Šalaš u Ḫepat ina ekallim* [*a*]*na i*[*d*]*irtim rabîtim ša Sumu-epuḫ wašbānu u Ḫammurapi naptanam maḫar ilāni iškun*.

The mention of the two goddesses can be explained easily. Šalaš was the Palaeo-Syrian paredra of Dagān, already mentioned at Ebla, while Aleppo was a major centre of the cult of Hepat. However, like e.g. in KUB 27, 13, Hepat should have been mentioned with Addu / Tešub of Aleppo in relation to the ceremony performed inside the palace in memory of Sumu-epuḫ. The letter thus seems to syncopate the mentions of the deities involved in the two events, recorded only in order to situate the provided information in a broader context.

The palace could nevertheless participate in the popular festival by giving some offerings. Administrative texts thus record *2* GÚ *7* MA.NA *lipî ša pagrā'ia*, "two talents and seven minas of tallow for the Ploughing-feast" (ARM 21, 147, 4-5), to be used obviously for the preparation of the food at the party. Also chosen cuts of meat were given, thus *1 malakum ša alpi ša pagrā'i* (ARM 21, 62, 1 and 4; 21, 76, 1-2), "one beef thigh for the Ploughing-feast", with an eventual total: *napḫar 1 alpum 8 malakū ša alpim ša pagrā'i* (ARM 21, 62, 43), "Total: one beef and eight beef thighs for the Ploughing-feast". Occasionally, a limited financial help was provided, thus one shekel of silver as *ikribātim ša ekallim inūma pagrā'i* (ARMT 23, 561, 15-16), "votive offerings of the palace at the time of the Ploughing-feast". Wealthy people could offer three sheep, and even more, at the occasion of the Ploughing-feast of Dagān (FlM 7, 51, 19-25).

An important text confirming the meaning of *pagrā'um* is a letter of Dam-ḫurāṣim, possibly a secondary wife of king Zimri-Lîm. She was sending letters to him from Terqa, expressing wishes for his victory and using various formulas, for instance: "may Dagān, the lord of Terqa, hand over your enemies and your foes to you" (ARM 10, 62, 9-12) or "may Dagān, the Master of Ploughing, and Itūr-Mēr, the king of Mari, hand over your enemies and your foes to you", *Dagān bēl pagrê u Itūr-Mēr šar Mari ajābīka u nakrīka ana qātika limallû* (ARM 10, 63, 15-19). She did certainly not call on "Dagān, the lord of the carcases" or "corpses", but used a major epithet of the deity. Since Dagān was the main god of agriculture, the basic living source of the Mari population, this epithet was obviously referring to this paramount quality of the god: "the Master of Ploughing".

Bibliography

AISTLEITNER, J. 1963: *Wörterbuch der ugaritischen Sprache* (Berichte über die Verhandlungen der Sächsichen Akademie der Wissenschaften zu Leipzig. Phil.-hist. Kl. 106/3), Berlin (1965²)

BODI, D. 1991: "Les expressions *pigrê malkêhœm* dans Ez 43, 7b. 9 et *pigrê gillûlêkœm* dans Lev 26, 30 à la lumière des termes akkadiens *pagrû*(*m*) et *maliku*(*m*) des textes de Mari", in Th. Römer (ed.), *Lectio difficilior probabilior? L'exégèse comme expérience de décloisonnement. Festschrift F. Smyth-Florentin* (Dielheimer Blätter zum Alten Testament 12), Dielheim, 87-101.

DE VAUX, R. 1960: *Les institutions de l'Ancien Testament* II, Paris.

DURAND, J.-M. 2008: "La religion amorrite en Syrie à l'époque des archives de Mari", in G. del Olmo Lete (ed.), *Mythologie et religion des Sémites occidentaux I. Ebla, Mari* (OLA 162), Leuven, 161-722.

LAESSØE, J. 1955: *Studies on the Assyrian Ritual and Series bît rimki*, Copenhagen.

LANE, E.W. 1863-93: *An Arabic-English Lexicon*, London.

LIPIŃSKI, E. 1973: "*SKN* et *SGN* dans le sémitique occidental du Nord", in *Ugarit-Forschungen* 5, 191-207.

NEIMAN, D. 1948: "*PGR*: a Canaanite Cult-Object in the Old Testament", in *Journal of Biblical Literature* 67, 55-60.

PODANY, A.H. 2002: *The Land of Hana*, Bethesda.

SEUX, M.-J. 1976: *Hymnes et prières aux dieux de Babylonie et d'Assyrie* (LAPO 8), Paris.

VINK, J.G. 1962: *Leviticus* (De Boeken van het Oude Testament II/1), Roermond-Maaseik.

ZIMMERLI, W. 1969: *Ezechiel* II. *Ezechiel 25-48* (Biblischer Kommentar. Altes Testament 13/2), Neukirchen-Vluyn.

MIDDLE BRONZE AGE RITUAL, SUBSISTENCE AND ENVIRONMENT AT TELL TWEINI INFERRED FROM BIOARCHAEOLOGICAL EVIDENCE

Elena MARINOVA[1], Veerle LINSEELE[1&3],
Patricia VANDORPE[2], Jan VAN DER VALK[3]

[1] KU Leuven
[2] Universität Basel
[3] Royal Belgian Institute of Natural Sciences, Brussels

Introduction

Bioarchaeological studies from funerary contexts provide important evidence on the rituals in the past and, related with this, on plant and animal products as part of festivities or offerings. The current study focuses on plant and animal remains recovered from Middle Bronze Age tombs at Tell Tweini and will discuss the question whether these bioarchaeological finds represent the remains of funerary rites. To fit them in the larger framework of the Middle Bronze Age environment and subsistence at that time, they will be compared with remains from settlement layers dated to the same period. Already several zooarchaeological analyses of such contexts are published for the Bronze Age of the Levant (e.g., Horwitz 2001, Vila 2004, Genz et al. 2010), while studies of archaeobotanical remains dealing with Bronze Age graves from the region are exceptional only (Genz et al. 2010, 200). Thus the current paper will for the first time emphasize information on the plants and their products involved in funerary rituals. A further innovative aspect of this study is the combination of both botanical and zoological data and the attempt to integrate the two lines of evidence.

Tell Tweini and its Middle Bronze Age burials

Tell Tweini is situated in the fertile Syrian coast plain, about 30 km south of the modern port of Lattakia (Fig. 1). Its main occupation dates between the Middle Bronze Age and the Iron Age (2600-550 BC) (see Bretschneider and Van Lerberghe 2008, 3-4). Two rivers run around the tell, one of which, the Rumailah, was navigable as recently as the early part of the 20th century.

Precipitation is, due to its regional and seasonal diversity and inter-annual fluctuations in its amount, the most important climatic factor in Syria (Wilkinson 2004). Most of Syria's Early and Middle Bronze Age sites lie in an area of 200 to 400 mm of modern mean annual precipitation, while mean annual precipitation at Tell Tweini could have been as much as 600-1000 mm (Wirth 1971, 31). Rain-fed agriculture should therefore have been easily possible near the site, even without serious losses in drought years. The natural vegetation in the study area belongs to the Mediterranean plant-geographical zone (Zhohary 1973, 73-79), which has today mostly degraded to cultivated areas, pasture land or maquis shrublands.

Based on cuneiform tablets from ancient Ugarit, modern Tell Tweini is most probably to be identified with the ancient city of Gibala, which must have been of considerable importance as it was in contact with great Bronze Age centers in the Levant and its coastal areas (van Soldt 1997, 703-744). Moreover interregional contacts with Egypt, Cyprus and the Hittite Empire are attested by the archaeological evidence. The presence at Tell Tweini of typical 'Middle Minoan II' ceramics, also called 'Kamares ware' underlines the commercial relations between the Aegean and the Levant during this period (Bretschneider and Van Lerberghe 2008, 20). The emergence of a series of small states during the Middle Bronze Age helped to develop complex commercial relations, and the royal houses of the new dynasties participated intensively (Akkermans and Schwartz 2003, 46-47).

Since excavations started in 1999, eleven burials from both the Bronze and Iron Ages have been unearthed in Field A. The majority, namely nine, can be dated to the Middle Bronze Age, mainly Middle Bronze Age II, and give a good insight on the burial customs of the period (Hameeuw and Jans 2008, 72-76).

Materials and Methods

Archaeobotany

The botanical dataset comprises 17 samples from different Middle Bronze Age contexts (see Tab. 1): floors, ovens, general cultural layers and installations, also from different types of contexts within the graves — like grave layers and jar contents. The plant materials were extracted from the sediment by machine floatation and identified using a stereo-microscope (magnification 6-50x) and modern reference collections. For identification also illustrated atlases (Cappers et al. 2006, Cappers et al. 2009), identification guides (Nesbitt 2006) and further publications (van Zeist and Bakker-Heeres 1982) were used. Apart from the absolute number of plant remains (Tab. 1) in each samples (#r) also density (#r/L), taxon richness (#t) and diversity (#t/#r) were calculated to give a general idea of the preservation and character of the archaeobotanical assemblages. The percentage of all samples in which a certain taxon is found, also called ubiquity, was calculated too in order to estimate the relative importance of the plant taxa. Further, the proportions of the most important plant remains, grouped by their economic or ecological importance, are calculated for the different types of studied contexts (Fig. 3). This was done in order to recognize differences in the function/origin of the plant remains deposited in burial and not burial contexts.

Archaeozoology

During excavations in Field A at Tell Tweini faunal remains have been systematically collected by hand. In addition, faunal remains were also retrieved from the floats and heavy fractions of sediments processed with the floatation machine (see above). No distinction will be made here between the different sample types obtained through floatation, nor is the volume of processed sediment they represent considered. They will only be used as an indication for what kind of animals are missed when sampling is limited to hand collection. As explained for the archaeobotanical remains, also the fauna was retrieved from different types of contexts. Faunal remains were studied on site during several field stays and with the permission of the Syrian Antiquities Service a selection of remains was exported to Belgium for analyses with appropriate reference collections. Tab. 2 and 3 summarize the number of identified specimens (NISP) per taxon, date and type of locus, with a distinction between hand collected (n=2452) and floated material (n=867). Vertebrate animals that probably did not end up at the site intentionally through human actions have been omitted. These intrusive faunal remains include more specifically turtles, various small birds and micromammals. Also shells have not been put in the summarizing table. Most of them are probably not anthropogenic either. Details on the fauna of the grave contexts are given in Tab. 4, including skeletal elements, fusion data of long bones, measurements, size estimates, etc.

Results

Description of the finds

Plant remains

The archaeobotanical assemblages are generally dominated by cultivated plants like wheat, pulses and especially fruits, namely grape and olive. The high amounts and abundance of grape and olive remains indicate clearly that they were of great importance for the plant economy of the site. Together with the remains of cultivated plants also a variety of wild growing plants, originating from wet environments, open habitats etc. was recorded (Tab. 1 and Fig. 3).

The inventory of cultivated plants found in the grave contexts does not differ qualitatively from that found in general cultural layers or oven contexts (see Tab. 1). However, the main emphasis of the samples from burial contexts is on fruits and pulses (Fig. 3). Further, in the grave jar samples wild growing plants are almost missing apart from a few common weeds like *Lolium* sp. and *Phalaris* sp. The latter two usually occur in crops that have already been cleaned, due to their adaptation strategy as weeds, passing through the sieves during crop processing together with the cereal crops. In grave jar from locus TWE-A-01070, also a concentration of the pulse crop bitter vetch (*Vicia ervilia*) was found, comprising of ca. 800 ml pure bitter vetch seeds. This sample is not given in Tab. 1 as it was processed without floatation and studied directly.

Animals

It is clear from Tab. 2 that floor levels contain only few faunal remains. Although floors are more reliable contexts than fill layers, chances to recover bone remains from them are usually low, as people normally kept those clean during habitation. For the fill layers the fauna has been grouped in Tab. 2 according to the date that was attributed to them. The groups discerned show differences in faunal composition, but we think they are artifacts of small sample size. All material from layers will therefore be discussed together. In general, the Middle Bronze Age fauna from Tweini shows many similarities with that of the Late Bronze and the Iron Age, although there are some diachronic trends (Linseele 2008).

As indicated earlier, shells have not been included in Tab. 2 and 3 and they will not be discussed in detail here. However, it is probably relevant to mention that shells are very common and represented by many different species, marine, freshwater as well as terrestrial. In general, there are very few indications that they were used by the site's inhabitants in some way. Tab. 3 shows that floatation has been mainly useful to collect fish remains that are otherwise overlooked. The lack of systematic sieving therefore results in an underrepresentation of fish and their economic importance must have been higher than can be judged from the number of identified specimens. Nevertheless, it is probably safe to say that fish consumption was much less important than meat consumption. This is true for all periods at Tweini, but is especially marked for the Middle Bronze Age. Marine, mainly coastal or estuarine, as well as freshwater fish is present. The latter includes Nile perch (*Lates niloticus*) that most have been brought to the site from Egypt in some way (Linseele et al. accepted). Trade in Egyptian fish is also evidenced at other, contemporary sites in the area (Van Neer et al. 2004, 107-109). The importance of Nile perch at Tweini shows an increasing trend through time (Linseele et al. accepted).

In general, hunted animals are rare in the faunal assemblages from Tweini. The species evidenced for the Middle Bronze Age are hare, red fox, fallow deer and boar, which are animals mainly from forested areas. In the later material also animals from steppe environments were identified, and it is possible that their absence in the Middle Bronze Age layers is not more than a consequence of smaller sample size. Domestic animals represent the bulk of the Middle Bronze Age fauna. Cattle and ovicaprines are most common. They occur in a ratio of about 2:1. Sheep is prevailing over goat. Domestic pig seems to be missing completely at Tell Tweini, as most measurable bones fall clearly within the size range of wild boar (cf. Payne and Bull 1988, 27-66). It seems thus that the animals that are found in the graves, are the species that were economically most important. Apart from cattle, sheep and goat, domestic dogs and probably also domestic equids are represented in the fauna from settlement contexts at Tell Tweini.

Discussion

Sources of plant and animal remains in the archaeological deposits

Most of the plant and faunal assemblages come from archaeological contexts, which were accumulated over a longer time period. They represent mixed assemblages coming from different paleo-economic activities, typically from waste disposal. The plant macrofossils in most cases are interpreted as residual from fuel of domestic hearths. The relatively high proportion of small seeds of grasses and leguminous crops is considered as an indication for dung fuel (Miller 1984, 77). The remains of grape and olive also should be considered as by-products of their processing, which subsequently were used as fuel and in that way had the chance to become charred (Marinova et al. 2011, 474).

Plants and animals in ritual contexts

The plant remains which could be considered as unambiguously belonging to the burial ritual is the pure concentration of pulses found in Middle Bronze Age II grave from locus TWE-A-01070. Similarly in the floatation samples from grave jar locus TWE-A-1085 and from grave layer TWE-A-169, both from the same occupation phase, concentrations of pulses were found. The occurrence in concentrations can be considered as proof for the fact that these plant remains were put intentionally in the graves. Another group of plant remains found in the graves are the fruit remains. Three of the samples coming from grave jars are dominated by fruits such as grape, fig and olive (Tab. 1). Those comprise over 50% of all of the charred plant remains found. Several of the samples collected out of burial contexts also contain higher amounts of grape seeds and olive fruit stone fragments. Thus these remains could originate from the general "background noise" sensu Bakels (1991, 284) of plant remains preserved in the cultural layers. The remains of olive and grape could come from corresponding vine and oil pressing residues used for fuel (Neef 1990, 297-300). Also the rather high concentration of such remains in the samples from ovens speaks for this interpretation (Tab. 1). The study of plant remains from Middle Bronze Age burial contexts from Tell Fadus (Genz et al. 2010, 200) also shows few archaeobotanical remains for which it was not clear whether they belonged to the burial ritual or those charred plants were deposited in the cultural layer through the settlement waste. Nevertheless apart from olive and grape remains also charred fig remains are very typical for the grave layers and those are much less present in the other studied contexts. Moreover, concentrations of grape are typical for the grave jars and there, in contrast to the other samples, very few wild plants are found, so that this grape concentration could also have been intentionally placed in the burial. Thus it is not excluded that fruits like fig and grape were part of the burial ritual and became mixed with other plant remains from the cultural layers. Further studies of carefully collected plant remains from graves are needed to understand better the role of such plants in the burial rituals.

Only few faunal remains have been recovered from the Middle Bronze Age graves at Tell Tweini — several yielded no fauna at all (Tab. 2) — compared to contemporary examples in more southern parts of the Levant (Horwitz 2001, Vila 2004). From the hand collected material only cattle, sheep and goat have been identified, with a clear predominance of the latter two and more particularly of sheep. The animal remains were usually found mixed with the human remains, although in one case (TWE-A-00934) a skull of a sheep or goat was found placed over the feet of the deceased [1] In general, various parts of the animals seem to have been included in the burials and sometimes (e.g., TWE-A-00934) several bones of the same individual were present. However, complete animals are missing. We agree with Vila (2004) that incomplete animals represent probably waste of sacrificed animals of which parts were put in the graves as food offerings for the dead, while the other parts were consumed elsewhere. Nevertheless, butchery marks have not been observed on any of the animal remains from burials at Tell Tweini. One unidentified bone fragment is worked. Among the samples processed with the floatation installation, fish bones were also present. Because of their low numbers and small sizes, we assume that they were not put in the tombs intentionally, although it has been shown that (complete) fish were being offered in Middle Bronze Age contexts in the Levant (Van Neer 2006, 86-95). Vila (2004, 172-174) observed at Sidon that mainly constructed graves contained animal remains, but there are too few such tombs from Tell Tweini to confirm this trend here, nor do we have sufficient data to make comparisons between grave types or between MBAI and MBAII tombs.

Subsistence at Tell Tweini during the Middle Bronze Age

The plant economy was based on annual crops like barley, wheat and several leguminous crops. Together with them several fruits especially grapes, olive and fig were of importance. Those general trends fit well with the tendencies observed for Middle Bronze Age agriculture in the region (Riehl 2009, 109-111). The faunal assemblages are largely dominated by domestics, mainly ovicaprines. The consumption of game and

[1] This skull could only be studied based on photographical material, but it is clear from Fig. 2 that an earlier preliminary identification as cow/oxen is incorrect (Hameeuw and Jans 2008, 76 and Figure I11.6.).

fish, among which Nile perch imported from Egypt, was limited. Despite of some small diachronic changes, this type of subsistence economy dominated by domestics, and especially ovicaprines, persisted into the Late Bronze Age and Iron Age, and seems to have been relatively similar over the whole of the Levantine coast (Chahoud and Vila, in press).

Environment of the site and its exploitation by the Middle Bronze Age inhabitants

The archaeobotanical evidence indicates only indirectly the environments in the surrounding of Tell Tweini and mainly those which were economically exploited. The main part of the non-cultivated plants found originates from the weed flora accompanying the fields. Besides them also evidence of open grasslands and fresh meadow to wetland habitats is visible. Most of the evidence for these plants originates from seeds, which passed through the digestion of the cattle and ovicaprines and were charred as components of the dung fuel used at the site, indicating which kind of divers habitats existed around the site during the Middle Bronze Age, like open grassland and open stony places, meadows, wetlands, etc.

The wild fauna is not very suited for local environmental reconstructions as there are indications that they were brought in from larger distances. The species present in the Middle Bronze contexts indicate the exploitation of forested areas, while in later periods also steppe animals are present. The exploitation of local aquatic resources seems to have been limited despite of the proximity of the sea and two rivers. Although cattle are relatively common at Tell Tweini in comparison with Late Bronze Age sites in the Levant for example (Chahoud and Vila in press), the predominance of ovicaprines over cattle in the herds may point to a lack of sufficient good grazing areas in the surroundings of Tell Tweini. However, cultural factors, such as the urban nature of the site, may also have determined herd composition.

Conclusions

The bioarchaeological remains found in the Middle Bronze Age graves of Tell Tweini graves should mainly be considered as food offerings. The clearest evidences for offerings are represented by finds like the sheep/goat skull near the feet of the deceased and the concentration of bitter vetch seeds accompanying a jar burial.

Leguminous crops and fruits of fig, grape and olive are the main components of the archaeobotanical finds in the graves at Tell Tweini, which reflects their importance for the subsistence of the site. Similarly, the archaeozoological finds are dominated by cattle, sheep and goat, the economically most important animals at Tweini. Thus the current study shows that the dead were offered the same food as eaten by the living.

Acknowledgements

This contribution is dedicated to Prof. Dr. Karel Van Lerberghe on the occasion of his 65th birthday. With this article, the authors would like to express their gratitude to him for inspiring and encouraging them for the research of ancient Gibala.

The authors would like to thank the directors of the excavation for the opportunity to study the material from Tell Tweini, the excavation team for providing the background information and Klaas Vansteenhuyse for valuable help on the dating of the loci of Tell Tweini. The field research would not have been possible without the funding of the Research Foundation Flanders (FWO), the Interuniversity Attraction Poles 6/34 and the *Onderzoeksteelagen* KU Leuven.

Bibliography

AKKERMANS, M. M. G. and G. M. SCHWARTZ 2003: *The Archaeology of Syria, From Complex Hunter-Gatherers to Early Urban Societies (ca. 16,000-300BC),* Cambridge.

BAKELS, C. C. 1991: “Tracing Crop Processing in the Bandkeramik Culture”, in J. Renfrew (ed.) *New Light on Early Farming. Recent Developments in Palaeoethnobotany*, Edinburgh, 281-288.

BRETSCHNEIDER, J. and K. VAN LERBERGHE 2008: *In Search of Gibala. An Archaeological and Historical Study Based on Eight Seasons of Excavations at Tell Tweini (Syria) in the A and C fields (1999-2007)* (Aula Orientalis-Supplementa 24), Barcelona.

CAPPERS, R. T. J., R. M. BEKKER and J. E. A. JANS 2006: *Digitale Zadenatlas van Nederland*, Groningen.

CAPPERS, R. T. J. R. NEEF and R. M. BEKKER 2009: *Digital Atlas of Economic Plants*, Eelde / Groningen.

CHAHOUD J. and E. VILA in press: “Faunal Exploitation in Rash Shamra “Maison aux Albâtres” during the Late Bronze Age — Northern Levant”, in M. Mashkour and M. Beech (eds.), *Archaeozoology of the Near East IX*.

GENZ, H., S. El-ZAATARI, C. ÇAKIRLAR, K. BADRESHANY and S. RIEHL 2010: “A Middle Bronze Age Burial from Tell Fadous-Kfarabida, Lebanon”, *Ägypten und Levante* 20, 184-205.

HAMEEUW, H. and G. JANS 2008: "Burial Customs at Tell Tweini – Field A" in J. Bretschneider and K. Van Lerberghe (eds.) In *Search of Gibala, An Archaeological and Historical Study Based on Eight Seasons of Excavations at Tel Tweini (Syria) in the A and C fields (1999-2007)* (Aula Orientalis-Supplementa 24), Barcelona, 75-86.

HORWITZ, L. K. 2001: "Animal Offerings in the Middle Bronze Age: Food for the Gods, Food for Thought", *Palestine Exploration Quarterly* 133, 78-90.

LINSEELE, V. 2008: "Faunal Remains from Tell Tweini. A First Report", in J. Bretschneider and K. Van Lerberghe (eds.) In *Search of Gibala, An Archaeological and Historical Study Based on Eight Seasons of Excavations at Tel Tweini (Syria) in the A and C fields (1999-2007)* (Aula Orientalis-Supplementa 24), Barcelona, 143-149.

LINSEELE, V., W. VAN NEER and J. BRETSCHNEIDER accepted: "The Mysteries of Egyptian Nile perch (*Lates niloticus*). The Case of Tell Tweini (Syria, Middle Bronze Age-Iron Age)" in B. De Cupere, V. Linseele and S. Hamilton-Dyer, *Archaeozoology of the Near East* X, Leuven.

MARINOVA, E., J. M. A. VAN DER VALK, S.-M. VALAMOTI and J. BRETSCHNEIDER 2011: "Experimental Approach for Tracing Olive Processing Residues in the Archaeobotanical Record with Preliminary Examples from Tell Tweini, Syria", *Vegetation History and Archaeobotany* 20, 471-478.

MILLER, N. 1984: "The Use of Dung as Fuel: An Ethnographic Example and an Archaeological Application", *Paléorient* 10, 71-79.

NEEF, R. 1990: "Introduction, Development and Environmental Implications of Olive Culture: the Evidence from Jordan", in: S. Bottema, G. Entjes-Nieborg and W. van Zeist (eds.) *Man's Role in the Shaping of the Eastern Mediterranean Landscape*, Rotterdam, 295-306.

NESBITT, M. 2006: *Identification Guide for Near Eastern Grass Seeds*, London.

PAYNE, S. and G. BULL 1988: "Components of Variation in Measurements of Pig Bones and Teeth and the Use of Measurements to Distinguish Wild from Domestic Pig Remains", *Archaeozoologia* 2, 27-66.

RIEHL, S. 2009: "Archaeobotanical Evidence for the Interrelationship of Agricultural Decision-making and Climate Change in the Ancient Near East", *Quaternary International* 197 (1-2), 93-114.

VAN NEER, W. 2006: "Bronze Age Fish Remains from Sidon", *Archaeology & History in the Lebanon* 24, 86-95.

VAN NEER, W., O. LERNAU, R. FRIEDMAN, G. MUMFORD, J. POBLOME and M. WAELKENS 2004: "Fish Remains from Archaeological Sites as Indicators of Former Trade Connections in the Eastern Mediterranean", *Paléorient* 30, 101-148.

VAN SOLDT, W. 1997: "Studies in the Topography of Ugarit (2), The Borders of Ugarit", *Ugarit Forschungen* 30, 703-744.

VAN ZEIST, W. and J. A. H. BAKKER-HEERES 1982: "Archaeobotanical Studies in the Levant 1, 2, 3 & 4", *Palaeohistoria* 24, 26, 27, 151-170, 247-315.

VILA, E. 2004: "Survey of the Remains of Mammals Recovered in the Middle Bronze Age Burials at Sidon (Lebanon) in 2001", *Levant* 36, 167-180.

VON DEN DRIESCH, A. 1976: *A Guide to the Measurement of Animal Bones from Archaeological Sites*, Harvard.

WILKINSON, T. J. 2004: "*On the Margin of the Euphrates. Settlement and Land Use at Tell es-Sweyhat and the Upper Lake Assad Area. Syria Excavations at Tell es-Sweyhat, Syria*", Oriental Institute 1, Chicago.
WIRTH, E. 1971: *Syrien: Eine Geographische Landeskunde*, Mainz.
ZOHARY, M. 1973: *Geobotanical Foundations of the Middle East*, vol 1, Stuttgart.

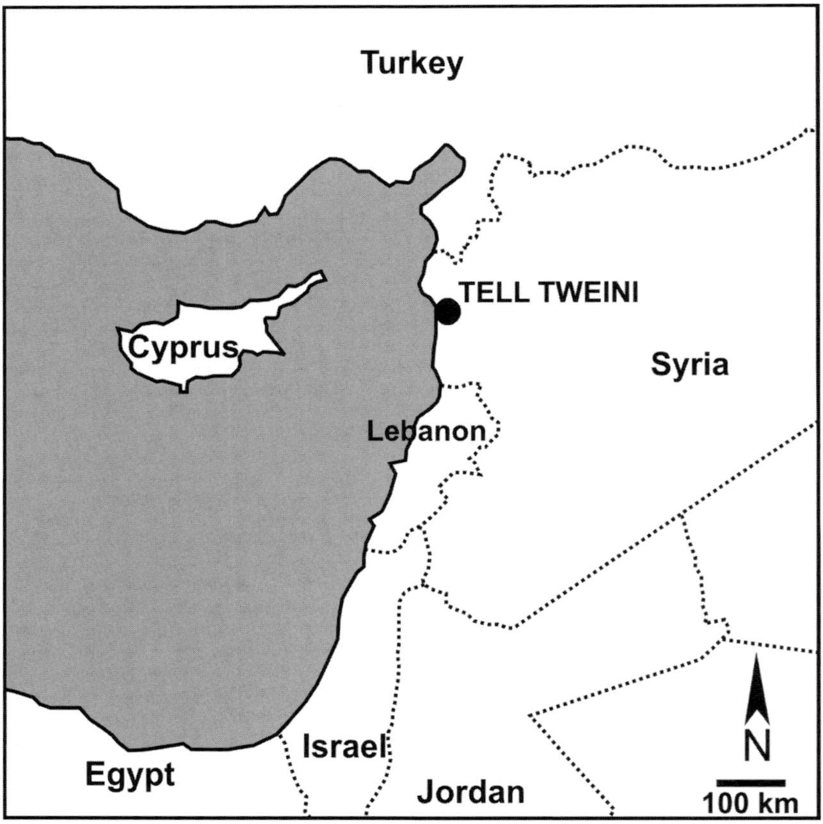

Fig. 1. Map of the study area and site.

Fig. 2. Picture of grave TWE-A-00934 with sheep/goat skull over the feet of the deceased (after Hameeuw and Jans 2008).

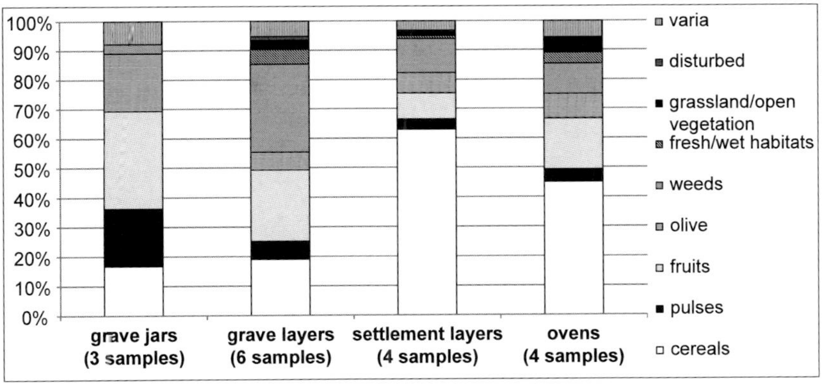

Fig. 3. Percentage proportions of the main groups of plant macrofossils from different Middle Bronze Age contexts.

Phase				MBA II	MBA II	MBA II	MBA II
Context type				gJ	gJ	gJ	gL
Locus n°				1070	1085	2542	166
Soil sample volume (L)				15	9	16	12
Year sampled				2007	2004	2005	2004
Absolute count remains (#r)		Total	2761	136	54	55	34
Density of remains (#r/L)		Avg.	6,8	9,1	6,0	3,4	2,8
Taxon richness (#t)		Avg.	16	10	7	9	11
Taxon diversity (#t/#r)		Avg.	0,16	0,07	0,13	0,16	0,32
Botanical name	**Common name**	**Part**	**Pres.**				
Cereal crops							
Hordeum distichon/vulgare	Pearl barley/Barley	Se/Fr	ch			2	
Hordeum distichon/vulgare	Pearl barley/Barley	Rachis	ch				1
Hordeum distichon/vulgare	Pearl barley/hulled Barley	Se/Fr	ch	2	1		
Triticum aestivum s.l./durum	Common wheat	Se/Fr	ch				
Triticum dicoccum	Emmer wheat	Se/Fr	ch		2	1	
Triticum dicoccum	Emmer wheat	HSB	ch				2
Triticum sp.	Wheat	Se/Fr	ch	5			
Cerealia indet.	cultivated cereals	Se/Fr	ch	12	12	4	2
Cerealia indet.	cultivated cereals	HSB	ch				
Cerealia indet.	cultivated cereals	Hano	ch				
Pulses							
Cicer arietinum	Chickpea	Se/Fr	ch				
Lathyrus sativus/cicera	Grass pea/Red pea	Se/Fr	ch			1	
Lens culinaris	Lentil	Se/Fr	ch	4		1	2
Vicia ervilia	Bitter vetch	Se/Fr	ch	41	28		
Vicia faba	Horse bean	Se/Fr	ch				
Fabaceae (cultivated) indet.	cultivated pulses	Se/Fr	ch	25			
Fruits							
Ficus carica	Common fig	Se/Fr	ch				6
Ficus carica	Common fig	Se/Fr	mi				
Pyrus sp.	Pear	Se/Fr	ch				
Vitis vinifera	Grape	Se/Fr	ch	38	18	16	
Vitis vinifera	Grape	Se/Fr	mi			9	
Vitis vinifera	Grape	Frfl	ch				
Vitis vinifera	Grape	Sti	ch				
Oil and fibre annual crops							
Olea europaea	Olive	Se/Fr	ch	17	16	15	5
Olea europaea	Olive	Em	ch				
Linum usitatissimum	Common flax	Se/Fr	ch				
Potential weeds				3	3	2	5
Fresh and wet habitats							5
Grasslands/Open vegetation							3
Disturbed habitats/Open vegeation							
Varia				13	2	4	3
Absolute count of remains (#r)				160	82	55	34

Table 1. Archaeobotanical samples from the Middle Bronze Age
(gJ — grave jar, gL — grave layer, L — settlement layer, O — oven, MB — Middle Bronze Age).

MBA II	MBA I	MBA I	MBA II	MBA II	MBA II	MBA I	MBA I	MBA	MBA	MBA		
gL	gL	gL	L	L	O	O	L	O	O	L		
178	179	2357	167	1628	2141	959	2537	863	864	866		
25	15	10	29	12	20	37	15	18	26	31		
2004	2004	2005	2004	2004	2004	2004	2005	2004	2004	2004		
167	64	68	67	37	61	768	290	194	128	91		
6,7	4,3	6,8	2,3	3,1	3,1	20,8	19,3	10,8	4,9	2,9		
20	16	13	12	9	18	31	9	21	17	20		
0,12	0,25	0,19	0,18	0,24	0,30	0,04	0,03	0,11	0,13	0,22		
											#r	Ubiquity (%)
					2	98		2	1		105	29
						1					2	12
						102				1	106	24
								3			3	6
2			9	3		6	174	8			217	53
1		1	5	1		1	4				16	47
11		2	7	5		51	46	5	9	14	173	71
27	5	7	6	2		187	23	17	17	4	400	94
						2					2	6
						3					3	6
											1	6
	1					6					13	29
				4	5	8		3			47	53
2			4	3		6				2	43	47
								3	1	1	5	18
1		2	2		3	9		4	1	1	59	65
13	16		7			18			1	3	143	53
						2			1	1	4	18
						1		1		1	3	18
	1	6	8	3	4	34		85	34	15	345	82
		9	1	2	2				1		24	35
						2					2	6
								4	8	2	14	18
	9	14	9	8		60	5	17	18	12	229	88
						1					1	6
						3					3	6
81	20	20	6	2	15	83	30	11	10	18	448	100
10	4				16	21	4	6		1	92	59
5	4			2	11	35	1	6	3	3	88	70
2	1	2	1			2	1	2	1	1	19	59
12	3	5	2	2	3	24	1	17	22	11	148	100
167	64	58	67	37	61	766	289	194	128	91	162	

Phase	MBA II	MBA II	MBA II (-EBA)	MBA II	MBA I	MBA II	MBA II	MBA II	MBA II	MBA	MBA?	MBA II	MBA II	MBA II	MBA I	MBA
Context type	Tomb with jar burial	Earth burial (collective)	Earth burial (collective)-floor tomb	Earth burial	Structural tomb	Tomb with jar burial	Tomb with jar burial	Tomb with jar burial	Tomb with jar burial	Earth burial	Earth burial	Floor	Floor	Layer	Layer	Layer
Loci	51	177	178	934	954	1070	1085	2542	2543	2544	2545	197	919	All MBA II	All MBA I	All MBA
Groupers etc. (Serranidae)	–	–	–	–	–	–	–	–	–	–	–	–	–	–	2	–
Gilthead see bream (*Sparus aurata*)	–	–	–	–	–	–	–	–	–	–	–	–	–	1	–	–
Breams etc. (Sparidae)	–	–	–	–	–	–	–	–	–	–	–	–	–	–	–	1
Mullet (Mugilidae)	–	–	–	–	–	–	–	–	–	–	–	–	–	–	–	1
Nile perch (*Lates niloticus*)	–	–	–	–	–	–	–	–	–	–	–	–	–	1	1	1
Unidentified fish	–	–	–	–	–	–	–	–	–	–	–	–	–	2	1	1
Fox (*Vulpes vulpes*)	–	–	–	–	–	–	–	–	–	–	–	–	–	2	–	–
Wild boar (*Sus scrofa*)	–	–	–	–	–	–	–	–	–	–	–	–	–	5	1	–
Fallow deer (*Dama mesopotamica*)	–	–	–	–	–	–	–	–	–	–	–	–	–	3	2	2
Dog (*Canis lupus* f. familiaris)	–	–	–	–	–	–	–	–	–	–	–	–	–	3	2	1
Sheep (*Ovis orientalis* f. aries)	3	–	2	3		–	–	–	–	–	–	1	1	26	8	4
Goat (*Capa aegagrus* f. hircus)	–	–	–	1	–	–	–	–	–	–	–	–	–	14	8	4
Sheep or goat	8	–	5	2	3	–	5	–	–	–	–	3	–	226	148	36
Cattle (*Bos primigenius* f. taurus)	–	–	–	–	2	1	–	–	–	–	–	–	2	93	93	43
Equid	–	–	–	–	–	–	–	–	–	–	–	–	–	1	8	4
Unidentified mammals	30	–	25	16	9	–	3	–	–	–	–	1	–	749	549	280
Total	**41**	**0**	**32**	**21**	**14**	**1**	**8**	**0**	**0**	**0**	**0**	**5**	**3**	**1126**	**823**	**378**

Table 2. Animal remains in the handpicked samples (NISP) from different Middle Bronze Age contexts. With one exception all graves are

Phase	MBA II	MBA II	MBA II (-EBA)	MBA II	MBA II	MBA II	MBA II	MBA I	MBA I	MBA
Context type	Tomb with jar burial	Earth burial (collective)	Earth burial (collective)-floor tomb	Tomb with jar burial	Tomb with jar burial	Tomb with jar burial	Layer	Layer	Installation	Layer
Loci	51	177	178	1070	1085	2542	All MBA II	All MBA I	2547	All MBA
Herrings etc. (Clupeidae)	–	–	–	–	1	–	2	–	1	–
Groupers etc. (Serranidae)	–	–	–	–	–	–	1	–	–	–
Jacks and pompanos (Carangidae)	–	–	–	–	–	–	1	–	1	–
cf. Carangidae	–	–	–	–	–	–	–	1	–	–
Parrotfish (Scaridae)	–	–	–	–	–	–	1	–	–	–
Mullet (Mugilidae)	–	–	1	–	–	–	1	–	–	–
Cyprinidae	–	–	–	–	–	–	–	–	2	1
Eel (*Anguilla anguilla*)	–	–	–	1	–	–	–	–	–	–
Unidentified fish	4	–	10	–	4	–	20	1	9	1
Hare (*Lepus europaeus*)	–	–	–	–	–	–	–	–	–	1
Sheep or goat	2	–	–	–	–	–	15	–	–	–
Unidentified mammals	102	52	165	4	–	82	268	31	–	81
Total	**108**	**52**	**176**	**5**	**5**	**82**	**309**	**33**	**13**	**84**

Table 3. Animal remains retrieved from sieved samples and the heavy fraction of floatation samples (NISP) from different Middle Bronze Age contexts.

Locus	Species	Element	Fusion data	n	Measurements/ren
51	Sheep	talus		1	GLL: 31.9, GLm: DL: 19.4, Bd: 20.6
51	Sheep	talus		1	GLL: 32.4, Glm: 3 DL: 18.3, Bd: 20.9
51	Sheep	talus		1	GLL: 30.6, Glm: 2 DL: 17.9, Bd: 21.8
51	Sheep or goat	femur	prox and dist NF	1	
51	Sheep or goat	femur	prox NF	1	
51	Sheep or goat	rib		4	
51	Unidentified mammal			30	
51-float	Unidentified mammal			4	
51-float	Sheep or goat	tooth		1	
51-float	Sheep or goat	lower premolar		1	
177				–	
177-float	Unidentified mammal			52	
178	Sheep	talus		1	GLpe: 34.9, Bp: 11 SD: 10.1, Bd: 10.6
178	Sheep	phalanx 1		1	GLL: 30.6, GLm: DL: 17.9, Bd: 21.8
178	Sheep or goat	upper molar		1	
178	Sheep or goat	lower molar		1	
178	Sheep or goat	rib		2	
178	Unidentified mammal			25	
178	Worked bone fragment			1	
178-float	Unidentified mammal			165	
178-float	Unidentified fish			10	
178-float	Mugilidae	caudal vertebra		1	SL: 5-10 cm
934	Sheep or goat	skull		1	not seen
934	Sheep or goat	femur	prox and dist NF	1	
934	Sheep	metacarpal	NF	2 (L & R)	Bp: 22.8, SD: 11.8

s	Species	Element	Fusion data	n	Measurements/remarks
	Sheep	humerus	prox NF, dist fusing	1	SD: 11.3 Bd: 28.3, BT: 25.5,
	Goat	talus		1	GLL: 29.2, GLm: 28.3, DL: 14.9, Bd: 18.1
	Unidentified mammal			9	
	Sheep or goat	upper premolar		1	
	Sheep or goat	phalanx 1		1	
	Sheep or goat	rib		1	
	Cattle	tibia	dist fusing	1	Bd: 63.1
	Cattle	thoracic vertebra		1	
)	Goat	metapodal	NF	1	
)-float	Unidentified mammal			4	
-float	Eel	precaudal vertebra		1	SL: 20-30 cm
5	Unidentified mammal			3	
5	Sheep or goat	ulna		1	
5	Sheep or goat	phalanx 2	NF	1	
5	Sheep or goat	pelvis		1	
5	Sheep or goat	cervical vertebra		1	
5	Sheep or goat	rib		1	
5-float	Clupeidae	precaudal vertebra		1	SL: 10-15 cm
5-float	Unidentified fish			4	
2				–	
2-float	Unidentified mammal			82	
3				–	
4				–	
5				–	

Table 4. Details on the animal remains found in Middle Bronze Age graves at Tell Tweini. NF: not fused L & R. Measurements (mm) are taken according to von den Driesch (1976). For fish estimates of the Standard Length (SL) are given.

IMAGES DE FAÏENCE DE TELL TUEINI ET DE RAS SHAMRA (SYRIE)

Valérie MATOÏAN
UMR 5133 (CNRS), Lyon

Une découverte faite en 2004 à Tell Tueini, lors des recherches menées sous la direction de Karel Van Lerberghe, a retenu notre attention en raison d'un parallèle qu'elle permet d'établir avec le matériel de Ras Shamra. L'objet en question est une figurine-plaquette en faïence, d'une hauteur de 8 cm, représentant une figure féminine nue (Fig. 1)[1]. La pièce faisait partie du riche mobilier d'une tombe construite collective datée du Bronze moyen IIB/C (vers 1700 av. J.-C)[2]. Technique et forme permettent de la rattacher à une série de figurines en faïence mises au jour sur le site de Ras Shamra dont nous offrons une présentation détaillée à Karel van Lerberghe, en souvenir d'excellentes relations de «voisinage littoral» et à titre amical.

Les découvertes de Ras Shamra

L'étude des matières vitreuses d'Ougarit a révélé la présence, dès la période du Bronze moyen, d'objets en stéatite glaçurée (scarabées), en bleu égyptien[3] et en faïence. Le corpus des objets en faïence, d'environ deux cents pièces, est de loin le plus important et le plus varié (Matoïan 2000a, 93-103, 225-229). Au sein de cet ensemble, les éléments de parure constituent le groupe le plus riche (environ ¾ du corpus), les récipients ne sont attestés que par dix spécimens[4], et les figurines représentent 1/7e du corpus (Fig. 2 et 3)[5].

[1] Hameeuw et Jans 2008, 83, fig. 9: TWE-A-00177-C-012. Nous remercions vivement Joachim Bretschneider pour les informations fournies au sujet de la figurine de Tell Tueini, ainsi que pour la photographie de l'objet.

[2] TWE-A-00170: Hameeuw et Jans 2008, 80-83; Bretschneider et Van Lerberghe 2008, 21-26, fig. 16-21.

[3] Matoïan 2000a, 304, cat. Bleu 1: perle en «bleu égyptien» faisant partie d'un collier de la tombe LVI [61] de la *Ville Basse ouest*.

[4] Caubet et Kaczmarczyk 1987, 4; Matoïan 2000a, cat. faïence 169-179; Matoïan 2007, 209-210, n° 201-202.

[5] Nous adressons nos sincères remerciements à V. Huyard pour la réalisation des figures 2 et 3.

Cette dernière catégorie apparaît dans les publications concernant la côte levantine dès 1962. À cette date, A. Kuschke publie une première figurine incomplète, rattachée au niveau II de Ras Shamra, provenant du sondage réalisé dans la cour III du Palais royal (Kuschke 1962, 253, pl. XVIII: 3). En 1980, L. Badre étudie un autre spécimen fragmentaire issu d'un sondage réalisé sur l'Acropole (niveau II) lors de la 14e campagne (Badre 1980, 382, n° 9, pl. LIX: 9) et, quelques années plus tard, A. Caubet publie quatre spécimens issus des fouilles de C. Schaeffer et conservés dans les collections du Louvre (Caubet 1985, 193-195, cat. 12, et 197, fig. 9). Enfin, en 2000, notre étude du corpus des matières vitreuses d'Ougarit permet d'établir un catalogue de vingt-six figurines en faïence à l'effigie d'une femme nue (voir tableau), provenant toutes sans exception du site de Ras Shamra (Matoïan 2000a, cat. faïence 143-168). Les exemplaires d'Ougarit sont tous fragmentaires, au contraire de la figurine de Tell Tueini qui est complète. La glaçure est de couleur bleu turquoise, le plus souvent altérée (décoloration, tressaillage); un décor peint en noir souligne systématiquement la zone pubienne et la coiffure, parfois les seins, les membres supérieurs ou les yeux.

Des objets en faïence

Différents termes ont été utilisés, dans les notes de fouille et dans les premières publications, pour décrire ces figurines. C. Schaeffer a parlé de «faïence» (RS 9.276, RS 14.8, RS 21.102), de «terre vernissée» (RS 10.115) ou encore de «fritte à couverte bichrome bleu-vert et noir» (RS 26.128); L. Badre et A. Caubet ont classé ces objets dans la catégorie des terres cuites à glaçure.

Dans le courant des années 1980, l'étude en laboratoire de cinq pièces du Louvre a apporté des éléments permettant de définir la technique employée pour façonner ces objets. Il s'agit de la faïence: le corps des objets, à base de silice, est recouvert d'une glaçure alcaline colorée au cuivre pur, sans association d'étain. La glaçure noire, utilisée pour le décor peint, est colorée par des oxydes de manganèse et de fer, accompagnés d'un peu de baryum et de nickel[6].

Description typologique

À l'exception d'une pièce, les spécimens de Ras Shamra appartiennent à la catégorie des figurines-plaquettes moulées. L'arrière est plat, ce qui

[6] Caubet et Kaczmarczyk 1987, 50; Caubet et Kaczmarczyk 1989, fig. 27.2; Kaczmarczyk 2007, 17-27; Matoïan 2007, 206-208, n° 196-200.

suggère l'emploi d'un moule univalve pour la production de ces objets. L'image féminine, traitée de manière schématique, se détache en général sur un fond, de largeur variable, parfois inexistant. Sur certains exemplaires, la partie supérieure forme un cadre cintré plus ou moins régulier (figurines 2, 7, 20, 26). Sur deux spécimens, on observe des «barbelures» de chaque côté des jambes (figurines 5 et 6) dont l'origine est probablement à rechercher dans l'emploi de la technique du moulage. La face arrière de certaines pièces peut présenter de légers bosselages (figurine 20) ou des traces de raclage (figurine 25). L'observation de variantes laisse supposer l'existence de plusieurs moules.

Seule la tête de la figurine 1 présente un rendu en relief sur ses deux faces et a peut-être été obtenue à l'aide d'un moule bivalve; à l'arrière, le cou montre trois lignes horizontales en creux.

Ces objets représentent une femme nue, bras pliés et mains posées sur les seins. Les jambes sont jointes, séparées par un mince sillon, à l'exception de la figurine 21 sur laquelle aucune incision n'apparaît. Les pieds sont traités en un bloc unique. Les hanches sont généralement bien marquées — à l'exception peut-être de la figurine 4 — et la zone pubienne toujours soulignée de noir. Le ventre de deux figurines (8 et 11) est légèrement bombé, cette caractéristique étant plus marquée sur la seconde.

Les bras sont pliés, l'emplacement des coudes formant un angle aigu ou un arrondi, et les mains sont posées sur la poitrine. Les seins sont marqués d'une tache noire sur trois exemplaires (figurines 3, 4, 10). Dans deux cas (figurines 9, 23), une ligne noire souligne, à l'extérieur, la courbure des bras.

Le rendu de la tête présente de nombreuses variantes. Quand elle se dégage sur un fond cintré, le visage est encadré d'une longue chevelure peinte en noir (figurines 2, 7, 20), sauf sur une figurine où la peinture noire se limite à une bande au-dessus du front (figurine 26). Sur les spécimens présentant une échancrure au niveau du cou, on observe, soit une bande noire horizontale au-dessus du front (figurine 4), soit un agglomérat informe de petites taches noires (figurine 10).

Le visage est traité de manière schématique. L'image féminine est souvent parée d'un collier rendu par une bande noire au niveau du cou (figurines 1, 10, 25, 26). Les oreilles sont toujours indiquées et parfois soulignées de noir, de même que les yeux.

Contextes de découverte et datation

Pour la majorité des figurines de Ras Shamra, nous ne disposons pas de données précises sur le contexte de découverte (cf. tableau). Deux pièces, déjà citées, ont été mises au jour dans des sondages stratigraphiques, l'un mené sur l'Acropole et l'autre dans le Palais royal. Les fouilleurs les ont attribuées au niveau II de Ras Shamra (Bronze moyen). Le même horizon stratigraphique est donné par C. Schaeffer pour la figurine 11, découverte en 1958[7].

Par ailleurs, un fragment (figurine 22), retrouvé dans le puisard de la Maison dite aux albâtres du Quartier résidentiel, à trois mètres de profondeur, pourrait provenir de terres remuées, associées à un niveau antérieur à celui de l'habitation (datée du Bronze récent).

La situation est plus complexe pour la figurine 21 qui provient d'une tombe de la Tranchée Sud-Acropole datée du Bronze récent (Marchegay 1999, 671, 678). On pourrait émettre l'hypothèse d'un objet conservé sur plusieurs générations ou d'un objet mis au jour dans les terres remuées lors du creusement de la sépulture.

L'homogénéité technique et typologique, l'association de plusieurs pièces au niveau II de Ras Shamra, ainsi que les parallèles établis avec le matériel anatolien du niveau Ib du *kārum* de Kültepe — Kaniš / Neša (voir *infra*)[8], nous avaient conduite à dater cette série du Bronze moyen II (Matoïan 2000a, 227-229). La découverte de Tell Tueni vient augmenter le corpus de la Syrie côtière, témoigner de la diffusion de ce type d'objets et confirmer cet horizon chronologique. Signalons enfin un exemplaire plus méridional issu du niveau XII de Megiddo (Loud 1948, pl. 241: 2).

Comparenda avec les faïences d'Anatolie

Des figurines en faïence représentant une femme nue, dont certaines sont très proches des exemplaires d'Ougarit, ont été retrouvées sur plusieurs sites d'Anatolie Centrale: à Kültepe — Kaniš / Neša, à Alişar Hüyük, à Karahöyük[9] et sont datées du XVIIIe siècle av. J.-C.

D'autres catégories d'objets en faïence (la vaisselle, la parure et la glyptique) de Ras Shamra permettent d'établir des parallèles avec le matériel anatolien. Dès 1936, C. Schaeffer (Schaeffer 1936, 122) avait indiqué un rapprochement entre deux bols à profil en S et au décor peint en noir, mis au jour dans une tombe de la *Ville Basse centre*[10], et une découverte

[7] Cf. notes de fouille inédites de C. Schaeffer (archives du Collège de France).

[8] Vers 1810-1740 av. J.-C. (Veenhof 1995, 862).

[9] Schmidt, 1932a, 36, fig. 27: 2296; Van Der Osten 1937, 193, fig. 230: d2971 et d2966; Özgüç 1986a, 201-204, pl. 41 et 42, ill. 3 à 8.

[10] Voir aussi: Peltenburg 1987, 15, fig. 1: 6; Caubet et Kaczmarczyk 1987; Matoïan 2007, n° 202, 209-210.

faite au niveau II d'Alişar (Schmidt 1932b, pl. III et X: b 1868)[11]. Plus récemment, nous avons attiré l'attention sur un ensemble de perles et de cachets en faïence (Matoïan 2000c), provenant des fouilles de 1931 sur le tell de Ras Shamra, dont plusieurs éléments — des perles zoomorphes et un cachet décoré du «signe Omega» (Fig. 4) — sont très proches de spécimens découverts en Anatolie (Kültepe - Kaniš / Neša, Alişar, Acemhöyük, Gordion, Karahöyük) ainsi qu'en Syrie du Nord (Hammam et-Turkman, Chagar Bazar)[12].

Comparenda avec les faïences d'Égypte

Bien que des différences formelles existent, un parallèle semble aussi pouvoir être établi avec une série bien connue de figurines féminines nues en faïence du Moyen Empire égyptien. La technique est similaire: la faïence, avec l'emploi d'un décor peint en noir sur fond de glaçure bleu. En revanche, les figurines égyptiennes sont représentées les bras le long du corps, tatouées et parées de bijoux, et sont souvent sans jambes. Leur profil est aplati mais il ne s'agit pas de figurines-plaquettes comme les pièces de Ras Shamra et de Tell Tueini. Leur signification serait liée à la sexualité et à la fertilité; elles ont été mises en parallèle avec des figurines égyptiennes fabriquées dans d'autres matériaux (argile, lin, bois, pierre) et déposées préférentiellement dans les sanctuaires d'Hathor, déesse de l'amour et de la renaissance (Pinch 1993, 198-234; Pierrat-Bonnefois 2005, 36-37, fig. 64-66).

Des spécimens proches sont connus jusqu'au Levant sud (Megiddo) (Loud 1948, pl. 241: 5: niveau IX) et central où des figurines similaires figuraient parmi les offrandes retrouvées dans les dépôts du Temple aux obélisques de Byblos (Dunand 1958, 764-765, n° 15362-15371, pl. XCIX).

Origine de la production

Selon T. Özgüç, les figurines de femme nue retrouvées sur les sites anatoliens proviendraient d'un même atelier ou d'ateliers étroitement liés, situé(s) dans une région s'étendant de la plaine d'Antioche au Khabur (Özgüç 1986b, 204).

[11] Plus récemment, un rapprochement a également été proposé avec une découverte d'Haradum, agglomération des XVIIIe-XVIIe siècles sur l'Euphrate (Kepinski-Lecomte 1992, 407, fig. 102, n° 8 et fig. 176; Kepinski-Lecomte 1995, 38, fig. 5: 3).

[12] Voir aussi Keel 1986 et 1989; Özgüç 1992.

Même s'il reste difficile d'être catégorique quant au lieu de production de ces objets, Ras Shamra paraît être un bon candidat et le nombre élevé des découvertes qui en sont issues pourrait se révéler un indice en faveur d'une production locale.

Il faut toutefois rappeler que certaines figurines anatoliennes en faïence n'ont pas de parallèle à Ougarit. Il s'agit de spécimens dont le traitement rappelle la célèbre figurine en ivoire de Kültepe (Aruz et al. 2008, 79-80, cat. 44): le corps est traité en ronde-bosse, la tête agrémentée d'une coiffe ronde, et le visage présente de grands yeux en relief.

La création du type attesté sur la côte syrienne a peut-être subi une influence des productions égyptiennes, tout en s'en démarquant. Des parallèles entre les spécimens de Ras Shamra et les productions égyptiennes du Moyen Empire égyptien sont possibles: emploi de la technique du décor peint sur fond de glaçure bleue et emploi de recettes similaires pour l'obtention des glaçures[13]. Toutefois, la forme, le style et les résultats des analyses en laboratoire suggèrent des productions différentes. Ainsi, la proportion de manganèse par rapport au fer est nettement plus élevée que dans les noirs contemporains du Moyen Empire. Pour le manganèse, la présence systématique de baryum dans les glaçures d'Ougarit indique l'utilisation de psilomélane comme source, alors qu'en Égypte la pyrolusite est préférée[14].

L'existence, à Ras Shamra, d'une autre catégorie d'objet en faïence, datée du Bronze moyen II, dont la forme témoigne elle aussi d'une influence de l'Égypte, doit aussi être mentionnée. Elle est représentée par la série des coupelles dont le manche se termine par une tête de canard retournée[15].

Enfin, se pose la question d'une éventuelle influence de certaines productions anatoliennes relevant du domaine de la métallurgie qui ont connu un développement à la période correspondant au niveau Ib du *kārum* de Kültepe. Il s'agit de la série des moules et des figurines en plomb (Emre 1971), au sein de laquelle on retrouve le type iconographique de la femme nue debout soutenant sa poitrine. Plus précisément, nous nous demandons si un lien pourrait être établi entre la figurine 1 de Ras Shamra dont

[13] Emploi du cuivre pour l'obtention de la couleur bleue et du manganèse et du fer pour la couleur noire.

[14] Caubet et Kaczmarczyk 1987, 48 et 50; Caubet et Kaczmarczyk 1989, fig. 27.2; Kaczmarczyk 2007; Matoïan 2007, 206-208, n° 196-200.

[15] Les gobelets en faïence décorés d'un visage féminin en relief représente une autre catégorie de récipient datée du Bronze moyen II, caractérisée par une influence de l'art égyptien et attestée en Syrie occidentale, à Alalakh et à Ebla (Mazzoni 1987). (Schaeffer 1938, pl. XXII: 2 et fig. 60; Matoïan 2004, 41, n° 22).

le cou présente, à l'arrière, trois lignes horizontales et les images de femmes nues, sur les moules et les figurines en métal d'Anatolie, ornées d'un collier composé de plusieurs rangs (Emre 1971, pl. II et III).

Fonction et symbolique

L'image de la femme nue, l'une des plus anciennes de l'iconographie proche-orientale, est aussi l'une des plus complexes à interpréter[16]. Les recherches menées sur le tell de Ras Shamra en ont fourni de nombreux témoignages depuis le Néolithique précéramique (Schaeffer 1962, 154, fig. 1; de Contenson 1992, vol. II, 164, fig. 155) jusqu'à l'âge du Fer (Stucky 1983, pl. 26).

Les figurines en faïence présentées ici offrent des représentations schématiques dont la qualité esthétique peut paraître minime. Leur valeur est probablement liée au matériau, la faïence, encore peu attestée sur la côte syrienne au début du IIe millénaire av. J.-C., aux couleurs qu'elles revêtent et à la symbolique qu'elles véhiculent. Le manque de données sur les contextes de découvertes à Ras Shamra limite considérablement l'interprétation. La découverte du spécimen de Tell Tueini et de nombreux spécimens anatoliens dans des sépultures pourrait conforter une symbolique funéraire, en rapport avec la fertilité, voire peut-être la renaissance.

L'absence de stabilité de ces objets en position verticale laisse supposer que les figurines étaient soit fichées dans un support, soit placées en position horizontale, c'est-à-dire couchées. Cette caractéristique permettrait peut-être de les rapprocher des spécimens de faïence égyptiens.

Ce type de figurines en faïence ne perdure pas à Ougarit au Bronze récent. Pour cette période, le corpus de la faïence, d'environ 18.000 pièces, n'a livré que de rares figurines anthropomorphes et aucune figurine de femme nue. Les images de femmes nues apparaissent sur d'autres supports, de préférence la terre cuite et les métaux (bronze et métaux précieux)[17]; on retiendra toutefois, dans le domaine des matériaux vitreux, deux figurines-plaquettes moulées en verre bleu (Matoïan 2000b, 29-32, fig. 6 et 7).

Conclusion

Avec le Bronze moyen, la Syrie côtière, qui fait alors partie du monde culturel amorrite, entre dans l'histoire et développe des contacts avec les

[16] Entre autres: Winter 1983; Cornelius 2004.

[17] Badre 1980, pl. LX: 11 à 30; Monloup 1987; Cornelius 2004; Dardaillon 2006.

régions qui l'environnent. Les archives de Mari éclairent le statut particulier d'Ougarit, ville frontière et place commerciale permettant les échanges entre deux mondes: l'Orient et la Méditerranée orientale[18], ce dont témoigne aussi la culture matérielle. Les découvertes faites sur les autres sites de la côte confortent cette position stratégique du Levant nord[19]. Ainsi, les fouilleurs de Tell Tueini signalent d'une part dans la tombe collective où fut retrouvée la figurine en faïence des importations céramiques chypriotes, et, d'autre part, associés à la sépulture, des aménagements en rapport avec le rituel du *kispum* (Bretschneider et van Lerberghe 2008, 21-22).

Les liens entre l'Égypte et la Syrie occidentale se développent aussi au cours de cette période. Au-delà des importations[20], les contacts se traduisent par une influence des productions égyptiennes sur certaines productions locales, dans les domaines de la glyptique (Teissier 1996), de la peinture murale (Taraqji 1999), de l'ivoirerie (Scandone Matthiae 1988), ou encore de la faïence, comme nous venons de le voir, entre autres, avec les figurines de Tell Tueini et de Ras Shamra.

Mais ces dernières sont aussi d'un grand intérêt pour l'étude des relations entre le Levant nord, l'Anatolie et la Syrie du Nord au Bronze moyen II, à l'époque du commerce assyrien en Anatolie[21], en particulier de son renouveau contemporain de Šamši-Addu, souverain du royaume de Haute-Mésopotamie, et de son fils Išme-Dagan. Il semble possible d'envisager une production locale, sur la côte du Levant nord, dont l'aire de diffusion, par des intermédiaires, aurait touché l'Anatolie centrale. En retour, Ougarit aurait pu recevoir des objets en faïence, comme le cachet décoré du signe oméga[22] et les perles zoomorphes mentionnés précédemment (Fig. 4), des figurines en plomb[23] ou encore des sceaux-cylindres en pierre. P. Amiet a identifié dans le corpus de Ras Shamra plusieurs importations anatoliennes (Amiet 1992, n° 5-7) pour lesquelles des parallèles

[18] Villard 1986; Durand 1999; Guichard 1999; Charpin et Ziegler 2003, 214-216.

[19] Pour Ras Shamra, voir notamment Caubet et Matoïan 1995; Al-Maqdissi et Matoïan 2008. Pour Tell Iris: cf. Al-Maqdissi et Matoïan 2008, 135, note 29. Pour Tell Sukas: Thrane 1978. Pour la céramique chypriote au Levant, voir la publication récente de L. C. Maguire (2009).

[20] Voir, entre autres: Schaeffer 1939, 19-22; Scandone Matthiae 2002; Al-Maqdissi 2006, notes 9 et 16; Grimal 2008; Lagarce 2008.

[21] Voir entre autres: Veenhof 1995; Michel 2001; Larsen 2008, 70-73.

[22] T. Özgüç considère ces cachets comme des productions nord-mésopotamiennes et syriennes, destinées à être vendues aux Anatoliens (Özgüç 1992).

[23] Un spécimen (RS 17.54), mis au jour dans le Quartier dit égéen ou résidentiel, est attesté à Ras Shamra (Dardaillon 2008, 211-212, fig. 39a; Dardaillon 2011, 228-229, fig. 7).

existent dans la glyptique de Kaniš (niveaux II et Ib). L'auteur signale aussi un sceau-cylindre, classé dans la série dite classique, qui présente encore de fortes affinités avec les modèles cappadociens. Son décor, réparti en colonnes, comporte entre autres une figure féminine nue représentée debout, bras plié au niveau du buste[24] (Fig. 5).

Il est possible que ces objets qui permettent aujourd'hui d'évoquer les goûts, voire les aspirations des habitants du Proche-Orient ancien, aient circulé à la faveur d'échanges commerciaux, en particulier ceux relatifs à la circulation des métaux qui tenait alors une place majeure comme en témoignent les textes.

Bibliographie

AL-MAQDISSI, M. 2006: «Notes d'archéologie levantine VIII. Stratigraphie du chantier B de Tell Sianu (plaine de Jablé)», *Syria* 83, 229-245.

AL-MAQDISSI, M. et V. MATOÏAN 2008: «La céramique découverte par C. Schaeffer dans le Palais royal d'Ougarit: remarques générales», in V. Matoïan (dir.), *Le mobilier du Palais royal d'Ougarit* (Ras Shamra — Ougarit XVII), Lyon, 127-155.

AMIET, P. 1992: *Corpus des Cylindres de Ras Shamra-Ougarit, II, Sceaux-cylindres en hématite et pierres diverses* (Ras Shamra — Ougarit IX), Paris.

ARUZ, J., K. BENZEL et J. M. EVANS (éds.), 2008: *Beyond Babylon. Art, Trade and Diplomacy in the Second Millenium B.C.*, New York.

BADRE, L. 1980: *Les figurines anthropomorphes en terre cuite à l'Age du Bronze en Syrie*, BAH CIII, Paris.

BOUQUILLON, A., A. CAUBET, A. KACZMARCZYK et V. MATOÏAN 2007: *Faïences et matières vitreuses de l'Orient ancien*, Gand-Paris.

BRETSCHNEIDER, J. et K. VAN LERBERGHE 2008: «Tell Tweini, ancient Gibala, between 2600 B.C.E. and 333 B.C.E.», in J. Bretschneider et K. Van Lerberghe (éds.), *In Search of Gibala, An archaeological and historical study based on eight seasons of excavations at Tell Tweini (Syria) in the A and C fields (1999-2007)* (Aula Orientalis-Supplementa 24), Barcelone, 11-68.

CALVET, Y. et G. GALLIANO (éds.) 2004: *Le royaume d'Ougarit, aux origines de l'alphabet*, Lyon.

CAUBET, A., 1985: «Poterie tournée à glaçure du Bronze Récent: Syrie et Chypre», in J.-L. Huot, M. Yon et Y. Calvet (éds.), *De l'Indus aux Balkans, Recueil Jean Deshayes*, Paris, 191-198.

CAUBET, A. et A. KACZMARCZYK 1987: «Bronze Age Faience from Ras Shamra (Ugarit)», in M. Bimson et I. C. Freestone (éds.), *Early Vitreous Materials* (BMOP 56), Londres, 47-56.

24 Amiet 1992, n° 27: RS 24.363 provenant de la Tranchée Sud-Acropole.

— 1989: «Trade and local production in Late Cypriot faience», in E. J. Peltenburg (éd.), *Early Society in Cyprus*, Edinburgh University Press, 209-215.

CAUBET, A. et V. MATOÏAN 1995: «Ougarit et l'Egée», in M. Yon, M. Sznycer et P. Bordreuil (éds.), *Le pays d'Ougarit autour de 1200 av. J.-C., Actes du Colloque International, Paris, 28 juin - 1er juillet 1993* (Ras Shamra-Ougarit XI), Paris, 99-112.

CAUBET, A. et G. PIERRAT-BONNEFOIS (éds.) 2005: *Faïences de l'Antiquité, de l'Égypte à l'Iran*, Paris.

CHARPIN, D. et N. ZIEGLER 2003: *Mari et le Proche-Orient à l'époque amorrite. Essai d'histoire politique* (Florilegium marianum V, Mémoires de N.A.B.U. 6).

CORNELIUS, I. 2004: *The Many Faces of the Goddess, The Iconography of the Syro-Palestinian Goddesses Anat, Astarte, Qedeshet, and Asherah c. 1500-1000 BCE* (Orbis Biblicus et Orientalis 204), Fribourg — Göttingen.

DARDAILLON, E. 2006: *Les productions métalliques dans les royaumes du Levant au deuxième millénaire av. J.-C.*, thèse de doctorat de l'Université Lumière-Lyon 2 (non publiée).

— 2008: «Images de métal», in M. Al-Maqdissi et V. Matoïan (éds.), *«L'Orient des palais». Le Palais royal d'Ougarit au Bronze récent* (Documents d'archéologie syrienne XV), Damas, 211-216.

— 2011: «Le plomb dans les productions métalliques d'Ougarit», in V. Matoïan, M. Al-Maqdissi et Y. Calvets (éds.), *Études Ougaritiques II* (Ras Shamra — Ougarit XX), Leuven, 221-239.

DE CONTENSON, H. 1992: *Préhistoire de Ras Shamra* (Ras Shamra-Ougarit VIII), Paris.

DUNAND, M. 1958: *Les fouilles de Byblos II.2*, Paris.

DURAND, J.-M. 1999: «La façade occidentale du Proche-Orient d'après les textes de Mari», in A. Caubet (éd.), *L'acrobate au taureau. Les découvertes de Tell el-Dab'a (Égypte) et l'archéologie de la Méditerranée orientale (1800-1400 av. J.-C.)*, Paris, 149-164.

EMRE, T. 1971: *Anatolian Lead Figurines and their Stone Moulds* (TTKY VI: 14), Ankara.

GRIMAL, N. 2008: «Quelques réflexions sur la géo-politique du Levant au deuxième millénaire av. J.-C.», in *Interconnections in the Eastern Mediterranean, Lebanon in the Bronze and Iron Ages* (Bulletin d'Archéologie et d'Architecture Libanaises, hors-série VI), 339-360.

GUICHARD, M. 1999: «Les mentions de la Crète à Mari», in A. Caubet (éd.), *L'acrobate au taureau. Les découvertes de Tell el-Dab'a (Égypte) et l'archéologie de la Méditerranée orientale (1800-1400 av. J.-C.)*, Paris, 165-177.

HAMEEUW, H. et G. JANS 2008: «Burial Customs at Tell Tweini — Field A», in J. Bretschneider et K. Van Lerberghe (éds), *In Search of Gibala, An archaeological and historical study based on eight seasons of excavations at Tell Tweini (Syria) in the A and C fields (1999-2007)* (Aula Orientalis-Supplementa 24), Barcelone, 75-86.

KACZMARCZYK, A. 2007: «Méthodes d'analyse. Caractérisations des compositions en fonction des époques et des régions», in A. Bouquillon, A. Caubet, A. Kaczmarczyk et V. Matoïan, *Faïences et matières vitreuses de l'Orient ancien*, Gand-Paris, 17-27.

KEEL, O. 1986: «A stamp seal research project and group of scarabs with raised relief», *Akkadica* 49, 1-16.

— 1989: «Die Ω-Gruppe. Ein mittelbronzezeitlicher Stempelsiegel-Typ mit erhabenem Relief aus Anatolien-Nordsyrien und Palästina», *in* O. Keel, H. Keel-Leu et S. Schroer (éds.), *Studien zu den Stempelsiegeln aus Palästina/Israel II* (Orbis Biblicus et Orientalis 88), 39-87.

KEPINSKI-LECOMTE, C., 1992: *Haradum I, Une ville nouvelle sur le Moyen-Euphrate (XVIII°-XVII° av. J.C.)*, Paris.

— 1995: «La polarité occidentale d'Haradum, Moyen-Euphrate irakien (XVIIIe-XVIIe s. av. J.-C.)», *Anatolica Antiqua, Aski Anadolu* III, Paris, 33-51.

KUSCHKE, A. 1962: «Bericht über eine Sondage im Palastgarten von Ugarit — Ras Shamra», *in* C. F.-A. Schaeffer (dir.), *Ugaritica* IV (Mission de Ras Shamra XV, BAH LXXIV), 251-299.

LAGARCE, B. 2008: «Réexamen des monuments du Palais royal d'Ougarit inscrits en hiéroglyphes égyptiens conservés au Musée national de Damas», *in* V. Matoïan (dir.), *Le mobilier du Palais royal d'Ougarit* (Ras Shamra — Ougarit XVII), Lyon, 261-280.

LARSEN, M. T. 2008: Notices, in J. Aruz, K. Benzel et J. M. Evans (éds.): *Beyond Babylon. Art, Trade and Diplomacy in the Second Millenium B.C.*, New York.

LOUD, G. 1948: *Megiddo II, Seasons of 1935-1939*, Chicago.

MAGUIRE, L. C. 2009: *The Cypriot pottery and its circulation in the Levant, Tell el-Dab'a* XXI, Vienne.

MARCHEGAY, S. 1999: *Les tombes de Ras Shamra-Ougarit (Syrie) au IIe millénaire avant J.-C.: architecture, localisation, relation avec l'habitat*, thèse de doctorat, Université Lumière/Lyon 2 (non publiée).

MATOÏAN, V. 2000a: *Ras Shamra-Ougarit et la production des matières vitreuses au Proche-Orient au second millénaire avant Jésus-Christ,* thèse de doctorat, Université de Paris I Pantéon-Sorbonne (non publiée).

— 2000b: «Données nouvelles sur le verre en Syrie au IIe millénaire av. J.-C.: le cas de Ras Shamra-Ougarit», in M.-D. Nenna (éd.), *La route du verre*, Maison de l'Orient Méditerranéen, TMO, Lyon, 23-47.

— 2000c: «Un cachet en 'faïence' décoré du signe-oméga à Ougarit», *Orient-Express* 2000-3, 61-63.

— 2004 : Notices, in Y. Calvet et G. Galliano (éds.): *Le royaume d'Ougarit, aux origines de l'alphabet*, Lyon.

— 2007 : Notices, in Bouquillon, A., A. Caubet, A. Kaczmarczyk et V. Matoïan: *Faïences et matières vitreuses de l'Orient ancien*, Gand-Paris.

MAZZONI, S. 1987: «Faience in Ebla during Middle Bronze Age II», in M. Bimson et I. C. Freestone (éds.), *Early Vitreous Materials* (BMOP 56), Londres, 65-77.

MICHEL, C. 2001: *Correspondance des marchands de Kanish*, Littératures anciennes du Proche-Orient, Paris.

MONTLOUP, Th. 1987: «Les figurines en terre cuite», in M. Yon (éd.), *Le Centre de la Ville, 38e-44e campagnes (1978-1984)* (Ras Shamra-Ougarit III) Paris, 307-328.

ÖZGÜÇ, T. 1986a: «Glazed Faience Objects from Kanish», *Bibliotheca Mesopotamica* XXI, 201-208.

— 1986b: *Kültepe-Kanish II, New researches at the trading center of the ancient Near-East*, Ankara.

— 1992: «New glazed faience objects from Kanish», in B. Hrouda, S. Kroll et P. Z. Spanos (eds.), *Von Uruk nach Tuttul eine Festschrift für Eva Strommenger Studien und Aufsätze von Kollegen und Freuden*, Munich - Vienne, 159-162.

PELTENBURG, E.J. 1987: «Early Faience: Recent Studies, Origins and Relations with Glass», in M. Bimson et I. C. Freestone (éds.), *Early Vitreous Materials* (BMOP 56), Londres, 5-29.

PIERRAT-BONNEFOIS, G. 2005: Notices, in A. Caubet et G. Pierrat-Bonnefois (éds.): *Faïences de l'Antiquité, de l'Égypte à l'Iran*, Paris.

PINCH, G. 1993: *Votive Offerings to Hathor*, Griffith Institute, Oxford.

SCANDONE MATTHIAE G., 1988: «Les relations entre Ebla et l'Egypte au IIIème et au IIème Millénaires av. J.-C.», in H. Hauptmann et H. Waetzoldt (éds.), *Wirtschaft und Gesellschaft von Ebla. Akten der internationale Tagung Heidelberg (Nov. 1986)*, Heidelberg, 67-73.

— 2002: «Art et politique: les images de pharaon à l'étranger», *Egypt and the Levant* XII, 187-193.

SCHAEFFER, C. F. A. 1936: «Les fouilles de Ras Shamra-Ugarit, Septième campagne», *Syria* 17, 105-148.

— 1938: «Les fouilles de Ras Shamra-Ugarit, Neuvième campagne (printemps 1937), Rapport sommaire», *Syria* 19, 313-327.

— 1939: *Ugaritica* I, Paris.

— 1962: *Ugaritica* IV, Paris.

SCHMIDT, E. F., 1932a: *The Alishar Hüyük Seasons of 1927, II* (OIP 7), Chicago.

— 1932b: *The Alishar Hüyük Seasons of 1928 and 1929, I* (OIP 19), Chicago.

STUCKY, R. 1983: *Ras Shamra, Leukos Limen*, Paris.

TARAQJI, A. F. 1999: «Nouvelles découvertes sur les relations avec l'Égypte à Tell Sakka et Keswé, dans la région de Damas», *Bulletin de la Société française d'Égyptologie* 144, 27-43.

TEISSIER, B. 1996: *Egyptian Iconography on Syro-Palestinian Cylinder Seals of the Middle Bronze Age* (Orbis Biblicus et Orientalis 11, Series Archaeologica), Friburg — Göttingen.

THRANE, H. 1978: *Sukas* IV, *A Middle Bronze Age Collective Grave on Tall Sukas*, Copenhague.

VAN DER OSTEN, H. N. 1937: *The Alishar Hüyük, Seasons of 1930-1932, II* (OIP 29), Chicago.

VEENHOF, K. R. 1995: «Kanesh: An Assyrian Colony in Anatolia», in J. M. Sasson (éd.), *Civilizations of the Ancient Near East* II, New York, 859-871.

VILLARD, P. 1986: «Un roi de Mari à Ugarit», *Ugarit-Forschungen* 18, 387-412.

WINTER, U. 1983: *Frau und Göttin, Exegetische unk ikonographische Studien zum weiblichen Gottesbild im Alten Israel und in dessen Umwelt* (Orbis Biblicus et Orientalis 53), Fribourg.

Fig. 1 a et b. Figurine en faïence (TWE-A-00177-C-012), Tell Tueini, H. 8 cm (© Mission de Tell Tueini).

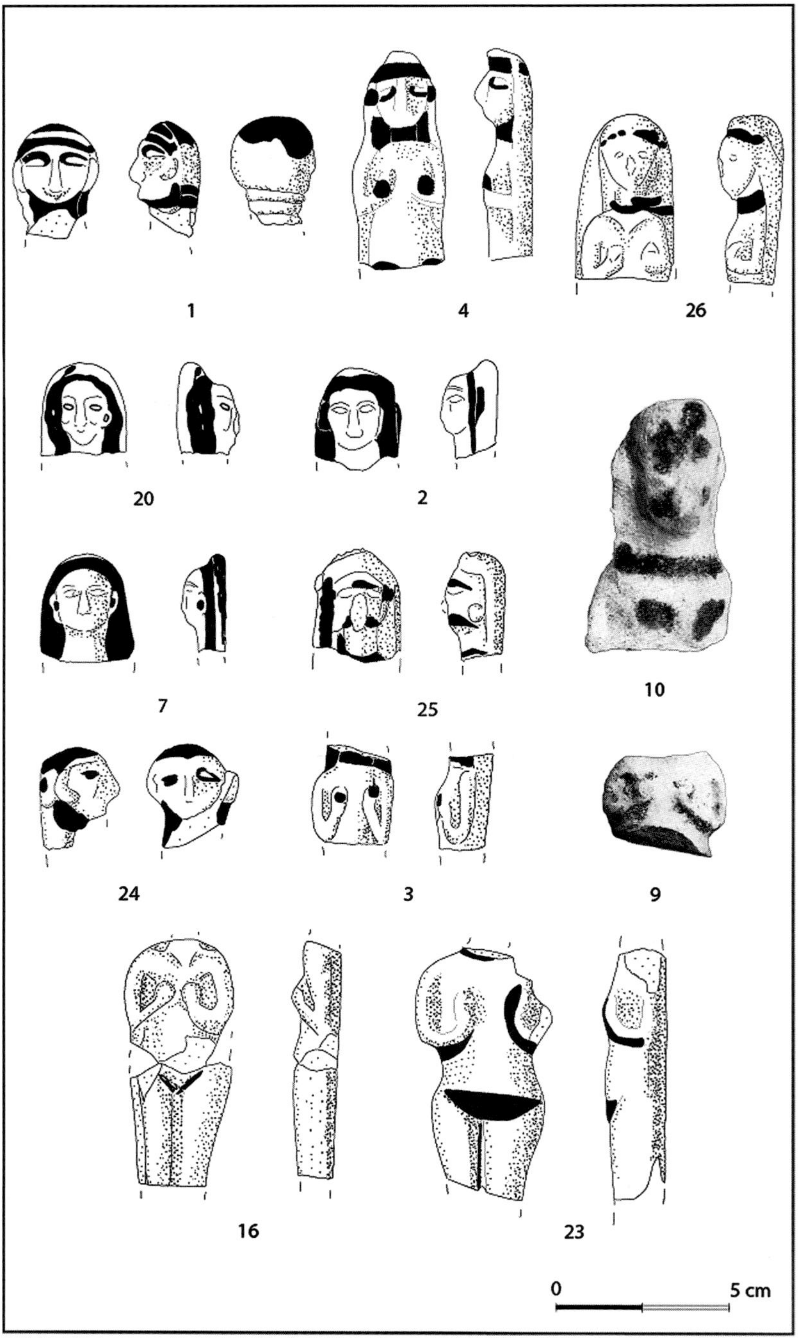

Fig. 2. Figurines en faïence, Ras Shamra, Bronze moyen II
(© Mission de Ras Shamra).

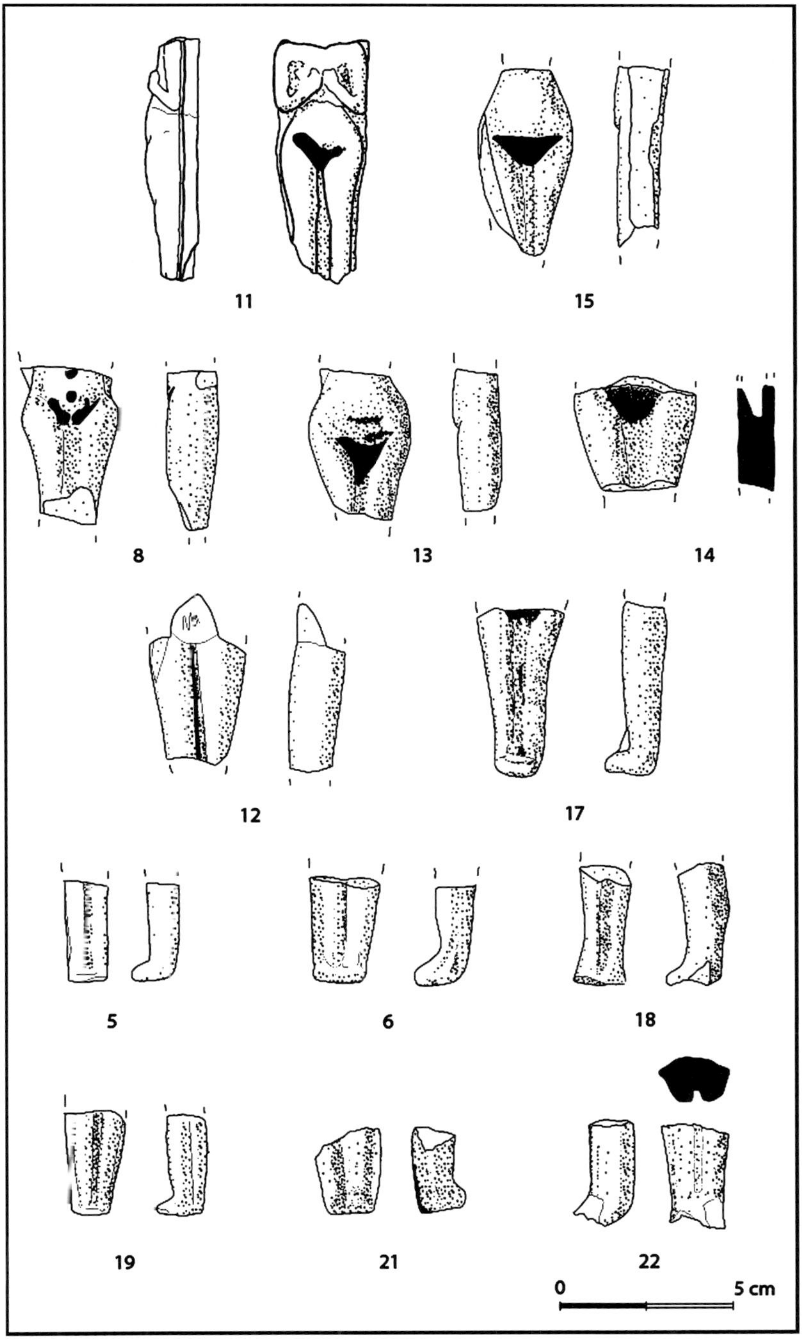

Fig. 3. Figurines en faïence, Ras Shamra, Bronze moyen II (© Mission de Ras Shamra).

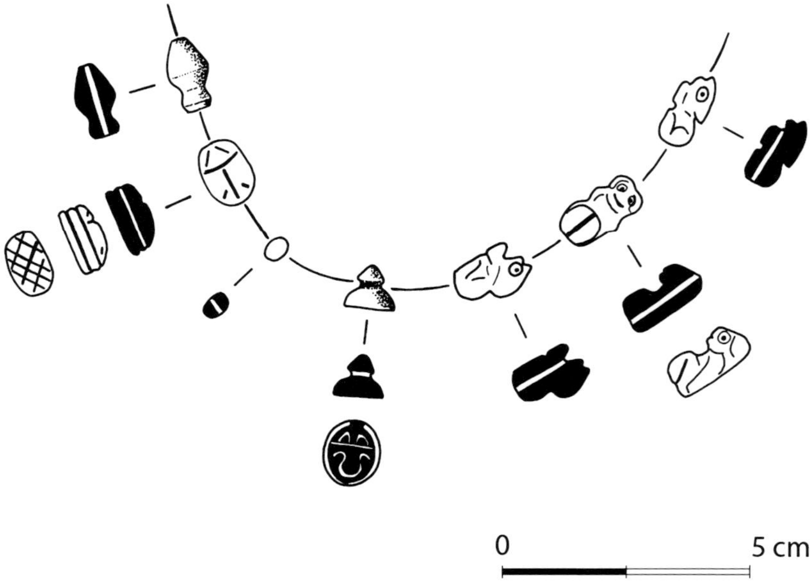

Fig. 4. Perles et cachets en faïence (Louvre AO 14831), Ras Shamra, Bronze moyen II (dessin C. Florimont © Musée du Louvre).

Fig. 5. Décor du sceau-cylindre RS 24.363, hématite, Ras Shamra (d'après Amiet 1992, © Mission de Ras Shamra).

	Description	Inv. RS / Musée	Faïence	Dimensions	Ras Shamra	Publications
1	Tête conservée	RS 9.276 Louvre AO 30682 / 83 AO 73	pâte siliceuse jaune pâle glaçure bleu turquoise décor peint en noir.	H. 2,75 cm la. 2,18 cm ép. 1,75 cm	1937 proba. *Butte nord-ouest*, S 433, –2,30 m	
2	Tête conservée	RS 9.276 Louvre AO 30683 / 83 AO 74 décor peint en noir	pâte siliceuse blanchâtre glaçure décolorée bleu pâle, traces couleur turquoise	H. 2,53 cm la. 2,1 cm ép. 1,45 cm	1937 proba. *Butte nord-ouest*, S 433, –2,30 m	
3	Buste sans tête conservé	RS 9.276 Louvre AO 30684 / 83 AO 75	pâte siliceuse blanchâtre glaçure bleu turquoise décor peint en noir	H. 2,7 cm	1937 proba. *Butte nord-ouest*, S 433, –2,30 m	
4	Partie supérieure conservée	RS 9.276 Louvre AO 30685 / 83 AO 76	pâte siliceuse blanchâtre glaçure bleu turquoise décor peint en noir	H. 5,17 cm la. 2,1 cm ép. 1,45 cm	1937 proba. *Butte nord-ouest*, S 433, –2,30 m	
5	Jambes conservées	RS 9.276 Louvre 83 AO 77	pâte siliceuse blanche glaçure bleu turquoise	H. 2,45 cm la. 125 cm ép. 1,1 cm	1937 proba. *Butte nord-ouest*, S 433, –2,30 m	
6	Jambes conservées	RS 9.276 Louvre AO 30687 / 83 AO 78	pâte siliceuse blanche glaçure bleu turquoise	H. 2,58 cm la. 1,74 cm ép. 1,35 cm	1937 proba. *Butte nord-ouest*, S 433, –2,30 m	
7	Tête conservée	RS 10.115 Louvre AO 30689 / 83 AO 80	pâte siliceuse jaune glaçure bleu turquoise décor peint en noir	H. 2,6 cm la. 2,1 cm ép. 1,3 cm	1938 proba. *Butte nord-ouest* SR 2066, –2,50 m	Caubet - Kaczmarczyk 1987, p. 50; Caubet - Kaczmarczyk — Matoïan 2007, 206, n° 196.

	Description	Inv. RS / Musée	Faïence	Dimensions	Ras Shamra	Publications
8	Bassin et cuisses conservées	Louvre AO 30714 / 83 AO 723	pâte siliceuse blanche glaçure turquoise	H. 3,9 cm la. 2,3 cm ép. 1,2 cm	1938 proba. *Butte nord-ouest* ER 1922	
9	Buste sans tête conservé	RS 14.8		H. 3,3 cm la. 2,8 cm	1950 *Acropole*, sondage 1 –2,10 m, niveau II.	Badre 1980, 382, n° 9, pl. LIX.
10	Buste conservé	RS 18.256 Damas 4987	pâte siliceuse glaçure vert turquoise irisée décor peint noir	H. 3,9 cm la. 2,3 cm ép. 1,3 cm	1954 *Palais royal*, cour III pt 1325, –3,45 m, sondage	Kuschke 1962, 253, pl. XVIII: 3.
11	Corps sans tête ni pieds conservés	RS 21.102 Damas 5858	pâte siliceuse fine glaçure turquoise irisée décor peint noir	H. 6 cm la. 2,4 cm ép. 1,27 cm	1958 Quartier dit résidentiel Pt 2039, –1,50 m	
12	Cuisses conservées	Louvre AO 30694 / 83 AO 85	pâte siliceuse jaunâtre glaçure bleu pâle décor peint en noir.	H. 4 cm la. 2,4 cm ép. 1,4 cm	1958-1959 Sud-est du *Palais royal*	
13	Bassin et cuisses conservés	Louvre 83 AO 86	pâte siliceuse blanche glaçure bleu turquoise décor peint en noir	H. 3,8 cm la. 2,5 cm ép. 1,4 cm	1958-1959 Sud-est du *Palais royal*	Caubet 1985, 195, n° 12.

14	Cuisses conservées	Louvre AO 30696 / 83 AO 87	pâte siliceuse blanchâtre glaçure bleu pâle décor peint en noir.	H. 2,7 cm la. 2,9 cm ép. 1 cm	1958-1959 Sud-est du *Palais royal*	Caubet 1985, 195, n° 12; Caubet - Kaczmarczyk 1987, 50; Kaczmarczyk 2007; Matoïan 2007, 208, n° 200.
15	Bassin et jambes conservés	Louvre AO 30697 / 83 AO 88	pâte siliceuse jaune pâle glaçure bleu pâle décor peint en noir.	H. 4,54 cm la. 2,38 cm ép. 1,4 cm	1958-1959 Sud-est du *Palais royal* Caubet 1985b, 195, n° 12.	
16	Buste et cuisses conservés	Louvre AO 30698 / 83 AO 89	pâte siliceuse jaune pâle glaçure vert pâle décor peint en noir.	H. buste 3,17 cm H. cuisses 3 cm la. max 2,68 cm ép. max 1,28 cm	1958-1959 Sud-est du *Palais royal*	Caubet 1985, 195, n° 12.
17	Jambes conservées	Louvre AO 30699 / 83 AO 90	pâte siliceuse blanchâtre glaçure décolorée, quelques traces bleu turquoise décor peint en noir	H. 4,06 cm la. 2,12 cm ép. 1,47 cm	1958-1959 Sud-est du *Palais royal*	
18	Partie inférieure des jambes conservée	Louvre AO 30700 / 83 AO 91	pâte siliceuse blanche glaçure bleu-jaunâtre pâle.	H. 3 cm la. 1,34 cm ép. 1,42 cm	1958-1959 Sud-est du *Palais royal*	
19	Partie inférieure des jambes conservée	Louvre AO 30701 / 83 AO 92	pâte siliceuse blanche glaçure bleu pâle.	H. 6 cm la. 1,62 cm ép. 1,3 cm	1958-1959 Sud-est du *Palais royal*	

	Description	Inv. RS / Musée	Faïence	Dimensions	Ras Shamra	Publications
20	Tête conservée	RS 26.128 Damas 4234	pâte siliceuse grise glaçure bleu-vert irisée décor peint noir	H. 2,3 cm la. 2,17 cm ép. 1,4 cm	1963 proba. *Sud acropole* tr. 7.22, W4234, –0,50 m	
21	Partie inférieure des jambes conservée	RS 26.485/1 Damas	pâte siliceuse blanchâtre glaçure vert-bleu irisée	H. 2,09 cm la. 1,6 cm ép. 1,2 cm	1963 Tranchée *Sud-acropole*, tombe 4253 [642]	Marchegay 1999, 678.
22	Partie inférieure des jambes conservée	RS 34.341 Lattaquié	pâte siliceuse blanc-beige glaçure bleu clair mate.	H. 2,6 cm la. 1,6 cm ép. 1,6 cm	1974 *Quartier résidentiel*, *Maison aux albâtres*, *locus* AM, puisard, –3 m	
23	Buste et bassin conservés	Louvre 83 AO 81	pâte siliceuse jaune pâle glaçure bleu turquoise décolorée décor peint en noir.	H. 6,1 cm la. 3,3 cm ép. 1,5 cm	Sans précision	Caubet - Kaczmarczyk 1987, 50; Matoïan 2007, 207, n° 197; Kaczmarczyk 2007.
24	Tête conservée	Louvre AO 30691 / 83 AO 82	pâte siliceuse jaune pâle glaçure bleu turquoise décolorée décor peint en noir.	H. 2,7 cm la. 2,4 cm ép. 2 cm	Sans précision	

25	Tête conservée	Louvre AO 30692 / 83 AO 83	pâte siliceuse jaune pâle restes de glaçure bleu turquoise décor peint en noir.	H. 2,8 cm la. 2,2 cm ép. 1,6 cm	Sans précision	Caubet - Kaczmarczyk 1987, 50; Matoïan 2007, 207, n° 198; Kaczmarczyk 2007.
26	Buste conservé	Louvre AO 30693 / 83 AO 84	pâte siliceuse jaune pâle glaçure décolorée bleu pâle décor peint en noir.	H. 4 cm la. 2,5 cm ép. 1,7 cm	Sans précision	Caubet - Kaczmarczyk 1987, 50; Matoïan 2007, 208, n° 199; Kaczmarczyk 2007.

Tableau: Catalogue des figurines de femme nue en faïence de Ras Shamra.

UNE NOUVELLE IMAGE DE L'ISHTAR *EBLAITU* PALÉOSYRIENNE

Paolo MATTHIAE
Sapienza University of Rome

Parmi les pièces du riche, même si fort abîmé, mobilier de culte et dans l'ensemble des monuments votifs qui appartenaient au Temple d'Ishtar (Aire D) de la Citadelle, s'est conservée une image, fort significative, de la grande déesse d'Ébla qu'on peut dater probablement au début du Bronze Moyen II (1800-1600 av. J.-C.) et qui se trouve dans l'un des registres de la face principale de la Stèle d'Ishtar, dont la base a été découverte, certainement réemployée, encore *in situ* dans le petit porche de la Chapelle D3 érigée sur le parvis du grand sanctuaire dynastique paléosyrien (Matthiae 2010a, 312-317, fig. 166-167, pl. XXIII). La déesse, vêtue d'un lourd manteau de *kaunakès*, qui cache presque complètement son corps sacré, apparaît debout dans un *naòs* ailé, érigé sur le dos d'un taureau et flanqué par deux hommes-taureaux qui soutiennent les ailes de la petite chapelle (Matthiae 1987). La même iconographie de la grande déesse éblaïte, usuellement connue dans le monde mésopotamien comme Ishtar *Eblaitu*[1], devait être présente aussi sur l'Obélisque d'Ishtar, un deuxième monument votif d'une structure fort pareille à celle de la Stèle d'Ishtar, qui lui aussi devait avoir été dédié à l'origine dans le Temple d'Ishtar de la Citadelle paléosyrienne (Matthiae 2010a, 324-326, pl. XXIV)[2].

[1] La divinité syrienne est mentionnée (*^{d}Eb-la-i-tu*) dans un rituel néoassyrien de rédaction médioassyrienne concernant le Temple du dieu Assur dans la ville d'Assur (Rawlinson and Smith 1870: 66), étudié par Frankena 1954, 1-22 et ensuite édité de nouveau, après de nouvelles collations, par Menzel 1981, T 122 (Texten 54: IX 19').

[2] Ce nouvel important monument votif paléosyrien du Temple d'Ishtar de la Citadelle, dont une première restitution a été préliminairement présentée tout récemment par Matthiae 2010a, 324-326, a pu être ultérieurement complété et partiellement restauré, car, dans la campagne de fouilles et d'études de 2010, par l'identification de deux autres fragments mineurs qui ont pu être joints au secteur inférieur du monument restitué en 2009, on a pu vérifier l'appartenance à l'obélisque de la base TM.66.D.156, trouvée en 1965 dans le vestibule L.213 du Temple d'Ishtar: Matthiae 1967, 112-123, pls. XXV 2-3, XXVII 2, XXVIII-XL 1. De la façon, alors que la dénomination d'obélisque dépend du fait que le monument, différemment de la typologie de la Stèle d'Ishtar, a une section presque exactement carrée, on a pu constater que, malgré cette variation morphologique, la Stèle et

La complexe image d'Ishtar de la stèle et de l'obélisque, qui étaient certainement des monuments votifs royaux qui célébraient la grande déesse surtout dans son rôle de patronne de la royauté éblaïte, était celle officielle, aulique et austère, par laquelle on montrait, en même temps, principalement son caractère astral et ouranien, mais aussi son domaine sur les eaux souterraines des abîmes, des sources et des fleuves et, surtout, sa protection sur la puissante royauté de l'Ébla palésoyrienne, pouvoir dominant en Haute Syrie avant l'essor du royaume de Yamkhad[3].

Il y a, pourtant, au moins un indice important que celle de la Stèle et de l'Obélisque d'Ishtar n'était pas la seule iconographie officielle de la déesse à Ébla. En fait, sur deux fragments, assez limités comme dimensions, trouvés dans la bouleversée cella du Temple d'Ishtar de la Ville Basse (Aire P), d'un bassin lustral en basalte de la typologie caractéristique des édifices religieux d'Ébla au Bronze Moyen I-II[4] s'est conservé un reste, malheureusement assez pauvre, d'une deuxième image de la déesse, tout à fait différente (Matthiae 1996): une figure féminine frontale ailée, fort probablement nue, représentée au centre de la face principale du bassin sculpté, probablement entourée de figures mythologiques et sacerdotales, desquelles presque rien s'est conservé (Matthiae 2010a, 298, fig. 155). Un deuxième fragment, qui devait appartenir à un secteur

l'Obélisque d'Ishtar étaient clairement, en ce qui concerne la structure et le programme figuratif, un couple d'objets votifs voués par un roi paléosyrien. En plus, la recomposition presque complète des secteurs inférieur et moyen de l'obélisque a permis d'établir qu'est dépourvue de fondement l'hypothèse de Matthiae 2010a, 326 que dans le dernier registre de la face principale était présente une scène d'acrobatie sur un taureau du genre étudié, dans les sceaux-cylindres paléosyriens, par Collon 1994 et, dans les peintures de Knossos et d'Avaris, par Bietak et al. 2007: la présence de la figure d'acrobate est confirmée, mais il n'y a aucun taureau au-dessous. L'Obélisque d'Ishtar sera publié dans une étude en préparation qui paraîtra dans la revue *Syria*.

[3] Les composants de l'iconographie paléosyrienne de la grande déesse éblaïte sur la Stèle d'Ishtar ont été analysés d'une façon préliminaire par Matthiae 1989. L'hypothèse que Ébla, ait été la puissance politique hégémonique de la Syrie avant les années de Yarim-Lim Ier de Yamkhad, peu après 1800 av. J.-C., est avancée dans Matthiae 2010a, 209-225, alors que sur la situation politique de la Syrie intérieure pendant le Bronze Moyen I-II est toujours valable la synthèse de Klengel 1992, 49-80.

[4] Comme on le sait bien, la typologie des rectangulaires bassins lustraux des temples d'Ébla à deux vasques carrées juxtaposées est considérée typique du mobilier sacré de la grande ville paléosyrienne et, en réalité, jusqu'à présent on ne connaît d'autres exemplaires de ce genre de pièces de mobilier trouvés dans des sanctuaires du Bronze Moyen I-II de Syrie: on doit observer, pourtant, que dans une toute récente visite à Tell Atshanah (été de 2010) l'auteur de ces lignes a pu voir abandonné tout près des restes de la maison de la Mission de Sir Leonard Woolley un bassin basaltique intact à deux vasques carrées, certainement inédit, tout à fait dépourvu de décorations sculptées, presque identique, comme structure et dimensions, aux bassins sacrés de Tell Mardikh.

latéral inférieur du même bassin, est significatif car il présente, presque entièrement, une petite figure féminine frontale nue avec les mains aux seins, qui était peut-être une hiérodule du sanctuaire (Matthiae 2010a, 298, fig. 156).

Ce bassin, qui est le seul d'Ébla à avoir une image divine au centre de la paroi principale, usuellement occupée par une scène de banquet dont est protagoniste le roi[5], devait, donc, présenter des figures du milieu, probablement divin et terrain, de la grande déesse d'Ébla, qui dans ce cas était montrée dans la nudité voluptueuse de son corps divin. Il paraît évident que dans l'image du Temple d'Ishtar de la Ville Basse Nord-Ouest, probable résidence et sanctuaire publique de la déesse, tandis que le Temple d'Ishtar de la Citadelle était le sanctuaire dynastique et privé de la famille royale (Matthiae 2010a, 265-270), ce qu'on soulignait était le caractère de l'Ishtar *Eblaitu*, identifiée à la planète Vénus, l'«étoile du soir et du matin» comme déesse de la fertilité, de l'amour et, peut-être, de la guerre[6].

On peut, donc, en déduire que dans l'Ébla paléosyrienne deux images de la déesse étaient courantes, l'une «austère», liée surtout à son rôle de patronne de la royauté, et l'autre «licencieuse», liée à son caractère dominant de dispensatrice de la fertilité (Matthiae 2010a, 297-300, 312-317).

En ce qui concerne cette dernière iconographie, qui avait une caractérisation assez marquée, tandis que l'autre était assez anonyme, la documentation fournie par le fragment de la face principale du bassin à deux

[5] Parmi les bassins lustraux, complets ou plus ou moins fragmentaires, découverts à Tell Mardikh ce sont le bassin en calcaire entier découvert en 1965 dans la cella du Temple d'Ishtar de la Citadelle (Aire D), le bassin en basalte presque complet trouvé avant le début des fouilles italiennes devant le Temple de Rashap de la Ville Basse Sud-Ouest (Aire B), le bassin fort fragmentaire récupéré en 1964 dans le puits du même Temple de Rashap qui présentaient une scène de banquet sur la face principale antérieure, tandis qu'on ne peut rien dire du bassin en calcaire trouvé dans le Temple de Shapash/Shamash en 1972 (Aire B) dans la Ville Basse Nord, car sa face antérieure est complètement perdue: en ce qui concerne la position de la figure de la déesse ailée en relation à la structure du bassin en basalte presque complètement perdu du Temple d'Ishtar de la Ville Basse Nord-Ouest (Aire P), on peut être sûr qu'elle se trouvait au centre de la face principale, car sur le côté postérieur du fragment est bien conservé un reste de la paroi de division entre les deux vasques, qui se trouvait toujours au centre car les deux vasques étaient de dimensions identiques: Matthiae 2006.

[6] Sur le caractère divin d'Inanna/Ishtar en Mésopotamie, et sur les contradictions de cette particulière figure divine on peut voir les considérations classiques de Jacobsen 1976, 135-143, alors que Albright 1968, 112-118 et Gese 1970, 156-164 donnent une bonne idée des connaissances antécédentes aux découvertes de la culture paléosyrienne d'Ébla. Dans l'exemplaire analyse de Durand 2008, 196-203 on trouve des notes significatives sur l'importance du culte d'Ishtar, sur la base des sources de Mari, dans la période d'Ur III et d'Isin et Larsa, dans la région de l'Euphrate et en Syrie Occidentale.

vasques, fort mal conservé, du Temple d'Ishtar de la Ville Basse Nord-Ouest (Aire P), est malheureusement trop partielle pour une restitution fiable de l'image originaire. Pour ne faire qu'un exemple, on n'a aucun indice de ce que la déesse tenait dans ses mains, alors qu'il est fort intéressant d'observer que les traces conservées des ailes sont suffisantes à faire comprendre que, dans cette image de l'iconographie «licencieuse», était souligné son caractère céleste exactement comme il arrivait dans l'iconographie «austère» par le moyen du *naòs* ailé[7].

Pour une restitution des images courantes dans les milieux religieux de l'iconographie «licencieuse» de la grande déesse de l'Ébla paléosyrienne a une particulière importance la découverte récente, dans un contexte de réemploi dans un mur tardif de l'époque perse-hellénistique près du Petit Palais de la période achéménide, d'un troisième fragment appartenant à une belle table de culte dont deux fragments avaient été trouvés, aux début de l'exploration de Tell Mardikh, dans la cella et dans le vestibule du même Temple d'Ishtar de la Citadelle. Cette remarquable pièce du mobilier sacré du principal sanctuaire de la Citadelle du Bronze Moyen I-II était une table ronde basaltique, soutenue par une sorte de trépieds composé de trois jambes verticales, assez larges et aplaties, probablement

[7] Malgré le fait qu'on connaît, dans le répertoire de la glyptique paléosyrienne, une assez large quantité d'images de la déesse nue frontale, avec un certain nombre de variantes, les images de la déesse nue ailée ne sont pas particulièrement fréquentes: Delaporte 1910, 255, n. 453 (déesse debout sur un lion avec 'guirlande'), pl. XXX; Delaporte 1920, 195-196, n. A.932 (AO.7296: déesse aux longs cheveux relevés en chignon et coiffé d'une tiare multicorne, qui tient dans chaque main par une jambe un personnage nu tête en bas), pl. 97 4; Eisen 1940, 62, n. 157 (Moore 170: dessin incertain par mauvaise gravure), pl. XV; Porada 1948, 129, n. 963 (déesse avec un bras étendu le long du corps et l'autre tenant une fleur de lotus); Buchanan 1966, 172, n. 880 (1913.553: déesse à la 'guirlande'), pl. 55; Buchanan 1981, 428-429, n. 1242 (NBC 7926: déesse avec 'guirlande'); Teissier 1984, 250-251, n. 493 (déesse, avec les ailes éployées d'une structure presque identique à celle du bassin du Temple P2, tenant dans chaque main une antilope); Hammade 1987, 88-89, n. 166 (M.4592: déesse avec deux scorpions); à présent voir aussi Otto 2000, 210, n. 157 (Louvre A.932), 226 (Ashmolean 880), 227 (Yale 1242), pl. 13, 18. Dans le large corpus des cylindres paléosyriens sont de particulière importance de rares sceaux qui permettent des liaisons entre les deux iconographies, «austère» et «licencieuse», de la grande déesse: c'est le cas, d'un côté, du cylindre von der Osten 1936, 14, n. 90, pl. IX, où la déesse avec la 'guirlande', frontale et en nudité comme il est la norme dans l'image «licencieuse», est insérée dans un *naòs* à arc avec quatre paires d'ailes déployées, structure qui, par contre, est typique de l'image «austère», ou, de l'autre, du sceau Delaporte 1910, 257-258, n. 457, pl. XXXI, où c'est la déesse nue frontale à apparaître dans un *naòs* rectangulaire avec deux courtes ailes monté sur le dos d'un taureau, exactement comme dans l'iconographie «austère» de la stèle et de l'obélisque du grand sanctuaire dynastique d'Ébla. D'un intérêt tout à fait particulier est le cylindre paléosyrien du British Museum BM 89122, où la déesse nue frontale apparaît sur le dos d'un taureau accroupi à l'intérieur d'un *naòs* à arc doué de deux ailes: Teissier 1996, 200, n. 109.

disposées à une distance régulière l'une de l'autre, décorées sur la face externe par une figure en relief assez marqué.

Le deux fragments trouvés en 1965 et en 1966 dans la cella L.202 et dans le vestibule L.213 du Temple d'Ishtar (Aire D) de l'Acropole (Matthiae 2010a, 419-422, fig. 228) étaient un secteur moyen de l'une des jambes verticales avec un reste d'une figure frontale en relief (Fig. 1)[8] et un segment périphérique de la table même, qui conservait, en haut, un trait de la superficie plate, avec une partie du bord légèrement rehaussé et, en bas, le secteur supérieur de l'une des jambes verticales avec l'extrême partie haute d'une figure frontale en relief avec des restes d'apparentes volutes au-dessus de la tête de cet être clairement mythique ou divin (Fig. 2)[9]. Il était clair que le premier fragment appartenait à une jambe différente de celle dont le deuxième fragment conservait l'extrême partie supérieure. Par conséquent, c'était seulement une conjecture que la figure présente sur le fragment de jambe conservée fût identique à celle dont le fragment de table conservait le secteur supérieur avec la tête d'un être surnaturel.

Le troisième fragment de la pièce du mobilier, découvert pendant la campagne de fouille de 2009 (Fig. 3)[10], a permis de résoudre le problème, car ce troisième fragment conserve un secteur moyen d'une deuxième jambe, douée d'une figure en relief tout à fait semblable à celle du premier fragment, qui se joint parfaitement à la cassure du reste supérieur de la jambe conservée dans le deuxième fragment (Fig. 4). De cette façon, d'un côté, on a rejoint la certitude que la table était soutenue par trois

[8] Il s'agit du fragment TM.65.D.265, trouvé dans le secteur antérieur, méridional, de la cella L.202: hauteur 11 cm; largeur 11 cm; épaisseur 5 cm: Matthiae 1966, 140-141, pl. LVI 1. L'hypothèse, erronée, qu'il s'agissait d'un reste d'une plaquette votive, dépendant des dimensions fort limitées du fragment, fut corrigée l'année suivante à la suite de la découverte du deuxième reste de la table offertoire (voir note suivante)

[9] Fragment TM.66.D.159, découvert devant le front du mur M.200+M.201, qui est le mur de périmètre Ouest du bâtiment sacré originaire: hauteur 15 cm; largeur 26,5 cm; épaisseur 19,5 cm: Matthiae 1967, 127-128, 131-132, pl. XLII 3. Le plan de la table, circulaire, est soigneusement lissé; le bord de la table, pour une épaisseur de 2,1 cm, lui aussi bien lissé, est surélevé de 0,5 cm en rapport au plan de la table à l'intérieur; la largeur de la partie inférieure de la jambe de ce fragment, qui est, de 11/12 cm, correspond parfaitement à celui de TM.65.D.265 et a permis, dès la découverte de ce deuxième reste, de comprendre que TM.65.D.265 et TM.D.66.D.159 ne pouvaient que appartenir à une seule sophistiquée pièce de mobilier conservé, à l'origine, dans la cella du Temple de l'Aire D: Matthiae 1967, 131.

[10] C'est le fragment TM.09.E.70, qu'on a trouvé remployé dans le mur M.9811 d'époque perse-hellénistique, dans le carré EiVI3iii dans le Secteur E Ouest de la fouille. Le fragment a une largeur de 10,7 cm et une épaisseur de 5,2 cm, alors que sa hauteur est de 9,7 cm.

jambes qui devaient avoir toutes la même décoration en relief d'une figure frontale nue (Fig. 5) et, de l'autre côté, on a pu restituer, en bonne partie, l'une de ces figures depuis la tiare jusqu'au début des jambes de l'être mythique.

Parmi les pièces du sophistiqué mobilier en basalte des temples et des palais de l'Ébla paléosyrienne on connaît la typologie si bien de la plus usuelle et plus raffinée table d'offrande employée dans les sanctuaires, documentée par les représentations sur les bas-reliefs des bassins à deux vasques sculptés des temples d'Ébla (Matthiae 2010a, 294-296, fig. 9, pl. XXII 1)[11], par les scènes incisées sur assez nombreux sceaux-cylindres[12] et par un splendide, même si incomplet, exemplaire en basalte du Temple d'Ishtar de la Ville Basse (Matthiae 1994, 173-177, fig. 3-4, pl. XVII a-b)[13], que d'un particulier bassin ronde sur haut trépieds à jambes sculptées en

[11] Cette table d'offrande est représentée sur les faces antérieures du bassin basaltique du Temple de Rashap (Aire B), découvert avant le début des fouilles italiennes à Tell Mardikh (Matthiae 1965, 71-81, pl. LXIX-LXX: dans cette contribution, sur la base de la comparaison avec une table d'offrande en basalte massif du Temple d'Alalakh I, mais sans doute plus ancien [AT/39/287: Woolley 1955, p. 243, pl. LII a] on avait supposé que la table fût carrée, plutôt que ronde]) et du bassin calcaire du Temple d'Ishtar de l'Acropole (Aire D), découvert en 1965 (Matthiae 1966, 113-129, pl. XLIV, XLV a). Il faut signaler que à Ébla une nouvelle représentation de la même table d'offrande des bassins se trouve sur un reste inédit de ce qui devait être le sommet d'un obélisque votif pareil à celui préliminairement publié tout récemment, qui avait été sans doute érigé dans le Temple d'Ishtar de l'Acropole: Matthiae 2010a, 324-326, pl. XXIV 1-2; cet important fragment d'obélisque sera publié par l'auteur dans l'article annoncé (note 2) en préparation pour *Syria*, où sera étudié l'Obélisque d'Ishtar après les dernières restitutions effectuées en 2010.

[12] La représentation de la table d'offrande éblaïte est relativement fréquente dans les empreintes des sceaux-cylindres des tablettes de Cappadoce de Kültepe II de style dit syro-cappadocien (Teissier 1994, 230-232, 234, n. 466, 491, 515, 551). Dans la glyptique paléo-syrienne, parmi les nombreux cas (28) de reproductions d'une table d'offrande catalogués par Otto 2000, 265, seulement un nombre fort limité (3) concerne la table d'offrande éblaïte, tandis que la plupart des tables reproduites sont d'un type clairement plus récent, à jambes courbes, sans support central à pattes de taureau et sans les colonnettes périphériques: n. 220 (Ashmolean n. 859), 255 (Baltimore, Walters Art Gallery n. WAG 42.414), 317 (Golénischef n. 121). Il faut aussi attirer l'attention sur le cylindre de la Collection Kelley de la Pierpont Morgan Library publié par Porada 1993, où la table d'offrande éblaïte est soigneusement reproduite devant un personnage assis sur un trône à haut dossier, qui paraît de la même typologie des sièges des statues votives des rois des temples paléosyrien d'Ébla: Matthiae 1992 et Matthiae 2006.

[13] Cette pièce du mobilier sacré (TM.91.P.717) du Temple d'Ishtar de la Ville Basse (Temple P2), même si conservé seulement dans le secteur inférieur, est un véritable chef-d'œuvre de sculpture, travaillé dans un basalte très fin et montre tous les détails sommairement reproduits dans les incisions des sceaux-cylindres, depuis la colonne centrale aux pattes sinueuses finissant par des socles de taureau et aux subtiles colonnettes qui soutenaient les bords de la table se fondant sur le sommet des socles de taureau: Matthiae et al. 1995, 504, 528, n. 469.

ronde bosse, dont on connaît au moins deux exemplaires, assez fragmentaires, découverts dans la salle de réception du Palais Septentrional de la Ville Basse (Matthiae 1994, 167-173, fig. 1-2, pl. XV b-c, XVI a-b).

La table avec les trois jambes verticales décorées de figures mythiques en relief du Temple d'Ishtar de la Citadelle partage avec la table du Temple d'Ishtar de la Ville Basse la forme du grand disque plat circulaire de la table proprement dite (Fig. 6) et avec le bassin du Palais Septentrional le schéma des trois jambes verticales périphériques[14]. En tout cas, les trois pièces de mobilier sacré et profane des deux sanctuaires d'Ishtar et du Palais Septentrional, probablement du Bronze Moyen II, sont la preuve de l'exubérante capacité d'inventer des formes de mobilier d'originale structure et de riche décoration sculptée.

C'était la face antérieure des jambes de la table d'offrande du Temple d'Ishtar de la Citadelle l'endroit où on avait sculpté celle qui apparaît une variante importante et officielle de l'image «licencieuse» de la grande déesse titulaire du temple dynastique. La déesse, comme on l'a dit, y est représentée nue et frontale dans l'attitude de soutenir deux longues tiges sur les bords mêmes de la jambe de la table, couronnées chacune par deux amples volutes qui arrivent à flanquer le visage frontal de l'être divin en se joignant au centre sur le sommet de sa tiare (Fig. 7)[15]. Une claire particularité du visage, humain par contre dans tous les détails, est la présence de deux proéminentes oreilles de vache[16]. La tiare est assez particulière: elle est formée apparemment par trois sortes de cornes droites, l'une centrale verticale et les deux autres latérales obliques. Cette

[14] Pour la configuration de la base de la table du Temple d'Ishtar de la Citadelle, étant donné que rien est conservé du secteur inférieur du meuble sacré, on peut faire trois hypothèses: les trois jambes étaient complètement libres; les bases des trois jambes se détachaient d'un disque de base, comme dans l'un (TM.87.P.260) des bassins circulaires du Palais Septentrional (Matthiae 1994, 169, fig. 1); les bases des jambes étaient mises en relation par des tronçons qui se suivaient en forment une sorte de sommaire cercle, comme dans le deuxième bassin circulaire du même édifice (TM.86.P.100: Matthiae 1994, 169, fig. 2).

[15] Déjà dans la première publication du fragment TM.66.D.159 (Matthiae 1967, 131) on avait individué les volutes végétales des tiges latérales soutenues par la déesse, en remarquant que seulement apparemment elles se joignaient aux cornes de la tiare divine. En plus dans le commentaire sur ces volutes on indiquait qu'elles ressemblent aux volutes des supports de symboles astraux de la glyptique paléosyrienne: Delaporte 1910, 263-264, n. 466, 467, pl. XXXI; Delaporte 1920, 194, n. A.920, pl. 96 10; Speleers 1943, 157, 165, 171-172, n. 676, 1482, 1460; Porada 1948, 120-121, n. 912, 920, pl. CXXXVII, CXXXIX.

[16] Cette particularité des oreilles de vache représentées dans une position horizontale est typique, dans la glyptique paléosyrienne, des relativement fréquentes images des têtes hathoriques frontales: Teissier 1996, 157-158.

typologie rare de la tiare doit fort probablement être interprétée comme un haut couvre-chef conoïdal pointu, flanqué par deux cornes de taureau libres en abrégée vision frontale[17]. D'une façon assez étrange, la partie centrale haute de la poitrine, au-dessous du cou, est cachée par une masse légèrement relevée en relief à base semi-circulaire comme une barbe, mais qui est sans doute un lourd collier[18].

Dans l'ensemble, donc, l'image de la déesse est celle d'une femme frontale nue aux oreilles de vache, ceinte d'une tiare à trois cornes et ornée d'un massif collier, qui tient dans ses mains deux longues tiges fleuries. S'il n'y a aucune allusion au caractère céleste de la déesse, clairement indiqué, au contraire, par les ailes si bien de l'image «licencieuse» conservé dans le bassin fort fragmentaire du Temple d'Ishtar de la Ville Basse que du *naòs* de celle «austère» du sanctuaire de la Citadelle, les bien évidentes oreilles de vache ne peuvent qu'être un emprunt de l'iconographie classique égyptienne de la grande Hathor, la vache céleste du panthéon de la vallée du Nil (Allam 1963). A ce propos, même s'il n'y a pas une certitude, il faut rappeler qu'il est probable que la déesse frontale du bassin du Temple d'Ishtar de la Ville Basse ait eu la typique chevelure hathorienne avec les deux larges boucles sur les épaules à la base du cou (Matthiae 2010a, 298, fig. 155).

Il est évident, d'autre part, que, dans les conditions de conservation des deux images fragmentaires de la déesse de la table du Temple d'Ishtar de la Citadelle, il n'y a aucune raison de supposer ou d'exclure la présence d'un animal sacré à la déesse — le lion ou le taureau — à la base de l'image, animal qui éventuellement aurait été le support de l'image de la déesse, comme dans l'iconographie «austère» du Temple d'Ishtar de la

[17] Il s'agit fort probablement d'une tiare ceinte si bien par des dieux que par des déesses, documentée par les figurines en bronze de l'aire syro-palestinienne, qui présente un élément central postérieur, toujours assez haut, de formes différentes, qui souvent assume une morphologie presque linéaire, comme dans les deux statuettes en bronze du Louvre (Negbi 1976, 166, n. 1378 et 1379, pl. 25), provenant de Tortose, AO.1464 (Bossert 1951, 177, n. 580; Collon 1972, 117, n. 22, fig. 3) et AO.11188 (Bossert 1951, 177, n. 579; Collon 1972, 117, n. 23, fig. 3) et deux cornes libres de taureau latérales: Negbi 1976, 163, 167, n. 1317 (Louvre AO.20160: déesse guerrière), 1319 (Louvre AO. 18511, provenant d'Ugarit, figure de Ba'l-Hadad) et 1390 (Louvre AO.22266: cfr. Bossert 1951, 176, n. 573, où les deux cornes libres sont bien évidentes).

[18] Ce détail est sans doute le plus singulier et bizarre de l'image, qui dans tous les autres éléments de la représentation ne présente pas des particularités difficiles à comprendre. L'aspect de la petite masse à base circulaire qui entoure la base du cou est certainement fort pareil à celui d'une barbe, mais il n'y a pas de doute que ce détail doive être interprété comme un lourd collier, d'autant plus que des colliers, assez massifs, sont toujours présents dans les images de la déesse nue dans une attitude tout à fait comparable des plaques en métal du Bronze Récent I et surtout II, mentionnées *ultra* à la note 24.

Citadelle, mais surtout dans plusieurs représentations de la glyptique paléosyrienne contemporaine[19].

En tout cas, l'image de la déesse qu'on avait voulu sculpter sur les jambes de la table du Temple d'Ishtar de la Citadelle était une image «licencieuse» de la divinité qu'on doit considérer un *unicum*, jusqu'à présent, dans le patrimoine iconologique de l'Ébla paléosyrienne. Sa présence dans le mobilier sacré du sanctuaire dynastique de l'Acropole est d'un particulier intérêt car elle permet d'exclure que l'image «licencieuse» de la déesse était réservée seulement au sanctuaire publique de la divinité — le Temple d'Ishtar de la Ville Basse — et celle «austère» à celui dynastique de la Citadelle. Évidemment, dans l'unité fondamentale de la figure divine de la grande déesse, était proéminent le caractère de dispensatrice de la fertilité, qui, par des variantes dans lesquelles gardait une valeur dominante l'image frontale nue de la divinité en raison de sa formidable efficacité visuelle, pouvait être représenté dans tous les lieux saints dédiés à la Ishtar *Eblaitu*, si bien dans le sanctuaire publique de la Ville Basse que dans la «chapelle» palatine et dynastique de la Citadelle.

La formule iconographique de la table d'offrande du Temple d'Ishtar de la Citadelle est d'un grand intérêt, car ses caractères les plus particuliers, même s'ils ne sont pas documentés dans la contemporaine culture figurative d'Ébla, se retrouvent rarement dans d'autres centres de culte de la grande déesse dans l'aire syro-palestinienne. Dans ce sens, l'élément le plus significatif est celui de la tiare à élément central haut et pointu[20] et deux cornes latérales libres qui se présente comme une tiare

[19] La déesse nue frontale, souvent avec la 'guirlande', est représentée fréquemment dans la glyptique paléosyrienne debout sur un taureau: Delaporte 1910, 258, n. 458, pl. XXXI; Delaporte 1920, 195, n. A.930, pl. 97 2; von der Osten 1936, 13, n. 85, pl. VII; Eisen 1940, 62, n. 156, pl. XV; Porada 1948, 125, n. 942, 943, pl. CXLII; Buchanan 1966, 173, n. 883, 884, 885, pl. 56; Buchanan 1981, 428-429, n. 124. Dans quelques cas le taureau sur lequel se tient debout la déesse est le taureau du dieu Hadad, représenté en face de la divinité féminine, comme, par exemple, dans Porada 1948, 130, n. 967, pl. CXLVI; Teissier 1984, 242-243, n. 477; Keel-Leu et Teissier 2004, 290, 460, n. 344. Voir aussi Matthiae 1989.

[20] Même s'il est clair qu'il n'y a aucune trace des cornes libres latérales, la structure de la tiare conoïdale allongée de la déesse de la table d'offrande éblaïte est certainement à comparer à celle de la déesse nue frontale avec 'guirlande' et deux oiseaux d'une assez rare figurine en argile d'Alalakh III (AT/39/240): Woolley 1955, 247, pl. LIV o. Cette figurine en argile, d'un point de vue iconographique, dépend clairement des moules en serpentine certainement du Bronze Moyen I, comme celle, de provenance inconnue, de la Collection von Aulock, attribuée au milieu de Kültépé: Özgüç 1950, 206, fig. 437 a-b, pl. LXVII; von der Osten 1957, 155, fig. 356; Emre 1971, 117, n. 51, pl. XI 4a-b.

à trois cornes[21], qui est documenté dans une moule, presque contemporaine, d'une figurine de déesse debout (Fig. 8: Dothan 1956, 21-22, pl. 6A-B; Negbi 1976, 64, 178, n.1352, fig. 78, pl. 39) trouvée sur les pierres du si-dit Haut Lieu du sanctuaire de Nahariyah en Palestine du nord pas loin de la Méditerranée (Dothan 1956 et 1957)[22]. Un autre élément, fort significatif, de la structure figurative du relief de la table d'offrande du temple de l'Acropole, mais lui aussi extrêmement rare dans les représentations de la déesse nue frontale de la glyptique paléosyrienne, est la position frontale du visage de la divinité, car la norme dans la glyptique est la position de profil de la tête divine: seulement un cas, pas absolument certain, peut être mentionné (Delaporte 1910, 255, n. 453, pl. XXX).

Or, si l'on considère les deux représentations monumentales de l'Ishtar *Eblaitu* dans la formule «licencieuse» documentée à Ébla, dans le bassin fort fragmentaire du Temple d'Ishtar de la Ville Basse et dans la table d'offrande du Temple d'Ishtar de la Citadelle, on peut constater que sont présents deux caractères iconographiques qui dans la glyptique de Syrie paraissent seulement au Bronze Récent I. Il s'agit, dans le premier cas, de la disposition des ailes qui, dans le relief sur le reste du bassin éblaïte, se courbent en bas vers les extrémités, tandis que dans toutes les représentations de la divinité de la glyptique paléosyrienne les ailes de la divinité sont levées en haut[23]. Dans le deuxième cas, il s'agit de la position frontale du visage de la déesse, pour laquelle il y a le témoignage, certain du point de vue si bien de la stratigraphie que du style et de la technique de l'incision, d'une empreinte d'Alalakh IV (Collon 1975, 118, n. 215).

Si, donc, deux caractères iconographiques de l'image monumentale de l'Ishtar *Eblaitu* — la disposition des ailes de la déesse, dans l'un cas, et le visage frontal dans l'autre — sont des éléments qui ne furent reçus par les graveurs des ateliers de la glyptique que, probablement, au début du Bronze Récent I, l'attitude générale de la déesse sur les reliefs de la

[21] L'un des très rares exemples de figurine masculine, certainement divine et de mauvais travail, qui présente une tiare à élément central et deux cornes latérales droites, comme sur la table d'offrande d'Ébla, appartenant au type usuellement dit du 'smiting god' (Collon 1972) est le petit bronze du Louvre AO.2247, haut seulement 9,0 cm, certainement provenant de Syrie, publié par Negbi 1976, 167, n. 1393, pl. 27.

[22] Mazar 1990, 212-213, 219-221.

[23] Le seul cas d'un cylindre de Syrie datable entre la fin du Bronze Moyen II et le début du Bronze Récent I dans lequel les ailes ont été représentées comme sur le relief du bassin du Temple d'Ishtar de la Ville Basse est Teissier 1984, 250-251, n. 493, daté par B. Teissier entre 1650 et 1500 av. J.-Chr.

table d'offrande du sanctuaire dynastique de la Citadelle est tout à fait typique des précieuses plaques, souvent en or, de Syrie du nord du Bronze Récent I et II. L'image de la déesse frontale nue qui tient à ses cotés deux tiges fleuries est, en fait, le sujet des plaques d'or des dépôts de Minet el-Beydah (Fig. 9), le port d'Ugarit, où, toutefois, il y a une variété de coiffures et de couvre-chefs qui peut évidemment être considérée une particularité typique des ateliers de la ville médiosyrienne de la côte méditerranéenne[24].

L'image «licencieuse» de l'Ishtar *Eblaitu* qui s'est conservée dans les deux versions du reste du bassin sculpté du Temple d'Ishtar de la Ville Basse et des fragments de la table d'offrande du Temple d'Ishtar de la Citadelle clairement soulignait, par la nudité frontale de la déesse, surtout son rôle de patronne de la fertilité universelle, par les ailes du relief du bassin lustral, son caractère astral comme planète Vénus et, par les tiges fleuries, son domaine sur le monde végétal. La présence des deux images sur des pièces importantes du mobilier sacré des deux sanctuaires de la déesse, assure que ces images étaient des variantes de l'iconographie officielle de la grande déesse éblaïte probablement dans les décennies entre la fin du Bronze Moyen I et une phase avancée du Bronze Moyen II, peut-être entre 1850 et 1650 av. J.-Chr.

Or l'introduction d'Ishtar comme patronne de la royauté d'Ébla dans le panthéon de la grande ville paléosyrienne peut fort probablement être datée par la formule de datation qui apparaît dans l'inscription du roi Ibbit-Lim, fils de Igrish-Kheb, qui, en 1968, a permis l'identification de Tell Mardikh à Ébla (Matthiae et Pettinato 1972). Malgré des incertitudes d'interprétation (Lambert 1981), il paraît assuré que la statue fut dédiée, probablement dans le Temple d'Ishtar de la Citadelle, l'huitième année après «la manifestation d'Ishtar» (Gelb 1984). Cet événement cultuel, évidemment d'extraordinaire importance, ne peut pas avoir été l'introduction du culte d'Ishtar à Ébla, car les textes des Archives Royales offrent une ample documentation du culte de la déesse déjà dans la ville protosyrienne du Bronze Ancien IVA, entre 2400 et 2300 av. J.-Chr.[25].

[24] Schaeffer 1929, 289-290,, pl. LIV 2 (Dépôt 11); Schaeffer 1932, 8-10 (Dépôt 213bis: AO.14716 et AO.14717); Negbi 1976, 191, n. 1698-1700, fig. 117-118, 128, pl. 54. Pour la diffusion, dans des formes simplifiées, de ces plaques médiosyriennes dans toute l'aire syro-palestinienne voir McGovern 1985, 29-35.

[25] Sur Ishtar à l'époque des Archives Royales on peut voir à présent Pomponio et Xella 1997, 63-67, Biga et Capomacchia 2008, 136-150 et Mander 2008, 58-59, alors que l'importance d'Ishkhara dans le culte de l'époque des Archives Royales a été mise en évidence par Archi 1993 et 2002.

Il est, donc, bien probable qu'ait été Ibbit-Lim même, peut-être tout au début du Bronze Moyen I, peu après 2000 av. J.-Chr, selon la conventionnelle Chronologie Moyenne, à avoir fait de l'Ishtar *Eblaitu*, possible résultat d'un syncrétisme entre Ishkhara, la grande déesse de l'époque des Archives Royales[26], et Ishtar même, la patronne de la royauté éblaïte (Matthiae 2003) de la ville qui aurait dominé la Syrie intérieure avant l'essor de Yamkhad au temps du grand Yarim-Lim I (Klengel 1992, 54-58).

L'image «licencieuse» de l'Ishtar *Eblaitu*, documentée à Ébla même dans la décoration de pièces du mobilier sacré des sanctuaires de la ville entre 1850 et 1650 av. J.-Chr., a eu des précédents au tout début du Bronze Moyen I, probablement entre 1950 et 1900 av. J.-Chr., qui sont attestés par des empreintes de style syro-cappadocien ou «syrien colonial» de Kültépé II (Teissier 1994, 233). Ces empreintes documentent que les deux iconographies, «austère» et «licencieuse», de la grande déesse d'Ébla étaient déjà formées au tout début du IIème millénaire av. J.-Chr.[27]

L'importance particulière de l'image «licencieuse» de l'Ishtar *Eblaitu* conservée par l'originale table d'offrande du temple de la déesse de la Citadelle d'Ébla est dans un nouvel témoignage significatif du rôle de premier plan que les ateliers royaux des temples de la grande ville paléosyrienne de la Syrie intérieure ont joué dans la création d'iconographies caractéristiques de la période médiosyrienne des siècles suivants et dans la transmission d'un remarquable et riche répertoire iconographique de l'époque protosyrienne de la deuxième moitié du IIIème millénaire av. J.-Chr. jusqu'aux siècles du Fer II au début du Ier millénaire av. J.-Chr. (Matthiae 1989).

[26] Prechel 1996, 5-22. En ce qui concerne l'élément iconographique représenté par les oreilles de vache dans l'image de la table d'offrande, il paraît nécessaire proposer une alternative à l'hypothèse présentée *supra* qu'il soit le résultat d'une influence égyptienne dérivant de Hathor: on ne devrait pas exclure, en fait, que cet élément dépende de l'élaboration syncrétistique entre Ishtar et Ishkhara, car dans l'iconographie protosyrienne d'Ishkhara qui a pu être identifiée sur un cylindre d'un haut dignitaire de la cour protosyrienne du roi Ishar-Damu, la déesse a des traits féminins unis à des éléments bovins: Matthiae 2010b. D'autre part, il est aussi possible que dans la conscience même des habitants de la ville paléosyrienne on était au courant que l'Ishtar *Eblaitu* était le produit d'un syncrétisme Ishtar/Ishkhara, si dans le prologue du poème bilingue hourro-hittite sur la destruction de l'Ébla paléosyrienne «Chant de la libération», avec Teshoub et Allani la seule autre divinité mentionnée est exactement Ishkhara, qui pourrait y paraître comme protectrice de la ville menacée par Teshoub de Kumme: Neu 1996, 30-31.

[27] Une étude détaillée des images de la déesse éblaïte dans le matériel glyptique de provenance et de production syriennes qu'on peut dater de l'époque de Kültépé II est en préparation par l'auteur de ces lignes pour un volume de contributions dédiées à la mémoire d'Adnan Bounni, qui paraîtra dans la série *Contributi e Materiali di Archeologia Orientale*.

Bibliographie

ALBRIGHT, W. F. 1968: *Yahweh and the Gods of Canaan. A Historical Analysis of Two Contrasting Faiths* (Jordan Lectures 1965), London.

ALLAM, S. 1963: *Beiträge zum Hathorkult (bis zum Ende des Mittleren Reiches)* (Münchner Ägyptologische Studien 4), Berlin.

ARCHI, A. 1993: «Divinités sémitiques et divinités de substrat: Le cas d'Išḫara et d'Ištar à Ebla», *M.A.R.I.* 7, 71-78.

— 2002: «Formation of the West Hurrian Pantheon: The Case of Išḫara», dans K. A. Yener, H. A. Hoffner Jr. (éd.) *Recent Developments in Hittite Archaeology and History. Papers in Memory of Hans G. Güterbock*, Winona Lake, 21-33.

BIETAK, M., N. MARINATOS et C. PALIVOU 2007: *Taureador Scenes in Tell el-Dab'a (Avaris) and Knossos* (Untersuchungen der Zweigstelle Kairo des Österreichischen Archäologischen Institutes 27), Wien.

BIGA, M. G. et A. M. G. CAPOMACCHIA 2008: *Il politeismo vicino-orientale*, Roma.

BOSSERT, H. Th. 1951: *Altsyrien. Kunst und Handwerk in Cypern, Syrien, Palästina, Transjordanien und Arabien von den Anfängen bis zum völligen Aufgehen in der Griechisch-Römischen Kultur* (Die Ältesten Kulturen des Mittelmeerkreises 3), Tübingen.

BUCHANAN, B. 1966: *Catalogue of the Ancient Near Eastern Seals in the Ashmolean Museum, I, Cylinder Seals*, Oxford.

BUCHANAN, B. 1981: *Early Near Eastern Seals in the Yale Babylonian Collection*, New Haven - London.

COLLON, D. 1972: «The Smiting God: A Study of a Bronze in the Pomerance Collection in New York», *Levant* 4, 111-134.

COLLON, D. 1975: *The Seal Impressions from Tell Atchana/Alalakh* (Alter Orient und Altes Testament 27), Neukirchen-Vluyn.

— 1994: «Bull-Leaping in Syria», *Ägypten und Levante* 4, 81-88.

DELAPORTE, L. 1910: *Catalogue des cylindres orientaux et des cachets de la Bibliothèque Nationale* (Fondation Eugène Piot), Paris.

— 1920: *Musée du Louvre. Catalogue des Cylindres orientaux, II. Acquisitions*, Paris.

DOTHAN, M. 1956: «The Excavations at Nahariyah. Preliminary Report (Seasons 1954/1955)», *Israel Exploration Journal* 6, 14-25.

— 1957: «Some Aspects of Religious Life in Palestine during the Hyksos Rule», *Antiquity and Survival* 2, 121-130.

DURAND, J.-M. 2008: «La religion amorrite en Syrie à l'époque des Archives de Mari», dans G. del Olmo Lete (éd.) *Mythologie et religion des Sémites Occidentaux, Volume I: Ébla, Mari* (Orientalia Lovaniensia Analecta 162), Leuven, 163-716.

EISEN, G. A. 1940: *Ancient Oriental Cylinder and Other Seals with a Description of the Collection of Mrs. William H. Moore* (Oriental Institute Publications 47), Chicago.

EMRE, K. 1971: *Anatolian Lead Figurines and Their Stone Moulds* (Türk Tarih Kurumu, Ser. VI, 14), Ankara.

FRANKENA, R. 1954: *Tākultu. De sakrale maaltijd in het Assyrische ritueel, met een overzicht over de in Assur vereerde goden*, Leiden.

GELB, I. J. 1984: «The Inscription of Jibbit-Lim, King of Ebla», *Studia Orientalia* 55, 213-229.

GESE, H. 1970: «Die Religionen Altsyriens», dans H. Gese, M. Höfner et K. Rudolph (éd.) *Die Religionen Altsyriens, Altarabiens und der Mandäer* (Die Religionen der Menschheit 10/2), Stuttgart, 3-232.

HAMMADE, H. 1987: *Cylinder Seals from the Collections of the Aleppo Museum, Syrian Arab Republic, 1. Seals of Unknown Provenance* (BAR International Series 335), Oxford.

JACOBSEN, Th. 1976: *The Treasures of Darkness. A History of Mesopotamian Religion*, New Haven.

KEEL-LEU, H. et B. TEISSIER 2004: *Die vorderasiatischen Rollsiegel der Sammlungen «Bibel+Orient» der Universität Freiburg Schweiz* (Orbis Biblicus et Orientalis 200), Fribourg. Göttingen.

KLENGEL, H. 1992: *Syria 3000 to 300 B.C. A Handbook of Political History*, Berlin.

LAMBERT, W. G. 1981: «The Statue Inscription of Ibbit-Lim of Ebla», *Revue d'Assyriologie* 75, 95-101.

MANDER, P. 2008: «Les dieux et le culte à Ébla», dans G. del Olmo Lete (éd.) *Mythologie et religion des Sémites Occidentaux, Volume I: Ébla, Mari* (Orientalia Lovaniensia Analecta 162), Leuven, 1-160.

MATTHIAE, P. 1965: «Le sculture in basalto», dans P. Matthiae (éd.) *Missione Archeologica Italiana in Siria. Rapporto preliminare della campagna 1964* (Serie Archeologica 8), Roma 1965, 61-80.

— 1966: «Le sculture in pietra», dans P. Matthiae (éd.) *Missione Archeologica Italiana in Siria. Rapporto preliminare della campagna 1965 [Tell Mardikh]* (Serie Archeologica 10), Roma, 103-142.

— 1967: «I frammenti di sculture in pietra», dans P. Matthiae (éd.) *Missione Archeologica Italiana in Siria. Rapporto preliminare della campagna 1966 [Tell Mardikh]* (Serie Archeologica 13), Roma, 111-138.

— 1987: «Una stele paleosiriana arcaica da Ebla e la cultura figurativa della Siria attorno al 1800 a.C.», *Scienze dell'Antichità* 1, 447-495.

— 1989: «Le temple et le taureau. Origine et continuité de l'iconographie de la grande déesse à Ébla», dans M. Lebeau et Ph. Talon (éd.) *Reflets des deux fleuves. Volume de mélanges offerts à André Finet* (Akkadica, Supplementum 6), Leuven, 127-135.

— 1992: «High Old Syrian Royal Statuary from Ebla», dans B. Hrouda, S. Kroll et P. Z. Spanos (éd.) *Von Uruk nach Tuttul. Eine Festschrift für Eva Strommenger* (Münchener Vorderasiatische Studien 12), München - Wien, 111-128.

— 1994: «Old Syrian Basalt Furniture from Ebla Palaces and Temples», dans P. Calmeyer, K. Hecker, L. Jacob-Rost et C. B. F. Walker (éd.) *Beiträge zur Altorientalischen Archäologie und Altertumskunde. Festschrift für Barthel Hrouda zum 65. Geburtstag*, Wiesbaden, 167-177.

— 1996: «Due frammenti di un nuovo bacino scolpito dal Tempio P2 di Ebla», *Studi Miscellanei* 30 (= *Studi in memoria di Lucia Guerrini*), 3-12.

— 2003: «Ishtar of Ebla and Hadad of Aleppo. Notes on Terminology, Politics and Religion of Old Syrian Ebla», dans P. Marrassini et al. (éd.) *Semitic and Assyriological Studies Presented to Pelio Fronzaroli by Pupils and Colleagues*, Wiesbaden, 380-402.

— 2006: «Old Syrian Statuary and Carved Basins from Ebla. New Documents and Interpretations», *Subartu* 17 (Festschrift J.-Cl. Margueron), 423-438.
— 2010a: *Ebla. La città del trono. Archeologia e storia*, Torino.
— 2010b: «The Seal of Ushra-Samu, Official of Ebla, and Ishkhara's Iconography», dans S. C. Melville et A. L. Slotsky (éd.) *Opening the Tablet Box: Near Eastern Studies in Honor of Benjamin R. Foster* (Culture and History of the Ancient Near East 42), Leiden - New York, 271-290.
MATTHIAE, P. et G. PETTINATO 1972: *Il torso di Ibbit-Lim, re di Ebla*, Roma.
MATTHIAE, P., F. PINNOCK et G. SCANDONE MATTHIAE 1995: *Ebla. Alle origini della civiltà urbana. Trent'anni di scavi in Siria dell'Università di Roma «La Sapienza»*, Milano.
MAZAR, A. 1990: *Archaeology of the Land of the Bible 10,000-586 B.C.E.* (The Anchor Bible Reference Library), New York - London.
MCGOVERN, P. E. 1985: *Late Bronze Palestinian Pendants: Innovation in a Cosmopolitan Age* (JSOT/ASOR Monograph Series 1), Sheffield.
MENZEL, B. 1981: *Assyrische Tempel, Band II. Anmerkungen, Textbuch, Tabellen und Indices* (Studia Pohl: Series Major 10/II), Roma.
NEGBI. O. 1976: *Canaanite Gods in Metal. An Archaeological Study of Ancient Syro-Palestinian Figurines* (Publications of the Institute of Archaeology 5), Tel Aviv.
NEU, E. 1996: *Das hurritische Epos der Freilassung, I. Untersuchungen zu einem hurritisch-hethitischen Textensemble aus Ḫattuša* (Studien zu den Boghazköy-Texten 32), Wiesbaden.
OTTO, A. 2000: *Die Entstehung und Entwicklung der Klassisch-Syrischen Glyptik* (Untersuchungen zur Assyriologie und Vorderasiatischen Archäologie 8), Berlin - New York.
ÖZGÜÇ, T. 1950: *Ausgrabungen in Kültepe. Bericht über die im Auftrage der Türkischen Historischen Gesellschaft, 1948 durchgeführten Ausgrabungen* (Türk Tarih Kurumu, Ser. V, 10), Ankara.
POMPONIO, F. et P. XELLA 1997: *Les dieux d'Ebla. Étude analytique des divinités éblaïtes à l'époque des archives royales du IIIe millénaire* (Alter Orient und Altes Testament 245), Münster.
PORADA, E. 1948: *Corpus of Ancient Near Eastern Seals in North American Collections, I, The Collection of the Pierpont Morgan Library, I-II, Text and Plates* (The Bollingen Series 14), Washington.
— 1993: «A Cylinder Seal for Discussion with Nimet Özgüç», dans M. J. Mellink, E. Porada et T. Özgüç (éd.) *Aspects of Art and Iconography: Anatolia and Its Neighbors. Studies in Honor of Nimet Özgüç*, Ankara, 535-537.
PRECHEL, D. 1996: *Die Göttin Išḫara. Ein Beitrag zur altorientalischen Religionsgeschichte* (Abhandlungen zur Literatur Alt-Syrien-Palästinas und Mesopotamiens 11), Münster.
RAWLINSON, H. C. and G. SMITH 1870: *The Cuneiform Inscriptions of Western Asia III, A Selection from the Miscellaneous Inscriptions of Assyria*, London.
SCHAEFFER, C. F. A. 1929: «Les fouilles de Minet-el-Beida et de Ras Shamra (campagne de printemps 1929). Rapport sommaire», *Syria* 10, 285-297.
— 1932: «Les fouilles de Minet-el-Beida et de Ras Shamra, troisième campagne (printemps 1931). Rapport sommaire», *Syria* 12, 1-14.

SPELEERS, L. 1943: *Catalogue des intailles et empreintes orientales des Musées Royaux d'Art et d'Histoire. Supplément*, Bruxelles.

TEISSIER, B. 1984: *Ancient Near Eastern Cylinder Seals from the Marcopoli Collection*, Berkeley - Los Angeles - London.

TEISSIER, B. 1994: *Sealing and Seals on Texts from Kültepe Kārum Level 2* (Uitgaven van het Nederlands Historisch-Archaeologisch Instituut te Istanbul 70), Leiden.

— 1996: *Egyptian Iconography on Syro-Palestinian Cylinder Seals of the Middle Bronze Age* (Orbis Biblicus et Orientalis, Series Archaeologica 11), Fribourg - Göttingen.

VON DER OSTEN, H. H. 1936: *Ancient Oriental Seals in the Collection of Mrs. Agnes Baldwin Brett* (Oriental Institute Publications 37), Chicago.

— 1957: *Altorientalische Siegelsteine der Sammlung Hans Silvius von Aulock* (Studia Ethnographica Upsaliensia 13), Uppsala.

WOOLLEY, C. L. 1955: *Alalakh. An Account of the Excavations at Tell Atchana in the Hatay, 1937-1949* (Reports of the Research Committee of the Society of Antiquaries of London 18), Oxford.

Fig. 1. Fragment de jambe de table d'offrande TM.65.D.265, basalte, face antérieure, Ébla, Temple D, cella L.202. Bronze Moyen II (env. 1800-1600 av. J.-Chr.).

Fig. 2. Fragment de secteur supérieur de table d'offrande TM.66.D.159, basalte, face antérieure, Ébla, Temple D, devant M.200 + M.201. Bronze Moyen II (env. 1800-1600 av. J.-Chr.).

Fig. 3. Fragment de jambe de table d'offrande TM.09.E.70, basalte, face antérieure, Ébla, Secteur E Ouest, Carré EiVI3iii, mur M.9811. Bronze Moyen II (env. 1800-1600 av. J.-Chr.).

Fig. 4. Recomposition des fragments TM.66.D.159 et TM.09.E.70, basalte, face antérieure. Bronze Moyen II (env. 1800-1600 av. J.-Chr.).

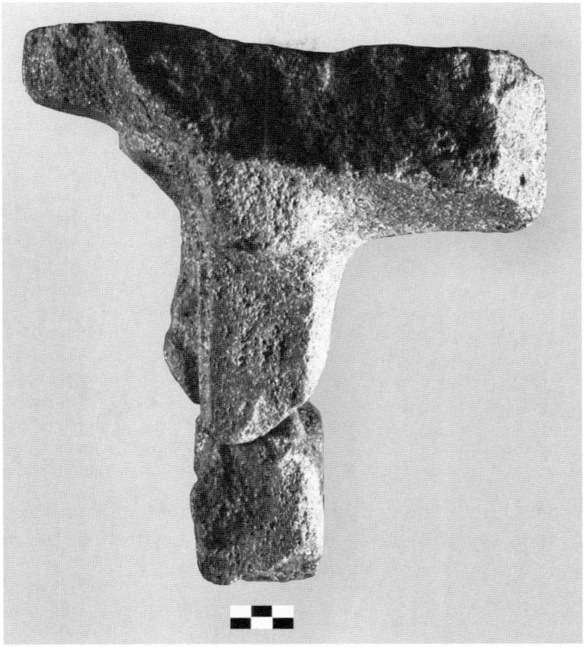

Fig. 5. Recomposition des fragments TM.66.D.159 et TM.09.E.70, basalte, vue latérale. Bronze Moyen II (env. 1800-1600 av. J.-Chr.).

Fig. 6. Fragment de secteur supérieur de table d'offrande TM.66.D.159, basalte, vue du plan de la table d'en haut. Bronze Moyen II (env. 1800-1600 av. J.-Chr.).

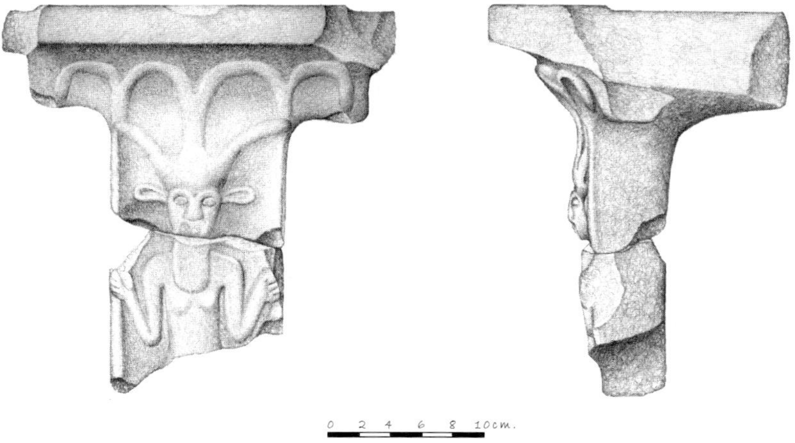

Fig. 7. Dessin de l'une des jambes et du secteur supérieur de la table d'offrande TM.66.D.159 + TM.09.E.70, vues frontale et latérale (dessin Tiziana D'Este).

Fig. 8. Moule d'une figurine de déesse nue debout avec tiare à cornes, stéatite, Nahariyah, Haut-Lieu, phase B, Jérusalem, Israel Museum (4460/4460a) (de Negbi 1976, pl. 39). Bronze Moyen II (env. 1750-1550 av. J.-Chr.).

Fig. 9. Plaque en repoussé avec figure de déesse nue frontale, or, Minet el-Beydah, dépôt 11 (de Schaeffer 1929, pl. LIV 2). Bronze Récent II (env. 1400-1200 av. J-Chr.).

SEAL IMPRESSIONS ON ADMINISTRATIVE TAGS FROM THE REIGN OF ŠU-AMURRU

Rudolf H. Mayr
Rosen Collection, New York

For Karel Van Lerberghe and Gabriella Voet, who seem as inseparable as the text and the seal impressions on the tablets they study.

In the study collection of the Cornell University Near Eastern Studies Department is a group of nine small clay tags that appear to date to an otherwise unknown dynasty in the early Old Babylonian period.[1]

These tags are flat, approximately triangular, and have string holes at the corners of the upper edge. Each tag bears a text dealing with the loss or disposal of a few small cattle, and is dated by a month and year name. Five surfaces of each tag are covered with seal impressions. As many as five different seals were used on each tag, partially obscuring or even obliterating the writing, but providing multiple partial impressions of several seals. In all, the author has reconstructed the portions of the inscriptions of eleven different seals. The inscriptions of these seals are of particular interest because they name two kings, *Nabi-Enlil* and *Šu-Amurru*, who appear to be otherwise unknown to scholarship.

Contents

In content, the tags are fairly uniform. Each states that a number of sheep or goats has been deducted from an owner's account, presumably on some master list. A different owner is specified on each tag. In most cases the animals are described as "dead" (ba-ug$_7$) which serves as the reason for the deficit (tags 1, 2, 4, 6, 7, 8, 9). On tag 3, the animals were not dead, but had been taken in charge by *Ibbi-Suen* (*i-bi*$_2$-^{d}*suen* i$_3$-dab$_5$). On tag 5

[1] I would like to thank Jonathan and Jeannette Rosen for permission to study and publish these tags. I also thank D. I. Owen for his assistance by collating the tags in person and offering numerous valuable suggestions. I am particularly indebted to Laura W. Johnson-Kelly for the photographs of the tags.

it appears they were to be fed to a lion. Tag 2 lists, in addition to five ewes that had died, four ewes taken to the kitchen.

Month Names

Seven different month names appear on the tags. Four of these are clearly legible, and all belong to the traditional calendar of Ur:

i	^{iti}še-kin-ku$_5$	(tag 8)
iv	^{iti}u$_5$-bi-ku$_3$	(tags 2 and 3)
v	^{iti}ki-sik$_2$-^{d}nin-a-zu	(tag 5)
xiid	^{iti}diri-me-ki-gal$_2$	(tag 7)

Two are somewhat less legible, but also appear to belong to the Ur calendar:

ii	^{iti}šeš!?-da-gu$_7$	(tag 6)
vii	^{iti}ezem-^{d}šul-gi (?)	(tag 4)

One is barely legible, but does not appear to belong to the Ur calendar:

(?)	^{iti} ezem-balag?	(tag 1)

Chronology

On the basis of the assemblages of seals impressed (see below), one can divide the tags into three groups, namely (1), (2, 3, 4, 5) and (6, 7, 8, 9). These are almost certainly chronologically distinct, but their correct sequence is uncertain. Nonetheless one may tentatively assume the tags that bear impressions of seals with inscriptions that name *Nabi-Enlil* are from the reign of that king, or at any rate pre-date the tags whose seal inscriptions name *Šu-Amurru*. There are six different year names, not counting one that is quite illegible (tag 9).

By this reasoning, three year names may be assigned to the reign of Nabi-Enlil:

The year the *Su-X-tum* canal was dug (tag 1)
The year the fortress *Dunnum*[2] on the Tigris was destroyed (tags 2, 3, 4)
The year after *Dunnum* was destroyed (tag 5)

[2] See Groneberg 1980 (RGTC 3), 57. This may be the town named in a year name of Manana, mu bad$_3$ du-nu-um ma-na-na ba-du$_3$, "Year Manana built the wall of Dunnum," or possibly the town referenced in "Year Dunnum and the canal Išartum were built" (Gungunum 22). The conquest of (another?) Dunnum was mentioned in the year name for Rim-Sin 29. See http://cdli.ucla.edu/tools/yearnames/

By the same logic, three year names presumably belong to the reign of *Šu-Amurru*:

The year he destroyed [...] Dunnum (tag 6)
The year after the year after Al-DAM^{ki} [3][...] (tag 7)
The year the Shining Cup canal was dug (tag 8)

The Seals

Each tag has five sealed surfaces. For convenience, the edges that follow the obverse and reverse are here called the *obverse edge* and *reverse edge* respectively. On some tags each surface bears the impressions of a different seal, while on others two or more surfaces were sealed with the same seal. Sometimes two seals were rolled side by side on the reverse of a tag. Interestingly, where impressions of the same seal appear on multiple tags (as is usually the case), that seal appears on the same surface of each of those tags. The seals of the highest ranking official present (seal J or K) appear on the reverse edge and the obverse. It appears that when these tablets were prepared, a group of mostly the same officials (or at least their seals) was present to apply their seals in the same order.

The seals were used in four distinct assemblages, which reflect the changing group of officials overseeing, or witnessing, the transactions that these tags record. The earliest assemblage of five seals (B, C, D, G, and J) appears only on tag 1. The second assemblage, four seals (A, C, F. and J), appears on tags 2, 3, 4. and 5. The third assemblage is three seals (B, I, and K) and appears only on tag 6. The fourth assemblage is four seals (E, H, I, and K), on tags 7, 8, and 9.

Regarding the owners of these seals, one can only speculate whether the "archivist" *Warad-Enlil* whose seal (K) was used in the later assemblages was identical to the "archivist" whose name is lost, but whose seal (J) was used in the earlier assemblages; or the scribe *Warad-Enlil* whose seal (C) was used in the earlier assemblages.

The impression of a seal on a tablet or tag serves a purpose similar to that of a signature on a modern document. Typically when seals were impressed on tablets and tags, only the inscription — or part of the inscription — was impressed. That is the case here; since very little of the scenes is preserved, the discussion focuses on the inscriptions. Seal design at this period consisted of a scene involving two or more figures, but very little of these scenes is preserved on these tags.

[3] Compare Al-Damua (^{iri} ^{d}da-mu-u$_2$-a^{ki}), RGTC 3, 11.

Autonomous Seals

The most common type of seal inscription gives the name of the seal owner, followed by his (or her) title and a familial relationship, most commonly a patronymic, describing the seal owner as the child of another person. This information was normally sufficient for establishing a person's identity at this period. The author has reconstructed the partial impressions of four seals of this type from these tags. One should note that most of these inscriptions are incomplete. Owing to the incomplete nature of what was impressed, it is possible, and indeed likely, that the missing last line of any of these inscriptions identified its owner as the slave of the king, making it a servant's seal rather than an autonomous one:

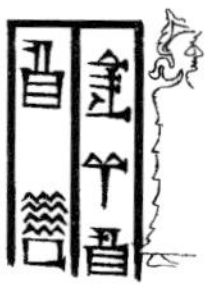

A
ar-wu-um
dub-sar

"*Arwum*, scribe." This inscription appears to be complete. Part of one figure, a *lamassu* goddess, is preserved at the right side of the inscription.

This seal was typically rolled twice on the obverse edge and then rolled repeatedly on the reverse of the tag, sometimes alongside seal G below.

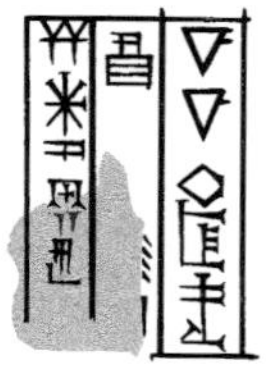

B
i$_3$*-li*$_2$*-ki-ib-ri*
dub-sar
dumu DINGIR.A. . .]

"*Ili-kibri*, scribe, son of ..." The inscription is reconstructed from two sets of impressions, both on tag 5. The seal owner's name appears only on the reverse of the tag, while the patronymic appears only on the obverse edge. Seal F, below, probably belonged to the same man.

This seal was rolled several times on the reverse and obverse edge of the tag.

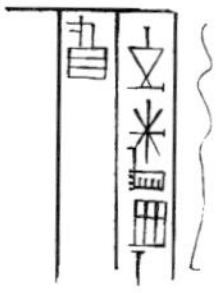

C
arad$_2$*-*^{d}*en-lil*$_2$
dub-[sar]
dumu [. . .]

"*Warad-Enlil*, scribe, son of …" The inscription is incomplete.

This seal was usually impressed twice on the upper edge of the tag. On one tag it was also impressed on the reverse edge.

D

eš$_4$-*tar*$_2$-DINGIR-[. . .]?

[. . .]

An impression of this seal appears on the obverse edge of one tag only (1). The preserved traces are extremely incomplete, and barely sufficient to distinguish this seal from the others.

Servant's Seals

In addition to autonomous seals, these tags bear the impressions of six seals whose inscriptions describe their owners as the "slave" of another person, usually the king. These are conventionally called "servants' seals." Inscriptions of this type are a common phenomenon on seals of the Ur III kingdom as well as its predecessor and successor states. But along with the obvious and explicit statement, that the seal owner was the "slave" of another person, these inscriptions carry a more subtle message about the seal owner's status, distinguishing three classes of slaves or, possibly, distinguishing true slaves from the king's servants and staff.

While there is little doubt that slavery did indeed exist at this period (Adams 2011), the inscriptions on the seals of the highest court officials indicate that they, too, were "slaves" of the king. Thus it is hard to believe that all of the people who were (according to their seal inscriptions) slaves of the king were indeed his slaves in a literal sense or, to be sure, all slaves in the same sense. On closer study, it appears that the composition and wording of the inscriptions contains coded information about the seal owner's status. While the words of these inscriptions literally state that these people were all slaves of the king, the format of the inscriptions distinguish three distinct classes of slaves of the king. For convenience, these are here classified as Type I, Type II, and Type III seal inscriptions, with Type I being the most humble, and the Type III the most prestigious type.

Type I

The most humble, and presumably the most common type of Servant's Seal inscription gives the seal owner's name and title as on an autonomous seal, followed by an expression of servitude very much like a patronymic.

E.

i_3-li_2-*k[i-ib-ri]*
dub-[sar]
arad$_2$ [^{d}. . .]

"*Ili-kibri*, scribe, slave of..."

This seal most probably belonged to the same owner as seal B above. Like B, it was rolled on the reverse and obverse edge.

F.
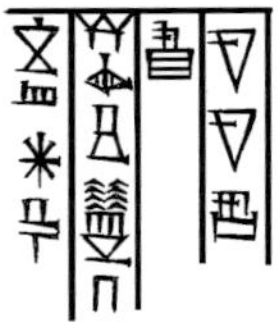
i_3-li_2-*ra-[pi]*
dub-[sar]
dumu *na-ap-li-i[s]*
arad$_2$ *šu-*^{d}*mar-[tu]*

"*Ili-rapi*, scribe, son of *Naplis*, slave of *Šu-Amurru*." Note that the king's name is written without a divine determinative.

This seal appears on the reverse of several tags alongside seal A above.

G.
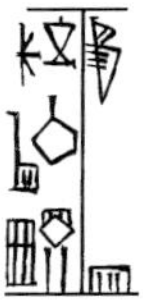
[illegible]
^{lu2}ašlag$_2$
arad$_2$ *na-bi*$_2$-~^{d}*en-lil*$_2$

"[illegible], fuller, slave of *Nabi-Enlil*." Note that the king's name is written without a divine determinative.

A single impression of this seal appears on the upper edge of tag 1.

H.

[. . .]
dub-sar
dumu *a-bu-ṭab-um*
arad$_2$ ^{d}*šu-*^{d}*mar-tu*

"[illegible], scribe, son of *Abu-tabum*, slave of *Šu-Amurru*."

This seal was impressed on the obverse edge of the tags.

Type II

The best known type of servant's seal bears a much more formal type of inscription, beginning with the name and titles of the seal owner's superior, who is typically the king or a city governor. The seal owner's name and title(s) appear next, very much as in an autonomous seal, followed finally by the phrase IR$_{11}$.ZU, "his servant."[4]

Impressions of seals of this type are ubiquitous on Ur III and early Old Babylonian tablets. One seal impressed on four of these tags probably belongs to this type (or to Type III):

I.

^{d}šu-^{d}mar-[tu]
lugal-kala-ga
^{d}suen-ba-ni
dub-sar
[dumu ...]?
[IR$_{11}$.ZU]

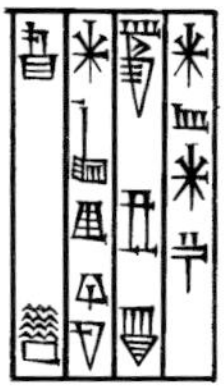

"*Šu-Amurru*, the mighty king; *Sin-bani*, scribe, [his servant]."

The inscription is incomplete, but probably no more than one or two lines are missing. No trace of the scene is preserved.

This seal was impressed one time one the upper edges of several tags.

Type III

The most elaborate type of servant's seal was the "royal gift seal," on which the inscription explicitly states that (the seal) was a gift from the king to his servant.

J.

[^{d}*na-bi$_{2}$]*
~^{d}en-lil$_{2}$
nita-kala-ga
dumu il$_{3}$-šu-ni-ga?
[...]
ša$_{13}$-dub-ba
arad$_{2}$-da-ni-ir
in-na-[ba]

[4] Schneider 1936, 109-116, read this phrase as a second person construction in Sumerian, "your servant," and introduced the term "dedication seals," (Widmungssiegel) for this type of inscription. The latter term is singularly unfortunate, since nothing akin to "dedication" takes place in these seal inscriptions, it is not addressed to the person named first, &c. No (other) second person construction is attested in seal inscriptions. The etymology of the phrase is troublesome, apparently involving the borrowing of an Akkadian noun complete with its possessive suffix, but its sense is certainly "his servant," in parallel with a number of third person constructions, such as dumu-ni, šeš-a-ni, lukur-a-ni (Owen and Mayr 2007, seal no. 14 on p. 431), geme$_{2}$-ni (same volume, seal nos. 58 on p. 435, 78 on p. 436) & c.

"*Nabi-Enlil*, mighty man, son of …, gave (this seal) to his servant [*Warad-Enlil*?], archivist."

The inscription is incomplete, missing part of the king's name and the seal owner's name. The former is restored with some confidence, based on the inscription of the following seal. With the latter, one cannot be so sure: At issue is the question whether this, rather than seal C above, was the earlier seal of *Warad-Enlil* (K). *Warad-Enlil* was presumably a common name, so it is not impossible that this and seal C belonged two different men with the same name.

The scene was presumably an audience scene, of which only part of the seated king is preserved.

This seal was impressed on the obverse and the reverse edge.

K.

^{d}*šu*-^{d}*mar*-~*tu*
lugal-kala-ga
dumu ^{d}*na-bi*-~^{d}*en-lil*$_{2}$
arad$_{2}$-^{d}*en*-~*lil*$_{2}$-*la*$_{2}$
ša$_{13}$-dub-ba
arad$_{2}$-da-[ni-ir]
in-[na-ba]

"*Šu-Amurru*, mighty king, son of *Nabi-Enlil*, gave (this seal) to his servant *Warad-Enlil*, archivist." Either seal C or J, above, may have belonged to the same owner.

The inscription is complete except for a few signs. The scene was presumably an audience scene, of which only part of the seated king is preserved.

This seal was impressed on the obverse, and sometimes the reverse edge, of several tags.

In conclusion, these nine tags bring to the attention of modern scholarship two kings, *Nabi-Enlil* and his son *Šu-Amurru*. Possibly *Nabi-Enlil's* father, AN.ŠU.NI.GA, also styled himself king. We do not know what city they ruled, but perhaps their use of the traditional calendar of Ur localizes their territory in the southern part of Sumer. The name *Šu-Amurru* suggests that this dynasty, like its contemporaries, was of

Amorite origin. We know nothing of the events of their rule, beyond that (like other early Old Babylonian kings) they devoted some of their energies to digging canals and destroying neighboring cities. The seal inscriptions that preserve their names suggest that these kings, like their contemporaries, organized their court along the same lines as the Third Dynasty of Ur.

Transliterations of the tags

1. 58-01-108

obverse
1. 1(diš) uz_3
2. $ba\text{-}ug_7$
3. ki $ki_2\text{-}ri_2\text{-}{}^{d}adad$

reverse
4. iti ezem-balag?
5. mu id_2 su-x-tum

~mu ba-al

Being the only one impressed with the first assemblage (seals B, C, D, G, and J) tag 1 is tentatively assumed to be the earliest of the nine tags studied here.

tag 1

2. 58-01-177

obverse
1. 5(diš) u_8
2. ba-ug_7
3. 4(diš) u_8 ku_9-ra-~e_2-muhaldim-$še_3$

reverse
4. ki a-bi-i-a
5. $^{iti}u_5$-bi-ku_3
6. mu bad_3 du-nu-um ~$ša_3$ gu_2 ^{id2}idigna ~ ba-hul

Impressed with the second assemblage (seals A, C, F, and J)

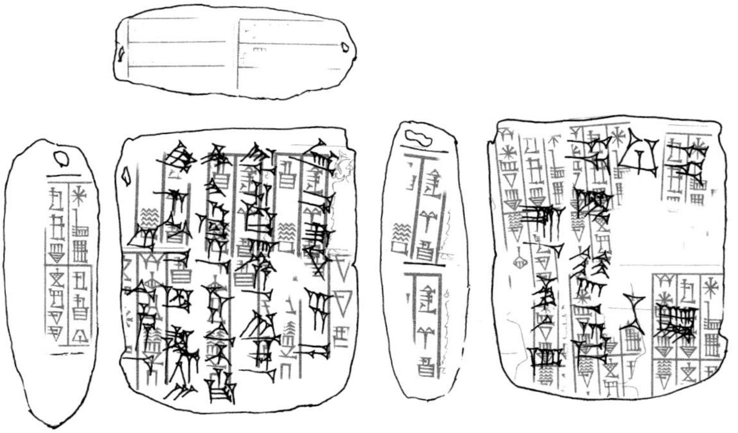

tag 2

3. 58-01-181

obverse
1. 1(diš) udu
2. i-bi_2-^{d}suen i_3-dab_5
3. ki dumu u-bar-um

reverse
4. $^{iti}u_5$-bi_2-ku_3
5. mu du-un!-nu-um ~ $ša_3$ gu_2 ^{id2}idigna ~ ba-hul

Impressed with the second assemblage (seals A, C, F, and J)

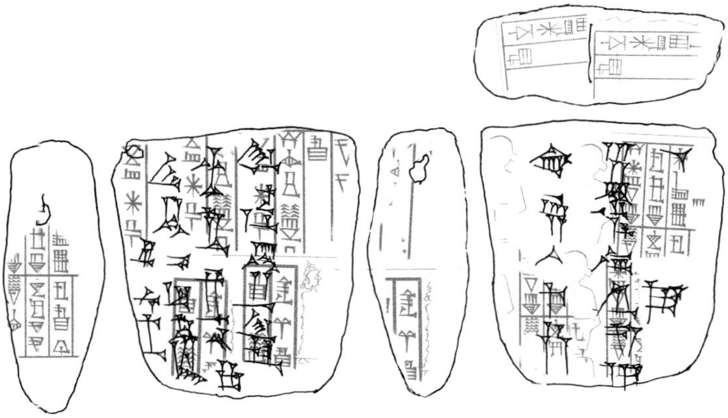

tag 3

4. 58-06-079

obverse

1. 1(diš) sila$_4$? X
2. ba-ug$_7$
3. ki bi$_2$-zu-ma-al

reverse

4. sa u$_4$ ka x ka
5. iti ezem-^{d}šul-gi
6. mu ċu-nu-um ~ba-hul

Impressed with the second assemblage (seals A, C, F, and presumably J, though it is illegible here).

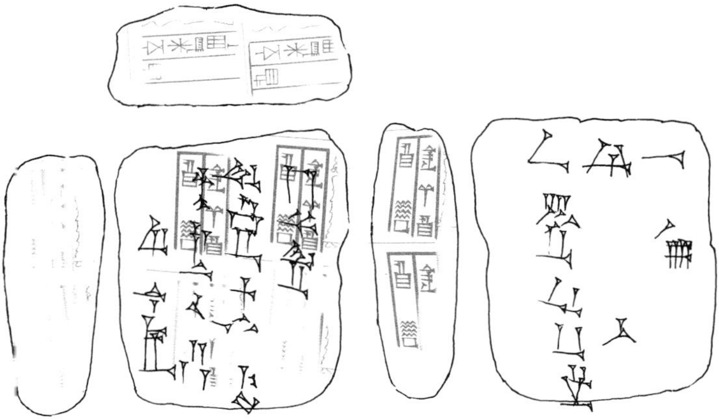

tag 4

5. 58-01-178

obverse
1. 1(diš) uz_3
2. ur-mah-$še_3$ in-$šam_2$
3. ki hu-ud-ra

reverse
4. ^{iti}ki-sik_2-^{d}nin-a-zu
5. mu us_2-sa ~ du-un-nu-um^{ki} ~ ba-hul

Impressed with the second assemblage (seals A, C, F, and J)

tag 5

6. 58-06-075

obverse
1. 1(diš) udu
2. ba-ug_7
3. ki i-pi_2-iq-x[-x?]

reverse
4. ^{iti}šeš!?-da-gu_7
5. mu gan_2-ne [?] ~ du-un-nu-um ~ mu-[hu]l?

Impressed with the third assemblage (seals B, I, and K).

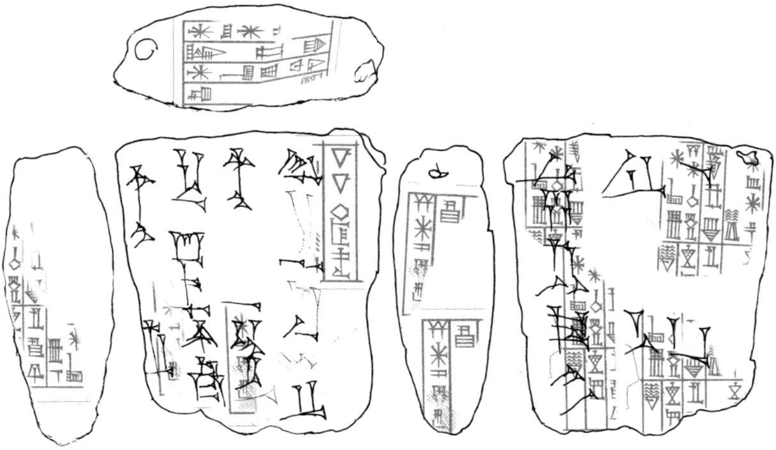

tag 6

7. 58-01-163

obverse
1. 1 u_8
2. ba-ug_7
3. ki na-ma-a

reverse
4. [iti] diri me-ki-gal_2
5. mu-us_2-sa iri-~^{d}dam^{ki} na- ~ [x-x]?~ [mu] us_2-sa-bi

Impressed with the fourth assemblage (seals E, H, I, and K).

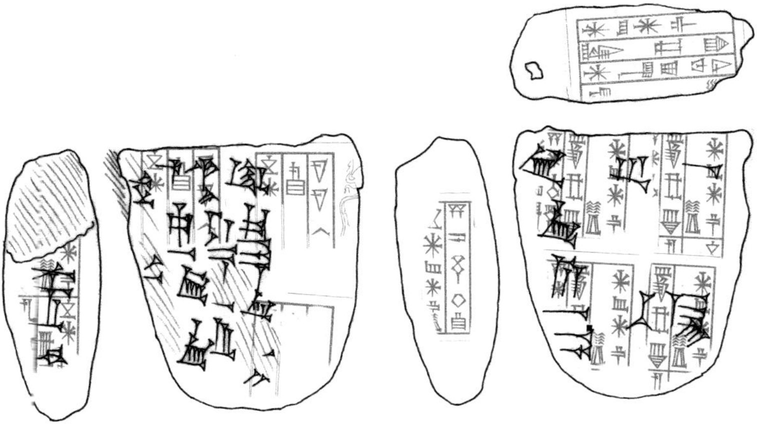

tag 7

8. 58-01-164

obverse

1. 2 sila$_4$-ga
2. ba-ug$_7$
3. ki ^{d}sin-mu-ba-~-li$_2$-<-it?>

reverse

1. ^{iti}še-kin-ku$_5$
2. mu id$_2$-gal-babbar ~ gub-a ~ mu-ba-al

Impressed with the fourth assemblage (seals E, H, I, and K)

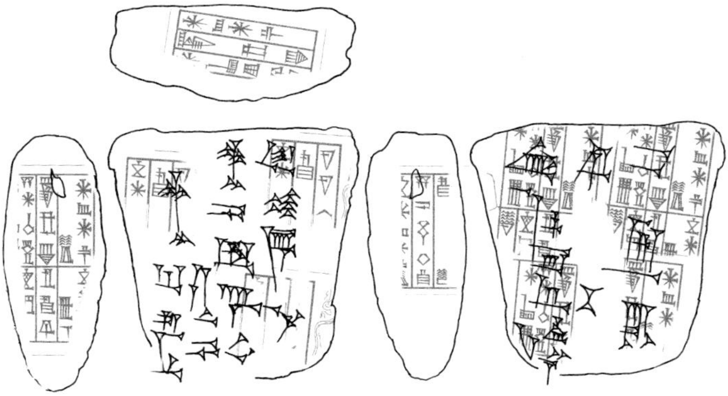

tag 8

9. 58-06-071

The tag appears to conform to the other tags in this group in all respects, but is quite illegible. It is impressed with the fourth assemblage (seals E, H, I, and K)

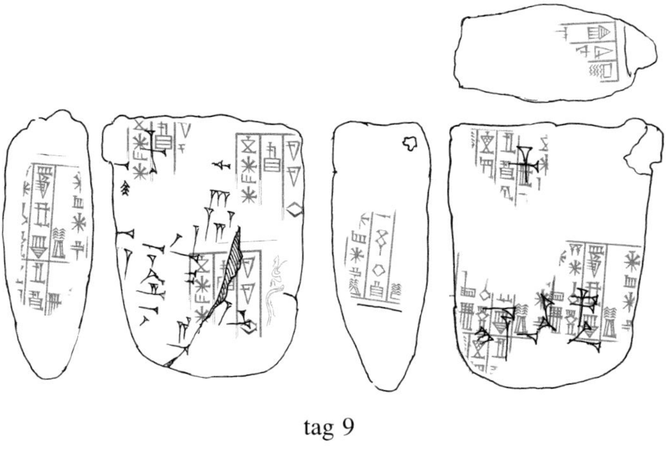

tag 9

Bibliography

ADAMS, R. M. 2011: "Slavery and Freedom in the Third Dynasty of Ur", in D. I. Owen, *Garšana Studies* (Cornell University Studies in Assyriology and Sumerology 6), Bethesda.

GRONEBERG, B. 1980: *Die Orts- und Gewässernamen der altbabylonischen Zeit* (Répertoire Géographique des Textes Cunéiformes 3), Wiesbaden.

OWEN, D. I. and R. H. MAYR 2007: *The Garšana Archives* (Cornell University Studies in Assyriology and Sumerology 3), Bethesda.

SCHNEIDER, N. 1936: "Die arad-zu, dumu-ni, und in-na-ba Siegel von Ur III", *Orientalia Nova Series* 5, 109-116.

THE PROMULGATION OF THE NAME OF THE THIRD YEAR OF RIM-ANUM OF URUK

Piotr MICHALOWSKI and Gary BECKMAN
University of Michigan, Ann Arbor MI

The purpose of this short study is to publish a new example of an Old Babylonian year-name promulgation-text.[1] This type of document consists of a full version of a Sumerian language year-formula, sometimes accompanied by an Akkadian translation; it is generally assumed that most of these were sent out by central authorities, providing local scribes with the official version of a new year-name. All preserved examples are inscribed on landscape-oriented cuneiform tablets. Scholars have known this kind of text for a long time; the first published exemplar — one that we will deal with below — was already provided by George Smith in 1875 (IV R 35 no. 8, republished in the second edition of 1891). In 1976 Marten Stol provided a list of all known promulgations (Stol 1976, 49), and Malcolm Horsnell edited all fourteen known First Dynasty ones, with hitherto unpublished additions.[2] There are only four promulgations from other dynasties: *UET* 5 872 = Rim-Sin I 27, possibly *YOS* 5 99 = Rim-Sin I 8,[3] *YOS* 5 226 = Rim-Sin II b, and IV R 35 no. 8 = Rim-Anum c. Until now, none of these promulgations has been attested in more than one exemplar.

While working in the Yale Babylonian Collection, Gary Beckman copied 16 tablets from the war-prisoner (*bīt asīrī*) archive of the Old Babylonian sovereign Rim-Anum, who ruled in Uruk for three years during the time of the Rim-Sin II rebellion against Samsuiluna of Babylon.[4] One of these was a new promulgation-text. He subsequently handed the copies over to Andrea Seri for inclusion in her comprehensive study of the reign of Rim-Anum (Seri 2012). Because the publication and philological analysis of the year name lay outside the analytical framework

[1] We are grateful to Marten Stol for comments on a draft and to Andrea Seri for providing us with a preliminary copy of her forthcoming monograph.

[2] Horsnell1999, 149–172. For comments and additions, see Hallo 2004 , 67–68.

[3] It is not certain that this is promulgation-text; see Hallo 2004, 68 n. 18.

[4] On this archive see, for the present, Rositani 2003, 1–36.

of her book, Andrea graciously asked us to deal with this particular document separately.

The tablet in question, NCBT 848, provides a complete version of the year-formula for Rim-Anum's year "c," undoubtedly the third and last year of his rule, and of his life as well.[5] This is welcome information, but this tablet has more importance: it duplicates, with variants, another promulgation-text for the same year, published long ago as IV R 35 no. 8, and thus this pair provides the first evidence for multiple copies of such documents.

The Yale tablet was purchased together with the other tablets from the *bīt asīrī* archive and therefore most probably originated in Uruk; as is the case with other texts in the Newell collection at Yale, no information is available as to its acquisition. It was therefore an internal document, sent from whoever was in charge of such matters to someone in control of the recording of the affairs of the prisoner of war center, probably Sin-šeme. The other exemplar, housed in the British Museum, has the registration number K. 4709, but it is certainly not from Kuyounjik. There is no evidence, at present, that Rim-Anum's control stretched anywhere beyond Uruk and its environs, and therefore one assumes that both tablets came from that city.

In economic texts Rim-Anum's last year is usually abbreviated simply as mu ri-im-^{d}a-nu-(um) lugal-e ma-da e-mu-ut-ba-lum (ugnim eš$_3$-nun-na), and therefore the long version can only be reconstructed on the basis of the two promulgation-texts.[6] The matter is complicated by the fact that the two duplicates differ in the sentence order of the second part, and, furthermore, the BM text is only partially preserved, with the lower right hand corner broken off. Older renditions of the year-name, based on the BM text (B below), are inaccurate and out of date.

There are interpretive and philological problems in both versions that will require further analysis and therefore the renditions proposed here must be viewed as preliminary at best. Nevertheless, the differences between the two versions of the same year-name raise serious questions about the function of the texts that have been labeled as "promulgations." If these are indeed matrix versions that were sent out to inform officials about the full official form of a new year-name, why is it that until now

[5] The reconstruction of the year-names of Rim-Anum follows the scheme established by Rositani 2003, 15. According to Seri 2012, chapter 1, his rule at Uruk spanned two years and four months.

[6] Rositani 2003, 15 n. 23 lists eight known documents from year "c."

not a single duplicate of any exemplar has been recovered, and the first such example contains such striking variants?

Our interpretation suggests that the armies of Larsa (Emutbalum), Eshnunna, Isin, and Kazallu approached Uruk, perhaps pretending to be allies (e-ne-bi-da/ta-gin$_7$); their march created an enormous dust cloud, but after it subsided, Rim-Anum's forces defeated them and forced them to withdraw. This internal strife among the anti-Babylonian rebels obviously did not serve them well, as documented in Samsu-iluna's tenth year formula, which proclaimed victory over Idamaraṣ, that is the Transtigridian territories that included Eshnunna and Emutbalum as well as Uruk and Isin; the next year was named after the destruction of the walls of Uruk and Ur.[7] Although details remain obscure, the battle described in this year-date is undoubtedly to be connected with the defection of Uruk from the coalition of rebels against Samsuiluna recognized by Seri in her close study of administrative records of Rim-Anum (Seri 2012, chapter 1).

The two tablets are:

A. NCBT 848[8]

1. mu ri-im-^{d}a-nu-um lugal-e
2. ma-da e-mu-ut-ba-⸢lum ugnim⸣ eš$_3$-nun-na i$_3$-si-in^{ki} ka-zal-lu e-ne-bi-ta-gin$_7$
3. unug^{ki}-šè mè-a in-ši-sug$_2$-eš-⸢am$_3$⸣
4. ⸢gar$_3$-dar⸣ erin$_2$-na-⸢bi⸣ mi-ni-in-ĝar-ra
5. niĝ$_2$-ul-du$_3$-a-⸢ta⸣ unug^{ki} sahar-ra la-ba-⸢dub$^?$-ab$^?$⸣-ba
6. sahar ba-dub$^?$-ba-a-ba ⸢mi-ni-in-šar$_2$⸣-šar$_2$-re
7. nam-a$_2$-ĝal$_2$-la-a-ni kalam-ma ⸢mi⸣-ni-⸢in-ri⸣-a

"[1]The year in which King Rim-Anum, [2]the (forces of) the land of Emutbalum, the armies of Eshnunna, Isin and Kazallu, as if all together (with him), [3]having presented themselves at Uruk for war, [4]inflicted a defeat upon their troops. [5]Since time immemorial Uruk had never experienced (such) a dust storm (raised by a foreign army), [6]but after the dust storm settled, he slaughtered (all of them) [7]and by his power ejected (them all) from the homeland."

[7] Stol 1976, 50 and 55. On these events, see now Charpin 2004, 340–342.

[8] Measurements: 52 × 74 × 27. Published with the kind permission of Benjamin Foster, Curator of the Yale Babylonian Collection. We are grateful to Ulla Kasten for arranging the photography.

B. K. 4709 (IV R 35 no. 8)[9]

Judging by the original copy, the tablet has deteriorated quite a bit since Rawlinson drew it; indeed the rendition of an Old Babylonian text in Sumerian is impressively accurate for the time. So many signs are now partly preserved that it makes no sense to use half brackets throughout. The transliteration reflects the copy, modified by information from the photograph. There is a clear line at the end of the obverse that is not indicated by the copy. There are traces of final signs on the left side of the reverse, which is otherwise completely destroyed. In general, when promulgation documents have such a line at the end of the obverse, the reverse, if inscribed, carries an Akkadian version of the year-name (Horsnell 1999, 149). It is difficult to ascertain if the Sumerian text ran over to the reverse, as seems more likely, or if a short version in Akkadian was inscribed on the reverse.

1. ⸢mu⸣ ri-im-^{d}a-nu-um lugal-e
2. ⸢ma⸣-da ja-mu-ut-ba-a-lum^{ki}
3. ⸢ugnim⸣ eš$_3$-nun-na^{ki} i$_3$-si-in
4. [ka-za]l-lu e-ne-bi-da-gin$_7$
5. [unug^{ki}-š]e$_3$ me$_3$-a in-ši-su$_8$-re-eš-am$_3$
6. [unug$^{ki?}$] niĝ$_2$-ul-ta sahar-ra la-ba-dub$^{?}$-a-ba
7. [...]-us$_2^{?}$[10]-am$_3$
8. [(...) nam-a$_2$-ĝa]l-a-ni-ta gar$_3$-dar-a-bi i$_3$-ni-in-ĝar-ra

Three or four broken lines on the reverse.

"^{1}The year in which King Rim-Anum, ^{2}the (forces of) the land of Emutbalum, ^{3}the armies of Eshnunna, Isin ^{4}and [Kazal]lu, as if all together (with him), ^{5}presented themselves a[t Uruk] for war. ^{5}[Uruk$^{?}$], since time immemorial, had never experienced (such) a dust storm (raised by a foreign army), ^{7}... ^{8}(...?) by his power he inflicted defeat upon them (...)

Commentary

While there are many difficulties in the understanding of these two texts, it is obvious that the year-name was composed by someone familiar with the rhetorical and lexical content of such formulae as used by the kings of Babylon, especially by Rim-Anum's contemporary, Samsuiluna.

[9] Collated on photographs kindly provided by Jonathan Taylor; official photos provided by the British Museum are reproduced below. Because of the temporary closure of the Student's Room of the British Museum we could not inspect the original in person.

[10] This according to the copy. Only the end of the sign is now preserved.

Words such as gar_3-dar(...ĝar), nam-a_2-$ĝal_2$, and perhaps even e-ne-bi-ta/da, are all part of this word hoard.

A2/B4. The final word, e-ne-bi-ta/da-gin_7, has no exact parallel anywhere, to our knowledge. Without the particle -gin_7, it occurs only a few times in Sumerian literary and historical texts, and is not attested lexically. The basic meaning seems to be "with him/her"; this is best exemplified by the passage in the myth of Inana and Bilulu 106–116 (Jacobsen and Samuel 1953, 176):

ku_3 ^{d}inana-ke_4 $eš_2$-dam-ma ba-ni-in-ku_4 [...]
ki-tuš-a ba-e-gub nam mu-ni-ib-tar-re
ĝen-na ba-ug_5-ge-en na-nam-ma-am_3 mu-zu ga-ba-da-ha-lam-e
^{kuš}$ummu_3$ a $šed_7$ $niĝ_2$-edin-na he_2-me-en
dumu-ni $ĝir_2$-$ĝir_2$-re e-ne-bi-da
^{d}udug edin-na ^{d}lama edin-na he_2-em-ma-da-me-eš-am_3

"Sacred Inana entered her Tavern (shrine),
"She took her place and determined their future:
"'Now, I will kill you and moreover will erase your name,
"So that you will be but a leather pouch with cool water in the desert,
"And you and your son Girgire, together
"Will be spirit and genie of the desert.'"

Important, for our purposes, is the occurrence of this word in the name of Samsuiluna's sixth year, which begins:

mu sa-am-su-i-lu-na lugal-e ^{d}utu ^{d}marduk e-ne-bi-da-ra nig_2-dim_2-dim_2-ma-bi al in-na-an-dug_4-uš-am_3

"The year that King Samsuiluna, for Shamash and Marduk, who had both together expressed a desire for fashioned objects ..."

Other occurrences include Enlil and Sud 141, Ishme-Dagan Hymn A + V A 150, Hammurabi Hymn D 8, Hammurabi Inscription 10 [E4.3.6.10: 12]). In all other cases it refers to the combination of two entities, and not to any more. Therefore, it is likely that the usage here, in tandem with the equative –gin_7, is intended to index Rim-Anum and the city coalition as two distinct elements.

A3/B6. The verbal form in B (in-ši-su_8-re-eš-am_3) is incorrect. The plural stem of "to stand" ends in /b/. The photograph reveals that the old copy is correct and that the following sign is indeed /ri/.

A4/B8. Although the rare gar$_3$-dar is attested already in the inscriptions of Entemena and UruKAgina, as well as in one Ishme-Dagan hymn, an inscription of Hammurabi, and in Angin 139, gar$_3$-dar…ĝar is otherwise known only from Hammurabi year-name 30. The only Akkadian equivalent is found in Angin 139, where gar$_3$-dar me$_3$ huš is translated as “smasher in fierce battle” (*sa-kip ta-ḫa-zi ez-zi*, Cooper 1978, 80–81).

A7/B8. nam-a$_2$-ĝal$_2$ is rare. It is known from year-names of Samsuiluna (14, 28) and Ammiditana (3=4), as well as from one royal inscription of the former king (Samsuiluna Inscription 8: 40, RIME4 3.7.8). It is at present unattested in the lexical corpus and the only literary attestation is in a fragmentary OB proverb (CBS 14213, reference courtesy G. Rubio):[11] a$_2$ aĝ$_2$-ĝa$_2$ diš-am$_3$ mu-e-[…], ša$_3$-zu ga-bi$_2$-ib-du$_{10}$ nam-a$_2$-ĝal$_2$-⸢ĝu$_{10}$ ga-e⸣-[x…].

A5-6/B6. The understanding of sahar dub is based on the lexical equivalence with Akkadian *tarbu’tu*, “dust, dust heap, sand dune, dust cloud”; the idea here is that the marching armies of the coalition raised an enormous, unprecedented dust cloud; after it subsided, Rim-Sin annihilated them.

There is some question concerning the reading of the SAHAR sign in this context. Lines A5 and B6 both have –ra following, suggesting sahar. Proto-Ea 250-251 (*MSL* 14 41) offers, among other possibilities, the readings sa-ha-ar and u$_2$-ku-um for SAHAR; in Proto-Izi I 316-317 (*MSL* 13 27) these are rendered in Akkadian as *e-pe-ru (var. -rum)* and *ta-ar-bu-uḫ$_2$-tum*.[12] Another Old Babylonian lexical version of Proto-Aa — a prism from Hammam et-Turkman — distributes the readings differently:[13]

[sahar]	⸢sa⸣-har	SAHAR	*e-pe$_2$-ru*$^{!}$(šu)	(dust)
[(u)kum]	ku-um	SAHAR	*tar-bu-uḫ$_2$-⸢tum⸣*	(dust, dust heap/cloud)
[(u)kum]			*ši-ba-ḫu-um*	(settling [dust])
[šen$_x$]	še-⸢en	SAHAR⸣	*šu-uḫ$_2$-tum*	(patina, rust)[14]

[11] This is a round tablet with the proverb written twice on the obverse (reverse not inscribed), Alster 1997, 304. Photograph available on CDLI (P 231685).

[12] The later version of the syllabary provides two readings for the sign with the meaning *tarbu’tu*, namely u$_2$-ku-um and sa-ha-ar-dub (Ea IV 85-86 [*MSL* 14 358]).

[13] II 26-29; van Soldt 1995, 281.

[14] Later written as URUDU.SAHAR(.URUDU).

The standard meaning of sahar dub is "to pile up earth/dust", (see Civil 1985, 36), which can be positive, as in Samsuiluna Inscription 8: 72 (RIME4 3.7.8): sahar-bi im-mi-in-dub, or negative as in LSUr 320 (Michalowski 1989, 56–57): unu_2-RI-ban_3-da ^{d}nanna-ka sahar ba-da-dub-dub, "dust/sand piled up in the UnuRIbanda." But it can also be used in the sense "to raise up a dust cloud," as well illustrated in Iddin-Dagan Hymn A 94:[15] udu-bi amaš-bi-a sahar mu-na-an-dub-dub-bu-uš, "Its sheep raise up clouds of dust in their fold."

B7-8. It is possible that B7 is an indented line. There is room for three or four signs at the beginning of B8, but no feasible restoration comes to mind. It is possible that the verb ended with the copula and that this was on the broken edge.

Bibliography

ALSTER, B. 1997: *Proverbs of Ancient Sumer: The World's Earliest Proverb Collections*, vol 1. Bethesda, MD.

CHARPIN, D. 2004: "Histoire politique de la Mésopotamie (2002-1595)" in D. Charpin, D. O. Edzard and M. Stol, *Mesopotamien: Die altbabylonische Zeit* (OBO 160/4), Fribourg, 25-480.

CIVIL, M. 1985: "On Some Texts Mentioning Ur-Namma" *OrNS* 54, 27-45.

COOPER, J. S. 1978: *The Return of Ninurta to Nippur: An-gim dím-ma* (AnOr 52), Rome.

HALLO, W. W. 2004: "Date Formula Promulgations" *NABU* 2004/4 no. 66, 67-68.

HORSNELL, M. J. A. 1999: *The Year-Names of the First Dynasty of Babylon*, Hamilton, ON.

JACOBSEN, T. and S. N. KRAMER, 1953: "The Myth of Inanna and Bilulu" *JNES* 12, 160-188.

MICHALOWSKI, P. 1989, *The Lamentation over the Destruction of Sumer and Ur* (MesCiv 1) Winona Lake, IN.

ROSITANI, A. 2003: *Rīm-Anum Texts in the British Museum* (NISABA 4), Rome.

SERI, A. 2012: *The House of Prisoners: Slavery and State in Uruk during the Revolt against Samsu-iluna* (SANER 2), Leiden.

STOL, M. 1976: *Studies in Old Babylonian History* (PIHANS 40), Leiden.

VAN SOLDT, W. H. 1995: "Three Tablets from Tell Hammām et-Turkmān" in Th.P.J. van den Hout and J. de Roos (eds.), *Studio Historiae Ardens: Ancient Near Eastern Studies Presented to Philo H.J. Houwink ten Cate on the Occasion of his 65th Birthday* (PIHANS 74), Leiden, 275-291.

[15] This has been translated in various ways; most recently, P. Attinger ("Iddin-Dagan A (2.5.3.1)," http://www.arch.unibe.ch/content/e8254/e9161/e9679/2_5_3_1_ger.pdf), p. 16 rendered it as "Devant elle, les moutons là-bas font! des tas de poussière dans leur bergerie."

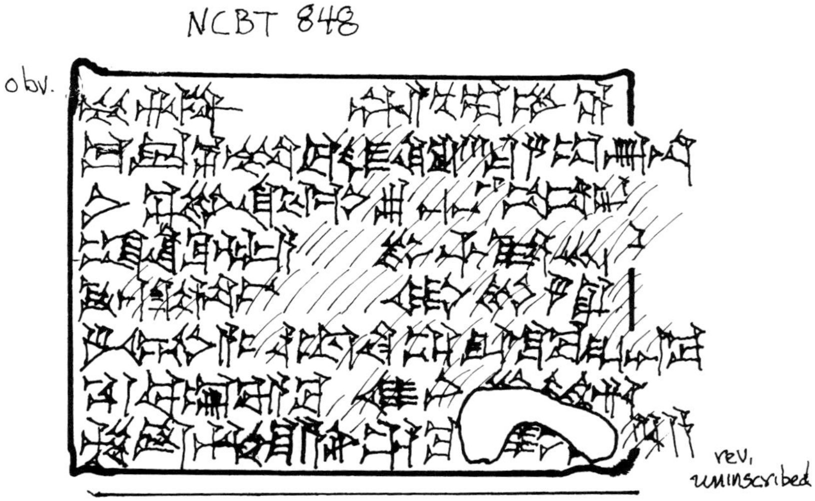

Fig. 1. NBCT 848, obverse (reverse uninscribed).
Hand copy by Gary Beckman.

Fig. 2. NBCT 848, obverse & right edge.

Fig. 3. K. 4709 (IV R 35 no. 8),
© Trustees of the British Museum.

EINIGE NEUSUMERISCHE TEXTE AUS UMMA ÜBER (OPFER-)LIEFERUNGEN (SÁ-DU$_{11}$)

Hans NEUMANN
Westfälische Wilhelms-Universität, Münster

In den 90er Jahren des vorigen Jahrhunderts sind mir die im folgenden in Kopie und Bearbeitung vorgelegten Verwaltungstexte aus der Zeit der III. Dynastie von Ur (2111-2003 v. Chr.) zur Kenntnis gelangt. Inhaltlich betreffen die aus Umma stammenden Texte (Opfer-)Lieferungen (sá-du$_{11}$)[1] für Gottheiten und vergöttlichte Könige der Ur III-Zeit. Dabei stehen die Urkunden Nr. 6-9, die alle aus dem I. Monat des Jahres IS 4 datieren, in einem Archivzusammenhang.

Der vorliegende Beitrag sei dem langjährigen Kollegen Karel Van Lerberghe anlässlich seines Ehrentages in freundschaftlicher Verbundenheit gewidmet.

Nr. 1

Privatbesitz Berlin (38 × 32 × 15 mm)
Umma (Š 25/VI und VII)

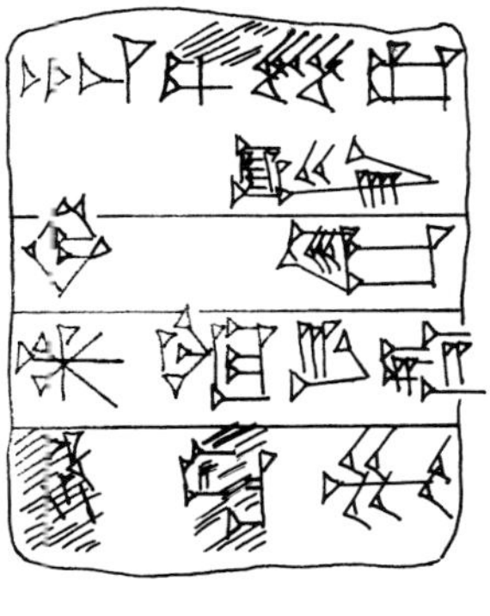

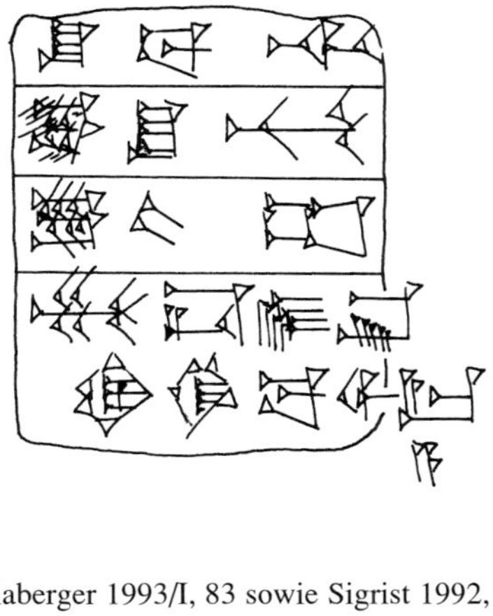

[1] Zu sá-du$_{11}$ „(Opfer-)Lieferung“ vgl. Sallaberger 1993/I, 83 sowie Sigrist 1992, 199-204 (“offrandes, livraisons régulieres”).

1 3.1.⸢2⸣ še gur-/lugal	3 Königsgur, 1 (Barig), 2 (Ban) Gerste,
2 sá-du$_{11}$-	Lieferung (an)
3 ^{d}Nin-ur$_{4}$-ra	Nin'ura,
4 ⸢Ḫa⸣-⸢la⸣-ĝu$_{10}$	(hat) Ḫalaĝu
5 šu ba-ti	in Empfang genommen.
6 iti-šu-numun	Monat:‚Šu-numun';
7 iti-min-èš	Monat:‚Min'eš'.
8 mu-ús-sa Kára-/ḫar^{ki} ba-ḫul-/a	Jahr nach dem Jahr, in dem Karaḫar zerstört wurde.

Nr. 2

Privatbesitz Berlin (36 × 37 × 15 mm)
Umma (Š 43/VII)

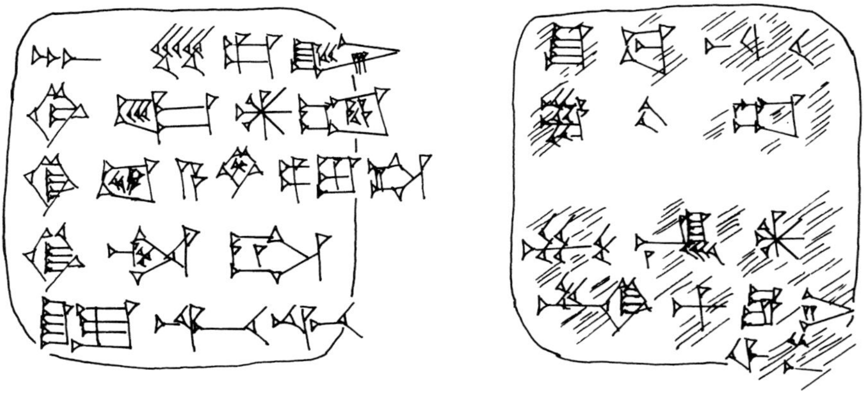

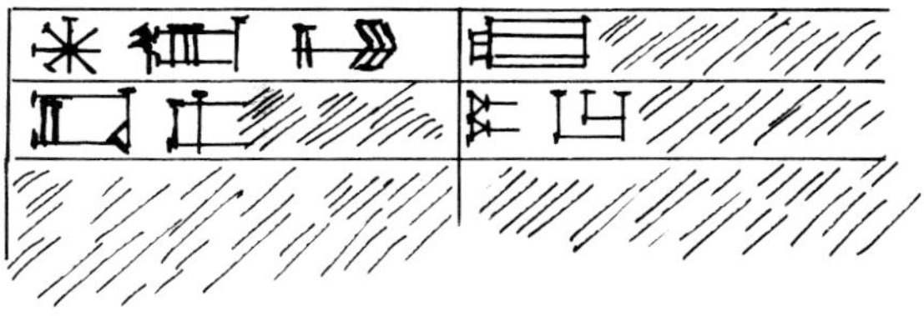

1 3 še gur-lugal	3 Königsgur Gerste,
2 sá-du$_{11}$-^{d}Nanše	Lieferung (an) Nanše,
3 ki-su$_{7}$-a-šà-sipa-ta	von der Tenne des Hirtenfeldes,
4 ki-Úrdu-ta	(hat) von Urdu
5 Niĝir-ti-ti	Niĝirtiti
6 šu ba-⸢ti⸣	in Empfang genommen.
7 iti-min-èš	Monat:‚Min'eš'.
8 mu en-^{d}/Nanna maš-e ì-/⸢pà⸣	Jahr:‚(Šulgi) bestimmte die En(-Priesterin) des Nanna durch Vorzeichen'.

Siegel: I	^{d}Šul-gi	Šulgi,
	nita-ka[la-ga]	der st[arke Mann],
	[lugal-Uri$_5^{ki}$-ma]	[der König von Ur],
	[lugal-an-ub-da-límmu-ba]	[der König der vier Weltgegenden],
II	Niĝir-[ti-ti]	Niĝir[titi],
	dumu-Ur-[x(-x)]	Sohn des Ur-[X],
	[x(-x)]$^{?}$	[X]$^{?}$,
	[úrdu-zu]	[dein Diener].

Die Tafelrückseite ist ziemlich stark zerdrückt und abgerieben.

Z. 3: Zum „Hirtenfeld" mit den dazugehörigen Tennen in der Provinz Umma vgl. Pettinato 1967/I-2, 166f.

Z. 5 mit Siegel: Niĝirtiti könnte mit dem gleichnamigen nu-bànda (BPOA 6, 273:5 [ŠS 1]) identisch sein. Der PN ist auch in Nisaba 11, 19 V 18 (Š 30) und SAT II 197, 4 (Š 38) bezeugt.

Z. 8: Zum Jahresnamen (Š 43 in der üblichen Kurzform) vgl. zuletzt Wu Yuhong 2010.

Nr. 3

Privatbesitz Berlin (30 × 26 × 15 mm)
Umma (Š 43/VIII)

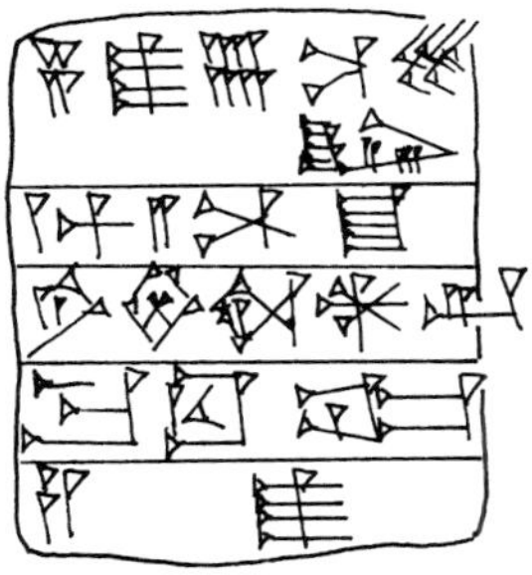

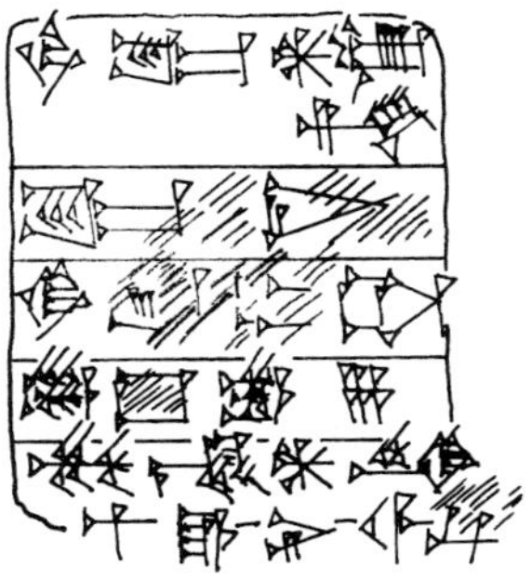

1 0.4.4.8 sìla še / lugal	4 Königs(-Barig), 4 (Ban), 8 Sila Gerste,
2 0 1.1.2 sìla zì	1 (Barig), 1 (Ban), 2 Sila Mehl,
3 ni-šà-te-An-né$^{!}$	‚Sache der Herzberuhigung' des/von An'e,
4 Ur$^{!}$-túl-saĝ	Urtulsaĝ;
5 0.3.0 zíz	3 (Barig) Emmer,
6 sá-du$_{11}$- ^{d}Šul-/gi	Lieferung (an) Šulgi,
7 Giri$_{17}$-zal;	Girizal;

8 ki-⸢x-x⸣-ta	von X.
9 iti-é-iti-VI	Monat:,E'iti-VI'.
10 mu en-^{d}Nanna / maš-e ì-pà	Jahr:,(Šulgi) bestimmte die En(-Priesterin) des Nanna durch Vorzeichen'.

Z. 3: Zu nì-šà-te vgl. Sallaberger 1993/I, 95 (mit Anm. 412) „,Sache (zur) Herzensberuhigung' (wörtlich:,-kühlung')". — Zu An-né in ähnlichen Zusammenhängen vgl. etwa die Texte BPOA 1, 8; 42; 46.

Z. 4: Zum PN vgl. Limet 1968, 290.

Nr. 4

Privatbesitz Berlin (36 × 38 × 14 mm)
Umma (Š 43/X)

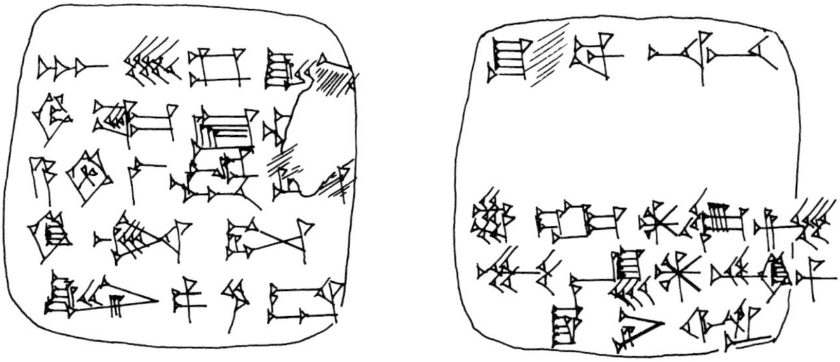

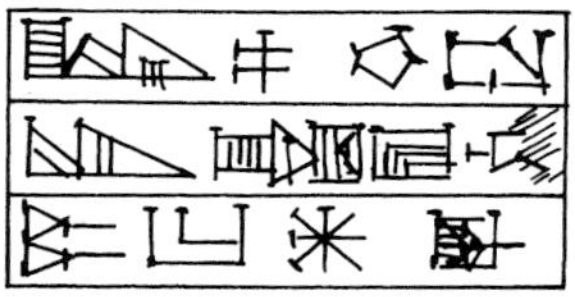

1 3 še gur-lugal	3 Königsgur Gerste,
2 sá-du$_{11}$-é-m[aḫ]	Lieferung (an) das Em[aḫ],
3 a-šà-lá-maḫ-⸢ta⸣	vom Lamaḫ-Feld,
4 ki-Úrdu-ta	(hat) von Urdu
5 Lugal-pa-è	Lugalpa'e
6 šu ba-ti	in Empfang genommen.
7 iti-ezem-^{d}Šul-gi	Monat:,Ezem-Šulgi'
8 mu en-^{d}Nanna maš-/e ì-pà	Jahr:,(Šulgi) bestimmte die En(-Priesterin) des Nanna durch Vorzeichen'.

Siegel: Lugal-pa-è	Lugalpa'e,
LÚ.ŠIM-é-ma[ḫ]	Brauer des Ema[ḫ],
dumu-Ur-^{d}Šára	Sohn des Ur-Šara.

Z. 2: Zum é-maḫ, dem Heiligtum des Gottes Šara in KI.AN^{ki} in der Nähe von Umma, als Empfänger von (Opfer-)Leistungen vgl. Sallaberger 1993/I, 84-85.

Z. 3: Zum a-šà-lá-maḫ in Umma vgl. Pettinato 1967/I-2, 49-53.

Siegel: Zu (LÚ.)ŠIM „Brauer" mit der Lesung $^{(lú)}$lunga vgl. Steinkeller 1989, 291. Zu Siegeln bzw. Siegelabrollungen von Brauern vgl. Neumann 1994, 324-325 Anm. 33; zum Siegel des Brauers Lugalpa'e vgl. Mayr 1997, 373 Nr. 516.1-3.

Nr. 5

Privatbesitz Berlin (36 × 35 × 13 mm)
Umma (Š 43/XII)

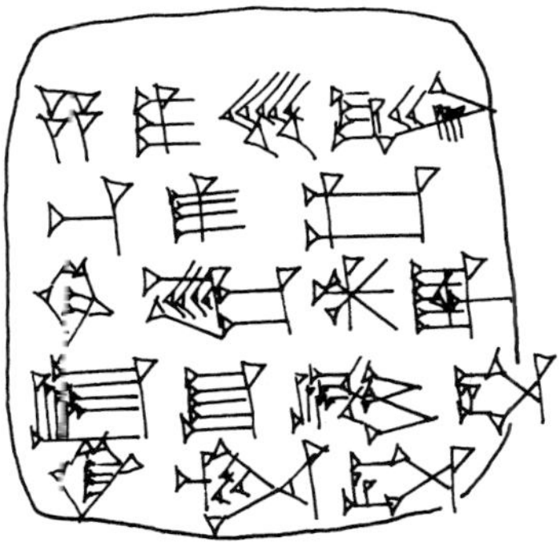

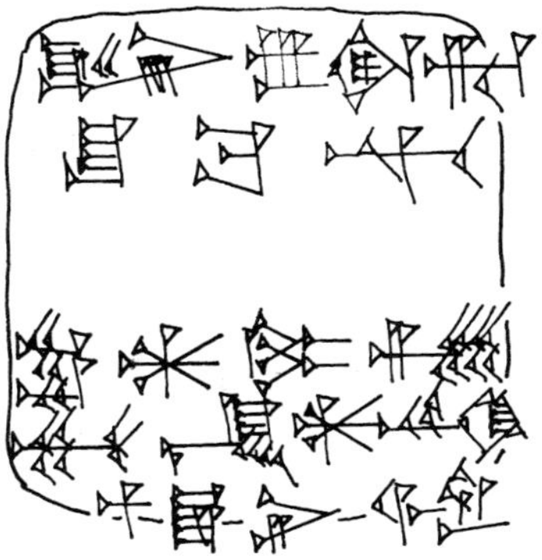

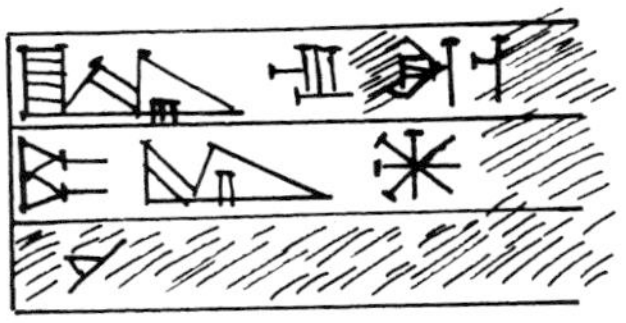

1 0.4.3 še lugal	4 Königs(-Barig), 3 (Ban) Gerste,
2 1.1.0 zíz gur	1 Gur, 1 (Barig) Emmer,
3 sá-du$_{11}$-^{d}Šára	Lieferung (an) Šara,
4 é-šu-tum-ta	aus dem Lagerhaus,
5 ki-Úrdu-ta	(hat) von Urdu

6 Lugal-má-gur$_8$-re	Lugalmagure
7 šu ba-ti	in Empfang genommen.
8 iti-^{d}Dumu-zi	Monat:‚Dumuzi'.
9 mu en-^{d}Nanna / maš-e ì-pà	Jahr:‚(Šulgi) bestimmte die En(-Priesterin) des Nanna durch Vorzeichen'.
Siegel: Lugal-má-⸢gur$_8$⸣-r[e]	Lugalmagur[e],
dumu-Lú-^{d}[ ]	Sohn des Lu-[X],
⸢nu⸣-[bànda(-gu$_4$)]	des In[spektors (der [Pflug-] Rinder)].

Siegel: Ergänzung nach den Zeichenspuren und Mayr 1997, 365 Nr. 493.

Nr. 6

Privatbesitz Berlin (43 × 41 × 15 mm)
Umma (IS 4/I)

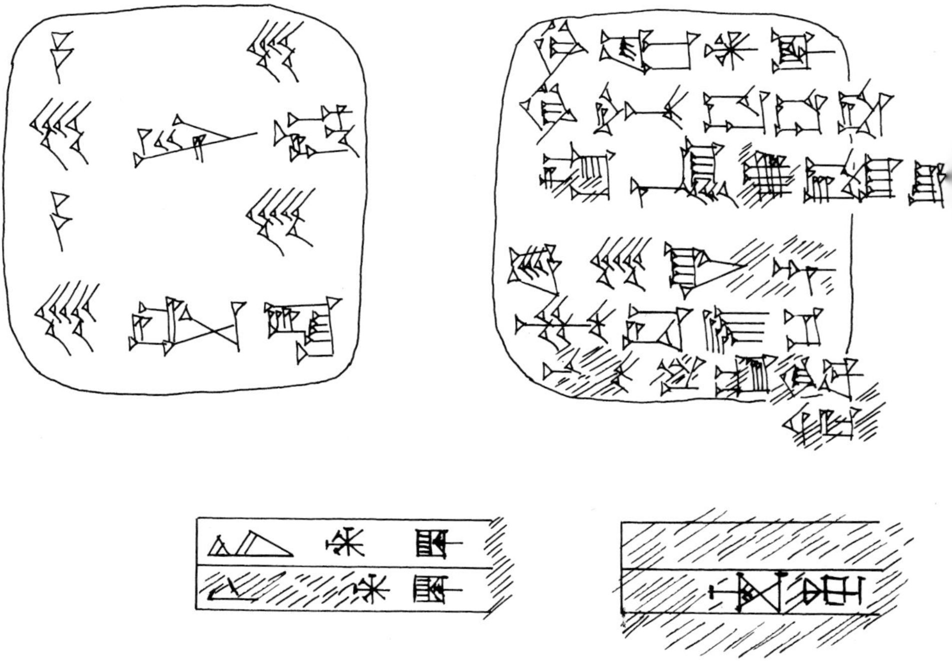

1 0.2.0 še	2 (Barig) Gerste,
2 še-lú-maḫ	Gerste des lumaḫ-Priesters;
3 0.2.0 še	2 (Barig) Gerste,
4 še-Al-la	Gerste des Alla;

5 sá-du$_{11}$-^{d}Šára	Lieferung (an) Šara,
6 ki-Gu-du-du-ta	von Gududu,
7 kišib-En-ú-šim-e	Siegel: En'ušime.
8 iti-še-KIN-ku$_{5}$	Monat: ‚Še-KIN-ku'.
9 mu-ús-sa *Si-/˹mu-ru˺-um*^{ki} ba-/ḫul	Jahr nach dem Jahr: ‚Simurrum wurde zerstört'.

Siegel: Vorhanden sind Siegelspuren, die gewiss verschiedenen Siegelinhabern zuzuweisen sind:

1: Ein erkennbares „Úrdu-dam" könnte zum Siegel des En'ušime gehören; vgl. Mayr 1997, 245 Nr. 151: En-ú-šim-e / dumu-Úrdu-dam / saĝĝa-^{d}Nin-e$_{11}$-e.

2: Zu erkennen ist darüber hinaus „Lú-^{d}Šára / ˹x˺-^{d}Šára" (s. Kopie). Bei Lu-Šara könnte es sich um den anderweitig belegten gleichnamigen lú-maḫ handeln,[2] so dass man Lú-^{d}Šára / ˹lú-maḫ˺-^{d}Šára zu lesen hätte. Das Siegel wäre dann mit dem lumaḫ-Priester in Z. 2 in Verbindung zu bringen.

Z. 2: Zur Priesterbezeichnung lú-maḫ vgl. Renger 1969, 126-129; Steinkeller 2003, 632-637.

Z. 6: Zu Gududu vgl. Dahl 2007, 81-83.

Nr. 7

Privatbesitz Berlin (41 × 39 × 13 mm)
Umma (IS 4/I)

1 0.2.0.4 sìla še	2 (Barig) 4 Sila Gerste,
2 sá-du$_{11}$-^{d}Nun-/gal	Lieferung (an) Nungal,
3 ki-Gu-du-du-ta	von Gududu,
4 kišib-Ab-ba	Siegel: Abba.
5 še-lú-maḫ	Gerste des lumaḫ-Priesters.
6 iti-še-KIN-ku$_{5}$	Monat: ‚Še-KIN-ku'.
7 mu-ús-sa *Si-/mu-ru-um*^{ki} / ba-ḫul	Jahr nach dem Jahr: ‚Simurrum wurde zerstört'.

Siegel: [Ab-ba]	[Abba],
dumu-Úrdu-dam	Sohn des Urdudam.

[2] Vgl. Steinkeller 2003, 633.

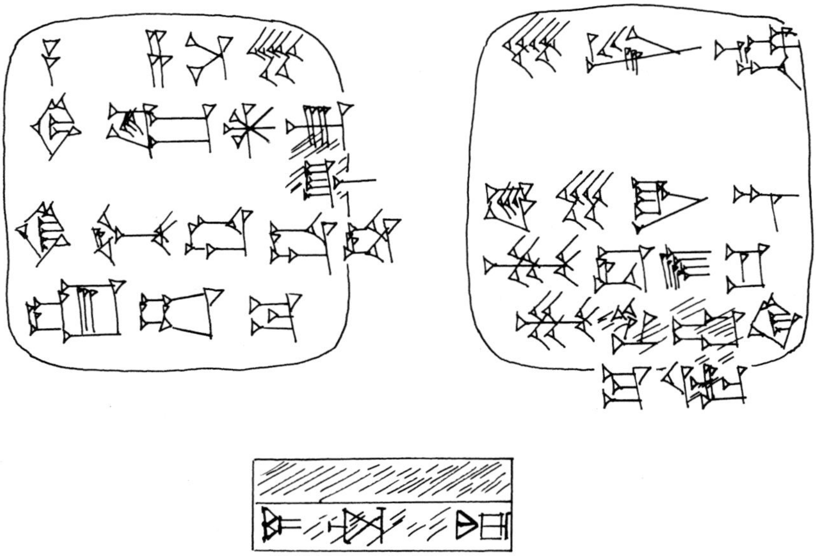

Nr. 8

Privatbesitz Berlin (41 × 38 × 13 mm)
Umma (IS 4/I)

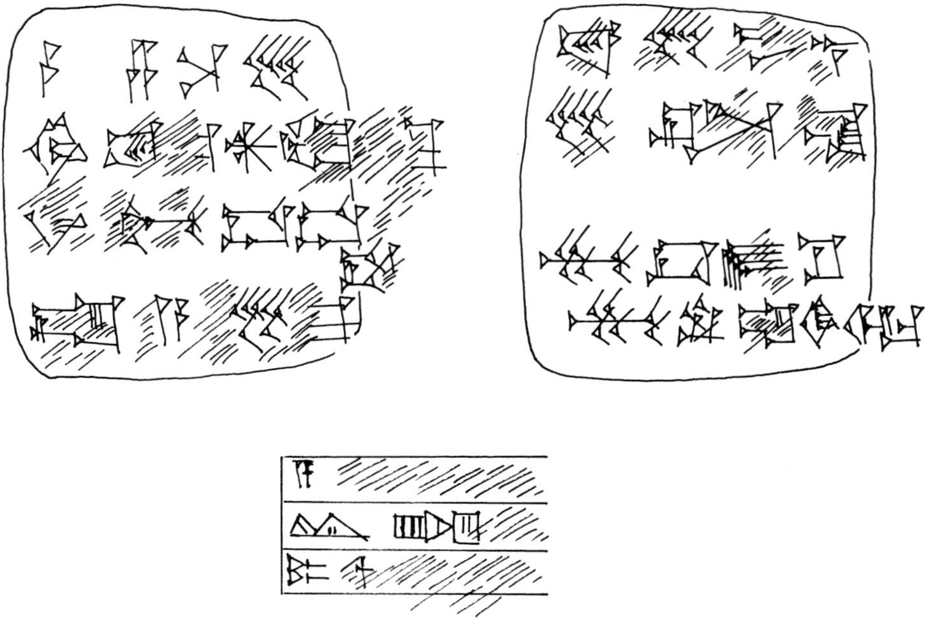

1 0.2.0.4 sìla še	2 (Barig) 4 Sila Gerste,
2 sá-⌜du$_{11}$⌝-^{d}Nin-[sú]n$^{?}$	Lieferung (an) Ninsun$^{?}$,
3 ⌜ki⌝-Gu-du-du-/ta	von Gududu,
4 kišib-A-⌜tu⌝	Siegel: Atu.
5 iti-še-⌜KIN⌝-ku$_5$	Monat: ‚Še-KIN-ku'.
6 še-Al-[l]a	Gerste des Al[l]a.
7 mu-ús-sa *Si-mu-ru-um*^{ki} <ba>-ḫul	Jahr nach dem Jahr: ‚Simurrum <wurde> zerstört'.
Siegel A-[tu]	A[tu],
LÚ.ŠIM [x(-x)]$^{?}$	Brauer [des/von x(-x)]$^{?}$,
dumu-⌜x⌝	Sohn des X.

Der Text ist stark zerdrückt.

Z. 2: Lesung des GN unsicher, aber möglich; zu (Opfer-)Lieferungen (sá-du$_{11}$) an die Göttin Ninsun in Umma vgl. Sallaberger 1993/I, 248 Anm. 1165.

Siegel: Vgl. oben zum Siegel von Text Nr. 4.

Nr. 9

Privatbesitz Berlin (41 × 40 × 14 mm)
Umma (IS 4/I)

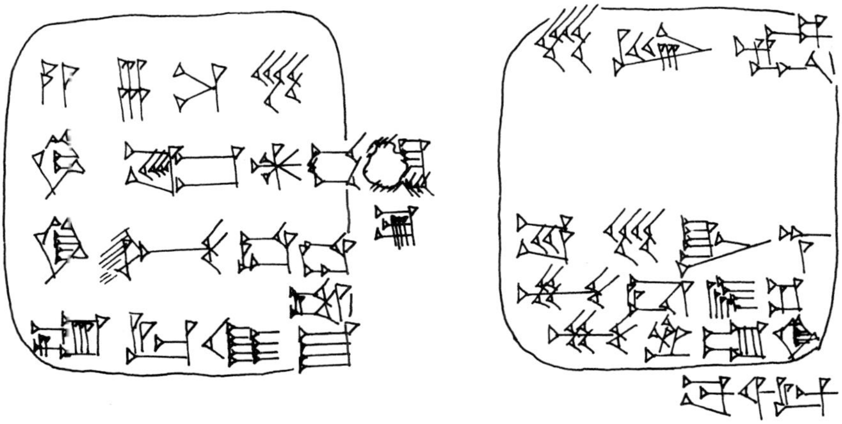

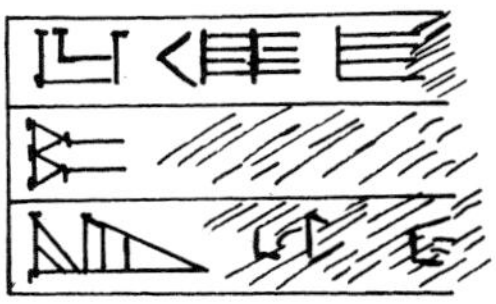

1 0.3.0.6 sìla še	3 (Barig), 6 Sila Gerste,
2 sá-du$_{11}$-^{d}Amar-[^{d}E]N./ZU	Lieferung (an) Amar-Su'[e]na,
3 ki-Gu-du-du-/ta	von Gududu,
4 kišib-Ur-ĝi$_{6}$-par$_{4}$	Siegel: Urĝipar.
5 še-lú-maḫ	Gerste des lumaḫ-Priesters.
6 iti-še-⸢KIN⸣-ku$_{5}$	Monat: ‚Še-KIN-ku'.
7 mu-ús-sa *Si-/mu-ru-um*^{ki} / ba-ḫul	Jahr nach dem Jahr: ‚Simurrum wurde zerstört'.

Siegel: Ur-ĝi$_{6}$-pa[r$_{4}$]	Urĝipa[r],
dumu-[ ]	Sohn [des X],
LÚ ⸢x x⸣	X.

Bibliographie

BPOA = Biblioteca del Próximo Oriente Antiguo, Madrid.
Nisaba = Nisaba. Studi Assiriologici Messenesi (Messina).
SAT = Sumerian Archival Texts (Bethesda).

DAHL, J.L. 2007: *The Ruling Family of Ur III Umma. A Prosopographical Analysis of an Elite Family in Southern Iraq 4000 Years Ago* (PIHANS 108), Leiden.

LIMET, H. 1968: *L'anthroponymie sumérienne dans les documents de la 3e dynastie d'Ur*, Paris.

MAYR, R. 1997: *The Seal Impressions of Ur III Umma*, Leiden.

NEUMANN, H. 1994: "Beer as a Means of Compensation for Work in Mesopotamia during the Ur III Period", in L. Milano (ed.), *Drinking in Ancient Societies. History and Culture of Drinks in the Ancient Near East* (HANE/S VI), Padova, 321-331.

PETTINATO, G. 1967: *Untersuchungen zur neusumerischen Landwirtschaft I/1-2*, Napoli.

RENGER, J. 1969: "Untersuchungen zum Priestertum der altbabylonischen Zeit, 2. Teil", *ZA* 59, 104-230.

SALLABERGER, W. 1993: *Der kultische Kalender der Ur III-Zeit* (UAVA 7/I-II), Berlin – New York.

SIGRIST, M. 1992: *Drehem*, Bethesda.

STEINKELLER, P. 1989: *Sale Documents of the Ur-III-Period* (FAOS 17), Stuttgart.

— 2003: "The Question of Lugalzagesi's Origins", in G.J. Selz (ed.), *Festschrift für Burkhart Kienast zu seinem 70. Geburtstage dargebracht von Freunden, Schülern und Kollegen* (AOAT 274), Münster, 621-637.

WU YUHONG 2010: "Differentiating Šulgi 43 and Amar-Suena 4", *Cuneiform Digital Library Notes* 2010:001.

THREE EARLY OLD BABYLONIAN ACCOUNTS

David I. OWEN
Cornell University, Ithaca NY

Karel Van Lerberghe, a friend and colleague I have known and admired for many years, takes particular delight in unusual Old Babylonian texts to whose interpretation and elucidation he frequently contributes. I take great pleasure in offering him the following three texts, none as obscure or as difficult as those he usually studies, knowing that he will likely manage to add more to their interpretation than provided herein.

Regrettably, the texts are without excavated contexts but even without context they provide new and important data that enhance our understanding of Old Babylonian economic issues. Those that believe that "context is everything" need to reconsider their conclusions.

Tablet 1 is in the Cornell University Collections[1] housed in the Jonathan and Jeannette Rosen Ancient Near Eastern Studies Seminar, Department of Near Easter Studies. The format of the text does not appear to have any parallels and the year name is otherwise unknown but perhaps *Gungunum* 16? or *Rim-Sîn* 4. It concerns large quantities of various types of wool and their silver and barley equivalent values.[2] The mention of the "replacement of Pašime," a city recently identified at Tell Abu Sheeja in Iraq, north of Amarah, about 50 km. southeast of Baghdad, and 7 km. from the Iran/Iraq border, on the western bank of the River Tieb,[3] is particularly interesting and unusual. There, an Old Babylonian temple and stratum were excavated in 2007. The identification is based on the

[1] Texts from these collections are being published in the series, Cornell University Studies in Assyriology and Sumerology (CUSAS), Bethesda: CDL Press, 2007ff.

[2] For the most up-to-date discussion of the role of wool in the Old Babylonian period see Stol 2004.

[3] Initially Altaweel et al. 2009: "The site of Tell Abu Shiija, just north of Amarah in Iraq, has been associated with ancient Bashime, as suggested by historical texts found from the site. These texts, which date to the third millennium BC, have been recovered from within a possible temple that likely dates to the Old Babylonian period. Some third millennium finds have been recovered from areas within the site, but most of the remains date to the second millennium BC. This paper will present some of the results of the first season of excavations at Tell Abu Shija, presenting evidence both for and against the possibility that Tell Abu Shiija can be associated with ancient Bashime." For a full report on the excavations, including the inscriptions, see Mohammad et al. 2010.

discovery of two texts, a fragmentary Sargonic period stele and an Ur III door socket. A seal inscription in the Walters Art Museum, identified by B. Studevent-Hickman via the *CDLI* (Mohammad et al. 2010, 58) belongs to a *Šalim-belī*, son of *Puzur*-Šuda, nu-bànda of Pašime. This may be the same *Šalim-belī* (no patronymic), a well-known royal messenger (lú-kíĝ-gi$_4$-a-lugal) at Iri-Saĝrig/*Āl-Šarrākī*.[4] These new data substantiate that Pašime is to be located in Iraq rather than in Iran, as hitherto thought. It alters, to some extent, our understanding of the geography of the late third and early second millennia in Babylonia and Iran.[5] The tablet may have originated in Larsa or Ur but perhaps also Pašime.

CUNES 55-01-008
Date: *Gungunum* 16?/v/- or *Rim-Sîn* 4/v/-
No seal
Tablet 124 × 58
No envelope
Provenance: Larsa, Ur or Pašime

(1)	88 gú siki-igi-saĝ-ĝá	88 talents of choice wool.
(2)	kar-gul-lá-bi 1 gú-šè 10½ gín-ta	Its market value is, for each talent, 10½ shekels (of silver).
(3)	kù-bi 15⅓ ma-na 4 gín	Its (total) silver value is 15⅓ minas 4 shekels;
(4)	50 gú siki-igi-saĝ-ĝá-libir	50 talents of choice old wool
(5)	1 gú-šè 8½ gín-ta	8½ shekels (of silver) for each talent (of choice old wool).
(6)	kù-bi 7 ma-na 5 gín	Its (total) silver (value) is 7 minas 5 shekels (of silver);
(7)	160 gú siki-gú-udu-gibil(NE×PAP)	160 talents of fresh wool (plucked) from the flanks of sheep.
(8)	1 gú-šè 9½ ma-na-ta	For each talent, 9½ minas (of silver).
(9)	kù-bi 25⅓ ma-na	Its (total) silver value is 25⅓ minas.
(10)	48 gú siki gú-udu-libir	48 talents of old wool (plucked) from the flanks of sheep.

[4] For *Šalim-belī* see my forthcoming, *Uprovenanced Texts Primarily from Iri-Saĝrig/Āl-Šarrākī and the History of the Ur III Period I-II* (Nisaba 15), Messina: Di.Sc.A.M., *passim*.

[5] For the implications of the location of Pašime/Bašime, cf. Mohammad et al. 2010, 56-59, the extensive discussion of P. Steinkeller, "On the Dynasty of Simaški: Twenty (or so) years After," *Stolper AV*, forthcoming (courtesy of the author) and Vallat 1993, 36, s.v. Bašime/Mišime, for previous location and bibliography.

Tablet 1. Obv. CUNES 55-01-008.

Tablet 1. Rev. CUNES 55-01-008.

(11)	1 gú-šè 8½ gín-ta	8½ shekels (of silver) for each talent (of old wool (plucked) from the flanks of sheep).
(12)	kù-bi 6⅔ ma-n[a] 8 gín	Its (total) silver value is 6⅔ minas and 8 shekels.
(13)	731 gú siki-gin	731 talents of ordinary wool.
(14)	1 gú-šè 8½ gín-ta	8½ shekels (of silver) for each talent (of ordinary wool).
(15)	kù-bi 1 gú 43½ ma-na ~ 3½ gín	Its (total) silver (value) is 43½ minas 3½ shekels.
(16)	{indent}1077 gú siki-hi-a	1077 talents of various (kinds of) wool.

rev.

(17)	kù-bi 2 gú 38 ma-na ~10½ gín	Their (total) silver (value) is 38 minas 10½ shekels.
(18)	é-kìšib-ba-ta	From the storehouse.
(19)	*Ilam-ku-ru-ub* ù ^{d}*Šamaš-tillatī*	*Ilam-kurub* and *Šamaš-tillatī*
(20)	gaba-ri dub-ba 1 šu ba-an-ti	received one copy of the tablet.
(21)	130 gú siki-gin	130 talents of ordinary wool (and)
(22)	1 gú-šè 17 še gur-ta	for each talent (of ordinary wool) 17 bushels of barley.
(23)	še-bi 2210.0.0. še gur	Its barley equivalent is 2210 gur.
(24)	1200.0.0. še gur ki-ba ĝar-ra Pá-ši-mé ~^{ki}	1200 bushels of barley, the "replacement" of Pašime,
(25)	tah$^{!}$ 1.0.0. gur-àm 10.0.0. gur-ta	being the addition of 1 gur (of barley) for each 10 gur (barley).
(26)	še-bi 200.0.0. gur ~ 3610.0.0. gur guru$_7$-šè	Its barley equivalent is 200 gur (a total of) 3610 gur (of barley) for the granary.
(27)	gaba-ri dub-ba 1	Copy of tablet one.
(28)	*Ilam-ku-ru-ub* ù ^{d}*Šamaš-tillatī* ~ šu ba-an-ti	*Ilam-kurub* and *Šamaš-tillatī* received it.
(29)	BLANK SPACE	
(30)	iti ne-ne-ĝar	The month of Nenegar,
(31)	mu é-^{d}Inana ba-dù	the year the temple of Inanna was built (= Gungunum 16? or *Rim-Sîn* 4).

Comments

Line 2: This is either an Akkadian loan from Sumerian, or a syllabic writing for kar(a)-kù-lá-bi, "its weighing out of silver at the quay." For *kargullu*, "market value," cf. CAD K 216, s.v., Leemans 1968, 191 and Charpin 1982, 55. The syllabic spelling here with -gul-lá is not otherwise attested. For market prices for wool in the Old Babylonian period see Stol 2004, 971 (§20.2.2.5).

Line 7: For síg-gú-udu, "*haltikku,*" cf. CAD H 53 s.v., where the reading and meaning were unknown, and Stol 2004, 963-964, "Berissenes Vlies (Wolle von der 'Seite'[gú] des Schafes)", based on the previous analysis by Waetzoldt cited there.

Line 15: Wool total of ll. 1, 4, 7, 9, 12.

Line 18: For the reading, *tillatī* for KASKAL.KUR, cf. Stol 1991, 192.

Line 19: Reading pointed out by M. Stol based on *ìl-lam-ku-<ru->ub* in YOS 5 133:18.

Line 22: The price of wool in this text appears to be standard for the Old Babylonian period. Cf. Waetzoldt 1972, 76 with notes 304-305 and more recently, Farber 1978, 46ff. and Charpin 1982, 31ff., 51 (references courtesy of H. Waetzoldt) and M. Stol, *loc. cit.*

Line 24: For ki-ba ĝar-ra, *pūhu*, "replacement," cf. CAD P 496 s.v. and Heimpel 2009, 137, for Ur III examples. Although the meaning of the phrase, ki-ba ĝar-ra, is established, its meaning in this context is not clear.

Line 25: Over erasure? saĝ or saĝ-bi is expected. The "tax" here would be 10%, cf. Veenhof 1985, especially 294-297.

Line 26: Equals the total of grain from ll. 23, 24, 25.

Tablet 2[6] is in the collection at Allegheny College[7] whose Ur III texts I had published two decades ago (Owen 1991). The text is related to Grant 1918, nos. 266 and 269, both dealing with *Āl-Warad-Sîn*. It concerns the receipt of ten kor of barley presumably pledged to the palace.

Allegheny 25
Date: *Rīm-Sîn* 23/vii/14
Two seals
Tablet 39×51
Envelope fragments
Provenance: unknown

(1)	10.0.0. še gur	10 gur of barley,
(2)	*ma-aš-ša-ar-ti ka-ri-im*	expenditures at the quay
(3)	*ša* iri^{ki}-árad-^{d}EN.ZU[8]	of *Āl-Warad-Sîn*,

[6] I would like to thank M. Stol for his helpful suggestions and additional references.

[7] The Allegheny tablet collection originally was brought to my attention by Professor Don Hobson who arranged for its loan that enabled me to study, copy and publish the collection.

[8] The city, *Āl-Warad-Sîn*, is poorly attested and its location unknown, cf. Groneberg 1980, s.v. for references.

(4)	šu-ti-a *ne-ru-ba-a-tim*	a receipt of a pledge?
(5)	*ša ki-ša-ad* i$_7$-idigna-an-ta	at the bank of the Tigris River
(6)	inim-ta ^{d}*ri-im*-^{d}EN.ZU-^{d}utu-*ši-ni*	at the order of *Rīm-Sîn-šamšīni*.
(7)	ĝìri *im-me-er*-diĝir dumu é-gal	Responsible (officials), *Immer-ilī*, "representative" of the palace,
(8)	*ù za-ku-re-e-lum*	and *Zakur-Elum*
(9)	kìšib-ba-ne-ne i[sic!]-íb-ra	who rolled their seals.
(10)	*šum-ma* é-gal-*lum*	If the palace
(11)	*ni-ik-ka-sà-am*	does not accept
(12)	*la im-ta-ḫa-ar*	the accounting
(13)	diš *im-me-er*-diĝir dumu é-gal	*Immer-ilī*, "representative" of the palace,
(14)	*ù za-ku-re-e-lum*	and *Zakur-Elum*,
(15)	šà guru$_7$ iri^{ki}-árad-^{d}EN.ZU	in the grain storage place of *Āl-Warad-Sîn*,
(16)	še ì-áĝ-e	they shall measure out the barley.
(17)	itu du$_6$-kù u$_4$-14- kam	The month of Duku, 14th day,
(18)	mu dug$_4$ ^{d}EN.ZU ^{d}en-líl	the year in which the righteous
	~ ^{d}en-ki-ga-ta	shepherd *Rim-Sîn*, by the order of
	~ i$_7$-buranun-na-bi di$_4$-lim-da	*Sîn*, Enlil, and Enki, dug (a canal)
	kù-ga ^{d}nanna-ke$_4$	
	~sipad-zi ^{d}*ri-im*-^{d}EN.ZU	towards the Euphrates, the holy cup
	~ mu-un-ba-al-lá	of Nanna.

Seal

im-me-er-diĝir	*za-ku-re-e-lum*
dumu *ḫa-ri-i*[*a*]	dumu *i-a-ku-nu-um*
árad AN-AN-MAR-TU	árad AN-AN-MAR-TU

Comments

Line 2 *maššartum*, "staples set aside in a household for specific periods to be processed by its craftsmen," CAD M/1 387 s.v. Additional references: Gordon Smith College 70:1, Sollberger 1980, 48, Nr. 117:5 (both with Birot 1969, 16:1-4); VAS 9, 37:4; ARM 28, 21:30, CBS 368:6 (both wool). Breckwoldt 1995-96, 76-77: "Expenditures for Storehouses: *maššartum ana bītim*"; Dyckhoff 1999, 35-38; Llop 2005, 48[71] ("Entnahmestelle," mAss).

Line 3: On the city *Āl-Warad-Sîn*, see Groneberg 1980 s.v. cf. SLB 1/2 38:13 and 63:11, Scheil 1915, 199 and TCL 10 123:26.

Line 4: For *nērubātum* cf. Robertson 1981, 246ff., UM 29-15-936: rev. 3 (caprids *ne-ru-ba-tum*, é-^{d}nin-maš). Cf. *še-am i-na ne-ri-ba-tim lu-ud-di-in*, Goetze 1958, 56, no. 30:16ff. Not entered in the dictionaries. Perhaps connected to Old Assyrian *erubātu*, "a pledge," CAD E 327 s.v.

(All 25)

obv. tab.

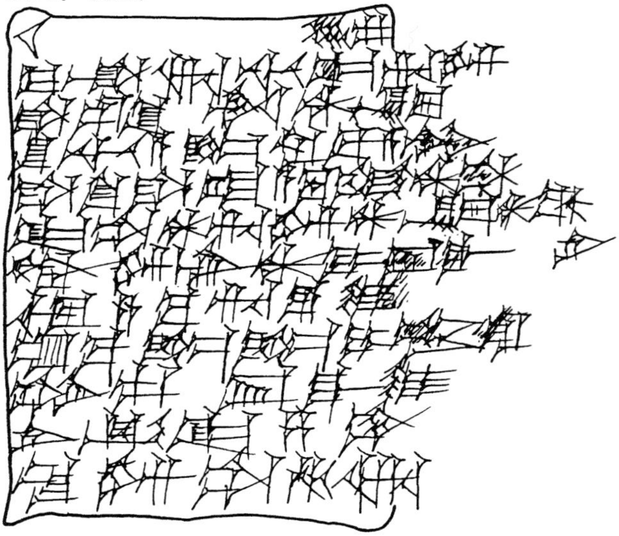

rev.

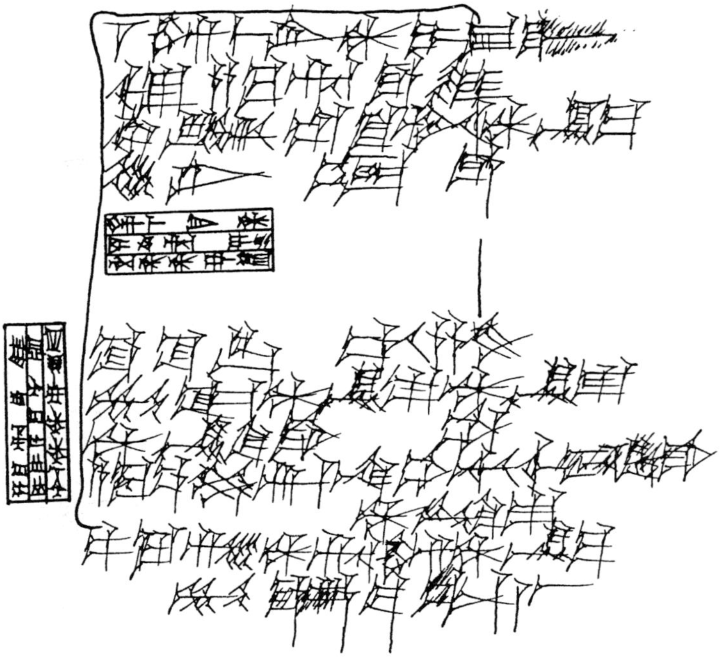

fragments of case preserved

Tablet 2. Obv. and Rev. Allegheny 25.

Line 6: For *Rīm-Sîn-šamšīni*, cf. Veldhuis 2008, 52, no. 4:5 with notes; also in Gordon Smith College 71 = AbB 9, 273:4!.

Line 7: *Immer-ilī* appears in Grant 1918, no. 269:12, 15 and as rá-gaba in Seri 2007, plate 15 (= CDLI P368395 = Kalamazoo Valley Museum 32.1178:4). The name also appears in AbB 6, 98:2; cf. Stol 2011.

Line 8: *Zakur-Elum* appears in Grant 1918, nos. 266:4, 269:14 (also seal). For the personal name, cf. Gelb 1980,128 s.v. ḎAKUR (UCP 10/1 no. 86:15).

Tablet 3 (JON-78) is in a private collection and is published with the kind permission of its owners in memory of their son Jonathan ז"ל. It is an early Old Babylonian loan contract concerning a substantial quantity of silver and contains unusual personal names. Its year name is unknown.

JON-78
Date: unknown
Sealed
Tablet 46 × 40
Provenance: unknown

1.	[n ma-na k]ù-babbar[9]	[n minas] of silver
	~ máš 1 m[a-na n gur š]e-ta	interest for one mi[na n kor] of barley each,
2.	ki *mu-na-a-a*	from *Munaya*
	~ dumu *a-di-hi-AN*	son of *Adihi-AN*
3.	šu ba-an-ti	was received (by *Iadihi-xx*).[10]
4.	igi *pa-za-i-a*	Witnessed by *Pazaya*
rev.		
5.	igi *me-en-hi-du-um*	Witnessed by *Menhidum*
6.	igi *ar-ga-da* nu-bànda	Witnessed by *Argada*, the captain
7.	BLANK SPACE – SEAL	Seal
8.	iti ne-ne-ĝar	Month of Neneĝar,
9.	mu *i-din!-*[d]*šamaš*[11] ba-ug$_7$	the year *Iddin-Šamaš* died.[12]

Seal

ì-a-di-hi-x-x	*Iadihi-xx*
dumu *za-an-ka-na-x*	son of *Zankana-x*

[9] The restoration assumes a substantial quantity of silver was loaned.
[10] Presumably the sealer of the tablet was the receiver of the interest bearing loan.
[11] The din seems to be written over an erasure. Together the sign looks like a gú.
[12] The year name appears to be new as does the name of a presumed king.

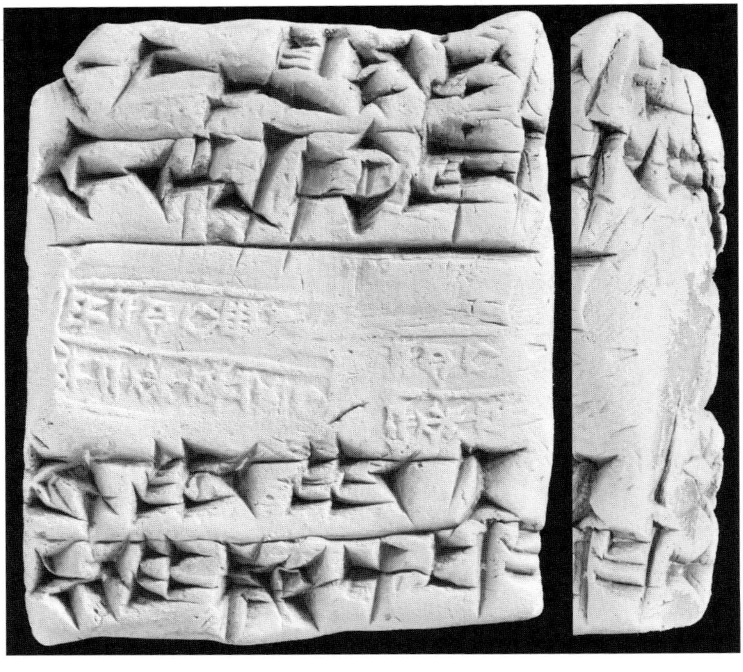

Tablet 3. Obv. and Rev. JON-78.

Bibiography

ALTAWEEL, M. A. et al. 2009: "Ancient Bashime Revealed? Results from the First Season of Excavations at Tell Abu Shiija" posted November 29, 2009. http://www.docstoc.com/docs/17933838/Mobile-pastoralists-are-one-of-the-most-elusive-segments-of-.

BIROT M. 1969: *Tablettes d'époque babylonienne ancienne* (TEBA), Paris.

BRECKWOLDT T. 1995-96: "Managment of Grain Storage in Old Babylonian Larsa", *AfO* 42-43, 64-88.

CHARPIN, D. 1982: "Marchands du palais et marchands du temple à la fin de la 1re dynastie de Babylone", *Journal Asiatique* 270, 25–65.

DYCKHOFF C. 1999, *Das Haushaltsbuch des Balamunamḫe I*, München. (Diss.)

FARBER, H. 1978: "A Price and Wage Study for Northern Babylonia during the Old Babylonian Period", *JESHO* 21, 1-51.

GELB I. J. 1980, *Computer-Aided Analyses of Amorite*, Chicago.

GOETZE, A, 1958: "Fifty Old-Babylonian Letters from Harmal", *Sumer* 14, 1-76.

GRANT E. 1918: *Cuneiform Documents in the Smith College Library* (Biblical and Kindred Studies, No. 1), Haverford.

GRONEBERG, B. 1980: *Die Orts- und Gewässernamen der altbabylonischen Zeit* (Répertoire Géographique des Textes Cunéiformes 3), Wiesbaden.

HEIMPEL, H. 2009: *Workers and Construction Work at Garšana* (CUSAS 5), Bethesda.

LEEMANS W. F. 1968: "Old Babylonian Letters and Economic History A Review Article with a Digression on Foreign Trade", *JESHO* 11, 171-226.

LLOP J. 2005: "Die königlichen "großen Speicher" (karmū rabi'ūtu) der Stadt Assur in der Regierungszeit Salmanassars I. und Tukulti-Ninurtas I.", *MDOG* 137, 41-55.

MOHAMMAD, A. et al. 2010, "Tell Abu Sheeja/Ancient Pašime: Report on the First Season of Excavations, 2007," *Akkadica* 131, 47-103.

OWEN, D. I. 1991: *Neo-Sumerian Texts from American Collections* (MVN 15), Rome.

ROBERTSON, J. F. 1981: *Redistributive Economies in Ancient Mesopotamian society: A Case Study from Isin-Larsa Period Nippur*, Philadelphia. (Diss.)

SCHEIL V. 1915: "Notules", *RA* 12, 193-201.

SERI, A. 2007: "The Mesopotamian Collection in the Kalamazoo Valley Museum", *Cuneiform Digital Library Journal* 2007/1, 1-45.

SOLLBERGER E. 1980: "The Cuneiform Tablets in the Chester Beatty Library", *RA* 74, 43-59.

STOL, M. 1991, "Old Babylonian Personal Names", *Studi Epigrafici e Linguistici sul Vicino Oriente Antico* 8, 191-212.

— 2004, "Wollertrag", in D. Charpin, D.O. Edzard and M. Stol (eds.) *Mesopotamien, Die altbabylonische Zetit* (OBO 160/4), Fribourg - Göttingen, 959-972 (§§20.2.2.1 – 20.2.2.6).

— 2011, "Altbabylonisch rá-gaba", in *Fs Attinger*. (forthcoming)

VALLAT, F. 1993: *Les noms géographiques des sources suso-élamites* (Répertoire Géographique des Textes Cunéiformes 11), Wiesbaden.

VELDHUIS, N. 2008: " Old Babylonian Documents in the Hearst Museum of Anthropology, Berkeley", RA 102, 49-70.

VEENHOF, K. R. 1985: "sag.íl.la = saggilû, "Difference Assessed" on Measuring and Accounting in Some Old Babylonian Texts", in J.-M. Durand and J.-R. Kupper (eds.) *Miscellanea Babylonica, Mélanges offerts à Maurice Birot*, Paris, 285-306.

WAETZOLDT, H. 1972: *Untersuchtungen zur neusumerischen Textilindustrie* (UNT), Rome.

WORD *VERSUS* DIRT

HISTORY AND ARCHAEOLOGY APPLIED TO PROTO-HISTORICAL SAGALASSOS

Jeroen POBLOME
KU Leuven

"*Carpe diem, quam minimum credula postero*" was Quintus Horatius Flaccus' (65-8 BC) poetic and clear opinion in his *Odes* 1,11: "*Seize the day, putting as little trust as possible in the future*". A little bit of poetry is never bad to open an honorific academic contribution, especially considering to whom this particular volume is dedicated. The future is unforeseen and unknown, and therefore it is best to enjoy the moment of now. Even though I wish Karel Van Lerberghe a lot more moments of now, preferably with good company and wine, the meaning of his life and work has little to do with now or the future, rather with all things of the past. Horace, however, does not offer much concerning the past. That is a little unfortunate, as the study of the past can do with a bit of advice. Indeed, whereas in traditional schemes of academic organisation every aspect of the world seems to be divided up among specific disciplines (e.g. gods go to theology, mixing explosive substances to chemistry and curing bodies to medicine), the past is not studied by one, but by two scientific disciplines: history and archaeology. Both disciplines claim their right to exist, as each deals with discipline-specific data types and source material, has particular theoretical frameworks, methods and techniques of analysis, and discipline-specific epistemologies leading to different frameworks of interpretation and explanation of the (same) past. To make matters worse, in their evolution, archaeology and history were not considered to be equal scientific partners. The Cambridge historian and medieval numismatist Philip Grierson expressed the potential contribution of archaeology as follows: "*It has been said that the spade cannot lie, but it owes this merit to the fact that it cannot even speak*" (Grierson 1959, 129). The Force is with the Word, and not with the Dirt. Clearly, 1959 is a long time gone, and it would be uncouth to reduce Philip Grierson's appreciation of archaeology to only this sentence, but as an active participant in the scene of historical archaeology, I sometimes wonder whether both disciplines can ever be considered truly equal.

In this paper, I intend to explain my pessimistic sentiment by focusing on a period and region where neither history nor archaeology have the upper-hand: the second millennium BC in the study region of ancient Sagalassos.

First, a prelude. Claudio Ottoni and colleagues recently published a study on the mitochondrial DNA of a mid Byzantine population group, part of the cemetery of which was excavated at the site of Sagalassos (SW Turkey) (Ottoni et al. 2011). In their own words: "*The purpose of this study is to estimate the maternal genetic signature potentially left in the Byzantine population from Sagalassos by the historic events impacting the Sagalassos region and South-Western Anatolia since the Bronze Age, and whether these events may have been associated to large population movements, to more restricted elite dominance or only to cultural diffusion.*" (Ottoni et al. 2011, 572). Of the 85 excavated skeletons, datable to the 11th-13th centuries AD, the mtDNA of 51 individuals could be analysed, revealing 39 haplotypes, which are considered to represent a fairly high diversity, and forming part of West Eurasian sequences. Comparison of Eurasian and African populations indicated that Sagalassos is very similar to samples from neighbouring populations in Turkey, the Balkans, Crimea, Cyprus and Iran, confirming the Anatolian peninsula's geographical strategic position for the movement of people. Genetic proximity was also noted with populations from Italian Campania and Puglia.

The affinity with current Anatolian populations is considered to result from similar historic and demographic trajectories. The genetic proximity with Balkan populations is partly explained by influences of the genetic signature of the Phrygians, originating from Balkan lands, and also admixtures with Macedonian and Seleucid blood in Hellenistic times. The Iranian link is explained from Persian Achaemenid interaction, whereas the Italian connection is seen to result from the foundation of a ring of veteran colonies in Pisidia in Augustan times. The Levantine component is considered to result from intense trade contacts resulting in a cultural *koinè* in these regions, possibly strengthened by outposting mercenaries. A Caucasian connection is also suggested, potentially as a legacy of the introduction of Luwian groups in the study region, around 2000 BC. The similarities to Central Asian Uygur and Uzbek populations are explained by the high frequencies of West-Eurasian specific aDNA characteristics in these groups, but a real connection is ruled out based on archaeological evidence of violent destruction at Sagalassos that suggests a hostile relationship with the Seljuks. In conclusion, this "*study provides new clues to pinpoint the impact of historical events, and correspondingly of the related population groups, on the maternal gene pool of the Byzantine population from Sagalassos*" (Ottoni et al. 2011, 575).

In other words, the explanatory framework for this high profile interdisciplinary study on the results of archaeological excavations is basically historical in nature. In this way, the genetic pool of the Byzantine population at Sagalassos is a palimpsest of the major stages of the region's historical trajectory.

Some archaeological edits are in place, perhaps. In this paper, only the suggested proto-historical Luwian connection will be examined in more detail. To be sure, Luwian was one of the first languages attested in writing in Anatolia at Middle Bronze Age sites, such as Kültepe, shortly after the end of the third millennium BC. Luwian did not originate in Asia Minor, but is an Indo-European language. Together with Hittite and Palaic, Luwian is actually one of the oldest documented Indo-European languages. Historical linguistics now traces this group of languages to the north Pontic steppes and the start of the dispersal process to around 4000 BC or the Late Chalcolithic period (Anthony 2007). The way these languages and the people who spoke them spread is much less clear (Melchert 2003, 23-26). Languages and people are two different things, however, and require substantial evidence to be linked in a meaningful way, especially when considered to have formed part of migration processes. When readable texts become available from the end of the Middle Bronze Age onwards, Luwian appears to be associated with settled communities (Sagona and Zimansky 2009, 244-247), which are considered to have formed different states (Marek 2010, 103-104). From the reign of Hattusili I (*c.* 1565-1540 BC) onwards, for instance, sources mention the Arzawa lands in western Asia Minor, which are not necessarily considered to be states as such, but to reflect "*the emergence of states or kingdoms in these regions*" (Bryce 2003, 32). In this way, a third ingredient is added to the cocktail, being political constellations.

As to the dispersal processes, for now, it seems appropriate to conclude, with Bleda Düring (2011, 261-3), that "*there is no convincing archaeological evidence at present for the migration of Indo-European-speaking groups into Asia Minor*". This does not mean that the dispersal of Indo-European languages in Asia Minor did not happen, but that archaeology cannot trace its chronology, speed nor mechanisms. In this respect it is better to be safe than sorry, not in the least because cases of migration in the past have been used in political and ethnic debates in the present. Be that as it may be, also closer to home, within the history of the archaeological discipline itself, the process of migration used to represent the golden formula to explain phenomena, such as 'dark ages' or sudden appearances of entirely new assemblages of material culture and ways of living (Trigger 1989, 150-155). Now that archaeological frameworks of interpretation are conceptually richer, migration is considered to form part of an ongoing variety of events of interregional interaction, along and possibly contemporary with, for instance, trade and exchange, and raids and conquest. Human interaction is complex and variable. Although models and typologies of migration and interaction have been developed (e.g. Gosden 2004), recent focus is also placed on the analysis of the parameters of interaction influencing acculturation at both group and individual levels. These parameters or variables include the number of people involved in the interaction, the duration of the interaction, the cultural distance between the groups involved, the segmentation of the population involved, the power balance between the groups involved and the level of pluralism and tolerance within these groups. Migration is considered to result in intense interaction bringing about instantaneous deep change in material culture assemblages and behavioural patterns, as expressed, for instance, in subsistence patterns and food habits, architecture, material culture production and consumption, as well as aspects of gender. Assaf Yasur-Landau (2010) recently applied the parameters of interaction to the study of Philistine migration, indicating that, when sufficient material is available, archaeology can provide answers to issues of migration. Unfortunately, such is not yet the case with the Indo-European, including Luwian, processes of dispersal.

Some of the effects of the dispersal can be documented, however. Early Hittite documents, for instance, refer to the lands of Luwiya as a territorial constellation, that was treated with respect. The sources stop short of identifying Luwiya as a single political entity, rather "*indicating a general region which was inhabited by peoples speaking a shared Indo-European language, but without territorial limits*" (Bryce 2003, 31). Luwiya extended into the western half of Anatolia. Even if overlap existed in the sources between a region and people speaking the same language, this need not imply ethnic connotations or forms of statehood. The same holds for the Arzawa lands. Arzawa came to replace Luwiya as a term for many of the same territories in the Late Bronze Age, containing five kingdoms that are attested in the sources. Luwian may have been an important language in these kingdoms, but it was not the only one, and Luwians were not the only population and/or ethnic group. Once again, archaeology seems speechless, however (Aro 2003, 285-288). The consideration that "*a nomadic or semi-nomadic existence probably characterized a large part of the Luwian population* (Bryce 2003, 31)" is particularly unhelpful, by making these groups archaeologically invisible. How is it possible to identify a site, its architecture and material culture as Luwian? Is a site in western Anatolia with Middle and Late Bronze Age remains, such as Beycesultan, automatically Luwian? Even in the event that a Luwian site and material culture could be defined, with documents indicating its inhabitants spoke Luwian, how is it possible to be sure that this community or members thereof were ethnically Luwian? There is no easy solution to these issues, while recent linguistic and archaeological research "*suggests that there was a high degree of micro-regionalism and diversity within western Anatolia in terms of both cultural traits and social practice*" (Mac Sweeney 2010, 8) — once more indicating that Luwian was only part of the package and that the archaeology of contemporary Asia Minor should be freed to some extent of a Hittite/text-driven perspective.

Moreover, it is important to consider that: "*languages can spread either through large-scale migrations of people, as in the colonisation of North America, or through foreign elites inducing language shifts among the populace, as occurred in much of colonial Africa* (Düring 2011, 262)". In the latter case, some advantage must have been appreciated by local groups to give up their language, or to add another language to their knowledge. In this way, social advantages and political shifts can be as effective mechanisms of language dispersal in local communities as population displacement following warfare and destruction of the homeland.

Therefore, as long as the mechanisms of Luwian language dispersal and/or the mentioned parameters of interaction are not documented in more detail, Luwian ancestry of the mid Byzantine population buried at the site cannot, at the moment, be considered 'proven'. The argumentation would take us beyond the scope of this paper, but the other steps in the suggested historical build-up of the aDNA profile of the Byzantine population of Sagalassos should be approached with similar caution. Ethnicity is not a creation based on historical interpretation of linguistic patterns or assemblages of archaeological material, but a process of active creation and cultivation by past communities (Jones 1997).

Can the archaeology of the study region in the second millennium BC provide other indications? Although the wider study region contains some major Early Bronze Age höyüks, such as at Kuruçay, Hacılar II, Karaçal and possibly at Kokar Pınar, perhaps territorially organised to some degree

(Vanhaverbeke and Waelkens 2003, 183-184), the Middle and Late Bronze Ages are hardly defined (Duru 2008, 178-181). The fact that the Bronze Age höyüks were abandoned by the start of the second millennium BC and that no highly diagnostic repertoire of material culture is available, as in Hittite contexts for instance, led to a series of explanations. These traditional explanations involve imploding settlement patterns including environmental change, demographic decline, (internal) warfare, a climate of insecurity caused by (Indo-European/Luwian) newcomers, an upsurge in nomadism, as well as the burial of older remains by continuing settlements (Vanhaverbeke and Waelkens 2003, 195-207). From lack of material and sites none of these mostly external factors of presumed societal decline (Tainter 2005) can be evaluated in any archaeological detail, however. The question should be asked, therefore, whether 'collapse' should be the right concept with which to approach this period, rather than gradual shifts in societal complexity and organisation that phased out the höyük communities. Admittedly, also for this interpretation, the archaeological material is lacking, but at least it connotates a less drastic scenario.

Some information is available on contemporary nature-society interactions. During the late Holocene, ecological change continued and human impact on the environment increased in the eastern Mediterranean. More specifically, the so-called Beyşehir Occupation Phase, the start of which is mostly dated in the transition towards the Late Bronze Age, was characterized by climate amelioration, forest clearance and the appearance of cultivated cereals and tree species in pollen diagrams. As a result, landscapes were more prone to erosion, especially during a relatively wet period in the Late Bronze Age (Dusar et al. 2011). Obviously, local circumstances and events could be different. For instance, in the study area, deciduous oak woodland had declined. This possibly resulted in a dry trend before the onset of the Beyşehir Occupation Phase, while cultivated tree species such as *Olea europaea* and *Juglans regia* were introduced, but never frequent, during that phase (Bakker et al. 2011). Although the evidence is patchy, the results are not indicative of drastic environmental changes, but rather of continuing or increased human impact on the landscape, which is not necessarily compatible with the scenario of societal collapse.

Additionally, some archaeological material is available, yet the absence of a stratigraphical reference framework makes it hard to define the evidence in any detail. New intensive survey campaigns in the southwestern part of the Burdur Lake plain resulted in the identification of some late third/second millennium BC pottery fragments of local fabrics (Kaptijn et al., in press). The assemblage to which this pottery belonged, albeit mostly Early Bronze Age in date, was associated with a hamlet or village. Late Bonze Age pottery was reported at the surface of Hacılar II (Birmingham 1964, 30). Contemporary, LH IIIA2/B (*c*. 1350-1200 BC) Mycenaean and other similar pottery was discovered along the northern side of Lake Yarışlı, near Düver-Yarımada (Mellink 1967, 164; 1969, 212), a major archaeological site located on a promontory in Lake Yarışlı. The find circumstances of this material are, unfortunately, unclear, but a funerary context of deposition seems likely, as the objects are well preserved. An Early Bronze Age cemetery with pithos burials was registered in the same area (Mellink 1969, 212). As Mycenaean pottery is well attested along the Aegean coast of Anatolia and similar products were made locally, the Düver finds need not have resulted from direct exchange with the Greek mainland, but nonetheless stand out in the archaeological record of the region. Christopher Mee (1978, 150) suggested a transit route along the Maeander valley. Recently, Middle and Late Bronze Age material, including LH IIIC (*c*. 1200-1050 BC) Cypro-Mycenaean fine wares, was found at the acropolis of Parha/Perge (Martini 2010, 21) suggesting a southward corridor as another option of connectivity for the study region.

In the western parts of the later town of Sagalassos, a limited amount of thick walled, wheel-made, red slipped rim sherds of shallow bowls and containers was picked up during the intensive urban survey in 2005. Unfortunately, a targeted control excavation of this location in 2009 did not result in the discovery of a stratigraphical context for this material. The fabric and finish of the small collection of sherds stood out as unusual, as these features could not be associated with pottery from any other documented period at ancient Sagalassos. Petrographic analysis identified a non-calacareous fabric with, amongst others, volcanic mineral fragments belonging to a regional volcanic-sedimentary group related to ophiolitic clays present in and around Sagalassos (Braekmans 2011). Mainly the deep red lustrous burnished surfaces on the exterior and interior are characteristic of this (possibly) local product. Dennis Braekmans (2011, 121) suggested an association for this fabric with Late Bronze Age Red Lustrous wheel made wares, datable between the 16th and early 12th centuries BC, with an abundant presence in the northern Levant and more generally in the eastern Mediterranean. The latter ware is a much finer fabric made into a range of typical and often closed shapes. The region of Kazaphani on northern Cyprus is a likely candidate for its production, although geologically related areas in southern Asia Minor cannot yet be ruled out (Knappett et al. 2005). Considering that we are dealing with surface material at Sagalassos, that the fabric is local, and that the quantities are small and the shapes inconclusive, it is perhaps best to be very prudent with this material at the moment.

This being the case, the so-called 'Indictment of Madduwata' (KUB XIV 1 and KBo XIX 38) mentioned a site named Sallawassa, for which an identification with later Sagalassos has been proposed (Freu 1987, 140-141, 147). The Hittite document was actually a letter written by Arnuwanda I (*c.* 1400-1375 BC) to his vassal Madduwatta, ruler of the Siyanta River Land, which was possibly located in the upper Sangarios river basin (Hawkins 1998, 22) and close to hostile Arzawa territories. The end of the document is lost, but clearly Madduwatta was not a simple, loyal vassal to the Hittite throne, who tried to make the most of his position through conquest of Arzawa lands. On one such occasion, things went wrong for Madduwatta, who escaped for his life into unspecified "mountains". Hittite armies came to the rescue and recovered Madduwatta's goods, wives, children and servants from the city of Sallawassa. They returned these, along with the same belongings of the Arzawa king that were also kept at Sallawassa, to Madduwatta and reinstated him. The contemporary political and historical geography has been discussed in detail by Marc Waelkens (2000), who (following Jacques Freu) identified Sallawassa with later Sagalassos. Based on the concept of cultural superposition, Marc Waelkens (2000) suggested a continuum of settlement from the second millennium BC onwards. There is insufficient evidence available to evaluate this, but the fact that we can now most probably situate the origins of the urban community of Sagalassos around the middle of the first millennium BC (Poblome et al., in press) makes this less likely. The discoveries at Düzen Tepesi in recent years (Vanhaverbeke et al. 2010) suggest that other settlement options were also available in the Ağlasun Valley, possibly placing the issue of continuity (yet to be fully proven, however) at the level of the *Siedlungskammer*. More fundamentally, however, the identification of Sallawassa with later Sagalassos should not be considered unequivocally 'proven'. The upper Sangarios basin and the neighbouring Arzawa lands, which Madduwatta had invaded and from which he had to flee, are at some distance from actual Sagalassos. David Hawkins (1998), using more recent documentary sources, considers Madduwatta during this particular Sallawassa episode to have seized the state of Hapalla (located roughly between Afyon and Konya). This possibly *"involved him with the ruler of Kuwaliya"* (Hawkins 1998, 25 and

Fig. 11). Kuwaliya is considered to have been located roughly between Afyon and Dinar, possibly with the site of Beycesultan as the principal city of that kingdom. Sagalassos seems to be located to the south of this action radius — making its identification with Sallawassa less likely, if at all.

The available evidence for the Middle and Late Bronze Ages in Sagalassos and in the study region, in general, is difficult to pin down, and the question arises whether the archaeological record of the study region *überhaupt* allows us to sketch some elementary features of second millennium BC society and settlement patterning. When considering the study region, Marc Waelkens (2000, 483) was of the opinion that: "*the creation of chiefdoms and states from the Middle Bronze Age onward may have introduced a new kind of society, no longer centred around höyüks*".

Indeed, instead of considering the mostly external factors related to scenarios of societal collapse discussed above (Vanhaverbeke and Waelkens 2003, 195-207), would it not be useful to consider changes in the social, economical, political, religious and military power structures of the Bronze Age communities in order to help framing the evidence? Could increased social complexity and differentiation, and political centralisation eventually have left the agricultural villages/höyüks of the Early Bronze Age without a function? Could the fact that the höyüks did not suffer destruction and that there are no signs of hurried evacuation be an indication for a gradual, but sure process of abandonment? To be clear, the excavations at Bademağacı höyük sufficiently indicated that höyük society was not egalitarian. The site lay-out followed a planned, radial logic that was retained in subsequent building phases — with large-hall-and-porch houses oriented towards a common courtyard that was filled at some point with a sizeable building (Duru 2008, 145-177). The finding of seals, a bulla and numerical tablets indicated that the site functioned within some sort of administrative system, possibly focused on landed property and its produce (Umurtak 2010). The Early Bronze Age village of Bademağacı höyük is considered to form part of a broader settlement tradition (Düring 2011, 281). No larger settlements, with fortification systems and extensive populations as in South-Central Asia Minor, are known in the study region. Recent intensive survey work in the Burdur plain, however, indicated that höyüks are only part of the settlement pattern that also included smaller units (Kaptijn et al., in press). One of these smaller units produced the mentioned possible Middle to Late Bronze Age material, as a matter of fact. Considering population totals of a couple of hundred in the höyük villages and even adding an unknown proportion from smaller settlement units, it seems fair to consider that the associated political impact of the höyüks may have been territorially limited to intra-mountainous basins or even less in the case of the Burdur plain (Vanhaverbeke and Waelkens 2003, Fig. 57).

When the fog of the second millennium BC disappeared, another political landscape is attested in the study region. In Archaic times (*c.* 750-546 BC), the archaeological record reveals the presence of major settlements within large agricultural plains, such as Düver-Yarımada in the southeast part of Burdur plain and Seydiköy in the western part of the neighbouring Çeltikçi plain. When considering the results of recent work at Uylupınar and Olbasa (Ekinci 2006; Çokay-Kepçe 2009), some general regional settlement characteristics become clear: location on a promontory in or near a lake of a central place within an extensive agricultural plain, surrounded by a monumentalised funerary landscape including tumuli and rock-cut tombs. In the study region, another type of site can be added: mountain sites or fortified kales overlooking large swathes of territory with adjoining settlement areas, such as near Hacılar Kalesi, Kepez Kalesi, Kayış and Taşkapı Kalesi. In a previous contribution, we argued that the mountain sites provided strategic control over the plains in which the central sites or principalities were located and that the geographical positioning of this settlement pattern along major natural thoroughfares between the Mediterranean coast and the Anatolian plateau was non-coincidental (Poblome et al., in press). Connectivity seems to have been an important factor in site and regional development during times of increased activity in the Mediterranean, which involved (amongst others) Greeks, Phoenicians and Cypriots. Complex exchange patterns of goods characterized these times, reflecting increasing social complexity that was translated into the organisation of towns and kingdoms and more abundant archaeological testimonies of class differentiation (Etienne 2010).

In comparison to the höyük landscape, increased social complexity and differentiation and political centralisation seem to be the key-words to explain the Archaic settlement pattern in the study region. Whereas the höyük communities shared more, yet smaller 'pieces of the cake', land ownership became a matter of the happy few. Principalities, from which the entire region was controlled, institutionalised centralised structures of power and ownership of the land. Düver-Yarımada can be considered in this role in Archaic times. Whether this site ever housed the seat of power of Madduwata, as suggested by Marc Waelkens (2000, 482), now seems unlikely, but also considering its later history, it seems worth wondering whether it could have played a key role in the development of the region in the second millennium BC. This is hinted at by the finding of Mycenaean and related pottery in an associated cemetery, but obviously more material and research is needed to answer this suggestive question. Clearly, the lack of relevant archaeological material does not allow us to make a strong point. Indeed, even if Düver-Yarımada started to take up a more central role in the area, it would still need to be proven that this process was in any sort of way related to the disappearance of the höyüks.

In other words, there is no option left but to conclude in an open way. Could it not be the case that we are actually dealing with a problem of archaeological visibility? The Bronze Age höyüks form the backbone of a recognizable archaeological landscape and so do the Archaic principalities. In the mean time, intensive survey research indicated for both periods that these type-sites are only part of the package. The actual settlement patterns also included some unexpected elements such as smaller Bronze Age sites. Was our pre-intensive-survey-understanding of the landscape an example of archaeologists finding what they were looking for? The associated thought is perhaps worse: as there is no clear pattern of archaeological expectancy of type-sites in the study region of the second millennium BC, are archaeologists not finding what they are not looking for? Is this the reason why the transition between systems of occupation of the land is obscured? The challenge at hand is to start looking at the unknown, preferably by applying an interdisciplinary camaraderie between history and archaeology (and a host of other disciplines). In this respect, a sufficient 'critical mass' of research has not yet been assembled in the study region. The intensive survey campaigns in the Burdur plain by the Sagalassos project are a step in the right direction and have already resulted in additional information on the second millennium BC (Kaptijn et al., in press). However, clearly more evidence and a different mental template of interpretation is needed. Bleda Düring (2010, 298) suggested that we frame our future research around the transition between a landscape of höyüks and one of principalities, which possibly occurred during (a part of) the second millennium BC in the study region, as follows: "*The pertinent question is... what induced people to give up a life of relative autonomy in favour of a way of life in which only a few people would have been able to join the elite class and the rest would have had to settle for the status of commoner. One possible mechanism that might explain this development is that everybody benefited from the process in that the standard of life was raised even for commoners.*" Hopefully, this perspective afforded the second millennium BC inhabitants of the region still sufficient scope to *Carpe diem*!

Acknowledgements

The research for this paper was supported by the Belgian Programme on Interuniversity Poles of Attraction (IAP 7/17), the Research Fund of the KU Leuven (BOF-GOA 13/04), Projects G.0788.09 and G.0562.11 of the Fund for Scientific Research Flanders (FWO) and a Methusalem Grant from the Flemish Ministry for Science Policy. J. Poblome was appointed as Francqui Research Professor for 2011-2014.

Bibliography

ANTHONY, D. W. 2007: *The horse, the wheel and language: how Bronze-Age riders from the Eurasian steppes shaped the modern world*, Princeton, NJ.

ARO, S. 2003: "Art and architecture", in H. C. Melchert (ed.) *The Luwians*, Leiden, 281-337.

BAKKER, J., E. PAULISSEN, D. KANIEWSKI, V. DE LAET, G. VERSTRAETEN and M. WAELKENS 2011: "Man, vegetation and climate during the Holocene in the territory of Sagalassos, Western Taurus Mountains, SW Turkey", *Vegetation History and Archaeobotany*, DOI 10.1007/s00334-011-0312-4.

BIRMINGHAM, J. 1964: "Surface finds from various sites", *Anatolian Studies* 14, 29-33.

BRAEKMANS, D. 2011: *The Archaic, Classical and Hellenistic ceramics in the later territory of Sagalassos and Düzen Tepe: the petrographic and geochemical evidence*, Unpublished Ph.D. Thesis, KU Leuven.

BRYCE, T. R. 2003: "History", in H. C. Melchert (ed.) *The Luwians*, Leiden, 27-127.

ÇOKAY-KEPÇE, S. 2009: "The pottery from Burdur Uylupınar necropolis", *Adalya* 12, 29-76.

DÜRING, B. S. 2011: *The prehistory of Asia Minor. From complex hunter-gatherers to early urban societies*, Cambridge.

DURU, R. 2008: *From 8000 BC to 2000 BC. Six thousand years of the Burdur-Antalya region*, Antalya.

DUSAR, B., G. VERSTRAETEN, B. NOTEBAERT and J. BAKKER 2011: "Holocene environmental change and its impact on sediment dynamics in the eastern Mediterranean", *Earth-Science Reviews* 108, 137-157.

EKINCI, H. A. 2006: "Rescue excavations at the Üç Tümülüsler in Karamanlı, Burdur", *Anadolu Akdenizi Arkeoloji Haberleri* 4, 143-145.

ETIENNE, R. (ed.) 2010: *La Méditerranée au VIIe siècle av. J.-C. Essais d'analyses archéologiques* (Travaux de la Maison René Ginouvès 7), Paris.

FREU, J. 1987: "Problèmes de chronologie et de géographie hittites. Madduwattas et les débuts de l'empire", in R. Lebrun (ed.) *Hethitica VIII. Acta Anatolica E. Laroche oblata*, Louvain-la-Neuve, 123-175.

GENZ, H. 2007: "The Iron Age in the Kızılırmak region", in H. Sivas (ed.) *The mysterious civilization of the Phrygians*, Istanbul, 127-140.

GOSDEN, C. 2004: *Archaeology and colonialism. Cultural contact from 5000 BC to the present*, Cambridge.

GRIERSON, P. 1959: "Commerce in the Dark Ages: a critique of the evidence", *Transactions of the Royal Historical Society* 9, 123-140.

HAWKINS, J. D. 1998: "Tarkasnawa King of Mira: 'Tarkondemos', Boğazköy sealings and Karabel", *Anatolian Studies* 48, 1-32.

JONES, S. 1997: *The archaeology of ethnicity. Constructing identities in the past and present*, London.

KAPTIJN, E., R. VANDAM, D. BRAEKMANS, J. POBLOME and M. WAELKENS, in press: "Changing Habitation in the Plain of Burdur. Results of the Intensive Survey of the Sagalassos Archaeological research Project (SW Turkey)", *Babesch. Annual papers on Mediterranean archaeology.*

KEALHOFER, L., P. GRAVE, B. MARSH, S. STEADMAN, R. L. GORNY and G. D. SUMMERS 2010: "Patterns of Iron Age interaction in central Anatolia: three sites in Yozgat province", *Anatolian Studies* 60, 71-92.

KNAPPETT, C., V. KILIKOGLOU, V. STEELE and B. STERN 2005: "The circulation and consumption of Red Lustrous Wheelmade ware: petrographic, chemical and residue analysis", *Anatolian Studies* 55, 25-60.

MAC SWEENEY, N. 2010: "Hittites and Arzawans: a view from western Anatolia", *Anatolian Studies* 60, 7-24.

MAREK, C. 2010: *Geschichte Kleinasiens in der Antike*, München.

MARTINI, W. 2010: *Die Akropolis von Perge in Pamphylien. Vom Siedlungsplatz zur Akropolis*, Stuttgart.

MEE, C. 1978: "Aegean trade and settlement in Anatolia in the second millennium BC", *Anatolian Studies* 28, 121-155.

MELCHERT, H. C. (ed.) 2003: *The Luwians* (Handbook of Oriental Studies. Section 1, The Near and Middle East 68), Leiden.

MELLINK, M. 1967: "Archaeology in Asia Minor", *American Journal of Archaeology* 71, 155-174.

MELLINK, M. 1969: "Archaeology in Asia Minor", *American Journal of Archaeology* 73, 203-227.

OTTONI, C., F.-X. RICAUT, N. VANDERHEYDEN, N. BRUCATO, M. WAELKENS and R. DECORTE 2011: "Mitochondrial analysis of a Byzantine population reveals the differential impact of multiple historical events in South Anatolia", *European Journal of Human Genetics* 19, 571-576.

ÖZDOĞAN, M. 1998: "Early Iron Age in Eastern Thrace and the megalithic monuments", in N. Tuna, Z. Aktüre and M. Lynch (eds.) *Thracians and Phrygians: problems of parallelism*, Ankara, 29-40.

POBLOME, J., D. BRAEKMANS, M. WAELKENS, N. FIRAT, H. VANHAVERBEKE, F. MARTENS, E. KAPTIJN, K. VYNCKE, R. WILLET and P. DEGRYSE, in press: "How did Sagalassos come to be? A ceramological survey", in *Festschrift for Levent Zoroğlu*, Antalya.

SAGONA, A. and P. ZIMANSKY 2009: *Ancient Turkey*, London.

STROBEL, K. 2005: "Aspekte eines neuen Bildes der Enticklung Anatoliens in der Frühen Eisenzeit", in A. Çilingiroğlu and G. Darbyshire (eds.) *Anatolian Iron Ages, 5* (British Institute at Ankara Monograph 31), London, 195-210.

TAINTER, J. A. 2005: "Dark Ages in archaeology/systems collapse", in C. Renfrew and P. Bahn (eds.) *Archaeology. The key concepts*, London, 54-58.

TRIGGER, B. G. 1989: *A history of archaeological thought*, Cambridge.

UMURTAK, G. 2010: "Questions arising from a bulla found in the EBA II settlement at Bademağacı", *Adalya* 13, 19-28.

VANHAVERBEKE, H. and M. WAELKENS 2003: *The chora of Sagalassos. The evolution of the settlement pattern from prehistoric until recent times* (Studies in Eastern Mediterranean Archaeology 5) Turnhout.

VANHAVERBEKE, H., M. WAELKENS, K. VYNCKE, V. DE LAET, S. AYDAL, B. MUŠIČ, B. DE CUPERE, J. POBLOME, D. BRAEKMANS, P. DEGRYSE, E. MARINOVA, G. VERSTRAETEN, W. VAN NEER, B. ŠLAPŠAK, I. MEDARIČ, H. A. EKINCI and M. O. Erbay 2010: "The 'Pisidian' culture? The Classical-Hellenistic site at Düzen Tepe near Sagalassus (southwest Turkey)", *Anatolian Studies* 60, 105-128.

VASSILEVA, M. 1998: "Thracian-Phrygian cultural zone", in N. Tuna, Z. Aktüre and M. Lynch (eds.) *Thracians and Phrygians: problems of parallelism*, Ankara, 13-17.

WAELKENS, M. 2000: "Sagalassos and Pisidia during the Late Bronze Age", in M. Waelkens and L. Loots (eds.) *Sagalassos V. Report on the survey and excavation campaigns of 1996 and 1997* (Acta Archaeological Lovaniensia Monographiae 11) Leuven, 473-488.

YASUR-LANDAU A. 2010: *The Philistines and Aegean migration at the end of the Late Bronze Age*, Cambridge.

A CLOSURE RITUAL AT TELL BEYDAR?

Alexander PRUSS
Ludwig-Maximilians-Universität, München

Karel Van Lerberghe helped to establish the archaeological mission at Tell Beydar and was for many years a helpful and very active colleague and partner. I am honoured to offer the following contribution on a peculiar Beydar context to him.

One of the surprising results of the recent excavation seasons at Tell Beydar was the discovery of the so-called Eastern Palace in Field P, in the eastern part of the Upper city of Beydar. The uncovering of a palatial building of the late EJZ 3b[1] outside the acropolis changed the view of the urban layout of Tell Beydar/Nabada.[2]

The Eastern Palace (level 5c of the local sequence of Field P; Table 1) was constructed as a representative residence for a member of the local or regional elite, but its use was changed after a short period of use. Several small-scale interventions (blocking of doors, parting of rooms with small walls, installation of small rooms in the courtyard, etc.) changed the syntax of the building completely. The building lost all its representative elements: the entrance to the building was moved to a small room in the western wing, the view on the buttressed façade of the banquet hall was obstructed, and the banquet hall itself saw the installation of four metallurgical kilns. The whole building had become a metal workshop (level 5a–b, Fig. 1), which however was still controlled by the central authorities of the town.[3] This is proved by the discovery of several impressions of an official seal already known from other spots within the site (Pruß 2011a, 126).

[1] The chronological terminology used here is the one defined by the ARCANE regional group 08 (Jezirah), see Lebeau 2011.
[2] See Pruß 2011a, 113-120 for a detailed description of the Eastern Palace.
[3] See Pruß 2011a, 121-128 on the metal workshop (level 5a–b).

Date BC (ca.)	JZ Period	Beydar Period	Acropolis	Field P
2340–2280	EJZ IVa	IVa	Early Akkadian	3
2425–2340	EJZ IIIb	IIIb	4 (post-palatial)	4
			3b	5a–b
			3a	5c
			2	6
				7
			1	

Table 1. Compared stratigraphy of Field P and the Acropolis at Tell Beydar.

The context of the finds

Some of the finds retrieved from the floors of level 5a–b seem not to fit into the context of the metal workshop. A plausible explanation of these objects is that they were used during a closure ritual connected with the abandonment of the building. These objects are:

- A group of small hand-made vessels, so-called 'decantation jars', found near the western wall of hall 16473 (Fig. 2).
- Several objects of unbaked clay, among them a miniature bowl with lid, an uninscribed tablet, an anthropomorphic figurine, and some tokens (?), all found in room 16160.
- A very unusual hollow terra-cotta figurine of a nude male, found in room 16160.
- A vessel with incised decoration which was smashed on the floor of the courtyard 16425. Some fragments of this vessel were found in adjacent rooms.

None of these finds alone would be very significant, but the evidence of these finds combined appears to be specific enough to consider a ritual use. All these objects were found in a rather small central part of the building (room 16160, the western part of hall 16473, and the northern corner of court 16425).

The 'decantation jars'

The so-called 'decantation jar' is a very characteristic element of the ceramic inventories of the Beydar IIIb (= EJZ IIIb) period.[4] These are

[4] Rova 2003, 400 (shape S.DV); Pl. 10; Rova 2011, 73-74, shape 71, fig. 5b.

wide-mouthed jars on a high pedestal base, provided with a hole and a wide spout at the bottom of the jar. This vessel type is found in many ceramic inventories at Tell Beydar,[5] normally once per inventory. These jars were obviously used to store a liquid which could be drafted from the bottom hole. Since impurities in water accumulate at the bottom of the container, it is very unlikely that the 'decantation jars' contained water. Beer would be an obvious candidate, since it regularly contained husk or other particles floating at the top.[6] The usual 'decantation jars' are 45–50 cm high. Body and pedestal were made separately on the wheel and then assembled; only the spout is handmade.

The three miniature 'decantation jars' from hall 16473 (Fig. 3) differ in a variety of elements from the Beydar standard: they are completely handmade, they are much smaller than usual (12.6, 13.7, and 14.8 cm), they occur as a group, and one of them was placed upside-down on the floor.

Despite its frequent occurrence in Tell Beydar, the 'decantation jar' is so far not attested at any other site (Rova 2011, 74). Considering the fact that the EJZ IIIb period is well known from many sites in the region (Lebeau 2011, 14, Table 2) this might be more than pure chance. It is thus possible that this shape had a symbolic value for the inhabitants of Nabada which influenced the choice of this particular shape for the miniature vessels used in hall 16473.

The miniature vessels were surely not used to store liquids but either as drinking or as libation vessels which held their content only for a very short time. Their placement on the floor, partly upside-down, must be the result of a deliberate action. Considering the possible symbolic value of the 'decantation jars', a ritual (of what specific nature ever) appears to be the most plausible explanation for this situation.

The unbaked clay objects from room 16160

The floor of room 16160 yielded a number of objects of unbaked clay. Some of them are easily explainable in the context of a metal workshop, e.g. a trial piece from a mould made in the lost-wax process, showing a bearded male face (Pruß 2011b, 192-194, fig. 11).

5 E.g., Lebeau 1997, 68, Pl. IV, 4-5. 7; Pruß 2007, fig. 4 and 10,1; Van der Stede & Devilliers 2011: fig. 24 and 55-56.

6 Several bottom fragments of 'decantation jars' were analysed for residues of their original content. The results were, regrettably, unspecific.

Other finds are more surprising. A miniature bowl has two piercings just below the rim which allowed the fixing of a matching lid (16259-M-9 and M-15; fig. 4, 1-2). Three small tetrahedral objects were found nearby, they might have been tokens (16259-M-5, M-18, and M-21, fig. 4, 3-5). A plano-convex object from the same context is interpreted as an uninscribed tablet in the typical shape of school tablets (16259-T-1; fig. 4, 6).[7] All these objects are made of carefully cleaned untempered clay. The fragment of an anthropomorphic figurine (16259-M-27; Fig. 4, 7) is, however, made of coarse uncleaned clay.

Fine almost pure clay is the usual material for tablets, sealings, and tokens. It is thus not surprising to have a tablet and tokens of this material in room 16160. There is, however, no evidence that any part of the administration of Nabada was actually situated in the metal workshop of level 5a–b. There are no other tablets and the sealings are — except for one container sealing — door sealings which were made with just two very similar Brak-style seals well attested at other parts of the site (Pruß 2011a, 126, fig. 2). These seals were obviously used by city officials to seal the doors of buildings controlled by the central administration. There is no indication that the owner(s) of these seals lived or worked in the Field P metal workshop. The tablet and the tokens are, on the other hand, not evidently linked with a possible ritual use. They are considered in this context since they were associated with other unbaked clay objects in the same room.

Due to its ductility, unbaked clay is — besides wax, dough, flour, bitumen, wood, and reed — a preferred material of magical rituals.[8] The small bowl with lid had no evident practical use, since its volume is minimal and its material is rather brittle. A ritual or symbolic use is, as for other miniature vessels, is the most likely explanation.

The anthropomorphic figurine fragment seems to be an ad hoc-production. It does not fit into the typological repertoire of Tell Beydar (Pruß in press). Due to the coarse clay, it is rather fragile and was probably not moved around a lot. A ritual or magic function is the most likely explanation of terra-cotta figurines;[9] it is even more plausible for an unbaked figurine. While animal figurines of unbaked clay are rather

[7] Milano in press, no. 238. I would like to thank Lucio Milano for providing the unpublished manuscript on the epigraphic finds of the 2004–2009 campaigns and for his permission to use the photograph of the tablet.

[8] Rittig 1977, 146, note 3, 224-226.

[9] See the recent discussion of the relevant literature by Strommenger 2010, 6-7.

common,[10] this material is very unusual for anthropomorphic figurines. Our figurine was thus most likely used for a peculiar purpose.

The 'Manneken Pis' figurine

The crudely modelled hollow male terra-cotta figurine 16259-M-2 (Fig. 5) was also found on the floor of room 16160. The arms are modelled and placed on the voluminous body: the right hand is placed on the chest, the left grasps the penis. The legs are not rendered; the figurine is standing on a concave base. The missing head had been reattached with bitumen of which traces are apparent at the neck. The cavity inside the figurine is linked to two holes, one through the penis, the other one on the left shoulder. When submerged, the figurine could be filled with liquid. The liquid remains inside the figurine until the index finger is lifted off the upper hole and the content is released through the genital (Fig. 6).

A similar piece was found by Mallowan in a grave a Germayir (Mallowan 1937: Fig. 9, 18). A group of small juglets with rims shaped as female heads, apparently all from the Middle Euphrates region,[11] provide a functional similarity. They all have a pierced base. Liquids could thus be transported in these vessels and released by the lifting of a finger (in case of the juglets the thumb). A ritual use of these objects appears to be very probable.

The use of a urinating figurine in room 16160 surely sent a strong symbolic message to all attendants of the ritual. It would fit well into the picture of a closing ceremony held before the abandonment of the building, symbolising the exposedness of the ruined building to malevolent forces.

The crushed decorated jar

The fragments of the incised jar 16464-C-1 (Fig. 7) were found scattered on the baked-brick floor 16424 in the north of court 16425. Single joining pieces were found in hall 16473 and room 16659. The decoration was incised before the burning. It consists of three horizontal lines which frame a zigzag band at the neck and a frieze of stylized trees. Below,

[10] At Tell Bi'a 34 of 216 animal figurines (16%) are made of unbaked clay: Rittig 2010, 51.

[11] See Strommenger 2010, 49-50, Pl. 45, 7–8 for two examples from Bi'a, as well as Tubb 1982 and Badre 1980, 398, Pl. 64, no. 45A on unprovenanced pieces in the British Museum and the AUB collection in Beirut. Sakal 2006 proposed Emar as possible origin of the British Museum vessel.

there is a row of animals, all facing to the right. The row starts with a bull and a smaller predator (a panther?) over his back. Both are followed by an equid, a deer (?), a lion, and at least three gazelles. Except for the first predator the animals are ordered by size, with the largest in front and the smallest at the end.

Two comparable jars were found at Beydar, both in late EJZ IIIb contexts in the Workshops of Field M.[12] Jars with incised decoration consisting of animal and plant motives were found at several Upper Mesopotamian sites, mostly in EJZ IIIb and EJZ IVa–b or contemporary Middle Euphrates contexts.[13] The contexts of these finds are ambiguous: some were found in burials, others in domestic or workshop contexts. Considering their unusual decoration, a peculiar (probably ritual) meaning of these vessels seems plausible, but such an interpretation has to be supported by the context of the objects.

The scattered find situation of the Field P jar fragments proves that the jar was deliberately smashed on the floor of court 16425. The sherds remained accessible for at least a short while which explains the find of joining fragments in adjacent rooms. Context and decoration thus seem to corroborate a ritual background of the find.

Fire traces in court 16425

Ritual burning has been described as a typical practice accompanying closure ceremonies (Bjorkman 1994). Fire traces are, of course, not surprising in the context of a metallurgical workshop and those around the metallurgical kilns or at a casting platform (Pruß 2011a, 123, fig. 29) are easily explainable by the activities in the workshop itself. A nearly circular area of ashes and fire traces on the baked brick-floor in the northern part of court 16425 (Fig. 8) are not evidently connected with any kind of metallurgical activity. These traces might be the remains of a ritual burning. The evidence is not unambiguous, however, since the fire could also be explained by the activity of squatters just after the abandonment of the building.

[12] Rooms 13302 and 13313. See Suleiman 2011, 79 for the context of these workshops.

[13] E.g. Oates 2001, 168, fig. 408, no. 368-374 (Brak M); Orthmann and Meyer 1989, fig. 41, 9-10 (Halawa A, level 3b-c); Orthmann and Pruß 1995, fig. 83, no. 82 and 88 (Khuera IE); Strommenger and Kohlmeyer 1998, 107, Pl. 133, 9 (Bi'a grave group 4); Margueron 2004, fig. 381, 5-10 (Mari, Ville III).

The urban context

The abandonment of the metal workshop inside the former Eastern Palace occurred at the same time as the abandonment of the Acropolis Palace (phase 3b), most temples (except for Temple A), and the city wall. The following, so-called 'post-palatial' final phase 4 of the Beydar IIIb occupation is restricted to the acropolis and its vicinity (Quenet 2011: 25, Table 2). As in Field P, level 4, these remains are best explained as a squatter occupation throughout the whole settlement. In other words, the city lost nearly all its urban features during this most significant break in the 3rd millennium occupation history of the site.

Considering this urban situation, it is probably significant that no traces of a deliberate infill were visible inside the former Eastern Palace. The objects related to the probable closure ritual were found on the very floors used by the metal workshop. After the deposition, the rooms remained open, they were filled with the usual brick collapse resulting of the normal disintegration of an abandoned mud-brick building (see Pruß 2011a: fig. 36). The large spaces of the former palace (court 16425 and hall 16473) received new floors on top of a brick collapse layer, the smaller rooms of the outer wings were not reused and continued to disintegrate.

The abandonment of the level 5a–b workshop in Beydar Field P is more or less contemporary with the closure rituals observed in the large official buildings FS and SS in Tell Brak/Nagar.[14] Contrary to the situation at Brak, the Beydar depositions did not include valuable materials or obvious sacrifices and they are not connected with a deliberate infill which might indicate the preparation of a rebuilding.

Who closed the building?

Accepting the mentioned indications as evidence for a closure ritual, one might ask who actually performed this ritual. The lack of valuable deposits might indicate that the Beydar depositions were not meant to appease natural or supernatural forces as in the case of the Brak closure rituals (Oates, Molleson & Sołtysiak 2008, 398). The deliberate smashing of the decorated vessel and especially the urinating male figurine seem to fit more to a cursing of the building than to the ritual protection of a

[14] On those, see Oates, Molleson and Sołtysiak 2008 and Oates, Oates and McDonald 2001, 90-91, 389-391. See for the Brak chronology Quenet 2011, 30-31, Table 4.

temporarily abandoned complex (as in Brak). The ritual actions emphasized a violent and ruthless attitude towards the building. Considering the fact that in the archaeological record of Tell Beydar there are no indications for a violent destruction or a military conquest of the site at the end of the 'palatial phase' of Beydar IIIb (= Acropolis phase 3c; Field P level 5), those responsible for the ritual were most probably not victorious invaders, but either inhabitants of Nabada itself or squatters who wanted to express their hostile attitude towards the institution which had administered the metal workshop and to prevent the reuse of the building.

Bibliography

BADRE, L. 1980: *Les figurines anthropomorphes en terre cuite à l'âge du bronze en Syrie* (BAH 103), Paris.

BJORKMAN, J. K. 1994: *Hoards and Deposits in Bronze Age Mesopotamia*, University of Pennsylvania Dissertation.

LEBEAU, M. 1997: "La céramique de la "Maison aux Tablettes" (chantier B)", in M. Lebeau and A. Suleiman (eds.), *Tell Beydar, Three Seasons of Excavations (1992-1994). A Preliminary Report* (Subartu 3), Turnhout, 65-87.

LEBEAU, M. (ed.) 2011: *Jezirah* (ARCANE I), Turnhout.

LEBEAU, M. and A. SULEIMAN (eds.) 2003: *Tell Beydar, the 1995-1999 Seasons of Excavations. A Preliminary Report* (Subartu 10), Turnhout.

— 2011: *Tell Beydar, the 2004/2 – 2009 Excavations, the 2004/2 – 2006 Seasons of Architectural Restoration. A Preliminary Report* (Subartu 29), Turnhout.

MALLOWAN, M. E. L. 1937: "Excavations at Tall Chagar Bazar and an archaeological survey of the Habur Region", *Iraq* 4, 91-177.

MARGUERON, J.-Cl. 2004: *Mari, Métropole de l'Euphrate au IIIe et au début du IIe millénaire av. J.-C.*, Paris.

MILANO, L. in press: "Third Millennium Cuneiform Texts from Tell Beydar (Seasons 2004-2009)", in M. Lebeau and A. Suleiman (eds.), *Beydar Studies II* (Subartu Series), Turnhout.

OATES, J. 2001: The Third-millennium Pottery", in Oates, Oates and McDonald 2001, 151-194.

OATES, J., Th. MOLLESON and A. SOŁTYSIAK 2008: "Equids and an acrobat: closure rituals at Tell Brak", *Antiquity* 82, 390-400.

OATES, D., J. OATES and H. MCDONALD 2001: *Excavations at Tell Brak, Vol. 2: Nagar in the third millennium BC*, Cambridge and London.

ORTHMANN, W. and J.-W. MEYER 1989: "Die Ausgrabungen in den Planquadraten L und M", in W. Orthmann, *Halawa 1980-1986* (Saarbrücker Beiträge zur Altertumskunde 52), Bonn, 63-84.

ORTHMANN, W. and A. PRUSS 1995: "Der Palast F", in W. Orthmann et al. (eds.), *Ausgrabungen in Tell Chuēra in Nordost-Syrien I. Vorbericht über die Grabungskampagnen 1986 bis 1992* (Vorderasiatische Forschungen der Max Freiherr von Oppenheim-Stiftung 2), Saarbrücken, 121-172.

PRUSS, A. 2007: "Tell Beydar 2002 – Field P", in M. Lebeau and A. Suleiman (eds.), *Tell Beydar, The 2000-2002 Seasons of Excavations, the 2003-2004 Seasons of Architectural Restoration. A Preliminary Report* (Subartu 15), Turnhout, 182-197.
— 2011a: "Excavations in Field P in the years 2004-2009", in Lebeau and Suleiman 2011, 111-175.
— 2011b: "Finds from Field P", in Lebeau and Suleiman 2011, 177-226.
— in press: *Figurines and Model Vehicles from Tell Beydar* (Subartu Series), Turnhout.
QUENET, Ph. 2011: "Stratigraphy", in Lebeau 2011, 19-47.
RITTIG, D. 1977: *Assyrisch-babylonische Kleinplastik magischer Bedeutung vom 13.-6. Jh. v. Chr.* (Münchener vorderasiatische Studien 1), Munich.
— 2010: "Theriomorphe Figuren", in Strommenger and Miglus 2010, 51-65.
ROVA, E. 2003: "The III Millennium Pottery Morphology. The Typological Principles, the Coding System and Some Preliminary Results", in Lebeau and Suleiman 2003, 395-489.
— 2011: "Ceramic", in Lebeau 2011, 49-127.
SAKAL, F. 2006: "Einige Anmerkungen über die Herkunft eines Gefäßes aus dem Bestand des British Museum", *Baghdader Mitteilungen* 37, 443-453.
STROMMENGER, E. 2010: "Anthropomorphe Figuren", in Strommenger and Miglus 2010, 2-51.
STROMMENGER, E. and K. KOHLMEYER 1998: *Die Altorientalischen Bestattungen* (Ausgrabungen in Tall Bi'a/Tuttul 1; WVDOG 96), Saarbrücken.
STROMMENGER, E. and P. A. MIGLUS 2010: *Altorientalische Kleinfunde* (Ausgrabungen in Tall Bi'a/Tuttul 5; WVDOG 126), Wiesbaden.
SULEIMAN, A. 2011: "Tell Beydar 2006-2009 — Chantier M: le Temple E", in Lebeau and Suleiman 2011, 77-92.
TUBB, J. N. 1982: "A Syrian 'Klepsydra' of the Third Millennium B.C.", *Levant* 14, 175-177.
VAN DER STEDE, V. and A. DEVILLERS 2011: "Le chantier B: résultats des campagnes 2004-2008", in Lebeau and Suleiman 2011, 15-76.

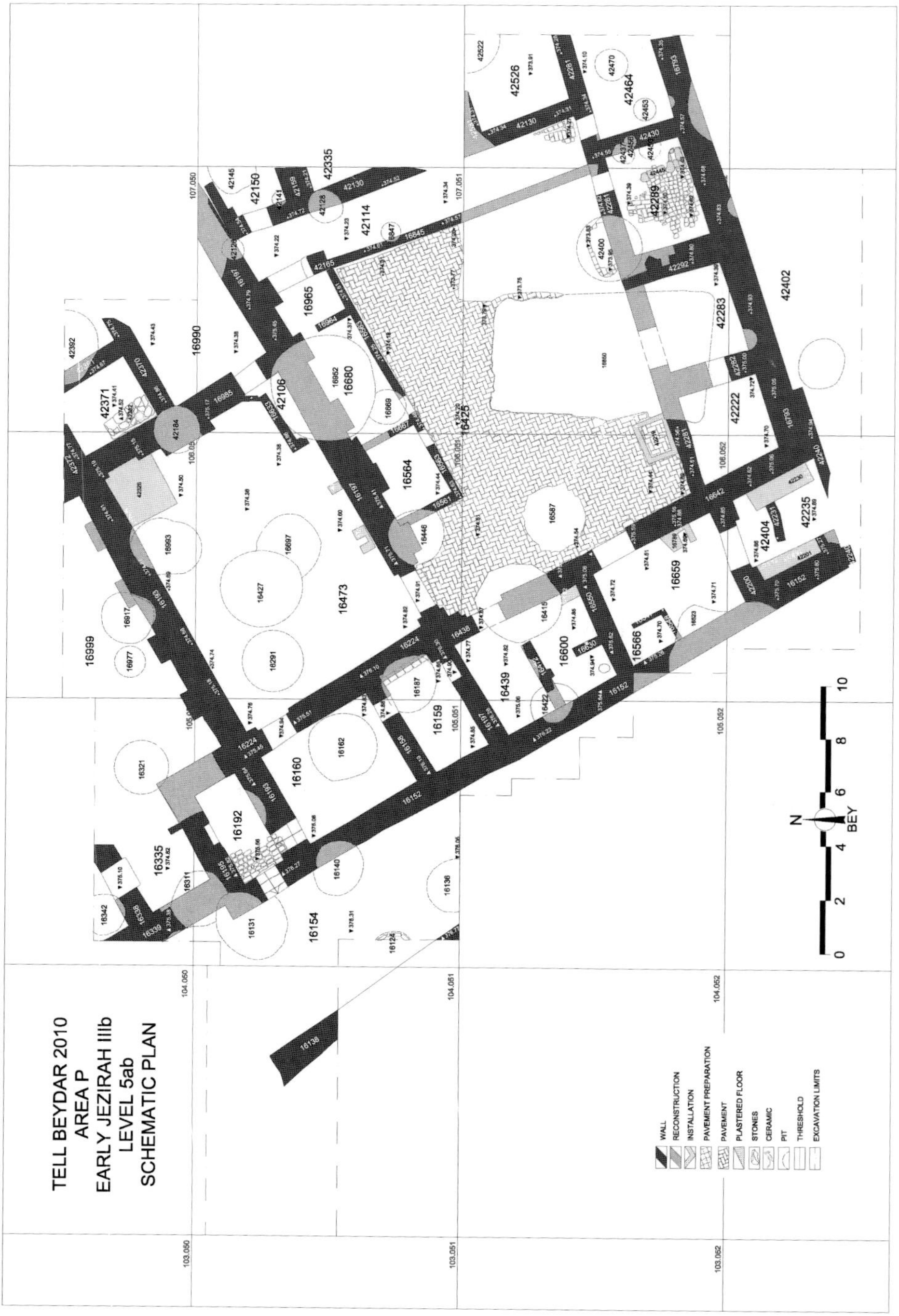

Fig. 1. Schematic plan of the

Fig. 2. Tell Beydar, Field P, level 5a-b, hall 16473, handmade 'decantation jars' in situ.

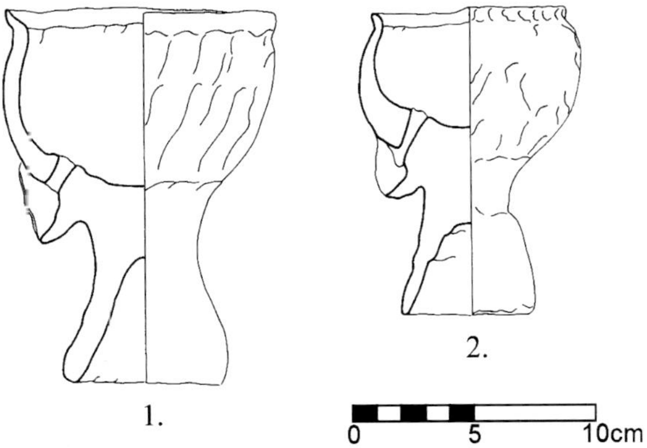

Fig. 3. Handmade 'decantation jars'; 1. 16458-C-6; 2. 16458-C-7; 3. 16458-C-16. Drawings made by A. Lebrun Nélis.

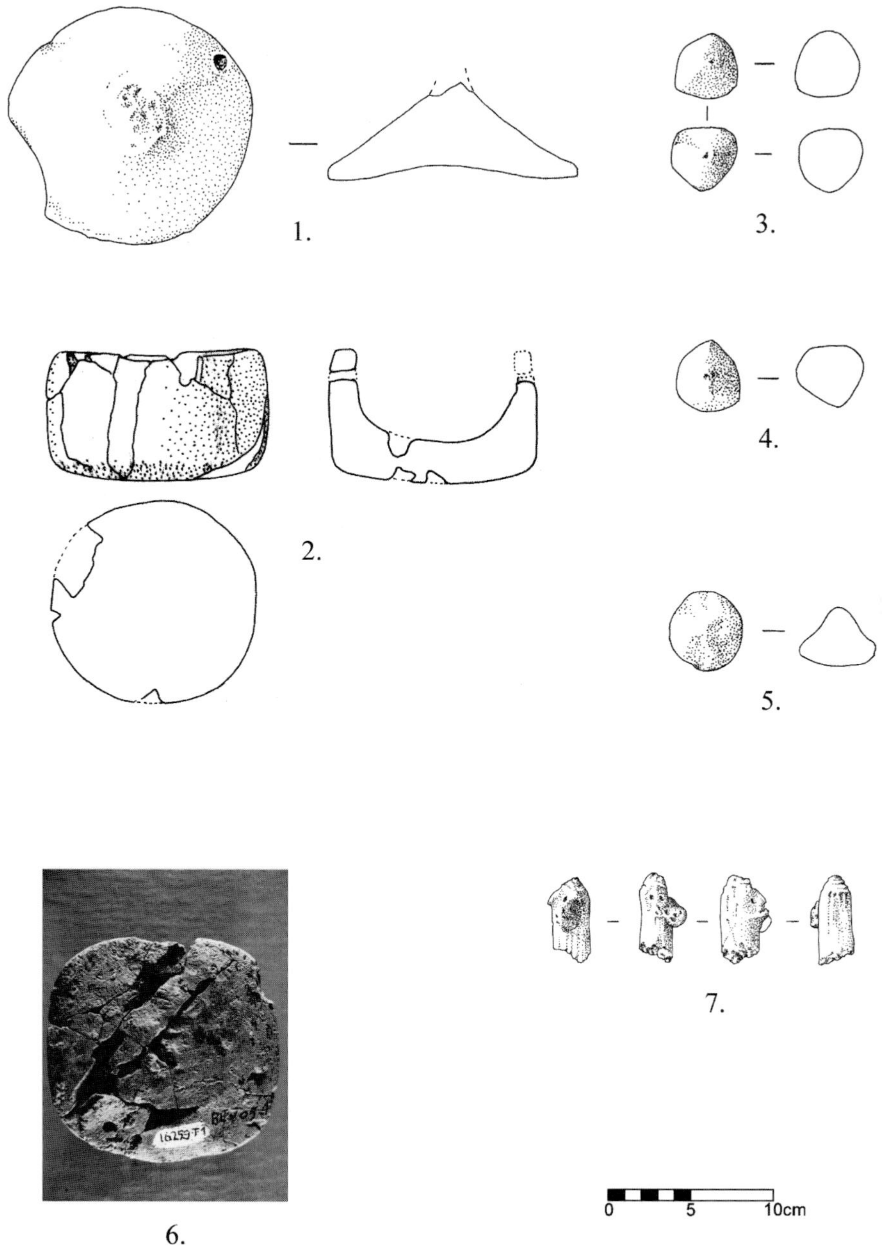

Fig. 4. Unbaked clay objects from room 16160; 1. Miniature lid 16259-M-9; 2. Miniature bowl 16259-M-15; 3. Token (?) 16259-M-5; 4. Token (?) 16259-M-18; 5. Token (?) 16259-M-21; 6. Uninscribed tablet 16259-T-1; 7. Head of an anthropomorph figurine 16259-M-27. Drawings made by A. Lebrun Nélis, Photo courtesy L. Milano.

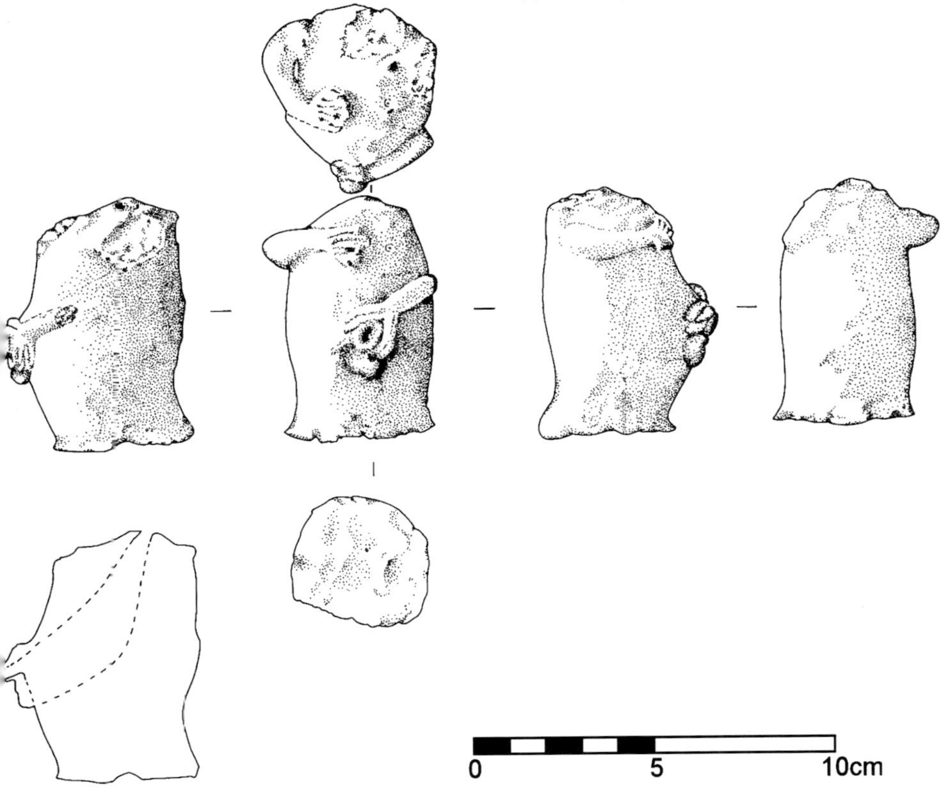

Fig. 5. Nude male terra-cotta figurine 16259-M-2.
Drawing made by M. A. Nuñez Villanueva.

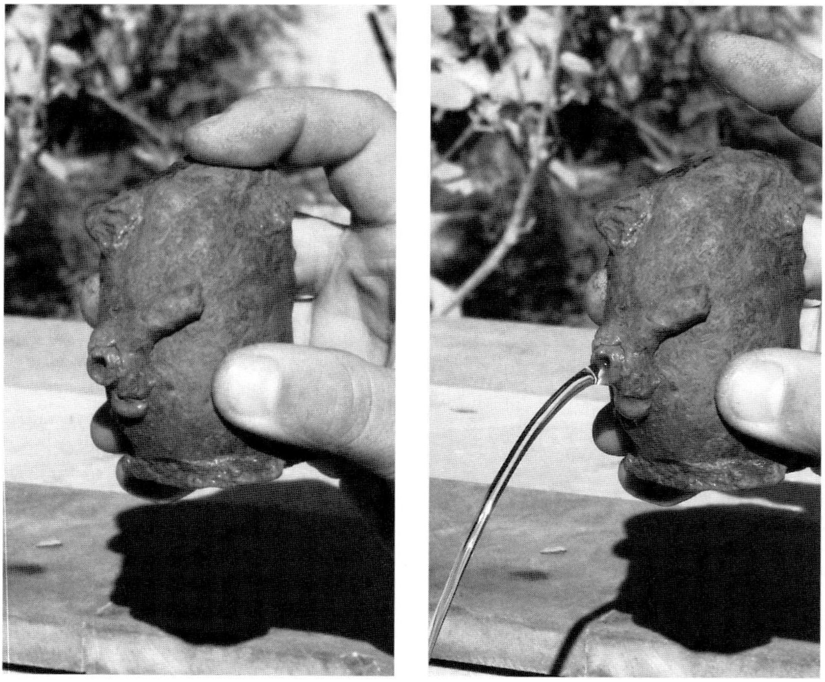

Fig. 6. Use of figurine 16259-M-2.

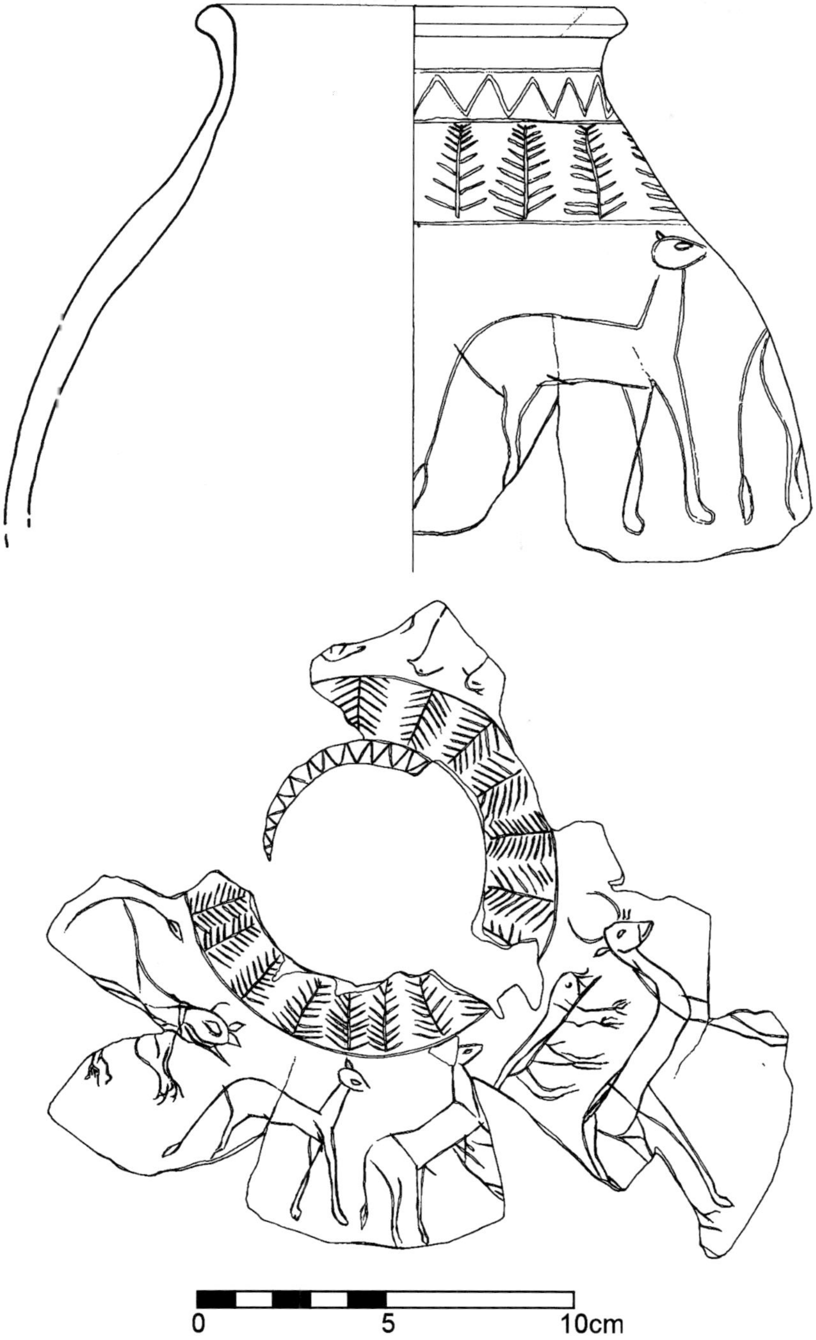

Fig. 7. Incised-decorated jar 16464-C-1. Drawing made by S. Zanetti.

Fig. 8. Northern corner of court 16425 with fire traces in the lower left.

BARING THE ESSENTIALS OF A DICTIONARY: SOME PRECURSORS OF *CDA*

Mervyn E. J. RICHARDSON
Leiden University

One's academic profile has customarily been evaluated by assessing the relative importance of teaching and research. Usually assessors have given prominence to the latter, but more recently these respective skills have come to be regarded as inseparable qualities, both demanding excellence to an equal degree. In other words, it is important always to allow the one to stimulate the other, and an ideal combination of skills will lead to a more excellent academic profile. Few I know embody such excellence as the one to whom this essay is offered with respect.

But those same combinations of skills were exemplified when Postgate and his team were making elaborate preparations for the publication of their concise dictionary of Akkadian. Only a year after the first publication it was replaced by a "2nd. (corrected) printing" (Postgate 1999 and 2000, henceforth *CDA*). It is well known that all three editors involved in the project shared a fine personal friendship and found it very easy to work together. So although it is carefully stated in the first sentence of the Preface that Postgate was the prime mover in the enterprise (without his initiative the dictionary may never have been engendered) he seems to have had no qualms about his name appearing last on the title page. It was he who secured the approval of von Soden "to produce a drastically abbreviated English translation of AHw", and who enlisted the co-operation of his co-editors.

His seven named assistants were clearly indispensable to the project, and recruiting them would not have been possible without securing external funding. It can be no coincidence that the three editors were affiliated to three of the most wealthy universities in England and then that the funds provided by the British Academy could be supplemented by their respective institutions: Cambridge gave support from Trinity College and the C. H. W. Johns Memorial Fund; Oxford from the Faculty of Oriental Studies and the Shillito Fund; SOAS presumably gave their support from central funds.

The editors' first task was to abbreviate the entries of AHw and then to translate what was left. Wisely the draft text was checked by both an English and a German native speaker. When dealing with single word definitions it is all too easy to garble the original meaning. The incorporating of *addenda et corrigenda* was more routine, except when it came to adjudicating between any divergent opinions found in *CAD*. This must have consumed much time and depended on mature, objective and independent considerations. At that time the last five volumes of *CAD* were yet to be published; now it is complete this aspect of their work needs to be updated.

Another routine task was the identification of lemmata where the original ordering of sub-meanings according to the semantic preferences of German was inappropriate for English. This problem arises whenever a translator comes face-to-face with how to express separate lexemes in the source language when the target language allows a wider semantic range for the most appropriate gloss. In fact the problem is inevitably linked to how to set out selected citations, and the decision not to provide a representative set of citations in *CDA* made it more complicated. Furthermore, without citations the relative frequency of a word within the language cannot be assessed and the context within which the word is used cannot be appreciated. This was a matter already anticipated in the Introduction; perhaps with hindsight it would have been better to provide some citations.

***

An aspect of this work which deserves to be more widely noticed is how it continues a long tradition in Semitic lexicography. Eminent scholars with well-established research profiles, who have spent years publishing their own advanced lexicographical studies, have subsequently realised the need for concise summaries to be prepared suited to the primary needs of a new generation of students. Sometimes they have taken this task upon themselves but more often it has been left to their successors to take the necessary steps. A glance through the publication histories of some dictionaries of the major languages of the ancient Near East highlights the different predilections of those who wished to strip a *magnum opus* down to its bare essentials.

As for Ancient Mesopotamia, outside the area of cuneiform studies, one of the most obvious languages which deserves to be considered is Syriac. Some, of course, would argue that Syriac does not really belong to the "ancient" world but to the world of "late-antiquity". This was the line taken in a recent book covering the languages of the ancient Near East from the viewpoint of an ancient historian. The editor explains in his foreword that the idea of the book had been conceived by his teacher D.O. Edzard (1930-2004), who had not been able to bring his project to completion before he died (Streck 2005). There is no doubt that the most appropriate translation of the word "alt" in the title would be "ancient". All the languages treated (Sumerian, Akkadian, Hittite, Hattic, Hurrian and Urartian, and Elamite) were dead or in mortal decline once Alexander had crossed the Bosphorus. No language attested only in or just before the Common Era, even though its roots may stretch back for many centuries, is mentioned. Furthermore, the editor has given the narrowest of narrow meanings to the word "Orient". Even if he had chosen "Vorder-Orient" the question arises of why he omitted ancient Canaanite languages and Syro-Palestine as a whole. So he has removed the possibility of having Syriac mentioned in this book.

From Leiden, in the year that *CDA* was first published, under the auspices of Ex Oriente Lux, a much respected and long established "town and gown" society in The Netherlands and Belgium, a clear and concise overview of ancient Near Eastern languages was published (Loose 1999). The editor gave pride of place to Egypt and Mesopotamia, but she also covered the whole region from Anatolia in the west to Iran in the east. In her introduction she does not attempt to define her choice of the word "oud" in the title, but in view of the contents of the book it would be rash to equate it with "ancient". That word implies a separation of the literature of the Middle East before the arrival of Alexander from that of the Hellenistic world of Late Antiquity, and this was not her intention. Biblical Hebrew from the Massoretic period and from Qumran was an important section of her book. Some other languages covered, though obsolescent at the turn of the era, also survived in restricted circles. For these purposes "oud" means "pre-modern", and so it is surprising that Syriac is virtually omitted from the survey. It is mentioned by Margaretha Folmer in passing (see p.115):

> *Edesseens* of *Oudsyrisch* (ook wel *Vroegsyrisch*) is de taal van de niet-christelijke inscripties van het Arabische koninkrijk Edessa (tegenwoordig Urfa in Zuid-Turkije), gesticht in 132 v. Chr. Het Edesseens was de officiële taal van dit koninkrijk en verschilt aanzienlijk van het latere Syrisch.

The title of a more recent book (Ehrlich 2009) was inspired by a phrase from a nineteenth-century English poet, Percy Bysshe Shelley (1792-1822), who had travelled to the Near East and who used the phrase "antique land" in his poem *Ozymandias* to refer to Egypt. It was one thing for him to use it then but the word is outdated in this context in the prose of today. That it is synonymous with "ancient" becomes clear from the Preface, in which the editor uses precisely that same word no less than three times in his first two sentences (p. xiii). He wrote primarily with the needs of the biblical scholar in mind, making the Hebrew Bible and the later Rabbinic tradition the focus of attention. Even so there is hardly any description of the ancient versions of the Bible, and the only reference to the Peshitta seems to be a brief comment saying that it is close to the Septuagint (p. 345). From what is said later in the book it can be inferred that, since Syriac is the language of later Aramaic literature, it was intentionally omitted (see p. 404):

> The ascendance of the Aramaic language from a language of some semi-nomadic groups to the common language of the ancient Near East affected also its use for the writing and recording of literature. It comes as no surprise that the religions, like Christianity or Mandaism, that appeared in the ancient Near East during the Roman era chose Aramaic as a language for their literature — in addition to Greek in the West.... Of course, this later literature written in Aramaic should be distinguished from the earlier "Aramaic literature" and thus will not be discussed here.

Postgate, by contrast, has shown that he is more open to the advent of Syriac into the Land between the Two Rivers. He was responsible for editing the proceedings of a meeting in London in 2003, which aimed to show how the territory we know today as Iraq had always been an area of linguistic diversity. This "study day" was arranged by the British School of Archaeology in Iraq, and his co-editors in *CDA* had both been invited to give presentations: Jeremy Black, who had been jointly responsible for organising the event, covered Sumerian (pp. 4-30), and Andrew George covered Akkadian (pp. 31-71). Aramaic was understandably too complex a topic for one author, so it was separated according to periods over three chapters. The second of these, "Aramaic in the medieval and modern periods" (pp. 95-113), was covered by Geoffrey Khan, who devoted section 2 (pp. 96-99) of his chapter to Syriac. Khan made no reference to the monumental *Thesaurus Syriacus* of Robert Payne Smith (Smith, R.P. 1879), published at the beginning of the last century and from which so much Syriac lexicography as we know it today has been derived. But this fits in with what appears to have been a general editorial policy: hardly any of the bibliographies in the book list dictionaries, even though they list grammars.

***

Robert Payne Smith (1819-1895) was the Dean of Canterbury Cathedral, a position which would hardly have allowed the holder the time to start let alone complete such a massive undertaking. So the bulk of the work must have been prepared during his time at Oxford, first as a Sub-Librarian in the Oriental section of the Bodleian Library and then as the Regius Professor of Divinity. The first volume of the *Thesaurus* was published in 1879, and the second in 1901 posthumously (Smith R. P. 1895). His daughter Jessie (1856-1933) had taken it upon herself to make her father's Latin manuscript ready for publication. A little while later she brought out in her own name an abbreviated and translated version of the work entitled *Compendious Dictionary* (Smith, J. P. 1903). In the Preface she clarifies that her father, whom she respectfully refers to as "Dean Payne Smith", had himself been preparing this abridgement and had in fact read the proofs of the first part of the book himself. We may therefore conclude that it was he who decided to compose a prayer in Syriac, befitting his position, which he set centrally on the first page of text, as an element in the heading for the first lemma:

> I begin to write this book in the strength of Jesus our hope, for the simplification of the Syriac language; may the mercy of Almighty God be on the writer, and on the owner, and on the reader, for ever and ever. Amen.

The second part of the proofs were read by her husband, the Arabist D.S. Margoliouth (1858-1940), who had been occupying the Laudian Chair of Arabic at Oxford since 1889, an Arabist of the old school, competent also in Hebrew and Syriac.

It is interesting to note that she refers to a problem facing Syriac lexicographers which also faced editors of *CDA*. In both Akkadian and Syriac there are words that are attested in ancient lexical compendia but not in any literary context. In one sense such words are superfluous to a dictionary designed to facilitate the reading of literature. But, because new texts and new text editions are regularly being published in Syriac as well as Akkadian, it seems better to err on the side of safety and include such words even in a concise dictionary. Who knows when and where they could turn up in the future, whether written in cuneiform or estrangela script? Jessie Payne Smith had the assistance of Rubens Duval (1839-1911) especially for this purpose. His translation of Bar Bahlul had recently been published in France between 1888 and 1901 (Duval 1888). Bar Bahlul was one of the most important native lexicographers. He worked in the mid-tenth century in Tirhan, close to Jebel Hamrin, a place referred to by Nestorian Christians as "Mt. Uruk". The other native lexical work she cites is Jesus Bar-Ali written in the ninth century. But only the first part of his treatise had been published at the time; two later volumes followed (Hoffmann 1874; Gottheil 1910 and 1928).

The sequencing of lemmata was changed from a "scientific" to an alphabetical one. The word "scientific" was used to indicate the traditional format of identifying a consonantal root as a lemma and listing under it all derived lexemes. This means, for example, that in the *Thesaurus* the substantive *maḥzyt'* "spectaculum, exemplum" is listed as a derivation of the verbal root *ḥz'* (p. 1237a) but in the *Compendious Dictionary* it is listed alphabetically and glossed "example, mirror" (p. 264a). It goes without saying that an Akkadian dictionary has to conform to an alphabetical scheme, but to fulfil the demands of critical semantics there is still a need to identify the consonantal roots from which Semitic words have been derived. *AHw* was careful to tabulate roots and their derivatives at the beginning of every new letter section. *CDA* realised their importance and was able to incorporate them into a single Index (pp. xvii-xxiv). A not unrelated issue, which it is all too easy to forget in the world of twenty-first century Assyriology, is that until *AHw* and *CAD* became the primary reference points for most (and now all) lexemes, the student was obliged to search through a Hebrew not a Roman sequence of letters: Delitzsch 1896 even had running heads in a Hebrew font; see also Muss-Arnoldt 1905 and Bezold 1926.

The most recent development in Syriac lexicography, like *CDA* involves translation, but unlike *CDA* does not abbreviate but enlarges. This is the English version of the second edition of Brockelmann's *Lexicon* (Sokoloff 2009; Brockelmann 1928). Sokoloff took important decisions about how much to deviate from the traditional Semitic principles Brockelmann (1868-1956) had laid out for himself since some of them are now to be less favoured. Whereas now frequency within particular literary contexts is one of the more important factors in identifying the primary element of the semantic range of a given lexeme, Brockelmann felt that comparative philology should dominate:

> Significationes quo ordine exponendae sint, linguarum cognatarum ratione habita discernere pro viribus studens primariis, quas dicunt, investigandis vel potius fingendis ad huc abstinui.

He felt also that ordering words according to their root was more fitting when prominence was given to the wider Semitic meanings.

> Vocabula disposui ex ordine radicalium quarum in peregrinis vicibus ternae priores literae consonantes funguntur.

Theodor Nöldeke (1836-1930), who had been Brockelmann's teacher, wrote a preface to the first edition of the *Lexicon*, in which he expressed his support for the decisions the author had taken. However, he was circumspect enough to admit that "those who devote themselves to these studies in the future may well feel differently about many matters" (following Sokoloff 2009, p. 1680). That circumspection is an echo (though probably an unwitting one) of the motto *dies diem docet* which was chosen by the succession of editors who have persistently kept the ground-breaking work of Wilhelm Gesenius for Biblical Hebrew in print and up-to-date.

***

Wilhelm Gesenius (1786-1842), without question the master of nineteenth-century Semitic lexicography, did not himself use that motto in the first editions of his *Handwörterbuch* (Gesenius 1810; 1815). But on the title pages of the many posthumous editions, often slightly modified from the original, it became an indelible imprint. It is found, for example, in the 7th edition (1868), prepared by Franz Ed. Christ. Dietrich (Marburg) under the title *Hebräisches und Chaldäisches Handwörterbuch über das Alte Testament von Wilhelm Gesenius*; in the 10th edition (1886) prepared by F. Mühlau and W. Volck (Dorpat) and supplemented by D.H. Mueller (Vienna) under the title *Wilhelm Gesenius' Hebräisches und Aramäisches Handwörterbuch über das Alte Testament*; and in the 16th edition (1915), prepared in Copenhagen by Frants Buhl, a Danish Semitist. He had been responsible for the four previous editions and announced that this would be his last. Finding a substitute for him took more than 60 years. There was a 17th edition (1962) but it was given the subtitle "unveränderter Neudruck der 1916 erschienenen 17 Auflage" (for 1916 read 1915 and for 17 read 16). The first substitute for Buhl's work was Rudolf Meyer (1909-1991) who in partnership with Herbert Donner began what is now the latest edition, the 18th (Meyer 1987). It has taken more than two decades to complete the six volumes but towards the end the pace of production quickened amazingly: I (1987), the only one Meyer lived to see in print; II (1995); III (2005); IV (2007); V (2009); VI (2010). That so many modifications have been required makes the original declamation, *dies diem docet*, seem quasi-prophetic.

This long gap which followed Buhl's work on Gesenius was being interpreted in the world of Biblical scholarship as interminable, and the rising horrors of anti-semitism plus the cataclysmic losses in the War deepened despair. That was the background against which Ludwig

Koehler (1880-1956) in Zurich decided to contact P. A. H. de Boer (1910-1989) in Leiden. He asked him to be an intermediary with the Leiden publishers, established since 1673 and known then as E.J. Brill but now corporately as Koninglijke Brill NV, to agree to publish a new Hebrew dictionary which he intended to produce as a replacement for Gesenius. The substance of the early negotiations between Koehler and Brill were not generally known until they were brought to the attention of a meeting of the "Alttestamentlichen Sozietät" of Bern on 12 January 1989 (Stamm 1989). On that occasion J. J. Stamm (1910-1993) delivered an address in which he traced the vicissitudes of the Koehler tradition, beginning with the initial discussions with de Boer and Brill, and his decision to include Walter Baumgartner (1887-1970) as his co-author. These discussions led to the publication of the first edition of his *Lexikon*, and eventually to the final stages of editorial activity for completing the most recent edition. Stamm's recollections of what he had been told were that it was Koehler's idea to perpetuate the name of Gesenius in his new work but that the publisher had demurred. The reasons Stamm gave for such reticence are more socio-political in nature than academic. So far as academic matters are concerned these are most obviously found in the different approach adopted to lexicography by Baumgartner from that of Koehler. That may well be why Baumgartner restricted himself to the Aramaic section of the *Lexicon* so no feathers were ruffled in the main bulk of the book. Stamm lived to complete the task he had inherited, though he died before the Aramaic volume was actually published. What is more, he had the vision to request that Walter Dietrich, who succeeded to his chair in Bern, flesh out the skeletal plans he had made for an abridged one volume edition. That is at the moment a work in progress and supported by Brill Academic Publishers.

The first edition of what has popularly come to be known as "K-B" was published as one volume (Koehler 1953). What is generally referred to as the second edition is in fact a supplementary volume prepared by Baumgartner alone after the death of Koehler (Koehler 1958). Almost twenty years later the third edition began to appear in separate volumes: for vol. I (1967) the responsibility rested with Baumgartner, assisted by Benedikt Hartmann and E. Y. Kutscher; for vol. II (1974, after the death of Baumgartner and Kutscher) with Hartmann, Ph. Reymond and Stamm; for vol. III (1983) and iv (1990) with Stamm, assisted by Ze'ev Ben Ḥayyim, Hartmann and Reymond; for vol. v (1995, "Aramäisches Lexicon") with Stamm (who had died in 1993) and Hartmann, assisted by Reymond; in 1996 a *Supplementband* was published, with the names of all the previous editors and assistants on the title page. Hartmann had written his introduction to this latest volume on 18th April 1991, and supplemented it with a note dated September 1996 which stated that Dr. Joost Holleman (an assistant to the publisher) "hat die Arbeit zügig und überlegt ausgeführt"; that "Arbeit" will have consisted of Stamm's draft of abbreviations and a German-Hebrew index.

It was clearly of primary importance for Gesenius to apply a comparative philological method to the language of the Hebrew Bible:

> Vor allen war es mein erstes und vorzüglichstes Bestreben, welches ich nie aus den Augen verloren zu haben glaube, den Sprachgebrauch des hebräischen Dialekts als solchen in seiner Selbständigkeit aufzufassen, und in ein richtiges Verhältniss gegen den Sprachgebrauch der verwandten semitischen Dialekte zu setzen. (p. iv)

This can be interpreted as a deliberate attempt to show that the business of understanding the meaning of any Hebrew word is as much the responsibility of a professor of humanities as it is of a professor of theology. But despite his enthusiasm for the comparative philological method he did not feel it was necessary to arrange lexemes according to their consonantal roots. He preferred an alphabetical order.

What is also noticeable about Gesenius's approach is that at this time he treats the Hebrew Bible as a literary unit, and places all the lexemes from Aramaic verses within the running order of the Hebrew lexemes. Such a procedure would now generally be considered so unusual that it would be wrong, and that is why very soon it became normal to place all the Aramaic lexemes from the Old Testament in a separate appendix after the Hebrew section. However, even now a case could be made for sticking with the original format of the *Handwörterbuch*. That case would be based on the strong influence of Biblical Hebrew on Biblical Aramaic, the relatively small amount of Aramaic prose within the Massoretic text, and the fact that traditional readers of the Hebrew Bible seem to have had no serious difficulty in understanding the Aramaic portions. Perhaps these first bicentennial years of Gesenius's first *Handwörterbuch* are an appropriate time to question whether future dictionary makers should continue to separate Biblical Aramaic lexemes from their cognates in Biblical Hebrew. After all, Akkadian lexicographers have always integrated Semitic and non-Semitic lexemes into one single sequence.

The task of translating the genius of Gesenius for the English-speaking world fell to two scholars in particular. Josiah W. Gibbs (1790-1861) was the first with his translation of the *Neues Handwörterbuch*, a translation which he subsequently abridged with the needs of students in mind

(Gibbs 1827; 1833). Gesenius had also prepared a comprehensive *Lexicon* in Latin (Gesenius 1833), from which the 1834 edition of his *Handwörterbuch* had benefited. This work was translated into English by Edward Robinson (1794-1863) of the Union Theological Seminary in New York (Robinson 1844). These were the earliest precursors to what is today the most widely read English distillation of the Gesenius method (Brown et al. 1906), a work that has been regularly reprinted, occasionally with slight revisions. Even though, to say the least, it is distinctly over-ripe for a drastic revision, a challenge which was taken up by several scholars in the later part of the twentieth century but which has so far always proved too demanding for them, it is a book that has always found a prominent place for more than a century on the shelf of almost every English-speaking Hebraist. It is likely that before long a substantial new edition will be published, either by the Oxford University Press or with its co-operation. But perhaps this will be too little too late, for what would now be a more viable project would be to produce an English version of Gesenius's latest *Handwörterbuch* (18th edition) now that that has been completed.

***

From these remarks it can be seen that there are several aspects of the decisions made by the editors of *CDA* which can be compared and contrasted with those made by their forbears. The question of listing Akkadian words unattested except in lexical lists was seen to be paralleled also in Syriac lexicography, and the decision that such words were not ignored is to be applauded. For Hebrew that precise problem does not arise. But one that is not altogether unassociated concerns personal names. The main argument for listing them in the body of the text is to identify the meaning of the different elements of a name. But, even when an element is correctly identified, its meaning within a name has a significantly different nuance from that of a common noun. Assyriologists exclude names from their dictionaries, and Gesenius set them apart as an *Einschluss*. The reason for keeping them in Biblical Hebrew seems to have more to do with theology than with linguistics.

We should also note that the editors of *CDA* were able to work together with the author of the work they were abridging, something shared with Jessie Payne Smith. For her it was more the intimate relationship between a daughter and her father rather than between a team of younger scholars and a world authority. The difference was that she had only one task to do, to abridge a more extensive original. Similarly Edward Robinson was concerned only with one task, that of translating. But it has been noted that he modified his source text where he considered that necessary (see Brown 1906, v):

> This broad-minded, sound, and faithful scholar added to the successive editions of the book in its English form from the newest materials and conclusions in the field of Hebrew word-study, receiving large and valuable contributions in manuscripts from Gesenius himself.

One of the noticeable differences between the revisions of Gesenius and Payne Smith is that there was never any question of omitting text references for Hebrew, but there was never any question of keeping them in for Syriac. Here *CDA* has towed the Syriac line and faced the difficulty of choosing an appropriate gloss without the luxury of defining that gloss more precisely by citing the word in context. It is obviously much more straightforward to keep citations for a closed corpus of literature like the Bible than it is for one that is continually subject to change. On this point it should be noted that the Gesenius lexicographical tradition insists on citing Semitic roots, and this is material which is also subject to change. While our forefathers had to rely on the permanency of the printed word to record such changeable documentation, we now have access to websites that not only cope with but welcome regular updating. So when it comes to recording an impermanent set of citations or philological cognates it is likely to become more helpful if publishers link their printed books to electronic databases: *dies diem docet.*

Bibliography

BEZOLD, C. 1926: *Babylonische-Assyrisches Glossar, nach dem Tode des Verfassers unter Mitwirkung von Adele Bezold zum Druck gebracht von Albecht Götze*, Heidelberg.

BLACK, J., A. GEORGE and N. POSTGATE 1999: *A Concise Dictionary of Akkadian*, Wiesbaden ("2nd (corrected) printing", 2000).

BROCKELMANN, C. 1895: *Lexicon Syriacum*, Berlin (2nd. ed., Halle, 1928; reprinted, Edinburgh 1995).

BROWN, F., S. R. DRIVER and C. A. BRIGGS 1906: *A Hebrew and English Lexicon of the Old Testament with an appendix containing the Biblical Aramaic based on the Lexicon of William Gesenius as translated by Edward Robinson*, Oxford.

CDA see Black.

DELITZSCH, F. 1896: *Assyrisches Handwörterbuch*, Leipzig.

DUVAL, R. (ed.) 1888-1901: *Lexicon Syriacum: voces syriacas graecasque cum glossis syriacas et arabicis complectens e pluribus codicibus: Hassanus Bar Bahlul* (3 vols.), Paris.

EHRLICH, C. L. 2009: *From an Antique Land. an Introduction to Ancient Near Eastern Literature*, Lanham.

GESENIUS, W. 1810-1812: *Hebräisch-Deutsches Handwörterbuch über die Schriften des Alten Testaments mit Einschluss der geographischen Nahmen und der chaldäischen Wörter beym Daniel und Esra*, I *aleph – kaph*; II *lamedh – taw*, Leipzig.

— 1815: *Neues Hebräisch-Deutsches Handwörterbuch über die Alte Testament mit Einschluss des biblischen Chaldaismus. Ein Auszug aus dem grössern Werke in vielen Artikeln desselben umgearbeit vornehmlich für Schulen*, Leipzig.

GIBBS, J. W. 1827: *A Hebrew and English Lexicon to the Old Testament including the Biblical Chaldee; edited with improvements from the German works of Gesenius*, London.

— 1833: *A Manual Hebrew and English Lexicon including the Biblical Chaldee; abridged with the latest improvements from the works of Professor W. Gesenius, and designed particularly for the use of students*, London.

GOTTHEIL, R. J. H. 1910-1928: *Bar 'Ali (Isho'). The Syriac-Arabic Glosses* (Atti della R. Accademia dei Lincei. Classe di Scienzi morali, storiche e filologiche Ser. 5, Vol. 13), Rome.

HOFFMANN, G. 1874: *Syrisch-Arabische Glossen. Erster Band. Autographie einer Gothaischen Handschrift enthaltend Bar Ali's Lexicon von Alaf bis Mim,* Kiel. (Reprinted 1886).

KOEHLER, L. and W. BAUMGARTNER 1953: *Lexicon in veteris testamenti libros*, Leiden.

— 1958: *Supplementum ad lexicon in veteris testamenti libros*, Leiden.

— 1967: *Hebräisches und Aramäisches Lexicon zum Alten Testament*, Leiden.

LOOSE, J. (ed.) 1999: *De Talen van het Oude Nabije Oosten* (MVEOL 32), Leuven.

MEYER, R. and H. DONNER 1987-2010: *Wilhelm Gesenius' Hebräisches und Aramäisches Handwörterbuch über das Alte Testament*, Berlin - Heidelberg.

MUSS-ARNOLT, W. 1905: *A Concise Dictionary of the Assyrian Language*, Berlin.

POSTGATE, J. N. (ed.) 2007: *Languages of Iraq*, London.

ROBINSON, E. 1844: *A Hebrew and English Lexicon of the Old Testament including the Biblical Chaldee translated from the Latin of William Gesenius*, London.

SMITH, R. P. 1879-1901: *Thesaurus Syriacus* (2 vols.), Oxford.

SMITH, J. P. (ed.) 1903: *A Compendious Syriac Dictionary founded upon the Thesaurus Syriacus of R. Payne Smith*, Oxford (Reprinted 1990).

SOKOLOFF, M. 2009: *A Syriac Lexicon. A Translation from the Latin, Correction, Expansion, and Update of C. Brockelmann's Lexicon Syriacum*, Winona Lake - Piscataway.

STAMM J. J. 1989: "Bericht über den Stand der Arbeit an der 3. Auflage des hebräischen und aramäischen Wörterbuches von Ludwig Koehler und Walter Baumgartner, mit einem Rückblick auf die 1. und 2. Auflage", *Theologische Zeitschrift* 45/4, 277-289.

STRECK, M. P. (ed.) 2005: *Sprachen des Alten Orients*, Darmstadt.

LIBBALI-SHARRAT OR NAQIA? ON QUEENS PORTRAYED ON ASSYRIAN RELIEFS

Arlette ROOBAERT
Liège University

The queen seated in front of Ashurbanipal on the famous banquet relief celebrating the king's victory on Teumman (BM 124920) from Room S of the North Palace at Nineveh, is generally identified with his wife Libbali-sharrat (Fig. 1).[1] Historical and stylistical considerations might suggest another identification.

The main argument for identifying Libbali-sharrat is the similarity between the figure seated in front of Ashurbanipal and the enthroned figure wearing a mural crown, carved on a broken stele from Ashur (Fig. 2). The Ashur stele was associated at the time of discovery with a cuneiform inscription naming Libbali-sharrat[2] the palace woman of Ashurbanipal (Andrae 1913, 7-8) (Fig. 2), hence the identification of the figure on the stele with Libbali-sharrat.

If there is no doubt that the figure carved on the Ashur stele represents a seated Assyrian queen, its identification with Ashurbanipal's first wife cannot be taken for granted. The stele, as stated by Andrae (1913, 8), was very damaged — only eighteen joining fragments of the upper part were found, the lower part was entirely lost — and there is no certainty that the fragmentary five-line inscription belonged to that part of the stele. Reade (2004, 464) already stressed the unsure position of the fragmentary inscription.

Thus, if Libbali-sharrat had undoubtedly a stele erected in Ashur, it might not be the one that was carved with the seated figure of a queen. Shammuramat herself had only an inscription engraved on her stele, without any figurative representation (Andrae 1913, 10). On the other hand, it has to be emphasized with Reade (2004, 464) that the Ashur stele portraying a queen is unique among all the Ashur steles.

[1] See among others: Parrot and Nougayrol 1956, 149; Hrouda 1965, 47-48; Albenda 1976, 61; 1987, 20; and more recently Melville 1999, 51; Ornan 2002, 462, 473. On the other hand, Grayson (1991b, 160) considers that she is "probably" the woman portrayed on the banquet scene.

[2] A more accurate reading than Ashur-sharrat, according to Deller and Postgate 1985, 73.

From the stylistical point of view, the figure on the Ashur stele and the one on the banquet scene are rather similar. The two ladies are seated on a throne, wearing rich embroidered garments, the same type of earring, a large necklace and a bracelet decorated with rosettes around the right wrist. The hairstyle with small curls on the forehead, a lock before the ear and heavy curls resting on the shoulders is also identical. The mural crown identifies them as queens. There are, however, differences in the details. If they are both holding a flower in the left hand, the figure on the stele raises her right hand, while the other on the banquet scene is holding a cup. The rendering of the crown also differs. On the Ashur stele, the crown is higher with only three towers represented and it hides the top of the head, while on the banquet scene, the crown looks more like a diadem with the representation of six towers. On the Ashur stele, the counterweight of a necklace seems to be partly visible. On the banquet relief, such a device is not visible. These discrepancies could be explained by the nature of the two monuments. The Ashur stele was intended as an official representation of a deceased queen, while the banquet scene was meant for a more private environment.[3]

Are there other arguments to identify the queen seated in front of Ashurbanipal with Libbali-sharrat? The evidence about Ashurbanipal's wives and about Libbali-sharrat in particular is unfortunately extremely scarce. We only know that she married Ashurbanipal when he was still crown prince, thus between 672 B.C. and 669 B.C., and had at that time precedence problems with Sherua-etirat, the eldest daughter of Esarhaddon (Weissbach 1928, 225; Ambos 2001, 661). The Ashur inscription implies that she became queen when Ashurbanipal ascended the throne in 669 B.C. As the crown prince, Ashur-etel-ilani, was rather young and apparently still a minor when he ascended the throne, some time between 630 B.C. (Brinkman 1998, 183) and 627 B.C. (Oates 1991, 167), it seems unlikely, as J. Oates (1991, 176) has observed, that Libbali-sharrat was his mother. So we cannot be sure that she was still first wife in 653 B.C. when Ashurbanipal celebrated his victory over Teumman.

However, among the Assyrian queens of the seventh century B.C., there is a strong personality whose presence on the banquet scene could be considered for both political and personal reasons, namely Naqia/Zakutu.[4] She was the wife of Sennacherib, the mother of Esarhaddon and the grandmother of Ashurbanipal.

[3] On the interpretation of the banquet scene, see Albenda 1976, 65.

[4] On Naqia see Lewy 1952, 264-286; Grayson 1991a, 138-140; Streck 1998-2001, 165; Streck 2001, 929-930 and especially Melville 1999.

She is depicted on a bronze plaque in the Louvre,[5] following her son, king Esarhaddon,[6] and identified by an inscription on her shoulder (Fig. 3). The Louvre bronze is quite unique, because it associates on the same relief, the queen mother and her son involved in a religious ceremony (Ornan 2002, 469).

As Melville (1999, 51) observed, Naqia on the Louvre bronze "is almost identical in terms of both style and accoutrements to the figure of Libbali-sharrat as seen on Ashurbanipal's banquet relief." She is represented with the same hairstyle, the same type of ear-ring. The mural crown she is wearing looks like its conterpart on the banquet scene, even if only four towers are represented (Hrouda 1965, 47). On the other hand, as on the Ashur stele, a possible counterweight is hanging down her back.

As far as style is concerned, it seems difficult to differentiate between those three representations of a seventh century B.C. queen. It is not surprising given that the Assyrian sculptors used a standard image to portray women and personalized them only by their garments, jewellery and other attributes. This is quite obvious on the relief of Ashurbanipal's banquet where the female fan bearers behind the seated queen have the same hairstyle and the same type of ear-ring as the queen, but wear only a headband (Fig. 1). The crucial point, however, is that, on the Louvre bronze, queen Naqia is identified by an inscription and that she is depicted in a way that is very close to the two other representations of a queen, especially the figure on the banquet relief.

Why should Naqia be portrayed in front of her grandson Ashurbanipal? Firstly for political reasons. In 669 B.C., after Esarhaddon's death, she was responsible for Ashurbanipal's accession to the throne, without trouble, by imposing a loyalty oath on his behalf, the so-called Zakutu treaty (Parpola and Watanabe 1988, 62-64). It lasted till 652, the year after the victory on Teumman, when Shamash-shumu-ukin rebelled against his brother. A document also unique, because it was not imposed by a king (Melville 1999, 86). More personal reasons might have played a role too. It is very likely that since 672 B.C., after the death of Esharra-hammat, most probably the mother of Ashurbanipal (Radner 1999, 406; Weissert 1998, 160-161), she also acted as queen mother for her grandson as she

[5] AO 20.185. Parrot and Nougayrol 1956, 147-160. Complete bibliography in Melville 1999, 99.

[6] This identification was made by J. Nougayrol (Parrot and Nougayrol 1956, 155) and seems the most convincing. J. Börker-Klähn (1982, nos. 220-221) considers that the king represented before Naqia is Sennacherib. Against this opinion see Melville 1999, 25-26.

did for her son. She seems to have been very close to Ashurbanipal whom she calls her "favourite grandson" in the Zakutu treaty (Parpola and Watanabe 1988, 62, line 11). Finally, as she had already been associated with a king, her son Esarhaddon, on public monuments, and had also her statue exhibited in the Nabu temple at Nimrud (Melville 1999, 46), why should her grandson, for whom she acted both as grandmother and queen mother, not have honoured her, as did his father, by associating her with him on a public monument? The presence of Naqia in the intimacy of the king — he does not wear a crown, but only a headband — surrounded by the symbols of his glorious deeds, which he could achieve thanks to her strong and effective support, could even be part of the royal propaganda.

There are thus political and personal reasons for her presence on the banquet relief.

From the chronological point of view, her presence does not seem impossible either. The precise date of her birth is not known, but, as she entered Sennacherib's harem at the end of Sargon's reign and as her son Esarhaddon was most probably born between 713 B.C. and 711 B.C. (Melville 1999, 13), she must have been in her seventies in 653 B.C. when Ashurbanipal defeated the Elamite king Teumman. A quite young age compared to Nabonidus' mother, Adda-Guppi, who, according to an inscription on a stele from Harran, "lived to the impressive age of 102 (or perhaps 104)" (Oates 1991, 167).

It is therefore likely that the queen seated in front of Ashurbanipal on the famous banquet relief was his grandmother Naqia.

Bibliography

ALBENDA, P. 1976: "Landscape Bas-Reliefs in the *Bit-Hilani* of Ashurbanipal", *BASOR* 224, 49-72.

— 1977: "Landscape Bas-Reliefs in the *Bit-Hilani* of Ashurbanipal", *BASOR* 225, 29-48.

— 1987: "Woman, Child, and Family, their Imagery in Assyrian Art", in J.-M. Durand (ed.) *La femme dans le Proche-Orient antique*, Paris, 17-21.

AMBOS, C. 2001: "Libālli-šarrat", *The Prosopography of the Neo-Assyrian Empire* 2,2, 660-661.

ANDRAE, W. 1913: *Die Stelenreihe in Assur,* Leipzig.

BÖRKER-KLÄHN, J. 1982: *Altvorderasiatische Bildstelen und vergleichbare Felsreliefs* (Baghdader Forschungen 4), Mainz.

BRINKMAN, J. A. 1998: "Aššūr-etel-ilāni", *The Prosopography of the Neo-Assyrian Empire* 1,1, 183-184.

DELLER K. and J. N. POSTGATE 1985: "Nachträge und Verbesserungen zu RGTC 5. Mittelassyrische Teil", *AfO* 32, 73.

GRAYSON, A. K. 1991a: "Assyria: Sennacherib and Esarhaddon (704-669 B.C.)", *The Cambridge Ancient History*, 2nd ed., III/2, 103-141.

— 1991b: "Assyria 668-635 B.C,: the reign of Ashurbanipal", *The Cambridge Ancient History*, 2nd ed., III/2, 142-161.

HROUDA, B. 1965: *Die Kulturgeschichte des Assyrischen Flachbildes*, Bonn.

MELVILLE, Sarah C. 1999: *The Role of Naqia/Zakutu in Sargonid Politics* (State Archives of Assyria Studies 9), Helsinki.

LEWY, H. 1952: "Nitokris-Naqî'a", *JNES* 1, 264-286.

OATES, J. 1991: "The Fall of Assyria (635-609 B.C.)", *The Cambridge Ancient History*, 2nd ed., III/2, 162-193.

ORNAN, Tallay 2002: "The Queen in Public: Royal Women in Neo-Assyrian Art", in S. Parpola and R. M. Whiting (eds.) *Sex and Gender in the Ancient Near East*, Helsinki, 461-477.

ORTHMANN, W. 1985: *Der alte Orient*, Berlin.

PARPOLA, S. and K. WATANABE 1988: *Neo-Assyrian Treaties and Loyalty Oaths* (State Archives of Assyria 2), Helsinki.

PARROT, A. and J. NOUGAYROL 1956: "Asarhaddon et Naqi'a sur un bronze du Louvre (AO 20.185)", *Syria* 36, 147-160.

RADNER, K. 1999: "Ešarra-ḫammat", *The Prosopography of the Neo-Assyrian Empire* 1, 2, 406-407.

READE, J. E. 2004: "The Historical Status of the Assur Stelas", in J. G. Dercksen (ed.) *Assyria and Beyond: Studies Presented to Mogens Trolle Larsen*, Leiden, 455-473.

STRECK, M. P. 1998 — 2001: " Naqi'a", *RlA* 9, 165.

— 2001: "Naqi'a", *The Prosopography of the Neo-Assyrian Empire* 2,2, 929-930.

WEISSBACH, F. H. 1928: "Aššuršarrat", *RlA* 1, 225.

WEISSERT, E. 1998: "Aššur-bāni-apli", *The Prosopography of the Neo-Assyrian Empire* 1,1, 159-163.

Fig. 1. Banquet relief of Ashurbanipal (BM 124920)
(after Orthmann 1985, 247).

Fig. 2. Queen depicted on an Ashur stele and fragment of inscription naming Libbali-sharrat (after Andrae 1913, Taf. X, 1).

Fig. 3. Fragment of a bronze relief depicting queen Naqia and king Esarhaddon (AO 20.185) (after Parpola and Watanabe 1988, 63 Fig. 20).

THE ANCIENT THEATRES OF SYRIA IN THEIR REGIONAL SETTING

Saraa SALEH
KU Leuven

As a former architect who worked for the DGAM in Syria, I participated in the Syrian-Belgian mission that worked on the theatre of Jebleh and Tell Tweini.[1] This gave me the great opportunity to meet Prof. Karel Van Lerberghe in the year 1999. With his help and supervision, I was able to come to Belgium and to complete a Master in Conservation of Historic Towns and Buildings and a Ph.D in Near Eastern Studies at the KU Leuven. I would like to take this opportunity to express my appreciation and sincere gratitude to Karel for his guidance and support.

1. Introduction

Modern Syria boasts the presence of eleven remaining ancient theatres.[2] Earlier work[3] described the architectural characteristics of the theatres of Cyrrhus, Jebleh, Apamea, Dura-Europos, Palmyra, Bosra, Der'a, Soueida, Qanawat, Sahr and Philippopolis.

The aim of this paper was to compare the ancient theatres in Syria with those of other regions and thus to situate their architectural characteristics in their regional setting. The first criteria for selecting comparable theatres from other regions were their historical provincial locations, especially because geographically, historically and culturally the region of modern Syria has always been, linked to the neighboring Eastern Mediterranean countries. Therefore, the theatres of the Levant and of Asia Minor were the first to be selected for the comparative study. Additionally, the theatres of the Levant will be compared to the two major types of ancient theatres, the Roman style of theatre and the Greek style of theatre (Fig. 1).

[1] This is an on-going project since 1999; it is a multi-disciplinary research program initiated at the behest of the DGAM. Project directors are Prof. Dr. Karel Van Lerberghe (KU Leuven, Belgium) and Prof. Dr. Michel Al-Maqdissi (DGAM, Syria).

[2] This enumeration is not absolute considering the fact that we know of a number of completely destroyed or still concealed theatres, see Saleh 2009, 1.

[3] Saleh 2009

2. The theatres of the Levant

In addition to the theatres remaining in present-day Syria, we know of several ancient theatres that were built in the Levant. Based on their historical locations, four groups can be distinguished: a first group is located in Palestine,[4] a second in Arabia,[5] a third in Syria Phoenicia,[6] and a fourth group in modern Hatay in Turkey (Fig. 1).[7] In what follows, we will list the remaining theatres of the Levant in four tables, including their building date, cavea diameter, orientation, function and historical background.

We know of eleven ancient theatres to have been built in Palestina (Table 1). Moreover, the southern extremity of present-day Syria has a number of remaining ancient theatres, i.e. the theatres of Bosra, Der'a, Qanawat, Philippopolis, Sahr and Soueida. During the Roman period, the cities of these theatres belonged to the Roman province of Arabia. In addition to these six theatres, several are also known to have been built in the province of Arabia (Table 2).

Under Septimius Severus, the province of Syria was divided into Syria Coele in the north and Syria Phoenicia in the south. Palmyra was located in Syria Phoenicia and Dura-Europos in Syria Coele. The region of modern Lebanon was entirely located in Syria Phoenicia.[8] At present, we know of four ancient theatres to have been built in this region (Table 3).

Historically, the province of the Hatay (Alexandretta) in present-day Turkey was Syrian territory until 1939. In that year, the French mandate in Syria gave the former Ottoman administrative district of Alexandretta, in which Antioch the ancient capital of Syria is located, to Turkey.[9] At present, we know of three ancient theatres to have been built in this region (Table 4).[10]

2.1. *Historical discussion*

The Roman theatres in modern Syria were built over a period of three centuries, from mid-first century BC to mid-third century AD.[11] For theatres

[4] Southern-western geographical area of the Levant

[5] Southern-eastern geographical area of the Levant

[6] Northern geographical area of the Levant

[7] During Roman time, the Levant was divided into three Roman provinces, Palestine (south-west), Arabia (south), and Syria (north and north-west); for more information see, Saleh 2009, 44-47.

[8] Ball 2000, 85

[9] Tibawi 1969, 335

[10] The information in these tables were obtained from: Sear 2006, 302-324, Segal 1995, 98-110, Rossetto and Sartorio 1994, Vol. 2, and Retzleff 2003, 115-138

[11] For more information on the history of the ancient theatres in Syria see, Saleh 2009, 50-70.

in the Levant at large, the case seems similar. Apart from the theatre of Byblus, which has an undated Hellenistic origin, the rest of the ancient theatres found in the Levant seem to have been built in the period between the mid-first century BC and the mid-third century AD.[12]

Seven of the ancient theatres found in present-day Syria, among them the two theatres found in Decapolis cities Qanawat and Der'a,[13] were built during the rule of the Antonine and Severan dynasties; Tables 1, 2, and 3, show that fifteen other theatres in the Levant were also built during the rule of the Antonine and Severan dynasties. Likewise, all the ancient theatres of the Decapolis were built in this period.

Among the ancient theatres found in present-day Syria, only one theatre, that of Laodicea, was built in the Augustan period of the early first century AD.[14] Tables 1, 2, and 3 show that two other theatres in the Levant, those at Daphnae and Sepphoris, were also built during this period. Unlike that of Laodicea, these two theatres survived, thanks to the rebuilding program applied to them in later Roman periods.[15]

Three ancient theatres in present-day Syria, those at Sahr (Nabataea), Damascus (Judea) and Palmyra (local kingdom of Palmyra)[16], were built during the rule of local authorities, As tables 1, 2, and 3 show, in the Levant, as a whole, we know of nine theatres to have been built during the rule of local authorities, five by Herod the Great and his son, and four by the Nabataeans. The Herodian theatres are among the earliest known ancient theatres in the Levant; all are completely destroyed at present. The earliest ancient theatre known to us in the Levant is the theatre of Byblus, which has an undated Hellenistic origin.

2.2. *Architectural discussion*

At present, we know of 49 theatres to have been built in the Levant. Almost half of them (24) were located in Roman Arabia, 11 in Roman Palestine, and 14 in Roman Syria, which included Syria Phoenicia. In total, more than two third of these theatres were concentrated in the southern half of the Levant, in the areas that were Nabataean and Judean before the Roman invasion.

12 See tables 1, 2, 3 and 4

13 We know of eighteen ancient theatres to have been built in Syria; only thirteen theatres of them provided us with sufficient information to estimate their building date, see Saleh 2009, 50-70

14 Saleh 2009, 220

15 Sear 2006, 307, 319

16 Saleh 2009, 218-220

In the author's PhD thesis, several architectural features were highlighted as differences or similarities between the theatres of Syria and the theatre of Arabia.[17] For the theatres found in the Levant as a whole, the following observations can be noted:

Function and size

In Roman Syria, eight out of nine remaining theatres are large urban theatres (Tables 1, 2, 3, and 4). We actually know of only two small ritual theatres to have been built in the province of Syria, i.e. Dura-Europos and Daphnae-Nymphaeum. To date, no odea[18] or medium-sized theatres have been discovered in Syria, Lebanon or the Hatay. Ninety percent of the theatres found in the province of Syria are large urban ones. Equally, in Palestine, six out of nine remaining theatres are large urban theatres, bringing percentage of the large urban theatres among the theatres discovered in the Province of Palestine to more than 65%. For the province of Arabia the percentage is lower: almost 30% of the theatres found in Arabia are large urban ones. On the other hand, 13 out of the 18 theatres found in Arabia are small or medium-sized (more than 70%); among them 4 odea and 9 ritual and urban ritual theatres. Based on these figures, it is evident that the theatres of Arabia present more variety in size and function in comparison with those of the other two provinces. One can partly understand this difference in view of the fact that at least 6 out of the 9 ritual and urban ritual theatres in Arabia were built by the Nabataeans. Indeed, the Nabataeans are known to have had a great impact on urban architecture, and they, especially excelled in religious architecture.[19]

In general, it seems that the northern Levant has a concentration of large urban theatres. It even has two theatres with a cavea[20] diameter larger than 110 m, which was not found in the south. Palestina also presents a considerable number of large urban theatres. This could be due to the Hellenistic influence, which was stronger in Syria and Palestina than in Arabia. Naturally, the Hellenistic influence was stronger in Syria because of the Seluiced origin of its cities. To the south, the Hellenistic influence on the culture in Judea was due to Herod's attempt to be part

[17] Saleh 2009, 290-292
[18] Small theatres located inside the city and was only used for musical concerts.
[19] Segal 1981, 118
[20] The part of the theatre where the audiences sit.

of the Greco-Roman world.[21] In Arabia, it seems, the influence of the local traditions on the theatre architecture was stronger, especially in relation to its function.

Proportional relation between the parts of the theatre

An attempt was made to understand the relation between the cavea diameter (D), the orchestra diameter (O) and the scaenae[22] length (S) of the ancient theatres found in modern Syria. The result showed that, in the theatres found in Roman Arabia, the plan was geometrically perfect. The proportional equation between D, S, and O was: $D = 1.5 \times S = 3 \times O$, $D = S = 4 \times O$, or $D = S = 2 \times O$. The plan of the theatres found in Roman Syria was less perfectly geometrical. The proportional equation there ranged between: $D = 1.6 - 2 \times S = 4 - 5.5 \times O$.[23] An analysis of the proportional relations between the parts of the Levantine theatres as a whole, show the same results. Most of the theatres of Roman Arabia and Palestina present a perfect geometrical equation. In Palestina, this equation was $D = S = 3 \times O$ for the theatres of Caesarea, Mamas, and Sebaste; and $D = 1.5 \times S = 3 \times D$, in Sepphoris. In Arabia, the equation was $D = S = 4 \times O$ for the theatres of Pella, Petra (the large theatres) and Philadelphia (the large theatres). Moreover, the equation was $D = S = 3 \times O$ for the theatres of Elusa and Gadara, and $D = 1.5 \times S = 3 \times D$ for the northern theatre of Gerasa.[24]

The Scaenae frons[25]

Apart from function and size, and the proportional relation between the parts of theatres, the architecture of stage building of the ancient theatres found in present-day Syria deserves attention. Interestingly, the theatres with developed scaenae building in Roman Syria had three doorways in the scaenae frons. While the theatres of developed scaenae building in Arabia had five.[26] This is also the case for the theatres of the Levant as a whole. Except for the theatre at Daphnae, which had three doorways in

21 For more information on the Herodian theatres see, Segal 1995, 4-6
22 The stage building
23 Saleh 2009, 242-246
24 Only theatres with reliable measurements were considered, therefore, the theatres of Lebanon and the Hatay could not be included in this proportional analysis.
25 The front façade of the stage building
26 Saleh 2009, 267-269

its scaenae frons, all the known ancient theatres found in Roman Syria (Palmyra, Apamea, Cyrruhs, and Jebleh) had a scaenae frons with five doorways. Furthermore, all the remaining ancient theatres of Roman Palestine and Arabia with preserved stage buildings, presented a scaenae frons with five doorways.

Building materials

As for the building materials used in the ancient theatres found in modern Syria, the theatres of Arabia were mainly built with basalt, whereas, the theatres of Roman Syria were mainly built with limestone.[27] This result was not applicable when we reviewed the theatres of the Levant at whole. Actually, the theatres of Palestina and southern Arabia were mainly built with limestone. The use of basalt was limited to the Hauran region, which covers northern present-day Jordan and southern present-day Syria. The Hauran is dominated by the range of volcanic hills known as Jabal Al Arab, and the area is covered in black basalt rock and lava flows.[28] It seems, overall, that the ancient theatres of the Levant were mainly built with local building materials (limestone, sandy-limestone, basalt, and mud bricks). All parts of the construction itself were of local stone while imported stones, marble, granite, and alabaster, were used for decorations.

2.3. *Roman characteristics in the Levantine theatres*

In spite of the differences between the ancient theatres of Roman Syria, Arabia, and Palestine, highlighted above, these theatres shared several architectural characteristics. In fact, in terms of layout, the theatres of the Levant were generally of the Roman style; or what is known as the western type of theatre.[29] Indeed, they showed the distinguishing characteristics typical of the Roman type of theatre: all of the remaining theatres in the Levant displayed unity in their plans. The stage building was joined to the cavea and rose to the same height, which transformed the theatre into a single closed architectural space. The Levantine theatres had a semicircular orchestra and cavea; and even when the cavea

[27] Saleh 2009, 281

[28] Ball 2000, 238

[29] For detailed information on the Roman (western) type of theatre, see Saleh 2009, 73-85, Sear 2006, 24-36, Bieber 1961, 167-189, Rossetto and Sartorio 1994, Vol. 1, 136-137

exceeded the semicircle, its analemmata[30] stayed parallel to the wall of the stage building. The aditus maximi,[31] were always vaulted galleries. The cavea, which was vertically divided into two or three sections, extended on top of the two aditus maximi. In most cases, the ima cavea[32] was partly built on a slope; only the theatres of Palmyra, Bosra, Jebleh, Dura-Europos, Elusa and Sahr were completely built on level land. Thus, the entire cavea, or at least the upper levels of it, were free-standing and supported by artificial substructure.[33] This substructure, mostly consisted of radial and semicircular vaulted galleries, and was used to facilitate circulation, allowing spectators to reach the interior of the theatre through vaulted passages (vomitoria). The cavea was bounded from the outside with a semicircular façade. Almost all the theatres had developed stage building, with a stage shaped as a long narrow rectangular. Only three theatres did not have a stage building, i.e. the small-ritual theatres of Sahr, Emmatha, and Dura-Europos. The pulpitum[34] front wall (proscenium) was closed and decorated with niches and it contained staircases at either end leading from the orchestra to the stage floor. The scaenae frons was sometimes rectangular, but more often it had doorways enclosed in niches. In most of the large and medium theatres, there was a colummatio in front of the scaenae frons wall. A corridor ran behind the scaenae frons, providing access to the stage doorways and leading to the exterior of the theatre (Fig. 2).

3. Comparing the theatres of the Levant with those of Greece and Asia Minor

The most important features of the Greek theatre were a circular orchestra, a curved seating that extended beyond a semicircle, and converging analemmata. Actually, theatres with converging analemmata continued to be built throughout the Roman imperial period in parts of Greece and Asia Minor.[35] Moreover, many of the Greek theatres in Greece and in Asia Minor were modernized in the Roman period. Yet, even when

30 The ends of the cavea

31 The two entrances, which permitted direct access to the orchestra from the outside

32 The lower horizontal section of the cavea

33 The theatres of Palmyra, Sahr and Elusa represented a special construction system, which could not be considered typically Roman. The theatre was built completely on level land, and the cavea was supported on an enclosed fill of stone structure.

34 The stage

35 For more information on the classical Greek Theatre see, Saleh, 2009: pp 23-26

modernized, the theatres kept their converged edges of the cavea. This could explain why the type of the ancient theatres found in Greece and Asia Minor was mostly related to the Greek style,[36] with a high trapezoidal pulpitum, and a mostly rectangular scaenae frons. The cavea and the orchestra exceeded a semicircle, and the analemmata were converged. The cavea was vertically divided into two zones and the seats were usually profiled. The two aditus maximi were unroofed; so the unity in the theatre plan featured in Roman theatres was not feasible in the Greek style.[37] Greece and Asia Minor had few late theatres of the pure Roman type, the most significant of which was the theatre of Aspendos in Asia Minor (late second century AD).[38] Also, in Greece there is the Roman theatre of Herodes Atticus of Athens (end of the first century AD) and the Roman theatre of Nicopolis (built in early first century AD and rebuilt in second/third century AD).[39]

Although the general layout of the theatres in the Levant was Roman in style, they shared few detailed architectural features with the theatres of Greece and Asia Minor. For example, unlike those of western theatres, the seats in almost all the Levantine theatres had profiles, as in the Greek/Asia Minor type of theatre. A study of the profiles by Barlest showed that theatres of Apamea, Palmyra and Cyrrhus had a seat profile similar to those at Aezani and Aspendos.[40] Also, the seats profile in the theatres of Jebleh, Apamea, Palmyra and Cyrrhus are similar, while the theatres of Qanawat, Soueida and Der'a present a variety of seat profile shapes.[41]

A number of theatres in the Levant, among them Der'a, the northern theatre at Gerasa, the medium theatre at Philadelphia, and Philippopolis, all had a rectangular scaenae frons, as was the case in the majority of the theatres in Greece and Asia Minor. In fact, these four theatres were located in Decapolis cities, which could explain the Hellenistic impact on their architectural style. It is noteworthy that the stage building of the Levantine theatres tended to be of the Roman type, although many theatres of them lack the basilicas, just like the theatres of Greece and Asia Minor. Moreover, the theatres of Roman Syria, Palmyra, Jebleh, Apamea,

[36] Sear 2006, 68, Bieber 1961, p 213

[37] For detailed information on the style of the theatres of Asia Minor see, Rossetto and Sartorio (ed.) 1994, Vol. 2, 120, Sear 2006, 24-25, 110-113, Bieber 1961, 213-220

[38] Sear 2006, 112

[39] Sear 2006, 115

[40] Barlet 1972, 148

[41] Saleh 2009, 257

and Cyrruhs all had five doorways in their scaenae frons, a number commonly found in the theatres of Greece and Asia Minor.

The bottom of the cavea in most of the Levantine theatres was bounded by a podium, rising to a height of approximately that of the pulpitum. This type of podium, which separated the cavea from the orchestra, was also commonly found in the theatres of Asia Minor. For example, it was found in the theatres of Troy, Ephesus, Myra, Hierapolis, and Side. Nevertheless, a number of the Levantine theatres presented a different type of cavea-orchestra relation. In Apamea, Caesarea, Petra, Dura-Europos and Soueida the cavea directly joined the orchestra floor, with no podium dividing the two areas. This kind of cavea — orchestra relation was normally associated with the Greek design of theatre, and was found in the majority of the known ancient theatres in Greece. It was also found in several theatres in Asia Minor, such as those of Aspendos, Aegae, Caunus, Nysa, Soli, and many others. A third variant of the cavea-orchestra relation was typically found in the Hellenistic theatres. In this type of theatres, the orchestra was encircled with a row of special seats, which were seats of honor. A passageway in the back of these seats separated them from the auditorium.[42] The same type of the cavea-orchestra relation was found in the Levantine theatres of Der'a and Scythopolis, which were both located in Decapolis cities. Here too the Hellenistic impact on the theatres is visible. The same type of the cavea-orchestra relation was found in old Greek theatres such as the theatre of Priene in Asia Minor, and the theatres of Delos in Greece. In the theatres of Palmyra and Daphnae, instead of a row of special seats, the orchestra was encircled with a freestanding podium. This is also the case in several Greek theatres and these features were modified in later Roman periods, as in the theatres of Dionysus, Athens, and Corinth.

The cavea of the vast majority of the Greek/Asia Minor theatres was entirely supported by a natural slope. However a number of these theatres, as for example those of the Levant, had the upper level of the cavea supported on an artificial substructure. Most of the theatres of this type in Greece and Asia Minor were late ones (second – third century AD). Among these were the theatres at Sagalassos, Side, Selge and Miletus in Asia Minor, and also the odeum of Corinth as well as the theatre of Patrae in Greece[43] (Fig. 2).

[42] Moretti 1997, 22
[43] Saleh 2009, 317

4. Conclusion

Overall, it seems that the history of the theatre building in Syria was part of a larger, similar tradition in the Levant. The earliest theatres in the Levant were built after Pompey's conquest of 64 BC: Antioch (Julius Caesar) and Laodicea (Augustus). However, it was Herod the Great who gave the initial and greatest impetus to theatre building in the region. He built theatres at Jerusalem, Jericho, Caesarea and Damascus. The second boom of theatre building in the region was to come in mid-second century AD and lasted until the mid-third century AD. Most of the ancient theatres of the Levant were built during this period, especially during the rule of the Antonine and Severan dynasties.

Architecturally, the percentage of the large urban theatres among the theatres found in Syria and Palestina was bigger than among the theatres found in Arabia. This could be due to the differences in the pre-Roman architectural influence, which was Hellenistic in Syria and Palestine, and Nabataean in Arabia. Also, the rigidity of basalt, which was the main building material in most of the cities in Arabia, might have had an influence on the size of the theatres there. Secondly, a proportional analysis between the parts of the theatres showed that most of the Roman Arabian and Palestinian theatres presented a perfect geometric equation, while the plan of the theatres found in Roman Syria was less perfect geometrically. The strictness of the architectural design of the southern theatres was also evident in the vertical division of the cavea and in the shape and the architectural details of the stage building.

It was also discussed that despite these differences, the theatres of the Levant shared several architectural characteristics. They mostly shared features in their layout that were related to the Roman type of theatre. On the other hand, they had few detailed characteristics drawn from the Greece/Asia Minor type of theatre, apart from some features of their own.

To sum up, the ancient theatres of the Levant, in general, and of present-day Syria, in particular, presented the following major architectural features:

- They were built in the period between the mid-first century BC and the mid-third century AD
- They were satiated with the Roman theatre architectural tradition. This included the unity in their plans, the stage building, which was joined to the cavea and rose to the same height, the semicircular orchestra and

cavea, the vaulted aditus maximi and the extension of the cavea over them, the partly or fully free-standing cavea, the use of the substructure that supported the cavea in the circulation, the outer façade of the cavea, the developed stage building, the wide and fairly low pulpitum, and the columnmatio in front of the scaenae frons wall.

- The influence of the Greek theatre architecture tradition was minimal. Although they shared a few architectural details with this type of theatre; among them, the profiled seats, the rectangular scaenae frons, which was found in a number of the Levantine theatres, the lack of basilicas, the five doorways in the scaenae frons, the well-cut masonry, and the cavea-orchestra relation.
- They presented unity and practicality in design.
- They displayed creativity and verity in their construction system. Only few theatres were completely built on a flat surface. In general, a natural slope was used to support the ima cavea where possible. The cavea was thus fully or partly supported on an artificial substructure, which consisted of a complex of barrel and radial vaults. The functional use of this artificial substructure facilitated public circulation.
- The function of the aditus maximi went beyond their traditional purpose of only connecting the outside with the orchestra. In several theatres of the Levant they also connected the stage with the vaulted galleries that supported the cavea.
- The orchestra was U-shaped and was usually paved with slab stones, which follow the cavea curve and form geometric patterns.
- The proscaenium usually presented an alternation of curved and rectangular niches
- The scaenae frons often had an indented profile with three or five doorways enclosed in niches
- The builders depended mainly on a supply of local building materials, which were limestone for most of the regions, and basalt for the Hauran region in the south. Marble and granite were used to decorate several large theatres.
- The theatres in the south, especially the ones built in basalt, are very symmetrical and have a simple and austere appearance.
- All theatres known to us in the Decapolis cities were built in basalt, during the rule of the Antonine or Severan dynasties. Moreover, they presented a number of similarities with the Hellenistic style of theatre, being the seat profile, the rectangular scaenae frons and the cavea orchestra relation.

Bibliography

BALL, W. 2000: *Rome in the east, the transformation of an empire*, London and New York.

BARLET, J. 1972: "Travaux au théâtre 1969-1972", in J. Balty and J.-C. Balty (eds.) *Apamée de Syrie: Bilan de recherches archéologiques 1969-1972* (Actes du colloque tenu à Bruxelles les 15, 17 et 18 avril), Bruxelles, 143-157.

BIEBER, M. 1961: *History of Greek and Roman Theatres*, Princeton University Press.

MORETTI, J. C. 1997: "Formes et destinations du proskenion dans les théâtres hellénistiques de Grèce," in B. Le Guen (ed.) *De la scène aux gradins. Théâtre et représentations dramatiques après Alexandre le Grand* (Pallas, Revue d'Etudes Antiques 47), Toulouse, 13-39.

RETZLEFF A. 2003: "Near Eastern Theatres in Late Antiquity Source", *Phoenix* 57, 115-138.

ROSSETTO P. C. and SARTORIO G. P. (ed.) 1994: *Teatri Greci e Romani, alle origini del linguaggio rappresentato*, Rome.

SALEH, S. 2009: *Architectural characteristics of ancient theatres in modern Syria, a contribution to a cultural heritage values and conservation*, unpublished Ph.D. dissertation, KU Leuven, Leuven. (promoter Prof. Karel Van Lerberghe – co-promoter Prof. Koen Van Balen).

SEAR, F. 2006: *Roman Theatres An Architectural Study*, Oxford University Press.

SEGAL, A. 1981: "Cities in the Province of Arabia", *The Journal of Architectural Historians* 40, No. 2.

SEGAL, A. 1995: *Theatres in Roman Palestine and Provincia Arabia*, Leiden, New York.

TIBAWI, A. L. 1969: *A modern history of Syria: including Lebanon and Palestine*, London.

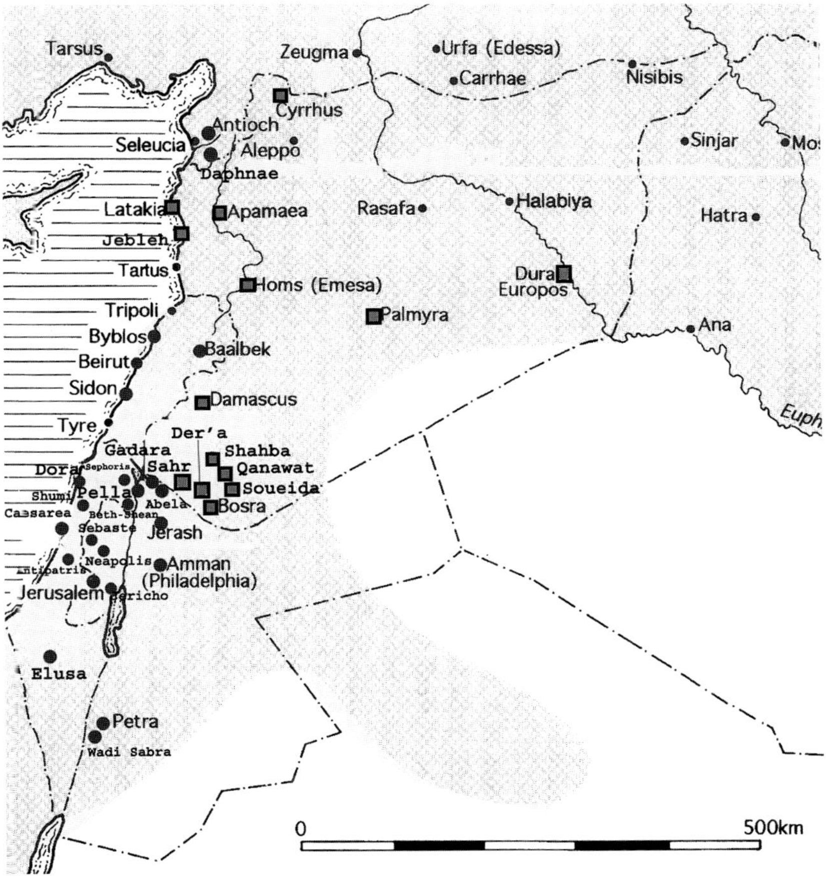
Tarsus
Zeugma
Urfa (Edessa)
Carrhae
Nisibis
Cyrrhus
Antioch
Seleucia
Aleppo
Daphnae
Sinjar
Latakia
Apamaea
Rasafa
Halabiya
Hatra
Jebleh
Tartus
Homs (Emesa)
Dura Europos
Palmyra
Tripoli
Byblos
Ana
Beirut
Baalbek
Sidon
Damascus
Tyre
Der'a
Gadara
Shahba
Dora
Sephoris
Sahr
Qanawat
Shumi
Pella
Soueida
Caesarea
Abela
Bosra
Beth-Shean
Sebaste
Jerash
Neapolis
Amman
Antipatris
(Philadelphia)
Jerusalem
Jericho
Elusa
Petra
Wadi Sabra
0
500km

Fig. 1.

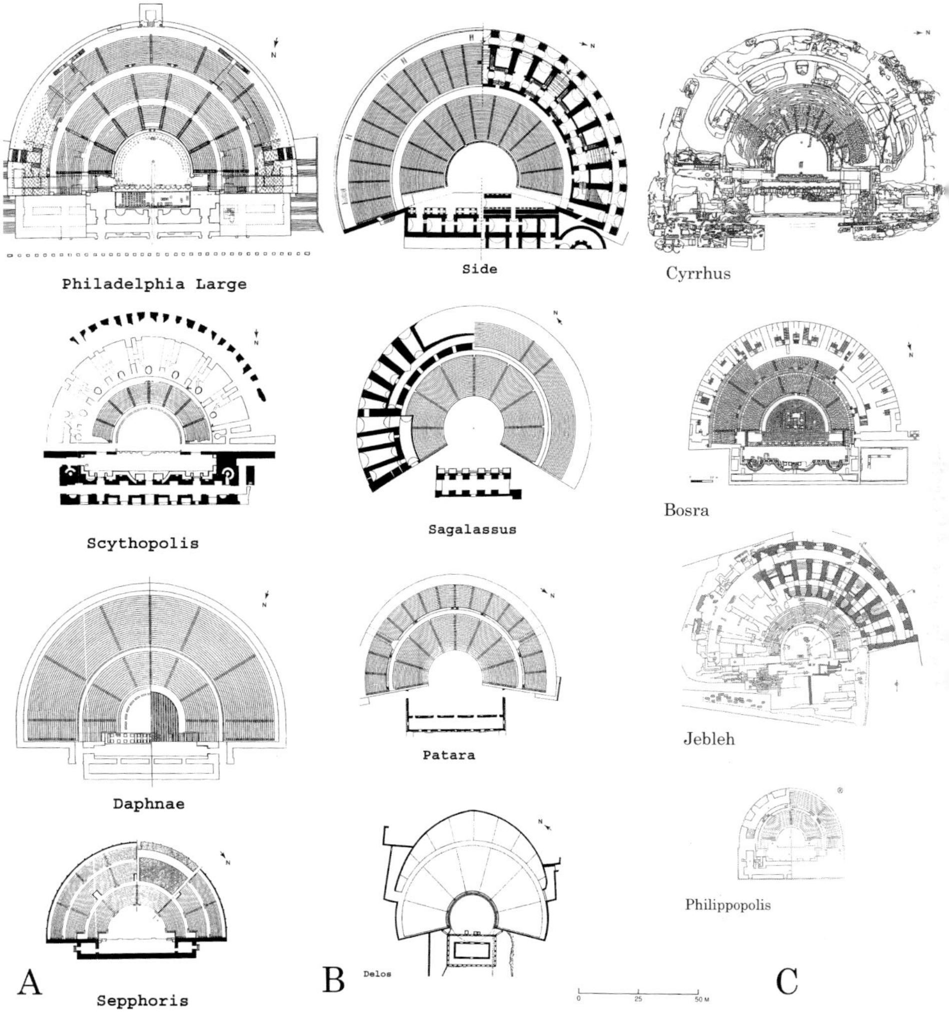
Philadelphia Large
Side
Cyrrhus
Scythopolis
Sagalassus
Bosra
Daphnae
Patara
Jebleh
Philippopolis
A
Sepphoris
B
Delos
0
25
50 M
C

Fig. 2.

The theatres of Palestina

Theatre name	Date	Cavea diameter / size category	Urban type / orientation	Historical background
Caesarea Maritima	Originally Herodian — existing theatre mainly from last quarter of 1st century, few remains of the 2nd and 3rd C. AD	Large - 100 m	Urban – northeast	Built by Herod the Great
Jericho	Late 1st C BC (Herodian)	–	–	Built by Herod the Great
Jerusalem	Completely lost, its existence is known on the basis of literary sources; built by Herod the Great in the 2nd half of the 1st century BC	Probably large	Urban	Built by Herod the Great
Scythopolis (Beth-Shean)	Late 2nd C. – early 3rd C. AD (Severan)	Large - 87 m	Urban – north	Built by the Romans in the Decapolis
Scythopolis (Beth-Shean)	–	Small – 24 m	Bouleuterion – east	Built by the Romans in the Decapolis
Antipatris (Tel Aphek)	360-363 AD	–	–	Built by the Romans (different regions)
Dora	Late 2nd C. – early 3rd C. AD (Severan)	Medium - 60 m	Urban – north	Built by the Romans (different regions)
Sepphoris	Early 1st C. AD, rebuilt in 2nd C. AD	Large – 74 m	Urban	Built by the Romans (different regions)
Mamas (Shumi)	Late 2nd C. – early 3rd C. AD (Severan)	Medium - 60 m	Urban Ritual – east	Built by the Romans (different regions)
Neapolis (Shechem)	1st half of 2nd C. AD	Large - 100 m	Urban – north	Built by the Romans (different regions)
Sebaste (Samaria)	Late 2nd C. – early 3rd C. AD (Severan)	Large - 65 m	Urban – north	Built by the Romans (different regions)

Table 1. The theatres of Palestina.

The theatres of Arabia outside present-day Syria				
Theatre name	Date	Cavea diameter / size category	Urban type / orientation	Historical background
Abela	Late 2nd C. – early 3rd C. AD (Severan)	*Large - 73 m*	*Urban*	Built by the Romans (different regions)
Emmatha	Late 2nd C. – early 3rd C. AD (Severan)	*Medium - 35 m*	*Urban ritual – north*	Built by the Romans (different regions)
Pella	Late 1st C. – early 2nd C. AD	*Medium - 38 m*	*Odeon – southeast*	Built by the Romans (different regions)
Petra	*Early 1st C. AD* (Nabataean)	*Large – 95 m*	*Urban ritual – northeast*	Built by the Nabataeans
Petra	*Late 1st C. – early 2nd C. AD* (Nabataean)	*Medium – 32 m*	*Urban ritual* – southwest	Built by the Nabataeans
Wadi Sabra	*Late 1st C. – early 2nd C. AD* (Nabataean)	*Medium – 39 m*	*Ritual – northwest*	Built by the Nabataeans
Elusa	*Early 1st* C. AD (Nabataean)	*Small - 28 m*	*Urban ritual – north*	Built by the Nabataeans
Philadelphia (Amman)	*2nd half of 1st C. AD, with Antonine additions*	*Large* - 102 m	*Urban – north*	Built by the Romans in the Decapolis
Philadelphia (Amman)	*2nd half of 2nd C. AD (Antonine)*	*Medium – 38 m*	*Odeon – west*	Built by the Romans in the Decapolis
Gadara (north)	*2nd half of 2nd C. AD (Antonine)*	*Large - 80 m*	*Urban – north*	Built by the Romans in the Decapolis
Gadara (west)	Late 2nd C. – early 3rd C. AD (Severan)	*Medium - 55 m*	*Urban – west*	Built by the Romans in the Decapolis
Gerasa (south)	1st C. AD – rebuilt 2nd C. AD	*Large* - 76 m	*Urban – north*	Built by the Romans in the Decapolis
Gerasa (north)	2nd half of 2nd C. AD (Antonine - Severan)	*Medium - 59 m*	*Odeon – north*	Built by the Romans in the Decapolis
Gerasa (birketein)	Late 2nd C. – early 3rd C. AD (Severan)	*Medium – 31 m*	Ritual – east	Built by the Romans in the Decapolis

The theatres of Syria Phoenicia outside present-day Syria				
Theatre name	Date	Cavea diameter / size category	Urban type / orientation	Historical background
Byblus	*Originally Hellenistic, modified in 1st half of 2nd C. AD*	–	–	Had a Hellenistic origin
Sidon	Herodian	–	–	Built by Herod the Great
Beirut	Originally built by Agrippa son of Herod	–	–	Built by son of Herod the Great
Heliopolis	Roman	*Large – approximate 100 m*	*Urban – north*	Built by the Romans (different regions)

Table 3. The theatres of Syria Phoenicia outside present-day Syria

The theatre of modern Hatay (Roman Syria)				
Theatre name	Date	Cavea diameter / size category	Urban type / orientation	Historical background
Antioch	Built by Julius Caesar 1st C. BC; modified in early 1st C. AD	*Probably large*	–	Built by the Romans (different regions)
Daphnae	*Late 1st*C. AD	*Large - 106 m*	*Urban – north*	Built by the Romans (different regions)
DaphnaeNymphaeum	*Hadrianic*	–	*Ritual*	Built by the Romans (different regions)

Table 4. The theatres of modern Hatay.

'*NOTHING SO SWIFT AS CALUMNY*': SLANDER AND JUSTIFICATION AT THE MARI COURT

Jack M. SASSON
Vanderbilt University, Nashville TN

Slander boldly, something always sticks[1]
The eyes of the slanderer always move around as shiftily as a spindle.[2]

Karel will surely know that the title of this paper comes from Cicero, who goes on to say, "Nothing is so swift as *maledictum*; nothing is more easily uttered; nothing more readily received; nothing more widely dispersed".[3] *Maledictum* is calumny. At its lightest it can be a taunt, an insult, meant to belittle; but as it takes on wings and achieves permanence, it slanders and defames. In English there is a large repertoire for this category of words, including defamation, calumny, libel, smear, slur, vilification, maligning, and disparagement. Each term has its own range of meanings, affected by whether it is oral or written, literary or legal. Intent also matters in differentiating between the propagation of malicious untruth and the dissemination of mischievous gossip.

No ancient or modern culture actively advocates defaming and slandering, even if, perniciously enough, the goddess Inanna was said entitled to dispense them.[4] Rather, in ancient records we have repeated remonstrance against practicing it, most often in Wisdom literature, but also in narratives, legal lore, royal edicts, prayers, and penitential or graveyard

[1] "*Audacter calumniare, semper aliquid haeret*"; Francis Bacon, *De dignitate et augmentis scientiarum* (1623), VIII/2. The French proverb, "Calomnions, calomnions, il en restera toujours quelque chose" is often wrongly assigned to a scene in Beaumarchais's *Barbier de Seville*.

[2] The instructions of Šuruppag (c.5.6.1: 65); accessed on January 12, 2012, at http://tinyurl.com/8a5358r.

[3] "Nihil est autem tam voluere, quam maledictum; nihil facilius emittitur; nihil citius excipitur, latius dissipatur"; Marcus Tullius Cicero, *Oratio Pro Cnoeo Plancio* (XXIII). The apothegm is widely cited in compilations of quotations and online.

[4] A hymn to Inana (Inana C): c.4.07.3, "To bestow the divine and royal rites, to carry out the appropriate instructions, slander, untruthful words, abuse, to speak inimically and to overstate are yours, Inana"; accessed on June 15, 2011, at http://etcsl.orinst.ox.ac.uk/section4/tr4073.htm.

confessions.[5] There is also advice not to leave it unchallenged, as well as prayers petitioning for the death of slanderers. One Neo-Assyrian parent, obviously fearing ridicule, names a child Nabu-karṣīya-ubāš, "May Nabu shame my slanderer' (ADD 912 I 3). Something similar may be behind the circumstances that earned a name for the patriarch Isaac (Gen 21:6-7).[6]

If we stay with Mesopotamia, we may notice that its documents provide us with an impressive vocabulary for this sort of tort. The evidence cuts across epochs and dialects, for scorn, slander, mortification, justification, and retaliations are impulses that are much too human to confine to any single period. But they are revealed thicker and juicier when they come from palace archives, especially when time restricted as are those from Mari on the Euphrates. There, many individuals, from kings to lowly administrators, are featured across a number of documents, allowing us a fuller portrayal of personalities and events as well as a rare entry into the emotional state of individuals four millennia removed from us.

In the Mari records, the vocabulary for scorn and slander includes a number of derivatives of *ṭapālum* (*ṭapultum*; *ṭuppulum, muṭappiltum*)

[5] Lore on slander is nicely attested in ancient Near Eastern literature. Sumerian wisdom (Šuruppag and Proverb collections) alerts against slanderers and exposure to potential slander; compiled at http://tinyurl.com/7ojkqhh. We are told that slander finds its way in the holiest places (B. Alster, cited from Hallo and Younger 1997, 564). The same can be said about Akkadian literature. The "Righteous Sufferer" (*ludlul bēl nēmeqi*), finding conspiracy everywhere even in heaven, defends himself against courtiers out to demean him, (B. Foster, cited from Hallo and Younger 1997, 487). In the collections of fables, it is told that "in the presence of a ruler, the maligner (*šaḫšaḫḫû*) speaks hostility, spins cleverly, and avows libel" (Lambert 1960, 218 iv:11-12). In a hymn to Ninurta (Lambert 1960, 119), slanderers are set between adulterers and abusers of the poor.

The vice is fairly represented in Egyptian literature. It is featured categorically among the negative confessions in the *Book of the Dead* (R. Ritner, cited from Hallo and Younger 2000, 60); but denial is normally limited to specific targets, such as when a courtier of Osorkon II claims, "I never slandered anyone to the captain of the land" (B. Porten, cited from Hallo and Younger 2000, 189-190 n. 8.) In his Testament, the Hittite king Ḫattusilis I repeatedly denounces slander and gossip-mongering (G. Beckman, cited from Hallo and Younger 2000, 79-81).

In Hebraic lore, slander (*rěkîlût*, among other terms) is attributed to the dullard (Prov 10:18). The offense is set within other immoral acts (Lev 19:16) and is condemned by the prophets (Jer 6:28, 9:3, Ezek 22:9) as well as by sages (Prov 11:13, 20:19, Ps 34:4). The Aramaic Carpentras stela praises a woman for not uttering disparaging words against anyone (Porten, cited from Hallo and Younger 2000, 189). The idiom used there, *krṣn 'mr*, seems to be a calque of Akkadian *karṣam akālum,* on which see below. See also Dan 3:8, 6:25.

[6] The playful Hebrew is often translated coyly. More likely the aged Sarah is saying, "The Lord has made laughter on me. Anyone hearing about it will laugh at me".

and *nuggurum*, verbs that have to do with insulting an individual.[7] We have the nouns *pištum,* "insult" and *erratum,* a "curse". When used in tandem (as in Gilgamesh, SB vi: 73, 85f) they express a slander that sticks. We frequently meet with *lā šāti* /*la šināti* (CAD Š/3, 40), literally, "not this/these", a phrase trimmed from a fuller expression that applies to pronouncements so vile as to be unworthy of repetition (Durand 1998, 452; note g. to # 704). But most often we meet with the noun *karṣum*, something "pinched or broken off" (*karāṣum*). With the verb *akālum*, "to eat or partake", *karṣum* creates an idiom (*karṣam akālum*) that approximate our notion of "slandering" and "defaming". (Admittedly, it is difficult to account how "eating something that is pinched off" could become "to slander".) As occurs often in Semitics, however, the phrase easily shades its meanings, and it applies also to scorning or ridiculing. In this paper, I group relevant attestations anecdotally rather than exhaustively under the rubrics: **Gifts, Kinship, Rivalry, Loyalty, and Envy**.

Gifts

The exchange of gifts among rulers, their families and administrators is a fairly attractive entry to our topic. In those days, the shuttle of gifts was regulated and formalized. The thought behind a gift mattered much less than a prompt and commensurate response. Gift-giving was a highly staged function, in which diplomats delivered presents worthy of their senders and returned with gifts worthy of their receivers, with some of them meant for themselves to keep. The value of such gifts is calculated by its contents in precious objects rather than by any artistic merit. Heaven forbid should the barter prove to be unequal: Too little would mean scorn;

[7] Note the contrast between *muštāltum* ("thoughtful") and *muṭappiltum* ("contemptuous") in ARM 26 380: 9-10, said of words attributed to Zimri-Addu and Ibal-pi-El; see CAD Ṭ, 48 and below. The noun *ṭapultum* occurs several times (see CAD Ṭ, 50), none as dramatic as when a daughter of Zimri-Lim was said to wield it against her father (ARM 26 312; see below). The fear is that an overlord may give credence to slander, as expressed by Arriyuk (ARM 28 155:10), "Look here, I have been slandered many [text: five] times before my lord. My father believes even when without confirmation (5-*šu ṭaplātiya maḫar abiya iškunūma abī išemme u šutakūnum ul ibašši*)". Ibal-Addu of Ašlakka openly worries that his own suzerain may be spreading the slander (ARM 28 60:37-38), "In the future, my lord must not spread rumor about me (*ana urram šēram bēlī ṭapultī la iqabbi*)". The idiom must not be confused with *awātum lā damiqtum* (hostile words) as in, e.g., LAPO 16 297 (M. 6060):21'; text published by Durand 1991, 50-53.

too much might open a bidding war that can bankrupt. A well-known document will illustrate my observations.

When the great Samsi-Addu of Šubat-Enlil arranged for his son ruling Mari to wed the daughter of Išḫi-Addu of Qatna, he sought to unite two great "Houses". Shortly afterwards, another of his sons, Išme-Dagan of Ekallatum, requested two horses from Qatna.[8] Special breeds of horses were still a rarity, then, fetching about five pounds of silver each. Imagine the shock of Išḫi-Addu when he received just twenty pounds of tin in return. Worth just about two pounds of silver, the yield was one fifth of Išḫi-Addu's investment.[9] Išḫi-Addu first met insult for insult, "How could you be a great king?" he asks. "Without doubt, when you sent this paltry amount of tin, you had no desire to have honorable discourse with me".

The offense was personal; but with ambassadors floating in and out of capitals, its sting will be carried far and wide. "What will anyone hearing this think?" continues Išḫi-Addu, "Will he not disdain us (*ul iṭappalannêti*)?" Išḫi-Addu might have inflated the worth of his beasts; but he felt blameless. "Had you sent me nothing, at all" he lectures, "I would have kept quiet". My notion is that Išme-Dagan did not have the wherewithal to respond in kind; yet he added injury to insult by making exactly the wrong move. However, the state of Išme-Dagan's treasury could not be of concern to Išḫi-Addu: You simply must not run with the pack unless you can maintain full wind. In fact, one of the saddest episodes in the Mari archives has a king (Ibal-Addu of Ašlakka, ARM 28 49) begging his suzerain (Zimri-Lim) to stop offering him presents because shame — and likely also dethronement — await his

[8] Letter King Išḫi-Addu of Qatna to the brother of his son-in-law, then ruling in Mari (ARM 5 20 = Durand LAPO 16 256):

> This matter ought not be discussed; yet I must say it now and vent my feelings. You are the great king. When you placed a request with me for two horses, I indeed had them conveyed to you. But you, you sent me (just) twenty pounds of tin. Without doubt, when you sent this paltry amount of tin, you had no desire to have honorable discourse with me. Had you planned sending nothing at all — By the god of my father! — I would be angry! Among us in Qatna, the value of such horses is six hundred shekels [= ten pounds] of silver. But you sent me just twenty pounds of tin! What would anyone hearing this say? Would he not mock us?
>
> This house is your house. What is lacking in your house that a brother cannot fulfill the need of his equal? Had you not planned to send me any tin, I should not have been in the least upset over it. Are you not the great king? Why have you done this? This house is your house!

[9] For the value of tin, which fluctuated according to relationship with Elam, see most recently Lacambre 2003; Joannès 1993, 99-100.

inability to respond in kind. Even messengers, he whines, are dismissing his gifts as too paltry for honorable acceptance. What is curious about the horse and tin correspondence, too, is that Išḫi-Addu's letter never reached its destination, as it was found in Mari. We can only guess on how well Išḫi-Addu endured the salt of an unanswered letter on an oozing wound.

This anecdote exposes the sensibility that prevailed in Old Babylonian palaces: the world was all ears and eyes, waiting for someone to be slighted, the better to relish the disgrace. A princess sent to Sippar as a *nadītum* is traumatized when her step-mother returns her gift? [10] A diplomat cannot endure the humiliation of not receiving the proper garment when visiting a foreign court.[11] We know of a sad sack (Yašub-El) who felt maligned by a superior (Sin-tiri, a general). His fear is that calumny would stick (verb: *maḫārum*) leading to a loss of face and a loss of

[10] Erišti-Aya, daughter of Zimri-Lim, writes ARM 10 43 = LAPO 18 1202 to her "mother" the queen. She is a *nadītu* in Sippar and feels deeply wounded, "Why did you not wear my garment but returned it, thus heaping on me insult (*pištum*) and injury (*erretum*)?" The paired words also occur in a famous Gilgamesh pun (at VI:73) about eating bread of insult (*pišātu*) and injury (*errētu*).

[11] Feeling insulted and slightest for not getting proper clothing is fairly well represented in the archives. The affront is made personal when the dispatch is done via improper channels. Ibbi-Ilabrat, who writes fawningly to Samsi-Addu in Šubat-Enlil (FM 9 35), is less respectful when addressing Yasmaḫ-Addu (FM 9 33 = ARM 5 76 = LAPO 16 10). He lectures him on for keeping two music specialists when his father has none and then demands worthy garments.

A whole nation may feel insulted when its diplomats are humiliated in foreign courts. A sharp example is in a letter La'um writes to Zimri-Lim (ARM 2 76 = LAPO 16 404). A "scribe of Amurru" (dub.sar mar.tu; ARM 27 151:9-10), and once a governor at Qattunan (FM 2 55-61), La'um headed a diplomatic mission to Babylon during ZL9'. There, he experienced the following (ARM 2 76 = LAPO 16 404):

> We entered to take a meal in Hammurabi's presence, having come into the Palace Court. Just the three of us — Zimri-Addu, I, and Yarim-Addu — were outfitted with garments, but members of the Yamḫad (delegation) that entered with us were all outfitted. As all the Yamḫadians were outfitted, but they did not outfit my lord's servants, the attachés (*ša sikkim*), I told Sin-bēl-aplim (Hammurabi's chief-of-staff) on their behalf, "why do you discriminate among us, as if we were the brood of a sow? Whose servants are we? And whose servants are these attachés? We are the servants of [a leading king], so why would you make right and left hostile (to each other)?" This is what I stressed to Sin-bēl-aplim.
>
> While I was arguing with Sin-bēl-aplim, my lord's servants, the attachés, got angry and stormed out of the Palace Court. Hammurabi was told of the matter and subsequently, (the attachés) were outfitted. Once they were outfitted, Ṭāb-eli-mētim and Sin-bēl-aplim [summoned me] and told me (what) Hammurabi said, "Since early morning, you ceaselessly launch provocative words toward me. Do you imagine now that you can dictate to my palace about garment (distribution)? Who pleases me, I outfit; who does not, I don't. I won't come back (on this): I will not outfit (mere) messengers at banquets!" This is what Hammurabi told me; my lord should know this.

favor (*ina libbim šūṣûm*). He took his case before Samsi-Addu himself (ARM 5 75 = LAPO 16 18), and while he found justification (ARM I 47 = LAPO 16 19), he nevertheless had to leave his post in Harran.[12]

Kinship

In addressing the boorish Išme-Dagan as his "brother", Išḫi-Addu was certainly not trying to mollify him. In our period, kinship contributed key metaphors for diplomacy. Kings are brothers to equals, fathers to vassals, and sons to suzerains. Slipping down the rung any further and they become "servants" (Lafont 2001, 232-238). Usurpers marry the daughters of suzerains, and thus become sons no less than sons-in-law. "The seat of the father" they claim to occupy, therefore, could be that of a sponsor as often as that of flesh and blood. It is all in the family, and we can chart the political fortunes of some rulers by the labels they use when corresponding with their contemporaries. Thus, two decades after insulting Išḫi-Addu with his paltry gifts, we find an Išme-Dagan so weakened that he is forced to address as "father" a ruler he once called his "servant" (compare ARM 26 384:53'-54'; ARM 2 119 = LAPO 16 351). In contrast, when Zimri-Lim of Mari moved up the influence ladder, Hammurabi of Babylon came to be his "brother" rather than "father". On the other hand, Hammurabi of Yamḫad addressed his father's vassal as "father"; but only temporarily, when he succeeded to the throne. From then on, they were "brothers" to each other. The protocol was highly formalized, with harsh retaliation for infraction; for in a world in which thrones are gained by a shrewd selection of sponsor, they can also be lost by impetuously inflating one's status. So when a king of Kurda dares to call Zimri-Lim "brother" rather than "father", the affront could not be left unanswered (Lafont 1994).

Diplomats too had to be sensitive to this finely calibrated protocol. Because they represented kings, diplomats share in the gift-giving and, presumably, the gift-returning, thus becoming wealthier than many local rulers. Before he was eventually proved venal, Sammetar, a *šukkallum* (a counselor) of Zimri-Lim, was highly favored. We have this delicious letter from him begging his lord to take away the palanquin he gave him because all but two kings he was visiting (those of Kurda and Razama) had to make do by travelling on chariots; some, even second quality

[12] On this episode, see Villard 1991, 83-84. Yašub-El found employment in Tuttul, Villard 1991, 87 and 89.

chariots at that. "Now I fear", he writes, "that were I to ride a palanquin, and these kings see (it), they will make a big fuss, saying, '(Is he) like us?'"[13] Sammetar is being modest; he knows he is better than these kinglets; in fact, one convention in the Mari age is that diplomats are but avatars for their kings and so must be treated as representing him bodily.[14] Still, it would not help his mission if blue blood watched him ambulating on the backs of slaves. In fact, it was dangerous. A diplomat (Yaduranum) was reported killed, together with his porters (ARM 26 512), no doubt for parading with *chutzpah*.

Rivalry

In a palace setting, thin skin was the disease of courtiers. It should not surprise us, therefore, that hardly any of its elite were immune from its ravages. Jean-Marie Durand may be right that scandalmongering was practiced by the state as a stimulus for information.[15] I rather think of it, however, as an investment against uncertainty, especially when bureaucrats forced to work together (say a provincial governor and a palace majordomo) reached their posts by different nominating processes, and so held divided allegiances; see Charpin 2010, 51 §1.

Officials and vassals write to seek assurance that the slander has not deceived the king (ARM 2 66 = LAPO 18 1251).[16] They may write

[13] A.868 cited from Arkhipov 2010. Sammetar writes Zimri-Lim,

> About the palanquin that my lord sent me; this palanquin has reached me. My lord has certainly granted me great prestige; the whole land has heard (about it). Yet my lord knows that that the kings of this land where I am about to go — aside from Buna-Ištar (of Kurda) and Šarraya (of Razama) who use a palanquin — they all ride a quality chariot. There are some who even ride an ordinary chariot.
>
> Now I fear that were I to ride a palanquin, and these kings see (it), they will make a big fuss saying, "(Is he) like us? — yet he sent his servant here by having him ride a palanquin!" They will make a big fuss here. Now if it suits my lord, since all the messengers no less than the whole land, have seen this palanquin, I plan to set the palanquin either in Qattunan or Saggaratum. If otherwise, my lord should write me whatever he wishes done.

On Sammetar, see van Koppen (2002). For more on palanquins and their constructions, see Arkhipov 2012, 147-149 and 2009.

[14] On this point, Charpin (2008, 161) cites a text in which the king of Aleppo expects his envoys to be treated as his clones (*kīma pagriya*) and so must not kowtow to Zimri-Lim.

[15] Durand 2010a, 656, "La 'calomnie' (mais peut-être vaudrait-il mieux parler de 'médisance', puisqu'elle doit s'en tenir au 'vrai') est un trait fondamental de la société amorrite, encouragé par l'État et l'on pourrait parler de 'l'art de la délation comme pratique de gouvernement'".

[16] Nigḫatum writes to Zimri-Lim, her 'brother, "I know that you are angry with me. Yatarum has slandered me and you have heeded his words. I have therefore discussed it

protectively, anticipating the slurs that will soon reach the king.[17] If desperate, they might offer bribes to the king's private secretary to rid themselves of a tormentor (ARM 27 36). Habitually, they expect to be slandered by people under their command.[18] So when they write, they expose souls on fire. Kibri-Dagan, governor of Terqa, reports on a crude exposition by a tribal chieftain (Ṣura-ḫammu, a Yaminite) before confessing, "I was ready either to *truss* this man or to pitch him into a ditch. But respect for my lord made me resist touching this man or answer him crudely (*awātum masiktum*). Just the same, this man has offended me, saying vile things to my face" (ARM 3 36 = LAPO 17 704).[19]

Even kings can be caught in this maelstrom. The same Yasmaḫ-Addu who did not appreciate Išḫi-Addu's daughter found himself unfavorably compared to Išme-Dagan, the older brother who had sent tin for Išḫi-Addu's horses. Why is he cavorting with harem women, his father had scolded, when his brother is out conquering cities? In truth, Yasmaḫ-Addu was the sensitive sort. He spoke a cultured Akkadian rather than a commoner's Amorite and had the most wonderful rapport with musicians, who happen to operate in the harems.[20] Naturally, Yasmaḫ-Addu

with Yawi-ila; he may or may not have reported (it) to you. Another matter; I have told my wish to Yawi-ila. In Qaṭna my sheep are depleted. If it is your pleasure, please assign me as many sheep as you could".

[17] I draw this example from the correspondence of Yamsum, Zimri-Lim's diplomat at the court of Ḫaya-Sumu of Ilanṣura (ARM 26 325):

> Kunnaman took along Elamites but did not retain Simat-ḫuluriš. He set him up in Šehna. So the entire area was agitated. All the kings provided their own troops. When troops under my command seized two Elamite informers at the border region, I said "they must make them reach my lord". Whether foe or friend, they must be sent away.
>
> Ḫaya-sumu sent (troops), and when they were brought back from two miles away, he told (me), "Why do you keep acting terribly against the city where I live?" I answered "soldiers on patrol seized the men. Now you can do whatever you want". I had answered him frankly; but right away he deprecated me to my lord when there is absolutely no fault my part. He told me just now, "Go, depart!" But I (said), "I can't leave until my lord writes me". This man is simply not forthright with my lord. My lord should know this. Just now, he has dispatched his troops and a general".

[18] Yakun-urubam, an official in Qattunan, writes Zimri-Lim (FM 2 54), "The town and district are safe. Since the 8th of the month, my lord had charged me to work on the fortification. I began to move earth since the 10th of the month. The work-team, the job having fallen to its members, has complained. Should they slander me, I hope that my lord will not listen. [Remaining lines not clear.]"

[19] See the collations and comments of Durand in his LAPO edition.

[20] The dossier on Yasmaḫ-Addu's attachment to music is published in Ziegler's wonderful 2007 volume. The letter that reveals this king's language limitation is A.3823, published in Ziegler and Charpin 2007, 60-62. The gist is in a quote Yasmaḫ-Addu attributes to his father, Samsi-Addu, "Within three days, I will get busy with taking the census. I will take their census and then come to my lord. My lord had written as follows, 'You will not be able

felt slandered by his palace officials, most of them reporting directly to his father who accused him of extravagance. Besieged, Yasmaḫ-Addu lashes back. To his father, he complains about defamation; to his brother, he warns against a denouncer (Abum-waqar) with an acid (*pariš* — but see CAD P, 180) and cursing tongue (ARM 5 4 = LAPO 16 20). Yasmaḫ-Addu takes his revenge on the informers by making their life miserable. He keeps some in limbo, while others (Mubalsaga) had to sustain his insults for three years running (ARM 1 61 = LAPO 16 35).[21] For good measure, he questions their competence. By doing so, however, he risks provoking defamation against his own protégés.

We have remarkable letters from officials who got caught on opposite ends of this war of nerves.[22] Yasmaḫ-Addu brings to Mari a *Kapellmeister* named Rišiya. Samsi-Addu hears about it and berates his son for appointing someone so unskilled as to result "in the death of music at Mari" (*nārūtum ina Mari uḫtalliq*). Better that another musician (FM 9 13), a native of Mari, be installed there. Smarting from a slur that originated on High, Rišiya wants to argue his competence before the great king himself. Yasmaḫ-Addu fears expansion of feuds and extracts from Rišiya this oath, (FM 9 16), "Even if they bring me out as a clown (*ana ḫuppimma ušeṣṣūninni*)" — he pledges — he will not reveal what he really feels".

But, as they say, "throw enough mud and some will stick", for we have a letter (Ziegler 2007, 17), in which (likely) the same Rišiya is forced to defend his expertise. "...My lord has written me, 'A lion does not plow; he hinders plowmen.'" In answer, Rišiya massages the aphorism, "As for me, have I not done good work in your House? (Therefore), the person who has slandered me is indeed the plowman and the lion who hinders plowmen is me! While I have done well by your House (the slanderer) has ruined the good in your House ever since he came here. When my lord enters Mari in good health, let him test my work and that of the person slandering me; he will promptly realize the good" (ll. 22'-41').

Tarim-šakim is another official who feels "the slings and arrows of outrageous fortune" (*Hamlet*, 3/1) in the war between father and son.

to speak Amorite with them. You ought not to go yourself; but do send La'um, Mut-bisir and Mašum to take census of them'. Is it not enough that I plan to learn to speak Amorite? ... Within days of sending this letter of mine, I shall take the census of the nomads".

[21] On Mubalsaga, majordomo of Yasmaḫ-Addu's estate in Ekallatum, see Villard 2001, 101-107.

[22] The rivalry among musicians is now nicely highlighted in Ziegler 2011, 290-294.

Seeking counsel from a colleague who has not yet been tainted by slurs (Ikun-pi-Sin), Tarim-šakim confides that Yasmaḫ-Addu no longer cites himself as "your lord" when writing, so withholding from him protection and confidence. Rather, he finds himself labeled a *munaggirum*, "a snitch". "Have I snitched on my lord Yasmaḫ-Addu?" he asks. "Have I snitched on a servant of my own class? Is this not a reprehensible accusation? You must know who is slandering me; so do please look into the matter" (ARM 5 34 = LAPO 16 21).[23] Here, we must keep in mind that in a society that depends on scribes for communication, nothing is private and palaces are echo chambers. So to have logged his misery on clay, Tarim-šakim must have been at wits' end. In fact, we know that he gets reassigned, but also that he dies soon afterwards; I expect from wounded pride.

In those circles, we are realizing, there is much investment in exporting malice and good certainty that it will reach its goal. We should likely discriminate between the gossip that titillates the hearers and the slander that destroys careers. Of the former, we have this juicy tidbit, extracted from a diplomat's otherwise sober reports on troop movements, "The wife of Sin-iddinam", he writes to Zimri-Lim, "has made the following attestation, 'Before Sin-iddinam could marry me, I agreed with father and son, so that whenever Sin-iddinam left his home, the son of Asqudum would notify me, 'I want to have you!' He kissed my lips and touched my vagina; but his penis did not penetrate it, for I thought, I will not sin so contemptibly against Sin-iddinam..." (ARM 26 488:29-41).[24]

Loyalty

We have many notices about feeling insulted and slandered, unfortunately not always with the needed details.[25] They tend to feature rivals, whether

[23] On Tarim-šakim see Villard 2001, 22-23. Tarim-šakim dies suddenly, who knows if not from a broken heart? The same letter also question Yasmaḫ-Addu's judgment about another official, Sin-ili.

[24] On this passage, see S. Lafont 1999, 56-59, 248, 268-69, 284-86, 498-99 [text citation], and Sasson 2003, 337-338.

[25] Queen Šiptu feels herself slandered before her brother and had Dadi-ḫadun, a Yaminite king of Abattum and a kin of her husband, defend her. Or so he tells her (ARM 10 156 = LAPO 18 1134):

> I have listened to the message you conveyed to me. I set before Hammurabi (of Yamḫad) a complete account of what you sent me and he seems satisfied. Here is more: I broached the matter by saying, "By Addu, the lord of Halab and (by) the god of your father: a year ago Ḫammi-dadum has ... as follows, saying, 'My lord Hammurabi has written that Šiptu cares little about him.' So I got very angry. On this matter, it is possible that she was slandered in your presence and embittered you

among vassals or within the palace, and since their clashes reach us through correspondence, they invariably involve the king, who is dragged into their wars willingly or otherwise. They couch their diatribes as tests of their loyalty; implying that slander weakens their effectiveness as vassals, advisors, or administrators. So, we must often read their protests of fidelity as a deflection of their true targets. The same Ibal-Addu I have just cited as falling into penury, once tried to control damage in this way (ARM 28 63).[26] He writes to Zimri-Lim:

> How much longer will Šubram keep on sending me such vile notes, ascribing to me unbelievable acts? While I give him advice to improve his lot, he only plots vile action. Just now by his deeds he has encouraged Išme-Addu (of Ašnakkum) to act. He has not yet given up his plans. Instead of collecting soldiers or moving out as a unit when the enemy of our lord (Zimri-Lim) remains whole, he spews insults. Because of his activity, the judgment of the land is hesitant and proceeds without resolution. Once I observed his deed, I decided not to go out of Ašlakka.
>
> Now then, my lord ought to hear his messages before trusting the words he keeps sending me. How much longer will I not be believed in the House of my lord? They certainly have reached me, all those slanders of the past year that have gone to my lord, claiming that 'Ibal-Addu is forcing the country out his control!'... Yet it is I who readily goes to his help. My lord can verify all these statements.

I have cited a good chunk of the letter, because it has all the elements in a classic justification. Ibal-Addu cast himself as a *juste souffrant*. His virtues are sterling: He is loyal, not just to his suzerain, but also to those who do not deserve it. His enemy is the opposite: He lacks civility, is ungrateful, and is a devoted *spinmeister*. He is also devious, using third parties to stir up hostility. Although, the adversary has the gall to boldly promote his lies, Ibal-Addu's faith is in his lord, for that lord cannot be fooled once alerted to injustice and deceit.

Envy

Such appeals to the king to arbitrate parochial disputes occur readily in our archives, with enough variations to keep us interested. I will share

> so". Said Hammurabi, "This is true: She was slandered in my presence and I got angry with her". So I have now appeased him and there is now no offence whatsoever. As I have taken up your cause, may Šamaš take up mine.

On this passage, see Wasserman 2012, 23-24.

[26] The apothegmatic nature of the final lines (36-37) is highlighted in Durand 2006, 12, 17.

two of them. They both feature magnates with impressive influence and showcase classic issues: Envy, self-promotion, quarrels over trivia, obsessive self-justification, and never ending quests for rewards. Let me focus first on the clash between Bannum and Asqudum.

Bannum and Asqudum

No tribal leader was more influential than Bannum, a Sim'alite *merḫum* — a tribal chieftain. There is reason to give him credit for capturing Mari before handing it to Zimri-Lim, who was then still in the Balikh area.[27] If so, it explains why Bannum writes bracing, even offensive, letters to Zimri-Lim. His vitriol targets many, but his chief nemesis is Asqudum, a diviner imported from Ekallatum in the days of Yasmaḫ-Addu.[28] For an outsider, Asqudum had prospered nicely, even marrying a daughter of a preceding king, Yaḫdun-Lim. Such unions with ex-nobility allowed reigning monarchs — often usurpers with minimal deference to the fallen dynasty — to reward mid-level careerists without bringing them too close to the ruling family. Nevertheless, his presence rankled the natives, among them elite administrators (La'um, Sin-iddinam, Šamaš-tillassu), who protested that no one was safe from his slander (ARM 26 4; ARM 2 28 = LAPO 17 830). It was a defensive tactic on their parts, for diviners were instrumental in consulting the gods on crucial affairs of state, including personnel decisions (Durand 2010a). True, most kings had a stable of diviners for such enterprises, and there were always ways to restructure questions and answers so that they end up matching preferred responses; but a clever and persuasive diviner can go far at court, especially when willing to rise on the corpses of rivals.

Asqudum was a survivalist and his fortunes soared on accession of Zimri-Lim, for he was now married to a sister (full or otherwise) of the new king. In those days of revolving thrones, mid-rank administrators generally retained their posts even as their patrons lost their heads. Outraged at the honors heaped at Asqudum, Bannum minces no words, "Can it be good that Asqudum keeps setting before you vile things and that you keep listening to him?" he asks the king. Bannum resents Asqudum's ability to charm the king into trusting him to rule a major town (Ḫišamta)

[27] On Bannum, see Villard 1994, 291-297 and Heimpel 1997, 68-70. Bannum's boldness is obvious from his cylinder seal where he is "Baninum [a variant of Bannum] of Mulḫan, servant of Yaḫdun-lim, who reinstated Yaḫdun-Lim's line".

[28] On Asqudum, fundamental is the dossier gathered by Durand in ARM 26/1. There is also now the nice study of Charpin 2011, where is reviewed the previous literature.

and into placing his buddy as its manager. "Asqudum", continues Bannum, "(was once) my own prisoner; but (now) he plots evil in his heart". Bannum's advice is blunt: Asqudum heads a fifth column, ready to surrender Mari to Zimri-Lim's enemy, Išme-Dagan (our tin man). At the very least, the king must select a diviner from the king's own tribe (Sim'al) in whom to confide (ARM 26 5).

Asqudum's response to Bannum's charges has not survived. But he was known to wield an acid tongue when defending his own turf (ARM 26 74).[29] In one developed case (A.337+M.8290, Durand 2010b), a merchant reports on Asqudum's uncouth behavior: He accepts gifts greedily but does not return them and his trading practices are judged so lamentable that they must be appealed before the emblems of the gods. Still, for the duration, Asqudum's life was charmed, for his nemesis Bannum died soon after posting his charges. Yet, even as Zimri-Lim was reading Bannum's indictment, he was entrusting Asqudum with some very delicate negotiations, among them brokering his marriage with Princess Šiptu, the daughter of the area's most powerful ruler, King Yarim-Lim of Aleppo. Asqudum continued to prosper before he drowned in a boating incident midway in Zimri-Lim's reign (ARM 14 4 = LAPO 18 1019).[30] We might imagine that by his brutal end the gods were signaling major disappointment with him; but when the palace acted on his vast estate, there is no hint that his misfortune was read as an infraction against king or god.

Zimri-Addu and Ibalpiel

The other cosmic rivalry pitted two old hands in Zimri-Lim's court. One was Zimri-Addu, a high official at Qaṭṭunan by the Ḫabur River, a man with proven administrative skills, but also with a history of contentiousness. He was believed to snitch on colleagues (ARM 27 117), to

[29] Writes Asqudum to Yassi-Dagan:

I have heard the tablet you have sent to me. You said, "People from Mišlan approached the king with the complaint, Asqudum is holding (our land)'". Much as a dog does not covet gold, I myself do not covet their field or (anything belonging) to them. As to you, why are you making problems before the king? You know well how unruly are their people. Now then, about the fields in Zarri on which you wrote me. Ṣura-ḫammu is now with the king and speaks (to him) whatever is on his mind. He has now accepted half of what is in the storeroom of the Multicolor Court just for the asking!

[30] Charpin (2011, 264), follows Durand in allotting his death to another Asqudum; yet Durand himself seems to have fudged his position in LAPO 18, pp. 190 and 239. Lion (2001, 148-149 n. 38) recognizes the existence of just one major player named Asqudum.

undercut trusted officers (ARM 27,108–109; 137–138), and to act impetuously (ARM 27: 116).[31] Not surprisingly, Zimri-Addu feels himself despised: "No one wants to approach me", he writes to his king, "and when I go out, no one joins me. Destitute, I move about like a cursed man" (ARM 27 151:100-102). So, with an ego to compensate for perceived snubs, Zimri-Addu was not a man to dodge a fight or to avoid the gutter.

Unfortunately for him, his chosen nemesis was one of Zimri-Lim's most trusted lieutenants, the *merḫum* Ibalpiel. Ibalpiel has left many letters written in an engaging prose, at once chatty and precise, with fine humor and irony. Ibalpiel was competent, a take-charge person who, like Karel, was also a fine reader of history; in fact, he was the first to describe the domino effect in regional politics.[32] Yet he was also stubborn and vainglorious, and the object of numerous complaints by diviners (ARM 26 101), commanders (ARM 26 380), and diplomats (ARM 26 126), who resented the way he clogged access to the king (ARM 27 137).

Zimri-Addu and Ibalpiel clashed when Zimri-Lim inexplicably assigned them both to lead one of four major contingents assisting Hammurabi in his war against Larsa. Zimri-Addu was to lead troops recruited from the main urban centers and Ibalpiel those of nomadic background. We have a nice comment (ARM 26 380) about their dispute by third party. Himself a lieutenant of Ibalpiel, Šarrum-ṣulūlī felt the need to alert the king about their conflict, allegedly because it displayed Mari negatively but likely also to broadcast his own good sense.[33] The two men exchanged

[31] See my portrait of Zimri-Addu in Sasson 2010.

[32] A.2119 = LAPO 17 442 is published in Charpin 1992. Writes Ibal-pi-el to Zimri-Lim,

> I have heard about the release of Yariḫa-abum from the (control of the) ruler of Ešnunna. My lord knows how full of deceit that House is. I fear that until it captures Andariq, it will keep my lord completely duped (*ruttumma uratta*). But as soon as it seizes Andariq, it will aim for Kurda. Subsequently, it will cross Mount Saggar [Sinjar], and all of Šubartum will shout 'Hail, my Lord' to it. This House is beginning to behave as did Samsi-Addu in progressively resetting his frontier. Seizing Ekallatum, it will [*move*] toward Qaṭṭara and Allaḫad. Once it seizes a town, it forces it under its control. This House is indeed full of deceit. Now before the burden becomes too heavy to bear, time is near when we must move against him. The Ḫana-nomads are eager for battle; the rulers of Idamaraṣ are gathered, together with their armies, and look only toward my lord for help. The royal agents (*sugāgū*) are gathered and have sent Anniti-El and Ḫanzan to my lord. My lord should consult with his servants and decide on heading here.

[33] His name is usually read Šarrum-andulli, but see Stol 1991, 193. Šarrum-ṣulūlī prided himself for knowing all that happens in Hammurabi's palace; see ARM 26 381:9.

charges (*muštālātum*) and insults (*muṭappilātum*) publically, endangering the mission. According to Šarrum-ṣulūlī, Ibalpiel browbeats officers and threatens to cut off their rations. In turn, these officers give distorted grievances to Zimri-Addu, who eagerly endorses their complaints.

That Šarrum-ṣulūlī was not exaggerating is confirmed by a long, incendiary letter Zimri-Addu wrote to catalogue his peeves against his rival (ARM 27: 151). The litany of grievance is long, mingling Ibalpiel's crimes against Zimri-Addu and against the palace. These include his illegitimate control (placing his seal) of the roster of recruits (ll. 5-17); his humiliation of Zimri-Addu (ll.18-23); his concealment of a report on missing soldiers (ll. 23-31); his launching of insults (32-41); his defiance of the king's military orders (42-68); his charging Zimri-Addu with theft (69-81), and his humiliation of nomadic troops (82-95). All these charges are distilled in a repeat at the tail end of the letter. If this were not enough, Zimri-Addu posted another letter (ARM 27 152), this time citing his humiliation at receiving lesser allocations than others. Incredibly, he reveals that he vented his frustration first to Ibalpiel. Either we are missing something, or Zimri-Addu is missing it all.

Ibalpiel, too, has left us his opinion (ARM 2 31 = LAPO 17 591). He opens on how Hammurabi consults with him on all matters, underscoring how other kings also esteem his judgment. Zimri-Addu, he claims, has no courage to discipline armies bent on looting, yet he still plots to subvert Ibalpiel's authority. "My lord should write to Zimri-Addu", he advises. "He may set (him) or remove him. As for me, I need for palace matters to be resettled, so that I could be ready at the time of the battle and assign the troops as best I know. Otherwise, this man will turn against me the army's opinion and I will not manage to have full security. I am now writing my lord for him to be fully aware. This man is turning the army's opinion against me, causing me much trouble. As far as I can observe, the army's opinion has already turned against me. My lord's army is safe".

Unlike the animosity between Bannum and Asqudum that ended with heaven giving it a merciful conclusion, recovering how matters turned out for Zimri-Addu and Ibal-pi-El is not yet within our grasp. Their dispute played out at the tail end of Zimri-Lim reign; but as far as I know they both outlasted their king, disappearing from our view. We do not read in the archives about any disciplinary measure taken against either of them. Perhaps Zimri-Lim had read them both correctly as overblown egos; yet he knew them to do his bidding just the same.

A Final notice

In this article, I have proposed that slander and scorn were deemed fair weapons by partisans and grave ethical lapses by victims. They must be deflected if not fought, confronted early rather than late, and tackled directly or through third party. Yet we have indications that they were also judged immoral if not sinful, with heaven as their arbitrator. A recently published protocol of oaths taken by Zimri-Lim's court officials opens on a pledge not to speak slander (*ṭapultī*), before moving to such mundane infractions as spying, subverting, betraying, looting, and stealing.[34] Bizarre for us to consider is the ordeal reported by a governor (A.1890) involving Aštabi-El, a deity treated as a venerated ancestor. An accusation was made and, to arrive at the truth, Aštabi-El's statue is laid out prone, with two experts conducting the interrogation.[35] How to explain the proceedings escapes me; luckily the denunciation proved false. Nonetheless, the god opted to let the slanderer go unpunished, vexing the governor who took matters in his own hands.

The clearest testimony for divine displeasure, however, is reported by a diplomat (Yamsum) at the court of vassal. Ḫaya-sumu of Ilanṣura had married Šimatum, one of Zimri-Lim's daughters. In their controlled world and far from Mari, the couple was acting beyond the pale, tormenting a loyal supporter of the king. The diplomat discloses the outrage, then adds (ARM 26 312:36'-39'; see CAD Ṭ, 50), "Another matter; about Šimatum who so slanders my lord (*ṭaplāt bēliya idabbubu*) that my lord faced God on her account, the god of my lord mutilated her fingers and epilepsy is plaguing her"). Here we reconstruct a series of allegations: a daughter who spread lies against a father, a father who makes divine inquiry to locate the source and dimension of the slander, and the proof of her guilt. Yet, because we also know about the circumstances, which involved the rejection of a sister of Šimatum married to the same vassal (Kirum), we might wonder whether the judgment of this diplomat was swayed by sympathy for the other princess no less than by indignation at the mistreatment of a colleague.

This little episode from the domestic life of Mari elite, with slander, accusation, and punishment as main ingredients, is a good place on which to end this paper. I have not sought to spice it by parallels with what might occur in own world, the academia and professional societies we

[34] Charpin 2010, 51 (§1). The clause is clear despite heavy damage.
[35] Text cited in Durand 2008, 456.

all know and love. Yet I dare hope that envy, malice, calumny, and distortions have never entered the universe of Karel, an old friend to whom I offer this study.

Bibliography

ARKHIPOV, I. 2009: "Nouveaux textes sur la fabrication de palanquins à Mari", *RA* 103, 31-36.

— 2010: "Les véhicules terrestres dans les textes de Mari. I. *le nūbalum*", in L. Kogan et al. (eds.) *Languages in the Ancient Near East* (Proceedings of the 53e RAI; Vol. 1, 2), Winona Lake, IN, 405-420.

— 2012: *Le vocabulaire de la métallurgie et la nomenclature des objets en métal dans les textes de Mari* (Archives Royales de Mari, 32; Matériaux pour le Dictionnaire de Babylonien de Paris, 3), Leuven.

CHARPIN, D. 1992: "De la vallée du Tigre au 'triangle du Ḫabur': Un engrenage géopolitique", in J.-M. Durand (ed.) *Recherches en Haute Mésopotamie. Tell Mohammed Diyab. Campagnes de 1990 et 1991* (Cahiers de NABU 2), Paris, pp. 97-102.

— 2008: "Chroniques bibliographiques 11. Se faire un nom: la louange du roi, la divinisation royale et la quête de l'immortalité en Mésopotamie", *RA* 102, 149-180.

— 2010: "Un nouveau 'protocole de serment' de Mari", in S. C. Melville and A. L. Slotsky (eds.) *Opening the Tablet Box: Near Eastern Studies in Honor of Benjamin R. Foster* (CHANE 42), Leiden, 51-77.

— 2011: "Patron and Client: Zimri-Lim and Asqudum the Diviner", in K. Radner and E. Robson (eds.) *The Oxford Handbook of Cuneiform Culture*, Oxford, 248-269.

DURAND, J.-M. 1991: "Précurseurs syriens aux protocoles néo-assyriens. Considérations sur la vie politique aux Bords-de-l'Euphrate", in D. Charpin and F. Joannès (eds.) *Marchands, diplomates et empereurs: études sur la civilisation mésopotamienne, offertes à Paul Garelli*, Paris, 13-72.

— 1997-2000: *Documents épistolaires du palais de Mari*, 1-3 (Littératures anciennes du Proche-Orient 16-18), Paris = LAPO 16 (1997); 17(1998); 18 (2000).

— 2006: "Dictons et proverbes à l'époque amorrite", *Journal asiatique* 294, 3-38.

— 2008: "La religion amorrite en Syrie à l'époque des archives de Mari", in G. del Olmo Lete (ed.) *Mythologie et Religion des Sémites Occidentaux, I: Ébla, Mari* (Orientalia Lovaniensia Analecta 162), Leuven, 163-716.

— 2010a: "Pouvoir et divination", *Annuaire* 109e année, Collège de France, Paris, mars 2010, 643-667; accessed on February 12, 2012 at http://annuaire-cdf.revues.org/181.

— 2010b: "Des dieux, un ministre et un coquin", in D. Shehata et al. (eds.) *Von Göttern und Menschen. Beiträge zu Literatur und Geschichte des Alten Orients: Festschrift für Brigitte Groneberg* (Cuneiform monographs 41), Leiden, 63-71.

HALLO, W. W. and K. L. YOUNGER (eds.) 1997-2003: *The Context of Scripture* (1, 1997; 2, 2000; 3, 2003), Leiden.

HEIMPEL, W. 1997: "Disposition of Households of Officials in Ur III and Mari", *Acta Sumerologica* (Japan) 19, 63-82.

JOANNÈS, F. 1993: "Metalle und metallurgie, A", *RlA* 8, 96-112.

KOPPEN, F. VAN 2002: "Seized by Royal Order: The Households of Sammêtar and other Magnates at Mari", *Florilegium Marianum* 6, 289-372.

LACAMBRE, D. 2003: "La région du Suḫûm (Moyen-Euphrate) et le commerce de l'étain à l'époque de Mari", NABU 2003/#29, 27-28.

LAFONT, B. 1994: "L'admonestation des anciens de Kurdâ à leur roi", in D. Charpin and J.-M. Durand (eds.) *Recueil d'études à la mémoire de Maurice Birot* (*Florilegium marianum* 2; Mémoires de N.A.B.U. 3), Paris, 209-230.

— 2001: "Relations internationales, alliances et diplomatie au temps des royaumes amorrites. Essai de synthèse", *Amurru* 2, 213-328.

LAFONT, S. 1999: *Femmes, droit et justice dans l'antiquité orientale* (Orbis biblicus et orientalis 165), Fribourg.

LAMBERT, W. G. 1960: *Babylonian Wisdom Literature*, Oxford.

LION, B. 2001: "Les gouverneurs provinciaux du royaume de Mari à l'époque de Zimri-Lîm", *Amurru* 2, 141-209.

SASSON, J. M. 2003: "Forcing Morals on Mesopotamian Society?" in G. Beckman et al. (eds.) *Studies in Honor of Harry A. Hoffner Jr., on the Occasion of his 65th Birthday,* Winona Lake, IN, 329-340.

— 2010: "Where Angels Fearlessly Tread: Mari Insights on Genesis 19", in L. Kogan et al. (eds.) *Languages in the Ancient Near East* (Proceedings of the 53e RAI; Vol. 1, 2), Winona Lake, IN, 1163-1183.

STOL, M. 1991: "Old Babylonian Personal Names", *Studi epigraphici e linguistici* 8, 191-212.

VILLARD, P. 1994: "Nomination d'un Scheich", in D. Charpin and J.-M. Durand (eds.) *Recueil d'études à la mémoire de Maurice Birot* (*Florilegium marianum* 2; Mémoires de N.A.B.U. 3), Paris, 291-234.

— 2001: "Les administrateurs de l'époque de Yasmaḫ-Addu", *Amurru* 2, 9-140.

WASSERMAN, N. 2012: *Most Probably: Epistemic Modality in Old Babylonian*, Winona Lake, IN.

ZIEGLER, N. 2007: *Les Musiciens et la musique d'après les archives de Mari* (*Florilegium Marianum* 9; Mémoires de NABU 10), Paris.

— 2011: "Music, the Work of Professionals", in K. Radner and E. Robson (eds.) *The Oxford Handbook of Cuneiform Culture*, Oxford, 288-312.

ZIEGLER, N. and D. Charpin: 2007: "Amurritisch Lernen", *WZKM* 97 (= *Festschrift für Hermann Hunger zum Gerburtstag gewidmet von seinen Freunden, Kollegen und Schülern*), 55-77.

THE AMBIGUITY OF ENJOYMENT IN QOHELETH*

Antoon SCHOORS
KU Leuven

Sometimes Qoheleth is called a "Preacher of Joy", for example by Whybray (1982), and in more recent commentaries and monographs I see a tendency to endorse that opinion. Thus Fischer (1997, 74-86; esp. 79) wonders whether Qoheleth considers joy as a narcotic or as God's fundamental answer to man's toilful existence: "Die Freude als Narkotikum oder als Antwort Gottes?" He is convinced that the second alternative is the correct one and that the recommendation of joy takes a central position in the theology of this book and must not be understood as a recommendation of a sour-sweet *carpe diem*. The Korean Exegete Pahk has given the lofty and theologically charged title "Il canto della gioia in Dio" to his book on Qoh 8,16-9,10, and already in his introduction he explains what he means by that: "Il 'canto della gioia' consente, infatti, di reperire, accanto di una forma di severo realismo, quello que a noi pare essere il contenuto effettivo dalla reflessione qoheletiana" (1996, 2). Such interpretations, of course, appeal to Christian readers who are familiar with some prophetical invitations to joy or with the importance of the theme of joy in some pericopes of Paul's letters, and they make of Qoheleth an interesting and exciting subject for preaching. But, is that really so? The fact that the use of Qoheleth in liturgy is limited to the extreme and that, at least according to my experience, the book is not often dealt with in sermons, raises questions about the message of that book being full of joy.

Seven times Qoheleth recommends enjoyment: in 2,24-25; 3,12-13. 22; 5,17-19; 8,15; 9,7-9; 11,8. This so-called sacred number might point out the importance of those recommendations, and, no doubt, they play an important part in the book. But, if we want to understand the sayings correctly, we must ask ourselves how they function in their context.

* This is a revised and updated version of an article which was published in Italian: "L'ambiguità della gioia in Qohelet", in G. Bellia and A. Passaro (eds.), *Il libro del Qohelet. Tradizione, redazione, teologia*, Milano 2001, 276-292. I am happy to offer it as a modest contribution to this *Festschrift* in honour of Karel Van Lerberghe, whom I highly appreciate as a very competent colleague and a friend.

When we look at the wording carefully, a number of features catch the eye. Although four of those sayings begin with the same words, literally "there is nothing good/better" (אין טוב), they, nevertheless, do not say exactly the same thing. The Hebrew text of Qoh 2,24 does not say "There is nothing better for a human than that he should eat and drink..." (*RSV*)[1], but אין־טוב באדם שׁיאכל ושׁתה, which means "It is not a good that good that is in (the power of) man that he should eat and drink", and this is confirmed further, where Qoheleth continues saying "it is from the hand of God". The translation which sticks to the Masoretic text, has been defended by such critics as Thilo, Tur-Sinai, Müller and Lohfink[2]. However, the *RSV* version of 2,24 tallies with 3,12: "I know that there is nothing better for them than to be cheerful and to enjoy themselves as long as they live"; 3,22: "I saw that there is nothing better than that man should enjoy (the fruits of) his work"; 8,15: "There is nothing better for man under the sun than to eat, drink and enjoy himself". In a non-comparative manner Qoh 5,17 says the same thing, viz. "that it is becoming to eat and drink and to enjoy the good things". All this makes it likely that also for 2,24 the first mentioned interpretation is the correct one, the more so that it is supported by the Peshitta, — normally a literal translation — and the Targum, and that the MT reading can be explained by haplography of the *mem*.

In 9,7-9 the introduction with "good" or "better" is lacking. It is a more detailed and direct exhortation, almost like a short poem, in which a number of pleasures are listed:

7 Come, eat your bread with enjoyment
and drink your wine with a merry heart;
for God is already favourable to your works.
8 Let your garments be white at all times
and let not oil be lacking on your head.
9 Enjoy life with a woman you love
all the days of your absurd life
which God gives you under the sun
during your absurd days.
For that is your portion in life
and in your toil at which you toil under the sun.

[1] Reading משׁיאכל instead of שׁיאכל; LXX supports MT: οὐκ ἔστιν ἀγαθὸν ἐν ἀνθρώπῳ ...; but the reading adopted by the *RSV*, is found in the Peshitta: ܠܝܬ ܕܛܒ ܠܒܪܢܫܐ ܐܠܐ ... and in the Targum: ... לית דשפיר בני אנשא אלהין.

[2] Thilo 1923, 33: "Nicht ein dem Mensch anhaftendes Gut ist es..."; Tur-Sinai 1968, 155: "אין זה ניתן בידי האדם שיראה טוב בחיים, אלא מיד האלהים הוא"; Müller 1968, 511; Lohfink 1980, 30.

The shorter exhortations can be seen as a summary of this poem. All of these sayings deal with eating, drinking, dressing, a woman, the good things (טוב[ה]), wealth and property. Therefore it is wrong to translate here the Hebrew root שׂמח by "happiness, be happy" or "joy, be joyous". The only correct rendering is here "enjoy" and "pleasure". Fox (1999, 115) adduces a few other convincing arguments in support of this view. Among other things, he states that Qoheleth himself had a great deal of שִׂמְחָה, as he testifies (2,10), but little happiness, as he shows. He also underlines that Qoheleth could not reasonably call happiness or joy inane, absurd and unproductive (2,1-2).

Two words in vs. 9 of the short poem 9,7-9 deserve particular attention עמל, "toil" and חֶלְקְךָ, "your portion". The latter will be elaborated on farther down. As for the first word, we see that enjoyment takes place "in your toil". The Hebrew preposition ב has a very broad range of meaning. The expression בעמלךָ can be understood as "at your toiling, while you are toiling", but it may also express means or instrument: "with/through your toiling", or the price or remuneration: "(in return) for your toil", or it may have a concessive force: "in spite of your toiling". It is striking that this expression returns a few times in the enjoyment sayings, viz. in Qoh 2,24; 3,13; 5,17-18; 8,15. According to the last cited text enjoyment will accompany man in his toil. That means that enjoyment is a help or support in toil, it lightens the burden or counterbalances it.

"Toil" (עמל) is a key word in Qoheleth: the verb occurs 22 times and the noun 13 times. The verb usually means "to work hard", whereas next to "hard labour" the noun may also refer to the result or profit of work, i.e possessions or wealth, and further to the strains of life in general[3]. As we have seen, in 8,15 עמל means toiling and even life's strains in general, and there is no reason why this would not be the case in the other texts mentioned. Therefore the sour-sweet interpretation of the enjoyment sayings cannot be excluded at all.

But we have to take a step further and look into the question of where Qoheleth precisely puts his exhortations to enjoyment. Qoh 2,24-25 is at the conclusion of the so-called royal fiction (Qoh 1,12-2,26), in which the author takes the guise of king Solomon. When at the end of this section he considers his search for wisdom, he arrives at clearly negative conclusions: in the end there is no difference between the fate of the wise

[3] Cf. Fox 1999, 97-102, esp. 101: "The scope of *'amal* is so broad in Qohelet that life's experiences in general can be subsumed under this heading".

person and that of the fool, since they both die (2,15). He hates life, for all its toil and burden leads to nothing (2,17-23). All his explorations again and again lead to the conclusion that "all is absurdity and vexation"[4]. After that follows the surprising saying "There is nothing better for a man than that he should eat and drink..." (2,24).

Qoh 3,12-13 follows after the catalogue of times and the following considerations on man's toiling. I cannot enter at length into the question what עלם in vs. 11 means and whether it is not a corruption of עמל, "toil" (this reading has been adopted by Ginsberg 1961, 74; Tur-Sinai 1968, 157; Fox 1999, 211). Whatever the solution to this problem, in vs. 9 the author speaks of toil that does not yield profit, and there is a failure in the fact that man cannot fathom what God does from beginning to end, i.e. in its totality. However, MT עלם is already attested in all ancient versions (LXX: τὸν αἰῶνα; Vg: *mundum*; Pesh: ܥܠܡܐ; Tg: עלמא). And in this context it can be understood as follows: God has put in the heart, i.e. in the cognitive faculty, of humankind a desire of insight into the unlimited time, in other words into all that happens from the remote past to the distant future, into the divine foundation of creation, but humans cannot fully fathom God's work. It remains completely opaque and people cannot do anything about it.

Verse 3,22 is the conclusion of a musing about death, in which man and animal are equal. This shows the absurdity of the whole course of life. "Individual existence is absurd, because all distinctions in life, even the difference between humans and other creatures, are obliterated" (Fox 1989, 197). Therefore nothing is better than that man should enjoy (the fruit of) his work, for who can bring him to enjoy[5] what will come after him?

[4] The correct translation of הבל is not "vanity", but in a few verses it means "ephemeral", for example in 11,10 "youth is *hebel*", and possibly in 6,12; 7,15; 9,9 "life of *hebel*" or "days of *hebel*". But in most of the texts it means "absurdity" in the sense this word has in existentialist philosophy: it refers to a disparity between two phenomena that are thought to be linked by a bond of harmony or causality but are actually disjunct or even conflicting. Absurdity arises from a contradiction between two undeniable realities. Absurdity means that one has the feeling that ideas, visions, convictions do not tally with the reality as it is experienced. Cf. Fox 1986, 409-427; 1989, 29-48; 1999, 30-42; further: Barucq 1968, *passim*; Michel 1989, 40-51; Lavoie 1992, 207-221.

[5] In Qoheleth, ראה ב or ראה טוב mean "enjoy", which is also the case here in 3,22 (cf. 2,1.24; 5,17; 6,6.9; 11,9). This has been remarked by the translators of the *RSV* and a long series of commentators, such as Ginsburg, Thilo, Whybray, Whitley, Strobel, Braun, Galling, Lauha, Podechard, Barton, Gorssen, Aalders, Buzy, Gordis, Wildeboer, Michel, Fox. Cf. Schoors, 1996, 228-230.

The somewhat more expanded exhortation of Qoh 5,17-19 concludes a pericope in which a grievous evil comes up, namely when stored up wealth is lost in an unfortunate business, so that the rich owner cannot leave behind anything for his offspring. At his death he can take nothing with him and also during his lifetime he goes through bad days. It is therefore becoming to eat and drink, to experience enjoyment in all one's toil. Qoheleth concludes this with an important consideration: "For then he will not much remember, — i.e. call to mind — the days of his life, because God keeps him occupied with his heart's pleasure". A number of scholars parse מענה as a hif. participle of ענה I, "answer", here in the sense of "answer for", hence "provide"[6]. But there is not one single uncontested attestation of the hif. of this verb in the Bible, and the root ענה III, "busy oneself", is typical of Qoheleth (cf. 1,13; 3,10 and the key word ענין , "business, occupation" in 1,13; 2,23. 26; 3,10. 4,8; 5,2. 13; 8,16). Therefore, and because it completely fits the context, it is beyond doubt that this is the root which is used in 5,19[7]. In other words, God, who imposes on humankind quite a few bad occupations (Qoh 1,13; 2,23. 26; 3,10-11; 4,8), here gives him the occupation of enjoying pleasure, in order that he may less call to mind his days. Qoheleth praises pleasure for keeping one's mind off the brevity of life or its frustrations. This, of course, means that enjoyment is meant as an antidote or a narcotic and that with "the days of his life" are meant the bad days. With enjoyment God allows man a great gift: oblivion (Fox 1999, 239).

The same idea is expressed in another way in Qoh 11,8: "Now even if a man live many years, he should take pleasure in them all, and remember that the days of darkness are many. All that comes is absurdity" (Fox). Since vs. 7 says that it is sweet and good to see the sun, in other words, to live, the days of darkness no doubt refer to death. If one thinks of death, he is urged to enjoy life and so divert his thougths from death. Here too, enjoying pleasure is a narcotic. This is repeated in a somewhat different key in the continuation of the text. The exhortation is addressed to a young man: "Rejoice, young man, in your youth, and let your heart

[6] E.g. Elster 1855, 90; Gordis 1951, 246; cf. Jastrow 1919, 219, who understands it in the sense that God approves of joy, litterally "God answers the joy of his heart".

[7] Cf. LXX: περισπᾷ αὐτόν; Pesh: ܡܥܢܐ ܠܗ; Rankin, 1956, 60; Müller 1968, 517; Lauha 1978, 108; Whitley 1979, 56; Whybray 1989, 103; Fox, 1999, 240. The emendation of מענה to מענהו, based on LXX and Pesh and suggested by *BHS*, Gordis, Lauha, Whitley, Fox and others, is not necessary. LXX and Pesh explicitly render the direct object, which is implicit in the MT.

give you cheer in the days of your youth… Remove vexation from your heart and banish pain from your body, for youth and the prime of life are fleeting" (vss. 9-10). And this thought of fleetingness is continued in the first verses of chapter 12, which refer to old age and death with three clauses that are introduced with עד אשר לא , "before" (12,1. 2. 6): before the days of unpleasantness come (vs. 1b), before the winter of life comes (vss. 2-5), before death comes (vss. 6-7). I fully endorse what Fox (1999, 316) has written about this pericope: "Although the theme of the unit is *carpe diem*, far greater attention is given to the negative — the somber limits on this opportunity — than to the positive enjoyment itself".

Just like Qoh 5,17-19, so the enjoyment saying Qoh 8,15 follows after another absurdity (הבל) which Qoheleth has experienced, viz. that act and consequence do not link up well with each other. Although traditional biblical wisdom promises a long life to the righteous and a short life to the wicked, reality is often different: "There are righteous people who are treated according to the conduct of the wicked, and there are wicked people who are treated according to the conduct of the righteous" (8,11-14).

The more expanded exhortation of Qoh 9,7-9 (cf. *supra*) follows after the description of a similar absurdity, viz. the fact that the same fate, i.e. death, comes to all, irrespective of their ethical or ritual behaviour or status (cfr. Schoors 1985, 196-199):

> (1) But all this I laid to heart, examining[8] it all, how the righteous and the wise and their deeds are in the hand of God; whether it is love or hate a human does not know. Everything before them is (2) absurd[9], since[10] one

[8] וְלָבוּר is an old *crux*. It can be parsed as an inf. constr. of בור, "make clear, clear up" (BDB, 101). However, בור may also be a parallel form of ברר (cf. 3,18; *HAL*, 111). Syntactically, the inf. constr. can be regarded "as an infinitive consecutive with the force of a finite verb" (Whitley 1979, 78; cf. GK §114 p). Gordis 1951, 289; Lauha 1978, 164; Whitley, *loc. cit.*, and Tur-Sinai 1968, 171 prefer the reading of the LXX: καὶ καρδίᾳ μου σὺν πᾶν εἶδεν τοῦτο, and Pesh: ܘܠܒܝ ܚܙܐ ܠܗ ܠܟܠ ܗܢܐ, which reflect Heb. וְלִבִּי רָאָה אֶת־כָּל־זֶה. I prefer the MT, with the remark that the conjunction ו could be not original, so that לבור would function as a gerund, subordinate to the main verb נתתי.

[9] הַכֹּל: LXX ματαιότης; Pesh ܗܒܠܐ, attaching it to verse 1, but still beginning verse 2 with ܟܠ (thus *lectio conflata*); Sym: *sed omnia coram eis incerta* (Jerome, *In Eccl.*, *ad loc.*). Jerome has adopted "incerta" in his Vulgate, but he interprets the end of verse 1 somewhat differently: "sed omnia in futuro servantur incerta".

[10] A number of critics have tried to save the MT by giving to כאשר a comparative meaning. Thus Gordis 1951, 290: "Everything is like everything". But once we follow the LXX, Pesh and Sym in reading הבל instead of הכל, כאשר is causal; cf. Ginsberg 1961, 113; Tur-Sinai, *loc. cit.* (he supposes that it should be read באשר, as does also *BHS*); Lauha 1978., 163; Schoors 1992, 145.

fate comes to all, to the righteous and the wicked[11], to the clean and the unclean, to him who sacrifices and him who does not sacrifice. As is the good man, so is the sinner; and he who swears is as he who shuns an oath. (3) This is an evil in all that is done under the sun, that one fate comes to all. Also the hearts of men are full of evil, and madness is in their hearts while they live, and after that[12]: to the dead!

And then it is too late, when one is dead everything is finished. It is good to enjoy life (vss. 7-9) and to take advantage of its possibilities (vs. 10), for that is one's portion in this life, and we do not have anything more, since death is final.

In my opinion, the conclusion is inescapable: Qoheleth puts each of his recommendations to enjoy the pleasures of life after having recorded an absurdity "under the sun": the fact that the same fate of death is awaiting the wise as well as the fools and even that man and animal are equal in death, that God puts an idea of "eternity" in the human mind without a human being able to ever fathom that fully, that somebody can be rich but is finally denied the possibility to enjoy his wealth, that reward and penalty are unjustly distributed in this life, and that, irrespective of their ethical behaviour, all must die. In the end death is the fundamental absurdity: man only lives the time of a breath (*hebel*), even if we can speak of a long life, thereafter nothing remains but the lasting emptiness of death. Thus, life comes to nothing, and the thought of that should incite people to enjoy the good things of this life. To me it is beyond doubt that for Qoheleth enjoyment is such a thing as a narcotic. He has no answer to the absurdities of life: he knows that the human mind cannot fathom either God's nature or his work (e.g. 3,11. 14-15; 6,10-12; 7,23-24; 8,16-17). Neither does he have a solution to the ethical absurdities in the form of evil that goes unpunished, wealth from which one does not benefit, the unreliability of popularity (4,13-16). He has, however, a practical solution in order to stick it out as good as possible in those absurd situations, and that consists in enjoying the good things that fall to our share. Qoheleth is not a preacher of joy, and to him "joy" is not the central message. He indeed recommends a *carpe diem*.

11 לטוב: dl. Cf. *BHS*; Ginsberg, *loc. cit*; Loretz 1963, 169; Strobel 1967, 134; Lauha 1978, 164. The ancient versions read "to the good and the evil" (LXX: καὶ τῷ κακῷ; Vg: et malo; Pesh: ܘܠܒܝܫܐ), but this is a later adaptation. It is hard to accept that טוב would occur twice in these antitheses.

12 According to Gordis (1951, 228), אחריו is an adverb with a fossilized suffix, comparable to יחדיו. This is correct, because the singular suffix does not match the plural suffixes in בלבבם בחייהם. Cf. Schoors 1992, 118-119.

On the other hand, this enjoyment is not just a banal medicine invented by Qoheleth as "opium of the people". Several times he explicitly states that enjoyment is a gift of God. Already in 2,24 he says that eating, drinking and enjoying are from the hand of God: גם־זה ראיתי אני כי מיד האלהים היא, "I realized that this is also from the hand of God". Some critics, such as Lauha (1978, 58), consider this clause an orthodox gloss, meant to give a religious foundation to the recommendation of enjoyment. However, the theme of the verse is God's giving also the possibility to enjoy the good things of life — not only the toil — and this is of paramount importance in Qoheleth. And in vs. 26 he puts that into a larger context, when he writes: "To the one who pleases him God gives wisdom and knowledge and pleasure, but to the one who is offensive he gives the business of gathering and amassing in order to give (the wealth) to the one who pleases God". This verse calls for some further comment. Here and in 7,26 we find the phrase טוב לפני האלהים/לפניו. The moral connotation of this expression is not undisputed. A number of commentators understand it in a strictly moral sense, and they can invoke the contrasting term חוטא, which in their opinion must be understood as "sinner" (cf. Artom 1976, 75; Delitzsch 1875, 258; Whybray 1989, 64-65). But there is a strong exegetical trend to interpret חוטא as the one who has missed the mark, the unfortunate, and טוב לפני האלהים then is the lucky one, whom God likes[13]. Fox (1999, 189) produces a decisive argument in favour of this view when he writes with regard to 2,26: "A true sinner toiling for the benefit of a God-favored man would not be *hebel* by any definition". However, he stresses that חטא always denotes a component of offensiveness to someone (e.g. Gen 40,1; 1 Kgs 1,21; 8,31; 18,9; Prov 20,2): "While most sages take it for granted that God is offended only by sin or moral folly, Qoheleth believes that God (like a human ruler) may treat a person as offensive for inexplicable reasons and not necessarily because of actual sin or folly" (1989, 189). Gordis (1951, 217-218) rightly points out that Qoheleth uses the conventional terms צדיק and רשע to express the concepts of conventional morality and piety. As for חוטא, he "rarely uses the word in the conventional sense of sinner (8,12 is a cited proverb, where incidentally it is explained by עשׂה רע, and in 9,2 its

[13] Carlebach 1936, 34: "Pechvogel"; Thilo 1923, 33 and 38; Blieffert 1938, 40-41; Hertzberg 1963, 94; Galling 1969, 92-93; Gorssen 1970, 298-9; Braun 1973, 51-53; Bonora 1992, 124: "chi ha la fortuna di essere gradito a Dio e di ottenere la sua protezione...chi invece è sfortunato, fallito"; Michel 1989, 39-40: "mit diesen Wendungen kann Qohelet im Kontext nur meinen: 'wer Gott genehm ist' und 'wer Gott nicht genehm ist', wobei das Kriterium für 'genehm' oder 'nicht genehm' allein bei Gott liegt".

meaning is clear from the contrast with כטוב)". But Gordis (1951, 94) still sticks to a certain moral sense even in 2,26 and 7,26: "Actually *ḥōṭē'* in these passages is used both in its non-moral sense of 'fool, one who misses the right path,' and in its religious connotation of 'sinner', as Qoheleth understands it, the man who violates God's will by failing to enjoy the blessings of God's world, as in the Talmudic parallels adduced above"[14]. In view of Qoheleth's scepticism vis à vis the traditional connection between a moral attitude and good fortune (*Tun-Ergehen-Zusammenhang*), we may conclude that in 2,26; 7,26 טוב לפני אלהים (and its opposite חוטא) does not have the traditional moral meaning but denotes an element of divine favour without an ethical connotation. According to Braun (1973, 51-53), this idea that some people are in God's favour without any previous moral achievement on their part is unknown in Israelite wisdom before Qoheleth. It seems to be connected with Hellenistic utterances from Qoheleth's time in which the *Tun-Ergehen-Zusammenhang* has been abandoned in favour of a somewhat fatalistic idea of a divine disposition. The expression טוב לפני האלהים may even be a Hebrew rendering of θεόφιλος.

According to Qoh 3,13, "that every man should eat and drink and take pleasure in all his toil" is a gift of God (מתת אלהים היא). The thought is the same as the one expressed in 2,24b. In both verses the idea is that man can do nothing about the good things of life, such as eating, drinking and other enjoyments, but accept them, for they are given by God. And since in this context נתן is closely connected with עשה (3,11.14), it means that God is the one who makes it possible and who has it within his control: one cannot enjoy life unless God makes it possible. The consequence is that the way of wisdom is to enjoy the goodness of life as long as it is granted by God. For, as Qoheleth says in 7,14, God makes the day of prosperity as well as the day of adversity[15].

The phrase מתת אלהים היא occurs again in 5,18, in a context similar to the one of 3,13, but worded somewhat differently, and in which the root נתן plays an important role (5,17-18):

[14] The Talmudic parallels he refers to are BErub 54a and esp. JKidd, end: "Every man must render an account before God of all the good things he beheld in life and did not enjoy".

[15] Müller 1968), 511: "der Mensch kann über die Lebensfreude nicht selbst verfügen"; Gorssen 1970, 299-300: "*Mtt* exprime l'action déterminante de Dieu"; Crenshaw 1987, 90 and 99; Isaksson, 1987, 111.

17 הִנֵּה אֲשֶׁר־רָאִיתִי אָנִי טוֹב אֲשֶׁר־יָפֶה לֶאֱכוֹל־וְלִשְׁתּוֹת וְלִרְאוֹת
טוֹבָה בְּכָל־עֲמָלוֹ ׀ שֶׁיַּעֲמֹל תַּחַת־הַשֶּׁמֶשׁ מִסְפַּר יְמֵי־חַיָּו [חַיָּיו] אֲשֶׁר־
נָתַן־לוֹ הָאֱלֹהִים כִּי־הוּא חֶלְקוֹ׃ 18 גַּם כָּל־הָאָדָם אֲשֶׁר נָתַן־לוֹ
הָאֱלֹהִים עֹשֶׁר וּנְכָסִים וְהִשְׁלִיטוֹ לֶאֱכֹל מִמֶּנּוּ וְלָשֵׂאת אֶת־חֶלְקוֹ
וְלִשְׂמֹחַ בַּעֲמָלוֹ זֹה מַתַּת אֱלֹהִים הִיא׃

The first occurrence of the root is in vs. 17, in a relative clause attached to the expression מספר ימי־חיו, "the few days of his life". Isaksson (1987, 83-84) discusses the question whether נתן should be translated by an English perfect tense or a present tense:

> "However, is the *nātan* to be considered as expressing a past decision concerning the predestined life span of a human being (= English perfect tense) or just the present fore-ordaining will of God (= English present tense)? This question cannot be answered by a grammatical analysis only. Instead, the world- and life-view of Qoheleth must be examined. Is he a determinist? Most commentators deny that, and I agree with them. Even if it might be argued that the eternal God must have pre-determined the *ʿittīm* already before the beginning of the world, that question is not the point of interest in the Book of Qoheleth... Twelve times in Qoheleth God is the subject of giving, and the meaning is that 'man should seize what God gives in every moment and be glad of the portion that God gives'. I conclude that *nātan* in 5:17 should be translated by the English present (or even the future) tense."[16]

I have a feeling that this comes close to hair-splitting. In my opinion both translations are acceptable, since, whether God has ordained the number of someone's days before the beginning of the world or he ordains that number now, in the end the result is the same: man's life span, like everything else in his life, completely depends on God and is within his control. The only convincing argument in favour of a present tense translation is the idea of *creatio continua* behind the verb עשה in the suffix-conjugation in Qoh 3,11. That God is the "giver" of man's lifetime, is again said in relative clauses in 8,15 and 9,9. As for the latter instance, some authors regard אשה as the antecedent of the relative clause: "...the woman whom he has given you" (Geier 1668, 353; Trapp 1660, 201; Ogden 1987, 153). But this is not the obvious interpretation, for in Hebrew the relative clause immediately follows the antecedent, in this case כל־ימי חיי הבלך, and so it has also been understood in the ancient versions (LXX: ἡμέρας...τὰς δοθείσας σοι; Vg: *diebus...qui dati sunt tibi*; Targ=MT; in Pesh the relative clause is missing).

[16] A number of commentators translate the verb in the present tense, e.g. Barton 1908, 126; Podechard 1912, 353; Zimmerli 1980, 134.

Verse 5,18 is almost tautological: "If *God gives* anyone wealth and property and enables him to partake of it and to take his portion and to get pleasure through his toil — *that is a gift of God*" (Fox). God's gift consists not only in the possession of wealth but also in the ability to enjoy it. The message is the same as in 2,24 and 3,13, but the distinction between the possession of wealth and the possibility to enjoy it deserves some attention, as appears from 6,2: there are cases where God gives a man wealth but lets a stranger consume it. The evil that Qoheleth resents (vs. 1) is that such cases exist, that life is unpredictable.

In sum, God brings about the whole world, he has fixed all that happens under the sun; thus he also gave humankind the desire to grasp this process. This sort of determinism of divine origin applies to good as well as to bad things, as well to the absurdities of life as to the possibility to enjoy good gifts. The fact that man disposes of this narcotic is also in God's plan. But it is not a supreme gift, it is a limited help to keep one's head above the water.

This also appears from the phrase "this is his/your portion (חֵלֶק)", which occurs a few times in the enjoyment sayings (3,22; 5,17-18; 9,9). Nowhere does Qoheleth explicitly speak of a portion that is given by God. Nevertheless, it must be understood as given by God. Rather than "part" the Hebrew word חלק specifically means "share, portion". In Qoheleth, a person's share is his or her potential of pleasure that is included in his or her possessions. This is expressed in the somewhat laborious sentence of 5,18: "Furthermore, every man to whom God has given wealth and property and enabled him to partake of it and to take his portion and to have pleasure in his toil — that is a gift of God" (cf. Fox 1999, 240-1). In order to reach enjoyment, God must give the resources for enjoyment *and* enable the recipient to enjoy them. He does not always do so. Sometimes he takes away the resources (5,12-16; 6,1-6). See, for example, 6,2 which is the negative counterpart of 5,18:

5,18 כל־האדם אשר נתן־לו האלהים עֹשר ונכסים והשליטו לאכל ממנו
6,2 איש אשר יתן־לו האלהים עֹשר ונכסים ... ולא־ישליטנו האלהים לאכל ממנו

But if it is given to someone to receive his "portion", than he himself should act to enjoy it. With the words of Fox (1999, 111): "God can give you a piece of the pie but *you* must eat it". However, the possibilities to do so completely depend on God. The fact that at a certain moment you can enjoy pleasure, that is your portion.

Qoheleth exhorts his readers to enjoy pleasure because that is their portion. But it does not bring them "profit", no abiding gain (יתרון). In

1,3 Qoheleth expresses his fundamental question: "What profit does man have in all his toil at which he toils under the sun?" Further in the book this question gets a negative answer[17]: "There is no profit under the sun" (2,11). This negative answer is also suggested a couple of times with a rhetorical question, thus in 3,9: "What profit has one who does something from what he toils at?" and in 5,15: "What profit is there for him who toils for the wind?". That does not mean that under the sun, i.e. in this sublunar life, there are no good things which one can enjoy. But it expresses that no human endeavour yields a net profit. Man does have a portion (חלק) indeed, but no final gain (יתרון). "For Qohelet, pleasure is a good portion (2:10). But since it is not, in his view, meaningful or truly productive — it "does" nothing, achieves nothing beyond itself (2:1f.) — it is not adequate remuneration for the effort invested in earning it (2:11)."[18]

In conclusion, my analysis has shown that Qoheleth is not a book with a message of joy. It is a book in which enjoyment or pleasure plays an important part, when it boils down to leading a livable life. Thus it is a good of which a person receives his or her share, but this enjoyment is not able either to cancel out the absurdities of human life or even make them transparent. The exhortation to enjoy pleasure is the practical counterbalance of a philosophy which describes absurdities everywhere in the world and is aware that the world, and man who lives in it, ultimately are unfathomable, because they are the unfathomable work of an unfathomable God.

Bibliography

ARTOM, E.S. 1976, *חמש מגילות מפרשות* (ספרי המקרא 13), Tel Aviv.
BARTON, G.A. 1912: *A Critical and Exegetical Commentary on the Book of Ecclesiastes* (ICC), Edinburgh.
BARUCQ, A. 1968: *Ecclésiaste, Qohéleth. Traduction et commentaire* (Verbum Salutis, AT 3), Paris.
BLIEFFERT, H.J. 1938: *Weltanschauung und Gottesglaube im Buche Koheleth*, Rostock.
BONORA, A. 1992: *Il libro di Qohelet*, Roma.
BRAUN, R. 1973: *Kohelet und die frühhellenistische Popularphilosophie* (BZAW 130), Berlin.

17 In Qoh 2,13 we read: "Wisdom has an advantage (יתרון) over folly as light has an advantage (יתרון) over darkness". Here יתרון does not mean profit/gain but a relative advantage in comparison to another subject.

18 Fox 1999, 113. On p. 109-113 we find a good discussion about חלק and יתרון, of which I have gratefully made use.

CARLEBACH, J. 1936: *Das Buch Koheleth*, Frankfurt.
CRENSHAW, J.L. 1987: *Ecclesiastes: A Commentary* (OTL), Philadelphia.
DELITZSCH, F. 1875: *Hoheslied und Koheleth* (Biblischer Kommentar über die poetischen Bücher des AT 4), Leipzig.
ELSTER, E. 1855: *Commentar über den Prediger Salomo*, Göttingen.
FISCHER, A.A. 1997: *Skepsis oder Furcht Gottes? Studien zur Komposition und Theologie des Buches Kohelet* (BZAW 247), Berlin.
FOX, M.V. 1986: "The Meaning of *hebel* for Qohelet", *JBL* 105, 409-27.
— 1989: *Qohelet and his Contradictions* (JSOTSup 71), Sheffield.
— 1999: *A Time to Tear Down and a Time to Build Up. A Rereading of Ecclesiastes*, Grand Rapids.
GALLING, K. 1969: *Der Prediger* (HbAT 1,18), Tübingen.
GEIER, M. 1668: *In Salomonis Regis Israel Ecclesiasten Commentarius*, Lipsiae.
GINSBERG, H.L. 1961: *קהלת* (פרוש חדש לתורה נביאים וכתובים), Tel Aviv.
GORDIS, R. 1951: *Koheleth — the Man and his World*, New York.
GORSSEN, L. 1970: "La cohérence de la conception de Dieu dans l'Ecclésiaste", *ETL* 46, 282-324.
HERTZBERG, H.W. 1963: *Der Prediger* (KAT XVII,4), Gütersloh.
ISAKSSON, B. 1987: *Studies in the Language of Qoheleth. With Special Emphasis on the Verbal System* (Studia Semitica Upsaliensia 10), Uppsala.
LAUHA, A. 1978: *Kohelet* (BKAT XIX), Neukirchen.
LAVOIE, J.-J. 1992: *La pensée du Qohélet: étude exégétique et intertextuelle* (Héritage et projet 49), Québec.
JASTROW, M. 1919: *A Gentle Cynic, being a Translation of the Book of Koheleth ... also its Origin, Growth and Interpretation*, London.
LOHFINK, N. 1980: *Kohelet* (Neue Echter Bibel), Würzburg.
LORETZ, O. 1963: *Gotteswort und menschliche Erfahrung. Eine Auslegung der Bücher Jona, Rut, Hoheslied und Qohelet*, Freiburg.
MICHEL, D. 1989: *Untersuchungen zur Eigenart des Buches Qohelet* (BZAW 183), Berlin.
MÜLLER, H.P. 1968: "Wie sprach Qohälät von Gott?", *VT* 18, 507-21.
OGDEN, G. 1987, *Qoheleth* (Readings — A New Biblical Commentary), Sheffield.
PAHK, J.Y.-S. 1996: *Il canto della gioia in Dio. L'itinerario sapienziale espresso dall'unità letteraria in Qohelet 8,16-9,10 e il parallello di Gilgameš Me. iii* (Istituto Universitario Orientale. Dipart. di Studi Asiatici, Series Minor 52), Napoli.
PODECHARD, E. 1912: *L'Ecclésiaste*, Paris.
RANKIN, O.S. 1956: "The Book of Ecclesiastes", in *The Interpreter's Bible* 5, Nashville, 3-88.
SCHOORS, A. 1985: "Koheleth: A Perspective of Life after Death?", *ETL* 61, 295-303.
— 1992: *The Preacher Sought to Find Pleasing Words: A Study of the Language of Qoheleth* (OLA 41), Leuven.
— 1996: "The Verb ראה in the Book of Qoheleth", in A.A. Diesel et al. (eds.) *"Jedes Ding hat seine Zeit ..." Studien zur israelitischen und altorientalischen Weisheit. Diethelm Michel zum 65. Geburtstag* (BZAW 241), Berlin.
STROBEL, A. 1967: *Das Buch Prediger (Kohelet)* (WeltBib, KK 9), Düsseldorf.

THILO, M. 1923: *Der Prediger Salomo, neu übersetzt und auf seinen Gedankengang untersucht*, Bonn.
TRAPP, J. 1660: *A Commentary upon the Books of Proverbs, Ecclesiastes and the Song of Songs*, London.
TUR-SINAI, N.H. 1968: *חמש המגילות וספרי דניאל, עזרא ונחמיה, איוב* (פשוטו של מקרא על ספר, IV, 2), Jerusalem.
WHITLEY, C.F. 1979: *Koheleth. His Language and Thought* (BZAW 145), Berlin.
WHYBRAY, R.N. 1982: "Qoheleth, Preacher of Joy", *JSOT* 23, 87-98.
— 1989: *Ecclesiastes* (The New Century Bible Commentary), London.
ZIMMERLI, W. 1980: *Prediger* (ATD 16,1), Göttingen.

THE SECRET OF GILGAMESH

Johanna SPAEY

I was 19 when I met Gilgamesh. In my Akkadian II class I deciphered sign by sign and word by word the tale of a brutal, selfish man who lost his hope in a happy ever after. As Professor Van Lerberghe was so smart to leave the epic only partially translated until now, I thought, like every young and naïve Assyriologist, that I was the first who unveiled the tragedy of that long-forgotten god-king-man. I disliked Gilgamesh at that time. I didn't know what to expect, so I read the story of a rude man who raped women, brutalised his own citizens, challenged the gods and only lost his arrogance when he discovered that life was just life, even for him, with a beginning and an end.

Perhaps the secret of my later fascination lay in my then clumsy, stubborn transcription of his tale. It never occurred to me at that time that the epic would demonstrate its real power when I grew older and lost my innocence, since with age illusions disappear and loved ones die, and everyone has an Enkidu in their life. I left university and Assyriology behind and found out that writing was my true calling.

In fact, many writers and poets transformed their fascination for this epic into literature. But the discrepancy in their interpretation is remarkable.

First, Scottish National poet Edwin Morgan takes Gilgamesh in *The Play of Gilgamesh* (2005) on a quest through a world that is inhabited by demons and political prisoners, gods and singing transvestites. Enkidu, the healthy child of nature, dies of a virus in the blood. The unspoken erotic attraction between the men becomes more obvious at latter stages in the play.

Canadian poet and Ancient Near Eastern-student Derrek Hines creates in *Gilgamesh* (2002) an energetic, very modern version of Gilgamesh. In streetwise slang, he tries to recapture for the modern reader the vigour and excitement the original audience must have felt. Gilgamesh, as the spoiled hip-hop boy, surrounded by the jeunesse dorée, who finally submits himself to his destiny. In his lament for Enkidu, Gilgamesh says:

> "Ah, Enkidu, we were the beginning of many things.
> Am I not the first to have watched myself die
> And lived to tell of it?"

Pulitzer Prize-winner Yusef Komunyakaa and theatre producer Chad Gracia created a wonderful, vital translation with *Gilgamesh: A verse play* (2006). Komunyakaa's other work is infused with loss, death and deep longing. His heartbreaking rendition of Gilgamesh's grief for Enkidu sounds like this:

> "And I sit here,
> And I sit here,
> And I sit here,
> till
> till one day
> turns into three
> and I cannot stop
> staring at Death
> till a maggot
> drops from Enkidu's
> nose.

Writer Philip Roth, on the other hand, uses a fictional character called Gil Gamesh in *The Great American Novel* (1973). The novel concerns a fictional American baseball league that becomes a communist organisation. Gil Gamesh is a brutal, very aggressive and uneducated player who becomes a spy for the Soviet Government. He is friendly with Stalin and Beria, but in the end he is executed as a double agent in old-fashioned Soviet tradition.

It is clear Gilgamesh still fascinates writers, poets and playwrights alike.

I wrote three novels on the First World War. Research is of great importance. But I'm not a First World War historian, so I can more easily intertwine facts with fantasy. I take a 'petit histoire' from 1915 and use it in 1917. It makes me blush, but not ashamed. It would probably take me ten years to write a 'Babylonian' novel and I would still feel insecure about every fact and name I use.

After all these years, I'm lucky that I know my original Gilgamesh. I didn't know then that my knowledge of Gilgamesh would make me a better writer. I transcribed his anger and pain slowly and meticulously. I know now why there is sometimes only silence in his life, why there are tears and madness. And why he is the father of all those fictional heroes who end as ordinary men. Gilgamesh is my secret weapon. In my novels Gilgamesh emerges as the big, silent warrior. The man who goes to war, any war, who battles and cries, who loses and rediscovers himself. Because in the end, the only thing every warrior finds is himself. Nothing less, nothing more.

Professor Karel Van Lerberghe introduced me to Gilgamesh. For 25 years I went to war with this epic god-king-man. And in the end, we both found out that life is just life. Therefore I'm extremely grateful. Thank you, Karel.

RENTING THE DIVINE WEAPON AS A PREBEND

Marten STOL
Nederlands Instituut voor het Nabije Oosten, Leiden

Babylonian gods had their "weapons" and other emblems. We are here interested in the roles these symbolic objects played in legal procedures during the Old Babylonian period. [1]

"Weapon" will stand for giš.tukul (*kakkum*) (once šíta)[2] and "emblem" for other *palladia*. Most frequent are "the weapon (*kakkum*) of god NN" and the emblem named "*šurinnum* of god NN".[3] More names are *pāštum* "axe", *ḫuḫārum* "bird-trap",[4] etc. The emblem can be indicated by a name inspired by its outer form (like "The Dog of Gula").[5] In general, it guarantees the truth. We read in a Mari letter about the city of Sippar: "Let them bring the Weapon of Šamaš and give a right judgment for (this) case (*a-wa-tim šu-te*(!)-*še-ra*), before the Weapon of Šamaš."[6] Accusations were investigated in the presence of the weapon or emblem and the result could be negative: "it was not confirmed" (*burrum*), a claimed good "is not there" (*bašûm*).[7] Such a divine symbol could be moved outside the temple (*warādum* "to descend"; *waṣûm* "to go out")

[1] Veenhof (2003a, 323-328) gave a thoughtful discussion of some aspects. Facts can be found in Dombradi 1996, I, 84-86 §112-113; II, 91-92 (notes). Corrections: (1) *iṣrat* (*ša Uraš*) (I, 85; II, 92 note 426) is urudu šen.tab.ba, the Sumerogram for *pāštu*, CAD P 266a; already seen by Walther 1917, 203 n. 1. (2) In note 423 "Ba 3:4" stands for Ba 2:34 (= VAS 22 28).

[2] BE 6/2 58:1 (= UET 5 256), with Walther 1917, 205 n. 1, Locher 1986, 251. CAD A/2 365b saw this sign in TCL 11 245:6. Read in TCL 10 4B:34 *ni-ka-sú*.

[3] The emblem: Van Lerberghe 1982, 253-256. Corrections to CAD Š/3 345b, *šurinnu*: (1) In CT 4 23a: 21, cancel what precedes (*maḫar šībī* ...) and translate "they *will* make a deposition". See Walther 1917, 206 n. 1. (2) Read in BE 6/1 10:10 (the judges) *i-na šu-ri-ni-*[*im ú-ki-in-nu*]. For *ana NN kunnum*, see Walther 1917, 223 n. 1. Not taken by CAD K! Walther overlooked the same expression in the related text Pinches Peek 13:17-21.

[4] A precious new reference is *ḫuḫārum saḫeštum*, "zuschnappende Vogelfalle", BM 122691:3; Farber 1981, 61. Also CT 53 43:14, with Deller 1984 90 [CAD M/2, 265b].

[5] Survey: Krecher 1969, 497-489.

[6] Durand 2010, 65 A. 337+:10.

[7] BE 6/2 58:4-6 (*ūl ubirraši*); CT 2 6:37 (*ūl ibašši*); TCL 10 4B:18, 34:15; V. Scheil, RA 12 (1915) 116:15.

to a place where the truth is to be established. The verb for establishing the truth by this means is *burrum*; extensive quotations are given in CAD B 127-130 (*bâru* A). For example, men were convicted by the Weapon of stealing pigs (*ina šarāqim bu-úr-ru-ú*, YOS 8 159:5-6), or this way a person was convicted of robbing divine robes (*ina ḫummuṣi bu-ú-úr*, TCL 11 245:32-34). The result of the procedure was written on a *tuppi būrtim* which could be shown as proof (AbB 6 181:20-22).

Since Walther 1917 (196-208) and Harris 1965, more texts about the weapon and its journey have been found and it is certain that many more remain unpublished. In the contracts of renting a weapon, the Journey is in most cases indicated by the Sumerogram kaskal, once by Akkadian *gerrum*, and this is confirmed by all evidence. In the second part of this contribution we will return to this renting.

A. General remarks

a. *The weapon on the road*

Some general remarks first. A Mari letter shows that a divine "weapon" (or symbol) "rests" (*rabāṣum*) on the place where it has to establish the truth: "After the harvest, let the Lightning (*Birqum*) of Adad and the Weapon of Šamaš rest in that field and let them establish the owner of the field on his field. If the field is yours, you take it; if it is mine, I will take it."[8] Many texts outside Mari say that the Weapon is "set up" (*šakānum* N) *in loco*.[9] The Journey takes place when an exact amount of barley or silver is to be established, or the dimensions of fields and houses. An example of the latter is Gautier Dilbat 13 (case: TLB 1 245+259+261). "They brought the Axe of Uraš to the house and checked (*sanāqum* D) (the dimensions of) the house, and the house exceeded (*watārum*) by 1 SAR, and PN (...) has paid 4 shekels of silver for the excess area (*tertum*) of the house." The reverse was the result in CT 2 45 (case in MHET II/2 183): "By the Saw of Šamaš the house was checked (case: they checked the house) and the house was 12 shekels less (*maṭûm*) than the text of the sale contract (indicated)." A few texts tell

[8] AEM 1/2 (1988) 260 no. 404:44-47. More examples of a god "resting" in a place: Durand 2009, 92:19, 24 (Itur-Mer, in the city gate); A. 747, Durand 2009, 93 (= Durand 2008, 456) (Aštabel).

[9] BM 108887 rev. 2 (copy by Irene Sibbing), see note 14; Scheil, RA 12 (1915) 116:10; TCL 10 4A:31, 4B:35; TCL 10 34:13; VAS 22 28:35, 41; YOS 8 76:6. In Mari: Florilegium Marianum 3 (1997) 54 II 7 (ritual of Ištar).

us that the weapon "circumambulated" (*saḫārum*) a house or garden (MHET II/1 49; Tell Sifr 71). In a similar way, the god Itur-Mer was taken around (*saḫārum* D) in order to find lost cattle (AEM 1/2 383 no. 458, with note by J.-M. Durand). In contracts, to be discussed later, the Weapon is characterized as "walking"; more precise: "walking in front" (*muttallikti panî(tim)*), "leading the way" (thus CAD M/2 305a)[10]. Sometimes, the emblem *šurinnum* is named *ālik maḫra*, "going in front" (CAD A/1 344b). Actually, leading the way is the role of the *šurinnum*: king Zimri-Lim "goes in front like an emblem" (*kīma šurinnim ippana illak*).[11]

Telling is this passage in a letter: "After (the work with) the (measuring) rope and reed, let the Axe of Ningišzida and the *ku-ku-ra-tum* of Ninurta go and check the garden; I will hold you responsible for any *iku* of field that is exceeding" (Kienast Kisurra 159:17-27). Judges forced herdsmen to make a sworn statement "at the gate of Marduk", before the priest (*ērib bītim*). Two witnesses have the unusual title "He of the Weapon" (*ša* giš.tukul). The weapon of Marduk? (TIM 4 35, with Sommerfeld 1982, 35 n. 3).

b. *Reasons for using the weapon*

Rivkah Harris summarized as follows. "The divine symbol or weapon might be transported for various reasons in view of the evidence of the Old Babylonian letters, legal texts, and contracts: to ensure the just collection of taxes and tithes and the fair distribution and storage of the harvest yield and to bring settlement of disputes by means of the oath taken in the presence of the sacred object" (Harris 1965, 224b). To be more specific, the weapon appears in the following situations.

1. At the partition of an inheritance

BE 6/2 49, with VAB 5 298; CT 2 9, with CT 45 23 and BAP 80; CT 2 47, with VAB 5 261 (oral depositions); CT 6 22a, case Aula Orientalis 15 (1997) 111 no. 13 (gift of gardens and field to sister); CT 8 3a, with VAB 5 194; CT 48 1, with VAS 8 71 (includes the dissolution of a society); CT 48 2 (a slavegirl of the family had been given away);[12] CT 48 5; Spaey 1993, 418, 420 Text 5 (CBS 1513);

[10] The masculine form *muttallik*, only in CT 4 29a, and taken seriously by CAD M, must be an error.

[11] Guichard 1999, 41 n. 92 (in the *Épopée de Zimri-Lîm*).

[12] The family had authority over house-born slaves. This example was not given by M. Stol 2004a, 915.

TCL 10 4B (ten minas of silver, the "take" [*ša leqe*] of PN); TCL 10 34 (*mimma ša leqe*, 14); TCL 11 173 (it includes a debt [*ḫubullum*] of the family);[13] VAS 9 130-131, with VAB 5 187.

2. Property or dimensions of houses

BIN 7 176 (sale); CT 2 45 = MHET II/2 183 (size); Gautier Dilbat 13, with VAB 5 275 (size); MHET II/1 49 (size); II/5 700; Scheil 1915, 116, with Malul 1988, 316-317; TIM 5 16 (splitting up a house); Pinches Peek 13; VAS 7 56, with Charpin, 1985, 277-278; Spaey 1993, 416-417, 420 Di 2122 (sale; the complaints are repeated here); UET 5 251, with Kraus 1955, 136; Malul 1988 316-317; VAS 22 28, with Charpin 1985, 275-276; YOS 12 73 (complete payment); Owen and Westbrook 1992, 205 (sale).

3. Property or dimensions of fields

AbB 4 40:29-36 (ownership), 118:24-31 (ownership of family property); AbB 12 64 (family property); AEM 1/2 260 no. 404:44-47 (ownership); Gautier Dilbat 35, with Walther 1917, 203 n. 1; MHET II/1 54 (sale), 119 (size) (read giš.tukul ^{d}EN.ZU in line 10); II/5 669; TCL 1 70; TLB 1 242 ("the boundary between them", 4. Read in 2 [*pa-a*]*š-tu-um ša* ^{d}Uraš).

4. Property of gardens

Arnaud 1976b, 76 no. 171 (L. 74.63); Kienast Kisurra 159; Jean Tell Sifr 71; YOS 8 76.

5. Lost property

CT 2 1 and 6 (goods of a *nadîtum*); CT 4 47a, with VAB 5 305 and AfO 15 (1945-51) 77 (case) (caravan donkey).

6. Suspicion of theft. The quantity of the stolen goods can be an issue.

AbB 4 79, with Harris 1965, 219-220 (a field with its harvest); AbB 8 12:47, after CAD N/2 83b; BE 6/1 103:32-33 (barley); Holma1914,

[13] Note the *ḫubullum* to be paid in the Journey CT 8 8c:13; Harris 1965, 220 n. 32.

no. 9 (silver), with Walther 1917, 58-59, Harris 1965, 220a ("taxes"), and Schwemer 2001, 326-327; TCL 11 245 (a garment of a goddess in her temple); YOS 8 159 (four pigs); UCP 10 no. 107, with Greengus 1986, 171 (theft); UET 5 248 with Kraus 1955, 136 (in fact, a woman had paid for something); UET 5 254, with Charpin 1986, 88 (temple theft); YOS 12 325.

7. Quantities of earth excavated in canals

AbB 9 194; AbB 13 115; BM 108887 rev. 1-4 (copied by Irene Sibbing).[14]

8. Number of bricks baked(?)

Birot Tablettes 19:1.

9. Legal status of persons.

ARN 174 (adoption); Van Lerberghe 1982, 247 (the man is not a slave); PBS 5 100, with Stol 2000, 174 (newborn son); PBS 8/2 264, with Charpin 1986, 169-173 (adoption); Tell Sifr 58 (adoption); Veenhof 2003a, 314-318 (child).

10. Other

AbB 6 181:16-20 (somebody had lived in the house of PN during three years), BE 6/2 58 (an accusation of having said insolent words proved to be unfounded)

11. Barley during and after the harvest: see below.

c. *A few remarks on the weapons and emblems.*

Often, *two* weapons are involved, as was stressed by Veenhof 2003a, 326-328. Note that Wilcke reads in TCL 11 245:6 "die beiden ... (Götter-waffen?) (AN-*ni-it-ti-an*) (zogen aus)" (Wilcke 1992, 59, 73 n. 59) (the word *nītum*, "axe"? See below). Add these examples: AEM 1/2 260 no. 404:44; CAD P 266a (in two unpublished texts); Durand 2008, 363-364; Holma 1914 no. 9:18; MHET II/5 700:5-6; TIM 5 16:13-14;

[14] Text: (rev. 1) giš.tukul *ša* [d]Marduk *l*[*i*]-*ša-ki-in-ma* (2) *i-na* giš.tukul *ša* [d]Marduk saḫar.ḫi.a (3) *ki-iš-da-ti-ja bi-ir-ra-am-ma* (4) *lu-sú-uḫ*.

UCP 10 no. 107:12-13; UET 5 251:24-25; VAS 9 130:6-7. *Three* weapons: AbB 6 181:17-18; CT 2 47:18-20; Greengus Ishchali 27:2-5 with Greengus 1986, 24; YOS 8 76. *Four*: Jean Tell Sifr 58:21-24, with Sommerfeld 1982, 55.

The weapon is often that of the chief god of a city, present together with the elders. Sometimes it is named simply "the god of the city" (AbB 4 40:32, 118:24, 30). A few times, the weapon or emblem is used by a city "ward" (*bābtum*) (BE 6/1 103:33; BE 6/2 58:2, with Locher 1986, 251; CT 2 1:30/6:40; OBTI 27:9, with Greengus 1986, 25; read *bābtum i*[*p-ḫu-ur-m*]*a*). In Sippar, the Weapons of Šamaš and Adad are used.

d. *Weapons or emblems that are not mentioned in earlier literature:*

(igi) ^{d}*Ḫābiš ša* ^{d}x x x, (igi) *gamlātim ša* ^{d}MAR.TU, TIM 5 16:13-14, with Durand 1983, 344.

giš.tukul *ša Išar-kidissu*, UCP 10 no. 107:13, with Greengus 1986, 171.

giš tukul *ša* ^{d}Zamama ^{d}*Kāmi-tāmišu*, VAS 22 28:40, with Charpin 1985, 276.

giš tukul *Labbi* (in the temple of Marduk), VAS 22 28:22, with Charpin 1985, 276.

Kukkuratum ša Ninurta, Kienast Kisurra 159:20. A vessel? Stol 2011, 248-249.

Kusarikku, Ellis 1989, 135.

Nikkassum, CAD N/2 229b (4.) Veenhof 2003a, 327 n. 37, translates "abacus", and he may have had in mind *nikkassu* B "(a measure of length)". One is reminded of the bronze bar with incisions in the Istanbul Museum; the "Nippurelle" published by Unger in 1916; lastly Powell 1990, 462b, "the Nippur Cubit".

Nītum, "axe", possibly in TCL 11 245:6. Wilcke 1992, 59, 73 n. 59: "die beiden … (Götterwaffen?) (AN *ni-it-ti-an*) (zogen aus)". The word is hardly attested in CAD N (see *nêtu* B) but is now well known from Mari (*ni-tum*) and Ebla (*ne-a-tu*; in an oath); Archi 2005. However, our text presupposes **nittûm*, not *nêtum*. Another possibility is the feminine form of *nûm* "ours": "both our goddess(es)."

^{d}*Ūmum ša* ^{d}*Bēl-gašer u* ^{d}*Šukurrum ša* ^{d}*Wēr*, Greengus Ishchali 27:2-5, with Greengus 1986, 24.

Šukurrum of silver, Owen and Westbrook 1992, 205:25.

Obscure names: AbB 6 181:18 (giš KU-*ul-tum ša* Dagan); TCL 11 245:6; see above, *Nītum*; YOS 8 159:2 (like NA_4 IG), with Wilcke 1992, 73 n. 60 (but his á.gál is never preceded by lú).

Emblems in Mari: note the list in ARMT 21 289, and the ritual of opening their mouths (CAD P 446-447), and the discussion in Durand 2008, 363-364

Veenhof, 2003a, 323-327 (with Van Lerberghe 1982, 255), gives these locations for swearing an oath within the holy precinct: *kilkillū*, *kippat qēmim*, *saparrum*, *šipārum*, *uṣurtum*.

B. After the harvest

Often, the Weapon appears in harvest time and Harris 1965 discussed the texts; see also Schwemer 2001, 324-327.[15] At harvest time, there was much work to do with the Weapon. In a Mari letter, the presence of (the emblem of) Itur-Mer was required for taking an oath, but this was impossible because the god was needed for the harvest: "It is harvest! They must not neglect his harvest and the harvest of the Palace." Elsewhere, the gods Ikšudum and Lagamal take care of "l'affaire du grain".[16] In a letter (already cited above), a cultivated field is claimed. "That field, I sowed it with barley, I want to harvest the barley, I want to have my stalks[17] dried. After the harvest, let the Lightning (*Birqum*) of Adad and the Weapon of Šamaš rest (*rabāṣum*) on that field and let them establish (*kânum* D) the owner of the field on his field."[18]

Most of the texts edited by Harris speak of the Journey "at the harvest of barley/sesame". Here is a list of these texts, and more, published later. In chronological order (not so no. 14). *M.* = *muttallikti panî*(*tim*) is added after (in two texts: before) the location.

[15] Major additions and corrections to Harris 1965: The witnesses are omitted everywhere. In CT 6 22a (p. 217 n. 9), the left edge, after the yearname, this is omitted: (30) igi ᵈutu-*en-nam ú-ki-in*. CT 8 19a:30, end (p. 218b n. 18), read *e-ma illikam* (coll. G.Th. Ferwerda). PBS VII 85 (p. 219 n. 22) is no more relevant; Veenhof 1985, 291 f.; now AbB 11 85. MAH 16147 (p. 222 n. 44) is not pertinent; see Charpin 1979, 187-188; new edition in this article. CT 4 23c (p. 223 n. 51): the witnesses Šamaš and Aja are omitted.

[16] ARM 27 116:46-48; Durand, 2008, 363 (M. 6607).

[17] Akkadian *ḫamū*. See AEM 1/2, 263, note (m), by Durand: "la partie supérieure de la tige, celle qui est coupée avec l'épi. Le français courant n'ayant pas d'équivalent exact de cette réalité, le terme 'paille' est ici à prendre dans un sens générique". He refers to A 2342 in AEM 1/1 42, now Durand 2000, 224 no. 1053, with note (d) (p. 226): "le chaume (du blé)". More in Veenhof 2003b, 701-702; Dalman 1924, 81-82: "Der Häcksel, das heißt, die Stücke des weicheren oberen Teiles der Getreidehalme (arab. *tibn*) werden geschieden vom Stroh, das heißt, den Stücken des härteren unteren Teiles der Halme (arab. *qaswal*). Dies geschieht beim Wörfeln."

[18] AEM 1/2, 260 no. 404:42-46

1. CT 8 8c (21.I Ha 1); Harris 1965, 220b (n. 32). In this early text no Weapon is mentioned. End of line 14: *i-pa-al*?
2. TCL 1 140 (8.XII Si 22); VAB 5 147; Harris 1965, 221a (n. 36); Schwemer 2001, 325.
3. OLA 21 no. 1 (25.I 33 Amd 33); Spaey 1993, 418-419. *M*.
4. OLA 21 no. 6 (21.VII Amṣ 5); Spaey 1993, 419. Sesame! *M*.
5. CT 4 29a (27.II Amṣ 5?); Harris 1965, 222b (n. 49). Pientka 1998, 98 n. 462. *M*.
6. TLOB 65a (+6.II Amṣ 6); p. 44. *M*.
7. CT 4 18c (1.VIII Amṣ 8). Sesame! Harris 1965, 221b (n. 41). *M*.
8. TLOB 65 (29.II Amṣ 10). *M*.
9. TLOB 65b (14.II Amṣ 11); p. 44 -45. *M*.
10. CT 4 23c (23.I Sd 5); Harris, 223a (n. 51); Pientka 1998, 223 n. 39. *M*. Witnesses: Šamaš and Aja.

Date lost:

11. OLA 21 no. 62; Spaey 1993, 419-420. *M*. Witnesses: Šamaš and Aja.
12. CBS 149. *M*.
13. BM 78393. Sesame! *M*.
14. YOS 12 442 (9.I Si 24) is somewhat aberrant: one axe (*pāštum*) of Šamaš, together with two persons, are rented for specific periods. First witnesses: Šamaš and Aja.

Unpublished: Di 821, Di 1674; Tanret 2010, 141.

The texts that explicitly speak of the "harvest of barley" are dated to months XII (no. 2), I (nos. 3, 10), II (nos. 5, 6, 8, 9); those on "the harvest of sesame" to months VII and VIII (nos. 4, 7). This fits the time of the harvests, or the period shortly after them. Many texts give a location: a city/village (uru; *ša* PN) or a canal (district) (íd). Most of these are little known. One text says "from A to B" (no. 2); another mentions two cities (no. 6), or a city and a canal (district) (no. 8), a canal (district) (nos. 1, 9).[19] Clearly, the Weapon followed a route, from village to village, from district to district. These areas may be identical with "the countryside" (*libbu mātim*) in one of the texts about the Journey (MAH 16147:5, Harris 1965, 222 n. 44; a new edition is given below). A fragmentary

[19] Note Kār Kutâ in no. 11 and Sippar-Amnānu in no. 4 (sesame) and in CBS 92, published here. Is Kār Kutâ a quay in the Sippar area? Also in BM 97521:6, the hire of a boat to be loaded with garlic (6.II Aṣ 14) (Sippar).

text shows that the Journey made a round (*siḫrum*) through "the country" ([*a-r*]*a ge-er-ri si-ḫi-ir ma-tim* (BM 80984:5, with Richardson 2002, II 218).

What was going on after the harvest? The owner and the tenant farmer of a field divide its yield. Both get their share, named *miksum*. The Sumerian Hymn to Ḫendursagga mentions this "share" (níg.ku$_5$) (197): "From the piled up and spread stacks, from the heaped up grain to be laid under the stick, he pays you a share."[20] In this situation, a problem can arise: "Together with the field of I., I cultivated another field and the barley was stored on óne spot. Let them establish by the Weapon of the god the barley as much as was grown on the field of I. and let them take the share (*miksam lilqû*)" (AbB 2 28:8-13, cf. *še'am makāsum* and *miksāt eqlim* in the related letter AbB 13 4 rev. 7, 12, 19). An early OB text: "The emblem of Šamaš descended and the sons of Kikīnum took their two-thirds; Mānum took the one-third. They will not raise claims to each-other (the oath follows)" (BDHP 36:1-7, with HG IV 1766, Suurmeijer 2010). They are the tenant farmers and the owner of a harvested field. Indeed, "the Journey (...) was most likely employed to insure the just distribution of the harvest between the lessors and lessees (...)" (Harris 1965, 223a).

Now, in a list of expenditures we read: "1 seah: Marduk went out together with the ZAG.ḪA" (CT 47 80:13, with Sommerfeld 1982, 99-100). This is the *mākisum*, the expert who assisted at the partition of the barley. He was in the State's service: "Ein Beamter oder Beauftragter der Obrigkeit, welcher für sie [the State] den Ernteanteil bzw. Pachtzins alles von ihr vergebenen Ackerlandes einhebt" (Kraus 1984, 244, 248). Institutional land! We can be more specific. Harris (1965, 224b) speaks about "the just collection of taxes and tithes". "Tithe" is based on *še'um aširtum* in MAH 16147:6, according to Harris "the tenth of the harvest" (Harris, 222).[21] And the tithe is a temple tax. Did the Weapon visit temple lands in various places? Unfortunately, the word cannot mean "tithe" (one expects **eširtum* and the word "tithe" actually is *ešrētum*). Still, the dictionaries link the word *aširtum* with temples: etwa "eine heilige Gabe" (AHw); (an offering or a pious gift to the gods) (CAD A/2 439b). Temple land! There are more indications that in Sippar the temple was

[20] After Civil 1994, 97.

[21] Accepted by van der Toorn 1996, 123 n. 23. However, his references concern the *aširtum* in silver that has been "made equal" (*ašārum*); "équilibré", see F. Joannès 1989, 144 (20).

behind the Journey. Three texts have as witnesses the gods Šamaš and Aja (nos. 10, 11, 14). The main persons, lessors and lessees, and the witnesses, are the temple priests *gudapsûm* and *ērib bītim* (Harris 1965, 223b). Once, the lessor is the head of the temple (sanga) of Aja (no. 4). The notes on the persons in CBS 92 (published below) will show how those priests were interrelated by family ties.

Survey of the main persons.

Lessor(s):

Ašqudum, son of Rīš-Gibil (no. 1), Awelātum, son of Ibbî, and Warad-Ebabbari, son of Warad-Kubi (8), Etel-pi-Nabium, sanga of Aja (4), Iddin-Marduk, son of Ḫunnātum (5), Iddin-Marduk, son of Ipqu-Antum (nos. 7, 13), Marduk-muballiṭ, *gudapsûm*, and Sîn-išmeanni, *ērib bītim* priest (the son of Ibni-Gibil)[22] (9), Marduk-muballiṭ, *gudapsûm*, Šumum-libši [...], and Attâ (12), Marduk-muballiṭ, Iddin-Marduk, Etel-pu, and Aḫuni, all four *gudapsûm* (10), Rīm-Adad, *gudapsûm*, and Ibni-Gibil, *ērib bītim* priest (3), Sîn-nādin-šumi, *gudapsûm*, and Rīš-Šamaš, son of Sîn-abi (11), Sîn-ḫāzir (2), Šamur-ezēssu, son of Šamaš-dajjān, and Atanaḫ-ili, son of Ipqu-Annunītum (6).

Lessee(s):

Atanaḫ-ili, son of Ipqu-Annunītum, and Šamaš-bani, son of Ibni-Gibil (3), Atâ, son of Bēlšunu (9), ... and Ibni-Gibil (12), Iddin-Marduk *gudapsûm*(?), and Iddātum, son of Bunene-iddinam (8), Ina-Esagila-zērum, PA erén. meš, son of Rīm-Adad (10), Ipqatum and Damiq-Marduk (1), Sinātum, son of Nannātum (2), Šamaš-bani, son of Ibni-Gibil (nos. 7, 13), Šamaš-bani, son of Ibni-Gibil, and Ipqu-Šala, son of Šamaš-... (11), Warad-Sîn, *gudapsûm*, son of Šamaš-tappašu (5), the same, [and ..., the son of] Rīm-[Adad] (4).

We can no longer avoid discussing a notoriously difficult text already mentioned before.

MAH 16.147, with Szlechter 1958, 122-123.

(1) íd kaskal *ge-er-ri-im*
šà *ma-tim*
a-na dumu.meš *ì-lí*
ù dumu.meš *iš-ta-ri*(!)

[22] So in CBS 149:16 f. (witness). Restore the seal inscription on TLOB 65b. accordingly. Line 6 was collated by Frans van Koppen (read *e-ri-ib* é).

ša i-na šà *ma-tim wa-aš-bu*
še-am a-ši-ir-tam
šu-ud-du-nim-ma
a-na UD.KIB.NUN ki *ba-ba-li*
^{P}*a-bu-um-wa-qar*
sanga Ištar(?)UD.KIB.NUN ki
^{P}ìr-é.gal.maḫ
i-gur-šu
i-na ša-la-am ge-er-ri-šu
2/3 gín kù.babbar *i-le-eq-qé*
(ruling)
igi *qùr-di*-Ištar sanga ...
igi ^{d}EN.ZU-*e-ri-ba-am* dub.sar
(ruling)
Date: 10.IV Ammi-ṣaduqa 14.

Translation:

"River (district), the route of the Journey, the countryside: in order to make the sons of the god and the sons of the goddess living in the countryside deliver the barley, the *aširtum*, and bring (it) to Sippar: Warad-Egalmaḫ hired Abum-waqar, the head of (the temple of) Ištar-of-Sippar. At the completion of his Journey, he will take 2/3 shekels of silver.

Before Qurdi-Ištar, the sanga ... Before Sîn-erībam, the scribe."

Notes.

See the remarks in the reviews of Szlechter 1958 by Finkelstein 1961, 131a; Kraus 1959, 124b. Later remarks: Renger 1973, 103; Kraus 1973, 66-67; Farber 1976, 125-126; Charpin 1979, 187-188.

(1) Some attempts at reading the first signs have been made: *a-na* (Szlechter, Kraus, Charpin), 1 *agrum* (ḫun?) (Finkelstein). We have learned above that the Journey often takes place in "river (districts)" (íd). This fits the copied signs. I cannot believe that *ge-er-ri-im* is a gloss to kaskal and suggest to read *ḫarrān gerrim*.

(6) *aširtum*: see above. I read in YOS 12 356:14 (Charpin 1986, 169, 512) *a-ši-<ir>-ti pur-šu-mi*. This is another text about the Journey; note *ša ebūri u libbi mātim* there (line 8).

(8) The transportation (*babālum*) of barley to a city is also mentioned in the Journey of Adad, YOS 12 48:5.

(10) nimgir *wa-ši-ib* (Kraus) is not good. We know Abum-waqar sanga Ištar(?) as first witness in OLA 21 no. 73:24 (Amṣ). Janssen (1992, 45) gave a

list of the sanga's in Sippar in some years of king Ammi-ṣaduqa. Here we meet with Abum-waqar, son of Utul-Ištar, sanga Ištar/ᵈInanna, in Di 1692 and Di 967 (Amṣ 12). This fits the traces in our text. Examples of "Ištar-of-Sippar" are rare: CTMMA I 55:2 (so!); possibly CT 2 43:3 (to be collated).

(11) Warad-Egalmaḫ (or: Ir-Egalmaḫ) probably is the sanga of the goddess Gula (Charpin).

(15) Qurdi-Ištar sanga *An-nu-ni-tum* is first witness in CTMMA I 53:12 (Amṣ 7). He is simply sanga in VAS 29 77:16 (Amd 20). Can we read sanga ᵈinanna a-[ga-d]è <ki>, a title known from CTMMA I 53:5 (Amṣ 7)?

I suggest that the "the sons of the god and the sons of the goddess living in the countryside" are found on the lands of god Šamaš and goddess Aja.[23] In our text, their fields have already been visited after the harvest. We are now in month IV and the *aširtum* barley is to be transported to the city. A collector (*mušaddinum*) is hired to take care of this "journey" and is paid in silver — not in barley or sesame oil, as in the other texts.

We now return to the fourteen texts about the Journey in harvest time.

The barley is to be paid either "in (the harbour of) Sippar" (nos. 1, 2, 7, 14), or the temples of the gods Sîn (3, 8, 9, 13); name of god lost (4); in the latest text Nabium (10). A temple of Nabium in Sippar is not known; Nabium is the god of Borsippa, near Babylon. We may witness here a change due to the political situation in the reign of Samsu-ditana.

Who profited from the "yield of the Journey" (gú.un *gerrim*)? Harris (1965) made several suggestions: the Šamaš temple (223a), the head of the temple (sanga) (223-224), the *gudapsûm* priests (223b), temple personnel or persons related to them (224b). Now, an unusual text records the solemn allotment of "one Journey, share (ḫa.la) of Ibni-Gibil" by casting lots "in water/in the ritual" (*ina isqim ina mê*), between colleagues (*tappû*); he has to pay to the sanga the yield of the Journey (Scheil, Sippar 287, with Harris, 223-224). The word *isqum* in Old Babylonian texts can refer to a prebend (van Driel 2002, 109) and more than once the *gudapsûm* is present when an *isqum* is at stake (Sippar).[24] In Ur, a transaction about a prebend (mar.za) is witnessed by the sanga and three *gudapsûm* priests "of Eridu" (PBS 8/2 255, with Charpin 1986, 188-189, 393-394). Renting the "Journey" looks like a prebend of the *gudapsûm* priests, and exactly that has been suggested by Maria deJong Ellis: "In fact, the underlying basis of those transactions — certainly of those

[23] Cf. the field name "Irrigation disrict of Those of Aja (*šūt ša Aja*)" in Sippar: a.gàr *šu-ut ša* ᵈA-a, MHET II/4 496:3, TLOB 6:1, YOS 13 12:2, 22, 28, rev. 6. Note a.šà *mala maṣû* a.gàr *Ašukum ina šūt ša Aja*, BE 6/1 83:3-4.

[24] CBS 414:8; Charpin 1988, 30:27; Wilcke 1983, 62:19.

which specify one year and possibly also some of those only mentioning the harvest — was not any specific journey of the weapon, but the right to conduct such journeys. In other words, the texts attest the leasing of a prebendary privilege, which presumably conferred a stipendiary income on the lessee, as well as yielding rental fees for the temple. This would explain both why the rank of the lessee, when known, is that of a *gudapsû*, and why the duration of the contract, when specified, is for the period of one year or one harvest-season (...)" (Ellis 1989, 132a). Wilcke sees parallels in the rituals (*parṣum*) about the *kezertum*-women in Kish (Wilcke 1976, 86).[25]

There are several indications that the prebendaries traded with their rights. It is likely that in this they did this business with each other. One text says that the payment in barley will be done to "the bearer of (this) contract" (OLA 21 no. 6:12; above, no. 11). Such transactions take place within a closed and trusted community (Stol 2004, 879-880, following Veenhof). Another text records an "interest-bearing loan" (*ḫubullum*) that is outstanding (CT 8 8c:13; above, no. 1). In the archive of Ba-a-a-mu in Ur, he and another person share the Journey of Adad in a commercial society, so it seems (YOS 12 354, with YOS 12 356; Charpin 1986, 167-169, 512).[26] The transportation of "the barley of the Journey of Adad" is organized in a commercial venture (YOS 12 48, with Schwemer 2001, 335-336). The Sippar text CBS 92 published below gives us a glimpse of how they traded in "the yield of the Journey".

C. A new text: CBS 92

Dimensions: 5,5 × 4,6 × 2,5 cm

Obv.	(1)	6 še.gur giš.bán ^{d}utu
		šà gú.un *ge-er-ri*
		UD.KIB.NUN^{ki}—*am-n*[*a*]*-nu-um*
		ša dumu.20.kam dumu *ib-ni-*^{d}marduk
	(5)	*e-li* ^{d}*bu-ne-ne—ga-mil*
		e-lu-ú
Edge		*a-na* mu.bal
		[*i*]*-na re-eš* níg.gur$_{11}$ (GA)

[25] Note in this group of texts the Journey named kaskal of a person, YOS 13 236:3; elsewhere named *ḫar-ra-an* PN, UMM G 18:4, with Yoffee 1998, 323.

[26] Charpin 1981, 542 and 547 Archives H (includes YOS 12 50).

Rev. [x še.g]ur giš.bán ^{d}utu
$^{p\,d}$*bu-ne-ne—ga-mil*
i-le-eq-qé
(ruling)
igi *ri-im*—^{d}iškur gudu$_4$.abzu
ig[i *t*]*a-ri-bu-ša* gudu$_4$.abzu
(ruling)
[itu še.KI]N.ku$_5$ u$_4$.25.kam
[mu] *am-mi—di-ta-na* lu[gal.e]
íd.da *am-mi—di-ta-na*
mu.un.ba.[a]l.la

Seal impressions:
1. [*ta*]*-ri-bu-u*[*m*]
gudu$_4$.[ZU].AB
[dumu] sig—*an-nu-ni-*[*tum*]
ìr níg é.[babbar.ra]

2. [...]—*ga*(?)*-mil*
[...].babbar.ra
[...] x x

Translation

"6 kor of barley in the seah-measure of Šamaš, from the yield of the journey of Sippar-Amnānum, is what Bunene-gāmil owes(?) to Mār-ešrê, the son of Ibni-Marduk. In the next year, Bunene-gāmil will take from the available assets [6(?)] kor of barley in the seah-measure of Šamaš.
Before Rīm-Adad, the *gudapsûm*.
Before Tarībuša, the *gudapsûm.*"

Date: 25.XII, year Ammi-ditana 22.

Remarks

(4-5) This Mār-ešrê is not known elsewhere. There is a priest *ērib bītim* with this name (BE 6/1 76:36, Ae kk; Van Lerberghe and Voet 1997, 152:27, Ae e). I cannot identify Bunene-gāmil. Note that in the hire of the axe of Šamaš (no. 14) a Bunene-abi is assistant (YOS 12 442:3). Bunene is the vizier of god Šamaš.

(5-6) One expects *ša* M. *eli* B. *i-šu-ú* "what B. owes to M." But we have to take *e-lu-ú* seriously. There is only one OB parallel, in an administrative text listing expenditures of bread and barley, summarized *ša Be-lí-ja-*<*tum*>

e-l[*i*] 30-*i*-[...] *e-lu-ú* (TCL 1 227:14-15).[27] One is reminded of Neo-Babylonian *ana muḫḫi elû* "to take over a charge, to enter upon an obligation" (CAD); "mit Ansprüchen auftreten", and: "(Zahlung) auf sich nehmen".[28]

(7) mu.bal is the Sumerogram for *šattum ēribtum*, "next year", CAD Š/2 201-202; *ēribu* adj., CAD E 293a. Cf. *erēbu* "to come (said of months, seasons, etc.)", CAD E 266b (e). A docket is dated to the third day of month 1 of what is provisionally called "the next year".[29] Charpin and Kraus stated that mu.bal can mean "the current year" ("l'année en cours", "das laufende Jahr"). Kraus gives no argumentation at all and Charpin adduces two passages.[30] However, there, and elsewhere, a prepayment for the coming year is meant. Payments in advance speaking of mu.bal occur more than once in field leases and house rentals; the coming year (for which no yearname was known as yet, of course) is here indicated by mu.bal or mu *e-ri-ib-tum*. In house rentals: *ša* mu *e-ri-ib-tum* (YOS 12 114:3), *ša ša-at-tim e-ri-ib-tim* (VAS 29 37:4-5), *ša* mu.bal (YOS 13 267:3). One house rental offers the unusual formula "in the new year", *ina* mu.1.kam *eš-ši-tim inaddin* (YOS 12 2:9-11). Sometimes the contract says that the prepayment will be "deducted" (*ḫarāṣum*) later, YOS 12 114:8 (house; here according to the exchange rate barley-silver: kar *ibbaššû* kù *iḫḫarraṣ*), and OLA 21 43:10-11 (field, *ina* gú.un a.šà-*ša ša* mu.bal *iḫḫarraṣ*). In one text, wool, valued as 1 shekel of silver, "*teqrūbatum* of 4 *iku* field of the coming year" (*ša* mu.bal), will be "given" when the (new) year begins, lit. "at the entering of the year" (*i-na e-re-eb ša-at-tim*) (BM 97257).

Remark. This text was cited in CAD T under *teqrūbatum* ("meaning unknown") and was published in transliteration by Seth Richardson in his dissertation.[31] It is my suggestion that *teqrūbatum* means "(partial) advance payment (of a field rent)" in the first three texts quoted by CAD.[32] It is possible that a letter refers to this kind of payment: "Let me advance to them (*luqerribšunūšim*) these ten shekels of silver and sometime I will take it from field or garden" (AbB 3 88:9-12). Petschow has pointed out the background of such advance payments; sometimes the full sum.[33]

[27] Edited in VAB 5 no. 40. Read in line 4: ninda *ù* dug.útul (*diqārum*, "dish"). Line 5: perhaps *a-na ḫa*-TI-*ip* giš/gada (=?). Line 14: Bēlijātum (emendated!) is well known in other texts from Paris; see Burggraaff, *Aula Or.* 13 (1995) 161-167 (he does not discuss this text).

[28] CAD E 125b; AHw I 207 f., meanings 5. d), and 7.

[29] Weitemeyer 1962, 56, 97 no. 112.

[30] Charpin 1986, 167; Charpin 1993, 186b ad AUCT IV 36:6 (elsewhere, Charpin translates mu.bal as "l'année suivante"; 209, UET 5 868:11); Kraus (1985, 538) on mu.bal.bi.šè in Sigrist 1984, 48-50 (his own examples are simple mu.bal in field rentals from Dilbat). Incidentally, mu.bal.bi.šè in the *sattukku* texts rather means "on account of its turn".

[31] BM 97257, CAD T 348a, Richardson 2002, II, 355 f.

[32] CT 8 19a:24, BM 97257:3, AbB 13 77:4, perhaps also in *teqrūbat aplūtim*, TLOB 86:3.

[33] Petschow 1984, 198-200; summarized by Stol 2004a, 850; Stol 2004b, 171a.

Another solution — to see in mu.bal not the calendar year, but the year stipulated by the contract — would fit "the current year" but this is hardly convincing.

For *ana šattim ēribtim* (*ana* mu.bal is frequent) on perhaps would expect not *ana* but *ina š. ē*. In early Old Babylonian, *ana* can be used in time indications, probably meaning "at a point of time in the future". It can live on in frozen expressions, like this one. The best known example is *ana ittišu*, studied by B. Landsberger. Another example is *ana ebūrim imaddad* in early texts.[34]

(8) *re-eš* níg. gur_{11}(GA). The correct reading for níg.ga is nì.gur_{11},[35] but up till now one often finds níg.ga in current literature, and for convenience's sake we shall follow here the old path. CAD N/1 231-232 sees in níg.ga the Sumerogram for Akkadian *namkūrum*, "possession(s)", and probably would interpret *re-eš* níg.ga as *rēš namkūrim*. It indeed gives the references for sag níg.ga, presumably *rēš namkūrim*, under *namkūru*. Added are two passages for sag.níg.ga.ra (with an extra.ra), introduced by the remark "Note also" (it looks like a meaningless variant).[36] However, I opt for the Akkadian reading *rēš makkūrim*, "available assets" (CAD), "etwa verfügbarer Bestand" (AHw). I prefer "the initial amount" (so A. Goetze).[37] In fact, níg.ga also stands for *makkūrum*, so *rēš makkūrim* is equally possible. The problem with *namkūru* is that in syllabic form it is so rare in Old Babylonian context: in two letters, at least one of them probably originating from Dilbat.[38] Syllabic *re-eš ma-ak-ku-ri* is better known, from the Mari texts and occasionally elsewhere.[39] Both options remain possible, however. "To have (a new) initial amount fixed"

[34] Landsberger 1966, 64-65, correcting "innerhalb (von)" of AHw 47b, *ana* 2.b, into "in". *Ana ebūrim*: BDHP 37:13; De Meyer 1978, 164-180; nos. 26:6, 27:6, 63:8 (*a-na* u_4.ebur.šè); TA 495-1930:5-6 (unpubl. Tell Asmar).

[35] Confirmed by the syllabic writing ni-in-gur for NÍG.GA; see Civil 1996, line 2.

[36] In the letter AbB 7 176:11 we meet the word *ma-kur-ri* which I interpret as "(fishing-) boat". "Take stock of the cargo of your boat (*re-eš* níg *ma-kur-ri-ka i-ši*); sell (it) for barley (or) silver and let them take (...) the fish." For *rēšam našûm*, see Veenhof 1985, 297-298; Stol 1993, 246a. Another interpretation was given S. Greengus 1981, 260.

[37] CAD M/1 136b (c), R 288-289; AHw II 975b (4.c) (*rēšum* means in itself "etwa verfügbarer Bestand"). RA 64 98:9 is now ARMT 23 556:9. Cf. Goetze 1950, 83 CUL 78:3 ("the initial amount").

[38] AbB 6 219:25 (in CAD "VAS 7 202"), where *pateḫ* is Dilbat dialect for *peti* ("opened"), cf. the Dilbat god Ipteḫ-bītam; Stol 1973, 221 n. 3; accepted in CAD P 341a. The other letter, AbB 9 183 = YOS 13 449, was published in an edition with many Dilbat texts.

[39] Only the syllabic passages were given in CAD M. More: Mari: ARMT 23 428:1, 429:1 (personnel). Elsewhere: AbB 12 190:17, Jursa 1997, 136:21 ("den genauen Umfang der Güter [kennen wir nicht]").

is in Akkadian *rēš namkūri rašûm* Š in the one letter, and *rēš makkūrim rašûm* Š in the other (AbB 9 183:16, AbB 4 141:10). The Dilbat letter is somewhat complicated. It begins with "That barley had a (fixed) initial amount (*še'ûm šû rēš namkūri išû*)". Here, barley had been stolen and it was decided that the amount should be fixed anew: "That barley should acquire a (new) initial amount (*še'ûm šû* sag níg.ga *liršî*)" (AbB 6 219:25, 31) (again the verb *rašû*).[40] Here, Sumerian sag níg.ga unexpectedly appears in line 31.

Von Soden was on the wrong track when he tentatively identified sag. níg.ga with *sannigû* (AHw s.v.).[41] The Sumerogram sag níg.ga.ra is well known from Southern texts, notably in the phrase sag níg.ga.ra šà.bi.ta.[42] Twice the variant sag.níg.ḪAR.ra šà.bi.ta; twice sag.níg.UL.ra šà.bi.ta.[43] Redundant is *rēš* in: *re-eš* sag níg.ga in BIN 2 68:25. In the texts on wool in the archive of princess Iltani the phrase *ana* sag níg.ga-*šu iṣṣabbat* is frequent.[44]

The witnesses

1. Rīm-Adad.
Rīm-Adad, *gudapsûm*, is attested in OLA 21 no. 1:4 (Amd 33), BDHP 15:2 (Amd -).

Two sons of him are known:

a. Ina-Esagila-zērum.
In another text about the Journey, a man appears at the end of a list of four *gudapsûms* and he may be his son: "Ina-Esagila-zērum, head of the workmen (PA erén.meš), son of Rīm-Adad" (CT 4 23c:9-10; above, no. 10; Sd 5). Anbar (1975, 119: BM 13596:11; Amṣ 15) draws attention to this unusual occupation when discussing Ina-Esagila-zērum PA MAR.TU,

[40] Cf. the warning threat "I have with me (a tablet mentioning) your initial amount" (sag.níg.ga-*ka našiāku*) (AbB 3 38:30).

[41] Only in Ḫḫ II 73a and uncertain; CAD S 26a, *sagniggarû*. Dalley (2009) accepts Akkadian *sannigû*.

[42] TCL 10 107:14, YOS 12 152:12, YOS 13 43:4, 19, 142:4. More in CAD N/1 231b.

[43] sag.níg.ḪAR.ra: Birot Tablettes 13:3, VAS 18 81:5. sag.níg.UL.ra: YOS 8 165:2, BM 16173:3 (transliteration distributed by Walker at a Rencontre Assyriologique). Cf. níg.UL.ra a.na.gál.la.àm, Wilson 2008, 179, Coll. Cotsen no. 78:14 f. Note the parallels in CAD M/1 134a s.v. *makkūru*; add giš šu.kára níg.ga a.na.gál.la in TCL 10 34:24 with coll. Arnaud 1976b, 85. And note níg.UL (of a god) for níg.ga in TIM 3 124:3, Kienast Kisurra no. 104:6 (thus according to the copies).

[44] BBVOT 1 5:13, 81:9 f., etc. See CAD Ṣ 23a (3), "included in the capital sum". Note *ana* sag.níg.*ga-ku-nu liṣṣabit* in AUAM 3204, cited by Gallery (1980, 13b with note 58); *ṣabtu*, Birot Tablettes 59:7 f.

first witness in a harvest labour contract. An "Ina-Esagila-zērum, son of Rīm-Adad(?)" is first witness in an expenditure of barley of the silo (De Graef 2002, 79 BM 97601:10; Amṣ 21).

b. Marduk-muballiṭ.
Another son is Marduk-muballiṭ *gudapsûm* (Charpin 1988, 30 = HG 96:27; Amṣ). Note Marduk-muballiṭ *gudapsûm* (no father's name is given) at the beginning of the list of four *gudapsûms*, just mentioned, where Ina-Esagila-zērum appeared at its end (CT 4 23c:5; Sd 5). And we see him again at the beginning of another list of persons in an unpublished text about the Journey (CBS 149:4). He is first witness in the rental of a Journey (TLOB 65:17; Amṣ 10). Mār-ešrê, son of Ilšu-ibni, owes bundles of garlic to a Marduk-muballiṭ *gudapsûm*; first witness is Ibni-Šamaš, a priest (*ērib bītim*) (OLA 21 no. 7:3, 10; Amṣ). He and Ibni-Marduk, a priest, are the first witnesses in a loan of silver from a *nadītum* (BBVOT 1 no. 138:9-10 [cf. no. 121; Colbow 1992, 148-149]; Sd 18).

Rīm-Adad as a father of [...] in a text about the Journey: OLA 21 no. 6:7 (Amṣ 5).

2. Tarībum, son of Ipiq-Annunītum (seal inscription 1).
Tarībum is the first in a list of six *gudapsûms*, all witnesses (BE 6/1 76:28; Ae kk); the second in a list of four *gudapsûms* (Van Lerberghe and Voet 1997, 152 Di 1851:23; Ae "e"); in both texts some "priests" (among whom a Mār-ešrê) follow. He is as *gudapsûm* a witness in CT 47 69:26, 69a:10 (Ae "h") and uses the seal of his father Ipiq-Annunītum, with the inscription "Ipiq-Annunītum, $gudu_4$ ^{d}utu, dumu Aḫam-arši [sic]" (seal 9). Another *gudapsûm* in this text also uses his father's seal; here the father again has the title $gudu_4$ ^{d}utu and he is "servant of (the temple) Ebabbar" (seal 7). Harris sees in the sequence $gudu_4$ — *gudapsûm* an "upward mobility in temple offices".[45] "The $GUDU_4$.ABSU ranks above the ordinary $GUDU_4$" (van Driel 2002, 102 n. 22).[46]

Later on, Tarībum, son of Ipiq-Annunītum appears as sanga of Ištar of Akkad (^{d}inanna a-ga-dè ki) (CTMMA I 53:5-6; Amṣ 7).

45 Harris 1975, 168, 170. She adds that Tarībum may be the father of the $gudu_4$ Bēlšunu in BE 6/1 104:5 (note 99).

46 Note that a text in Isin seems to show the reverse: the father is *gudapsûm* and the son $gudu_4$ (BIN 7 212:24-27). Renger (1969, 145) identifies the *gudapsûm* Abba in BIN 7 212:27 (no date) with Abba, son of Ikun-pi-Damu (no title is given), who buys the prebend nam.$gudu_4$ (BIN 7 66:7 f.; Damiq-ilišu year 6). However, the latter Abba has the title šà.tam in Nougayrol 1979, 80 AO 11143 rev. 5-6 (Damiq-ilišu year 5) (three $gudu_4$'s follow).

Bibliography

ANBAR, M. 1975: "Textes de l'époque babylonienne ancienne", *RA* 69, 109-136.

ARCHI, A. 2005: "Minima eblaitica 22: the symbolism of the axe (*ni'tum*) in the death", *NABU* 2005 no. 69.

ARNAUD, D. 1976a: "TCL X et XI: ajouts et corrections", *RA* 70, 84-92.

— 1976b: "Larsa. Catalogue des textes et des objets inscrits trouvés au cours de la sixième campagne", *Syria* 53, 47-79.

CHARPIN, D. 1979: "À propos d'une consultation oraculaire", *RA* 73, 186-187.

— 1981: "La Babylonie de Samsu-iluna à la lumière de nouveaux documents", *BiOr* 38, 517-547.

— 1985: "Un quartier de Babylone et ses habitants sous les successeurs d'Hammurabi", *BiOr* 42, 265-278.

— 1986: *Le clergé d'Ur au siècle d'Hammurabi (XIXe-XVIIIe siècles av. J.-C.)*, Genève-Paris.

— 1988: "Sippar: deux villes jumelles", *RA* 82, 13-32.

— 1993: review of M. Sigrist, *Old Babylonian account texts in the Horn Archaeological Museum* (1990), *RA* 87, 185-187.

CIVIL, M. 1994: *The Farmer's Instructions* (Aula Orientalis-Supplementa 5), Barcelona.

— 1996: "Sin-iddinam in Emar and SU.A = Šimaški", *NABU* 1996 no. 41.

COLBOW, G. 1992: "Einige Abrollungen aus der Zeit Ammiditanas bis Samsu-ditanas im Louvre", *RA* 86, 121-157.

DALLEY, S. 2009: *Babylonian tablets from the First Sealand Dynasty in the Schøyen Collection* (Cornell University Studies in Assyriology and Sumerology 9), Bethesda.

DALMAN, G. 1924: *Orte und Wege Jesu* (Schriften des Deutschen Palästina-Instituts 1), Gütersloh.

DE GRAEF, K. 2002: "Two Ilšu-ibni's, two ugula gidru's", *Aula Or.* 20, 61-97.

DELLER, K. 1984: "Akkadische Lexikographie: *CAD* M", *OrNS* 53, 72-124.

DE MEYER, L., "Documents épigraphiques paléo-babyloniens provenant des sondages A, B et D", in: *Tell ed-Dēr II. Progress reports (first series)* (1978), Leuven, 147-184.

DOMBRADI 1996: *Die Darstellung des Rechtsaustrags in den altbabylonischen Prozessurkunden* (Freiburger Altorientalische Studien 20), Stuttgart.

DURAND, J.-M. 1983: *Textes administratifs des salles 134 et 160 du palais de Mari Transcrits, traduits et commentés* (Archives Royales de Mari 21), Paris.

— 2008: "La religion amorrite en Syrie à l'époque des archives de Mari", in: G. del Olmo Lete (ed.), *Mythologie et religion des Sémites occidentaux* (Orientalia Lovaniensia Analecta 162), Leuven, 163-716.

— 2009: "Un conflit diplomatique évité", in: D.A. Barreyra Fracaroli and G. del Olmo Lete (eds.), *Reconstruyendo el pasado remoto: estudios sobre el Próximo Oriente antiguo en homenaje a Jorge R. Silva Castillo* (Aula Orientalis-Supplementa 25), Barcelona, 93-96.

— 2010: "Des dieux, un ministre et un coquin", in: D. Shehata, F. Weiershäuser and K. V. Zand (eds.), *Von Göttern und Menschen. Beiträge zur Literatur und Geschichte des Alten Orients. Festschrift für Brigitte Groneberg* (Cuneiform Monographs 41), Leiden, 63-72.

ELLIS, M. DEJONG 1989: "An Old Babylonian *kusarikku*," in: H. Behrens, D. Loding and M. T. Roth (eds.) *DUMU-E$_2$-DUB-BA-A. Studies in honor of Åke W. Sjöberg* (Occasional Publications of the Samuel Noah Kramer Fund 11), Philadelphia, 121-135.
FARBER, W. 1976: review of Kraus 1973, *WdO* 8, 124-128.
— 1981: "Zur älteren akkadischen Beschwörungsliteratur", *ZA* 71, 51-72.
FINKELSTEIN, J.J. 1961: review of Szlechter 1958, *JCS* 15, 129-131.
GALLERY, M. 1980: "The office of the šatammu in the Old Babylonian period", *AfO* 27, 1-36.
GODDEERIS, A. 2002: *Economy and society in Northern Babylonia in the early Old Babylonian period (ca. 2000-1800 BC)* (Orientalia Lovaniensia Analecta 109), Leuven.
GOETZE, A. 1950: "Sin-iddinam of Larsa. New tablets from his reign", *JCS* 4, 83-118.
GREENGUS, S. 1981: review of C.B.F. Walker, *Cuneiform texts from Babylonian tablets in the British Museum, Part 52* (1976), *JAOS* 101, 257-260.
— 1986: *Studies in Ishchali documents* (Bibliotheca Mesopotamica 19), Malibu.
GUICHARD, M. 1999: "Les aspects religieux de la guerre à Mari", *RA* 93, 27-48.
HARRIS, R. 1965: "The journey of the divine weapon", in: *Studies in Honor of Benno Landsberger on his seventy-fifth birthday April 21, 1965* (Assyriological Studies 16), Chicago, 217-224.
— 1975: *Ancient Sippar. A demographic study of an Old-Babylonian city (1894-1595 B.C.)* (Uitgaven van het Nederlands Instituut voor het Nabije Oosten te Leiden, 36), Leiden.
JANSSEN, C. 1992: "Inanna-mansum et ses fils: relation d'une succession turbulente dans les archives d'Ur-Utu", *RA* 86, 19-52.
JOANNÈS, F. 1989: "La culture matérielle à Mari (IV): les méthodes de pesée", *RA* 83, 113-152.
JURSA, M. 1997: "Als König Abi-ešuḫ gerechte Ordnung hergestellt hat": eine bemerkenswerte altbabylonische Prozessurkunde", *RA* 91, 135-145.
KRAUS, F.R. 1955: "Neue Rechtsurkunden der altbabylonischen Zeit", *WdO* 2, 120-136.
— 1959: review of Szlechter 1958, *BiOr* 16, 120-129.
— 1973: *Vom mesopotamischen Menschen der altbabylonischen Zeit und seiner Welt* (Mededelingen der Koninklijke Nederlandse Akademie van Wetenschappen, afd. Letterkunde, Nieuwe Reeks 36, 6), Amsterdam.
— 1984: *Königliche Verfügungen in altbabylonischer Zeit* (Studia et Documenta 11), Leiden.
— 1985: "Eine altbabylonische Buchhaltung aus einem Amtsarchiv in Nippur", *BiOr* 42, 526-542.
KRECHER, J. 1969: "Göttersymbole. Nach sumerischen und akkadischen Texten", *RlA* III/7, 495-498.
LANDSBERGER, B. 1966: "Einige unerkannt gebliebene oder verkannte Nomina des Akkadischen", *WdO* 3, 48-79.
MALUL, M. 1988: *Studies in Mesopotamian legal symbolism* (Alter Orient und Altes Testament 221), Kevelaer-Neukirchen-Vluyn.
NOUGAYROL, J. 1979: "Tablettes diverses du Musée du Louvre", *RA* 73, 63-80.

OWEN, D.I. and R. WESTBROOK 1992: "Tie her up and throw her into the river! An Old Babylonian inchoate marriage on the rocks", *ZA* 82, 202-207.

PETSCHOW, H.P.H. 1984: "Die §§45 und 46 des Codex Hammurapi. Ein Beitrag zum altbabylonischen Bodenpachtrecht und zum Problem: Was ist der Codex Hammurapi?", *ZA* 74, 181-212.

PIENTKA, R. 1998: *Die spätaltbabylonische Zeit* (Imgula 2), Münster.

POWELL, M.A. 1990: "Masse und Gewichte", *RlA* VII/7-8, 457-517.

RENGER, J. 1969: "Untersuchungen zum Priestertum der altbabylonischen Zeit. 2. Teil", *ZA* 59, 104-230.

— 1973: "mārat ilim: Exogamie bei den semitischen Nomaden des 2. Jahrtausends", *AfO* 24, 103-107.

RICHARDSON, S. 2002: *The collapse of a complex state* (Dissertation Columbia University, New York).

SCHEIL, V. 1915: "Le terme put bîti ullulu en droit babylonien", *RA* 12, 115-116.

SCHWEMER, D. 2001: *Wettergottgestalten*, Wiesbaden.

SIGRIST M. 1984: *Les sattukku dans l'Ešumeša durant la période d'Isin et Larsa* (Bibliotheca Mesopotamica 11), Malibu.

SOMMERFELD 1982: *Der Aufstieg Marduks* (Alter Orient und Altes Testament 213), Neukirchen-Vluyn.

SPAEY J. 1993: "Emblems in rituals in the Old Babylonian period", J. Quaegebeur (ed.), *Ritual and sacrifice in the Ancient Near East* (Orientalia Lovaniensia Analecta 55), Leuven, 409-420.

STOL, M. 1973: review of J.J. Finkelstein, *Late Old Babylonian documents and letters* (1972), *JCS* 25, 215-233.

— 1993: "Biblical idiom in Akkadian", in M.E. Cohen, D. C. Snell and D. B. Weisberg (eds.), *The Tablet and the Scroll. Near Eastern Studies in honor of William W. Hallo*, Bethesda, 246-249.

— 2000: *Birth in Babylonia and the Bible* (Cuneiform Monographs 14), Groningen.

— 2004a: "Wirtschaft und Gesellschaft in altbabylonischer Zeit" in D. Charpin, D. O. Edzard & M. Stol, *Mesopotamien: Die altbabylonische Zeit* (OBO 160/4), Fribourg - Göttingen, 643-975.

— 2004b: "Pacht. B. Altbabylonisch", *RlA* X/3-4, 170-172.

— 2011: "An Old Babylonian list of objects", in L. Vacín (ed.), *Studies in Memory of Blahoslav Hruška*, Dresden, 247-252.

SUURMEIJER, G. 2010: "A new couple and two orphans", *NABU* 2010 no. 3.

SZLECHTER, E. 1958: *Tablettes juridiques de la 1re Dynastie de Babylone conservées au Musée d'Art et d'Histoire de Genève*. Deuxième Partie: *transcription — traduction — commentaire*, Paris.

TANRET, M. 2010: *The seal of the sanga* (Cuneiform Monographs 40), Leiden–Boston.

VAN DER TOORN, K. 1996: *Family religion in Babylonia, Syria and Israel* (Studies in the History and Culture of the Ancient Near East, 7), Leiden–New York–Köln.

VAN DRIEL, G. 2002: *Elusive silver. In search of a role for a market in an agrarian environment. Aspects of Mesopotamian society* (Uitgaven van het Nederlands Instituut voor het Nabije Oosten te Leiden, 95), Leiden.

VAN LERBERGHE, K. 1982: "L'arrachement de l'emblème *šurinnum*", in: *Zikir šumim. Assyriological studies presented to F.R. Kraus* (Studia Francisci Scholten Memoriae dicata, 5), Leiden, 245-257.

VAN LERBERGHE, K. and G. VOET 1997: "A poor man of Sippar", *AOF* 24, 148-157.

LOCHER, C. 1986: *Die Ehre einer Frau in Israel* (Orbis Biblicus et Orientalis 70), Freiburg-Göttingen.

VEENHOF, K.R. 1985: "sag.íl.la = saggilû", J.-R. Kupper and J.-M. Durand (eds.), *Miscellanea babylonica: Mélanges Maurice Birot*, Paris, 285-306.

— 2003a: "Fatherhood is a matter of opinion. An Old Babylonian trial on filiation and service duties", in: C. Wilcke, W. Sallabergher, K. Volk and A. Zgoll (eds.), *Literatur, Politik und Recht in Mesopotamien. Festschrift für Claus Wilcke* (Orientalia Biblica et Christiana 14), Wiesbaden, 313-332.

— 2003b: "Three unusual Old Assyrian contracts.", in: G. Selz (ed.), *Festschrift für Burkhart Kienast zu seinem 70. Geburtstag dargebracht von Freunden, Schülern und Kollegen* (Alter Orient und Altes Testament 274), Münster, 693-705.

WALTHER, A.: *Das altbabylonische Gerichtswesen* (Leipziger Semitistiche Studien VI), Leipzig.

WEITEMEYER, M. 1962: *Some aspects of the hiring of workers in the Sippar region at the time of Hammurabi*, Copenhagen.

WILCKE, C. 1967: "Inanna/Ištar", *RlA* V/1-2 (1976) 74-87.

— 1983: "Nachlese zu A. Poebels Babylonian Legal and Business Documents From the Time of the First Dynasty of Babylon Chiefly From Nippur (BE 6/2) Teil 1", *ZA* 73, 48-66.

— 1992: "Diebe, Räuber und Mörder", in: V. Haas (ed.), *Außenseiter und Randgruppen* (Xenia 32), Konstanz, 53-78.

WILSON, M. 2008: *Education in the earliest schools*, Los Angeles.

YOFFEE, N. 1998: "The economics of ritual at Late Old Babylonian Kish", *JESHO* 41, 312-343.

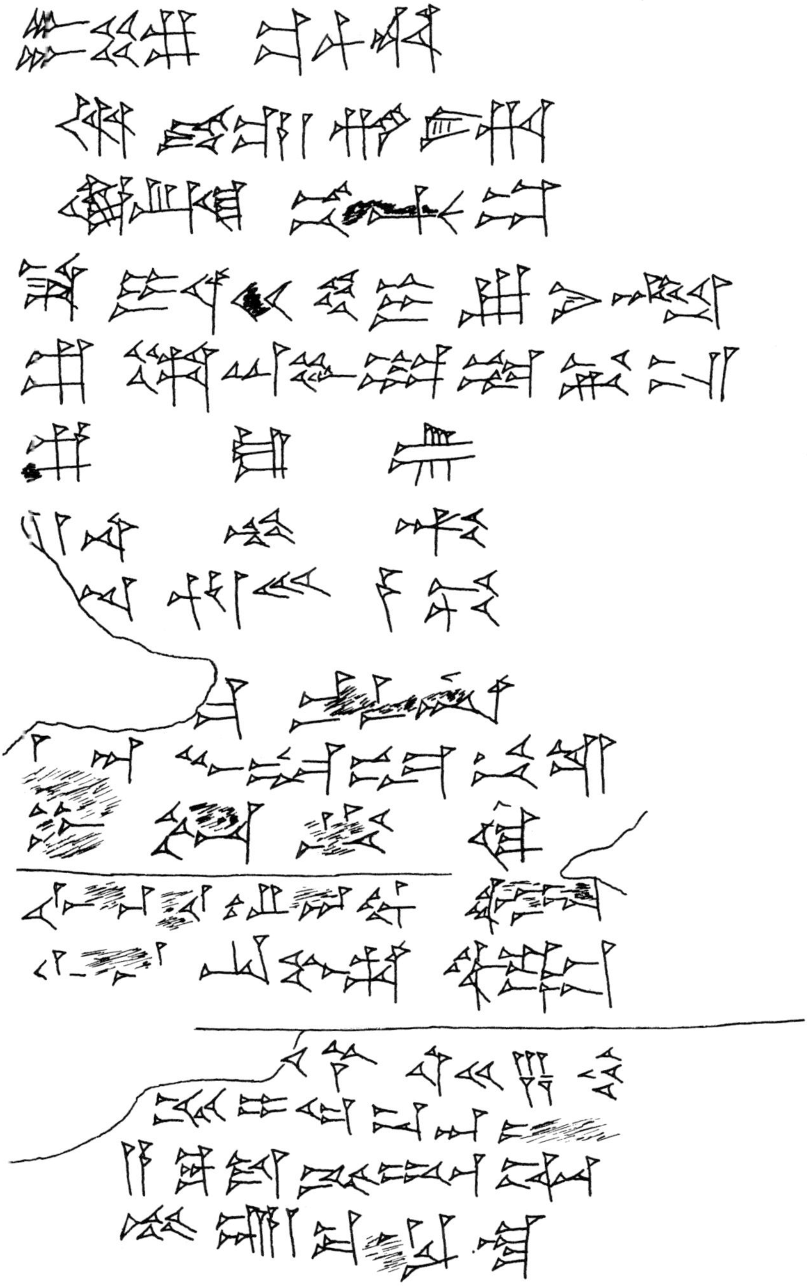

CBS 92

OF WILLS AND BILLS…

ON INHERITED DEBTS IN THE UR-UTU ARCHIVE

Michel TANRET
Ghent University

It is a pleasure to dedicate these few pages to Professor Karel Van Lerberghe as a token of appreciation and friendship now lasting for a good fourty years, since our first lessons of Akkadian taught by L. De Meyer, our stays in Tell ed-Dêr and our collaboration in the long standing IAP project.

A testing inheritance

The quarrels and lawsuits between the chief-dirge singer Ur-Utu and his brothers about the inheritance of their father Inana-mansum, the former Chief Dirge Singer, are well known since the article of C. Janssen (1992).

The events unfolded as follows. At the end of 1547[1], the fourth year of king Ammi-ṣaduqa, after 41 years in office, Inana-mansum "transmits his sceptre" to his son and successor Ur-Utu[2]. Other than that, according to a letter from Ur-Utu (Di 1194, published in Janssen 1992, 22-24), he did not want to divide his inheritance during his lifetime. His three other sons, Kubburum, Ili-iqīšam and Ḫuzalum then must have feared that they would not receive their fair share, probably because Ur-Utu, favoured by his father, already had the office and the income related to it while they still had received nothing and did not know how long it would be before Inana-mansum would pass away.

[1] We use the New (ultra-short) Chronology as exposed by Gasche, Armstrong, Cole and Gurzadyan (1998).

Abbreviations used for royal names in dates: Ad = Ammi-ditana, Aṣ = Ammi-ṣaduqa.

[2] We can confirm the proposal of C. Janssen (1992, note 1) as to the date of the transmission of the office and add some precision. The study of the archive has revealed that the last text in which Inana-mansum is mentioned as chief dirge singer is not Di 1232, dated Aṣ 4/11/8 but the harvest labourer contract Di 1110, dated Aṣ 4/12 diri/15. This confirms that the month name of Di 990, the first text in which Ur-Utu holds the title must indeed be 12 diri making it Aṣ 4/12 diri/30. The 'transmission of the sceptre" must thus have taken place between the 15th and the 30th day of the intercalary 12th month of that year.

Kubburum bribes an official, probably from Babylon, in order to exert pressure on Inana-mansum to divide the inheritance. The answer of the father is remarkable. He describes the three sons, not as sons of himself or his wife but of some other often lowly person, arguing that, because of this, he will not let them inherit anything. We must stress that these words of Inana-mansum are 'cited' by Ur-Utu, still in the same letter (Di 1194). Some subjectivity may thus be at play here and we cannot know whether Inana-mansum really said this and if he did whether he said it in such a disparaging way. What is important is that Ur-Utu wants to convey in writing that he is the only heir and that this is in full agreement with his father's wishes. The fact that he kept a double of this letter in his own archive, a rather exceptional practice, is not unimportant in this context. His intention is clear: at a certain point in time Ur-Utu wanted his father to disinherit the other sons. Such a procedure would normally require a trial with proof of (repeated) wrongdoing (Codex Ḫammu-rabi § 170-71) but such proof might have been difficult to furnish. On the other hand, during his lifetime, the father could give part of his property to his preferred son. Such a gift would be kept out of the inheritance (Codex Ḫammu-rabi § 165) and this is what he did with his office. The brothers will no doubt have feared that more would go this way and that when the inheritance would finally be divided nothing much would remain. A much simpler and more radical way to proceed was to state that the brothers in fact did not belong to this family at all, and thus had no rights on the inheritance. This was an emotional argument, not a juridical one. Indeed, in all of the texts Kubburum, Ili-iqīšam and Ḫuzalum are simply said to be the sons of Inana-mansum and even if they were the biological descendants of other persons, they must have been adopted by the chief dirge singer and an adopted son had as much a right to the inheritance as a biological one.

C. Janssen (1992, 34) had interpreted these disparaging remarks as a spiteful action by the father, angered by the quarrels between his sons, threatening to disinherit the troublemakers and to give everything to his favourite (eldest?) son Ur-Utu. L. Barberon (2005) came up with another explanation. She started from the observation that Inana-mansum's wife, Ilša-ḫegalli, was a *qadištum*-priestess and that these priestesses were not allowed to bear children. Taking this into account, the words of the father 'cited' by Ur-Utu suddenly gained credibility: Inana-mansum could not have had children with his wife. Going back to the text, L. Barberon, pointed at a difference in the alleged filiations:

> Kubburum is said to be the son of Warad-Mamu, a servant of Esagila-[mansum]
> Ili-iqīšam is said to be the son of the sister of the daughter in law of Ku[...]ia
> Ḫuzalum is said to be the son of a female tenant of a house belonging to a servant of the sanga of Ṣarpanītum

We can add that there is something very odd with the way these three are presented. Only one parent is cited, with a name when this is the father but without one when it is the mother. Adding to the oddity is the fact that this parent is then further characterised vis à vis another person (as his servant, sister of his daughter in law or tenant of his house). This last person is always male and in two instances there is a clear reference to Marduk and/or Babylon. There is more at play here than meets the eye. The aim is clearly not only to state that they had a parent outside of the chief dirge singer family, the name of the parent would have sufficed for this, but also and even more, to be disparaging. The presentation is what one could imagine that a lowly person would say of himself in order to claim some social importance, building a chain of relations leading in some way to a person of high standing. Ur-Utu (or his father if these were really his words) use this in a reverse way, to ridicule his brothers.

In any case it appears that only for Kubburum a father is given, the two other ones are defined as sons of their respective mothers. L. Barberon logically deduced that, since in other documents these three sons appear as sons of Inana-mansum, since Inana-mansum could not have children with his wife Ilša-ḫegalli and since one other parent is given for each of them, they must have been adopted. Why then make a difference and cite a father for Kubburum and mothers for the other two? L. Barberon goes a step further and proposes that Ili-iqīšam and Ḫuzalum may have been sons of Inana-mansum and two other women, concubines in her words. Kubburum would then have no blood ties at all with Inana-mansum or his wife. This interpretation fits in very well with the fact that in the different texts documenting the quarrels between the brothers, Kubburum is always cited as the first of the three or even the only one. Since he is 'fully' adopted, he might have feared he stood weakest, fearing for his share in the inheritance.

After the father's death at the end of Aṣ 5 (1546) (Janssen 1992, 43), the inheritance is divided but the quarrel still goes on. This will last no less than seven years, until, in Aṣ 12 (1539) the parts of the inheritance are specified and the dispute ends.

Settling the father's estate: will and bill

During this time Ur-Utu has taken over from his father, and, as C. Janssen remarks, a few texts document this transition (Janssen 1992, 44), showing that the sons reimbursed the outstanding debts of the father.

– *No rite no pay*

The first one is Di 1784, given in transcription, translation and with commentary by C. Janssen (1992, 35-36.). The beginning of the text is broken but we can reconstruct the events. Šamuḫtum, the wife of Adad-mušallim must have been authorized by Inana-mansum to perform the rites of Annunītum (see Tanret and Van Lerberghe 1993) and she paid him 7 sheqel of silver for this purpose. We can deduce that the rites were not performed, which may have been due to the transition of the office to Ur-Utu or some obstacle on Šamuḫtum's side, but the silver was never reimbursed. As the text states, after the death of Inana-mansum, Šamuḫtum claims the silver from his four sons. Three of them, Kubburum, Ili-iqīšam and Ḫuzalum answer that, since Inana-mansum gave his inheritance (to be understood here as his office as suggested by C. Janssen) to Ur-Utu, it was up to the new Chief Dirge Singer to return the 7 sheqel of silver, and so it happened. The date of the text is lost, so it is impossible to know how long after the father's death it is to be situated but in good logic it must have been quite close to it. There seems to be agreement between the brothers (the text states that they decided *ina mitgurtišunu*, in common agreement) and Ur-Utu does not seem to resent the fact that he has to return the 7 sheqel, which he must indeed have received together with the assets linked to the office of chief dirge singer, from his father. Since Inana-mansum died at the end of Aṣ 5, this text could have been dated in Aṣ 6 or 7. It can be noted that the rites were planned and paid for when Inana-mansum still was Chief Dirge Singer, this is before the very end of Aṣ 4 but the reimbursement was done only two years later. We can imagine that Šamuḫtum may have claimed her money earlier but that payment was put off by the ageing, maybe ailing Inana-mansum. When he passed away the sons were asked to pay, Ur-Utu finally did.

An interesting point is that, whereas the Chief Dirge Singers' archive contains many documents about the remainder of (the cost of) the *parṣum*-rites, not telling us what the total cost was, this text exceptionally reveals the whole amount: 7 sheqel of silver, unfortunately the name of the rite is not preserved.

– *Rites again*

Another document, Di 1287, also referring to the execution of the *parṣum*-rites, was only briefly referred to by C. Janssen, and we now give it in full, as far as it is preserved.

Di 1287 (IM 82036) Aṣ 05/03/17

Obv.	1.	2 gín kù.babbar
	2.	íb.tag' kù.babbar *qú-ul-mi-i*
	3.	⌜*ša*⌝ ^{d}inana-ma.an.sum ⌜gala.maḫ *an-nu-ni-tum*⌝
	4.	[…] *sà-bi-tum* dam dumu-ud.20.kam
	5.	mu gibil.égir sipa búru.na
	6.	*ú-še-pí-šu*
	7.	*a-na* ur-^{d}utu gala.maḫ *an-nu-ni-tum*
Lo.E.	8.	⌜^{I}⌝dumu-ud.20.kam *ka-ni-kam*
	9.	*ú-ri-ku*
	10.	*a-na* itu.1.kam
Rev.	11.	*a-na ma-ri-i*
	12.	kù.babbar ì.lá.e
	13.	igi ìr-^{d}*ul-maš-ši-tum* sanga ^{d}EN.ZU
	14.	igi *ú-tul*-iš$_{8}$-tár sanga iš$_{8}$-tár
	15.	igi *šu-mu-um-li-ṣi* ⌜dub.sar⌝
		seals
	16.	itu sig$_{4}$.a ud.17.kam
U.E.	17.	mu *am-mi-ṣa-du-qá* lugal
	18.	alam.a.ni maš.igi.du (*sic*)
	19.	ù alam.a.ni šùd.dè
	20.	ab.bi.a
L.Edge		

Seals

The document is sealed by the third witness and his seal has a legend: Šumum-liṣi/dumu Bēlšunu/ìr Ninsiana ù ^{d}[…]. Two other seals have no legend and could not be identified. We would expect one of them to belong to Mār-ūm-ešrê and the other one to one of the other witnesses.

Translation

Two sheqel of silver, remainder of the silver of the 'ax' rite

that Inana-mansum chief dirge singer of Annunītum, let Sabitum, wife of Mār-ūm-ešrê, execute in the year Aṣ 3.

(concerning which) for Ur-Utu, chief dirge singer of Annunītum, Mār-ūm-ešrê 'extended' the tablet,

Within one month he will pay the silver to the fatteners

Before (the witnesses) Warad-Ulmaššītum, sanga of Sîn, Utul-Ištar, sanga of Ištar, Šumum-liṣi, the scribe

Fourth month, 17th day of the year Aṣ 5

Interpretation

This would be a run of the mill 'parṣum' text (see Tanret and Van Lerberghe 1993), in which the remnants of the contributions to a ritual have to be delivered to the animal fatteners of the storehouse of Sippar-Amnānum, were it not for lines 7-9. Their meaning is clear: Inana-mansum, who managed these rites, authorized Sabitum to perform them[3], but his son Ur-Utu, having taken over the office in the meantime, takes over the responsibility. The text states that Sabitum's husband, Mār-ūm-ešrê, who has to pay the remainder of the rites, 'extends' the tablet to Ur-Utu. The D stem of the verb *arākum* is used to express this, which is an otherwise unattested use of this verb in this stem. M. Stol kindly (as ever) informed us that there are more D stem attestations of *arākum* than the (very old) volume A of the CAD accounts for. Often a prolongation in time is meant. In accordance with this, here the meaning must be that the subject matter of the tablet, originally concerning Inana-mansum, now applies to Ur-Utu. The reason for this 'extension' is given by including the year name indicating when the rite was performed: this was in Aṣ 3, whereas the text is written in the third month of Aṣ 5.

[3] Sabitum, wife of Mār-ūm-ešrê is also attested in MHET I, 52, a list of quantities of emmer followed by (mostly nameless) wives of persons with a title (galamaḫ, sanga, ugula.gidri..). She also appears in a summary list of persons who executed the *parṣum*-rites and the remainder they had to pay. It would have been nice if this reference would have been the summary of Di 1287 but is not. It refers to her execution of the *muqabbirūtum*-rite, for which she owes 1 sheqel of silver. It is not often that we find the same person executing the rites more than once.

In contrast with the preceding text, not only was the silver paid, but the rite was performed, so no reimbursement of the original payment is required here. The performer or his representative have to pay the remainder of the original payment to the fatteners of the storehouse of Sippar-Amnā-num. We note that, here too, there is a time lapse of two years before repayment is due.

In this case Inana-mansum was still alive (he dies at the end of Aṣ 5) but his son Ur-Utu had taken over the office at the very end of Aṣ 4. This shows that no payment was expected in the year the rites were performed (Aṣ 3), nor in the next year, when Inana-mansum was still in office. Payment is requested in the third month of the year after that. One may wonder why the text has to be 'extended' to Ur-Utu, since his father had the rite executed and payment of the remainder is not due to the Chief Dirge Singer himself but to the fatteners. The reason is that, although he does not receive it, this payment has to be recorded on the account of the Chief Dirge Singer. It was important that this payment should be registered by the fatteners as coming indirectly through him. We know their office entailed fixed large yearly payments to the storehouse of their town and having the remainder of the rites paid to the fatteners must have helped in the completion of their dues. So it is in order to prove that payment indirectly came from them that Inana-mansum, and after him Ur-Utu, kept lots of these documents in their archives, although they only appear in them as authorising the execution of the rites, not paying anything, nor receiving anything. They even have their scribe draw up tablets summarizing these individual executions of rites in lists.

In the context of the quarrel between the brothers, we see that Ur-Utu has taken over his father's office and all responsibilities involved even before his father has crossed in the great beyond. The debt does not stay with the father but goes with the office. Just as in Di 1784, this is a cultic matter — and its financial corollary — and so Ur-Utu is concerned, not his brothers, even if the inheritance will not be settled for many years to come.

– *An agricultural debt*

A third document concerns a longstanding debt of the family. Although some crucial passages are broken, the general meaning of the text is clear. For our purpose here, the date of the text is important.

Di 837 IM 81586 Aṣ 13/06/30

Obv. 1. 6 gín kù.babbar šám 6.0.0.0 še.gur ^{giš}bán ^{d}utu
2. gú.un 1.0.0 iku a.šà a.gàr *bu-ša*
3. *ša la-ma-sà-ni* lukur ^{d}utu dumu.munus ^{d}AMAR.UTU-*mu-ša-lim*
4. ša ^{d}inanna-ma.an.sum gala.maḫ *an-nu-ni-tum*
5. *i-ri-su-ma*
6. *še-am* gú.un a.šà *la id-di-nu-ma*
7. 6 ⸢gín⸣ kù.babbar šám 6 še.gur ^{giš}bán ^{d}utu
8. gú.un 1.0.0 iku a.šà a.gàr *bu-ša*
9. ⸢dumu⸣.meš ^{d}inanna-ma.an.sum ⸢gala⸣.[maḫ *an*]-⸢*nu*⸣-*ni-tum*
10. *i-*⸢*na-di?-...*⸣ [...]
11. 4 ½ gín ⸢...⸣ [...]
12. *aš-šum* ^{I}*ku-ub-bu-rum* ⸢*ì-lí-i*⸣-[*qí-ša-am*]
13. *ù ḫu-za-lum* dumu.meš ^{d}inanna-ma.an.sum
14. ^{I}ur-^{d}utu gala.maḫ *an-nu-ni-tum*

Lo.E. 15. ⸢*a-na*⸣?...
16. ⸢*id-di-in*⸣

uninscribed seal

Rev. 17. *iš-tu* 1 1/2 gín kù.babbar šà 6 gín kù.babbar
18. *ki-iš-da-at* ur-^{d}utu *a-ḫi-šu-nu*
19. *ḫa-ar-ṣú*
20. 4 1/2 gín kù.babbar *ku-ub-bu-rum*
21; ^{I}*ì-lí-i-qí-ša-am ù ḫu-za-lum*
22. *a-na na-ši ka-ni-ki-šu-nu* ì.lá.e.meš

---

23. igi *ib-ni-*^{d}EN.ZU dumu ^{d}EN.ZU-*i-din-nam*
24. igi ^{d}ŠEŠ.KI-ma.an.sum di.kud dumu SIG-*an-nu-ni-tum*
25. igi ìr-^{d}EN.ZU dumu ^{d}EN.ZU-*i-din-nam*
26. igi ^{d}EN.ZU-*na-ṣi-ir* dumu SIG-*an-nu-ni-tum*

---

27. itu kin-^{d}inana ud.30.kam
28. mu *am-mi-ṣa-du-qá* lugal.e
29. urudu.ki.lugal.gub ì.maḫ.a
30. ḫur sag didli.a íd.da ì.me.eš.a.bi

Seals:

On the upper edge there are two seals. The one with a legend reads: Warad-Amurrim/dumu Sîn-erībam/ìr ^{d}... and it is also impressed on the top of the left edge where it is overwritten with a kišib to the name of Kubburum. The other seal on the upper edge has only one figure: the god Adad. It cannot be attributed but must have been used by one of the brothers, maybe Ili-iqīšam since he is second in the text. There are three other seals on the left edge: the second one has a religious legend (^{d}ak en.gal/^{d}lagamal/^{d}šeš.ki en.. ní.tuku...) and might have been used by Ḫuzalum, the third one has figures only and may be used by a witness, the fourth one has faint traces of an inscription between its figures but cannot be identified either. It could also belong to a witness.

On the lower edge there is an unidentified seal with figures only, which could belong to a witness. On the reverse, between the last witness and the date we find the seals of witnesses 2 and 3: Ibni-Sîn uses the seal of his father: Sîn-iddinam/ dumu Nuratum/ìr Ḫammu-rabi[4], witness three seals with his own seal: Nanna-mansum/dumu *i-pí-iq-an-nu-ni-tum*/ìr [Ammiditana].

If this is correct then the three brothers would have sealed and the four witnesses.

The tablet was kept by Ur-Utu to ensure that he had already paid and that the remaining 4 ½ sheqel of silver would have to be paid by his three brothers.

Translation

6 sheqel of silver, corresponding to 6 gur of barley in the *parsiqtu* measure of Šamaš

being the yield of a 1 bur field in the watering district of Buša

belonging to Lamassāni, *nadītum*-priestess of Šamaš, daughter of Marduk-mušallim

that Inana-mansum, Chief Dirge Singer of Annunītum

had cultivated and

the barley, yield of the field he had not given (to her)

6 sheqel of silver, corresponding to 6 gur of barley in the *parsiqtu* measure of Šamaš

being the yield of a 1 bur field in the watering district of Buša

the sons of Inana-mansum, Chief Dirge Singer of Annunītum

will give ....

4 This seal was drawn, published and discussed by G. Voet and the beneficiary of this Festschrift (Voet and Van Lerberghe 1989, 533 and *passim*).

4 ½ sheqel ....
because of Kubburum, Ili-iqīšam
and Ḫuzalum, children of Inana-mansum
Ur-Utu, Chief Dirge Singer of Annunītum
for/to....
gave
after 1 ½ sheqel of silver out of the 6 sheqel of silver
the acquisition[5] of Ur-Utu their brother
has been deducted
Kubburum, Ili-iqīsam and Ḫuzalum
will pay to the bearer of their tablet
Before Ibni-Sîn, son of Sîn-iddinam
Nanna-mansum, judge, son of Ipiq-Annunītum
Warad-Sîn, son of Sîn-iddinam
Sîn-nāṣir, son of Ipiq-Annunītum

Sixth month, thirtieth day
Thirteenth year of king Ammi-ṣaduqa

Interpretation

The general meaning of the text is clear. Inana-mansum had rented a field from Lamassāni and had failed to pay the standard rent of six sheqel of silver for 1 bur of rented field. He must have died in the meantime since his four sons will each pay 1 ½ shequel to reimburse the owner of the field, Lamassāni.

This *nadītum*-priestess of Šamaš, daughter of Marduk-mušallim, is attested in the Ur-Utu archive from Ad 29 to 32 only. She lends out 4 gur of barley, is involved in sheep herding and leases out a field to Inana-mansum. Her father is the son of Ibni-Sîn and he is sanga (name of deity broken[6]) according to the only text in which he is mentioned: Di 1921.

[5] According to the CAD, sub K p. 453a, *kišdātu* means "acquisition, assets". In the example it quotes from CT 4, 11a, a distinction is made between property from an inheritance and *kišdātu*, own acquisitions.

[6] It is impossible to restore the name of the deity because we know a Marduk-mušallim sanga of Aja under Abi-ešuḫ, but he is the son of Sîn-erībam (Tanret 2009, 17). There is a sanga of Annunītum of this name, but he is the son of Nūr-ilīšu (Di 979 Ad 37).

The rent for the field is slightly low for this period. When it is expressed, since the reign of Abi-ešuḫ a fixed amount of barley per bur is stipulated in advance. During the Old Babylonian period, in Sippar, in a very general way, the rent went down from 18 gur per bur under Ḫammurabi and Samsu-iluna to 6 gur per bur under Abi-ešuḫ and Ammi-ditana but rises again under Ammi-ṣaduqa to 8 gur per bur. With the 6 gur per bur we are somewhat lower than the normal rate but this amount is the second most frequent rent for this period.

The original document?

The archive of the Chief Dirge singers contains an unusual document (Di 1921 date not preserved) which seems to be a copy of two tablets concerning transactions of Lamassāni daughter of Marduk-mušallim. The first one[7] is her entrustment of cattle to a shepherd (Ili-iqīšam sipa) during one year (from the first day of the first month until the thirtieth day of the twelfth month, being one year). The first line of the second one is broken, then we have:

Lo.E. 10. šà.bi gú.un a.šà
11. *ša* ^I^*la-ma-sà-ni* lukur ^d^utu
12. dumu.munus ^d^AMAR.UTU-*mu-ša-lim* sanga [...]
Rev. 13. *ša* ^d^inana-ma.an.sum ⌜gala⌝.[maḫ...]
14. *i-na* a.gàr lú mar.tu
15. *ù ir-ṣi-it* ud.kib.nun^KI^-[...]
16. i-na mu bàd *iš-ku-un*-^d^[AMAR.UTU...]
16. *i-ri-šu*

(...) out of the yield of the field
belonging to Lamassāni, *nadītum*-priestess of Šamaš
daughter of Marduk-mušallim sanga-priest of ....
that Inana-mansum, Chief Dirge Singer (of Annunītum)
in the irrigation district Awīl-Amurrim
and the territory of Sippar-[...]
in the year Ad 32
had cultivated

[7] It is in this part that Marduk-mušallim is mentioned as son of Ibni-Sîn on line 3, and as sanga [...] on line 12.

This informs us that, in the year Ad 32 Inana-mansum had rented a field from this same Lamassāni. It is unfortunately very improbable that this is the rental referred to in Di 837, twenty years later. In that case Lamassāni would have had to wait for a very long time. It is more probable that Inana-mansum rented this field more than once, but even if we assume that what prevented him from paying his dues was his demise at the end of Aṣ 5, Lamassāni had to wait no less than eight years before receiving her 6 sheqel of rental money, not a negligible sum.

The reason she had to wait was no doubt the quarrels and lawsuit between the sons of Inana-mansum concerning his inheritance. This was over in Aṣ 12/5/2 according to Di 932. A little more than a year later Lamassāni received her 6 sheqels. It is not astonishing that after such a long time, she did not receive the barley to which she was entitled but its value in silver.

A notable difference with Di 1784 and Di 1291 is that this is not a cultic but a private matter and in this all brothers have to participate in equal parts, which indicates that, notwithstanding the words to the contrary of Inana-mansum, according to Ur-Utu at least, they must have inherited equal parts of the fatherly estate. What Ur-Utu had more, was the office of Chief Dirge Singer and all the perks this entailed, religious, social and financial. Furthermore, since all had to pay, Lamassāni had to wait until the inheritance dispute was settled before she could have her money back.

Conclusions

The texts above show that when sons inherited from their father, they did not only divide his properties but also his debts. As can be seen, these are neatly divided in equal parts between the sons, except when an inherited office is concerned. In that case, the son who inherited the title (and its perks) was sole responsible for the debts related to it.

Another remarkable conclusion is the slowness of the recovery of debts. It could take years before a creditor would see her or his silver.

Finally, even if the creditor has to insist, the payment of a father's debts is not something exceptional. The way it is presented in the texts shows that it was a normal thing to do. Never do the sons protest that they are not responsible for their father's arrears. They accept the bills with the wills.

Bibliography

BARBERON, L. 2005: "Quand la mère est une religieuse", *N.A.B.U.* 2005 n° 89, 94-95.

GASCHE, H. J. A. ARMSTRONG, S.W. COLE and V.G. GURZADYAN 1998: Dating the Fall of Babylon. A Reappraisal of Second-Millennium Chronology (MHE Series II, Memoirs IV), Gent.

JANSSEN, C. 1992: "Inanna-mansum et ses fils: relation d'une succession turbulente dans les archives d'Ur-Utu", *RA* 86, 19-52.

MHET I = VAN LERBERGHE, K. and VOET, G. 1991: *Sippar-Amnānum. The Ur-Utu archive* (MHE Series III, Texts I), Gent.

TANRET, M. 2009: The Seal of the Sanga. On the Old Babylonian sangas of Šamaš of Sippar-Jaḫrūrum and Sippar-Amnānum (Cuneiform Monographs 40), Leiden-Boston.

TANRET, M. and VAN LERBERGHE, K., 1993: "Rituals and Profits in the Ur-Utu Archive" in Quaegebeur, J. (ed.), *Ritual and Sacrifice in the Ancient Near East. Proceedings of the International Conference Organized by the Katholieke Universiteit Leuven from the 17th to the 20th of April 1991* (OLA 55), Leuven, 435-449.

VOET, G. and VAN LERBERGHE, K. 1989: "A Long Lasting Life", in H. Behrens and D. Loding (eds.), *DUMU-E2-DUB-BA-A, Studies in Honor of Åke W. Sjöberg*, Philadelphia, 525-538.

DE L'USAGE DES FIGURINES ET STATUETTES ANTHROPOMORPHES DANS LES SÉPULTURES DU BRONZE ANCIEN ET MOYEN EN SYRIE

Véronique VAN DER STEDE
Université de Liège

Pour quelles raisons et dans quelles circonstances des figurines ou autres statuettes anthropomorphes ont-elles été déposées dans des sépultures? Voilà une question qui taraude les spécialistes du Proche-Orient ancien depuis longtemps et multiples sont les interprétations qui ont été proposées[1]. Ainsi, pour certains, il ne s'agit là que de simples jouets accompagnant de jeunes défunts dans leur dernière demeure (Woolley 1955, 222-223), tandis que pour d'autres il se pourrait que de tels objets aient eu un rôle à jouer dans le rituel funéraire (Katz 2003, 204-205 et 208-209; Scurlock 2002, 1-6).

La préparation de la publication finale des tombes mises au jour à Tell Beydar-Nabada a été l'occasion de rouvrir cet épineux dossier en l'envisageant à la lumière des nouvelles attestations mais aussi en considérant l'ensemble des données disponibles, ce y compris celles issues des sources documentaires. Notre enquête est loin d'être close mais une première synthèse, reprenant les attestations d'effigies anthropomorphes en contexte funéraire au Bronze ancien et moyen en Syrie, peut déjà être proposée ici. Les quelques réflexions qui vont suivre susciteront, nous l'espérons, l'intérêt du Prof. Karel Van Lerberghe sans qui les fouilles de Tell Beydar n'auraient pas été les mêmes et dont le soutien sans faille nous a permis, tout au long de ces années, de persévérer dans la voie de la recherche.

[1] Une synthèse sur le sujet, prenant uniquement en compte les figurines en terre cuite et essentiellement consacrée aux attestations du 1er millénaire av. n. è., a été présentée par A. Pruβ (Pruβ et Novak 2000, 184-195) dans le cadre d'un séminaire ayant trait aux rituels funéraires en Mésopotamie. À la liste des sites mentionnés dans cet article, il faut rajouter celui de Tell Knēdig où une figurine féminine paraît associée à une tombe datée de la période néo-assyrienne (Klengel-Brandt et al. 2005, 301 et pl. 195).

I. Les sources matérielles

Le dépouillement de la documentation actuellement disponible montre que des figurines ou statuettes anthropomorphes ont été retrouvées en contexte funéraire dans onze sites syriens[2].

1. *Les attestations du Bronze ancien*

À Tell Beydar-Nabada, dans la région du Haut-Khabour au nord-est de la Syrie, c'est dans une tombe monumentale, aménagée sous la cella de la phase EJ IV du temple A, l'un des plus grands bâtiments cultuels identifiés à ce jour dans la ville haute, que fut découverte une petite figurine asexuée en terre crue d'une quinzaine de centimètres de hauteur[3]. Cette figurine modelée à main libre est des plus schématiques: le corps se résume à un simple rectangle auquel deux moignons, non conservés, devaient s'accrocher à hauteur du cou à la manière de ceux d'une figurine de type «bonhomme de neige» trouvée parmi les vestiges de l'occupation EJ IV du temple A (Debruyne et al. 2003, 207 et pl. IX). Le cou, court et massif, porte une tête arrondie dont le visage, aux traits sommaires, est marqué par deux cavités qui matérialisent à la fois le nez et les yeux.

Le matériel funéraire disposé dans la chambre sépulcrale de la T. 58550, une tombe monumentale formée de trois espaces distincts, se répartit en trois grands groupes. Le premier (groupe 1) est constitué des objets directement placés au contact du défunt, le second (groupe 2) des objets déposés à sa gauche et le troisième (groupe 3), dont fait partie la figurine, des

[2] Certaines découvertes de figurines ou statuettes anthropomorphes en contexte funéraire sont soit trop douteuses, soit trop peu documentées pour être prises en compte dans cette synthèse. À Hama, une tombe datée du Bronze ancien II aurait, selon Thuesen (1988, 102-103), été associée à une «idole» en argile (4 B 603). Cet objet énigmatique a été retrouvé à côté de la tombe en jarre 34/1934, attribuée à la phase K7 du site. L'hypothèse qu'il s'agisse d'une idole a en premier lieu été évoquée par Ingholt (1940, 21 et pl. V) qui décrit néanmoins l'artefact comme un couvercle lustré en forme de cloche. C'est aussi la description proposée par Fugmann (1958, 35 et fig. 37). Cet objet, dont la fonction reste incertaine, est mentionné ici à titre indicatif. Sept figurines ou fragments de figurines en terre cuite ont également été collectés dans des tombes de Mari datées de la période des Shakkanakku (Akkad et Ur III). Ces figurines, placées dans des sépultures individuelles en fosse, en jarre ou à sarcophage, ne sont malheureusement ni décrites, ni illustrées (Jean-Marie 1999, 10, 12, 14). À cela, il faut ajouter deux figurines en argile (n°s 2 et 14) découvertes à Tell Mozan (Wissing 2009, 27 et 29-30) qui, faute de temps, n'ont pas pu être prises en considération dans cet article.

[3] Tombe T. 58550: 58192-M-13 (Bretschneider et Cunningham 2007, 99-158; Van der Stede, à paraître).

objets se répartissant dans la moitié sud-est de la pièce. En effet, la chambre funéraire est clairement divisée en deux secteurs: le secteur interne réservé à la dépouille et aux deux premiers groupes d'objets et le secteur externe où les objets du troisième groupe se répartissent en plusieurs ensembles. L'un d'eux, situé du côté nord-est de la pièce, est formé d'objets rassemblés autour de la figurine qui a été retrouvée brisée en deux morceaux et partiellement recouverte d'une dague.

Dans la région du Moyen-Euphrate syrien, dix-neuf statuettes ont été retrouvées à **Selenkahiye** et **Wreide** dans des sépultures remontant au Bronze ancien IV[4]. À l'exception de l'une d'elles[5], façonnée en argile et cuite, toutes ont été taillées dans de la pierre calcaire. Ces statuettes, mesurant entre 7 et 22 centimètres de hauteur, sont pour la plupart travaillées de manière sommaire et l'absence de détails empêche de déterminer leur sexe. Le corps se résume à un simple rectangle généralement dépourvu de bras et de jambes. Il est surmonté d'une tête massive, parfois cylindrique, reposant directement sur les épaules. Quant au visage, il n'est animé que par de petits yeux circulaires et un nez aquilin qui le coupe en deux.

Dans la plupart des cas, le nombre de statuettes retrouvées dans chacune de ces tombes à inhumations multiples correspond au nombre de défunts qui y ont été déposés. Toutefois, chaque squelette n'est pas systématiquement associé à une statuette. Ainsi, dans la tombe W13 TbI, abritant trois individus, les statuettes ont été placées dans le remplissage au-dessus du dernier défunt déposé dans la sépulture. Dans les tombes Q26 TbI, N et P, elles étaient placées à proximité de l'un de leurs deux occupants. Enfin, dans la tombe W054, une sépulture formée de trois chambres et logeant au total six individus, toutes les statuettes étaient rassemblées dans la chambre C, les deux autres chambres (A et B), hébergeant chacune un défunt, en étant totalement dépourvues. Il est également à noter que si l'une des statuettes se situait à proximité de l'un des quatre occupants de la chambre C, les autres étaient mêlées à la poterie disséminée sur son sol.

[4] Tombe Q26 TbI: SLK 74-X3 et 74-X5 (Van Loon & Meijer 2001, 201; Van Soldt 2001, 459 et pl. 9.11). Tombe Q26 TbV: SLK 74-H205 (Van Loon et Meijer 2001, 202). Tombes W13 TbI et Tb II: SLK 75-S23, 75-S24 et 75-S25 (Van Loon & Meijer 2001, 210-212; Van Soldt 2001, 460 et pl. 9.12 a-b). Tombe U22 TbIX: SLK 75-S26 et 75-S27 (Van Loon et Meijer 2001, 207; Van Soldt 2001, 460 et pl. 9.12 c-d). Tombe K: WRD 67-451 (Van Loon et Meijer 2001, 157 et fig. 4A.9A: 17). Tombe N: WRD 67-504 et 67-505 (Van Loon et Meijer 2001, 162 et fig. 4A.10A:31). Tombe P: SLK 67-806 et 67-805 (Van Loon et Meijer 2001, 167-168 et fig. 4A.12A:31-32). Tombe W054: W54C: 77 à 82 (Orthmann et Rova 1991, 16-33). Le secteur du cimetière de Wreide a également livré vingt et une statuettes retrouvées hors contexte. Cf. Orthmann et Rova 1991, 63-70.

[5] SLK 74-H205 (Van Loon et Meijer 2001, 202).

À **Jerablus-Tahtani**, toujours dans la région du Moyen-Euphrate syrien mais plus au nord, près de la frontière syro-turque, une dizaine de figurines en terre crue, plus ou moins bien conservées, ont été identifiées dans deux tombes du site remontant au Bronze ancien III (Peltenburg et al. 1996, 11-12 et fig. 13)[6]. Selon les données disponibles, il semblerait que la tombe 1036, une tombe construite abritant quatre individus, dont un homme et un enfant, contenait cinq figurines portant des attributs sexuels masculins. De facture grossière, ces figurines au corps ovale et allongé étaient pourvues de petits bras repliés sur la poitrine et de courtes jambes se terminant à angle droit par des pieds aux orteils rendus par de courtes incisions. La tête arrondie, reposant sur un cou épais et court, est dotée d'un visage, qui, à l'exception d'une incision marquant la bouche, est matérialisé par de simples pincements. La tombe 2845, une tombe en fosse ne contenant plus de restes humains, a également livré des figurines en argile. Au nombre de quatre, ces figurines, dont le triangle pubien est matérialisé par des incisions et une ponctuation, sont clairement féminines.

Enfin, à l'extrémité opposée de la région du Moyen-Euphrate syrien, en aval du barrage de Tabqa, la nécropole du site d'**Abu Hamed,** utilisée au Bronze ancien III-IVA, a livré des figurines anthropomorphes en terre cuite se répartissant dans trois tombes[7]. Deux d'entre elles (GHA-90-Z19 et GHA-90-J80) sont de petites figurines au corps cylindrique s'évasant vers le bas pour former une base circulaire. Leurs bras, en forme de nageoire, sont repliés sur le thorax et l'une d'elles porte à hauteur des mains de longues incisions horizontales représentant très probablement les doigts. Leur grosse tête repose sur un cou allongé et se termine par une coiffure semi-circulaire de section aplatie décorée de perforations. Le visage est coupé en deux par un nez proéminent surmontant une petite bouche circulaire et séparant les yeux rendus au moyen de simples trous. La troisième figurine (GHA-90-J58) est d'un autre type. Son corps, en forme de cône, est surmonté d'un long cou supportant une tête caractérisée par un nez démesurément allongé et deux petits yeux circulaires. Elle porte une coiffure de section aplatie et en forme de croissant ornée de perforations disposées en arc de cercle. Un petit orifice, localisé à la base du cou et s'ouvrant sur l'intérieur creux de la figurine, conduit les fouilleurs à y reconnaître un hochet.

[6] Tombe 1036: SF 1152, 1153, 1213 et 1212. Tombe 2845: SF 3140, 3133, 3148 et 3149. Cf. http://www.arcl.ed.ac.uk/arch/jerablus/archivepage.htm au 28.07.2011.

[7] Tombe Z5: GHA-90-Z19 (Falb et al. 2005, 113, 61-62, fig. 41/8 et pl. VI), Tombe J9: GHA-90-J58 (Falb et al. 2005, 113, 41, fig. 26/4 et pl. VI), Tombe J10C: GHA-90-J80 (Falb et al. 2005, 104, 42 et fig. 29/4).

Dans la tombe à puits d'accès à cavité latérale Z5, la figurine (GHA-90-Z19) était placée sur le sol du puits d'accès entre une maçonnerie et une pierre de fermeture scellant la cavité latérale. Dans la tombe à ciste J9, elle (GHA-90-J58) se trouvait sur le sol à proximité immédiate du défunt. Quant à la figurine (GHA-90-J80) retrouvée dans la tombe à ciste J10C, faisant partie d'un complexe funéraire comprenant trois chambres, elle paraît également avoir été placée sur le sol de la sépulture à côté d'autres objets et de restes d'ovi-caprinés.

2. *Les attestations du Bronze Moyen*

À **Chagar Bazar**, dans la région du Haut-Khabour au nord-est de la Syrie, trois figurines anthropomorphes en terre crue ont été identifiées dans une tombe à puits d'accès à cavité latérale[8]. Ces figurines étaient déposées dans la moitié est de la cavité latérale avec d'autres objets parmi lesquels quatre poteries, un filtre de chalumeau en bronze et une lame (poignard ou dague) en cuivre. La cavité latérale contenait également des ossements d'animaux. En revanche, aucun reste humain n'a pu y être repéré et il est fort probable qu'aucun cadavre n'y ait jamais été inhumé.

Les figurines de Chagar Bazar, modelées à main libre sans souci du détail, ont un corps en forme de losange de section ovale mesurant de 11 à 12 centimètres. Les pointes supérieure et inférieure du losange forment respectivement la tête et les jambes de chacune des figurines tandis que les pointes latérales matérialisent les bras qui ne sont rien d'autre que des moignons étirés latéralement. Les jambes, légèrement écartées, sont également atrophiées. Quant au visage, il est rendu par un simple pincement central qui définit du même coup les yeux et le nez. Deux de ces figurines (CB 4936 et 4937) se caractérisent par la présence au niveau de l'entrejambe d'un motif rendu par deux pincements et qui paraît reproduire une vulve. Il est donc fort probable qu'il s'agit de représentations féminines.

Dans la vallée de l'Oronte, à **Hama**, quatre tombes, appartenant à la période H du site et remontant au Bronze moyen IB, contenaient des figurines féminines en terre cuite[9]. Plus ou moins bien conservées,

[8] T. 88: CB 4935, 4936 et 4937. Je remercie le Prof. Tunca de m'avoir permis de mentionner ces figurines inédites. Elles seront publiées courant 2013 dans un rapport final consacré aux tombes mises au jour à Chagar Bazar. Tunca et Baghdo, à paraître; Léon, à paraître.

[9] Tombe T. I: Hama 5 A 806 et 5 A 805 (Badre 1980, 164/12 et 165/18; Pruβ 2010, 51); tombe T. II: Hama 5 A 846, 5 A 847 et 5 A 848 (Badre 1980, 164/13 et 15; Pruβ

ces figurines, que Badre intègre à son «type classique» de la région de l'Oronte, ont les jambes jointes et des bras en moignon étirés latéralement. Leur tête, au visage en bec d'oiseau, est caractérisée par de grandes oreilles présentant des perforations et est surmontée d'une coiffure en peigne (Badre 1980, 45)[10]. Une figurine d'un autre type, celui des cavaliers en char, a, quant à elle, été identifiée dans une tombe mise au jour à **Murek**, un village situé immédiatement au nord de Hama[11].

Les tombes à inhumation de Hama n'ayant pas encore été publiées, la localisation exacte des figurines au sein de chaque sépulture n'est pas connue. Dans un rapport préliminaire, Ingholt précise néanmoins que le matériel funéraire était placé sur le sol des chambres sépulcrales auprès du défunt (Ingholt 1940, 50 et note 2). Le nombre de figurines recensées par tombe est variable. Ainsi, la tombe T. II en contenait trois, les tombes T. I et T. VI deux et les tombes T. X et T. M une seule. Cette variation est-elle à mettre au compte du nombre de défunts inhumés dans chaque sépulture? Dans l'état actuel de la documentation, il est difficile d'en être certain.

À **Nebi Mend-Qadesh**, autre site de la région de l'Oronte, deux tombes en fosse, remontant au Bronze moyen IIA, renfermaient chacune une figurine en terre cuite[12]. De la première, seule la tête pointue au visage en bec d'oiseau est conservée (Badre 1980, 191; Pruß 2010, 85). Ses yeux, marqués par des pastilles perforées, sont surmontés d'épais sourcils réalisés au moyen de bandes appliquées. La seconde figurine, quant à elle complète, représente un personnage portant une cruche. Elle est dotée d'un corps en colonne surmonté d'une tête arrondie pourvue de l'habituel visage en bec d'oiseau.

L'information disponible sur le contexte de découverte de ces figurines est, cette fois encore, plus que maigre. M. Pézard précise simplement que la première était placée dans une tombe renfermant un seul individu (tombe 2), tandis que la seconde était associée à l'un des trois défunts présents dans la sépulture (tombe 1).

Toujours dans la vallée de l'Oronte, à **Tell Atchana-Alalakh**, une tombe en fosse, datée du Bronze moyen IIB (niveau VII) et abritant deux

2010, 51-52); tombe T. VI: Hama 5 B 160 et 5 B 199 (Badre 1980, 164/14 et 167/26; Pruß 2010, 51), tombe T. X: Hama 6 A 355. Voir aussi Fugmann 1958, pl. X. Pour la datation de ces figurines: Marchetti 2001, tab. 3.6.

[10] Au sujet de ce type de figurines, voir aussi Marchetti 2001 et Pruß 2010, 50-56.

[11] Tombe T. M (Ingholt 1940, 8-9): Hama 8 M 7 (Ingholt 1940, 57 et pl. XVII/1; Badre 1980, 186/109; Pruß 2010, 64).

[12] Tombes 1 et 2. Pézard 1931, 73 et pl. XXXVII/1, XXX/2: 1.

individus, une femme et un enfant, contenait une figurine féminine en terre cuite également assignable au style «classique» de la vallée de l'Oronte[13].

Une figurine attribuable au même style a encore été retrouvée dans une tombe en fosse de **Tell Mardikh-Ebla**, au nord-ouest de la Syrie[14]. Datée du Bronze moyen IA, cette sépulture abritait deux sujets adultes. Une autre figurine en terre cuite, dont seule la tête est conservée, était associée à un crâne disposé dans le puits funéraire P.8680, un tombeau collectif utilisé au Bronze moyen II[15]. Selon les fouilleurs, cassée dans l'Antiquité, elle y aurait été placée déjà fragmentaire.

À une dizaine de kilomètres au nord d'Ebla, à **Tell Afis,** c'est également une figurine en terre cuite du type «classique» de la région de l'Oronte qui a été identifiée dans une tombe en fosse remontant au Bronze moyen IIA.[16] Parée de boucles d'oreilles et d'un collier en argent, cette figurine était placée avec d'autres objets au côté du défunt.

Enfin, sur la côte syrienne, à **Tell Tweini**, deux tombes datées du Bronze moyen II ont chacune livré une figurine[17]. La première (TWE-A-00177-c-012), une figurine féminine, a été retrouvée dans une tombe construite à inhumations multiples formée d'un puits, d'un dromos et d'une chambre funéraire. La figurine se trouvait parmi d'autres objets à proximité de l'entrée du dromos. La seconde était placée dans une tombe en fosse aménagée sous le sol d'une maison et logeant une femme et un jeune enfant.

II. Les sources documentaires

Les textes peuvent-ils nous éclairer sur la fonction des effigies anthropomorphes retrouvées en contexte funéraire ou offrent-ils des témoignages de l'usage de tels objets lors des funérailles? Selon certains chercheurs ce serait le cas. Ceci étant, est-il vraiment approprié, compte tenu du cadre chronologique et géographique de cette enquête, de faire appel à des sources textuelles? En effet, les documents susceptibles d'être pertinents pour notre propos sont pour la plupart nettement plus récents que

[13] Tombe AT G/46/15: AT/46/238 (Woolley 1955, 222-223).

[14] Tombe D. 6979: TM. 97. AA. 440 (Baffi Guardata 2000, 59 et fig. 7: 2; Marchetti 2000, fig. 1; Marchetti 2001, fig. 4).

[15] Puits funéraire P.8680, niveau 6c (Mogliazza et Polcaro 2010, 436 et 439).

[16] Tombe US 5604 (Aletta 2005, 34 et fig. 31:13).

[17] Tombe TWE-A-00170: TWE-A-00177-c-012 (Hameeuw & Jans 2008, 80; Hameeuw et al. 2008, 146) et TWE-A-00934 (Hameeuw & Jans 2008, 77 et Hameeuw et al. 2008, 144).

les tombes dont il est question ici sans parler du fait qu'ils sont issus de la tradition lettrée mésopotamienne qui n'évoque certainement pas les croyances locales ou populaires syriennes[18]. Bien que la démarche puisse donc, de prime abord, paraître totalement anachronique, elle n'en reste pas moins indispensable et cela essentiellement pour deux raisons. Premièrement, étant donné que les inventeurs des figurines n'hésitent pas à faire appel aux sources documentaires ou plutôt à l'interprétation qui en est proposée pour expliquer leur découverte, il ne paraît pas inutile de les examiner afin de tester leur validité[19]. Deuxièmement, même si les analogies ethnographiques ne sont pas à négliger, les textes restent à ce jour la meilleure source de données disponible pour élaborer des modèles interprétatifs relatifs à la fonction des effigies anthropomorphes en contexte funéraire. Il serait donc dommage de s'en passer surtout si la règle de base, qui veut que chaque modèle soit mis à l'épreuve des données archéologiques, est respectée.

Suite au décès d'un individu, outre son cadavre qu'il convient d'enterrer avec soin, il subsiste une entité désignée par les anciens sous le terme générique d'*eṭemmu* et que les assyriologues qualifient tour à tour d'esprit, d'âme ou encore de fantôme. Au moment du décès, cette entité se libère du corps pour rejoindre le monde des morts et la mise au tombeau, accompagnée des rituels funéraires adéquats, constitue une étape capitale de ce dernier voyage. En effet, la mise en terre du corps est perçue comme une procédure de première importance dont le non-respect peut engendrer des conséquences négatives tant pour le défunt que pour les vivants car celui qui ne reçoit pas de sépulture se voit condamné à errer comme une âme en peine et devient une source de troubles et de maux divers[20].

Pour J. A. Scurlock, le temps des funérailles est, par conséquent, une période délicate car, si l'*eṭemmu* s'est déjà détaché du corps, tant que celui-ci n'aura pas été enseveli, il existe un risque qu'il devienne un fantôme errant et, de ce fait, insatisfait. Pendant cette période et afin que le défunt puisse bénéficier de ses offrandes funéraires, l'*eṭemmu* aurait donc été momentanément transféré dans un support susceptible de prendre la forme de différents objets (Scurlock 2002, 1-6). Des statues auraient ainsi été utilisées à cet effet lors des funérailles de personnages importants comme le montre notamment la tablette VIII de l'épopée de Gilgameš dans laquelle le héros demande à ses artisans de réaliser une statue en

[18] À ce sujet, voir Moorey 2005, 6-7.
[19] Voir notamment Hockmann 2010, 81.
[20] À ce sujet, voir notamment Bottéro 1983, 162-169.

matériaux précieux représentant son ami décédé (Gilgameš VIII 65-72, cf. George 2003, 656-657 et 287). Au terme de la cérémonie funèbre, ces statues auraient été enfermées dans les tombes pour assurer aux défunts la bonne réception perpétuelle de leurs offrandes alimentaires. C'est en tout cas ce que donnerait à penser un texte néo-assyrien narrant la mise au tombeau d'un roi dont le nom reste à ce jour inconnu (McGinnis 1987, Rev. Col. II' 11'). Tout le monde n'ayant pas les moyens de s'offrir une statue, celle-ci pouvait, selon J. A. Scurlock, être remplacée par un autre objet, en l'occurrence une chaise qui, de la même façon, servira de siège provisoire à la partie volatile du défunt[21]. S'il est vrai que les témoignages en faveur d'une telle hypothèse se multiplient, celle qui voudrait que des statues aient eu ce rôle demeure, en revanche, peu fondée. En effet, jusqu'à preuve du contraire, rien ne prouve que la statue d'Enkidu, commanditée par Gilgameš, n'était pas simplement une de celles qui étaient déposées dans les temples suite au décès d'un souverain ou d'un personnage de haut rang. Par ailleurs, s'il est exact que le texte décrivant les obsèques d'un roi néo-assyrien mentionne une statue parmi les autres objets supposés être placés dans la tombe, il faut bien reconnaître, comme le souligne très justement K. Veenhof (2008, 117), que rien ne prouve qu'il s'agisse de la statue du défunt. Même si c'est très tentant, il faut donc se garder de déduire du postulat de J. A. Scurlock que les gens du commun remplaçaient les statues par de simples figurines anthropomorphes en argile.

L'hypothèse selon laquelle des effigies anthropomorphes étaient utilisées dans le cadre du rituel funéraire concomitant des obsèques est également envisagée par D. Katz[22]. En effet, selon elle, le texte littéraire paléo-babylonien connu sous le titre de «*Lulil and his Sister*» fait état d'un rituel dont l'objectif était, d'une part, de libérer «l'esprit» de la dépouille mortelle et, d'autre part, de procéder à l'activation du culte des ancêtres en fournissant au défunt ses premières offrandes alimentaires. Pour ce faire, on avait recours à une statue, incarnation du trépassé, qui, après avoir été placée sur une chaise, parée d'un vêtement et ointe d'huile parfumée, se voyait présenter du pain et offrir une libation d'eau. Bien que cette interprétation du texte soit des plus séduisantes, elle n'en reste pas moins très fragile, pour ne pas dire bancale. La raison en est

[21] Au sujet de l'usage d'une chaise comme support provisoire de l'*eṭemmu*: voir aussi Veenhof 2008, 115-117.

[22] Katz 2007, 168-169; Katz 2003, 204-205 et 208-209; Katz 2005, 62-64; Katz 1999, 109-118.

simple: elle repose pour une grande part sur un seul mot, si-la-ah ou si-im-la-ah, qui n'existe ni en sumérien, ni en akkadien mais qui, selon D. Katz, doit être rapproché du terme élamite si-i-la signifiant «statue». Nul doute d'ailleurs que le rituel ne soit exécuté à l'aide d'une statue puisqu'un texte contemporain, intitulé «*The Messenger and the Maiden*» et décrivant un rituel en tout point similaire mais, celui-là, effectué lors du culte régulier des ancêtres, ferait pareillement mention de l'usage d'une figurine ou é-gar$_8$ en sumérien. En réalité, c'est aller un peu vite en besogne car le terme é-gar$_8$ a fait couler beaucoup d'encre et sa signification est loin d'être assurée. Ainsi, à la traduction de «figurine», A. C. Cohen (2005, 71, note 9) préfère celle de «corps», ce qui signifie que, pour lui, le rituel évoqué dans le second texte s'appliquerait, non pas à une figurine, mais à la dépouille mortelle qui se voyait frottée avec du pain et parfumée au moyen d'huile odorante. Pour J. A. Scurlock également, il n'est nulle part question d'effigies anthropomorphes dans ces deux textes (Scurlock 2002, 3). Sur base du contexte, elle comprend le terme si(m)lah du premier document comme faisant référence à l'entité impalpable qui se libère du corps au moment de la mort et qui se voit provisoirement transférée dans une chaise où elle sera à même de recevoir des offrandes funéraires. La multiplicité des interprétations proposées pour les deux textes longuement évoqués ci-dessus reflète combien ils sont compliqués et cela tant sur le plan de la traduction que de la compréhension. Il est donc prématuré de les présenter comme les témoins par excellence du rôle joué par les effigies anthropomorphes dans le cadre du rituel funéraire ou du culte des ancêtres et cela d'autant plus que les arguments en faveur d'une telle hypothèse sont plutôt maigres.

Dans l'état actuel de la documentation, il ne semble donc pas y avoir de sources documentaires évoquant sans ambiguïté l'utilisation d'effigies anthropomorphes dans le cadre d'un rituel funéraire et encore moins de textes évoquant leur dépôt dans la sépulture au côté du défunt. Il est, en revanche, question du dépôt de telles effigies dans des tombes ou des succédanés de tombes à l'occasion de procédures exorcistiques. En effet, dans son ouvrage consacré aux traitements des maladies dues à des fantômes, J. A. Scurlock (2006, 49-53) recense vingt et une prescriptions d'époque néo-assyrienne qui préconisent d'enterrer rituellement les défunts malfaisants sous la forme de figurines et ceci bien sûr dans le but de les expédier dans le monde des morts. Au cours d'un simulacre d'enterrement, les figurines, généralement réalisées en argile, seront tantôt placées dans le tombeau familial, tantôt dans une fosse spécialement creusée pour l'occasion.

III. Synthèse

Si l'on excepte l'opinion d'E. Peltenburg (Peltenburg et al. 1996, 12), pour qui les figurines en terre crue de Jerablus-Tahtani ne sont rien d'autre que des offrandes funéraires réalisées expressément pour être déposées dans les tombes, deux grandes tendances peuvent actuellement être décelées en ce qui concerne l'interprétation du statut et de la fonction des effigies anthropomorphes en contexte sépulcral. Sans surprise, pour les uns, ces objets représentent, voire incarnent le défunt auprès duquel ils ont été déposés, tandis que pour les autres, bien qu'ils personnifient également un trépassé, il ne s'agit pas de l'occupant de la tombe.

Parmi les tenants de la première théorie figurent les fouilleurs de Selenkahiye qui, tout en se gardant bien d'expliquer la raison de la présence de statuettes en pierre dans certaines sépultures de l'établissement, s'accordent à dire qu'elles peuvent être perçues comme des symboles de l'esprit du défunt (Van Loon et Meijer 2001, 220; Meijer 2003, 57)[23]. Pour les inventeurs de la tombe monumentale de Tell Beydar, la figurine en terre crue, qui y a été abandonnée, doit également être appréhendée comme une représentation de l'esprit du trépassé. Selon eux, compte tenu de son état, il faut envisager la possibilité qu'elle ait volontairement été cassée et cette hypothèse serait, d'ailleurs, d'autant plus probable qu'une dague la recouvrait partiellement. La figurine aurait donc fait l'objet d'une procédure de type apotropaïque visant à se protéger du défunt (Bretschneider et Cunningham 2007, 107-108), en l'occurrence un soldat mort au combat et inhumé loin des siens, susceptible de ne pas bénéficier du culte funéraire adéquat et, par conséquent, potentiellement dangereux.

Au nombre des partisans de la seconde théorie se trouve notamment C. Falb (Falb et al. 2005, 41 et 62) pour qui les figurines en terre cuite récoltées à Abu Hamed étaient utilisées au cours de rituels magiques mis en œuvre lors de funérailles et visant à expulser des fantômes. C'est également l'opinion de B. M. Nasrabadi (1999, 158) qui, au sujet d'une figurine trouvée dans une tombe néo-assyrienne d'Assur, évoque l'idée qu'elle y a été placée à l'occasion d'un simulacre d'enterrement organisé dans le cadre d'un rituel magique et impliquant la réouverture de la tombe. Quant à D. Hockmann (2010, 81), il évoque, entre autres choses, la possibilité que les quelques figurines découvertes en contexte funéraire à Assur aient servi de substitut au corps d'individus décédés dans des circonstances particulières et dont la dépouille aurait été perdue.

23 À ce sujet, voir également Cooper 2006, 222.

Aussi séduisantes soient-elles, il faut bien convenir que toutes ces théories sont loin d'être étayées par des données observables sur le terrain. Ceci n'a du reste rien d'étonnant puisque, dans la plupart des cas, le chercheur se trouve bien démuni face à ce type d'objets dont la seule présence dans la sépulture ne permet évidemment pas d'élucider sa raison d'être. Une chose est cependant certaine, il ne faut pas chercher d'explication unique au dépôt d'effigies anthropomorphes dans les sépultures car, d'une période à l'autre, d'une région à l'autre, voire même d'un site à l'autre, cet acte peut avoir un objectif totalement différent.

Le dépôt d'effigies anthropomorphes en contexte funéraire est rare. De fait, seuls quelques sites sont concernés par cette pratique et, au sein de chacun d'eux, seul un nombre réduit de tombes en témoigne. Dans l'état actuel de la documentation, loin de constituer une norme, elle fait donc plutôt figure d'exception et force est de constater qu'il ne devait être fait usage de ce type d'objets qu'à l'occasion de procédures exceptionnelles. Mais n'est-ce pas là déjà forcer l'interprétation car, après tout, la présence d'une figurine dans une tombe n'implique pas toujours, comme explicité ci-dessous, qu'elle ait fait l'objet de manipulations rituelles.

Certaines des effigies anthropomorphes trouvées en contexte sépulcral, et plus particulièrement les figurines en terre cuite du Bronze moyen attribuables au style «classique» de la vallée de l'Oronte, dont la moitié des exemplaires connus ont été trouvés dans des quartiers d'habitation (Badre 1980), n'ont manifestement pas été fabriquées à des fins funéraires. A. Pruβ (Pruβ et Novak 2000, 185) a donc peut-être raison de suggérer que, si certaines d'entre elles ont échoué dans des sépultures, c'est avant tout parce qu'il s'agit d'objets populaires, produits à grande échelle et utilisés de manière intensive en contexte domestique. En d'autres termes, il faut envisager la possibilité que certains défunts aient choisi d'emmener ces objets d'usage courant dans leur dernière demeure pour des raisons qui leur sont propres, mais qui n'ont rien à voir avec des croyances en matière d'au-delà ou un quelconque rituel funéraire. Gardons-nous cependant de ranger toutes les figurines en terre cuite dans le même sac en les considérant systématiquement comme faisant partie de la catégorie «objet favori» du défunt. De fait, il faut tenir compte de la possibilité que certaines d'entre elles aient été recyclées avant de se voir attribuer une nouvelle fonction. C'est, en tout cas, ce que suggère la localisation de l'une des figurines en terre cuite d'Abu Hamed qui, contrairement au reste du matériel funéraire, n'a pas été déposée auprès du défunt dans la cavité latérale, mais a été abandonnée dans le fond du puits d'accès qui y mène sans qu'il soit malheureusement possible d'en préciser la raison.

D'autres effigies anthropomorphes, comme celles en pierre de Selenkahiye ou celles en terre crue de Jerablus Tahtani, Tell Beydar et Chagar Bazar, réalisées sans souci du détail et de facture plutôt grossière, ne semblent pas avoir été conçues pour être exposées aux regards. Qui plus est, le fait que l'on n'ait pas pris la peine de cuire les figurines en argile laisse supposer que l'on ne cherchait pas à les rendre aisément manipulables et E. Peltenburg (Peltenburg et al. 1996, 11) ne se trompe probablement pas en affirmant que, compte tenu de leur fragilité, elles devaient être fabriquées peu de temps avant usage. Il n'est donc pas déraisonnable de postuler que ces objets avaient dès le départ une fonction funéraire. Ceci étant, est-il envisageable d'aller plus loin en se prononçant sur leur statut et leur raison d'être? Ce n'est pas exclu puisque le contexte de découverte de ces objets offre un faisceau d'indices qui permet pour le moins de proposer des hypothèses de travail.

Dans la plupart des tombes de Selenkahiye, le nombre de statuettes équivaut à celui des squelettes; une situation qui, a priori, constitue un solide argument pour étayer l'idée que chacune d'elles représente un défunt. À cela, il pourrait bien sûr être objecté qu'une telle situation n'implique en rien que la statuette «représente» ou «incarne» le mort et cela serait entièrement vrai si la répartition de ces artefacts au sein de chaque tombe ne plaidait pas, elle aussi, en faveur de cette hypothèse. En effet, loin d'être chacune directement associée à l'un des occupants de ces sépultures à inhumations multiples, les statuettes sont généralement regroupées à proximité de l'un d'eux, probablement le dernier à avoir été inhumé comme c'est clairement le cas dans la tombe TW13 TbI. Si le nombre de statuettes correspond à celui des trépassés, c'est donc très vraisemblablement parce que chacun d'eux, pour une raison qui nous échappe, se devait d'être représenté par une «image» à l'occasion des funérailles clôturant l'emploi de la tombe.

Le cas de Chagar Bazar est particulièrement intéressant car nous sommes en présence d'une tombe qui ne contient pas de corps et qui paraît avoir été aménagée à l'unique intention de trois figurines anthropomorphes en terre crue. Dans la mesure où cette tombe abritait du mobilier funéraire et est aménagée à l'identique des autres sépultures à puits d'accès à cavité latérale de l'établissement, on est en droit de se demander si ces figurines n'avaient pas pour fonction de se substituer au corps de trois défunts dont la dépouille n'était pas disponible. Mais pourquoi avoir recours à de tels «substituts corporels». Ne serait-ce pas avant tout parce que la mise en terre du cadavre était perçue comme une étape capitale du processus funéraire permettant d'introduire le défunt dans le monde des morts[24]. Afin de pouvoir remplir cette condition, les trois défunts de Chagar Bazar auraient donc été inhumés sous la forme de figurines, à l'instar de ce qui est préconisé dans les rituels visant à se débarrasser de morts malfaisants. Au-delà de cette nécessité d'inhumer le cadavre, l'usage de «substituts corporels» pourrait également s'expliquer par un autre impératif. En effet, d'après les sources documentaires, il est clair que les morts continuent à fonctionner avec un corps dans l'au-delà et, dès lors, il ne peut être question d'en être privé[25]. Mais il y a plus important! Être démembré ou spolié d'une partie de son anatomie ou totalement privé de corps, c'est courir le risque de ne plus pouvoir être reconnu, de perdre son identité; en d'autres termes de ne plus exister.

Le cas de Tell Beydar est tout aussi exceptionnel. En effet, la figurine en terre crue, trouvée dans la partie externe de la tombe T. 58550, était entourée par différents groupes d'objets qui, pour la plupart, se trouvaient encore en place au moment de leur découverte et qui, puisque la sépulture n'a pas fait l'objet d'une réouverture, témoignent, chacun, de l'une des étapes d'un rituel célébré durant les funérailles. Le décor de la cérémonie reste donc planté et, bien que cela ne soit pas chose aisée, il est possible d'en décrypter certaines modalités.

Une analyse détaillée de la répartition du matériel dans la tombe permet d'emblée d'écarter la possibilité que ce rituel ait été d'une autre nature que funéraire[26]. En effet, des objets, qui devaient initialement être placés à la gauche du défunt et qui, au premier degré, peuvent être perçus comme ses biens personnels, ont manifestement été prélevés afin d'être transférés dans la partie externe de la chambre sépulcrale, un acte qui ne laisse planer que peu de doute sur le fait que le rituel avait pour centre d'intérêt le trépassé. Ceci étant établi, il y a évidement une forte probabilité pour que la figurine soit l'image de la personne décédée, un substitut du défunt peut-être mis en œuvre pour des raisons de facilité.

L'étude de la symbolique des objets rassemblés dans la partie externe de la chambre sépulcrale permet quant à elle d'identifier les objectifs de la procédure ou tout au moins deux d'entre eux. La présence de jarres de tailles différentes, susceptibles d'avoir contenu nourriture et boisson, mais aussi celle de bouteilles syriennes, probablement destinées à renfermer des huiles ou autres onguents parfumés, indique que le rituel avait notamment pour fonction de marquer la fin du deuil pour les participants

[24] À ce sujet, voir Van der Stede 2007, 72-74.
[25] À ce sujet, voir Van der Stede 2007, 109-115.
[26] Cette analyse sera prochainement publiée dans Van der Stede, à paraître.

aux funérailles et le retour à la vie. Un autre aspect du rituel concerne le défunt qui lui se verra contraint de rejoindre la foule des trépassés. Pour rappel, il semblerait qu'un certain nombre d'objets aient été prélevés du groupe d'artefacts rangés à la gauche du défunt; artefacts qui, pour des raisons qu'il serait trop long d'évoquer ici, symbolisent à la fois la vie et la nature humaine. Si l'objectif du rituel n'était certainement pas de dénier au défunt son statut d'être humain, en revanche, tout porte à croire que le prélèvement d'une partie de ces objets, symboles de vie, visait à entériner son nouveau statut d'habitant du monde des morts. En d'autres termes, par cet acte, le défunt se voyait définitivement retiré du monde des vivants, une situation qui, au terme du rituel, était probablement rendue définitive par la destruction de la figurine.

Comme précisé au début de cet article, il ne s'agit ici que de la première étape d'une recherche qui, à l'avenir, devrait être élargie tant sur le plan géographique que chronologique. Malheureusement, dans bien des cas, faute de données, le travail se borne à constater la présence de figurines ou de statuettes dans les tombes. Des découvertes du type de celles faites à Selenkahiye, Chagar Bazar ou encore Tell Beydar permettent néanmoins de progresser et il est aujourd'hui évident que les effigies anthropomorphes trouvées en contexte funéraire ne peuvent pas toutes être cantonnées dans le rôle «d'objet favori» que le défunt aurait choisi d'emmener dans sa dernière demeure. Au contraire même, tout semble indiquer que l'on pouvait avoir recours à ce type d'objets dans les circonstances les plus diverses, qu'il s'agisse de remplacer le corps disparu d'un trépassé ou de se substituer à la dépouille d'un autre dans le cadre d'un rituel funéraire.

Bibliographie

ALETTA, G. 2005: «Le sepolture dell'età del Bronzo Medio», *Egitto e Vicino Oriente* 28, 33-37.

BADRE, L. 1980: *Les figurines anthropomorphes en terre cuite à l'Age du Bronze en Syrie* (BAH 103), Paris.

BAFFI GUARDATA, F. 2000: «Les tombes du Bronze Moyen dans le secteur des fortifications à Ebla», in P. Matthiae et al. (eds.), *Proceedings of the First International Congress on the Archaeology of the Ancient Near East. Rome, May 18th – 23rd 1998*, 2 vols., Roma, 55-78.

BOTTÉRO, J. 1983: «Les morts et l'au-delà dans les rituels accadiens contre l'action des 'revenants'», *ZA* 73, 153-203.

BRETSCHNEIDER, J. et T. CUNNINGHAM 2007: «An Elite Akkadian Grave on the Acropolis at Tell Beydar», in M. Lebeau et A. Suleiman (eds.), *Tell Beydar. Rapport préliminaire sur les campagnes de fouilles 2000-2002 et les campagnes de restauration architecturale 2003-2004* (Subartu XV), 99-158.

COHEN, A. C. 2005: *Death Rituals, Ideology, and the Development of Early Mesopotamian Kingship. Toward a New Understanding of Iraq's Royal Cemetery of Ur* (Ancient Magic and Divination VII), Leiden-Boston.

COOPER, L. 2006: *Early Urbanism on the Syrian Euphrates*, London, 2006.

DEBRUYNE, M. et al. 2003: «Small Finds from the Acropolis (Field F)», in M. Lebeau et A. Suleiman (eds.), *Tell Beydar. Rapport préliminaire sur les campagnes de fouilles 1995-1999* (Subartu X), 203-224.

FALB, C. et al. 2005: *Gräber des 3. Jahrtausends v. Chr. im syrieschen Euphrattal. 4. Der Friedhof von Abu Hamed*, Saarwellingen.

FUGMANN, H. 1958: *Hama. Fouilles et recherches 1931-1938 II,1. L'architecture des périodes pré-hellénistiques*, Copenhagen.

GEORGE, A.R. 2003: *The Babylonian Gilgamesh Epic. Introduction, Critical Edition and Cuneiform Text* (2 vols.), Oxford.

HAMEEUW, H. et G. JANS 2008: «Burial Customs at Tell Tweini — Field A», in J. Bretschneider et K. Van Lerberghe (eds.), *In Search of Gibala. An Archaeological and Historical Study based on eight Seasons of Excavations at Tell Tweini (Syria) in the A and C Fields (1999-2007)* (Aula Orientalis – Supplementa 24), Barcelona, 75-86.

HAMEEUW, H. et al. 2008: «Living with the Dead. Tell Tweini: Middle Bronze Age Tombs in an Urban Context», in J. Cordoba et al. (eds.), *Proceedings of the 5th International Congress of the Archaeology of the Ancient Near East (3-8 April 2006)*, 3 vols., Madrid, 143-151.

HOCKMANN, D. 2010: *Gräber und Grüfte in Assur I. Von der zweiten Hälfte des 3. bis zur Mitte des 2. Jahrtausends v. Chr.* (WVDOG 129), Wiesbaden.

INGHOLT, H. 1940: *Rapport préliminaire sur sept campagnes de fouilles à Hama*, Copenhagen.

JEAN-MARIE, M. 1999: *Tombes et nécropoles de Mari* (Bibliothèque archéologique et historique CLIII), Beyrouth.

KATZ, D. 1999: «The Messenger, Lulil and the Cult of the Dead», *RA* 93, 107-118.

— 2003: *The Image of the Netherworld in the Sumerian Sources*, Bethesda.

— 2005: «Death they Dispensed to Mankind. The Funerary World of Ancient Mesopotamia», *Historiae* 2, 55-90.

— 2007: «Sumerian Funerary Rituals in Context», in N. Laneri (ed.), *Performing Death. Social Analyses of Funerary Traditions in the Ancient Near East and Mediterranean*, Chicago, 163-188.

KLENGEL-BRANDT, E. et al. 2005: *Tall Knēdig. Die Ergebnisse der Ausgrabungen des Vorderasiatischen Museums Berlin in Nordost-Syrien von 1993 bis 1998* (WDOG 113).

LÉON, S. à paraître: *Chagar Bazar (Syrie) VI. Les tombes de l'âge du Bronze. Les objets*, Leuven.

MARCHETTI, N. 2000: «Clay Figurines in the Middle Bronze Age from Northern Inner Syria: Chronology, Symbolic and Historical Relations», in: P. Matthiae et al. (eds.), *Proceedings of the First International Congress on the Archaeology of the Ancient Near East. Rome, May 18th – 23rd 1998*, 2 vols., Roma, 839-867.

— 2001: *La Coroplastica Eblaita e Siriana nel Bronzo Medio. Campagne 1964-1980.*

McGinnis, J. 1987: «A Neo-assyrian Text Describing a Royal Funeral», *SAA Bulletin* 1/1, 1-11.

Meijer, D. J. W. 2003: «Some Thoughts on Burial Interpretation», *Altorientalische Forschungen* 30, 51-62.

Mogliazza, S. et A. Polcaro 2010: «Death and Cult of Dead in Middle Bronze Age II Ebla: An Archaeological and Anthropological Study on Shaft Tomb P.8680, near Southern Palace (Area FF)», in P. Matthiae et al. (eds.), *Proceedings of the 6th International Congress on the Archaeology of the Ancient Near East*, Wiesbaden, 431-445.

Mocrey, P. R. S. 2005: *Ancient Near Eastern Terracottas: with a Catalogue of the Collection in the Ashmolean Museum, Oxford.*

Nasrabadi, B. M. 1999: *Untersuchungen zu den Bestatungssitten in Mesopotamien in der ersten Hälfte des ersten Jahrtausends v. Chr.* (Baghdader Forschungen 23), Mainz am Rhein.

Orthmann, W. et E. Rova 1991: *Gräber des 3. Jahrtausends v. Chr. im syrieschen Euphrattal. 2. Ausgrabungen in Wreide.*

Peltenburg, E. et al. 1996: «Jerablus-Tahtani, Syria 1995: Preliminary Report», *Levant* 28, 1-25.

Pézard, M. 1931: *Qadesh: Mission archéologique à Tell Nébi Mend 1921-1922*, Paris.

Prub, A. 2010 : *Die Amuq-Terrakotten. Untersuchungen zu den terrakkotafiguren des 2. und 1. jahrtausends v. Chr. Aus den grabungen des oriental institute Chicago in der Amuq-Ebene* (Subartu XXVI), Turnhout.

Prub, A. et M. Novak 2000: «Terrakotten und Beinidole in sepulkralen Kontexten», *Altorientalische Forschungen* 27/1, 184-195.

Scurlock, J. 2002: «Soul Emplacements in Ancient Mesopotamian Funerary Rituals», in L. Ciraolo et J. Seidel (eds.), *Magic and Divination in the Ancient World* (Ancient Magic and Divination II), Leiden – Boston – Köln, 1-6.

— 2006: *Magico-Medical Means of Treating Ghost-Induced Illnesses in Ancient Mesopotamia*, Leiden-Boston.

Thuesen, I. 1988: *Hama. Fouilles et recherches de la fondation Carlsberg 1931-1938 I. The Pre-and Protohistoric Periods*, Copenhagen.

Tunca, Ö. et A. M. Baghdo (eds.) à paraître: *Chagar Bazar (Syrie) IV. Les tombes de l'âge du Bronze*, Leuven.

Van der Stede, V. 2007: *Mourir au pays des deux fleuves. L'au-delà mésopotamien d'après les sources sumériennes et akkadiennes* (Lettres orientales 12), Leuven.

— à paraître: *Les pratiques funéraires à Tell Beydar – Nabada. Étude des tombes mises en place entre l'Early Djezireh II et l'Early Djezireh IV* (Beydar Studies II), Turnhout.

Van Loon, M. N., D. J. W. Meijer 2001: «Graves and their Contents», in M. N. Van Loon (ed.), *Selenkahiye. Final Report on the University of Chicago and University of Amsterdam Excavations in the Tabqa Reservoir. Northern Syria, 1967-1975*, 127-221.

Van Soldt, W. H. 2001: «Stone objects», in M. N. Van Loon (ed.), *Selenkahiye. Final Report on the University of Chicago and University of Amsterdam*

Excavations in the Tabqa Reservoir. Northern Syria, 1967-1975, 447-478.

VEENHOF, K. R. 2008: «The Death and Burial of Ishtar-Lamassi in Karum Kanish», in R. J. van der Spek (ed.), *Studies in Ancient Near Eastern World View and Society presentend to Marten Stol on the Occasion of his 65th Birthday, 10 november 2005, and his Retirement from the Vrije Universiteit Amsterdam*, Bethesda, 97-117.

WISSING, A. 2009: «Die Tonobjekte», in A. Bianchi et A. Wissing (eds.), *Ausgrabungen 1998-2001 in der zentralen Oberstadt von Tall Mozan/Urkeš. Die Kleinfunde*, Wiesbaden.

WOOLLEY, C. L. 1955: *Alalakh. An Account of the Excavations at Tell Atchana in the Hatay 1937-1949*, Oxford.

BIRD FEATHERS FOR CEREMONIAL USE IN HELLENISTIC TIMES AT TELL BEYDAR, SYRIA?

Wim VAN NEER[1,2] and Bea DE CUPERE[1]
1. Royal Belgian Institute of Natural Sciences Brussels
2. KU Leuven

Faunal studies at Tell Beydar began in 1997 when Karel Van Lerberghe set up an environmental study programme and invited the authors to take part in the project. Archaeozoological analyses were carried out in the field during two excavation seasons but dealt with the faunal remains from several years (Van Neer 2000; Van Neer and De Cupere 2000; De Cupere and Van Neer, accepted). Collaboration within the field of archaeozoology continues at the site of Tell Tweini (Linseele 2008; Linseele and De Cupere, in prep.). In the present contribution attention is focussed on an enigmatic deposit of bird bones that was discovered in a Hellenistic context at Tell Beydar in 1998 and that was only briefly mentioned thus far in a paper intended for publication in the proceedings of a conference held in 2006 (De Cupere and Van Neer, accepted). The osteological remains are described and possible explanations, both natural and anthropogenic, are formulated in an attempt to understand the peculiar skeletal element distribution that is observed.

Tell Beydar is a site of the Kranzhügel type located in northern Syria at about 35 km northeast of Hassake (Lebeau 1997). Excavations in different areas of the tell (Fig. 1) have shown that the site was occupied between the 3rd millennium BC and Hellenistic times. Traces of the final, Hellenistic, occupation have been found in various excavation areas. The faunal remains of that period are typically derived from refuse layers and from the fill of pits that are associated with Hellenistic structures. Bone material was found in Hellenistic pitfills of the central and most elevated part of the tell (Field F), in the southeastern part (Field E), and in more northerly located areas of the tell (Fields A, C and I). The assemblage that is described in this paper comes from a circular pit (locus 2301) near a Hellenistic house discovered in Field B (Bluard et al. 1997). A total of 16 such pits, with an average diameter of 2 m at the top and 2.50 m at the bottom, were found on a surface of about 400 m^2 in the upper city, between the palace of Field F and the houses of Field B. They were identified as storage units or containers for cereals (Sténuit and Van der Stede 2003, 230). After they were abandoned as cereal containers, nine of these pits were re-used as dumping places: they contained broken pottery, spindle whorls, loom weights, grinding stones, pestles, oil lamps, fragments of zoomorphic and anthropomorphic figurines, as well as animal bones and ashy sediment. The faunal remains consist of left-overs of human food, but besides this domestic waste, six of these pits also yielded more or less complete skeletons of a variety of animal species, mainly dogs and equids (donkey and mule or hinny). This seems to suggest that some kind of ritual behaviour took place (De Cupere and Van Neer, accepted).

The faunal remains from the Hellenistic pit (locus 2301) discussed here are dominated by rock dove (*Columba livia*), represented by a total of 144 bones. The other animal taxa are pig, sheep/goat, and an unidentified song bird. There are only seven remains of pig, most likely corresponding to human consumption refuse. The suid material consists of the left and right canine of a female animal, three metapodials, and two mandibles. The tooth wear of the last molar indicates that one of these lower jaws belongs to a pig between 2 and 3 years of age, whereas the other one was older than 3 years of age. The sheep/goat bones include a mandible, 14 ribs, a humerus and a radius, all from a single foetus that was apparently disposed of in the pit. The dimensions of the long bones (greatest length of radius 37 mm and greatest length of humerus 29 mm) indicate an ovicaprine foetus that was aborted about 3 months after conception (cf. Habermehl 1975). Sheep and goat are usually born around 4 ½ months after conception. Because the still poorly developed skeletal elements do not allow a distinction between sheep and goat, and also because there is some variability in the birth season of each species, the material does not allow the establishment of the season in which the carcass was deposited. The remains of an unidentified song bird (size of a sparrow *Passer domesticus*) include a skull, a clavicula, a sternum, two humeri, two ulnae, a tibiotarsal and a tarsometatarsal of the same individual. It is unclear if this small bird ended up naturally in the pit, or if it was also intentionally deposited. In addition to these animal bones, some very fragmented human remains were found among which only a partial femur, a metapodial fragment and a talus were recognisable. The heavily weathered nature of the human remains suggests a different taphonomic history. Possibly they are reworked remains that came originally from one of the human graves in the adjacent Field F?

The rock dove is represented by a piece of skull, and by numerous bones of the wing, namely a single ulna, five first, anterior phalanges of the second digit and 137 remains of carpometacarpals (Fig. 2). The carpometacarpals correspond to a MNE (minimum number of elements) of 67 left and 56 right specimens, indicating an MNI (minimum number of individuals) of 67 pigeons.

The ulna, carpometacarpal and anterior phalanges are the bones to which the distal series of large flight feathers of the wing are attached (Fig. 3). The peculiar skeletal distribution observed in locus 2301 is indicative of humans being interested in the feathers as a raw material. Other explanations are less convincing: alternatively, the wing bones could be seen as waste from food preparation involving the removal of the distal wings prior to cooking and eating the birds. However, in that case one would expect the radius and the ulna to be also proportionally present. Moreover, such kitchen refuse would normally also include skulls and feet (cf. Serjeantson 2009, 153), whereas the assemblage from locus 2301 yielded only one skull. It also seems unlikely that the assemblage corresponds to an accumulation by birds of prey. The manipulation of avian preys by raptors and subsequent digestion of bone can result in deposits showing very specific signatures, with certain skeletal elements being over-represented. A high proportion of carpometacarpals has been recorded in the pellets and food remains of several birds of prey (Laroulandie 2002; Bochenski 2005), but in each case there were also remains of various other skeletal elements, not represented in the Tell Beydar assemblage. Similarly, it seems very unlikely that other predators, such as mammalian carnivores, are responsible for this peculiar deposit.

Thus, the most plausible explanation for the accumulation of the carpometacarpals is that they represent the remains of wings that have been collected by man for their feathers. Bird feathers are indeed often used as decoration and examples are readily found in ethnographic objects. However, since feathers are made of keratin, they have poor chances of being preserved in the archaeological record and their use or application remains largely unknown. There are some rare publications on the use of feathers in former times (e.g. Russell and Mc Gowan 2003; Gál 2007; Peresania et al. 2011), but none related to this area and/or period.

The skeletal element distribution of the pigeon bones indicates which part of the wing was deposited in the Hellenistic pit at Tell Beydar (cf. Proctor and Lynch 1993). The ulna, of which only one specimen was present, carries the so-called secondaries or secondary remiges (Fig. 3). In pigeons, there are 15 such flight feathers attached to the ulna. An additional

10 flight feathers, the so-called primaries or primary remiges, are attached to the carpometacarpal and the first phalanx. Judging from the rarity of ulnae, it appears that only the anterior part of the wing is represented in the pit. It is possible that the secondaries were less used than the primaries. Since there is little or no difference in shape between the two types of remiges, this choice is maybe dictated by practical rather than by aesthetic reasons. The 'forearm' of the wing, with the radius and ulna, is fleshier than the carpometacarpal area (the 'hand') which makes it less suitable for drying. The 'hand' of the wing, on the contrary, can easily be dried and this may explain why this part of the wing preponderates in the deposit at Tell Beydar.

Compared to the carpometacarpals, the phalanges are heavily underrepresented. The sediment of the pit was not sieved and it is therefore not excluded that these smaller elements may to some extent have been overlooked. If the underrepresentation of the phalanges, compared to the carpometacarpals, is not due to loss during sampling, the wings must have been prepared in such a way that only the proximal 'hand' part was left with its attached feathers. The primaries differ in shape depending on their position in the wing: the outer ones (on the first phalanx) are relatively narrow and stiff while the inner primaries (on the carpometacarpal) are broader (Fig. 3 and 4). If the skeletal distribution reflects a deliberate choice, rather than a taphonomical artefact, this would mean that only the broadest feathers were retained for aesthetic reasons (Fig. 4).

The mean length of the carpometacarpals is 31.5 mm and there is a minimum of 113 carpometacarpals. If aligned, they correspond to a length of more than 3.5 metres of wing bases with attached feathers. If the outer part of the wing was also used, i.e. including the phalanges, the length must have been even greater. It is unclear how this raw material was used but obviously it must have served as some kind of decoration or adornment, possibly in a ritual, symbolic or ceremonial context. Apparently, no particular arrangement of the pigeon bones was noted during excavation that would indicate that they were draped along the edge of the circular pit. Its diameter being about two metres, somewhat more than six metres of wing bases would have been needed to adorn the whole circumference of the pit. Alternatively the pigeon wings may have been used to cover or ornament some of the pit content (the ovicaprine foetus?), but it may also have had no association at all with any of the objects or animals deposited in the pit. It cannot be excluded either that the feathers were used for personal adornment or that they were part of some kind of clothing. There are no doubt various other ways pigeon wings or feathers may have been used and, in order to allow the reader to further speculate on this, we made a collage (Fig. 5[1]) of various ways the use of pigeon feathers and pigeon wings is illustrated on the internet. For the time being we do not dare to speculate if, or to what extent, there is any parallel with uses in Hellenistic times. Nor do we want to suggest that such humble feathers would be sufficient laurels for celebrating Karel.

Bibliography

BLUARD, C., I. POINOT and P. QUENET 1997: "Un quartier d'occupation dynastique archaïque (chantier B)", in M. Lebeau and A. Suleiman (eds.) *Tell Beydar, three seasons of excavations (1992-1994). A preliminary report* (Subartu 3), Turnhout, 47-58.

BOCHENSKI, Z. M. 2005: "Owls, diurnal raptors and humans: signatures on avian bones" in: T. O'Connor (ed.) *Biosphere to lithosphere*, Oxford, 31-45.

DE CUPERE, B. and W. VAN NEER (accepted): "Consumption refuse, carcasses and ritual deposits at Tell Beydar (northern Syria)" in L. Limano and F. Bertoldi (eds.) *Proceedings of the International Symposium Methods and perspectives applied to the study of food practices in the ancient Near East, Venice 14-17/6/2006.*

GÁL, E. 2007: "Bird remains" in A. Whittle (ed.) *The Early Neolithic on the Great Hungarian Plain: investigations of the Körös culture site of Ecsegfalva 23, Co. Békés* (Varia Archaeologica Hungarica 21), Budapest, 361-375.

HABERMEHL, K.-H. 1975: *Die Altersbestimmung bei Haus- und Labortieren*, Berlin-Hamburg.

LAROULANDIE, V. 2002: "Damage to Pigeon long bones in pellets of the Eagle Owl *Bubo bubo* and food remains of Peregrine Falcon *Falco peregrinus*: zooarchaeological implications", *Acta zoologica cracoviensia* 45 (special issue), 331-339.

LEBEAU, M. 1997: "La situation géographique, la topographie et les périodes d'occupation de Tell Beydar", in M. Lebeau and A. Suleiman (eds.) *Tell Beydar, three seasons of excavations (1992-1994). A preliminary report* (Subartu 3), Turnhout, 7-19.

LINSEELE, V. 2008: "Faunal remains from Tell Tweini. A first report", in J. Bretschneider and K. Van Lerberghe (eds.) *In search of Gibala, An archaeological and historical study based on eight seasons of excavations at Tel Tweini (Syria) in the A and C fields (1999-2007)* (Aula Orientalis-Supplementa 24), Barcelona, 143-149.

[1] Collage based on pictures taken from the internet:
http://3.bp.blogspot.com/_lirt8srIYAI/SmYsxXvBjQI/AAAAAAAAEXg/YuT7Jr-p8LNU/s400/pigeon+feather+headband.jpg; http://i.cocoperez.com/wp-content/uploads/2010/11/kelly-brook-at-dior-private-dinner-in-a-feathery-dress__oPt.jpg;
http://justsickshit.com/wp-content/uploads/2008/08/feather-piercing.jpg;
http://thepandorian.com/wp-content/uploads/2009/09/001.jpg.

PERESANIA, M. I. FIOREB, M. GALAB, M. ROMANDINIA and A. TAGLIACOZZO 2011: "Late Neandertals and the intentional removal of feathers as evidenced from bird bone taphonomy at Fumane Cave 44 ky B.P., Italy", *PNAS* 108, 3888-3893.

PROCTOR, N. S. and P. J. LYNCH 1993: *Manual of Ornithology: Avian Structure and Function*, New Haven.

RUSSELL, N. and N. J. MCGOWAN 2003: "Dance of the Cranes: Crane symbolism at Çatalhöyük and beyond", *Antiquity* 77, 445–455.

SERJEANTSON, D. 2009: *Birds* (Cambridge Manuals in Archaeology), Cambridge.

STÉNUIT, M.-E. and V. VAN DER STEDE 2003: "Du palais au quartier de maisons privées (jonction entre le chantier F et le chantier B — campagnes 1997-1999)", in M. Lebeau and A. Suleiman (eds.) *Tell Beydar, The 1995 to 1999 Seasons of Excavations. A Preliminary Report* (Subartu 10), Turnhout, 225-231.

VAN NEER, W. 2000: Faunal remains from an Akkadian grave in Tell Beydar, in K. Van Lerberghe and G. Voet (eds.) *Tell Beydar Environmental and Technical Studies* (Subartu 6) Turnhout, 61-63.

VAN NEER, W. and B. DE CUPERE 2000: Faunal remains from Tell Beydar (excavation seasons 1992-1996 and 1997 partim), in K. Van Lerberghe and G. Voet (eds.) *Tell Beydar Environmental and Technical Studies* (Subartu 6), Turnhout, 69-115.

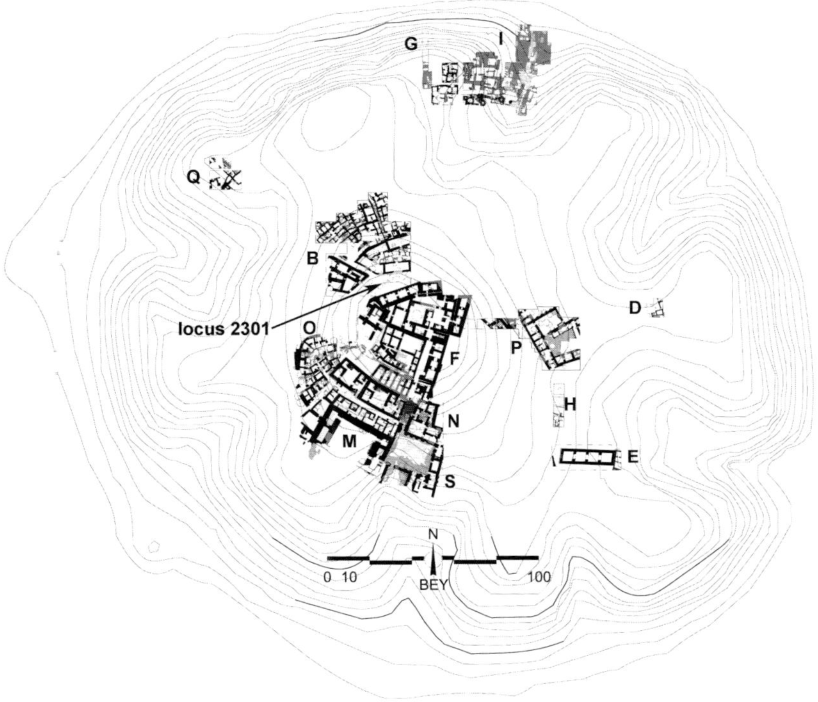

Fig. 1. General view of Tell Beydar with indication of the excavated fields (situation 2009) and the area where locus 2301 is located.

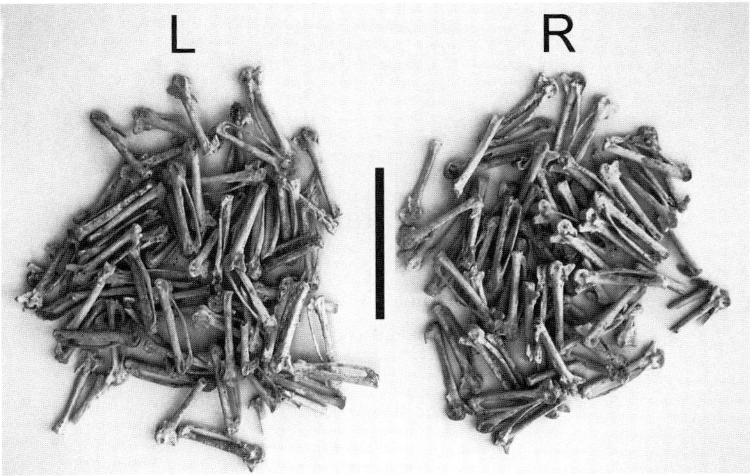

Fig. 2. The left and right carpometacarpals of rock dove found in locus 2301. The scale bar is 5 cm.

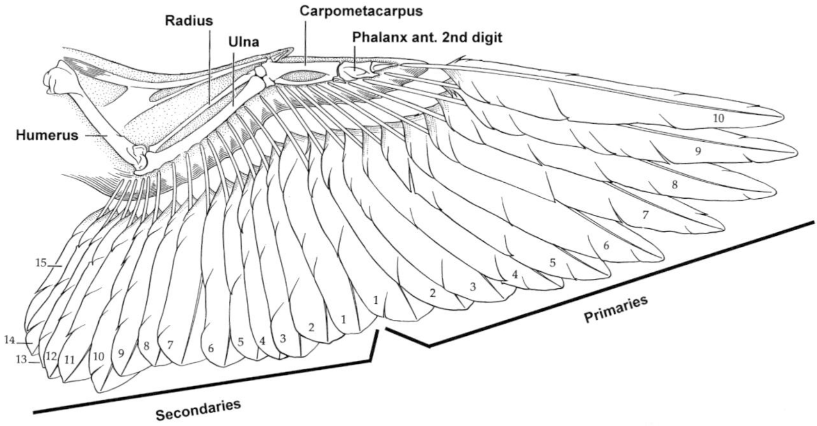

Fig. 3. View on the ventral part of a pigeon wing, with the coverts removed and the bones made visible (after Proctor and Lynch 1993).

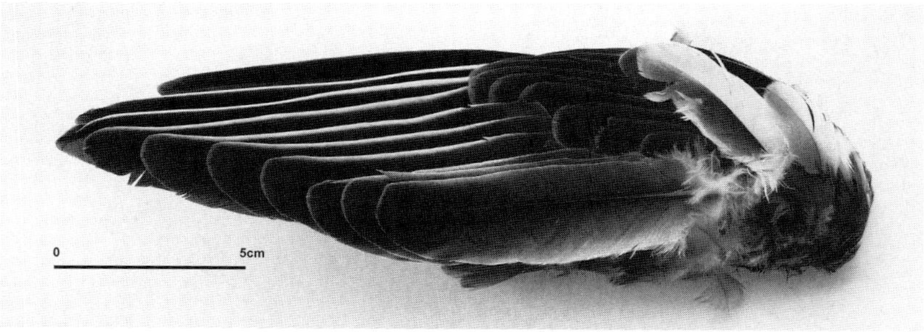

Fig. 4. Dorsal view of a modern pigeon wing, showing the ten primaries that were apparently selected at locus 2301.

Fig. 5. Pigeon wings and feathers for adornment and clothing.

AN OLD BABYLONIAN LAWSUIT ON THE PROPERTY OF A PRIESTESS

Klaas R. VEENHOF
Leiden University

in collaboration with Eva Dombradi

This tablet from Sippir, in the British Museum, published here by kind permission of its Trustees, was studied by the writer long ago. He made it available to Eva Dombradi for inclusion in a planned corpus of OB judicial records, whereupon she prepared a commented edition of it in German that we discussed. Since the publication of the corpus has not been realized, I publish it here, as a tribute to an old friend to whom we owe the knowledge of so many important OB records. Separate publication allows adding more comments than would otherwise be possible and they are necessary, because this record raises several questions, while its formulation is at times laconic. Because Eva Dombradi could not join me in writing this article, I explicitly mention some of her points of view, also by quoting from her old manuscript, and I insert some references to her book on the Old Babylonian judicial procedures (Dombradi 1996). Several years ago Frans van Koppen helped me with some collations and he also obliged me by providing me with excellent photos of the tablet.

1. *The text*

BM 97067 (1902-10-11, 121; 10.0 × 5.2 × 2.5 cm)

0,0.6 IKU A.ŠÀ *i-na* A.GÀR KÁ ^{d}*Na-bi-um*	6 *iku* field in the Bāb-Nabium polder,
i-ta A.ŠÀ *Ha-zi-rum*	next to the field of Hazirum
ù i-ta A.ŠÀ ^{d}URAŠ-*qar-ra-ad*	and next to the field of Uraš-qarrād,
a-di KASKAL *Im-gur-*^{d}UTU	reaching until the Imgur-Šamaš road;
0,0.5 IKU A.ŠÀ *i-na Im-gur-*^{d}UTU	5 *iku* field in Imgur-Šamaš,
i-ta A.ŠÀ DUMU.MEŠ *Qàr-ba-nim*	next to field of the sons of Qarbānum
ù i-ta A.ŠÀ *Li-wi-ra-šum*	and next to the field of Liwwiraššum;
1 SAR É.DÙ.A *i-na* AN.ZA.QÀR-^{d}EN.LÍL	1 built house of 36 m^2 in Dimat-Enlil,
DA É *A-hu-la-ap-*^{d}MARDUK	next to the house of Ahulap-Marduk;
1 ÁB ^{d}*Na-b*[*i*]-*um-ša-am-ši*	1 cow, called Nabium-šamšī -
$^{\text{p}\langle\text{d}\rangle}$UTU-*ša-ta-ka-l*[*i*]-*im*	Šamaš-ša-takālim had given to

	a-na Ni-ši-ni-šu NIN.DINGIR ^{d}*Na-bi-um*	Nīši-inišu, *ugbabtu*-priestess of Nabium,
	id-di-in$^{!}$*-ma i-ga-ru-um* [DUMU.MÍ.A.NI	his daughter, but (since) a/the wall
	i-na mu-[*u*]*h-hi tup*-pí nu-du-un-ne-ša*	was in excess over what her dowry
	[*wa-a*]*t-ru-ma* ^{p}*Li-wi-ra-šum*	record stated, Liwwiraššum
e.	[A].ŠÀ É$^{!}$ *ù* ÁB ^{p}*Ni-ši-i-ni-šu*	claimed Nīši-inišu's field,
	[*i*]*b-qú-ur-ši-i-ma*	house and cow from her. Thereupon
	^{p}*Ha-ia-ab-ni*-DINGIR *ù* DI.KU$_5$.M[EŠ]	they appealed to Hajabni'el and the
rev.	*ik-šu-<<ud>>-du-ma a-wa-ti-šu-nu*	judges who evaluated their case.
	i$^{!}$*-mu*$^{!}$*-ru* ^{pd}*Na-bi-um-ma-lik ra-bi-a-nu-*[*um*]	They fetched the mayor Nabium-mālik
	ù ši-bu-ut URU *Ha-bi-bi it-ru-nim-ma*	and the elders of the town Habibi
	ši-bu-sú-nu ki$^{!}$*-ma i-ga-ru*	and these declared as their testimony
	i-na mu-uh-hi DUB *nu-du-un-ne-ša*	that the wall was in excess over what her
	[*wa-at-r*[*u*]	[dowry record stated and they
	iq-bu-ú ù ki$^{!}$*-ma* ^{p}*Li-wi-ra-šum i-na*	also told that Liwwiraššum had previous-
	[*pa-ni-tim*	[ly raised a claimed against her
	ib-qú-ru-ši-ma DI.KU$_5$ KÁ.DINGIR.RA^{ki}.	and that the judges of Babylon had then
	di-nam ú-ša-hi-zu-šu-nu-ti-ma [MEŠ	passed a verdict for them and had indeed
	A.ŠÀ É *ù* ÁB *a-na Ni-ši-i-ni-šu-ma*	assigned field, house and cow to Niši-
	[*id-di-nu-ma*	[inišu, whereby
	qá-ti Li-wi-ra-šum na-as-ha-at iq-bu-ú	Liwwiraššum's claim was dismissed.
	ù Li-wi-ra-šum k[*i-m*]*a* DI.KU$_5$.MEŠ KÁ.	And Liwwiraššum admitted that the jud-
	[DINGIR.RA^{ki}	[ges of Babylon had passed
	di-nam ú-ša-hi-zu-ú-šu iq-bi-ma	a verdict for him. Then, on the basis
	a-na qá-bé-e ra-bi-a-nim ši-bu-ut URU^{ki}	of the declaration of the mayor, the town
	ù Li-wi-ra-šum A.ŠÀ É *ù*$^{!}$ ÁB	elders and Liwwiraššum himself they
	ša ^{d}UTU*-ša-ta-ka-lim a-bu-ša*	confirmed field, house and cow that
	a-na Ni-ši-i-ni-šu DUMU.MÍ.A.NI *id-di-nu*	Šamaš-ša-takālim, her father, had given
	ú-bi-ru-ma a-na Ni-ši-ni-ni-šu id-di-nu	to his daughter Niši-inišu and assigned
		[(them) to Niši-inišu.
e.	^{p}*Li-wi-ra-šum ar-nam i-mi-du*	On Liwwiraššum they imposed a penalty,
	DUB*-pí la ra-ga-mi ú-še-zi-bu-ú-š*[*u*]	they made him issue a no-claim record.
	ú-ul i-ta-ar-ma ^{p}*Li-wi-ra-šum*	Liwwiraššum will not again
l.e.	I *aš-šum* A.ŠÀ É *ù*$^{!}$ ÁB	raise a claim against Nīši-inišu
	a-na Ni-ši-i-ni-šu	because of the field,
	ú-ul i-ra-ga-am	the house and the cow.
	II MU ^{d}UTU ^{d}MARDUK	They swore the oath by Šamaš,
	ù Sa-am-su-i-lu-na	Marduk and
	it-mu-ú	Samsu-iluna.
	III [*di-i*]*n Nu-ra-tum*	Verdict of Nūratum
	ù DI.KU$_5$.MEŠ	and the judges
	ZIMBIR^{ki}	of Sippir.

Notes on the text

Some signs are rather cursive, such as Ù, written as U+ŠU in lines 2, 16 and 32; ÁB looks very much like U plus a broad-headed BAD. The combination DINGIR + UTU has become one complex sign in lines 11 and 33, which looks like TA.

Some signs are written over erasures, in line 13 the scribe changed *id-di-nu* into *id-dī-in*, and *ik-šu-ud-du* in line 19 is an impossible form. The writing of the 'Personenkeil' is irregular, since it occurs twice also in the middle of a line (lines 15, 20), as is the position of MEŠ in l. 25, after the place name, instead of after "judges", as in l. 29. See for the verbal form written *ú-bu-ru* in line 20 below.

10. The feature of OB cows with names – also attested during the Ur III period — was treated by Farber (1982) (see for three additional names YOS 14, 321 I:15, 17 and II:21). It is probably not accidental that the name of the cow in this text mentioned Nabium, whose priestess Nīši-inišu was.

11-15. The syntax of these lines is a problem, because the beginning of l. 11 is not clear, *ša*[!] [<d>]UTU- or [p<d>]UTU-, and the scribe changed the subjunctive *iddinuma* in l. 13 into *iddinma,* but maintained the subjunctive *watru* in l. 15. This *watru,* with connective *–ma*, probably with explanatory force ("and therefore"), leads to a sequence of three verbs in the apodosis, *ibquršima.... ikšud*[!]*-ma... īmurū*[!]. I assume that the scribe's second thought of turning the relative protasis of line 11, with lines 1-10 as fore-grounded object, into a main narrative clause (*iddinma*) to introduce the case, was not carried through by writing *watarma* or inserting a causative conjunction (e.g. *aššum... watruma*). The translation assumes that a conjunction was omitted at the end of l. 14, but whatever the best solution, these irregularities fortunately make little difference for the understanding of the issue.

19. The ambiguous *ik-šu-ud-du* must emended and the plural is more likely, assuming that the scribe by adding *–du* turned *ik-šu-ud* into a plural, without erasing the final *-ud*. If so, both parties together submitted their case to the court, as in the comparable VAB 5 (=Schorr 1913), 317:20-21. (Si. year 18), where in a fight about the size of a house-plot the parties *dajjānī Sippir ikšudū awātišunu imurū.* But there are also examples where the party who raised the claim is its subject, e.g. in TCL 1, 104:6-7 (Ha. year 39) A got into a conflict with B and C, *idīmma* ("started a lawsuit") *dajjānī šarrim ikšud*, and in CT 47, 24:14-15 (Ha. year 14) R. *irgum šarram imhur*. See for the verbs used and various formulations Dombradi (1996, § 80-83).

20. The emendation of *ú-bu-ru* into *i-mu-ru,* to obtain the well-known expression *awātim amārum*, "to evaluate the case", the first activity of judges when appealed to (Dombradi 1996, § 102), is unavoidable; cf. VAB 5 no. 317:21, quoted above. *Ubburum*, "to accuse", makes no sense and should have appeared as *ubbirū*.

25. Note the abnormal spelling with MEŠ not after DI.KU$_5$, but after of the combination.

The lack of witnesses and a date is remarkable and may indicate that the text was a draft.

2 *The structure of the text*

Eva Dombradi points out that that the formulary deviates from what is normal in not offering a chronological, narrative report of what had happened before, but presenting the result of the earlier legal action in the form of a testimony by the local authorities of Habibi. And this testimony appears not, as usual, in the form of a quotation in direct speech (cf. Dombradi 1996, 1, §117,e), but "mit den objektiv stilierten Vermerken des Formulars "Zivilprozesse", die syntaktisch den Vermerken über die Aussagen (Z. 28, 30) subordiniert sind". She also observes that in this way "eine erhebliche Straffung des Protokolls erreicht wird. Diese Tendenz zur Verschachtelung und zur Verwendung komplexer syntaktische Strukturen an Stelle von einfachen aufeinander gereihten Hauptsätzen, die sich in der altbabylonischen Periode zunehmend bemerkbar macht, reflektiert wohl Versuche logische Zusammenhänge sprachlich starker zum Ausdruck zu bringen und durch die Verwendung von abstrakten *terminci technici* zugleich inhaltlich zu charakterisieren." She adds: "Bei dem Experiment mit der Neugestaltung des Formulars waren wohl Schwierigkeiten zu bewältigen, die sich in dieser Urukunde in der Korrektur van Z. 13 spiegeln."

The more complex syntactice structure, for which she refers to Deutscher (2000, 181-182), brings along the use of "the factive complementizer" *kīma*, attested with the verb *qabûm* in lines 22 and 24 and documented in Deutscher 2000, Ch.7.4, with examples from OB letters. It also features in CT 8, 6b = VAB 5, 268 = MHET II (=Dekiere 1994-1997), 378 (tablet and case, Sippir, Si. year 3), which is in many ways similar to our text and was discussed in Stol 1998, 432, C, 1. To find out about a disputed field of a *nadītum* the judges, appealed to by the plaintiff, probably because there is no record to prove it, use the testimony of the mayor and elders of Halhalla. And they testified that (*kīma..... iqbû*) the plaintiff had illegally enjoyed the usufruct of a field, which they now assign to her.[1]

3. *The persons involved, the location of the property and the origin of the tablet*

Nīši-inišu, the lady whose property is under attack, is called NIN.DINGIR of the god Nabium. This title can be the equivalent of *entum*, "high priestess", but Stol (2000, 461) has shown that NIN.DINGIR occurs in

[1] Lines 8'-14', *kīma*... A.ŠÀ *ša* A B *ana la idim išriquma īkulu šibussunu* (so with the envelope) *iqbûma*....., followed (on the tablet) by A.ŠÀ.... (18) *ana* A. *ubirrūma iddinū*. The tablet in the first part writes [*šibūss*]*unu kīma*.... *eqel* A-*ma iqbû*, where –*ma* marks the predicate of a nominal sentence, which is embedded in the *kīma*... *iqbû* phrase. A minor difference is that while this text writes *šibussunu* immediately before *iqbû*, our record writes in lines 22-24 *šibussunu kīma*.......*iqbû*. Cf. also TCL 1, 157:42-45, where people interrogated *kīma*... *ilqû šībūssunu mahar dajjānī*... *iqbû*.

Sippir (and probably also in Kish) as equivalent of *nadītum*. Where equation with *entum* is unlikely, NIN.DINGIR designates a priestess and *ugbabtum* is its Akkadian equivalent (also in Old Assyrian). Referring to CT 48, 44, "nach der eine *nadītum* eindeutig den Status einer *ugbabtum* hat", he explains the word as "tabuierte (Klosterfrau)" and the tabu would be the bearing of children. This may apply in our text too, for the fact that her father gave her a *nudunnûm*, the equivalent of a dowry for a girl married off, implies that she remained unmarried and had to provide for herself.

Liwwiraššum, who is not identified by his father's name, contested Nīši-inišu's property. He owned a field bordering on that of Nīši-inišu (l. 7) and claimed a wall (l. 13) presumably owned by her. I assume that both had acquired part of the property of Šamaš-ša-takālim, Nīši-inišu by donation, Liwwiraššum as heir, probably not as son (the failure to identify him as "her brother" would be remarkable), but as close relative. The contested property was located about halfway between Sippir and Babylon, in the area where the Arahtum branches off from the Euphrates and the town Dimat-Enlil, where she had a house (l. 8), has to be situated, as shown by Steinkeller (2010). The village Imgur-Šamaš (lines 4-5), the polder Bāb-Nabium and the town Habibi must all be located in this area. This explains why the persons locally involved (mentioned in lines 2-4, 6-9, 11 and 21) are not attested in other sources from Sippir.

The discovery of this record in Sippir suggests that Nīši-inišu, having acquired it as confirmation her rights, preserved it in her house there, but no temple or shrine of Nabium, where she would have served, is known from Sippir.[2] Since the area where she owned land and a house also comprised a polder named Bāb-Nabium (l. 1) and had a mayor named Nabium-mālik (l. 21; note also the name of her cow, Nabium-šamšī), the shrine to which she was attached most probably was located there. She may have lived in the house in Dimat-Enlil given her by her father. The discovery of this record in Sippir then might indicate that she had moved there (in old age?), but if it was a draft it could also have surfaced in the

[2] It is unknown into which temple the throne of Nabium, mentioned in the name of Hammurabi's 16th year, was brought and the only evidence for a "temple of Nabium", in CT 4, 23c:17, from Sd. year 5, mentioned in Harris 1975, 147 note 31, is late; see on this text and Nabium, M. Stol, elsewhere in this volume, and for Nabium in the OB period in RlA 9 (1998-2001), 17, §3.1. George 1993 does not list a temple or shrine of him in Sippir and the dates of those attested for Babylon, some in Esagila, are unknown. Whether the letter AbB 5, 168:16'-17', which invokes the blessing of Šamaš and Marduk and mentions "the *akītu*-festival of Marduk and Nabium", originates from Sippir is uncertain, see Sommerfeld 1982, 92 note 2.

house of the main judge or the scribe of the court in Sippir, where the second trial was conducted.

4. *Liwwiraššum's claim*

The first claim made before the court in Babylon is only known from the testimony by the authorities of Habibi. It may have been a more general one, in which Liwwiraššum, perhaps as a frustrated prospective heir of Šamaš-ša-takālim, tried to regain the property donated to the lady. If it had only been a well-founded (lines 22-23) claim on (part of) a wall of her house it could have been solved easily, as shown by verdicts concerning houses sold that proved to be bigger or smaller than the relevant records stated. In such cases (see below under c) supplementary payments or the transfer of a piece of soil could solve the problem. Conflicts about "party walls" were solved in comparable ways or by the transfer or sharing of the ownership. A creative solution occurs in YOS 12, 557, where a man builds a house on a plot he had bought five years earlier from his neighbour. When the seller claimed that it was too big and encroached on his property, the buyer compensated him by making the encroaching wall "a party wall inside your house".[3] In VAB 5, 295, when a man claimed that his brother had obtained from the inheritance more (*watar*) than he was entitled to, it was taken away from (*šamāṭum itti*) his brother and assigned it to him.

Nothing similar happened in our case in Babylon. The claim that was rejected (l. 28, *qati* L. *nashat*)[4] is not specified, but the fact that the judges confirmed Nīši-inišu's right to fields, house and cow (l. 27) suggests that Liwwiraššum had claimed more than just (a piece of) a wall, as he did again in the second trial (lines 16-17). There are several examples, mentioned below under c), where a claim concerns a house or field that is too big or too small, but the record does not write that the plaintiff "filed a claim because of a house or field against a person" (*aššum... ana* PN *irgum*, the terminology also used in lines 39-41 of our text; see

[3] Lines 7-9, *eli 3* SAR IGI.5.GÁL É *ša addinakku bītam watram tēpuš*; 17-20, *watar bītim ša ēpušu lū igār birītim ina libbi bītika*. A still unpaid part of the purchase price (lines 10-11, *izibti kaspim ša šīm bītim ina qatika ibašši*) will count as compensation for the cost of building this wall, which becomes the property of the seller, but on which also the buyer may rest his beams.

[4] See for this expression and its different forms, "Partei-Fassung", "Richter-Fassung", and "stativische Fassung", Dombaradi 1996, §§132-133. and 453-455. See for more examples of *qātum* as the subject of the stative, not mentioned by her, CAD Q 12, a, 2'.

Dombradi 1996, §§58 and 65), but simply states that he claimed (*ibqur*) the house or field.[5] This apparently is a short way expressing that he disputed (*baqārum*) the full ownership of the house or field. Our text, accordingly, could have written *igāram ibqurši*, "he claimed the wall from her", but we read only that "he claimed fields, house and cow". This is contesting the donation as such and this the courts did not accept. The reason why the court in Babylon rejected his claim and no arrangement in line with the examples mentioned above was worked out is unknown.

That "a wall was in excess over the record of donation" and that this was the reason for (the function of the *–ma* after *watar*) the claim is only mentioned in connection with his second claim, filed in Sippir. When the authorities of Habibi confirm this fact, this acknowledgment — introduced in l. 24 by a second *kīma*, preceded by *ù*, "and in addition", and concluded by a second *iqbû* in l. 28 — is distinguished from their testimony about what the court in Babylon had done. The argument of the wall may not have been advanced in Babylon and have been presented in Sippir to buttress a new attempt to fight the donation to Nīši-inišu.

The somewhat opaque statement that "a/the wall is in excess"[6] allows different interpretations. It must have concerned a wall of or adjoining Nīši-inišu's house in Dimat-Enlil and Liwwiraššum's claim suggests that he owned a house or house plot adjoining hers, although our text mentions only Ahulap-Marduk (l. 9) as her neighbour.[7] The wording of the claim does not reveal what was at stake and contracts and conflicts about walls and especially party walls suggest that it could mean three things:

[5] According to San Nicolò 1974, 159, the plaintiff claimed the whole house "aus prozessualtechnischen Gründen", but it is not clear which and Dombradi 1996, §§380-383 does not accept this view.

[6] The phrase *ina muhhi pī ṭuppim watar* is noteworthy, because OB normally uses *eli* in such statements; in VS 7, 16:24-26, "the excess (surface) of a house" (*watarti bītim*) is defined as x shekels *ša eli 1* SAR *watru*, and YOS 12, 557:7-9 has *eli 2 5/6* SAR É... *bītam watram tēpuš*. Our text, defining the excess in relation to what the record stated, is comparable to CT 8, 9a:16-18, *watartašu* / [*ša*] *elēnu ṭuppi zittišu*, "his excess, which surpassed (what is stated in) the record of his share". But constructions vary, for in CT 8, 9a:12, *watartum ina ṭuppi zittim... watru*, uses the preposition *ina* (as does Old Assyrian, where TC 2, 11:8-12 mentions that the surface of a house can be too little or too big compared the size mentioned, *ina šalāš šubātim batiq* / *īter*). Other texts referring to a record whose data are referred to usually write *ana pī ṭuppim*, e.g. CT 2, 45:11, *ana pī ṭuppāt šīmātim imṭi*.

[7] He might have owned an un-built plot or a ruined house next to hers and have maintained his claim on an adjoining wall.

a) The wall as such did not figure in the record. This could mean that one wall of Nīši-inišu's house belonged to Liwwiraššum, although this was not stated in the record of donation. Or the claim concerned a separate wall, perhaps one adjoining the house, but not really part of it. Such a wall may occur in CT 6, 7b, since the purchase of "a 1 5/6 SAR house plot together with the wall" (*bītum qadum igāri*, l. 11), in lines 1-8 is specified as "an un-built house plot (É BUR.BALA) of 1 2/3 SAR and one wall (*1 igārum*) measuring 18 by 1 2/3 cubits". This wall could have been part (the remainder?) of a ruined building, as may have been the case in VS 22, 14:1-3, where a small empty lot (É KI.ŠUB.BA), "together with the walls" (*qādu* É.SIG$_4$.HI.A) that line its long and short sides, is exchanged. A separate wall may also occur in CT 4, 37d, an agreement about a wall 9 cubits long, called "the party wall of E. and Š.", on which both can rest their beams. But its description as "next (DA) to Š.'s house"[8] leaves unclear who of the two was its owner and makes it likely (as suggested by Lautner 1939, 84) that it was located somewhere between the houses of E. and Š. Eva Dombradi also refers me to MHET II, 200, where a *nadītum* buys a large house and lines 2-3 explicitly mention "the walls of the long side(s) that are party walls" *(igārātum ša šiddim ša birītim)*, but they probably were walls of the house, explicitly mentioned because neighbours normally shared only one party wall. She also refers to *ana ittišu* 7 III:34-39, where an adoptive parent who repudiates his son "looses house and wall" *(ina bītim u igārim itelli)*, where the separate mention of the wall, extremely rare in actual adoption contracts (but see TIM 5, 4:10-11) surprises.

b) Liwwiraššum may have meant that record of donation failed to state that the wall that Nīši-inišu's house shared with his was actually a party wall. Party walls with joint ownership were common, as we know from agreements and conflicts about them (see Lautner 1939). Such records create, claim[9] or confirm the right to rest beams on them, based on the payment of a proportional share in the cost of its building or repair to its owner.[10] One would expect that if a house with such a party wall was

[8] É.SIG$_4$ *ša* DA É Š. *1/2* NINDA *3* KÙŠ UŠ É.SIG$_4$ DAL.BA.<NA> *ša* E.... *ù* Š.

[9] *Igāram ana erištim erēšum*, according to Lautner 1939, 93, "etwas fordern worauf man einen Anspruch zu haben vermeint".

[10] See Lautner 1939. The "proportional share" (IGI.TE(N).BI) is mentioned in BE 6/2, 14:7, cf. MSL 1, 218. There are now more references for such features. *Tell Sifr* 92 (= Charpin 1980) contains a stipulation about (re)building and a possible future raising (*šuqqûm*? damaged; *Tell Sifr* 87, also from Ur, uses *ullûm*, as does TLB 1, 246:15, 21) of a party wall and measuring the (added) height. In UET 5, 125 one of the joint owners

sold or inherited this was mentioned to prevent future problems, but I do not know OB deeds of sale of houses that contain that information. There are also records that deal with walls not identified as "party walls", but for which an agreement about its use by a neighbour existed. Such contracts may end with the explicit statement that the wall belongs to one party and that the other has no property rights on it (*ana igārim ul awassu*).[11] Some at the end explicitly state or repeat who is its owner, e.g. CT 4, 14b:8-9, "the wall belongs to A". While the claim or right to use a neighbour's wall can apply to a whole wall (CT 33, 42b:1-3, *igār* N. *adi gamrišu*), it may also concern part of it, presumably if the adjacent houses were not of equal size or had a different shape or orientation. In TCL 1, 193, A is entitled to use 5 cubits of B's wall, to which the contract adds: "The whole wall belongs to B". TCL 10, 19 first mentions that a wall of 5 by 11 cubits[12] is a party wall and then specifies the walls of the main room (16 cubits) and its entrance (*nērebum*, 5 cubits), to which this did not apply, but it is difficult to visualize the situation.

c) There were also conflicts about the length of a wall that is not said to be a party wall. In BE 6/1, 60[13] A raised a claim about a wall against B, whereupon the judges inspect it, establish its size as it runs between (connects) two other walls and establish that it belongs to B. Such fights are comparable to those about the correct size of a house or field, e.g. when a house built "encroaches upon" (*erēbum ana*) a neighbouring house plot, its size is checked and its owner pays for the "excess" (*watartum*).[14] In VAB 5, 275 (from Dilbat), because the actual size of a house proves to be too big (*īter*) compared with what is stated in the deed of sale, the new owner pays some silver to the previous one "for

will be refunded by the other if he rebuilds the wall, and UET 5, 236 mentions the tearing down and rebuilding of such a wall (see for both texts Charpin 1986, 55-56 and 100-102). An original formulation occurs in MHET II, 355, where the shared ownership is indicated by stating that each of the two neighbors owns half of the width (2/3 cubit) of the wall, a situation created by the fact that "they piled the wall up jointly" (*igāram mithariš išpukū*, lines 9-10; cf. MHET II, 808:6-7, two women *mithariš šitpukā*, with a reciprocal Gt-stem); MHET II, 402:5-6 uses the normal formulation, *ahum mala ahim mānahtam iš*[*kunū*].

[11] See already Lautner 1939, 92 with note 36, on CT 33, 44b:9-10, TCL 10, 21:1 has *ul awatašu*!; Riftin 45 (in Sumerian) states that the A's "wall belongs to him alone (IZ.ZI *ramanišu*), B has no right on it", cf. TCL 1, 87/88:4-5, *igār ramanišuma ša* N.

[12] Probably not a massive wall 2,5 m. thick, but a long and a short (ÚS and SAG.KI) stretch on both sides of a corner.

[13] VAB 5, 286, cf. CAD I/J 35, 1,b',1'.

[14] "They gave x shekels of silver for the 5 ½ (surface) shekels that, when checked, proved to be in excess over the ½ SAR" (*ša eli* ½ SAR *ina sunnuqim īteru*, 28-29).

the excess of the house" (*ana terit*[15] *bītim*). In VAB 5, 317 (from Sippir), the son of the seller claims that the buyer "had bought a small(er) house and has in her possession a big(ger) one" (*bītam īṣam išâmma mādam ṣabtat*, lines 17-18), but her ownership is confirmed (*kunnum*) by inspection of the original deed of sale *(ana pī ṭuppiša labīri)*.[16]

The choice is difficult, because the record of donation that may have contained a more detailed description of the house given to Niši-inišu is not quoted[17] and the architectural situation on the spot is of course unknown.[18] As mentioned, the claim of Liwwiraššum, who owned land in the same general area, suggests that he also owned a house or house plot next to Nīši-inišu's (which he had inherited or otherwise acquired[19] as part of Šamaš-ša-takālim's real property), with which it shared (part of) a wall. His claim could be that it was a party wall of which he was co-owner or that she owned only part of a longer wall and that her father had failed to mention this in the record of donation. The disputed wall may also have been one adjoining the house, as in the cases mentioned under a). The use of the verb *watārum* with the preposition *ina muhhi* and the cases mentioned under c) make it most likely that it was the length or location of the wall that was in dispute.

[15] This noun must be a derivative of *watārum*, presumably *itertum* that has lost its initial *i-*. CAD A, s.v. *atāru* mentions a derivative *tirtum*, listed in *AHw* 1350a as *tertum*, but it does not figure in CAD T. *Itertum* is well-known from OAss as "what is extra"; its listing in CAD I/J as *itartum* is not correct, for the only evidence for middle *-a-*, in KTS 24:27, has to be read *ītardam*, "he has come down".

[16] In VAB 5, 278, where a check of the size of the house shows that it is 12 shekels less than the deed of sale states, the new owner receives an additional piece of soil; in VAB 5, 276 the ownership of an excess (*watartum*) is secured by an additional payment. In MHET II, 149 a check showed that the size of a house was correct, conform the deed of sale (*bītam usanniqma ša pī ṭuppi ša* N. *išāmu šalim*, case: 5-9).

[17] As happened in MHET II, 200, quoted under 1). In MHET II, 290, to which Eva called my attention, where two neighbors fight about the ownership of a party wall (*igārum ša birīt* I. *u* S. *bitqurū*; the case has *igār baqrī* [*irtaši*]) and S. had made I. stop the work (on building or repairing it, lines 6-8, I. *šipram ušaddi*). Since S. proved unable to show the deed of purchase as proof of his ownership (read lines 8-11 of the case: DUB *šīmātim ša Libūram* / *ku-li-ma-ni-ni-šu* / *bi-ir-ma li-qí*; cf. lines 16-19, *ūm* S. / *īterbam* – tablet*: ina erēbišu - ul ukallim*), the wall counted as I.'s wall. The original deed would have made clear who owned the party wall.

[18] Jahn 2005 does not deal with the walls of houses, although some of situations recorded in the texts quoted above might be reflected in the architecture.

[19] But if he had bought the field and house after Šamaš-ša-takālim's death, he would have seen to it that the property had been carefully described in the deed of sale and he would have been able to prove his right by submitting the deed of sale to the judges.

5. *The judicial procedure*

Our text reveals the history of the case by quoting the testimony given by the authorities of Habibi, summoned by the court in Sippir, perhaps at the instigation of Nīši-inišu. Their testimony must have been necessary in the absence of records of the first trial; no interrogation of the parties is mentioned, although this does not mean that it did not take place. It only mentions Liwwiraššum's claim,[20] that the court reached a decision *(dīnam šūhuzum)* on it,[21] that the property was assigned to Nīši-inišu, and that Liwwiraššum's claim was rejected (l. 28, *qāti L. nashat*).[22] No arguments for this decision are mentioned.

The second trial took place in Sippir, because both parties (if the reading *ikšudū* in line 19 is correct) had appealed there. No records are mentioned and their absence must have been the reason why the testimony of the local authorities of Habibi was needed. They may have been involved in the first lawsuit as local informants on the disputed wall and apparently were well aware of what had happened. This absence of records about the verdict of Babylon may have prompted Liwwiraššum to try again. The choice the court of Sippir may have been due to an administrative change or to the fact that Nīši-inišu had moved there. For Liwwiraššum a different court must have been attractive, but we do not know whether a plaintiff in a village in a case of civic law could choose the city where he would make his appeal, for the rules are not clear, as is shown by the observations in Dombradi 1996, §§ 295-299. This issue needs a special investigation, which can use observations made on individual cases[23] and has to take into account the status of the parties, the issues at stake and the dates of the conflicts, because there may have been developments over time.

In Sippir Liwwiraššum filed a new complaint *de eadem re*, a type of lawsuit treated in Dombradi 1996, §§251-256. He may have done so because, as the local authorities of Habibi admitted (lines 22-24), his

[20] The testimony does not say that Liwwiraššum himself had appealed to the court in Babylon, but this seems more likely than that the local authorities of Habibi had transferred the case to Babylon.

[21] See for the meaning of *dīnam šūhuzum* now Dombradi 2004.

[22] See for this expression and it different forms, "Partei-Fassung", "Richter-Fassung", and "stativische Fassung", Dombaradi 1996, §§132-13-24 and 453-455. See for more examples of *qātum* as the subject of the stative, not mentioned by her, CAD Q 12, a, 2'.

[23] Stol 1998, 432-433, discussing CT 8, 6b, suggests that the conflict that played in Halhalla may have been submitted to the judges of Babylon and Sippir, because the thief in question was the son of Halhalla's mayor, who otherwise might have had to pass a verdict on his own son.

claim about the wall had substance and this may also have been the reason why it was accepted for trial in Sippir, after evaluation (lines 19-20). Eva Dombradi notes that verdicts in such cases usually are based on the "tablet of forbearance" (*ṭuppi lā ragāmim*), which the losing party had issued after the first trial. The failure to mention such a tablet suggests that it was not available, another fact that may have encouraged Liwwirašsum to try again. She assumes that the fact that the local authorities had acknowledged that the wall was indeed "in excess", "vermutlich deshalb in der Urkunde hervorgehoben wurde, weil die Rechtslage in diesem Punkt zu Gunsten des Klägers stand, seine Klage aber trotzdem abgewiesen wurde. Darum war es besonders wichtig festzuhalten, dass dieser (widersprüchliche Punt) bei der Rechtsfindung bekannt und bei der Entscheidung berücksichtigt wurde, um weitere diesbezüglichen Klagen vorzubeugen."

Liwwirašsum's second attempt also failed. The court in Sippir apparently did nothing more than obtain a testimony (*šibūtum*, l. 22) about the earlier verdict and make Liwwirašsum himself confirm it. *Dīnam šūhuzum* by the court in Sippir is not mentioned, presumably because this had already been done in Babylon. The statements of the authorities of Habibi and Liwwirašsum himself (Nīši-inišu is silent) come in the place of reading the relevant records that apparently were not available in Sippir. The Sippir court simply confirms Babylon's decision, "was gegen eine Hierarchie der Gerichte mit den Richtern von Babylon als übergeordnetes Gericht im Sinne einer Berefugunsinstanz spricht". It imposed a penalty (*arnum*) on Liwwirašsum (see Dombradi 1996, §§ 134 and 458-465), presumably because he had ignored the previous rejection of his claim, but there is no *aššum* clause as "punishment reationalization" stating this.[24] We are not told what kind of penalty it was, presumably not a public, humiliating, corporal punishment as in cases of un-founded (*ina la idim*) claims by persons who had violated their written promise not to do so again, but rather a fine, since no violation of a *ṭuppi la ragāmim* issued by Liwwirašsum is mentioned. The penalty may not have been specified, because there were standard penalties for groundless claims, called *aran bāqirā*[*nim*] in VS 7, 152:4 (from Dilbat), and there existed a royal decree on this matter, mentioned in AbB 1, 14:22-26.[25]

[24] See for this feature Roth 2001, esp. 410-412, with examples from OB court records, where the *aššum* clause mentions a repeated claim as reason for the penalty.

[25] See Veenhof 2001, 66-68. VS 7, 152: 2'-5', the broken case of a tablet, says more than I mentioned: if the looser claims again *eqlam kīma eqlim* [*inaddin*] *u aran bāqir*[*ānim*]

6. *The authorities handling the case*

In Sippir Liwwiraššum turns to "Hajabni'el and the judges" and the last lines of our record call the result "a verdict of Nūratum and the judges of Sippir". Hajabni'el is known as a man of authority, for in AbB 11, 49:7 an Assyrian trader in Sippir, concerned about an endangered commercial capital, "put his case before him" (*mahar* H. *iškun*), a verbal expression known from the judicial sphere.[26] He occurs alongside "overseers of the traders" as recipient of commercial shipments in a record from Sippir and is probably identical to the anonymous "governor of Sippir" (*šāpir Sippir*) who figures, also as recipient, in a closely related text from the same year, around the beginning of Samsu-iluna's reign.[27] We can probably identify him with "Hajabni['el], son of *I-zi-na-*[*bu-ú*?], servant of Hammura[bi]", whose seal is impressed on OLA 21, 66 (dated to Ha. year 42!), and AbB 2, 63 and 13, 49 are letters of king Samsu-iluna addressed to him.[28]

A "governor of Sippir" occurs in a few judicial records from the reign of Samsu-iluna, according to Harris 1975, 128, "as the presiding officer of the court", because, as she states on p. 77, "[t]he *šāpiru* may have succeeded the *rabiānu* or mayor as such". Harris lists four different "governors of Sippir", from Si. years 17, 18, 25 and 27, in which Dombradi (1996, § 312) with note 1368, follows her, adding a fifth one, from Si. year 10. Only three of them, however, are acceptable,[29] but we can add "Zimri-arah, governor of Sippir", to whom and to the judges of Sippir plaintiffs appeal in MHET II, 459:16 (reign of Si., year lost). His occurrence with this title is interesting, because in CT 47, 63:45-46, from Si.

immidūsu, of which the tablet, VS 7, 7, only mentions the first part, which means a penalty equal to the (value of the) item involved.

26 Cf. its use in AbB 4, 17:6; 75:8-9; 6, 181:6' (all three *mahar bēlia aškun*, without *awātam*, but with the case described immediately before as virtual object); CT 47, 63:58 (*mahar* S. *ù kārum Sippir*); cf. CT 4, 7a (VAB 5, 310):20-21.

27 Veenhof 1991, 289, texts B:4, 18 and 22, and C, I:3, II:9, and IV:10.

28 Identity with the first judge of this name, who belongs to a group of five "judges of Babylon" in CT 29, 41-43:19 (undated) is uncertain. An earlier namesake, son of Sumuhabnu, occurs under Sabium (MHET II, 26:11; 29:18-19, first witness in a judicial record), and Apil-Sîn (CT 48, 68: 23-24); cf. also CT 2, 26:3 and MHET II, 109:2-3 (both from the reign of Sîn-muballiṭ).

29 Sîn-nādin-šumi, the writer of AbB 7, 116, probably is the governor of that name. (H)adanšu-likšud of CT 45, 37:8, 11, is *a šāpir rēdī*, and as for Awīl-Ištar of Riftin 48:11, Si. year 10, added by Dombradi, we do not know what may have followed *ša-pí-*[.....], and he is the second (preceded by the *mu'errum*) of four men who handle the case. A possible addition to the list could be Sîn?-iddinam, from MHET II:613:8, but its date is lost and the context is unclear.

year 14, he features as "mayor (*rabiānum*) of Sippir", alongside *kārum* Sippir, as authorities who inspect records and decide an issue. And when this same record reports on a later phase of the case, the appeal is made to another *rabiānum*, Sîn-išme'anni, (l. 71) and *kārum* Sippir.[30] If Ms. Harris' idea, that the role of *rabiānum* was taken over by the "governor", is correct MHET II, 459 must be later than Si. year 14, and since Zimri-arah apparently was "promoted" from *rabiānum* to "governor", his period of office could mark the transition. Hajjabni'el in our text has no title, but his role (lines 18-19) is the same as that played by the *rabiānum* and subsequently the "governor of Sippir".

Whatever the exact function of Hajabni'el, the "Gerichtsvermerk" (Dombradi 1996, § 224-227) of our text calls the decision a "verdict of Nūratum and the judges of Sippir" and not one of Hajabni'el. The formula "*dīn* PN" is rare compared with the much more frequent and earlier *dīn bēt Šamaš (ina Ebabbar)* and Dombradi (1996, note 917) mentions only two cases, both from Sippir and from the reign of Hammurabi: CT 6, 47b (VAB 5, 266):24, from Ha. year 24, "a verdict of Išar-līm", the mayor (*rabiānum*, see l. 17-18) together with the overseer of the traders, and of three other men; and the rather similar CT 47, 31: 35-37 // MHET II, 162:41-42, from Ha. year 5, "a verdict of Sin-iddinam", the mayor of Sippir, together with the overseer of the traders, and of two other men. Nūratum, who figures as the main judge in our text, was the son of Ipqu-Annunītum and, as discovered by Voet and Van Lerberghe (1989, 530-531), belonged to a family that held high positions in Sippir over five generations. He also appears as the second addressee of the letter of king Samsu-iluna on "the hungry *nadītums*", sent to the authorities in Sippir (see Janssen 1991, 11). He figures, with his seal impression (he uses a seal that had belonged to his grandfather) in several texts dated between Ha. 42 and Si. 36,[31] nearly always as first witness. This position in judiciary records identifies him as the main judge or chairman of the court, but he is never designated as "mayor", which would be understandable if by that time the *rabiānum* had ceded his place to the *šāpir Sippir*. In this connection the above-mentioned CT 47, 63:72 (from Si. year 14) is

[30] See for this text also Charpin 2000, 75-76, no. 34.

[31] Voet and Van Lerberghe mention OLA 21, 95; CBS 1255; CT 8, 6b = MHET II, 378, Di 700 and 1173. Janssen 1991, 11 note 34, also mentions CT 48, 11:17 (Ha. 42), CT 47, 67:20 (Si.), and BM 80638 rev. 6' (fragm., Si. [y?], first witness; courtesy B. Ferwerda). I can add CT 48, 5:23 (Si. 21), where the plaintiffs appeal to Nūratum, Ipiq-ilišu and the judges of Sippir, and he may occur in AbB 13, 104:17, as one of "the servants of the king", alongside Šamaš-bāni (presumably the overseer of the merchants) and *kārum* Sippir.

interesting, because our Nūratum features here as second witness,[32] after the *rabiānum*, which is somewhat surprising, since we meet him as first witness already in Ha. year 42 (CT 48, 11:17). The system was apparently not rigid and in particular cases the *rabiānum* or *šāpir Sippir,* on the basis of his administrative capacities functioned as chairman of the court, while in others a *primus inter pares*, such as Nūratum, acted as chief judge. Moreover, the authorities appealed to by the plaintiffs are not always identical to those who pass the judgment. When there is a "governor of Sippir", the appeal is usually to him (and the judges). VAB 5, 286 writes that the judges do their job "in the presence of (*mahar*) Š., the governor of Sippir" and the governor does not appear among the judges who seal the record. He therefore seems (the number of attestations is still limited) to function more as a chairman or supervisor than as a judge.

Our record does not answer the questions it raises about the nature of the claim, the judicial procedure and the persons involved as parties or judges. Narrative descriptions of what happened during a trial vary considerably in reporting procedural details, and we can also not exclude the possibility that the text, as suggested by the unusual absence of witnesses and a date and by several textual mistakes, was a draft. But even if this is the case, it still provides us with interesting data and calls for some observations that we hope will meet the interest of the jubilarian to whom this volume is dedicated.

Bibliography

CHARPIN, D. 1980: *Archives familiales et propriété privée en Babylonie ancienne. Étude des documents de "Tell Sifr"*, Genève.

— 1986: *Le clergé d'Ur au siècle d'Hammurabi (XIXe-XVIIIe siècles av. J.-C.)*, Genève-Paris.

— 2000: "Lettres et procès paléo-babyloniens" in F. Joannès (ed.) *Rendre justice en Mésopotamie*, Saint-Denis, 69-111.

DEKIERE L. 1994-1997: *Old Babylonian Real Estate Documents (Mesopotamian History and Environment*, II. Texts), Ghent.

DEUTSCHER, G. 2000: *Syntactic Change in Akkadian. The Evolution of Sentence Complementation*, Oxford.

DOMBRADI, E. 1996: *Die Darstellung des Rechtsaustrags in den altbabylonischen Prozessurkunden*, I-II (Freiburger Altorientalische Studien 20,1-2), Stuttgart.

[32] In the deed of sale CT 8, 9b:20 (Si. year 30) he also is the second witness, after Warad-Sîn, the priest of Šamaš. See for him also the damaged CT 45, 62 and VS 9, 116:7-9.

— 2004: "Notizen zur Deutung von *dīnam šūhuzu* in den altbabylonischen Prozessurkunden", *Welt des Orients* 34, 23-39.

FARBER, G. 1982: "Rinder mit Namen", in G. van Driel et al. (eds.) *Zikir Šumim. Assyriological Studies Presented to F.R. Kraus on the Occasion of his 70th Birthday*, Leiden, 34-36.

GEORGE, A. 1993: *House Most High. The Temples of Ancient Mesopotamia* (Mesopotamian Civilizations 5), Winona Lake.

HARRIS, R. 1975: *Ancient Sippar. A Demographic Study of an Old-Babylonian City*, Istanbul.

JAHN, B. 2005: *Altbabylonische Wohnhäuser. Eine Gegenüberstellung philologischer und archäologischer Quellen* (Orient-Archäologie 16), Rahden Westfalen.

JANSSEN, C. 1991: "Samsu-iluna and the Hungry *nadītums*", North Akkad Project Reports 5 (MHE series I), Ghent.

LAUTNER, J. G. 1939: "Rechtsverhältnisse an Grenzmauern. Studien zum Miteigentum im altbabylonischen Recht, I", in *Symbolae ad iura orientis antiqui pertinentes Paulo Koschaker dedicatae*, Leiden, 76-95.

ROTH, M. T. 2001, "The Because Clause: Punishment Rationalization in Mesopotamian Laws", in W. H. van Soldt et al. (eds.) *Veenhof Anniversary Volume*, Leiden, 407-412.

SAN NICOLÒ, M. 1974: *Die Schlussklauseln der altbabylonischen Kauf- und Tauschverträge*, 2. durchgeshene Auflage, München.

SCHORR, M. 1913: *Urkunden des altbabylonischen Zivil- und Prozessrechts* (Vorderasiatische Bibliothek - VAB 5), Leipzig.

SOMMERFELD, W. 1982: *Der Aufstieg Marduks* (Alter Orient und Altes Testament 213), Münster.

STEINKELLER, P. 2010: "On the Location of the Towns of Ur-Zababa and Dimat-Enlil and on the Course of the Arahtum", in J. C. Finke (ed.) *Festschrift für Gernot Wilhelm anlässlich seines 65. Geburtstages am 28. Januar 2010*, Dresden, 369-382.

STOL, M. 1998: "Die altbabylonische Stadt Ḫalḫalla", in M. Dietrich and O. Loret z (eds.) *Dubsar anta-men. Studien zur Altorientalistik. Festschrift für Willem H. Ph. Römer* (Alter Orient und Altes Testament 253), Münster, 415-445.

— 2000: "Titel altbabylonischer Klosterfrauen" in J. Marzahn and H. Neumann (eds.) *Assyriologica et Semitica. Festschrift für Joachim Oelsner* (Alter Orient und Altes Testament 252), 457-466.

VEENHOF, K. R. 1991: "Assyrian Commercial Activities in Old Babylonian Sippar", in D. Charpin and F. Joannès (eds.) *Marchands, diplomates et empereurs. Études sur la civilisation mésopotamienne offertes à Paul Garelli*, Paris, 287-303.

— 2001: "The Relation between Royal Decrees and 'Law Codes' in the Old Babylonian Period", JEOL 35-36 (1997-2000, publ. 2001) 49-83.

VOET, G. and VAN LERBERGHE, K. 1989: "A Long Lasting Life", in H. Behrens et al. (eds.) *DUMU-E$_2$-DUB-BA-A. Studies in Honor of Åke W. Sjöberg* (Occasional Publications of the Samuel Noah Kramer Fund, 11), Philadelphia, 525-538.

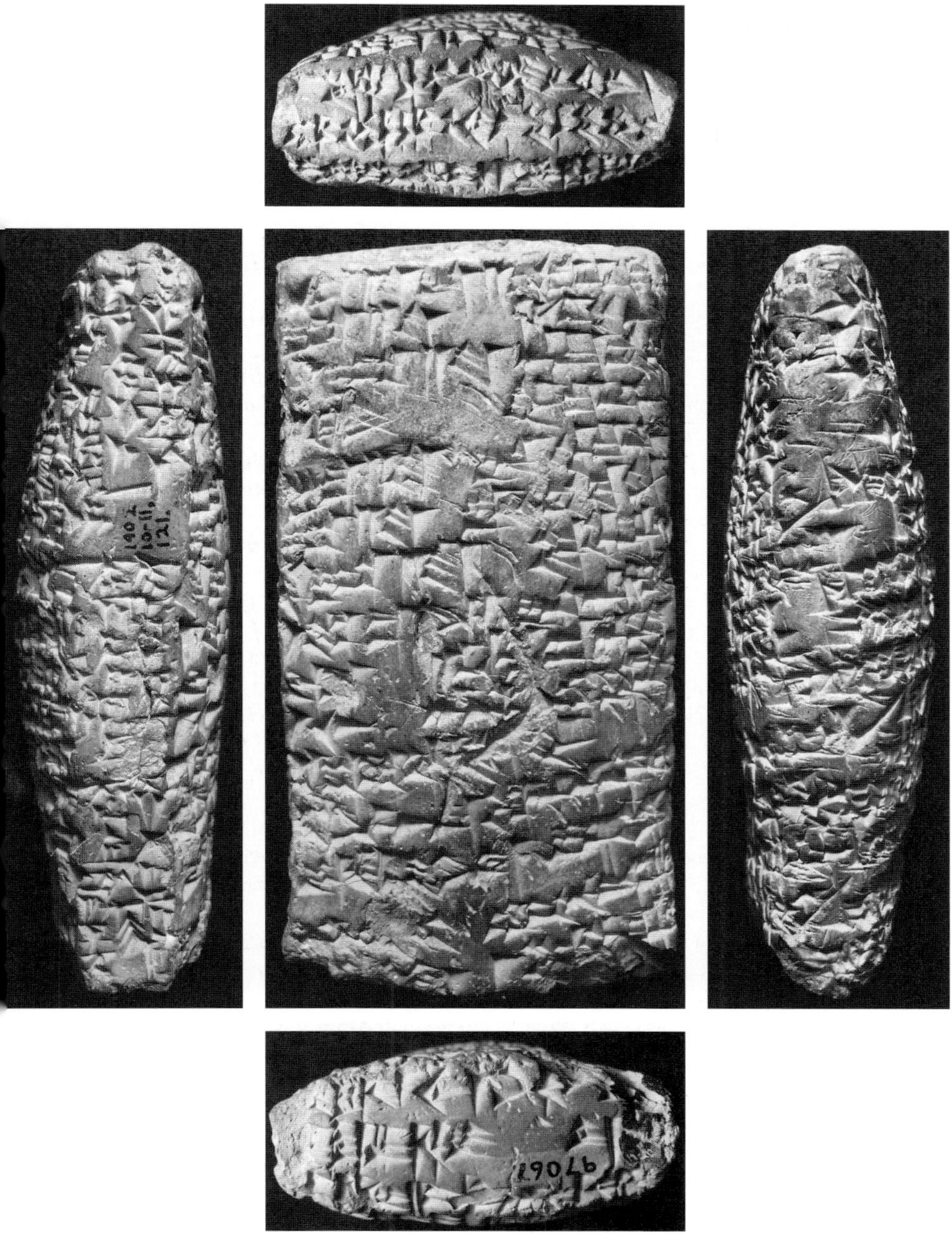

BM 97067, obverse.

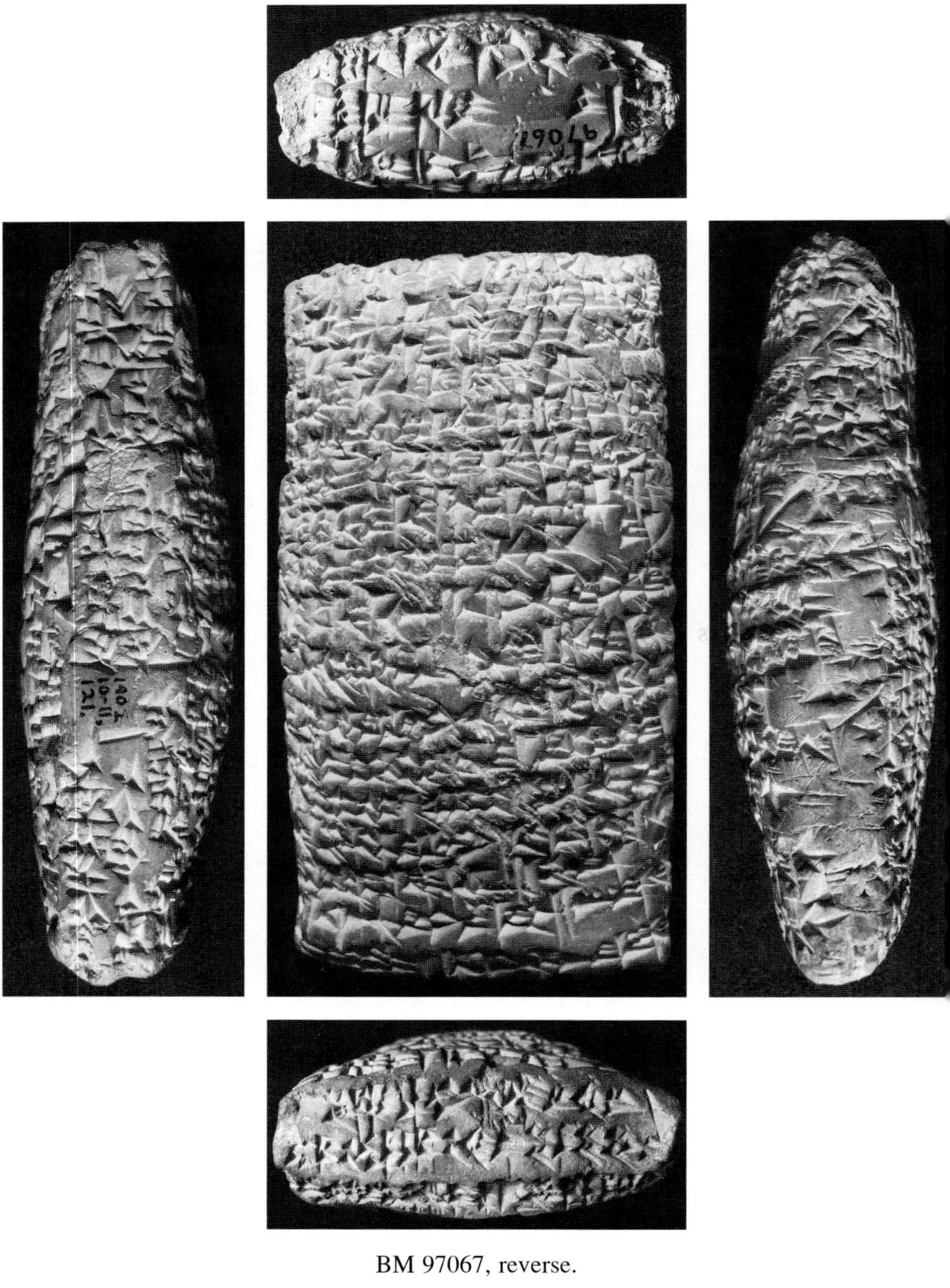

BM 97067, reverse.

THE SCRIBAL EXERCISE RS 16.265 FROM UGARIT IN ITS NEAR-EASTERN CONTEXT

Juan-Pablo VITA
CSIC – CCHS, Madrid

The Mesopotamian cultural tradition strongly pervaded, as is well known, the world of Ugaritic scribes[1]. Along with local scribes, there was the almost certain presence in this kingdom of scribes whose mother tongues were Babylonian and Assyrian, who contributed for decades to maintaining, reinforcing and updating that tradition as part of the human and professional training of Ugaritic scribes[2]. Nonetheless, the local cultural tradition, which had its own character, perfectly differentiated from that of Mesopotamia, was equally strong and influential on the scribes' training and production, the most apparent feature in this sense being the use of the cuneiform alphabet[3].

A new analysis of the Ugarit tablet RS 16.265 (= KTU 5.9; photo: Virolleaud 1957, pl. VII), which is the subject matter of the following lines, allows us to continue to explore the human, cultural and professional ties linking Ugaritic scribes to their Mesopotamian colleagues. Found in 1952 in room 73 of the royal palace of Ugarit, it is housed in the National Museum of Damascus (Bordreuil and Pardee 1989, 112). Virolleaud (1957, 39-40) published the tablet in 1957 and classified it as a 'private letter'. More recently, RS 16.265 has rightly been considered a scribal exercise[4].

[1] Concerning the various cultural traits of Mesopotamian origin existing in Ugarit see, amongst others, Nougayrol 1962, Eissfeldt 1962, Arnaud 1979, Xella 1982, van Soldt 1995, Malbran-Labat 1999, 2004, 82, Pardee 2004, Hawley 2008a.

I'm very grateful to Professor Dennis Pardee (The Oriental Institute of the University of Chicago) for having allowed me to reproduce his own handcopy of the tablet RS 16.265. I'm also grateful to him for agreeing to read and comment on an earlier draft of this article. Needless to say, any possible inconsistencies are entirely my own responsibility.

[2] Malbran-Labat 1999, 100, van Soldt 2001, 2002. On the training of the Ugaritic scribes see mainly van Soldt, 1995 and Hawley 2008a.

[3] Amongst the vast existing bibliography on the Ugaritic alphabet, see for example Dietrich and Loretz 1988; Tropper 2000, 13-80, Bordreuil and Pardee 2009, 21-22. Regarding the interaction between the Mesopotamian and Ugaritic cultural traditions, see also Hawley and Roche 2004.

[4] See, for instance, van Soldt 1991, 162, 749, Dietrich, Loretz and Sanmartín 1995, 491, Dietrich and Loretz 1988, 182, 185, Pardee 2002, 115, Hawley 2008a, 63.

According to Pardee (2002, 115), it may be dated to "the very last days of the kingdom of Ugarit".

RS 16.265 actually contains texts of quite different genres (see Fig. 1 for general outline) which we shall briefly comment on next. The recto and the bottom margin of the tablet contain the following epistolary text[5]:

1-6) [t]ḥm iṯtl l mnn. ilm tǵrk. tšlmk tʿzzk. alp ym w rbt. šnt b ʿd ʿlm

-----

7-8) iršt. aršt l aḫy. l rʿy

9-16) w ytnnn l aḫh. l rʿh rʿ ʿlm. ttn. w tn w l ttn w al ttn tn ks yn w ištn

-----

Pardee (2002, 115, 2007, 185) points out, after the collation of the text, that its palaeography shows that the letter was written by a skilled scribe and offers the following translation of it:

> 1-6) "[Me]ssage of ʾIṯṯēlu to MNN: May the gods guard you, may they keep you well, may they strengthen you, for a thousand days and ten thousand years, through the endless reaches of time. 7-16) A request I would make of my brother, my friend, and may he grant it to his brother, his friend, (his) friend forever: May you give, and give!, and may you indeed give, and will you not certainly give?, give (me) a cup of wine that I might drink!".

The introductory formula is more elaborate than usual in Ugaritic letters[6], and both the content and the tone of the message itself clearly illustrate that it is but an exercise[7]. Lines 9 to 16, in particular, seem to be variations on the verb *ytn* "to give"[8] and the last line, "give (me) a cup of wine that I might drink!" reveals even a humorous aspect to this text[9]. As in Mesopotamian literature, including some texts specifically designed for the training of scribes (D'Agostino 2000), in Ugaritic literature some passages of a humorous nature can also be identified, or they could be perceived as such in our current understanding[10]. Nevertheless, the letter

[5] Transcription by Pardee 2007, 185.

[6] All the epistolograhic particulars of this letter were analyzed in depth by Hawley 2003.

[7] Hawley 2008a, 63 n. 47: "Note the unusually elaborate benediction, the frivolity of the 'message'"; Pardee 2002, 115: "a practice letter, in which the scribe shows off his command both of epistolary formulae and of verbal conjugation".

[8] Pardee 2002, 115: "The scribe runs through the four principal volitive forms, the jussive, the imperative, the imperfective with asseverative *l*, and the imperfective with emphatic *ʾal*...". del Olmo and Sanmartín 2003, 46 translate: "you give, give, do not give, may you give".

[9] See also Pardee 2007, 184: "we are dealing with a bit of scribal humor".

[10] See, for instance, the mythical passage where the god Ilu rejoices when he sees his wife Aṯiratu approaching from a distance (RS 2.[008]+: IV:27-30 = KTU 1.4:IV:27-30).

RS 16.265 is not a fragment of a literary text: it rather reflects the spontaneous humour and personal ease of a scribe at the time of practising the writing of a letter. Mesopotamia does not lack instances of more or less improvised humour in non-literary texts: see, for instance, a clerical document of the Sargonic period recently published by Maiocchi (2009, 171-172), a balanced account of wool where a scribe records, amongst other garments, two turbans weighing over eight kilos each. The end of the document indicates that certain number of kilos of wool "on a rung are availa[ble], the arrears (being) 18.87 kg of wool: the innkeeper singer (is the supervisor)" (Maiocchi 2009, 172). Foster (2010, 141) comments in this respect that it is "an interesting school exercise giving a fantastic balances account for woollen garments..., and a huge arrears is humorously charged to a tavern singer".

Besides this full letter, tablet RS 16.265 contains the beginning of a new letter on the verso: *tḥm d̠mn l it̠tl* "[Me]ssage of Oimenu to 'It̠tēlu"[11]. Another Ugaritic text, RS 94.2273, which also contains the beginning of a letter, completes the list of practice letters yielded by Ugarit so far[12]. The two Ugaritic texts RS 16.265 and RS 94.2273 thus can be added to the few known instances of Mesopotamian practice letters[13]. It is not known with certainty at what point in their training the Mesopotamian scribes learned to write letters (Waetzoldt and Cavigneaux 2009, 300), although, according to Waetzoldt and Cavigneaux (2009, 302), "Die Briefe scheinen zum Teil parallel zu den Namenlisten im Elementarunterricht unterrichtet worden zu sein". As for the case of Ugarit, as demonstrated by Hawley (2008a, 61), this type of documents may have belonged to the third stage in the structure of the alphabetic scribal curriculum, after the lists of signs and the thematic lists of words. This scribal curriculum, in terms of learning the Ugaritic alphabet, could have the same structure

See considerations by D'Agostino 2000, 14-20, on the possibility of grasping, from our modern view, the humour used in texts of pre-classical and classical Antiquity.

[11] Lines IV:1-3 in the publication by Dietrich, Loretz and Sanmartín 1995, 492.

[12] Pardee 2002, 115: "[Mess]age of 'Abniya to 'Urtet̠ub: [I] fall at the feet of my brother. Here from afar I fall; seven times, eight times, I fall. May the gods guard you, may they ke[ep you well]". The text will be published shortly by P. Bordreuil, R. Hawley, and D. Pardee in a volume of the series "Ras Shamra-Ougarit".

[13] Michel 2010, 255: "les textes scolaires présentant des modèles de lettres sont plutôt rares en Mésopotamie, en raison du caractère peu stéréotypé de ce type de textes, contrairement aux contrats, par exemple, qui pour l'essentiel suivent un cadre rigide". See examples of Mesopotamian practice letters in, for instance, Kraus 1959-1962, 18 (Si. 441), 31 (1924, 559), Finkelstein 1963 (see comment by Kraus 1959-1962, 39), Westenholz 1974-1977, 96 no. 5 (MAD 5 no. 91) and Van Lerberghe in Van Lerberghe and Voet 1991, 99 (no. 67, Di 279; a text which was re-studied and commented on by Tanret 2002, 113-114).

as that of the curriculum designed in Ugarit for learning Mesopotamian cuneiform (Hawley 2008a, 59). The direct link between the Mesopotamian scribal tradition and the local Ugaritic tradition could be established by virtue of the aforementioned text of RS 94.2273: one side of this tablet, as we have seen, contains the beginning of a letter written in alphabetic cuneiform while the other side, however, contains "two parallel extracts (probably master and student) from the Mesopotamian exercise Silbenalphabet A" (Hawley 2008a, 63 n. 48), which suggests "that the training in the alphabetic and Mesopotamian traditions was parallel, not successive" (Hawley 2008a, 64).

The verso of tablet RS 16.265 contains texts of a different nature written by the same skilled hand as that of the letter on the *recto*. Unlike this letter, written downwards on the tablet, the texts on the verso are arranged horizontally. The surface of the verso is thus divided into two sections lengthwise by means of a separating line. The scribe divided also the top part of the verso into three columns separated by two vertical lines. The left and central columns contain two words each with no apparent connection with one another[14]; with one exception[15], the meaning of these terms is uncertain[16]. It is, in any event, a type of scribal exercise also known in Mesopotamian texts[17]. The right column shows the beginning of the aforementioned letter. The bottom part of the verso contains three lines of text whose exact meaning and interpretation have not yet been established[18]. As the available space in the *recto* and *verso* of the tablet had been used up, the remaining free spaces were the top, left and right margins. These three margins bear signs in a different hand, this time a

[14] Lines I:19-20 and III:1-2 in edition by Dietrich, Loretz and Sanmartín 1995, 491 and 492.

[15] *ʿbd* "slave". Line I:19 in edition by Dietrich, Loretz and Sanmartín 1995, 491.

[16] *qrq* (del Olmo and Sanmartín 2003, 711), *prṯ* (del Olmo and Sanmartín 2003, 684), *pṯ* (del Olmo and Sanmartín 2003, 687: "probably a spelling mistake or a pseudomorpheme"). Hawley 2008b, 228: "pourrait-on considérer la face avec les mots et phrases éparpillés comme étant l'exercice principal?".

[17] Cf. for instance text no. 15 in Westenholz 1974-1977, 104.

[18] Lines II:1-3 in edition by Dietrich, Loretz and Sanmartín 1995, 491: *q n ṣ ṣ. b ṣ ṣ ṣ p n* [...] / *d d n. d ḥ l m*[...] / *d d w a ṯ d*[...] (Hawley 2008b, 226 transcribes the last line as *d d w* ⸢*n*⸣ *ṯ* ⸢*b*⸣ [...]). Márquez Rowe 1996, 459-462, pointed out the existence of the same sign sequence *q n ṣ ṣ b ṣ ṣ* in the *verso* of the syllabic text from Ugarit RS 20.136, whose *recto* contains an excerpt of the Weidner God List. This author proposes that that sequence of signs on both tablets should be interpreted as "a school paradigm of the Ugaritic scribal curriculum" which could be understood as *qn ṣṣ bṣṣ* "the reed of the salt marsh (is) in/from the salt marsh"; other alternatives are that this sentence could stand "for the incipit of an incantation", or else it could be "a conventional orthographic alliterative exercise" (Márquez Rowe 1996, 461-462). See also comment in this respect by Hawley, 2008b, 227 n. 48.

beginner's (Pardee 2002, 115), to write the beginning of the Ugaritic alphabet three times[19]: the right and left margins show the first eleven letters of the Ugaritic alphabet (*a b g ḫ d h w z ḥ ṭ y*), the top margin includes only the first five letters (*a b g ḫ d*). Alphabets in Ugarit were part of the first stage of the learning ("lists of signs") in the alphabetic scribal curriculum (Hawley 2008a, 61).

To make the maximum use of the available surface, the Ugaritic tablet RS 16.265 presents a complex combination of texts of different genres. The common denominator of these diverse texts is that they are all scribal exercises which are part, moreover, of different training levels of the alphabetic scribal curriculum. The presence on one and the same tablet of such heterogeneous school material could indicate, as Hawley points out (2008a, 64), the existence at Ugarit of some cases of "a sequential connection between category 1 (list of signs) and category 3 (model documents)". Nonetheless, we must bear in mind that the complexity of the textual ensemble constituted by RS 16.265 is increased by the presence of two well differentiated scribal hands, one more experienced than the other, which show the joint use of tablets by scribes of different levels of training although a teacher-pupil relationship between them may not be established with certainty.

The Ugaritic texts of RS 16.265 illustrate at least two different levels of the alphabetic scribal curriculum, whose structure, in the case of Ugarit, was similar to that followed by scribes in the learning of the Mesopotamian syllabic script. In fact, various types of data allow us to claim that every Ugaritic scribe had to learn both scripts and cultural traditions simultaneously. Beyond the limits of Ugarit itself, the Ugaritic letter contained in the *recto* of RS 16.265 joins the few Mesopotamian instances of practice letters and its author shows the same playful and humorous attitude as some of his Mesopotamian colleagues. The Ugaritic tablet RS 16.265 should, in our opinion, be taken into consideration in any comprehensive analysis of the scribal world of the Ancient Near East.

My hope is that the above lines will serve as testimony of my respect, gratitude and friendship for Professor Karel Van Lerberghe, whose pupil I had the good fortune to be at the KU Leuven.

[19] Ever since Virolleaud's *editio princes*, all editions of the text have produced only the two alphabets of the right and left margins. Nonetheless, the tablet has also another beginning of an alphabet on the top margin; see, regarding this, Pardee 2002, 115, and Hawley 2008b, 226 (fig. 7) and 228. They are Type II alphabets in Hawley's 2008b, 226-228 classification ("Abécédaires associés à d'autre types de textes").

Bibliography

ARNAUD, D. 1979: "La culture suméro-accadienne", *Supplément au Dictionnaire de la Bible*, vol. 9, Paris, 1348-1359.

BORDREUIL, P. and D. PARDEE 1989: *La trouvaille épigraphique de l'Ougarit. 1. Concordance*, Paris.

BORDREUIL, P. and D. PARDEE 2009: *A Manual of Ugaritic*, Winona Lake.

D'AGOSTINO, F. 2000: *Testi umoristici babilonesi e assiri*, Brescia.

DEL OLMO, G. and J. SANMARTÍN 2003: *A Dictionary of the Ugaritic Language in the Alphabetic Tradition*, 2 vols., Leiden.

DIETRICH, M. and O. LORETZ 1988: *Die Alphabete. Die phönizisch-kanaanäischen und altarabischen Alphabete in Ugarit*, Münster.

DIETRICH, M., O. LORETZ and J. SANMARTÍN 1995: *Cuneiform Alphabetic Texts from Ugarit, Ras Ibn Hani and Other Places*, Münster.

EISSFELDT, O. 1962: "Mesopotamische Elemente in den alphabetischen Texten von Ugarit", *Syria* 39, 36-41.

FINKELSTEIN, J. J. 1963: "The Antediluvian Kings: A University of California Tablet", *JCS* 17, 39-51.

FOSTER, B. 2010: "Clothing in Sargonic Mesopotamia: Visual and written evidence", in C. Michel and M.-L. Nosch (eds.) *Textile Terminologies in the Ancient Near East and Mediterranean from the Third to the First Millennia BC.*, Oxford, 110-145.

HAWLEY, R. 2003: *Studies in Ugaritic Epistolography*, Ph.D. diss., Chicago.

— 2008a: "On the Scribal Curriculum at Ugarit", in R. D. Biggs, J. Myers and M. T. Roth (eds.) *Proceedings of the 51st Rencontre Assyriologique Internationale Held at the Oriental Institute of the University of Chicago, July 18-22, 2005*, Chicago, 57-67.

— 2008b: "Apprendre à écrire à Ougarit: une typologie des abécédaries", in C. Roche (ed.) *D'Ougarit à Jérusalem. Recueil d'études épigraphiques et archéologiques offert à Pierre Bordreuil*, Paris, 215-232.

HAWLEY, R. and C. ROCHE 2004: "Entre tradition mésopotamienne et fonds culturel local", in *Ougarit. Aux origines de l'alphabet* (Dossiers d'archéologie, hors-série n° 10), Dijon, 40-43.

KRAUS, F. R. 1959-1962: "Briefschreibungen im altbabylonischen Schulunterricht", *Jaarbericht Ex Oriente Lux* 16, 16-39.

VAN LERBERGHE, K. and G. VOET 1991: *Sippar-Amnānum. The Ur-Utu Archive. Volume 1*, Ghent.

MAIOCCHI, M. 2009: *Classical Sargonic Tablets Chiefly from Adab in the Cornell University Collections*, Bethesda.

MALBRAN-LABAT, Fl. 1999: "Langues et écritures à Ougarit", *Semitica* 49, 65-101.

— 2004: "Langues et écritures d'Ougarit", in Y. Calvet and G. Galliano (eds.) *Aux origines de l'alphabet. Le royaume d'Ougarit*, Paris-Lyon, 81-83.

MÁRQUEZ ROWE, I. 1996: "Syllabic and Alphabetical Texts. A Further Note on Scribal Education at Ugarit", *UF* 28, 457-462.

MICHEL, C. 2010: "review: C. Roche (ed.), *D'Ougarit à Jérusalem. Recueil d'études épigraphiques et archéologiques offert à Pierre Bordreuil*", *Journal Asiatique* 298, 249-256.

NOUGAYROL, J. 1962: "L'influence babylonienne à Ugarit, d'après les textes en cunéiformes classiques", *Syria* 39, 28-35.

PARDEE, D. 2002: "Scribal Exercises", in W. W. Hallo and K. Lawson Younger, Jr. (eds.) *The Context of Scripture*, vol. 3: *Archival Documents from the Biblical World*, Leiden, 115.

— 2004: "Aux origines de l'alphabet", in *Ougarit. Aux origines de l'alphabet* (Dossiers d'archéologie, hors-série n° 10), Dijon, 34-39.

— 2007: "The Ugaritic Alphabetic Cuneiform Writing System in the Context of Other Alphabetic Systems", in C. Miller (ed.) *Studies in Semitic and Afroasiatic Linguistics Presented to Gene B. Gragg*, Chicago, 181-200.

TANRET, M. 2002: *Per aspera ad astra. L'apprentissage du cunéiforme à Sippar-Amnānum pendant la période paléobabylonienne tardive*, Gand.

TROPPER, J. 2000: *Ugaritische Grammatik*, Münster.

VAN SOLDT, W. H. 1991: *Studies in the Akkadian of Ugarit. Dating and Grammar*, Neukirchen-Vluyn.

— 1995: "Babylonian Lexical, Religious and Literary Texts and Scribal Education at Ugarit and its implications for the alphabetic literary texts", in M. Dietrich and O. Loretz (eds.) *Ugarit. Ein ostmediterranes Kulturzentrum im Alten Orient. Ergebnisse und Perspektiven der Forschung. Band I. Ugarit und seine altorientalische Umwelt*, Münster, 171-212.

— 2001: "Naḫiš-šalmu, an Assyrian Scribe working in the 'Southern Palace' at Ugarit", in W. H. van Soldt, J. G. Dercksen, N.J.C. Kouwenberg and Th.J.H. Krispijn (eds.) *Veenhof Anniversary Volume: Studies Presented to Klaas R. Veenhof on the Occasion of Hus Sixty-fifth Birthday*, Leiden, 429-444.

— 2002: "The Orthography of Ugaritic Words in Texts Written by the Assyrian Scribe Naḫiš-šalmu", in O. Loretz, K. A. Metzler and H. Schaudig (eds.) *Ex Mesopotamia et Syria Lux. Festschrift für Manfried Dietrich zu seinem 65. Geburtstag*, Münster, 685-697.

VIROLLEAUD, Ch. 1957: *Le Palais Royal d'Ugarit* II, Paris.

WAETZOLDT, H. and A. Cavigneaux 2009: "Schule", *RlA* 12, 294-309.

WESTENHOLZ, A. 1974-1977: "Old Akkadian School Texts", *AfO* 25, 95-110.

XELLA, P. 1982: "L'influence babylonienne à Ougarit, d'après les textes alphabétiques et divinatoires", in H.-J. Nissen and J. Renger (eds.) *Mesopotamien und seine Nachbarn*, Berlin, 321-338.

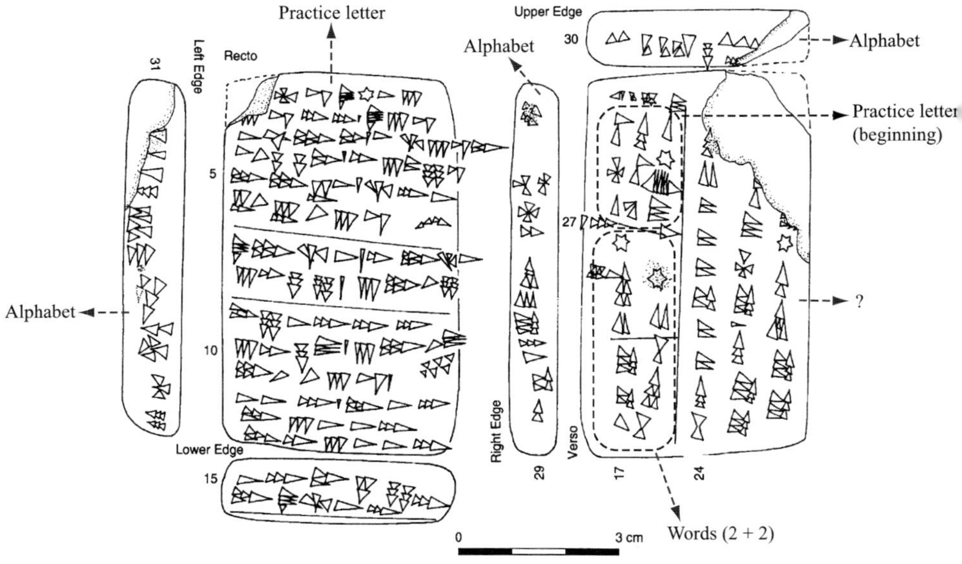

Fig. 1. RS 16.265 (Hand-copy: Dennis Pardee).

HAPPY DAYS: THE BABYLONIAN ALMANAC IN DAILY LIFE

Caroline WAERZEGGERS*
University College London

The *Babylonian Almanac* was one of the most popular items of learning circulating in first millennium BC Mesopotamia.[1] Over sixty copies of the text, or of its parts, are reported to be still in existence today.[2] In its fullest form, the *Almanac* offered guidance about the favorable or unfavorable nature of all 360 days of the year, with instructions about actions to be undertaken or avoided on those days. One of the best-known representatives of the full text is V R 48-49, a heavy, twelve-column tablet presumably from Achaemenid Babylonia now kept in the British Museum.[3] Many handy excerpts of the *Almanac* were in circulation, and BM 95163, the text presented here, is a good example of this tradition.[4]

The text

BM 95163 (1901-10-12, 816)
measurements: 4,6 cm (length) × 2,2 cm (width)
obv.

1. *u*$_4$-*mu*.meš dùg.ga
2. [*šá*] ^{iti}du$_6$ *u* ^{iti}apin
3. ud.1.kam ud.2
4. ud.4 ud.6
5. ud.6 ud.7

* I wish to thank the Trustees of the British Museum for permission to publish BM 95163 and to cite unpublished cuneiform tablets in their care. This article was written and researched within the framework of ERC Starting Grant Project "Babylon".

[1] Labat 1941; Labat 1952; Matouš 1961; George 1988, 151-5; Livingstone 1993, 1998 and 2000; Isma'el and George 2002; Robson 2004; Livingstone 2007.

[2] Livingstone 1998, 60 ("seventy or so relevant sources"); Livingstone 2000, 385 ("fifty-two manuscripts"); Livingstone 2007, 86-9 ("63").

[3] Labat 1941; for a photo of the text (BM 32641) see the British Museum's online catalogue (http://www.britishmuseum.org/research/search_the_collection_database.aspx).

[4] Other examples can be found in the Sippar collection of the British Museum. BM 67304, published by George 1988 no. 2, contains an excerpt of month IV; BM 52757 and BM 64359 (George 1988, 152 n. 5) deal with VII; and VAT 3 (MIO 5 pl. XII) pertains to month VIII. BM 29162 is a list of favorable days in month I from Borsippa; the entry of this tablet in Zadok 2009: 199 should be adapted accordingly.

6.	ud.7	ud.9
7.	ud. 8 1/2	ud.11
8.	ud.9	ud.13
9.	ud.11	ud.15
rev.		
10.	ud.13 1/2	ud.18
11.	ud.14	ud.20.1.lá
12.	ud.17	ud.22
13.	ud.20.1.lá	ud.24
14.	ud.21 ud.22	ud.26
15.	ud.23	ud.<<10>>.28
16.	ud.26.<<1>>	ud.30
17.	ud.28	
18.	ud.29	

The favorable days [of] month *tašrītu* — 01, 04, 06, 07, 08 at midday, 09, 11, 13 at midday, 14, 17, 19, 21, 22, 23, 26, 28, 29 — and of month *arahsamna* — 02, 06, 07, 09, 11, 13, 15, 18, 19, 22, 24, 26, 28, 30.

BM 95163 is published here with the kind permission of the Trustees of the British Museum. The small, oblong tablet contains a list of favorable days in the months of *tašrītu* and *arahsamna*. The list is excerpted from columns VII and VIII of the *Babylonian Almanac* as represented in its best-known exemplar V R 48-49.[5] It transmits only the essence of the *Almanac* (Which days are favorable?) and leaves out all information about the nature of a day's auspiciousness or about the activity to be undertaken on that day. For instance, for 22-VIII the *Almanac* predicts "Happiness" and for 28-VII it proscribes "Achieve an aim," but in the excerpt both days are simply said to be "favorable". Handy extracts like BM 95163 have been published in the scholarship before and an edition of all hemerological texts from Mesopotamia is in preparation by A. Livingstone.[6] The aim of this contribution is to discuss the social context in which this particular copy was produced and to investigate the correlation, if any, between the *Almanac*'s regulations and the rhythms of its keepers' daily lives.

[5] BM 95163 fails to mention days 25-VII and 20-VIII but it otherwise corresponds to V R 48-49.

[6] Cf. Livingstone 1998, 59 n. 1; 2007, 85-6.

Archival and social context

BM 95163 can be attributed to late 7th to early 5th century BC Borsippa on the basis of its museum context. It was purchased by the British Museum in 1901 from Élias Géjou together with c. 1,500 other clay tablets and items (collection 1901-10-12). All datable Late Babylonian tablets in this collection come from Borsippa and there can be no doubt that our text does too. At the time when Géjou sold these items to the British Museum, uncontrolled diggings at the site of Birs Nimrud had been going on for some time and many hundreds of tablets had already entered the Museum's collections at that point. Géjou's collection contained elements from seven major archives: Ahiya'ūtu, Atkuppu, Ea-ilūtu-bani, Huṣābu, Iddin-Papsukkal A, Iliya A, and Rē'i-alpi.[7] All these archives belonged to local families whose men worked in the Ezida temple as prebendary priests during the late 7th and early 5th centuries BC (Waerzeggers 2010). To which of these archives does our hemerological text, BM 95163, belong? As the tablet has no colophon, it is impossible to attribute it with absolute certainty; however, a case can be made that it belonged to the Iliya A archive based on the following two observations. First, BM 95163 is situated in a cluster of tablets from this achive in 1901-10-12;[8] given the size of Géjou's collection, archival patterns may still be reflected in the internal distribution of the texts. Second, there is independent evidence that members of the Iliya family were interested in the hemerological tradition of the *Almanac*. The text's most famous copy, V R 48-49, was produced by Nabû-le'i of the Iliya family, a brewer of Nabû. This clearly situates V R 48-49 in the city of Borsippa, where the Iliya family owned a prominent share of the brewer's prebend of Nabû (Waerzeggers 2010, 153-95), even if it is uncertain, indeed unlikely, that the tablet was actually found in that city.[9] The scribe of V R 48-49 can perhaps be identified with Nabû-le'i (son of Nabû-mukīn-apli) of the Iliya family who wrote

[7] See Waerzeggers 2005, 350 on the provenance of Neo-Babylonian tablets in the 1901-10-12 collection of the British Museum.

[8] BM 95162, BM 95182, BM 95183, BM 95185, BM 95187 are all part of the Iliya A archive.

[9] V R 48-49 belongs to the 76-11-17 collection which predates both Rassam's exploration of Borsippa in the early 1880ies, which led to the discovery of a number of monumental inscriptions and scholarly texts dating from the Neo-Assyrian until the Seleucid period, and the unauthorized activities on the site in the 1890ies, which resulted in the discovery of a large number of archival texts dating from the late 7th to early 5th centuries BC.

several contracts in Borsippa in the early Persian period and who is probably attested as an active brewer of Nabû.[10]

The *Almanac* and daily life in Borsippa

Hemerologies like the *Babylonian Almanac* were based on the belief that certain days of the year were particularly favorable or unfavorable for certain activities. The *Almanac* provides guidance in all areas of life that were of interest to "the common man" (Livingstone 1993, 102), including food, health, travel, business, climate, law, security, and the state of a man's relations to his god, king, wife, relatives, and slaves.[11] Evidence has been collected to prove that the *Almanac* was used and consulted at the court and in centres of high learning. The Assyrian kings and their consultants referred to the *Almanac* when planning major building works, military campaigns and festivals (Robson 2004, 63-8; Livingstone 2007, 92-4), and scholars throughout the Assyrian realm kept copies of this work in their professional libraries (Livingstone 2007, 94-9). But did other people turn to the *Almanac* for advice on how to organize their lives as well?

BM 95163 offers an opportunity to investigate this matter. On its own, this small tablet is of little interest. It does not add new information to the text tradition of the *Almanac*; on the contrary, excerpts like BM 95163 are common in the Neo-Babylonian corpus and this particular copy is corrupt.[12] But its value lies in its context. BM 95163 was found in a deposit of private archives documenting thousands of transactions that took place in the realms of law, agriculture, business, and marriage between the late 7th and early 5th centuries BC.[13] The same subjects are treated by the *Almanac*, and as the archival texts are dated by year, month and day, this allows us to investigate whether or not there is a correlation between the prescriptions of the *Almanac* and real-life activities. Concerns of the *Almanac* that cannot be matched with the archival data are food instructions,[14] advice about travel routes and methods,[15] recommendations

[10] Attestations as scribe: BM 26757, BM 27960, BM 82667, dated in the reigns of Cyrus and Cambyses; attestation as brewer: BM 94585, without family name.

[11] See Livingstone 1993, 102 and Livingstone 2007, 87-8 for the various categories of prescriptions given by the Alamanac.

[12] Two favorable days of months *tašrītu* and *arahsamna* were forgotten; see note 5 above.

[13] There are about 1,600 dated texts that can be used in our inquiry. This includes the Iliya A archive, to which I suspect BM 95163 belongs.

[14] E.g. "eat no fish," "eat pig meat," etc.

[15] E.g. "do not walk down a familiar road," "do not travel by boat," etc.

in the sphere of personal religion,[16] warnings for eclipses and fires, and some others.[17] The observations that follow relate to the realms of law, business, and marriage.

On days when the *Almanac* recommends or prohibits specific actions there is usually a good match between what is proscribed and what happened in daily life. For example, 14-I was a day "favorable in a lawsuit," and BM 29105 shows that on that day in the twelfth year of king Šamaš-šuma-ukīn a lawsuit took place. On 08-VI, the *Almanac* implores that "one must not quarrel," and on that day in the eighth year of king Kandalānu a family fight was resolved (Ellis 1984 no. 9). Day 22-III is labeled "inheritance" in the *Almanac*, and two brothers paid their deceased father's deputy that day (BE 8 117). Marriages, lawsuits and oaths were never planned on days that were considered unfavorable for such activities; only in the realm of the monetary economy did one sometimes fling the *Almanac*'s advice in the wind.[18] In the category of recommended actions, there is a 71% match between the *Almanac* and the archival records,[19] and in the category of discouraged actions, there is a 91% match. The evidence is presented in the appendix.

Many entries of the *Almanac* refer to moods and events instead of activities. Here, the results of our inquiry are less consistent. For instance, on the one hand there is no or very little recorded activity on days when the *Almanac* predicts the occurrence of "accidents",[20] while on the other hand business continued as usual on days of "weeping".[21] Days of "dishonesty" were, in spite of the *Almanac*'s warnings, days when important decisions were made. For example, on 07-I a business partnership was negotiated and a boat lease concluded among other transactions, while

[16] E.g. "release a bird," "bow down before (a certain) god," etc.

[17] E.g. the professional activities of the doctor (17-I), the killing of a snake (20-II), wearing new clothes (12-IX).

[18] The *Almanac*'s prohibition "not to deal in silver" on 13-II is neglected in three silver debt notes, of which two bear interest (BM 102003, Kand 13-II-[x]; BM 94613, Dar 13-II-04; BM 96248, Dar 13-II-12). The prohibition "not to pay silver to a businessman" on 12-VIII is respected in so far that no transactions with professional traders (*tamkāru*) are recorded, but the corpus contains one receipt of house rent (paid in silver) that is dated on that day (BM 26789, Dar 12-VIII-30).

[19] A "match" is counted when the corpus yields at least one real-life transaction that corresponds to the *Almanac*'s entry for that day.

[20] No documents were drafted on 30-VII and 30-XI. Only two texts were drafted on 14-II after a busy period (6 texts are preserved for 11-II, 8 for 12-II and 13 for 13-II).

[21] 19-I: seven recorded transactions, 02-IV: two (this is in general a period of limited activity, see below), 03-V: four, 02-X: five.

on 21-II several property transfers were made.[22] Such transactions were based on mutual trust and the *Almanac*'s warning for "treachery" might have served a sobering purpose. Perhaps the same effect was reached when a certain Tattannu agreed to stand surety for two men on a day when the *Almanac* warned for "denounciation" (BM 96205, Dar 27-II-25).

The best correlation between the *Almanac* and daily life is in the realm of marriage. The corpus counts thirty-six marriage contracts and dowry-related texts, of which thirty-one were drafted on days described by the *Almanac* as "happiness", "(happy) news", "completely favorable", or "favorable". Only one text about a woman's dowry was drafted on an "unfavorable" day (BM 26487) – and there is indeed good reason to doubt whether the transfer was a happy occasion in this case.[23] The other four texts were drafted on days with minor prohibitions and they all concern complicated or contested dowry transfers.[24] This data suggests that happy occasions were scheduled on "happy" or "(entirely) favorable" days, while difficult negotiations took place on unfavorable or otherwise negative days. In the corpus of marriage contracts edited by M. Roth (1989) another significant pattern emerges. The majority of fully dated texts were written on days of "happiness" or other auspicious days, but there are some exceptions. In all these cases, however, one or both wedding partners were non-Babylonian. The marriages concluded on a day of "grief" (27-IX) and on a day "unfavorable in court" (11-II) had West-Semitic brides; the marriage concluded on 17-I, when "a doctor should not treat a patient", took place within the Syrian exilic community from Neirab (nos. 11, 17, 26). Planning a marriage on a "happy day" was clearly a concern of Babylonian couples but not of non-Babylonian ones.

Many of the *Almanac*'s entries in the second half of the year only state whether a day was favorable or unfavorable without giving further explanations or instructions. It is difficult to correlate these parts of the *Almanac* with the archival material. Sometimes one can observe a drop in activity on "unfavorable" days,[25] but this is by no means a general

[22] VS 6 100, VS 5 48, VS 5 6, AchHist 15 no. 4.

[23] In BM 26487 (Nbk 21-VIII-22; "unfavorable") a grandfather exerted pressure on his son-in-law to assign property to his daughter and granddaughter in return for the dowry silver that he had given his daughter upon her marriage.

[24] Camb 120 (Camb 03-VII-02; "eat no fish"), BM 94555 (Camb 18-V-04; "take no oath"), BM 26586 and duplicate (Camb 06-XI-04; "do not cross a familiar street"), and BM 82655 (Nbk 06-XI-[x]; *idem*) all record disputed or complicated dowry transfers.

[25] For instance, 13 texts were written on 02-VI ("favorable"), 3 on 03-VI ("favorable"), 2 on 04-VI ("unfavorable"), 12 on 05-VI ("favorable"), 4 on 06-VI ("unfavorable"), 6 on 07-VI ("favorable").

rule, and often there is no clear difference between the nature or scale of activity carried out on "favorable" or "unfavorable" days.[26]

Conclusions

The most important conclusion to be drawn from our inquiry is that there is a good match between specific predictions, recommendations, and prohibitions found in the *Babylonian Almanac* and real-life activities recorded in the archival texts from Borsippa from the late 7th to early 5th century BC, especially in the realm of marriage. The generic labels "favorable/unfavorable" on the other hand do not correspond to any particular pattern of behavior recorded in the archival texts.

Appendix

Day	Recommended Action	Corresponding real-life transaction
10-I	seizure of a field	– cultivation contract of date palm garden (BM 26524) – property transfer of date palm gardens (BM 82619)
14-I	favorable in a lawsuit	– lawsuit held in Ššu 12 (BM 29105)
16-I	achieve an aim	– inheritance division among brothers (TuM 2/3 5)
18-I	wrongdoing will depart	this is the busiest day of month Nisan (12 texts in total); several problematic situations were resolved that day: – a dispute about an outstanding debt (TCL 12-13 115) – a contested slave sale (BM 82671) – a prebend acquired by proxy (AchHist 15 no. 171)
06-II	who marries will become old	[–] no marriages recorded
10-II	favorable in court	[–] no court cases recorded

[26] For instance, 7 texts were drafted on 20-VIII ("favorable") including sales of land and prebends, while 8 texts were drafted on 21-VIII ("unfavorable") including a cancellation of a land sale and an exchange of prebends.

Day	Recommended Action	Corresponding real-life transaction
12-II	favorable in the street	with 8 texts, this is the busiest day of month II so far; in keeping with the reference to the "street," one finds mostly business records on this day (debt notes and receipts); BM 27813 relates to the beer trade
15-II	grain harvest	– lease of a grain field (BM 27854) – property transfer of agricultural land (VS 4 176)
22-II	favorable in a lawsuit	very busy day (10 recorded transactions), especially for legal transactions: – two inheritance divisions (BM 17657, BM 26532) – two sales of date palms/groves (BM 26499, Amherst 256) – house rent contract (BM 29291); *urāšu* contract (BM TCL 13 173)
03-III	give grain; a god's ill will toward a man will be undone	a day of major business transactions: – creation of a joint venture (TEBR 75) – land sale (EAH 212) – house rent contracts and receipts (BM 29036, BM 82714, VS 4 191) – debt note of 10.5 minas of silver (*Bard* 2) – smithing contract (Joannès 1989: 250)
22-III	inheritance	– two brothers pay their deceased father's deputy (BE 8 117)
17-IV	good day at home, obedient slave	– slave pledged (*TuM* 2/3 55)
27-IV	good day in court	[–] no court cases recorded, but one prebend sale (AchHist 15 no. 170)
08-VI	one must not quarrel	– end of dispute within family (Ellis 1984 no. 9)
09-VI	seizure of a field	– six *imittu* texts
17-VI	inheritance, happiness	[–] no matching records
29-VI	desire fulfilled	– end of dispute between relatives (BM 96102)
07-VII	good day in court	[–] no matching records
09-VII	good day in court	[–] no matching records
28-VII	desires fulfilled	[–] no matching records

Day	Recommended Action	Corresponding real-life transaction
21-VII	favorable for grain	– debt note barley (TuM 2/3 75) – work contract of the baker's prebend (AchHist 15 no. 97)
25-X	friendship	– suretyship (BM 17644) – declaration by witness about contested slave (BM 17725)
12-XII	success of enterprise	– land and house sale (BM 82656, BM 87347) – two disputes are resolved (BM 25633, BM 102321)
24-XII	one should donate a share[27]	– marriage contract (BM 28852)

Recommended actions in the *Babylonian Almanac* and corresponding transactions in real life from Borsippa.

Day	Discouraged actions	Real-life transactions
02-I	do not go to law	no court cases recorded; 7 texts in total
12-I	do not barter grain	no grain transactions recorded; 9 texts in total
13-I	do not acquire a wife	no marriage or dowry transfers recorded; 4 texts in total
15-I	do not take an oath	no oaths recorded; 5 texts in total
03-II	do not barter grain	no grain transactions recorded; 4 texts in total
04-II	do not receive grain	no grain receipts, but one debt note of barley (TuM 2/3 81); 4 texts in total
05-II	do not acquire a wife	no marriage or dowry transfers recorded; 5 texts in total
11-II	unfavorable in court	no court cases recorded; 6 texts in total
19-II	do not take an oath	no oaths recorded; 4 texts in total
25-II	do not acquire a wife	no marriage or dowry transfers recorded; 3 texts in total
06-III	do not buy a slave	no slave sales recorded; 4 texts in total
26-III	do not acquire a wife	no marriage or dowry texts; 4 texts in total

[27] This is according to the Sippar library copy edited by Isma'el and George 2002, 258.

Day	Discouraged actions	Real-life transactions
29-III	bad day in court	no court cases recorded; only 1 text in total
25-IV	do not take an oath	no oaths recorded; 6 texts in total
30-IV	do not deliver grain	no grain transactions recorded; 2 texts in total
18-V	do not take an oath	no oaths recorded; 7 texts in total
27-V	loss of grain	no grain transactions recorded; 3 texts in total
24-VI	do not take an oath	no oaths recorded; 10 texts in total
25-VI	do not buy anything	no sales recorded; 11 texts in total
15-VII	do not acquire a wife	no marriage or dowry transfers recorded; 5 texts in total
03-VIII	do not deliver grain	no grain transacted; 4 texts in total
05-VIII	do not acquire a wife	no marriage or dowry transfers recorded; 6 texts in total
03-IX	do not barter grain	no grain transacted; 4 texts in total
06-IX	do not buy a slave	no slave sales recorded; 5 texts in total
28-IX	do not acquire a wife	no marriage or dowry tranfers recorded; no texts
04-X	loss of property	no property transactions recorded; 1 text in total
06-X	do not acquire a wife	no marriage and dowry transfers recorded; 3 texts in total
16-X	do not barter grain	no grain transactions recorded; 6 texts in total
19-X	a slave will escape, silver will go missing	no slave or silver transactions recorded; 1 text in total

Discouraged actions in the *Babylonian Almanac* and corresponding transactions in real life from Borsippa.

Bibliography

ELLIS, M. DEJONG 1984: "Neo-Babylonian Texts in the Yale Babylonian Collection", *JCS* 36, 1-63.

George, A.R. 1988: "Babylonian Texts in the Folios of Sidney Smith, Part ONE", *RA* 82, 139-162.

JOANNÈS, F. 1989: *Archives de Borsippa: La famille Ea-ilûta-bani: Étude d'un lot d'archives familiales en Babylonie du VIII*[e] *au V*[e] *siècle av. J.-C.*, Genève.

ISMA'EL, K.S. and A.R. GEORGE 2002: "Tablets from the Sippar Library XI. The Babylonian Almanac", *Iraq* 64, 249-258.
LABAT, R. 1941: "Un almanach babylonien (V R 48-49)", *RA* 38, 13-40.
— 1952: "Un calendrier cassite", *Sumer* 8, 17-36.
LIVINGSTONE, A. 1993: "The Case of the Hemerologies: Official Cult, Learned Formulation and Popular Practice", in E. Matsushima (ed.) *Official Cult and Popular Religion in the Ancient Near East*, Heidelberg, 97-113.
— 1998: "The Use of Magic in the Assyrian and Babylonian Hemerologies and Menologies", *SEL* 15, 59-67.
— 2000: "On the Organized Release of Doves to Secure Compliance of a Higher Authority", in A.R. George and I.L. Finkel (eds.) *Wisdom, Gods and Literature. Studies in Assyriology in Honour of W.G. Lambert*, Winona Lake, 375-387.
— 2007: "The Babylonian Almanac: A Text for Specialists?", in B. Groneberg and H. Spieckermann (eds.) *Die Welt der Götterbilder* (BZAW 376), Berlin and New York, 85-101.
MATOUŠ, L. 1961: "L'almanach de Bakr-Awa", *Sumer* 17, 17-59.
ROBSON, E. 2004: "Counting the days: scholarly conceptions and quantifications of time in Assyria and Babylonia, c. 750-250 BCE", in R. Rosen (ed.) *Time and Temporality in the Ancient World*, Philadelphia, 45–90.
ROTH, M.T. 1989: *Babylonian Marriage Agreements 7th-3rd Centuries BC* (AOAT 222), Neukirchen-Vluyn.
WAERZEGGERS, C. 2005: "The dispersal history of the Borsippa archives", in H.D. Baker and M. Jursa (eds.) *Approaching the Babylonian Economy: Proceedings of the START Project Symposium Held in Vienna, 1-3 July 2004* (AOAT 330), Münster, 343-363.
— 2010: *The Ezida Temple of Borsippa: Priesthood, Cult, Archives* (Achaemenid History 15), Leiden.
ZADOK, R. 2009: *Catalogue of Documents from Borsippa or Related to Borsippa in the British Museum I*, Messina.

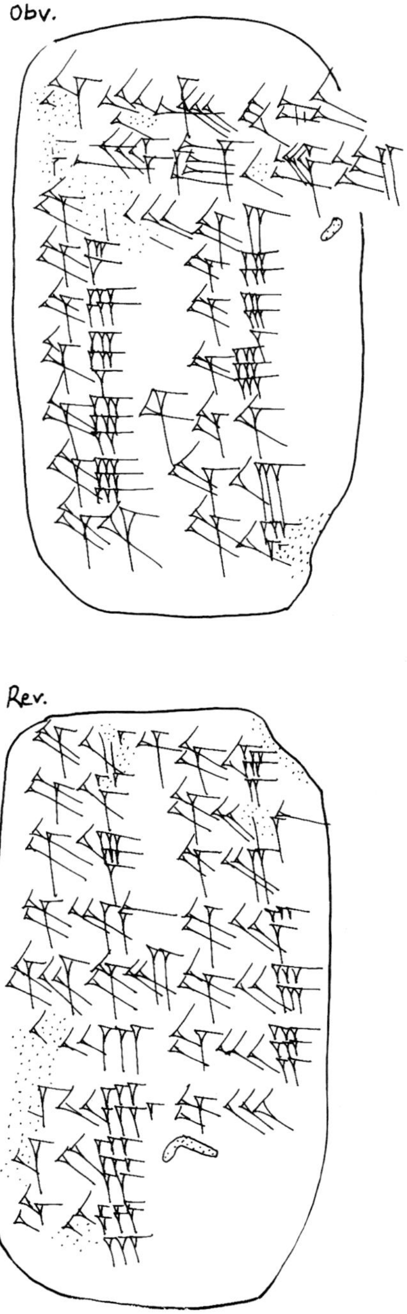

BM 95163

THE ARCHAEOLOGICAL LANDSCAPE OF THE TELL BEYDAR REGION: AN UPDATE USING SATELLITE IMAGERY

Tony J. WILKINSON and Emma CUNLIFFE
Durham University

Introduction

The Tell Beydar area is no ordinary area and we must be grateful to Karel Van Lerberghe, Marc Lebeau and Antoine Suleiman who had the vision to see the site and its region holistically. As a result, Tell Beydar is one of those rare sites where there exists a strong record from cuneiform texts, art history, environmental studies, excavations and archaeological survey.[1] The present note, dedicated to Karel Van Lerberghe, is intended to provide an update on settlement patterns in the Beydar area as a result of the increased availability of high-resolution satellite imagery since the original survey was conducted.

In 1997 and 1998 a team sponsored by the Oriental Institute of the University of Chicago were invited to undertake landscape and environmental surveys in the region around Tell Beydar with a view to understanding the processes that led to the rise of urbanism in the region, and to describe and interpret the full record of landscape features. Within a 12 km radius of Tell Beydar (i.e. 450 sq km) a total of 83 sites were surveyed (including Tell Beydar), and numerous features were recorded.[2] However, because the project was initiated at a time of rapid change in the availability of satellite imagery, the original survey has required significant updating as new generations of imagery became available.

The initial survey consisted of a traditional vehicle based survey aided by GPS and SPOT imagery. In addition, numerous wadi sections and other cuts were investigated to provide geoarchaeological control; transects

[1] This paper is dedicated to Karel Van Lerberghe, who acted as a catalyst for the Tell Beydar Survey and provided considerable help and support during fieldwork and after. The remote sensing research forms part of the AHRC (UK)-funded Fragile Crescent Project (Durham University). Thanks also go to Eleanor Wilkinson and Jason Ur for their processing of much of the original field data.

[2] Wilkinson 2000; Nieuwenhuyse and Wilkinson 2008; Ur and Wilkinson 2008.

were walked to gain a rough idea of the nature of archaeological material and features away from major sites, as well as on the basalt plateau to the west. However, there was insufficient time to conduct formal off-site sampling of archaeological materials and it was quite evident that after the first two seasons there was a need for much more survey. Although the release of CORONA satellite imagery in 1995 occurred before the Beydar Survey commenced, it took some time for the relevant imagery to be acquired and processed: consequently the field survey did not benefit as much as it should have from its release. Moreover, the increased availability of free satellite imagery through platforms such as Google Earth occurred after the project was completed. The release of CORONA and the launching of Google Earth have therefore necessitated the re-examination of the surveyed area through remote sensing methods.

The Beydar landscape is currently being re-examined as part of the Fragile Crescent Project, a major AHRC (UK) funded project conducted by Durham University. Aided by satellite imagery, sites discovered during earlier field campaigns are being re-interrogated with the central aim of re-constructing long-term trends in settlement across northern Mesopotamia and the Levant (Galiatsatos et al. 2009). A key research question for the Tell Beydar area is what has changed since 1998 and what has remained essentially the same? More significantly, how do these new discoveries impact our interpretations of the archaeological landscape?

The broad mandate of the Tell Beydar Project is reflected in the wide range of synthetic studies that have been conducted, either as a direct result of the field project, or from the activities of its members. Since the original survey report (Wilkinson 2000) the following are but a sample of the emerging results to appear:

- Use of the Beydar area as the underpinning of a programme of agent-based modelling of an early Upper Mesopotamian community (Wilkinson et al. 2007a and b; Christiansen and Altaweel 2006).
- The re-evaluation of survey and textual evidence using historical and archaeological sources (Sallaberger and Ur 2004; Ur and Wilkinson 2008; Nieuwenhuyse and Wilkinson 2008; Wilkinson 2002; Ur 2003).
- Further interrogation of textual sources leading towards insights into the regional agricultural economy (Van Lerberghe 1996; Widell 2004).
- Re-evaluation of sites using satellite images to assess various forms of damage to the site (Cunliffe in press).
- Finally, surveys of the basalt plateau to the west of the site have yielded new information on rock art, several new archaeological sites, and hunting features such as kites (Van Berg et al. 2003 and 2004).

In addition, results from the survey have contributed more generally to our understanding of environmental change and landscape development in the Khabur basin (Deckers and Riehl 2008; Ur 2010).

Most of the above publications have, quite understandably, been focussed upon the record of Tell Beydar society and landscape in the Bronze Age. Although there has been some investigation of the later landscapes, particularly those of the Iron Age (Wilkinson and Barbanes 2000; Wilkinson et al. 2004), discussion of the record of the later periods of settlement has been limited. Here, for reasons that will become evident, we are shifting the focus to the post Late Bronze Age landscapes.

The Tell Beydar area

Tell Beydar falls within the western Khabur basin where the valley of the Wadi 'Awaidj flows to the east of an extensive basalt plateau. The mean annual rainfall of approximately 300 mm is subject to a considerable inter-annual variation and the ability of the local soils to absorb and retain this moisture can mean the difference between a successful and a failed crop. During the Early Bronze Age most settlement was concentrated upon the three north south wadis where deep and fertile clay-rich *calcic-xerosol* soils retained sufficient moisture to produce successful crops in most years. However, as we know from the recent run of dry years in northern Syria, crop failure can occur even on these deeper soils. The soils on the gentle interfluves to the east of the 'Awaidj and fringing the basalt plateau are probably less water retentive than those along the main valley, and such soils are also more distant from water sources. Most marginal, in terms of both rooting depth and moisture retention, are the basalt soils of the Harra plateau to the west which were not settled during the Early Bronze Age (although there were significant amounts of other activities), and were only slightly settled during the Iron Age. These basalt soils seem to have been open land for much of the Holocene, where they functioned as pasture for flocks as well as the domain of mobile pastoralists or local shepherds who left traces in the form of hunting traps (kites), rock art and other activities. Significantly, the move toward mechanized cultivation in the last 30 years has resulted in even this marginal land being ploughed up for agriculture.

The long occupation history of the Beydar region dates back to the Pre-Proto-Hassuna sites of the early 7th millennium BC (Nieuwenhuyse and Wilkinson 2008, fig. 10) through to early Islamic times, when much of the area was abandoned until the re-settlement of the area during the 20th century AD.

The Oriental Institute survey of the Tell Beydar area took place in three weeks in September 1997 supplemented by a further three weeks in August 1998. The original survey employed SPOT satellite images from August 1991 to provide a basic mapping framework which detailed major topographic features, villages and land use zones. Subsequently this data base has been supplemented by two sets of declassified Corona satellite photographs taken during May 1965 and August 1969 and which provided a further record of topographic features. These two sources of imagery provided a useful basis for archaeological reconnaissance of sites and off-site features in the field (Wilkinson 2000).

A crucial structuring element in the landscape was the tell. During the third millennium BC prominent fortified tells were the dominant form of settlement especially along the three main north south wadis, but by the early second millennium BC most of the area was abandoned, perhaps reverting to the domain of mobile pastoralists who dominated the western Khabur basin during the period of the Mari letters (Lyonnet 1998; Wilkinson 2002; Ristvet 2008). Following a gap covering most of the second millennium BC, during which most of the mounds were unoccupied, re-settlement came in the form of rare small settlements together with one or two lower towns that grew up around the bases of tells during the Late Bronze Age. Although it is tempting to see this resettlement as corresponding to the period of re-expansion during the Middle Assyrian period, this still needs to be confirmed, and alternatively some may relate to the period of the Mittanian state. By the Iron Age the pattern of dispersed rural settlements had spread over virtually the entire area, including parts of the basalt plateau, either as a result of Neo-Assyrian administration policies, spontaneous settlement by Aramean nomads or perhaps as a result of settlement within estates parcelled out during the Neo-Assyrian period (Wilkinson et al. 2005). Although it is currently impossible to say what happened in the Beydar area at the collapse of the Neo-Assyrian empire in 612 BC, this predominantly dispersed pattern of settlement continued during the Hellenisitic, Partho-Roman, Sasanian-Byzantine and early Islamic periods, until the area was deserted during the 2nd millennium AD.

In summary the basic pattern of settlement consisted of:

- an early prehistoric phase of dispersed settlement with perhaps some minor tells,
- followed by a dominance of fortified tells during part of the 4th and 3rd millennium BC (continuing into the early 2nd millennium at two

sites in the very north of the area) and trace occupations on perhaps one or two other sites;
- followed by a pattern of dispersed, low or even flat settlement from the Late Bronze Age to the Islamic period.

This sequence is fundamental to the interpretation of the newly discovered sites because it can be inferred that if all the newly discovered sites are low mounds or flat and dispersed sites — that is they are not tells — there is a high probability that the sites belong to the later phase of imperial settlement during the last three millennia BC. However, some may also belong to the pre-fourth millennium BC phases of Late Neolithic settlement.

New discoveries

Satellite imagery is becoming more common in archaeological prospection (Donoghue 2001; Parcak 2009; Kouchoukos 1998; Philip et al. 2002), in part because relict landscapes that are hard to see from the ground, and in some cases no longer exist, can be identified and mapped. In the Near East the most commonly utilised imagery is that of the CORONA series, which shows the Near Eastern landscape on the cusp of agricultural and urban expansion. In addition, Google Earth[3] displays SPOT imagery, and high resolution Geoeye imagery. The new imagery, combined with the overview of the 1960's landscape via CORONA, has enabled the detection of sites and features which were not visible during the original survey.

The interpretation of satellite imagery can depend upon a number of factors. These include atmospheric conditions or poor weather which can obscure the ground on the image. Even if the ground is visible, land cover in the form of certain crops can obscure sites, and these factors can change from year-to-year, meaning sites can become more or less visible over time. Therefore the most reliable identifications of sites are those that are visible on multiple images.

The available CORONA imagery of the area consisted of a mosaic of five images from three different missions. The location of the image within the larger CORONA photograph affects the resolution, which means that the images can vary spatially. One image is from the 1021 mission in May 1965 (resolution 4 × 4 m), two are from the 1102 mission in December

[3] Available at time of writing, October 2011.

1967 (resolution 4 × 4 m), and two are from the 1105 mission in November 1968 (resolution 3 × 3 m). In order to compare images, it is necessary to place them within the same geographical coordinate systems a system known as georeferencing. The five images were georeferenced in ArcGIS using a polynomial geometric model with nearest neighbour sampling from a mosaic of three ETM panchromatic Landsat images (2002 — 2004, 15 m resolution), and converted into the WGS 84 coordinate system. The images from the CORONA missions were taken over a number of years during different seasons: sites identified on images from different missions are not directly comparable in terms of visibility. Sites are more visible on the 1102 imagery as there was less atmospheric dust at the time of image acquisition, and it was taken later in the year, when ground conditions were wetter, and many fields had been ploughed, increasing the visibility. The 1021 mission was also taken at the end of the rainy season. However, the resolution is slightly better on the 1105 mission imagery. Where effective, spectral enhancements were used to augment the images. The exact date of the SPOT imagery in the Tell Beydar area is unknown, but it is part of a mosaic of images taken over three years around 2004, and has a resolution of 2.5 m (Astrium Geo-Information Services 2008). Without knowing the acquisition date, the influence of factors such as seasonality, and the likely moisture content of the ground, on site visibility cannot be accounted for. As a result, the CORONA missions and the SPOT images are not directly comparable, but the Geoeye imagery dates from June (for the north) and August and October (for the south) 2010, and has a resolution of between 0.4 metres and 1 metre. The SPOT imagery was taken just before or just after the harvest, as many fields were covered with ripe crops or chaff, but the Geoeye was taken as the fields were being ploughed.

Sites recorded in the Tell Beydar area were predominantly mounded, being mainly composed of mud-brick, cultural layers and ash. In addition to tells there were occasional khirbet-type sites consisting of low, extensive often multiple mounds of post-Bronze Age date. Most sites are visible on the CORONA images as darker, paler or mottled patches standing out against the background of the natural *calcic xerosol* regional soils. Tell sites in particular have a characteristic signature, being roughly circular with a very pale half and a very dark half, the former receiving the full light of the sun, the latter being the shaded side of the mound. On the later colour imagery, sites are visible as crop marks in fields, or as areas of mounding disrupting the plough lines.

Potential sites were given an identification certainty of "high", "medium" or "low", indicating their likeliness to be an archaeological site. This depended on clearness of the site signature, and proximity to other features which leave similar aerial signatures (for example, relict wadi soils often leave pale traces on the SPOT images, therefore a pale patch in a field near a relict wadi is less likely to be a site than a pale patch with no other obvious cause). Only potential sites visible on at least two imagery types were recorded as "high" or "medium". Features that were visible on only one of the two images were also recorded but given a "low" certainty.

Fifty-six possible sites have so far been identified, of which fourteen have a "high" certainty (Figs. 1, 2 and 3).[4] As more imagery is analysed, certainty of correct identification increases. A further sixteen had a "medium" certainty, and twenty-six features were only visible on one image type, and were given a "low" certainty. An enclosed depression was apparent at one site (TBSI 9), but otherwise the identification of features were limited.

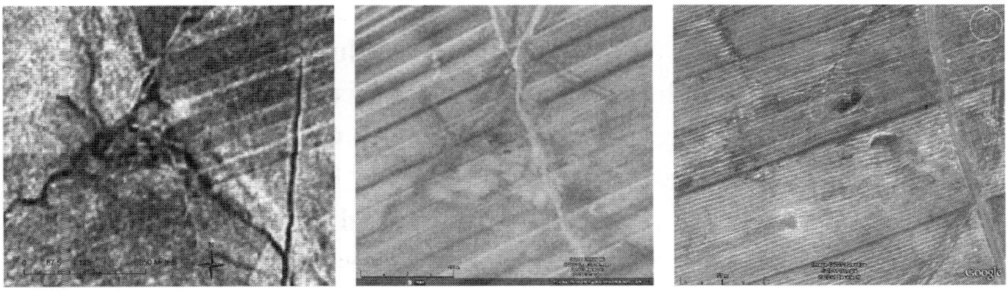

Figs. 1-3. Site TBSI 12. Fig. 1 (left). 1102 CORONA (1967), Fig. 2 (centre). SPOT imagery and Fig. 3 (right). Geoeye Imagery (June 2010). Note the crop mark, and the way the plough lines are disturbed.

The southwest of the survey area is occupied by the basalt plateau: archaeological features were much more common there than long-term occupation sites, and are not shown on the map (Van Berg et al. 2003; 2004). These sites, which include kites, necropolises, settlements and several thousand carved rocks and rock art sites, dating from the 5th millennium to the 3rd century AD, tend not to be visible on the satellite imagery. However, due to the increase in available imagery resolution, several features

[4] As an interim measure the newly discovered sites are referred to as TBSI to distinguish them from those discovered in the field (TBS numbers).

and sites are now visible on satellite imagery (Figs. 4 and 5), but only sites on the fringe of the basalt are still visible, and it is possible many have been destroyed as a result of the ploughing of the plateau soils and the recent agricultural intensification.

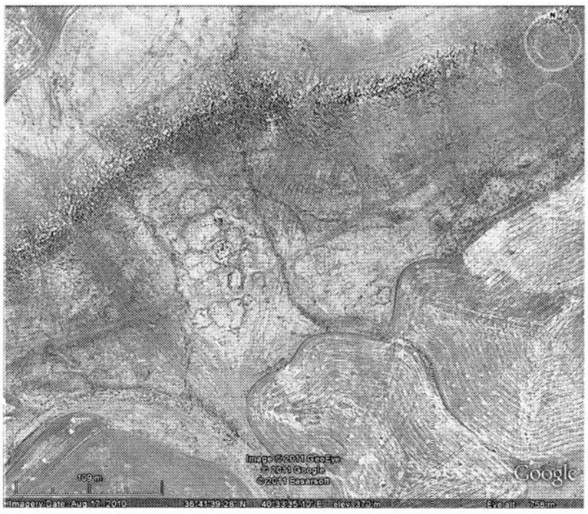

Fig. 4 (left). TBSI 31 on the edge of the basalt — the evidence of mounding is indicated by plough lines, Fig. 5 (right). TBS 69 — Khisham, surveyed by Van Berg et al. (2004).

In some cases the plough lines visible on the Geoeye imagery give some indication of height (Fig. 5), and suggest the presence of archaeological features. In the flat Jazira plain, elevated sites are more easily visible, and are more likely to have been located during the original survey. Those identified on imagery are almost all within crop fields and are probably low or flat sites which would have been easier to miss in the field, especially because the original survey took place when there was still much crop waste on the surface (the original survey notes make many references to chaff obscuring identified sites at the time).

The increased use of plough agriculture in recent years could potentially bring evidence of buried sites to the surface, but most "low" certainty sites were only visible on the CORONA imagery, suggesting that if they were sites they may have been damaged by agriculture instead. Many sites appear to have become less visible over time, despite the increase in imagery resolution. All small sites that were recorded as partly ploughed during the survey are now entirely ploughed. The resumption of agriculture when the region was resettled after the 1940s, and the later intensification initiated by the construction of the Hasseke dam in the late 1990s, has damaged many of the sites, with the associated loss of archaeological information. Moreover, the repeated ploughing will almost certainly have distorted the field scatters which are used to estimate manuring areas and site catchment areas (Ur 2010, Wilkinson 1982). Some sites, such as Tell Hassek (TBS 4 / Lyonnet (2000) site 28), show clear damage (Figs 6 and 7). This large tell site has a complex series of lower mounds extending to its north. Much of this lower town, dated between the Late Bronze Age and Late Antique periods, is no longer evident, except where small parts are visible as bends in the plough lines, or faint soil marks. Even the south eastern side of the tell appears to have been bulldozed to extend the fields.

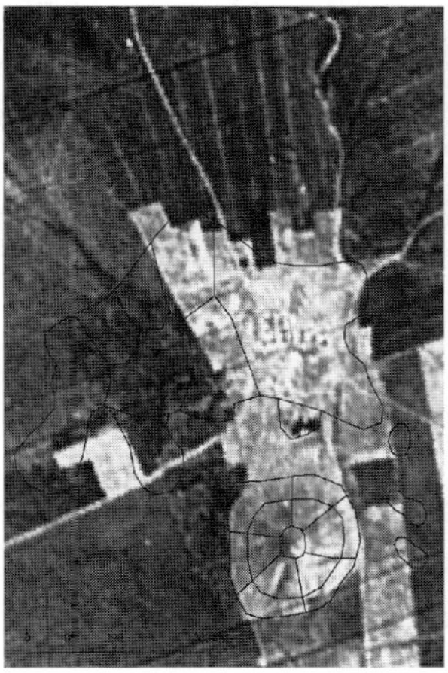

Fig. 6 (left). Tell Hassek (TBS 43 / Lyonnet 28) on CORONA image (left) and Fig. 7 (right). on GeoEye images. The thin black lines indicate the original survey subdivisions of the site (note how much smaller the tell is to the south, and the lack of obvious mounding to the left of the village.).

Of course, the existence and extent of new sites is unconfirmed until they can be visited in the field: there can be many reasons for the "site" signatures evident on the imagery. Moreover, without dating evidence, sites cannot be assigned to a particular period. The newly-discovered sites' signatures are small, and do not appear to be tell sites. Nevertheless, some do extend over relatively large areas, the largest being approximately 350 m by 250 m; most, however, are less than 100 m in diameter. Because most Early Bronze Age sites have been shown to be tells, this argues against a third millennium date for the new discoveries, and instead it is likely that they belong to a period of dispersed settlement, from the Late Bronze Age or later.

Discussion

As stated in an earlier article (Wilkinson et al. 2004), tells not only form the more prominent features of the Tell Beydar landscape, they also were those sites that were consistently occupied during the Early Bronze Age. On the other hand the low or flat sites tended to be either earlier (i.e. prehistoric) or post Late Bronze Age. Because most of the new discoveries belong to the latter category, it is unlikely that the original survey missed many tells and therefore EBA sites. This suggests that the original landscape interpretations, particularly those pertaining to the economic landscape of the area still hold (Ur and Wilkinson 2008). On the other hand, we have probably significantly under-estimated the number of sites of the later imperial periods, and may also have under-estimated, perhaps to a lesser degree, the earlier prehistoric sites. Without firm dating evidence, however, the possibility of the reoccupation of earlier sites also cannot be ruled out. Surveys of Late Bronze Age sites elsewhere in the Jazira (Ur 2010) found that 20% (or less) of sites were newly founded and most were reoccupied earlier settlements. Verifying these discoveries and unravelling their chronology must be the task of future field seasons.

We can now compare the revised estimate of archaeological sites from the Beydar survey with earlier estimates in Wilkinson et al. 2004 and Ur 2010. Many of the newly discovered sites identified fall within the "empty" areas between the main wadi channels in the north and east of the survey area. Fig. 8 shows the distribution map of sites drawn up after the 1998 survey season, and Fig. 9 is a map including sites with a "high" or "medium" degree of certainty. As can be seen, the settlement pattern now appears more evenly dispersed. Eighty-three sites were identified in the original survey, which covered approximately 450 km^2, giving a settlement density of 0.18 sites per km^2. Including the new sites of "high" certainty, the area can be seen to now have a settlement density of 0.22 per km^2, rising to 0.25 sites per km^2 including the medium certainty sites, and 0.31 sites per km^2 if the "low" certainty features were confirmed as sites. This increase in the number of sites or probable sites brings the Tell Beydar survey into closer alignment with other surveys in the greater Khabur region. In comparison with other surveys, both the Land of Nagar (Brak) and North Jazira surveys had site recovery rates per sq. km of nearly 0.40, whereas the small and very intensively surveyed Hamoukar region had a recovery rate of over 0.50 (Ur 2010, 40-42). Nevertheless, it is important to take into consideration that roughly one third of the survey

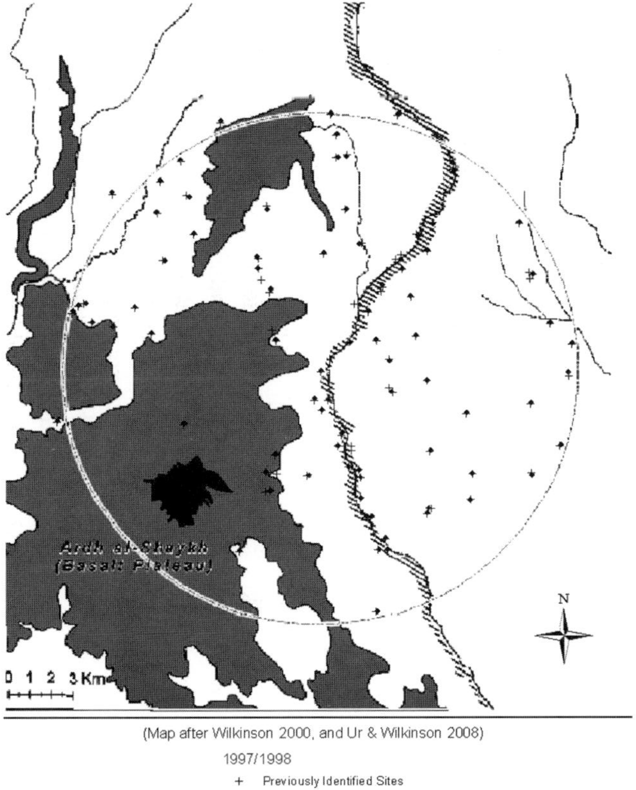

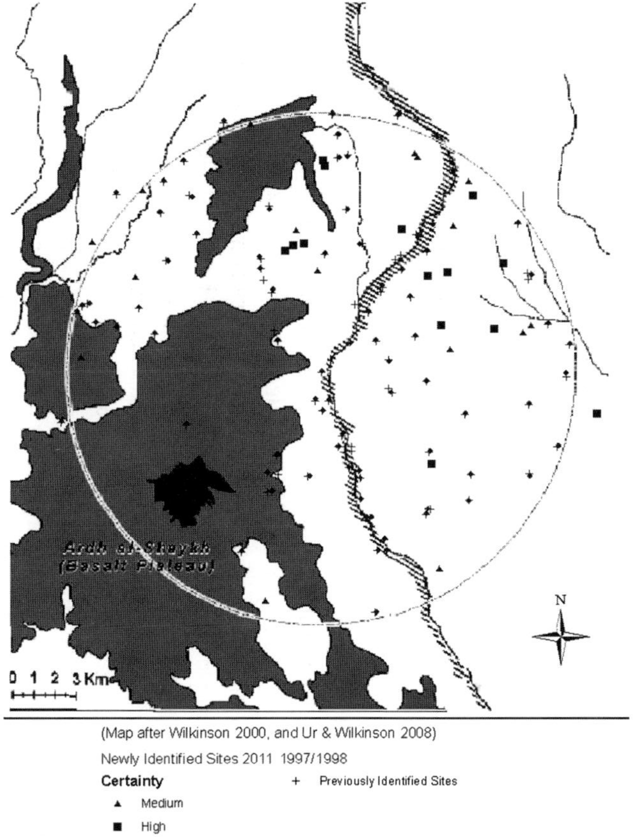

Figs. 8 and 9. The original pattern of settlement as it was recorded after fieldwork (to left) and the newly discovered sites (with High and Medium certainty sites shown).

area falls within the basalt plateau, and although settled by occasional sites and used for numerous other activities, was not as densely populated as the remainder of the area.

Of the 83 original sites, 20 were tells, of which 14 had lower towns; 56 were small dispersed rural settlement and 6 were marginal, nomadic or semi-nomadic sites. It is likely that most of the newly identified sites are small rural settlements, although further analysis of the plateau could reveal more sites of nomadic or semi-nomadic pastoralists. However, the extent of damage across the area and ensuing invisibility of some known sites suggests that more small sites remain, and that some of the "low" certainty sites which were visible on earlier imagery may now simply be damaged beyond recognition.

As noted above, the present results do not appear to have invalidated the original analyses of the economic landscapes of Tell Beydar. The analysis of site catchments in the Beydar area suggests that the larger Early Bronze Age sites were under producing cereals whereas the smaller sites, had, to some degree, some spare capacity. In other words, the smaller sites may have been sending agricultural products in the form of cereals perhaps as tribute to the nearby centres. This suggests that it was necessary for many sites to be producing more than they required for strictly subsistence purposes. This notion has formed the basis of estimates of site carrying capacities made by Deckers and Dreschler (2011) to suggest that if significant quantities of tribute were being extracted from subsidiary sites, then the Khabur communities were not only stressing the local cultivation systems, they were also "squeezing out" to some degree the local flocks that would have relatively meagre areas of grazing (Deckers and Dreschler 2011). Here, the Beydar area with its extensive spread of plateau to the west, was at an advantage because this area provided an ideal area for pasturing the local flocks, as well as perhaps for some degree of hunting and other non-agricultural activities.

Conclusions

The discovery of additional sites in the area around Tell Beydar has the potential to change our understanding of settlement patterning in the area, specifically increasing the number of later sites that relate to the periods of the later territorial empires. These new sites need to be confirmed in the field and surveyed for evidence of their periods of occupation before any definitive statement can be made about the density of settlement in the Tell Beydar area at any particular time. Such information will provide an important context for other occupation periods at Beydar such as the

Late Bronze Age and Iron Age lower town as well as the important discoveries of the Hellenistic palace and settlement on the Tell (Galán 2007). This 2nd and 1st century BC settlement, with its extensive views over the surrounding plains, seems to represent a re-assertion of earlier notions of Tell Beydar as a prominent feature of the local landscape. As a result of the present re-investigation of the Beydar survey, it appears that those lands that were probably pasture or waste during the Bronze Age were even more densely settled over the past 3000 years or so.

It is also important to emphasize that the record of archaeological sites is not stable. There is a "taphonomic" sample bias in the sites we are studying because sites must survive to be examined and we are starting from an incomplete record which becomes more damaged as time passes. Features such as linear hollows (i.e. hollow way tracks) are now near-invisible, and off-sites features such as cairn necropolises have been largely cleared for irrigated fields. The CORONA imagery also highlights the numerous geomorphological changes which have taken place over the millennia. Relict channels of the Wadi 'Awaidj and the associated sequences of erosion and deposition will doubtless have disturbed and buried sites with equal frequency, leaving us with only a partial record to study. The use of multi-period satellite imagery can however begin to correct the imbalance in our records, allowing us access to a past landscape that is already lost today.

Although the re-study of the Beydar area raises as many new questions as answers, it will allow the analysis of the site and its area to move forward. In future it will therefore be necessary to undertake the following:

- ground control of the newly discovered sites to determine whether they are indeed sites and what were their dates of occupation.
- Further work on off-site field scatters to establish whether they are present and whether they can be used as a proxy indicator of ancient agriculture.
- The integration of the investigations of the basalt plateau by Van Berg and colleagues within the broader Tell Beydar Survey database.
- The integration of the Tell Beydar survey area within a broader landscape of the land of Nagar and the western Khabur Basin.

Bibliography

ASTRIUM GEO-INFORMATION SERVICES 2008: *Spot Image Corp. Introduces New Services For Google Earth Users:* Http://Www.Spot.Com/Web/Sicorp/2229-Spot-Image-Corp-Introduces-New-Services-For-Google-Earth-Users.Php (Accessed 12 04 2011)

CHRISTIANSEN, J.H., M.R. Altaweel 2006: "Understanding ancient societies: A new approach using agent-based holistic modeling", *Structure and Dynamics: eJournal of Anthropological and Related Sciences* 1(2). http://repositories.cdlib.org/imbs/socdyn/sdeas/vol1/iss2/art7/.

CUNLIFFE, E. (in press): "Satellites, Surveys And Site Destruction: Using Satellite Imagery To Monitor Damage To Archaeological Sites In Syria", in: F. Borrell, M. Bouso, A. Gómez, C. Tornero. & O. Vicente (eds.) *Broadening Horizons 3. 3rd Conference Of Young Researchers Working In The Ancient Near East*, Universitat Autònoma De Barcelona.

DECKERS, K. and S. RIEHL 2008: "Tells of the Upper Khabur: their hydrological and agrarian context", *Paléorient* 34.2, 173-89.

DECKERS, K. and P. DRESCHLER 2011: "Spatial analysis of Early Bronze Age settlements and resource exploitation in the Upper Khabur (NE Syria)", in K. Deckers (ed.) *Holocene Landscapes through Time in the Fertile Crescent* (Subartu 28), Turnhout, 17-32.

DONOGHUE, D. N. M. 2001: "Remote Sensing", in D. R. Brothwell and A. M. Pollard (eds.) *Handbook of Archaeological Sciences*, Chichester, 555-63.

GALÁN, R. M. 2007: "The Hellenistic palace of Tell Beydar", in M. Lebeau and A. Suleiman (eds.) Tell Beydar: The 2000-2002 Seasons of Excavations; the 2003-2004 seasons of architectural restoration. A Preliminary Report (*Subartu* 15), Turnhout 211-225.

KOUCHOUKOS, N. 1998: "Satellite Images And Near Eastern Landscape", *Near Eastern Archaeology* 64, 80-91.

LYONNET, B. 1998: "Le peuplement de la Djéziré occidentale au début du 3e millénaire, villes circulaires et pastoralisme: questions et hypothèses", in M. Lebeau (ed.) *About Subartu. Studies devoted to Upper Mesopotamia* (Subartu 4), 179-93.

LYONNET, B. (ed.) 2000: *Prospection archéologique du haut-Khabur occidental (Syrie du N.E),* Beyrouth.

NIEUWENHUYSE, O. and T. J. WILKINSON 2008: "Late Neolithic Settlement in the area of Tell Beydar (NE Syria)", in M. Lebeau & A. Suleiman (eds.), *Beydar Studies 1,* (Subartu 21), Turnhout, 268-303.

PARCAK, S. 2009: *Satellite Remote Sensing for Archaeologists*, London and New York.

PHILIP, G., F. JABOUR, A. BECK, M. BSHESH, J. Grove, A. Kirk and A. Millard 2002: "Settlement And Landscape Development in the Homs Region, Syria: Research Questions, Preliminary Results 1999-2000 and Future Potential", *Levant* 34, 1-23.

Ristvet, L. 2008: "Legal and Archaeological Territories of the Second Millennium BC in Northern Mesopotamia", *Antiquity* 82, 585-99.

Sallaberger, W. and J. A. Ur 2004: "Tell Beydar / Nabada in its Regional Setting", in: L. Milano, W. Sallaberger, P. Talon and K. Van Lerberghe (eds.), *Third Millennium Cuneiform Texts from Tell Beydar (Seasons 1996-2002)* (Subartu 12), Brepols, Turnhout, 51-71.

UR, J. A. 2003: "Corona Satellite Photography And Ancient Road Networks: A Northern Mesopotamian Case Study," *Antiquity* 77, 102-115.

— 2010: *Urbanism and Cultural. Landscapes in Northeastern Syria. The Tell Hamoukar Survey, 1999-2001. Tell Hamoukar Volume 1,* OIP 137, Chicago.

UR, J. A. and T. J. WILKINSON 2008: "Settlement and Economic Landscapes of Tell Beydar and its Hinterland, in: M. Lebeau and A. Suleiman (eds.), *Beydar Studies 1* (Subartu 21), Turnhout, 305-327.

VAN BERG, P.-L. and V. PICALAUSE 2003: "Structures archéologiques et art rupestre à Khishâm (Hassake, Syrie): campagne 1999", in M. Lebeau and A. Suleiman (eds.) Tell Beydar, the 1995- 1999 Seasons of Excavations. A Preliminary Report, *Subartu* 10, Turnhout, 555-568.

VAN BERG, P.-L., N. CAUWE, S. LEMAITRE, V. PICALAUSE, and M. VANDER LINDEN 2004: Desert-Kites of The Hemma Plateau (Hassake, Syria), *Paléorient* 30/1, 89-99.

VAN LERBERGHE, K. 1996: "The Livestock", in F. Ismail, W. Sallaberger, P. Talon and K. Van Lerberghe (eds.), *Administrative Documents from Tell Beydar (Season 1993-1995)* (Subartu 2), Turnhout, 107-117.

WIDELL, M. 2004: "Some Observations on the Administration, Agriculture and Animal Management of Tell Beydar", *Ugarit-Forschungen* 35, 717-733.

WILKINSON, T. J. 1982: "The Definition of Ancient Manured Zones by Means of Extensive Sherd-Sampling Techniques", *Journal of Field Archaeology* 9 (3), 323-333.

— 2000: "Archaeological Survey of the Tell Beydar Region, Syria 1997", in K. Van Lerberghe & G. Voet (eds.), *Tell Beydar: Environmental And Technical Studies* (Subartu 6), Brepols, Turnhout, 1-37.

— 2002: "The Settlement Transition of the Second Millennium BC in the Western Khabur", in L. al-Gailani Werr, J. Curtis, H. Martin, A. McMahon, J. Oates and J. Reade (eds.) *Of Pots and Plans: Papers on the Archaeology and History of Mesopotamia and Syria Presented to David Oates in Honour of his 75th Birthday* (Nabu Publications), London, 361-372.

WILKINSON, T. J. and E. BARBANES. 2000: "Settlement and settlement patterns in the Iron Age: The Syrian Jazira", in G. Bunnens (ed.) *Essays on Syria in the Iron Age* (Ancient Near Eastern Studies supplement 7), Louvain, 397-422.

WILKINSON, T. J., J. A. UR and J. CASANA. 2004: "From Nucleation to Dispersal. Trends in Settlement Pattern in the Northern Fertile Crescent", in J. Cherry and S. Alcock (eds.) *Side-by side survey Survey*, Oxford, 189-205.

WILKINSON, T. J., E. B. WILKINSON, J. A. UR, and M. ALTAWEEL 2005: "Landscape and settlement in the Neo-Assyrian Empire", *Bulletin of the American Schools of Oriental Research* 340, 23-56.

WILKINSON, T. J., M. GIBSON, J. H. CHRISTIANSEN, M. WIDELL, D. SCHLOEN, N. KOUCHOUKOS, C. WOODS, J. SANDERS, K.-L. SIMUNICH, M. ALTAWEEL, J. A. UR, C. HRITZ, J. LAUINGER, T. PAULETTE and J. TENNEY 2007: "Modeling settlement systems in a dynamic environment: case studies from Mesopotamia", in T. A. Kohler and S. E. van der Leeuw (eds.) *The Model-Based Archaeology of Socio-Natural Systems*, Santa Fe New Mexico, 175-208.

WILKINSON, T. J., J. H. CHRISTIANSEN, J. A. UR, M. WIDELL and M. ALTAWEEL 2007: "Urbanization within a Dynamic Environment: Modeling Bronze Age Communities in Upper Mesopotamia", *American Anthropologist* 109(1), 52-68.

ORIENTALIA LOVANIENSIA ANALECTA

1 E. Lipiński, Studies in Aramaic Inscriptions and Onomastics I.
2 J. Quaegebeur, Le dieu égyptien Shaï dans la religion et l'onomastique.
3 P.H.L. Eggermont, Alexander's Campaigns in Sind and Baluchistan and the Siege of the Brahmin Town of Harmatelia.
4. W.M. Callewaert, The Sarvāṅgī of the Dādūpanthī Rajab.
5. E. Lipiński (ed.), State and Temple Economy in the Ancient Near East I.
6. E. Lipiński (ed.), State and Temple Economy in the Ancient Near East II.
7. M.-C. De Graeve, The Ships of the Ancient Near East (c. 2000-500 B.C.).
8. W.M. Callewaert (ed.), Early Hindī Devotional Literature in Current Research.
9. F.L. Damen, Crisis and Religious Renewal in the Brahmo Samaj Movement (1860-1884).
10. R.Y. Ebied, A. Van Roey, L.R. Wickham, Peter of Callinicum, Anti-Tritheist Dossier.
11. A. Rammant-Peeters, Les pyramidions égyptiens du Nouvel Empire.
12. S. Scheers (ed.), Studia Paulo Naster Oblata I. Numismatica Antiqua.
13. J. Quaegebeur (ed.), Studia Paulo Naster Oblata II. Orientalia Antiqua.
14. E. Platti, Yaḥyā ibn ʿAdī, théologien chrétien et philosophe arabe.
15. E. Gubel, E. Lipiński, B. Servais-Soyez (eds.), Studia Phoenicia I-II.
16. W. Skalmowski, A. Van Tongerloo (eds.), Middle Iranian Studies.
17. M. van Mol, Handboek Modern Arabisch.
18. C. Laga, J.A. Munitiz, L. Van Rompay (eds.), After Chalcedon. Studies in Theology and Church History.
19. E. Lipiński (ed.), The Land of Israel: Cross-Roads of Civilizations.
20. S. Wachsmann, Aegeans in the Theban Tombs.
21. K. Van Lerberghe, Old Babylonian Legal and Administrative Texts from Philadelphia.
22. E. Lipiński (ed.), Phoenicia and the East Mediterranean in the First Millennium B.C.
23. M. Heltzer, E. Lipiński (eds.), Society and Economy in the Eastern Mediterranean (1500-1000 B.C.).
24. M. Van de Mieroop, Crafts in the Early Isin Period: a Study of the Isin Craft Archive from the Reigns of Išbi-Erra and Šū-Ilišu.
25. G. Pollet (ed.), India and the Ancient World. History, Trade and Culture before A.D. 650.
26. E. Lipiński (ed.), Carthago.
27. E. Verreet, Modi Ugaritici. Eine morpho-syntaktische Abhandlung über das Modalsystem im Ugaritischen.
28. R. Zadok, The Pre-Hellenistic Israelite Anthroponomy and Prosopography.
29. W. Callewaert, M. Lath, The Hindī Songs of Nāmdev.
30. A. Shisha-Halevy, Coptic Grammatical Chrestomathy.
31. N. Baum, Arbres et arbustes de l'Égypte ancienne.
32. J.-M. Kruchten, Les Annales des prêtres de Karnak (XXIe-XXIIIe dynasties) et autres textes relatifs à l'initation des prêtres d'Amon.
33. H. Devijver, E. Lipiński (eds.), Punic Wars.
34. E. Vassilika, Ptolemaic Philae.
35. A. Ghaith, La Pensée Religieuse chez Ǧubrân Ḫalil Ǧubrân et Miḫâʾîl Nuʿayma.
36. N. Beaux, Le Cabinet de curiosités de Thoutmosis III.
37. G. Pollet, P. Eggermont, G. Van Damme, Corpus Topographicum Indiae Antiquae. Part II: Archaeological Sites.
38. S.-A. Naguib, Le Clergé féminin d'Amon thébain à la 21e dynastie.
39. U. Verhoeven, E. Graefe (eds.), Religion und Philosophie im Alten Ägypten. Festgabe für Philippe Derchain zu seinem 65. Geburtstag.

40. A.R. GEORGE, Babylonian Topographical Texts.
41. A. SCHOORS, The Preacher Sought to Find Pleasing Words. A Study of the Language of Qohelet. Part I: Grammatical Features.
42. G. REININK, H.E.J. VAN STIPHOUT (eds.), Dispute Poems and Dialogues in the Ancient and Mediaeval Near East.
43. C. TRAUNECKER, Coptos. Hommes et dieux sur le parvis de Geb.
44. E. LIPIŃSKI (ed.), Phoenicia and the Bible.
45. L. ISEBAERT (ed.), Studia Etymologica Indoeuropaea Memoriae A.J. Van Windekens dicata.
46. F. BRIQUEL-CHATONNET, Les relations entre les cités de la côte phénicienne et les royaumes d'Israël et de Juda.
47. W.J. VAN BEKKUM, A Hebrew Alexander Romance according to MS London, Jews' College no. 145.
48. W. SKALMOWSKI, A. VAN TONGERLOO (eds.), Medioiranica.
49. L. LAUWERS, Igor'-Severjanin, His Life and Work — The Formal Aspects of His Poetry.
50. R.L. VOS, The Apis Embalming Ritual. P. Vindob. 3873.
51. Fr. LABRIQUE, Stylistique et Théologie à Edfou. Le rituel de l'offrande de la campagne: étude de la composition.
52. F. DE JONG (ed.), Miscellanea Arabica et Islamica.
53. G. BREYER, Etruskisches Sprachgut im Lateinischen unter Ausschluß des spezifisch onomastischen Bereiches.
54. P.H.L. EGGERMONT, Alexander's Campaign in Southern Punjab.
55. J. QUAEGEBEUR (ed.), Ritual and Sacrifice in the Ancient Near East.
56. A. VAN ROEY, P. ALLEN, Monophysite Texts of the Sixth Century.
57. E. LIPIŃSKI, Studies in Aramaic Inscriptions and Onomastics II.
58. F.R. HERBIN, Le livre de parcourir l'éternité.
59. K. GEUS, Prosopographie der literarisch bezeugten Karthager.
60. A. SCHOORS, P. VAN DEUN (eds.), Philohistôr. Miscellanea in honorem Caroli Laga septuagenarii.
61. M. KRAUSE, S. GIVERSEN, P. NAGEL (eds.), Coptology. Past, Present and Future. Studies in Honour of R. Kasser.
62. C. LEITZ, Altägyptische Sternuhren.
63. J.J. CLÈRE, Les Chauves d'Hathor.
64. E. LIPIŃSKI, Dieux et déesses de l'univers phénicien et punique.
65. K. VAN LERBERGHE, A. SCHOORS (eds.), Immigration and Emigration within the Ancient Near East. Festschrift E. Lipiński.
66. G. POLLET (ed.), Indian Epic Values. *Rāmāyaṇa* and its impact.
67. D. DE SMET, La quiétude de l'Intellect. Néoplatonisme et gnose ismaélienne dans l'œuvre de Ḥamîd ad-Dîn al-Kirmânî (X^e^-XIe s.).
68. M.L. FOLMER, The Aramaic Language in the Achaemenid Period. A Study in Linguistic Variation.
69. S. IKRAM, Choice Cuts: Meat Production in Ancient Egypt.
70. H. WILLEMS, The Coffin of Heqata (Cairo JdE 36418). A Case Study of Egyptian Funerary Culture of the Early Middle Kingdom.
71. C. EDER, Die Ägyptischen Motive in der Glyptik des östlichen Mittelmeerraumes zu Anfang des 2. Jts. v. Chr.
72. J. THIRY, Le Sahara libyen dans l'Afrique du Nord médiévale.
73. U. VERMEULEN, D. DE SMET (eds.), Egypt and Syria in the Fatimid, Ayyubid and Mamluk Eras I.
74. P. ARÈNES, La déesse sGrol-Ma (Tārā). Recherches sur la nature et le statut d'une divinité du bouddhisme tibétain.
75. K. CIGGAAR, A. DAVIDS, H. TEULE (eds.), East and West in the Crusader States. Context – Contacts – Confrontations I.
76. M. BROZE, Mythe et Roman en Égypte ancienne. Les Aventures d'Horus et Seth dans le papyrus Chester Beatty I.

77. L. DEPUYDT, Civil Calendar and Lunar Calendar in Ancient Egypt.
78. P. WILSON, A Ptolemaic Lexikon. A Lexicographical Study of the Texts in the Temple of Edfu.
79. A. HASNAWI, A. ELAMRANI, M. JAMAL, M. AOUAD (eds.), Perspectives arabes et médiévales sur la tradition scientifique et philosophique grecque.
80. E. LIPIŃSKI, Semitic Languages: Outline of a Comparative Grammar.
81. S. CAUVILLE, Dendara I. Traduction.
82. C. EYRE (ed.), Proceedings of the Seventh International Congress of Egyptologists.
83. U. VERMEULEN, D. DE SMET (eds.), Egypt and Syria in the Fatimid, Ayyubid and Mamluk Eras II.
84-85. W. CLARYSSE, A. SCHOORS, H. WILLEMS (eds.), Egyptian Religion. The Last Thousand Years.
86. U. VERMEULEN, J.M. VAN REETH (eds.), Law, Christianity and Modernism in Islamic Society.
87. U. VERMEULEN, D. DE SMET (eds.), Philosophy and Arts in the Islamic World.
88. S. CAUVILLE, Dendara II. Traduction.
89. G.J. REININK, A.C. KLUGKIST (eds.), After Bardaisan. Studies on Continuity and Change in Syriac Christianity in Honour of Professor Han J.W. Drijvers.
90. C.R. KRAHMALKOV, Phoenician-Punic Dictionary.
91. M. TAHTAH, Entre pragmatisme, réformisme et modernisme. Le rôle politico-religieux des Khattabi dans le Rif (Maroc) jusqu'à 1926.
92. K. CIGGAAR, H. TEULE (eds.), East and West in the Crusader States. Context – Contacts – Confrontations II.
93. A.C.J. VERHEIJ, Bits, Bytes, and Binyanim. A Quantitative Study of Verbal Lexeme Formations in the Hebrew Bible.
94. W.M. CALLEWAERT, D. TAILLIEU, F. LALEMAN, A Descriptive Bibliography of Allama Muhammad Iqbal (1877-1938).
95. S. CAUVILLE, Dendara III. Traduction.
96. K. VAN LERBERGHE, G. VOET (eds.), Languages and Cultures in Contact: At the Crossroads of Civilizations in the Syro-Mesopotamian Realm.
97. A. CABROL, Les voies processionnelles de Thèbes.
98. J. PATRICH (ed.), The Sabaite Heritage in the Orthodox Church from the Fifth Century to the Present. Monastic Life, Liturgy, Theology, Literature, Art, Archaeology.
99. U.VERHOEVEN, Untersuchungen zur späthieratischen Buchschrift.
100. E. LIPIŃSKI, The Aramaeans: Their Ancient History, Culture, Religion.
101. S. CAUVILLE, Dendara IV. Traduction.
102. U. VERMEULEN, J. VAN STEENBERGEN (eds.), Egypt and Syria in the Fatimid, Ayyubid and Mamluk Eras III.
103. H. WILLEMS (ed.), Social Aspects of Funerary Culture in the Egyptian Old and Middle Kingdoms.
104. K. GEUS, K. ZIMMERMANN (eds.), Punica – Libyca – Ptolemaica. Festschrift für Werner Huß, zum 65. Geburtstag dargebracht von Schülern, Freunden und Kollegen.
105. S. CAUVILLE, Dendara. Les fêtes d'Hathor.
106. R. PREYS, Les complexes de la demeure du sistre et du trône de Rê. Théologie et décoration dans le temple d'Hathor à Dendera.
107. A. BLASIUS, B.U. SCHIPPER (eds.), Apokalyptik und Ägypten. Eine kritische Analyse der relevanten Texte aus dem griechisch-römischen Ägypten.
108. S. LEDER (ed.), Studies in Arabic and Islam.
109. A. GODDEERIS, Economy and Society in Northern Babylonia in the Early Old Babylonian Period (ca. 2000-1800 BC).
110. C. LEITZ (ed.), Lexikon der ägyptischen Götter und Götterbezeichnungen, Band I.

111. C. LEITZ (ed.), Lexikon der ägyptischen Götter und Götterbezeichnungen, Band II.
112. C. LEITZ (ed.), Lexikon der ägyptischen Götter und Götterbezeichnungen, Band III.
113. C. LEITZ (ed.), Lexikon der ägyptischen Götter und Götterbezeichnungen, Band IV.
114. C. LEITZ (ed.), Lexikon der ägyptischen Götter und Götterbezeichnungen, Band V.
115. C. LEITZ (ed.), Lexikon der ägyptischen Götter und Götterbezeichnungen, Band VI.
116. C. LEITZ (ed.), Lexikon der ägyptischen Götter und Götterbezeichnungen, Band VII.
117. M. VAN MOL, Variation in Modern Standard Arabic in Radio News Broadcasts.
118. M.F.J. BAASTEN, W.Th VAN PEURSEN (eds.), Hamlet on a Hill. Semitic and Greek Studies Presented to Professor T. Muraoka on the Occasion of his Sixty-Fifth Birthday.
119. O.E. KAPER, The Egyptian God Tutu. A Study of the Sphinx-God and Master of Demons with a Corpus of Monuments.
120. E. WARDINI, Lebanese Place-Names (Mount Lebanon and North Lebanon).
121. J. VAN DER VLIET, Catalogue of the Coptic Inscriptions in the Sudan National Museum at Khartoum (I. Khartoum Copt.).
122. A. ŁAJTAR, Catalogue of the Greek Inscriptions in the Sudan National Museum at Khartoum (I. Khartoum Greek).
123. H. NIEHR, Baʿalšamem. Studien zu Herkunft, Geschichte und Rezeptionsgeschichte eines phönizischen Gottes.
124. H. WILLEMS, F. COPPENS, M. DE MEYER, P. DILS, The Temple of Shanhûr. Volume I: The Sanctuary, The *Wabet*, and the Gates of the Central Hall and the Great Vestibule (1-98).
125. K. CIGGAAR, H.G.B. TEULE (eds.), East and West in the Crusader States. Context – Contacts – Confrontations III.
126. T. SOLDATJENKOVA, E. WAEGEMANS (eds.), For East is East. Liber Amicorum Wojciech Skalmowski.
127. E. LIPIŃSKI, Itineraria Phoenicia.
128. D. BUDDE, S. SANDRI, U. VERHOEVEN (eds.), Kindgötter im Ägypten der griechisch-römischen Zeit. Zeugnisse aus Stadt und Tempel als Spiegel des Interkulturellen Kontakts.
129. C. LEITZ (ed.), Lexikon der ägyptischen Götter und Götterbezeichnungen, Band VIII.
130. E.J. VAN DER STEEN, Tribes and Territories in Transition.
131. S. CAUVILLE, Dendara V-VI. Traduction. Les cryptes du temple d'Hathor.
132. S. CAUVILLE, Dendara V-VI. Index phraséologique. Les cryptes du temple d'Hathor.
133. M. IMMERZEEL, J. VAN DER VLIET, M. KERSTEN, C. VAN ZOEST (eds.), Coptic Studies on the Threshold of a New Millennium. Proceedings of the Seventh International Congress of Coptic Studies. Leiden, August 27 - September 2, 2000.
134. J.J. VAN GINKEL, H.L. MURRE-VAN DEN BERG, T.M. VAN LINT (eds.), Redefining Christian Identity. Cultural Interaction in the Middle East since the Rise of Islam.
135. J. MONTGOMERY (ed.), ʿAbbasid Studies. Occasional Papers of the School of ʿAbbasid Studies, Cambridge, 6-10 July 2002.
136. T. BOIY, Late Achaemenid and Hellenistic Babylon.
137. B. JANSSENS, B. ROOSEN, P. VAN DEUN (eds.), Philomathestatos. Studies in Greek Patristic and Byzantine Texts Presented to Jacques Noret for his Sixty-Fifth Birthday.

138. S. HENDRICKX, R.F. FRIEDMAN, K.M. CIAŁOWICZ, M. CHŁODNICKI (eds.), Egypt at its Origins. Studies in Memory of Barbara Adams.
139. R. ARNZEN, J. THIELMANN (eds.), Words, Texts and Concepts Cruising the Mediterranean Sea. Studies on the Sources, Contents and Influences of Islamic Civilization and Arabic Philosophy and Science.
140. U. VERMEULEN, J. VAN STEENBERGEN (eds.), Egypt and Syria in the Fatimid, Ayyubid and Mamluk Eras IV.
141. H.T. DAVIES, Yūsuf al-Shirbīnī's Kitāb Hazz al-Qūḥuf bi-Sharḥ Qaṣīd Abī Shādūf ("Brains Confounded by the Ode of Abū Shādūf Expounded"). Volume I: Arabic text.
142. P. VAN NUFFELEN, Un héritage de paix et de piété. Étude sur les histoires ecclésiastiques de Socrate et de Sozomène.
143. A. SCHOORS, The Preacher Sought to Find Pleasing Words. A Study of the Language of Qoheleth. Part II: Vocabulary.
144. M.E. STONE, Apocrypha, Pseudepigrapha and Armenian Studies. Collected Papers: Volume 1.
145. M.E. STONE, Apocrypha, Pseudepigrapha and Armenian Studies. Collected Papers: Volume 2.
146. M. CACOUROS, M.-H. CONGOURDEAU (eds.), Philosophie et sciences à Byzance de 1204 à 1453. Les textes, les doctrines et leur transmission.
147. K. CIGGAAR, M. METCALF (eds.), East and West in the Medieval Eastern Mediterranean I.
148. B. MICHALAK-PIKULSKA, A. PIKULSKI (eds.), Authority, Privacy and Public Order in Islam.
149. E. CZERNY, I. HEIN, H. HUNGER, D. MELMAN, A. SCHWAB (eds.), Timelines. Studies in Honour of Manfred Bietak.
150. J.-Cl. GOYON, C. CARDIN (eds.), Proceedings of the Ninth International Congress of Egyptologists. Actes du neuvième congrès international des Égyptologues. Grenoble, 6-12 septembre 2004.
151. S. SANDRI, Har-pa-chered (Harpokrates). Die Genese eines ägyptischen Götterkindes.
152. J.E. MONTGOMERY (ed.), Arabic Theology, Arabic Philosophy. From the Many to the One: Essays in Celebration of Richard M. Frank.
153. E. LIPIŃSKI, On the Skirts of Canaan in the Iron Age. Historical and Topographical Researches.
154. M. MINAS-NERPEL, Der Gott Chepri. Untersuchungen zu Schriftzeugnissen und ikonographischen Quellen vom Alten Reich bis in griechisch-römische Zeit.
155. H. WILLEMS, Dayr al-Barshā Volume I. The Rock Tombs of Djehutinakht (No. 17K74/1), Khnumnakht (No. 17K74/2), and Iha (No. 17K74/3). With an Essay on the History and Nature of Nomarchal Rule in the Early Middle Kingdom.
156. J. BRETSCHNEIDER, J. DRIESSEN, K. VAN LERBERGHE (eds.), Power and Architecture. Monumental Public Architecture in the Bronze Age Near East and Aegean.
157. A. CAMPLANI, G. FILORAMO (eds.), Foundations of Power and Conflicts of Authority in Late Antique Monasticism.
158. J. TAVERNIER, Iranica in the Achaemenid Period (ca. 550-330 B.C.). Lexicon of Old Iranian Proper Names and Loanwords, Attested in Non-Iranian Texts.
159. P. KOUSOULIS, K. MAGLIVERAS (eds.), Moving Across Borders. Foreign Relations, Religion and Cultural Interactions in the Ancient Mediterranean.
160. A. SHISHA-HALEVY, Topics in Coptic Syntax: Structural Studies in the Bohairic Dialect.
161. B. LURSON, Osiris, Ramsès, Thot et le Nil. Les chapelles secondaires des temples de Derr et Ouadi es-Seboua.
162. G. DEL OLMO LETE (ed.), Mythologie et Religion des Sémites occidentaux.

163. N. BOSSON, A. BOUD'HORS (eds.), Actes du huitième congrès international d'études coptes. Paris, 28 juin - 3 juillet 2004.
164. A. BERLEJUNG, P. VAN HECKE (eds.), The Language of Qohelet in Its Context. Essays in Honour of Prof. A. Schoors on the Occasion of his Seventieth Birthday.
165. A.G.C. SAVVIDES, Byzantino-Normannica. The Norman Capture of Italy and the First Two Invasions in Byzantium.
166. H.T. DAVIES, Yūsuf al-Shirbīnī's Brains Confounded by the Ode of Abū Shādūf Expounded (Kitāb Hazz al-Qūḥuf bi-Sharḥ Qaṣīd Abī Shādūf). Volume II: English translation, introduction and notes.
167. S. ARGUILLÈRE, Profusion de la vaste sphère. Klong-chen rab-'byams (Tibet, 1308-1364). Sa vie, son œuvre, sa doctrine.
168. D. DE SMET, Les Épîtres sacrées des Druzes. Rasā'il al-Ḥikma. Volumes 1 et 2.
169. U. VERMEULEN, K. D'HULSTER (eds.), Egypt and Syria in the Fatimid, Ayyubid and Mamluk Eras V.
170. W.J. VAN BEKKUM, J.W. DRIJVERS, A.C. KLUGKIST (eds.), Syriac Polemics. Studies in Honour of Gerrit Jan Reinink.
171. K. D'HULSTER, J. VAN STEENBERGEN (eds.), Continuity and Change in the Realms of Islam. Studies in Honour of Professor Urbain Vermeulen.
172. B. MIDANT-REYNES, Y. TRISTANT, J. ROWLAND, S. HENDRICKX (eds.), Egypt at its Origins 2.
173. J.H.F. DIJKSTRA, Philae and the End of Ancient Egyptian Religion. A Regional Study of Religious Transformation (298-642 CE).
174. I. UYTTERHOEVEN, Hawara in the Graeco-Roman Period. Life and Death in a Fayum Village.
175. P. KOUSOULIS (ed.), Ancient Egyptian Demonology. Studies on the Boundaries between the Demonic and the Divine in Egyptian Magic.
176. A. KARAHAN, Byzantine Holy Images – Transcendence and Immanence. The Theological Background of the Iconography and Aesthetics of the Chora Church.
177. J. NAWAS (ed.), 'Abbasid Studies II. Occasional Papers of the School of 'Abbasid Studies, Leuven, 28 June - 1 July 2004.
178. S. CAUVILLE, Dendara. Le temple d'Isis. Volume I: Traduction.
179. S. CAUVILLE, Dendara. Le temple d'Isis. Volume II: Analyse à la lumière du temple d'Hathor.
180. M. ZITMAN, The Necropolis of Assiut.
181. E. LIPIŃSKI, Resheph. A Syro-Canaanite Deity.
182. C. KARLSHAUSEN, L'iconographie de la barque processionnelle en Égypte au Nouvel Empire.
183. U. VERMEULEN, K. D'HULSTER (eds.), Egypt and Syria in the Fatimid, Ayyubid and Mamluk Eras VI.
184. M. IMMERZEEL, Identity Puzzles. Medieval Christian Art in Syria and Lebanon.
185. D. MAGEE, J. BOURRIAU, S. QUIRKE (eds.), Sitting Beside Lepsius. Studies in Honour of Jaromir Malek at the Griffith Institute.
186. A. STEVENSON, The Predynastic Egyptian Cemetery of el-Gerzeh.
187. D. BUMAZHNOV, E. GRYPEOU, T.B. SAILORS, A. TOEPEL (eds.), Bibel, Byzanz und Christlicher Orient. Festschrift für Stephen Gerö zum 65. Geburtstag.
188. J. ELAYI, A.G. ELAYI, The Coinage of the Phoenician City of Tyre in the Persian Period (5th-4th Century BCE).
189. F. HAGEN, J. JOHNSTON, W. MONKHOUSE, K. PIQUETTE, J. TAIT, M. WORTHINGTON (eds.), Narratives of Egypt and the Ancient Near East. Literary and Linguistic Approaches.
190. V. VAN DER STEDE, Les pratiques de stockage au Proche-Orient ancien du Natoufien à la première moitié du troisième millénaire avant notre ère.

191. W. CLAES, H. DE MEULENAERE, S. HENDRICKX (eds.), Elkab and Beyond. Studies in Honour of Luc Limme.
192. M. MARÉE (ed.), The Second Intermediate Period (Thirteenth-Seventeenth Dynasties). Current Research, Future Prospects.
193. I. JACOBS, Aesthetic Maintenance of Civic Space. The 'Classical' City from the 4th to the 7th c. AD.
194. H. KNUF, C. LEITZ, D. VON RECKLINGHAUSEN (eds.), Honi soit qui mal y pense. Studien zum pharaonischen, griechisch-römischen und spätantiken Ägypten zu Ehren von Heinz-Josef Thissen.
195. I. REGULSKI, A Palaeographic Study of Early Writing in Egypt.
196. S. CAUVILLE, Dendara XIII. Traduction. Le pronaos du temple d'Hathor: Façade et colonnes.
197. M. KUHN, Koptische liturgische Melodien. Die Relation zwischen Text und Musik in der koptischen Psalmodia.
198. B. SNELDERS, Identity and Christian-Muslim Interaction. Medieval Art of the Syrian Orthodox from the Mosul Area.
199. V. VAN AALST, K. CIGGAAR (eds.), East and West in the Medieval Eastern Mediterranean II.
200. E. LIPIŃSKI, Studies in Aramaic Inscriptions and Onomastics III.
201. S. CAUVILLE, Dendara XIV. Traduction. Le pronaos du temple d'Hathor: Parois intérieures.
202. K. DUISTERMAAT, I. REGULSKI (eds.), Intercultural Contacts in the Ancient Mediterranean.
203. F.S. JONES, Pseudoclementina Elchasaiticaque inter Judaeochristiana. Collected Studies.
204. D. ASTON, B. BADER, C. GALLORINI, P. NICHOLSON, S. BUCKINGHAM (eds.), Under the Potter's Tree. Studies on Ancient Egypt Presented to Janine Bourriau on the Occasion of her 70th Birthday.
205. R.F. FRIEDMAN, P.N. FISKE (eds.), Egypt at its Origins 3.
206. S. DORPMUELLER (ed.), Fictionalizing the Past: Historical Characters in Arabic Popular Epic.
207. G. CONTU (ed.), Centre and Periphery within the Borders of Islam.
208. B. MAHIEU, Between Rome and Jerusalem: Herod the Great and his Sons in their Struggle for Recognition.
209. M.M. BAR-ASHER, A. KOFSKY, Kitāb al-Maʿārif by Abū Saʿīd Maymūn b. Qāsim al-Ṭabarānī. Critical Edition with an Introduction.
210. M. DE MEYER, Dayr al-Barshā Volume II. First Intermediate Period Restoration of Old Kingdom Tombs.
211. R. EL-SAYED, Afrikanischstämmiger Lehnwortschatz im älteren Ägyptisch.
212. P. VAN DEUN, C. MACÉ (eds.), Encyclopedic Trends in Byzantium?
213. S. CAUVILLE, Dendara XV. Traduction. Le pronaos du temple d'Hathor: Plafond et parois extérieures.
214. L. EVANS (ed.), Ancient Memphis, "Enduring is the Perfection".
215. V. KLEMM, N. AL-SHAʿAR (eds.), Sources and Approaches across Disciplines in Near Eastern Studies.
216. A.M. BAGG, Die Assyrer und das Westland. Studien zur historischen Geographie und Herrschaftspraxis in der Levante im 1. Jt. v.u. Z.
217. B. BADER, M.F. OWNBY (eds.), Functional Aspects of Egyptian Ceramics in their Archaeological Context.
218. F. HAGEN, An Ancient Egyptian Literary Text in Context: The Instruction of Ptahhotep.
219. I. REGULSKI, K. DUISTERMAAT, P. VERKINDEREN (eds.), Seals and Sealing Practices in the Near East. Developments in Administration and Magic from Prehistory to the Islamic Period.

PRINTED ON PERMANENT PAPER • IMPRIME SUR PAPIER PERMANENT • GEDRUKT OP DUURZAAM PAPIER - ISO 9706

N.V. PEETERS S.A., WAROTSTRAAT 50, B-3020 HERENT